C0-AYF-601

Measuring and Evaluating Educational Outcomes

David A. Payne
University of Georgia

Merrill, an imprint of
Macmillan Publishing Company
NEW YORK

Maxwell Macmillan Canada
TORONTO

Maxwell Macmillan International
NEW YORK OXFORD SINGAPORE SYDNEY

Cover art: Marsha McDevitt
Editor: Linda A. Sullivan
Production Editor: Constantina Geldis
Cover Designer: Robert Vega
Production Buyer: Pamela D. Bennett

This book was set in Garamond and was printed and bound by R. R. Donnelley & Sons Company. The cover was printed by Lehigh Press, Inc.

Copyright © 1992 by Macmillan Publishing Company, a division of Macmillan, Inc. Merrill is an imprint of Macmillan Publishing Company.

Printed in the United States of America.

All rights reserved. No part of this book may be reproduced or transmitted in any form or by any means, electronic or mechanical, including photocopy, recording, or any information storage and retrieval system, without permission in writing from the Publisher.

Macmillan Publishing Company
866 Third Avenue
New York, NY 10022

Macmillan Publishing Company is part of the
Maxwell Communication Group of Companies.

Maxwell Macmillan Canada, Inc.
1200 Eglington Avenue East, Suite 200
Don Mills, Ontario M3C 3N1

Library of Congress Cataloging-in-Publication Data

Payne, David A.
Measuring and evaluating educational outcomes / David A. Payne.
p. cm.
Includes bibliographical references (p.) and index.
ISBN 0-02-392401-2
1. Educational tests and measurements. 2. Educational tests and measurements—Design and construction. I. Title.
LB3051.P336 1992
371.2'6—dc20 91-21424
CIP

Printing: 1 2 3 4 5 6 7 8 9 Year: 2 3 4 5

Love does not need to be measured or evaluated.

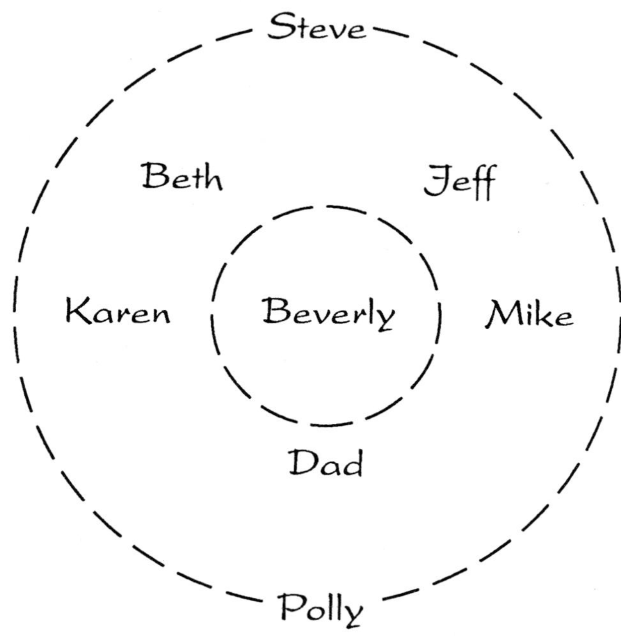

AN INSTRUCTOR'S LAMENT

My face is lined, my hair is gray
Though I'm but five and twenty;
I'll tell you how I got this way
My friends, I've been through plenty.

My principal once took a course
In measurement and testing
And since that God-forsaken day,
We've none of us been resting.

Each term begins the same old way,
We give tests diagnostic;
I once believed there was a God,
Now I'm a grim agnostic.

When all the papers have been marked
With data tabulated,
They're stored away till Judgment Day
Berated, hated, fated.

And then we give Achievement Tests
To find the children's level;
I fear my faith in life now rests
A-shattered with the devil.

We take them home and through the night
Work out the correlations,
We seek deficient coefficients
And those obscure relations.

And then without a breathing spell
We test to find IQ's,
Like soldiers shocked by shrieking shell
We seek out those M.A.'s.

Each day, each week, each month, we test
No matter what the weather,
For teaching there's no time at all
To ever get together.

The Mid-terms come, the Finals too,
And tests with other labels,
We're working now with fevered brows
Computing phoney tables.

The end has come, our principal
Now gives the figures study.
His face lights up, he shakes each hand,
He even calls me "Buddy."

"In one short term, our children
  gained
Three years," he cries, "that's plenty."
But he forgets to mention us—
His teachers—we've lost twenty.

Author Unknown

Preface

The perspective of *Measuring and Evaluating Educational Outcomes* is on preservice and in-service teachers, but the book is also for professionals who have a broader need for educationally relevant data. It is imperative that educators at all levels have a basic understanding of instrument development, analysis, and interpretation if they are to understand and make intelligent applications of the data from educational tests and measurements. The book will be very useful not only to the classroom educator, but also to the school principal, central office curriculum director, and state department person. Anyone interested in instrument development will find practical information and helpful techniques. Examples and illustrations are drawn not only from the classroom, but from the principal's office, the curriculum director's files, and the superintendent's agendas. Being both technique- and concept-oriented, the book will serve a reference need as well.

Measuring and Evaluating Educational Outcomes reflects a philosophy of testing that emphasizes the role of the test in facilitating communication within the teaching-learning situation that is embedded in a methodological framework referred to as *educational assessment.* In contrast to the denotations and connotations of the terms *measurement* and *evaluation,* assessment concerns itself not only with the inputs and outputs of an instructional system, but also with the transactions within it.

The samples of behavior represented by a test, and our evaluations of them, should communicate meaningful information to both instructor and student. The importance of educational objectives cannot be overemphasized, for it is typically by specifying expected and anticipated outcomes that an instructor can best teach, a student can best learn, and both can best rationally evaluate. Modest weight is therefore given to the specification of both cognitive and affective variables, and their roles in learning and assessment.

Achievement in school involves progress toward a specified set of multiple educational goals. Historically, these goals have emphasized the development of intellectual skills and abilities in conjunction with the acquisition of information. Information acquisition has, unfortunately, dominated educational curricula. Within the last several decades professional educators have moved away from the stultifying emphasis on recall of specific facts and information. Where appropriate, efforts have been made in this book to illustrate how higher-order mental abilities and skills can be measured with relative efficiency.

Organization of the Text

The book's 20 chapters are divided into seven broad groupings, as follows:

Part	*Chapters*
1. Overview of Concepts and Issues in Measurement and Evaluation	1–3
2. Planning for Instrument Development	4–5
3. Constructing Measuring Instruments	6–9
4. Summarizing Data and Instrument Development	10–13
5. Standardized Measures	14–16
6. Measuring Affective Educational Outcomes	17–18
7. Applications of Measurement Data	19–20

An overview of the frame of reference for educational measurement, evaluation and assessment, criticisms of testing, ethical and legal concerns, and the relationship of testing and teaching is given in the first three chapters. Chapters 4 through 9 describe the actual test development process from a variety of perspectives, and Chapters 10 through 13 present test analysis, refinement, and interpretation techniques. Standardized norm-referenced and criterion-referenced measurements and approaches to interpretation are explored in Chapters 14 through 16, and affective objectives and measurement techniques are considered in Chapters 17 and 18. Finally, applications of measurement data are focused on marking and reporting (Chapter 19), and curriculum evaluation and school effectiveness (Chapter 20).

Features of the Text

Among the major features of the text are the following:

- *Integrated Case Studies.* At the conclusion of fourteen chapters the student will find an integrated and continuing set of exercises, which can be used to develop, analyze, and apply the results of a midterm exam for a reading education course. Sample responses to the Case Study Application can be found in the Instructor's Manual.
- *Content Review Statements.* Each chapter contains a summary of major content topics presented and discussed. These summaries could be used for review or preview. Instructional objectives are implied.

- *Suggested Readings.* An annotated list of both contemporary and classic references are to be found at the conclusion of each chapter.
- *Speculations.* A set of thought-provoking questions that can be used for initiating classroom discussions are included in each chapter.
- *Glossary.* A 190-item glossary is presented at the end of the book to aid the student in mastering the vocabulary of measurement and testing.

Other content and organizational features include (a) a two-chapter focus on affective outcomes; (b) a general concern throughout the book on the evaluation process in addition to measurement; (c) an overall organization emphasizing the sequence of steps involved in instrument development, refinement, and application; and (d) excerpts from a teacher's diary as she progresses through a course where the text is being used.

Acknowledgments

Many "significant others" contributed to the preparation of the manuscript. The author is indebted to Dr. Jeanne Swafford of Texas Tech University for preparation of material upon which the Case Study Applications are based. The many marvelous magic fingers of the following helped in manuscript preparation: Michelle Bennett, Susan Berryman, Donna Bell, Sharon Cox, and Stephanie Jordan. A special thanks to these women for undertaking many tedious tasks.

Several colleagues and fellow professionals contributed meaningful reviews of manuscript during its gestation period. Among these were: Carl J. Huberty, University of Georgia; Robert L. Lissitz, University of Maryland; William Deaton, Auburn University; Stephen Dunbar, University of Colorado-Boulder; Louise Jernigan, Eastern Michigan University; Ronald Marso, Bowling Green State University; Darrell Sabers, University of Arizona; James Terwilliger, University of Minnesota-Minneapolis; Kinnard White, University of North Carolina-Chapel Hill; David Young, SUNY-Cortland; and William Stallings, Georgia State University. If I have misinterpreted their suggestions I apologize, and I thank them for their highly relevant input.

Brief Contents

Contents

Five Standardized Measures

Bev's Diary

I, Beverly L. Dean, being of sound mind and body, do attest that the following entries from my professional diary are a true and accurate picture of my experiences as an English instructor at Creston High School, home of the Polar Bears. I have been so engaged for the last two years since receiving a bachelor's degree from Michigan State University, home of the Spartans. I enjoy very much the challenges of teaching, but, wow—it's a tough job! I respect the dedication of my colleagues here at CHS, home of the poor (but the brave), and wish to continually increase the knowledge and improve the skills necessary to do a good job.

My responsibilities here at CHS are primarily to teach freshman English. Several times a year I teach both remedial and advanced composition, and an American literature course.

At the beginning of school this year my principal, Mr. Pappas, threw me a challenge:

Part One

Overview of Concepts and Issues in Measurement and Evaluation

"If you are really interested in improving your courses, why don't you gather some relevant data and undertake an evaluation or hone your testing skills?" I have no background in measurement and evaluation. This seemed like a very reasonable idea since I was now fairly well settled into the job and my undergraduate preparation in measurement was almost nonexistent—which, I understand, is typical. In fact, I had been toying with the idea of taking some courses at the University and maybe even working on an advanced degree. It was the proverbial multiple bird-single stone opportunity, not that anyone would wish to intentionally hurt one of our feathered friends. So it was not without some trepidation that I enrolled in a measurement and evaluation course with Dr. Sig Nificant. I am hoping that our textbook, *Explorations in the Universe of Measurement Truth* by Seymour Clearly, will reveal to me many insights in the area of applied educational measurement and evaluation.

Chapter 1

A Perspective on Educational Measurement and Evaluation

Everyone has attitudes about tests. Some may be positive about those tests on which they did well. Some may be negative about those on which their performance was less than optimal. Some tests are seen as fair and equitable, others as biased and discriminatory. Tests, defined (in the very generic sense) as samples of performance or opinion, touch our lives directly and indirectly every day. Students are tested, service personnel are certified, competencies of health care professionals are assessed, and products are measured against standards. We are a society that devours information, data, and statistics. It is no wonder, then, that we demand the best data available.

In our public schools this demand for data is ever-increasing. It is human nature to want to know how well you did or are doing on a task or lesson. Hundreds of decisions in and about school and schooling are made each day. We need the best information available, but technical adequacy must be balanced by practical considerations. If tests are abandoned, as some adherents would have it, negative consequences could result. One might be that distinction between the competent and less competent individuals would be very difficult to identify. Our society needs as

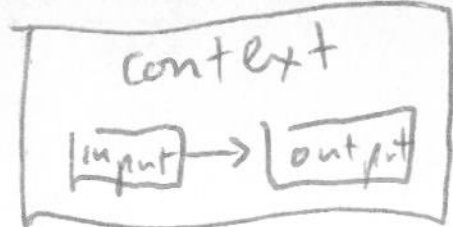

many competent individuals as possible if we are to compete successfully with other countries in terms of business, research, and education. If we did not have tests, evaluation of achievement would be based on less than solid evidence. Access to educational opportunity would be based on influence or background rather than achievement and aptitude; programs would be evaluated on appearance rather than efficiency and effectiveness.

Preparing these tests requires expenditures of considerable time, effort, and resources, but considering the importance of the data such expenditures are justified.

The thoughtful and intelligent application of educational assessment principles and devices can profoundly improve the quality of education. Measurement's primary relevance is, of course, to the activities of student and instructor, but its applicability to administration, curriculum development, counseling, and supervision should not be overlooked.

A Context for Educational Measurement and Evaluation: Educational Assessment

Educators, particularly college professors, love those things called paradigms or models. Although frequently overelaborate, a paradigm (graph or representation of a model) can help us see the forest *and* the trees. The framework (and corresponding paradigm) used to view the measurement process is similar to Bloom's (1970) discussion of *assessment*. His idea relates very directly to the complexity of the educational process and the interdependence of components involved in the process. Bloom was concerned with the description of relationships between task requirements (inputs), criterion behavior (outputs), and the environment (context). The inclusion of the environmental element distinguishes assessment from other tasks and activities—such as measurement and testing—associated with evaluating teaching-learning situations.

Educational assessment is difficult to define. English and English (1958) define assessment as "a method of evaluating personality in which an individual, living in a group under partly controlled physical and social conditions, meets and solves a variety of lifelike problems, including stress problems, and is observed and rated . . ." (p. 44). Kind of sounds like a school setting, doesn't it? This statement describes the procedures used by the military to select staff for the Office of Strategic Services (a forerunner of the Central Intelligence Agency) during World War II (OSS Assessment Staff, 1948). This intense process utilized a variety of data-gathering techniques, such as (a) observations, (b) stress interviews, (c) performance measures, (d) group discussions, (e) individual and group tasks, (f) peer ratings, (g) projective techniques, and (h) various kinds of structured tests. Cronbach (1960) notes three principal features of assessment: (a) the use of a variety of techniques, (b) reliance on observations in structured and unstructured situations, and (c) integration of information. These characteristics and the foregoing definition are readily applicable to a classroom situation. The term *personality* as used above refers to the totality of an individual's characteristics—cognitive, affective, and psychomotor. The classroom seting is social and provides for both structured and unstructured phases. Finally, problem solving is a major learning task. Obviously, a variety of instruments are needed to measure the myriad of relevant variables. Appraisal of the totality of the student, his or her environment, and his or her accomplishments is the objective of educational assessment.

The following statement by Bloom (1970, p. 31) admirably summarized the process of educational assessment:

> Assessment characteristically begins with an analysis of the criterion and the environment in which the individual lives, learns, and works. It attempts to determine the psychological pressures the environment creates, the roles expected, and the demands and pressures—their hierarchical arrangement, consistency, as well as conflict. It then proceeds to the determination of the kinds of evidence that are appropriate about the individuals who are placed in this environment, such as their relevant strengths and weaknesses, their needs and personality characteristics, their skills and abilities.

Assessment concerns itself with the totality of the educational setting, and is the more inclusive term, that is, it subsumes measurement and evaluation. It focuses not only on the nature of the learner, but also on what is to be learned and how. Stake (1967) has drawn attention to the importance of what he calls the "transactions" of the classroom: the countless interactions between student and teacher, student and instructional material, and student and student that constitute the process of education. In a very real sense, educational assessment is diagnostic in intent. Those with responsibility for overseeing education are concerned not only with the strengths and weaknesses of an individual learner, but also with the effectiveness of the instructional materials and curriculum. (See Chapter 20.)

A representation of the concept of educational assessment is found in Figure 1-1. It can be seen that all three components require measurement: inputs, context, and outputs. We are called upon to evaluate the relationships among these three elements in the system. Assessment is the aggregate of all three relationships and, at the school or school system level, is related directly to educational effectiveness. An example of task requirements (*input*) might be a set of performance objectives or standards expressed in terms of mastery or an expected test score. A *context* measurement might be observation of a teaching strategy or a description of the physical or socio-emotional climate of a classroom. *Outputs* might be test scores, products, or performance.

Assessments are made continuously in educational settings. Decisions are made about, for example, content and specific objectives (inputs), the nature of student faculty, and staff morale or attitudes (context), and the extent to which student performances meet standards (outputs). A typical example of how assessments can be used in decision making is described by Guerin and Maier (1983):

1. The teacher reviews a work sample, which shows that some column additions are in error and there are frequent carrying errors.
2. The teacher assigns simple problems on preceding pages; these reveal consistent

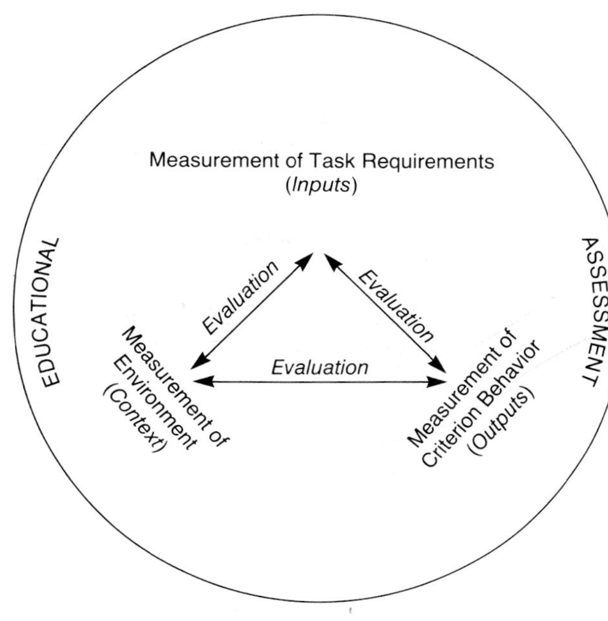

Figure 1-1

Components of educational assessment system

addition errors in some number combinations, as well as repeated errors in carrying from one column to another.

3. The teacher gives instruction through verbal explanation, demonstration, trial, and practice.
4. The student is successful in calculations made in each preparation step after direct teacher instruction.
5. The student returns to the original page, completes it correctly, and is monitored closely when new processes are introduced.

The intimate association of assessment and instruction is well illustrated in this example. The data useful in decision making may be related from informal assessments (e.g., brief observations from interactions) or from teacher-made or selected commercial standardized tests.

The benefits of informed decision making in education are obvious. The enhancement of student learning and development is foremost. The evaluation of feelings of competence in regard to academic skill and the sense of one's perception of being able to function effectively in society is mandatory. The affective side of development is equally important. Such personal dimensions as feelings of self-worth and mental health lead to better overall life adjustment.

The Nature and Place of Measurement in Assessment

The primary component of educational assessment is data collection—specifically, data collection through measurement. Measurement is the backbone of any educational process, as it provides information for decision making. Decisions are made continually about objectives, materials, the cost-effectiveness of the instructional system, student progress, and other similarly important questions.

Educational measurement is a process of gathering data that provides for a more precise and objective appraisal of learning outcomes than could be accomplished by less formal and systematic procedures. But why be concerned with precision at all? It may be enough to say, as Churchman (1959) does, that precise information is desirable because it can be applied to a wide variety of problems and decision-making activities.

There are probably as many definitions of measurement as there are measurers and testers. All definitions, although qualitatively different, involve the systematic assignment of numerals to objects, events, places, processes, or phenomena. Such a definition is not sufficient, because it allows enumeration and classification to be considered an aspect of measurement. Measurement is more than counting or sorting. It is the comparison of something with a unit or standard amount or quantity of that same thing, in order to represent the magnitude of the variable being measured. Data can be gathered, however, by either quantitative or qualitative means. A synonym for measurement might be "quantification," specifically, the quantification of *properties* of objects, not the objects themselves or the assignment of numerals to represent objects, properties, individuals, performance, dimension, variables, and so forth. Quantification is both the process and the result of measurement. The alternative to measurement is verbal description, but attempts—however systematic—to describe phenomena verbally tend to be laborious and inefficient, and the results tend to be rather vague and inexact.

Four major benefits deriving from measurement may be summarized as follows:

Assistance in interpretation. We can not only identify and describe individual differences, but we can also order individuals with respect to the variable measured, and describe individual differences; we can also order individuals with respect to the variable measured, and thereby derive an interpretation based on relative position or performance against a standard.

Data reduction. The introduction of metric (numerical) terms allows for the application of useful mathematical and statistical procedures to summarize large numbers of observations.

Descriptive flexibility. The application of measurement procedures allows us to discriminate between individuals and to describe individual differences.

Identification of patterns. Descriptive flexibility allows for the identification and measurement of individual differences in a number of different behaviors, which may then be interrelated in meaningful ways.

The four characteristics described above serve to summarize the "why" of measurement. The remainder of this book addresses itself to the "what" and "how" of educational measurement.

Tests, Measurements, and Evaluation

Words in common parlance often take on new and sometimes esoteric meanings when used by specialists. Such is the case with the terms *test, measurement,* and *evaluation.* As commonly used, they are interchangeable. In an educational assessment situation, however, this can lead to confusion. Within the umbrella category "assessment," *evaluation* is the most inclusive term. It describes a general process for making judgments and decisions. The data used to make evaluations may be quantitative or qualitative. A teacher may draw upon classroom exams, anecdotal material, scores from standardized tests, and informal observations in arriving at a decision on the promotion of a pupil.

Evaluation may be used *formatively* to help improve a program by using information gathered along the way as the student progresses or the curriculum unfolds. It also may be used *summatively* in making terminal end-of-experience judgments of worth, value, appropriateness, or goodness (e.g., as summarized in a final course grade). Measurement, on the other hand, is concerned with the systematic collection, quantification, and ordering of information. It implies both the process of quantification and the result. Measurement may take many forms, ranging from the application of very elaborate and complex electronic devices, to paper-and-pencil exams, to rating scales or checklists. A test is a particular form of measurement. Implicit in the current usage of the term is the notion of a formal standardized procedure in which the examinee is aware that he is being tested for a particular purpose at a specified time. A test might be defined as a systematic method of gathering data for the purpose of making intra- or interindividual comparisons. It is a sample of behavior.

Examples of our three key terms are as follows:

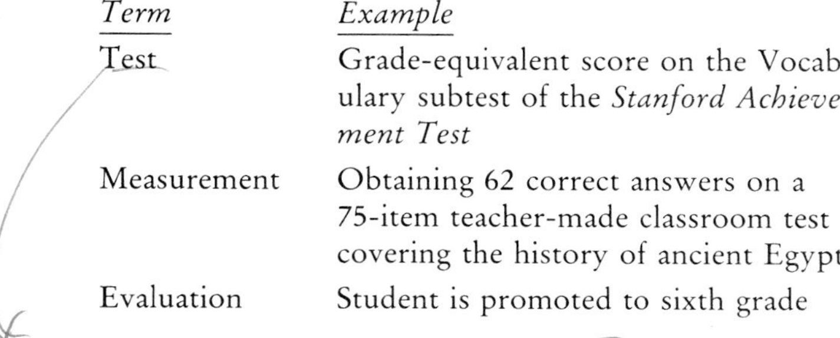

Term	*Example*
Test	Grade-equivalent score on the Vocabulary subtest of the *Stanford Achievement Test*
Measurement	Obtaining 62 correct answers on a 75-item teacher-made classroom test covering the history of ancient Egypt
Evaluation	Student is promoted to sixth grade

Tests might further be characterized as (a) *informal* (teacher-made) or *standardized* (specialist-made); (b) *oral* or *written;* (c) *mastery* (of basic knowledge and skills), *survey* (of general achievement), or *diagnostic* (of specific disabilities and deficiencies); (d) *speed* (in responding to items of approximately equal difficulty) or *power* (in responding to items of increasing difficulty, with speed deemphasized); and (e) *verbal, nonverbal,* or *performance* (requiring manipulation of objects). Many other types of classifications are possible, depending upon the needs and philosophy of the developer or user. Because written mastery, survey, and diagnostic tests have, in general, proved to be the most useful in assessing learning outcomes, the emphasis in this book is on paper-and-pencil tests.

A Brief Historical Perspective on Measurement

The forces that have shaped the current state of testing and measurement in the United States read like a United Nations roster (Payne, 1982b). DuBois (1970), for example, notes that as early as 115 B.C., during the Chou dynasty in China, candidates for public office were subjected to formal examinations involving an assessment of such basic skills as archery, horsemanship, arithmetic, writing, and music. The process became decentralized to the district level, and eventually a competitive civil service-type system evolved. Out of this experience came an appreciation for objectivity in scoring, uniformity in testing conditions, and the relevance of the test tasks for the nature of the decision to be made. In addition, the liberal use of oral examination techniques, with the advantage of the diagnostic possibilities allowing for the assessment of process as well as product, is still prevalent in education today.

German behavioral scientists also contributed directly and indirectly to the measurement movement. The "brass instruments" period of development in the middle and late 1800s focused concern on physiological and psychophysical measurement. This period of development was characterized by concern for measurement precision and the use of the scientific method to identify characteristics that are true of most individuals, the nomothetic philosophy (concern with characteristics that are true of groups of individuals).

Whereas German psychologists such as Wundt were interested in "universal characteristics," British scientists such as Darwin and Galton were more concerned with describing those characteristics that differentiated individuals—the idiographic approach (characteristics that distinguish among individuals). The effect, for example, of Darwin's *Origin of Species* on psychology and education, apart from biology, may never be fully appreciated. This concern for describing individual differences raised some problems with regard to methods useful in analyzing such data. The statistical tools developed by Sir Ronald Fisher, Karl Pearson, and Charles Spearman all contributed significantly to the quantitative development and refinement of psychometric devices.

In France, Alfred Binet and his colleagues constructed procedures to assess intellectual performance. The appearance in the early 1990s of "intelligence scales" both in France and in the United States, in the form of the Stanford-Binet, served as milestones in the assessment of cognitive development. The Stanford-Binet, with the concepts of mental age and intelligence quotient (IQ), thanks to the efforts of Lewis Terman and Maud Merrill (1937), became a standard against which other group and individual intelligence tests are still measured. Although the IQ has at times proved useful, its developer, the German psychologist Wilhelm Stern, himself urged educators to bury the concept. Contemporary Russian scientists have made contributions in the areas of operant conditioning and psychophysics.

All of these multicultural influences coalesced into a force that influenced education in the United States. This country was considered a psychometric melting pot and experienced psychometric and edumetric simmerings as early as the mid-1800s. The 154-question survey made in the Boston public schools was among the first recorded instance of curriculum evaluation (Caldwell & Courtis, 1971). It covered such basic areas as vocabulary, grammar, science, arithmetic, and geography. The results were less than had been hoped for, and reforms were instituted. An even earlier classic illustration of early mass test administration took place in 1895 and is attributed to the efforts of J. M. Rice (1914), who developed and administered a comprehensive spelling test to more than 16,000 students in grades four and eight. Rice even developed variations on his spelling test—such as spelling in context (sentences)—and added measures of basic arithmetic skills.

Interestingly enough, both World Wars I and II contributed significantly to the development of measurement in the United States. The classification problems posed by hundreds of thousands of military personnel required the creation of new and efficient measuring devices, particularly of the so-called general intellectual aptitude variety. Not only were newer tests being developed, but the availability of a large "captive audience" allowed large quantities of very basic psychometric research to be conducted.

Two major policy issues are currently having a significant effect on educational practice. The first of these is embodied in the National Assessment of Educational Progress (NAEP) (Greenbaum, Garet, & Solomon, 1977) and relates to society's need for and legislative response to accountability. NAEP is a cyclical testing program in which tests in 10 areas are alternated annually. Tests in the areas of music, reading, writing, art, citizenship, mathematics, science, social studies, literature, and occupational development are administered to carefully selected samples of individuals at four age levels: 9, 13, 17, and from 26 to 35. Results in the form of item data are reported by age, sex, geographic region, race, type of community, and parents' educational status. Many benefits have been derived from NAEP, not the least of which is the refinement of methodologies for implementing large-scale exercise development and data collection activities. It is hoped that the data have influenced school administrators and federal and state legislators to make rational decisions about the allocation of money for educational programs—and we know that politicians need all the help they can get.

A second contemporary event may result in significant changes on the face of measurement and the challenge it confronts. This event was the 1983 report by the National Commission on Excellence in Education entitled *A Nation at Risk: The Imperative for Educational Reform*. Test data were used to build an argument for change (e.g., decline in Scholastic Aptitude Test scores). Data were also requested to help demonstrate that new programs were effective. One of the problems in assessing the impact of such reform movements is that there is a clear and present danger that a demand for excellence will be gained at the expense of equity for *all* those entitled to education.

Another series of events, legal in nature, have had an impact on the way tests are used in special education settings. Several decisions, for example, *Larry P.* v. *Riles* (1979, 1980), have had the effect of banning the use of intelligence tests for placement purposes. The "mainstreaming" of special education students in the regular classroom required by Public Law 94–142 has placed difficult measurement demands on the teacher as well. A set of protracted litigations in *Debra P.* v. *Tulington* (1979, 1984) required the courts to decide on issues of test and instructional validity. Legal challenges can both help and hinder the future development and uses of testing and measurement. See Chapter 2 for an extended discussion of the implications of legal challenges of testing practices.

Applications of Educational Measurement Data

The kinds of outcomes considered important in American schools appear to be ever changing. Two different emphases or trends are currently evident. On the one hand, society appears to be pushing the schools to engage exclusively in a basic skills development orientation. The heated rhetoric about reading and mathematics and minimum competencies attests to this public concern. On the other hand, the schools appear to be assuming many of the educational responsibilities that were historically considered the prerogative of parents and other socializing segments of society. Such areas as sex education, human relations (including marriage), and values, morality, and ethics are now addressed in the schools. These affective concerns require evaluation; they pose many methodological measurement problems.

It is perhaps in the understanding of the teaching-learning process that measurement has made its greatest contributions to education. In particular, measurement data have been found useful in the diagnosis of learning difficulties and the evaluation of their treatments. The use of broadband survey batteries, particularly of the achievement variety, has gained both historic and contemporary acceptance in the public schools. These tests are seen as useful in directing curriculum emphasis, providing valuable information for a variety of administrative decisions, stimulating and motivating student learning, and aiding in the academic and vocational guidance of students.

On the contemporary education scene, tests continue to be used in traditional ways. Achievement tests are being applied throughout the grade range, and diagnostic tests in the early grades and in special education settings. Selection and admission tests are being used at institutions of higher education with undergraduate, graduate, and professional school students.

An increasing use of tests is found in the area of program and project evaluation. With "accountability" rampant in education and with virtually all funding agencies, especially at the state and federal levels, requiring documentation of progam effectiveness, great numbers of educational and psychological measurements are being made.

Six broad-use categories can be identified for educational measurements:

1. Selecting, appraising, and clarifying instructional objectives
2. Determining and reporting pupil achievement of education objectives
3. Planning, directing, and improving learning experiences

4. Accountability and program evaluation
5. Counseling
6. Selection

Selecting, Appraising, and Clarifying Instructional Objectives

Achievement in school involves movement toward a specified set of objectives. When teachers sit down to develop an instrument for the collection of data to be used in evaluating progress toward these objectives, they are forced by the very nature of the task to define and review this instruction. Ideally, the specification of objectives will be accomplished before instruction begins, and will continue as the curriculum is modified to meet individual student needs. It may even be desirable to administer an achievement test to reveal deficiencies at the beginning of a course of study. The original objectives may then be modified, enlarged upon, or discarded, as decreed by the data.

Determining and Reporting Pupil Achievement of Education Objectives

Educational measurement is most frequently used in assessing the level of pupil achievement in school subjects. The application of measurement procedures yields more objective data on achievement than does subjective appraisal. Such information is obviously of critical importance to the student, as it provides him or her with some perspective on the student's position relative to acceptable educational standards. These standards may be those of the school, society, or teacher, or they may be the student's own standards.

Many other individuals, in addition to the instructor and student, are interested in individual pupil status with respect to learning. School administrators are obviously concerned. College admissions personnel find high-school grades useful in making decisions. Despite the proliferation of national admissions and scholarship testing programs, previous academic performance remains the single best predictor of future performance.

Planning, Directing, and Improving Learning Experiences

The diagnostic use of measurement data can be extremely helpful. Tests can serve a valuable function by identifying strengths and weaknesses in the achievement of individual pupils or classes. If the teacher and student can identify the areas in which achievement is less than adequate, individual learning efforts—and for that matter, teaching—can be directed more efficiently.

In the improvement and facilitation of learning, data on the sequence, continuity, and integration of learning experiences can be of great value. For example, the requisite skills and knowledge for certain courses or units can be identified. The effectiveness of selected instructional practices can also be evaluated. This use of measurement is becoming more important each year with the appearance of new curricula, particularly in science, mathematics, and social studies. This essentially involves the use of tests for research. A teacher might compare the results of a new device or program to previous educational outcomes with the same class, outcomes obtained in control groups, or outcomes commonly obtained by similar classes.

Accountability and Program Evaluation

Educational assessment can make a significant contribution to today's schools in the area of "accountability." Alkin (1972) has defined accountability as "a negotiated relationship in which the participants agree in advance to accept specified rewards and costs on the basis of evaluation findings as to the attainment of specified ends." The key is probably the term *negotiated,* which suggests a dialogue among teachers, parents, administrators, and students. One common type of negotiated relationship is a contract, and the performance contract has already emerged as one of the most frequently used methods of implementing accountability. A performance contract is, basically, an agreement to bring about specified changes in individuals or groups. Criteria are detailed and the level of payment is correlated with performance. Obviously, the measurement of performance is critical. There are a number of technical problems associated with performance contracts, for example, regression effects and unreliable gain scores. But accountability is necessary at multiple levels, not just the classroom. We are concerned with school system responsibility as well.

Another dimension of accountability comes from the many innovative programs and projects that are continually being implemented in our schools. Implementation of these activities requires evaluation: evaluation in the formative sense where data are used to improve the program or project, and also in the summative sense where an overall judgment of worth is made and reported to the responsible funding agency or institution.

Counseling

With increasing frequency our public schools are emphasizing a "human resource development" educational goal. There is a desire to help the individual student assess his or her strengths and weaknesses in the context of academic and vocational guidance. A variety of measures from all three human resource domains (cognitive, affective, and psychomotor) are available. In particular, specialized aptitude measures, and self-report personality and adjustment inventories are valuable sources of information. More and more elementary schools are developing counseling programs to help students build psychological adjustment mechanisms useful throughout the developmental years and over the entire lifespan.

Selection

Whether for academic or vocational purposes, tests can provide information which will aid individual and institutional decision making. Schools, colleges, and universities must select those students most likely to benefit and succeed in their programs. Vocational training institutions are forced to make similar kinds of decisions. Tests can help describe general individual differences and the extent of mastery of basic knowledge and skills. These two general areas of test application lead to two approaches to measurement described in the following section.

Two Approaches to Measurement: Norm- and Criterion-Referenced

The multiple purposes of measurement mentioned in the previous section of this chapter require different measurement methodologies. The term methodology as used here includes everything from the specification of objectives, to construction, to analysis and interpretation. In the case of monitoring individual student progress in a course of study, we might want a limited sample of objectives that are similar in content or process. If we were interested in surveying the math achievement of all tenth graders in the school system with regard to a variety of skills (e.g., basic skills algebra, geometrics, etc.), a heterogeneous sample of different outcomes with different kinds of questions might be desired.

In 1963 an essay by Robert Glaser paved the way for the formal differentiation of two general approaches to test construction and interpretation. These methodologies are referred to as criterion-referenced and norm-referenced measurement. Popham (1990) suggests the following general definitions.

> *Criterion-Referenced Measurement (CRM):* A criterion-referenced test is used to ascertain an individual's status with respect to a defined assessment domain. (p. 27)
>
> *Norm-Referenced Measurement (NRM):* A norm-referenced test is used to ascertain an individual's status with respect to the performance of other individuals on that test. (p. 26)

One of the important distinctions between these two measurement approaches rests on the specification and description of the *domain* to be sampled. The concept of domain is broadly described in terms of learner behaviors. The specification of the instructional objectives associated with these behaviors is central to criterion-referenced measurement. The criterion is performance with regard to the domain. In some respects current classroom testing practice of writing items for objectives is kind of like a CRM. The difference rests on a tighter, more complete, definition of the domains being sampled, and in some cases a specification of a performance standard. The performance standard may take the form of specifying the number of items to be answered correctly or the number of objectives to be mastered (which usually refers to the number or percentage of correctly answered items).

Popham (1990) sees two major differences between CRM and NRM. The first relates to the above discussion of domain, with CRM focusing mostly on relatively homogeneous sets of objectives (words spelled, problems solved, periods of history, species of trees, etc.) and NRM focusing more on general content or process domains such as reading comprehension or knowledge about elements of biology or geography. The second major difference relates to interpretation. CRM usually employs percentages (of items or objectives) achieved; NRM uses scoring that compares a tester's performance to other tests taken. Percentiles and standard scores are used in conjunction with tables of norms (numerical collections or summaries of the performances of specified groups of individuals, e.g., a national sample of fifth graders). In this regard classroom tests are most like CRM and standardized tests are like NRM. The distinction, however, is not pure: classroom tests can be, but are usually not, norm-referenced.

Areas of Application for CRM and NRM

Six broad-use categories have been detailed previously in this chapter. Below is an indication as to whether or not a particular measurement approach—CRM or NRM—is predominantly relevant (+) to a given test purpose or application.

Purpose	*CRM*	*NRM*
Clarifying Instructional Goals and Objectives	+	
Determining and Reporting Student Achievement	+	
Planning, Directing, and Improving Learning Experiences	+	
Accountability/Program Evaluation	+	+
Counseling		+
Selection	+	+

The first three classifications are self-evident. CRM is a better approach for assessing individual instructional treatment effectiveness and progress. Accountability, however, can be oriented toward individual students, teachers, schools, or systems. We frequently engage in program or project evaluation and, depending on the nature of attendant activities, we may therefore desire CRM or NRM. We cannot make, however, very solid inferences regarding teaching quality from student achievement data aggregated at the classroom level, particularly at the upper end of teacher performance levels (Millman, 1981; Millman & Darling-Hamond, 1990). Counseling applications are primarily made in the areas of personality/mental health and vocation/career guidance. Measures in these areas are primarily available from commercial publishers and therefore NRM applies. As noted previously, selection of individuals for programs, projects, or training may be on the basis of (a) meeting a minimum knowledge or performance standard, or (b) discrimination among members of a qualified group. In the case of minimum standard selection, such as meeting licensure or certification requirements, a CRM would be most appropriate. If one must fill a limited number of openings, positions, or slots, then spreading the qualified applicants out to spot the best is most effectively accomplished with NRM.

How does one proceed to develop measures to meet the projected applications? With the CRM and NRM approaches there are both unique and common procedures. The unique and common requirements, adjustments, modifications, and embellishment are highlighted throughout the remainder of the book.

These two major approaches to measurement, with their different emphases on the source of standards, imply different kinds of tests. These different kinds of tests vary in the nature of the referent they use to help interpret the resulting scores.

Referencing Systems for Educational Tests

There are multiple purposes for measuring and evaluating. These purposes require not only different kinds of measures but also different frames of reference for interpreting results. Worthen and Sanders (1987) have described four general approaches to test development. Below is a brief description of the purposes and emphases of these four approaches.

Objectives-Referenced Measurement (*ORM*): The key to this approach is to develop or select test tasks that maximally match a specified set of objectives, usually behaviorally stated objectives. Interpretation is based on the number or percentage of items in a particular set that are answered correctly or the number of possible points garnered. We have been doing this in classroom ever since the first test (in the Garden of Eden?). The result of using this approach is a description of student or class performance. Nowadays almost everybody at least uses objectives as a basis for test development.

Criterion-Referenced Measurement (*CRM*): Like the ORM, the CRM approach seeks maximum relevance of item to curricular objective. The difference lies in the interpretive base. The standard for CRM measures is absolute. Did the student(s) answer enough questions correctly to have met a predetermined criterion or standard? Evaluation standards may apply to either individual student or class.

Domain-Referenced Measurement (*DRM*): A homogeneous universe or domain of content or behavior is specified. Specifications are very detailed. An item pool is collected and tests are constructed by random sampling from the pool. Meaningfulness is based on percentage of items answered correctly. Descriptive data may be used for instructional purposes. (See Hively, Patterson, & Page, 1968; Hively, 1974.)

Norm-Referenced Measurement (*NRM*): Our old friend NRM relies on a relative standard, "You did as well as or better than _____% of the students who took this test" (during the standardization). An attempt is made to create tasks that maximize individual differences. NRM achievement measures are based on content objectives that are in common to most curricula. The interpretive implication is that a higher percentile rank (or standard score or grade equivalent) is better.

You are likely to find NRM used where selection and/or classification of students (classes, schools) is the objective in testing. Academic progress in specified curricula is generally implied by the other three approaches. You cannot tell if a test is one of the four described types simply by looking at it. The method used in development and the guidelines for interpretation must be examined.

Outline of the Test Development Process

The term *education,* as used throughout this book, is defined as the process of creating changes in the cognitive, affective, and psychomotor characteristics of individuals. How does this process relate to construction of a test? How does the testmaker begin to construct his instrument? Presumably, he could simply sit down and begin to write test questions about the material that has been taught. If the instructor is writing the test, the types of questions that easily come to mind are those that address outcomes high on his or her list of priorities. If the test is to be a fair one, the instructor will have to examine the test to be sure that content and behavioral applications are covered in the proportion intended. This is the beginning of a deliberate analytic to test building, whose sequence of steps is approximately as follows:

1. Specify the ultimate goals of the education process.
2. Derive from these the goals of the portion of the system under study.
3. Specify these goals in terms of expected student behavior. If relevant, specify the acceptable level of successful learning.
4. Determine the relative emphasis or importance of various objectives, their content, and their behaviors.
5. Select or develop situations that will elicit the desired behavior in the appropriate context or environment, assuming the student has learned it.
6. Assemble a sample of such situations that together represent accurately the emphasis on content and behavior previously determined.
7. Provide for the recording of responses in a form that will facilitate scoring but will not so distort the nature of the behavior elicited that it is no longer a true sample or index of the behavior desired.
8. Establish scoring criteria and guides to provide objective and unbiased judgments.
9. Try out the instrument in preliminary form.
10. Revise the sample of situations on the basis of tryout information.
11. Analyze reliability, validity, and score distribution in accordance with the projected use of scores.
12. Develop test norms and a manual, and reproduce and distribute the test.

This sequence of steps describes the ideal process usually followed in the development of standardized tests. The intent if not the letter of the recommendations implicit in the steps should be adhered to in the construction of any custom-made measuring instrument whether for classroom or commercial purposes.

The importance of educational objectives in the first stages of test construction cannot be overemphasized. Objectives, ideally in behavioral form, guide and shape the total process. The development and application of tests and measurements can be a revealing and professionally satisfying activity. But, like most worthwhile activities, it requires concentrated time, effort, and patience.

Content Review Statements

1. The process and results of educational assessment constitute a very powerful force that can be used to improve the effectiveness of teaching-learning situations.
2. The term *educational assessment* refers to the collection and evaluation of data involving inputs to, transactions within, and outputs from an educational system.
3. The diagnosis of learning difficulties and their implications for remedial procedures is one of the major intents of educational assessment.
4. The chief inputs to an educational assessment decision-making system derive from measurement and evaluation procedures.
5. A test is a means of measurement characterized by systematic administration and scoring procedures, formalized objectives, and applications aimed at intro- or interindividual comparisons.
6. Measurement is the process of collecting, quantifying, and ordering information on an individual, attribute, or object.
7. Evaluation is the process of making value judgments about measurement data.
8. Tests may be categorized as standardized, informal (teacher-made), oral, written, mastery, survey, speed, power, verbal, nonverbal, or performance.
9. Contemporary measurement has international origins. Our heritage includes:
   a. German concerns for instrumentation and precision.
   b. British focus on individual differences and statistics.
   c. French contribution to intelligence testing.
10. The late 1800s saw mass administration of achievement tests in U.S. public schools aimed at curricular reform.
11. Federal and legal activities currently impact measurement practice to a significant extent.
12. Measurement data can be used to help:
    a. Select, appraise, and clarify instructional objectives.
    b. Describe and report pupil progress toward, or achievement of, educational objectives.
    c. Plan, direct, and improve learning experiences.
    d. Provide a basis for assessing accountability.
13. The processes of instruction and evaluation are intimately related.
14. An educational assessment system should be responsive to relevant cognitive, affective, and psychomotor educational objectives.
15. Educational measurement and evaluation involve the following stages:
    a. Specifying goals and objectives.
    b. Designing the assessment system.
    c. Selecting data-gathering methods.
    d. Collecting relevant data.
    e. Analyzing and summarizing data.
    f. Contrasting data and objectives.
    g. Feeding back results.

16. Educational measurements should be specifically applicable to the instructional field, area, discipline, or course in which they are used.
17. Educational measurements should yield reliable, consistent, and replicable results.

Speculations

1. In what ways does the concept of "educational assessment" make more sense than the individual process of measurement and testing?
2. How have particular tests and measurements influenced your life?
3. What are the essential ways in which criterion-referenced and norm-referenced measurement are different? In what ways are they alike?
4. What is the relationship of the terms *test, measurement,* and *evaluation?*
5. What kinds of decisions can tests help us make?
6. Would you want your neurosurgeon to have graduated from the Norm-Referenced College of Hard Knocks or the Criterion-Referenced University of Competencies? Why?

Suggested Readings

DuBois, P. H. (1970). *The history of psychological testing.* Boston: Allyn and Bacon. A fascinating survey of important events and an introduction to significant people and research.

Guerin, G. R., & Maier, A. S. (1983). *Informal assessment in education.* Palo Alto, CA: Mayfield. A comprehensive overview of *nontest* approaches to assessment. Includes consideration of surveys, interviews, questionnaires, case studies, and checklists.

Haertel, E., & Calfee, R. (1983). School achievement: Thinking about what to test. *Journal of Educational Measurement, 20,* 119–131.

Haney, W. (1984). Testing reasoning and reasoning about testing. *Review of Educational Research, 54*(9), 557–654. An outstanding brief history of testing leading to a discussion of contemporary trends and issues particularly regarding the impact of testing on policy and practice.

Jaeger, R. M. (1987). Two decades of revolution in educational measurement? *Educational Measurement: Issues and Practice,* 6(4), 6–14.

Linn, R. L. (1989). Current perspectives and future directions. In R. L. Linn (Ed.), *Educational Measurement* (3rd ed. pp. 1–10). New York: Macmillan.

Rudman, H. C. (1987). The future of testing is now. *Educational Measurement: Issues and Practice.* 6(3), 5–11. A projected measurement landscape for the 21st century.

Stiggins, R. J., Conklin, N. F., & Bridgeford, N. J. (1986). Classroom assessment: A key to effective education. *Educational Measurement: Issues and Practice,* 5(2), 5–17.

Wood, R. (1986). The agenda for educational measurement. In D. K. Nuttal (Ed.), *Assessing educational achievement.* London: Falmer Press.

Wittrock, M. C., & Wiley, D. E. (Eds.). (1970). *The evaluation of instruction: Issues and problems.* New York: Holt, Rinehart & Winston. A collection of highly original symposium papers.

Chapter 2

Testing and the Concerns of Individuals, Society, and the Measurement Profession

Testing: Criticism and Response
External Testing Programs
Invasion of Privacy—Ethical Considerations
Legal Challenges to Testing Practices
Monitoring of Testing Practices by Professional Organizations
Content Review Statements
Speculations
Suggested Readings

A considerable volume of intense critical comment on educational and psychological testing is published each year. Illustrative is the flood of magazine and newspaper articles on testing problems, as well as books (Haney, 1981). These publications reflect public antipathy, uneasiness, distrust, concern, and lack of knowledge about tests and testing. They are written by professionals and laypersons alike. Many of the criticisms are justified; most are not. As is often the case with observations on technical or social phenomena—particularly those related to education—intended for public consumption, the views expressed are often narrowly defined and emotionally charged. It is hoped, therefore, that this chapter provides the reader with a balanced view of the present state of the art and science of testing.

Two initial comments are in order. First, the critics of testing are saying nothing new. They offer no unique words of wisdom or new insights. They have not exposed long-forgotten or suppressed psychometric skeletons in the testers' closets. Secondly, criticism focuses on an unethical, or at least ignorant, minority of the psychological profession—the self-appointed testers trying to make a quick profit. Unfortunately, the public is likely to assume that these criticisms apply to tests and testers in general.

What can be said in support of the critics? The potential positive effects of their judgments can readily be discerned. First, they reemphasize the inadequacy of certain testing practices. Second, their comments should serve to caution both professionals and laypersons against the misuse of tests. Third, they have joined with professional testers in demanding better training for those who administer, interpret, and use tests. Lastly, they have made a significant contribution by identifying issues in need of research. The latter contribution is, however, directly related to a distinctly negative outcome: The critics, both directly by influencing professional educators and indirectly through parents, may tend to deter schools from participating in the much-needed research in testing. Furthermore, the brunt of criticism falls on the tests, instruments, methods, or devices themselves, when all too often the users are at fault.

Most observers would agree that the need for improving communications between the testing profession and the public is being acknowledged. Continued vigilance is necessary on the part of professional and lay groups to expose quacks and incompetents, and to press for higher standards in the test-publishing industry and more intensive preservice and in-service training in measurement.

Testing: Criticism and Response

Criticisms and controversies periodically draw attention to the many problems associated with standardized educational and psychological tests. Some of these are longstanding, while others have arisen out of changes in society. Below is a list of 13 criticisms of testing (Holmen & Docter, 1972). Each criticism is followed by a response that might typically be made by a representative of the testing profession. Most of the following comments are aimed at standardized tests, but many would apply to classroom and other locally developed tests.

CRITICISM: *Tests are biased against some individuals.*

RESPONSES: A growing body of literature suggests that this may be the case in particular situations. However, an extensive survey by Kirkpatrick and others (1968) of test and criterion data on some 1200 persons—including whites, blacks, and Puerto Ricans—indicates that many of the tests perform equally well in different ethnic groups. In some cases, given tests work best with particular groups. It is argued by some that it is not the test but the unresponsive society that discriminates. It will be argued by all testing professionals that the use of any test that has no demonstrable job-related validity is inexcusable. There is evidence that certain tests are biased in selecting individuals, particularly in employment situations. If such differentiation can be shown to be a function of the relationship between test content and criterion performance, there are no grounds for objection. Such a test distinguishes between those who have and have not achieved, and between those who are and are not likely to be successful. If, on the other hand, the test discriminates on the basis of variables unrelated to validity, it should not be used. Cultural factors (e.g., socioeconomic condition) can operate to decrease the validity of any test. Some of the issues central to this problem have been highlighted by Cole and Moss (1989), Berk (1982), and Bond (1981).

Bias, as used in a testing context, refers to a cultural or societal discrimination where factors unrelated to the test, influence the scores. Such bias may operate to systematically inflate or decrease an individual's score. Quality of education could be used as an example. If quality of education is high and some individuals have access to it, bias may be positive. If the instruction is of inferior quality then it may operate to depress an individual's scores. Reynolds and Brown (1984) have summarized six major types of objections to the use of educational and psychological tests with minorities because of the possible influence of potentially significant bias.

Type of Objection	*Description*
Inappropriate Content	Lack of background or experience inhibits performance.
Innappropriate Standardization	Standardization samples do not reflect proportional representation in population with which test is used.
Examiner Bias	Use of only standard English may operate to intimidate minority examinees.
Compounded Consequences	Bias in test coupled with already existing disadvantages compound plight of minority test taker.
Construct Validity Error	Because of background differences and language problems, test may not measure same construct for majority and minority.
Predictive Validity Error	It may be the case that both test *and* criteria are biased.

There are some very complex issues here and many legal challenges have been raised. Some of these will be treated later in the chapter. The main thrust should be toward research and validity studies into sound construction practices and applications of results.

CRITICISM: *Tests become standards.*

RESPONSE: Some uninformed users of standardized tests regard the distribution of scores derived from nationwide population samplings as goals to be achieved by each of their students. National norms may serve a useful function by providing "benchmarks" to judge students' overall progress, but they should never serve as the sole criterion of program effectiveness or pupil progress. Failure to take into account the educational philosophy of local teachers, administrators, and the community, and the socioeconomic and ability level of the school population, can lead to gross misevaluations. A related danger is that the tests may begin to determine the nature of the instructional program. A school and its teachers should not be evaluated exclusively on the basis of students' performance on standardized achievement tests. Nor should standards for a local school district be determined by blind consultation of norms tables. Furthermore, a standardized achievement test should never be the sole source of data for marking or promotional decisions.

CRITICISM: *Intelligence and achievement tests measure the same thing.*

RESPONSE: In a very real sense, intelligence and achievement tests measure the same thing: the ability to perform selected tasks at a specified point in time. Although achievement tests measure abilities acquired under relatively controlled conditions, and intelligence tests measure abilities acquired under relatively uncontrolled conditions, a cursory review of standardized achievement and intelligence tests reveals significant overlap. The content of the two types of tests is quite similar, and the correlations between scores are usually in the .50s and above. The tests do differ, however, in the ways in which results are used. We tend to use achievement tests to measure past performance or describe how well certain learning tasks have been accomplished, and intelligence tests to predict future performance. In schools and colleges today, however, achievement tests are playing an increasingly important role in prediction.

CRITICISM: *Standardized tests only measure recall of facts.*

RESPONSE: Most standardized achievement tests do emphasize recall, but it can legitimately be argued that one must have a large fund of information at his command in order to reason, argue, solve problems, or function effectively in society. As we have said, most reputable achievement tests do measure such higher-order abilities as comprehension, application, and problem solving. Test publishers are increasingly emphasizing the measurement of "higher-order" outcomes as curriculum emphases and instruction are moving in that direction. The user must remember that even the highest-quality achievement test cannot measure an entire subject-matter area. Such tests can only sample types of learning. Similarly, users should be very cautious in interpreting the multiscore profiles that many survey batteries provide. Test experts have demonstrated that, because of the high degree of relationship between subtests, the differences reflected in such profiles are highly unreliable.

CRITICISM: *Tests predict imperfectly.*

RESPONSE: Agreed: All instruments are fallible. In many instances, however, the use of test data is preferable to reliance on subjective judgment alone. In most cases some data are better than none. In combination with other kinds of information, tests can do a very creditable job. The fallibility of test scores can in part be traced to the fact that humans are fallible. People are inconsistent in responding to tests, thereby raising problems of the reliability of measurement. In addition, the criteria we use for test validation are less than perfect. It is no wonder that we fall somewhat short of perfection.

CRITICISM: *Tests rigidly classify individuals.*

RESPONSE: This criticism would be more appropriate if applied to the users of tests. The classification of individuals into broad categories is useful, efficient, and enhances our understanding of people and their behavior. The failure to recognize that (a) people are ever-changing and that (b) test results are only approximations of human characteristics does not reflect best current professional thought. The use of test scores to label individuals permanently is indefensible and patently unacceptable.

CRITICISM: *Tests imply the measurement of innate characteristics.*

RESPONSE: The author does not know of a single educational or psychological test publisher who would claim that its tests measure innate human characteristics. Some individual users ignorant of the concepts of validity and reliability may make this claim, but such beliefs in "fixed scores" and the capacity of tests to measure native intelligence are naive, scientifically unsound, and socially detrimental.

CRITICISM: *Tests provide the basis for self-fulfilling prophecies.*

RESPONSE: There is no doubt that expectations play an important role in the relationship between teacher and student. Test scores help mold those expectations because they describe important dimensions of a student's ability, proficiency, accomplishments, and personality. When test scores act to rigidify a teacher's thinking about students and predetermine evaluations of their performances, serious problems can result. We need to know more about the factors that shape teacher expectations. There are studies, however, that teachers tend *not* to be overly influenced by test scores (Kellaghan, Madaus, & Airasian, 1982; Salmon-Cox, 1981).

CRITICISM: *Tests have a harmful effect on a student's cognitive style.*

RESPONSE: There is little or no evidence that exposure to particular kinds of tests, for example, multiple-choice or true-false, adversely affects the development of an individual's style of thinking or problem solving.

A recent review of the literature has suggested some of the variables that may be contributing, however, to the impact of testing on students (Natriello, 1987). Natriello found that:

1. Students who were provided information about the criteria for performance on their assignments showed highest levels of skill, self-efficacy, and speed of problem solving.
2. Teachers who hold high standards for their students tend to find student effort and performance at the higher expected level.
3. Individual competitive (vs. cooperative) standards tend to produce superior academic performance.

4. More frequent testing tends to yield better achievement.
5. If students do not perceive the evaluation as being credible, performance and acceptance of results are depressed.
6. Personalized feedback to students about their performance has a very positive effect on acceptance of results and future performance.

CRITICISM: *Tests shape school curricula and inhibit educational change.*

RESPONSE: There is a real danger that this can happen. However, such an occurrence reflects a misuse of tests, rather than a shortcoming of the tests themselves. The critical question is whether or not the teachers' objectives are the same as those of the test items. If they are, there is no problem. If, however, the content of the test becomes the determining criterion, serious distortion of the educational process can result.

CRITICISM: *Tests distort student self-concept and level of aspiration.*

RESPONSE: It can be argued that, quite to the contrary, tests help individuals to see themselves, their capacities, and their accomplishments more realistically. We strive to assure that the tests provide fair and valid results, which are communicated by a trained professional skilled in test interpretation. This is an area in which school guidance and counseling personnel can make a significant contribution.

CRITICISM: *Tests select homogeneous educational groups.*

RESPONSE: This criticism should perhaps more accurately be leveled at the practices of grouping and ability tracking, rather than at tests. If tests were not used to select groups, other and less reliable measures—grades, teacher ratings, and the like—would probably be substituted. In any event, research does not support effectiveness of grouping on the basis of general intelligence as an organizational scheme, but perhaps using achievement in a particular subject area may prove beneficial.

CRITICISM: *Tests invade privacy.*

RESPONSE: This criticism is aimed primarily at measures of personality, values, and attitudes. If these kinds of measures have little relevance to a meaningful criterion, for example, school performance or job success, they should not be used. But if such information can be shown to be useful to the institution and the individual, it can legitimately be gathered.

Many of the criticisms of testing stem from the use of external tests, for example, those used by organizations outside the school primarily for selection, and placement decision (e.g., college admissions). Following is a discussion of these kinds of tests—their uses, advantages, and disadvantages.

External Testing Programs

Within the last few decades the number of external tests administered to high-school students has spiraled dramatically. Explanations of this phenomenon are varied, but primarily involve college admissions and the granting of scholarships. Objections to external tests are voiced by many local school administrators, because the burden of proving the legitimacy and validity of such programs frequently falls on their shoulders. External tests are characterized by three distinctive features: (a) their results are used primarily by an institution or organization other than the high school, (b) the local school is unable to choose whether or not their students take such tests, and (c) responsibility for security of the tests is assumed by the test publisher. Three tests widely used for selection purposes are the College Entrance Examination Board's Scholastic Aptitude and Achievement Tests, the American College Testing Program tests, and the College Qualification Test. The National Merit Scholarship Qualifying Test and the Preliminary Scholastic Aptitude Test are used to select recipients of scholarships. In addition, some states have their own selection testing programs.

The administration of these tests to hundreds of thousands of students each year has generated considerable controversy. Following is a list of major criticism of external testing programs and possible responses or solutions to each:

Criticism of External Testing	*Response or Possible Solution*
1. Not all important outcomes are measured.	1. Those variables of primary importance to college work are assessed. If important variables are ignored they may not have been defined clearly enough.
2. Only facts and knowledge are measured.	2. Within the last several years external tests have stressed the ability to use information. Command of useful knowledge is important.
3. External tests are unfair to some students.	3. Measuring instruments are fallible. Common essential outcomes are emphasized.
4. The use of objective (e.g., multiple-choice) items is discriminatory.	4. If these items are relevant to the criterion of college success, they are valid. Choice making is an aspect of all human activities.
5. External tests adversely influence curriculum innovation and educational change.	5. There is danger that this will be the case. Test developers work with curriculum experts and educators in establishing objectives.

6. Tests do not predict perfectly.	6. Tests, as well as individuals, are fallible. Successful predictions far outnumber mispredictions. It is impossible to assess all relevant variables in advance.
7. There is too much duplication of testing.	7. Development of general-purpose equivalency tables would help.
8. Too much time and money are expended for tests.	8. Considering the potential payoff and the importance of the decisions to be made, the investment is minimal.
9. The advantaged can secure coaching that helps insure success on tests.	9. Research indicates that coaching does on the whole have a modest effect. If coaching also improves school performance, so much the better. The validity of the test is not undermined. As well, the opportunity for coaching should be made available to all.
10. The use of external tests invites invidious comparisons between schools.	10. Scores should be reported only to target institutions and individual students.
11. Exposure to external testing situations adversely affects students' emotional stability and mental health.	11. There is little or no evidence that this is true.
12. External test scores determine college entrance.	12. Nothing could be further from the truth. An entrance decision is made on the basis of a collection of relevant data, never on a single test score.

Efforts are underway to revise external tests used for college admissions. Such innovations are the (a) inclusion of writing samples, (b) application of computerized adaptive testing (see Chapter 5), (c) inclusion of problem-solving and critical-thinking measures as part of the regular testing program, and (4) use of specific subject area tests.

The overall positive contribution of external testing programs is evident. In addition to the potential advantages to the individual, society benefits by identifying and training the students best qualified to make contributions. The voluntary nature of the testing system is another point in its favor. It promotes initiative. Problems within the system should be worked out cooperatively by test specialists, college faculties and admissions officers, test publishers, and school administrators.

Invasion of Privacy—Ethical Considerations

The right to privacy is the precious birthright of all members of a free democratic society. There must be a compelling justification for tests to invade that privacy.

Congressional hearings have been held to investigate the possible misapplication of specific tests (e.g., an older version of the *Minnesota Multiphasic Personality Inventory*) in situations relating to federal employment. Gallagher (1965) has presented a typical summary of charges.

1. Some federal job applicants were required to take personality tests as part of the employment screening process.
2. No effective appeal procedure was available.
3. Personality testing represented a form of "searching the minds of federal employees and job applicants."
4. Tests improperly excluded desirable people from jobs they deserved to hold.
5. The reliability and validity of score patterns on the personality tests used was an "unsettled controversy."
6. Personality-test questions inquired into highly personal and intimate matters.
7. The tests were utilized by personnel workers who were unqualified to do so.
8. Test reports were retained; they tended to follow a person through his career.
9. Test records were not kept confidential, as promised.
10. Personality tests raised questions about applicants that tended to cause personnel decisions to be made against them.
11. Personality testing was required of many federal job applicants in some agencies, but was not required of top-level federal employees.

This list highlights some of the potential problems with regard not only to the misuse of tests in federal government, but also at other governmental levels and in business and industry as well.

Obviously, the implications of these charges transcend the application of personality tests in federal employment. The invasion-of-privacy issue touches a number of fields in which tests are used. Most personality assessment in the public school is on a referral basis to a school psychologist or by individual request to a counselor. Inasmuch as tests are used extensively in educational settings (a) to diagnose and guide, (b) to make academic selections and employment decisions, and (c) to conduct human research, potential dangers may arise from the misapplication of tests in a variety of settings (Messick, 1980, 1981).

Legal Challenges to Testing Practices

We live in a litigious society so it is not surprising that when some individual or organization feels discriminated against by a test or application of test results the initial response is to go to court. The last several decades have seen a number of significant court cases where precedents have been set and the application of standard test development procedures reaffirmed. An overview of some of these landmark cases can be found in Table 2-1.

Whenever there is an apparent conflict between social policy objectives and accepted professional and administrative practices, governmental agencies are found to increase their attacks. Nowhere is this more evident than in several employment selection discrimination cases that can be traced directly to Title VII of the 1964 Civil Rights Act, which requires employers to hire individuals without regard to race, religion, national origin, or sex. Title VII and the resulting Equal Employment Opportunity Commission Guidelines (1966, 1970, 1978) have resulted in clearer perspectives on what are acceptable testing practices under the law.

The history of the *Griggs* v. *Duke Power Company* which spread over the years 1968–1970 reflects the joint efforts of the testing profession and the court to find reasonable guidelines to help both test users and developers. The bottom line was that forevermore it is necessary to empirically demonstrate job-relatedness (usually in the form of criterion-related validity) of any test used for personnel selection or the evaluation of training.

Misapplication of any test can result in legal action. It was charged in the just noted *Griggs* v. *Duke Power Company*, and *United et al.* v. *Georgia Power Company*, that tests were used in discriminatory ways. Title VII of the 1964 Civil Rights

Table 2-1 Summary of Court Cases Challenging Tests and Testing Procedures

Litigations	**Result**
Griggs v. *Duke Power Company* (1968)	Required test user to demonstrate job relatedness of scores.
Baker v. *Columbus Municipal Separate School District* (1971)	National Teacher Examination was held to be racially biased in terms of specifying a cut-off score.
United States v. *State of South Carolina* (1977)	Held NTE was acceptable measure of impact of academic training and could be used for certification and salary decisions.
Debra P. v. *Turlington* (1979)	Upheld instructional/content validity of Florida's minimum competency graduation test.
Larry P. v. *Riles et al.* (1979)	Placement in special education classes not allowed solely on basis of intelligence test if results in racial imbalance.
Parents in Action on Special Education v. *Hannon* (1980)	Upheld use of individually administered intelligence tests for placement purposes.
Golden Rule et al. v. *Washburn et al.* (1984)	Procedure agreed upon in out-of-court settlement did not appreciably increase minority pass rate.

Act, which requires employers to hire individuals without regard to their race, religion, national origin, or sex led to the establishment of the Equal Employment Opportunity Commission. EEOC has established guidelines for testing and other selection procedures. In writing the Supreme Court's unanimous opinion in *Griggs* v. *Duke Power Company,* Chief Justice Burger noted that:

> The Act proscribes not only over discrimination but also practices that are fair in form, but discriminatory in operation. The touchstone is business necessity. If an employment practice which operates to exclude Negroes cannot be shown to be related to job performance, the practice is prohibited . . . Nothing in the Act precludes the use of testing or measuring procedures; obviously they are useful. What Congress has forbidden is giving these devices and mechanisms controlling force unless they are demonstrably a reasonable measure of job performance. Congress has not commanded that the less qualified be preferred over the better qualified simply because of minority origins. Far from disparaging job qualifications as such, Congress has made such qualifications the controlling factor, so that race, religion, nationality and sex become irrelevant . . . Congress has placed on the employer the burden of showing that any given requirement must have a manifest relationship to the employment in question.

In an educational context the National Teacher Examination was also subjected to the similar scrutiny with the decision being that it was not considered to be a measure of teaching effectiveness (*Baker* v. *Columbus Municipal Separate School District,* 1971), but did reflect the impact of academic training (*United States* v. *South Carolina,* 1977).

Cultural bias was the basis for the *Larry P.* v. *Riles* case revolving around the assignment of students to classes for the educable mentally retarded. Larry P. defined an unbiased test as one which yields "the same pattern of scores when administered to different groups of people," an unreasonable criterion at best. It flies in the face of the whole notion of individual differences and their measurement. Fortunately Judge Grady's decision in *Parents in Action or Special Education* v. *Hannon* (1980) upheld the use of individually administered intelligence tests for special education classification purposes.

The Golden Rule Insurance Company recently challenged the Illinois Department of Insurance and Educational Testing Service claiming racial bias in the licensing tests for insurance underwriters (*Golden Rule et al.* v. *Wasburn et al.,* 1984). In an effort to work out a conciliation rather than force a confrontation ETS President Anrig agreed to an out-of-court settlement which was later renounced as unsound and ineffective (Anrig, 1987; Linn & Drasgow, 1987). The agreed-upon procedure required the selection of items where answer rates of black and white examinees differ by no more than 15 percent and exceed 40 percent of the items. The procedure did not improve pass rates. With the exception of applying the Golden Rule procedure in Illinois, ETS now uses a sophisticated item bias detection method (Mantel & Haenszel, 1959) with success. The basis of the procedure rests on the assumption that test takers who have the same knowledge base should have equal or similar chances of responding correctly regardless of their race, sex, or ethnic background. The usual test/item review procedures are still employed.

It is frequently the case, however, that questions of test validity and use are overshadowed and subverted because of perceived adverse test effects on discriminated-against groups. The use of dual standards in making selection decisions is a case in point. The admission criteria for the dominant cultural group are ranked for each criterion, and a decision is made. The same procedure is followed independently for minority group members. The *Bakke* v. *Regents of the University of California* (regarding nonminority admission to medical school) opinion has pointed out the potential legal problems in using a quota system for making educational or training decisions. In addition to the need for guidelines for the use of tests in employment selection and admission decisions, additional measurement issues can be traced to the use of test data to allocate funds for educational programs. The economic implications of the "truth in testing" legislation now in effect in the state of New York with regard to tests used for college admission—where copies of the tests must be made available to examinees—are staggering. Beyond the obvious economic effect is the influence on the test security of external testing programs and test validity. The spate of well-intentioned state and federal legislation is aimed at curbing abuses of tests. It would probably be best if the testing profession could police its own ranks, but what procedures are available for curbing the misuses of educational and psychological tests? There is, of course, now a legal precedent requiring proof of validity for tests used for selection purposes. Tightening state licensing and certification laws for those who are charged with the responsibility of administering and scoring tests is another avenue for improvement. Voluntary restrictions on the sale and distribution of tests by test publishers is yet another possibility. Perhaps the most powerful pressure for improved testing practices can be exerted within the profession. Preservice and in-service training programs should be expanded and updated.

As Bersoff (1981) points out, all the legal hassles and harassment have not been without some redeeming social consequences. Public and professional awareness to sensitive testing issues has been addressed, accountability has been reaffirmed, and needed research stimulated. But perhaps more important is the underscoring of the use of already acceptable test development procedures and standards (American Psychological Association et al., 1985).

Minimum Competency Testing: Be Prepared for Legal Attacks

Like any good Boy or Girl Scout will tell you, in order to survive you need to be prepared. Fisher (1980) has cautioned that if you are designing and implementing a minimum competency testing program, for example, where tests are used to certify academic performance, you may face legal challenges on several fronts. You need to have a well-designed program, one which meets the highest professional standards. It is particularly critical for minimum competency exams used in the public schools to be of the highest quality as they frequently are used as exit exams from high school. In addition, some school systems also use them to help make grade-to-grade promotion decisions.

Much controversy and several significant legal battles have been joined over the installation of minimum competency testing programs. The chief claims for such programs are the establishment of egalitarian and uniform standards. Minimum competencies are perceived as representing realistic goals for educational programs under local control. On the negative side are such factors as long-term startup and phase-in time, the possibility of the discriminatory use of the tests, the control and setting of standards, overemphasis on minimums with a corresponding deemphasis on maximums, and curricular concerns surrounding what the treatment should be for those who fail, that is, when and how remediation should take place.

Many test development issues present during the design and construction stage of any test are amplified for a minimum competency test. Chief among these is the question of whether test items match both curriculum and instructional objectives; in other words, do the test items measure not only the professed educational goals of the system, but also what is actually taught? The demonstration of acceptable types and levels of reliability is also important. It is particularly crucial that the developer of a minimum competency test be able to demonstrate that the test is measuring lasting general characteristics of the examinee.

Test security may also be an issue as many public groups, the board of education, special interest groups, and/or the media may exert political pressure on the local systems or state board of education to release the test items for public perusal. The Freedom of Information Act and "sunshine" laws can also be invoked. The adverse effect on the usefulness of postrelease data is obvious. Needless to say, it would behoove anyone involved in developing or implementing a minimum competency testing program to work closely with an attorney at all times, document all steps used in the development of the instrumentation, and make sure that sound and acceptable practices are used at all stages of instrument development and application.

What procedures are available for curbing the misuses of educational and psychological tests? Greater adherence to the recommendations of state and national professional organizations must be secured.

Monitoring of Testing Practices by Professional Organizations

The kinds of ethical responsibilities that need to be assumed by those engaged in testing are illustrated by sets or collections of principles published by various organizations where the use of tests represents a major professional responsibility.

Ethical Principles of Psychologists

The American Psychological Association (1981) has published a set of principles that helps guide both the practitioner and the consumer of psychological services. The original 10 principles deal with such diverse but critical areas as responsibility, competence, confidentiality, and research with human subjects. A principle titled

"Assessment Techniques" describes guidelines related to such basic issues as reliability, validity, and administration. Specific recommendations are as follows:

1. In using assessment techniques, psychologists respect the right of clients to have full explanations of the nature and purpose of the techniques in language the clients can understand, unless an explicit exception to this right has been agreed upon in advance. When the explanations are to be provided by others, psychologists establish procedures for ensuring the adequacy of these explanations.

2. Psychologists responsible for the development and standardization of psychological tests and other assessment techniques utilize established scientific procedures and observe the relevant APA standards.

3. In reporting assessment results, psychologists indicate any reservations that exist regarding validity or reliability because of the circumstances of the assessment or the inappropriateness of the norms for the person tested. Psychologists strive to ensure that the results of assessments and their interpretations are not misused by others.

4. Psychologists recognize that assessment results may become obsolete. They make every effort to avoid and prevent the misuse of obsolete measures.

5. Psychologists offering scoring and interpretation services are able to produce appropriate evidence for the validity of the programs and procedures used in arriving at interpretations. The public offering of an automated interpretation service is considered a professional-to-professional consultation. Psychologists make every effort to avoid misuse of assessment reports.

6. Psychologists do not encourage or promote the use of psychological assessment techniques by inappropriately trained or otherwise unqualified persons through teaching, sponsorship, or supervision.

Standards for Educational and Psychological Testing

A second set of guidelines that have been developed to help both the producer and the consumer of educational and psychological tests are the *Standards* (American Psychological Association et al., 1985). The *Standards for Educational and Psychological Testing*, which first appeared in 1954, represent an outstanding example of how a profession can monitor its own behavior and positively influence technological practices. Although they lack the mechanism for enforcement, the *Standards* represent best accepted professional practice in the areas of test development and application. Below is an outline of the *Standards* categories.

Part I Technical Standards for Test Construction and Evaluation

1. Validity
2. Reliability and Errors of Measurement
3. Test Development and Revision
4. Scaling, Norming, Score Comparability, and Equating
5. Test Publications: Technical Manuals and User's Guides

Part II Professional Standards for Test Use

6. General Principles of Test Use
7. Clinical Testing
8. Educational Testing and Psychological Testing in the Schools
9. Test Use in Counseling
10. Employment Testing
11. Professional and Occupational Licensure and Certification
12. Program Evaluation

Part III Standards for Particular Applications

13. Testing Linguistic Minorities
14. Testing People Who Have Handicapping Conditions

Part IV Standards for Administrative Procedures

15. Test Administration, Scoring, and Reporting
16. Protecting the Rights of Test Takers

The *Standards* have three levels of requirements: Primary, Secondary, and Conditional. *Primary Standards* are those that must be in place before a test is operational. These criteria are essential. *Secondary Standards* are those that are highly desirable, but may be beyond reasonable expectation. As one might expect *Conditional Standards* are peculiar to particular situations, and vary according to the application.

Although aimed primarily at commercially available so-called "standardized" tests, the *Standards* have many applications to classroom teacher-made tests, particularly as regards the developmental process (Frisbie & Friedman, 1987).

Following is a sample Standard from the section Reliability and Errors of Measurement (American Psychological Association et al., 1985, pp. 20–21).

> **Standard 2.3:** Each method of estimating a reliability that is reported shall be defined clearly and expressed in terms of variance components, correlation coefficients, standard errors of measurement, percentages of correct decisions, or equivalent statistics. The conditions under which the reliability estimate was obtained and the situations to which it may be applicable should also be explained clearly. (Primary)

Comment: Because there are many ways of estimating reliability, each influenced by different sources of measurement error, it is unacceptable to say simply, "The reliability of test X is .90." A better statement is, "Based on the correlation between alternate test forms A and C administered on successive days to a sample of 100 tenth-grade students from a middle-class suburban public school in New York, the alternate form reliability is estimated to be .90, with an approximate 95% confidence interval of (.85–.93)."

A Code of Fair Testing Practices in Education

In 1986 a Joint Committee on Testing Practices (JCTP) was formed with representatives from the American Educational Research Association, American Psychological Association, and the National Council on Measurement in Education, American Association for Counseling and Development/Association for Measurement and Evaluation in Counseling and Development, and the American Speech-Language-Hearing Association. JCTP was to develop guidelines for use in protecting the rights of test takers of standardized tests. The resulting *Code* of the Joint Committee on Testing Practices specified essential principles of good practice and the obligations of those who develop, administer, and use educational tests. The *Code* is organized into four areas (a) Developing/Selecting Tests, (b) Interpreting Scores, (c) Striving for Fairness, and (d) Informing Test Takers. The *Code* serves to amplify and supplement the *Standards,* and was created to meet the needs of professionals *and* the general public. See box for the *Code* in its entirety.

National Commission on Testing and Public Policy

It is estimated that testing in our public schools involves 20 million school days and requires an expenditure of perhaps somewhere between 700 and 900 million dollars a year. Because of this amount of time, effort, and money being expended on testing, a three-year study was undertaken of testing practices with a view to making recommendations for significant changes (National Commission on Testing and Public Policy [NCME], 1990). Among the major current deficiencies identified in current testing practice were the following:

Tests may mislead as indicators of performance.
Testing can result in unfairness.
There is too much educational testing.
Testing practices can undermine social policies.
Tests are subject to insufficient public accountability.

The reforms called for are summarized in the following recommendations.

1. Testing policies and practices must be reoriented to promote the development of all human talent.
2. Testing programs should be redirected from overreliance on multiple-choice tests toward alternative forms of assessment.
3. Test scores should be used only when they differentiate on the basis of characteristics relevant to the opportunity being allocated.
4. The more test scores disproportionately deny opportunities to minorities the greater the need to show that the tests measure characteristics relevant to the opportunities being allocated.

5. Test scores and implied measures should not be used alone to make important decisions about individuals, groups, or institutions; in the allocation of opportunities, individuals' past performance and relevant experience must be considered.
6. More efficient and effective assessment strategies are needed to hold institutions accountable.
7. The enterprise of testing must be subjected to greater public accountability.
8. Research and development programs must be expanded to create assessments that promote the development of talents of all our people.

CODE OF FAIR TESTING PRACTICES IN EDUCATION

A Developing/Selecting Appropriate Tests*

Test developers should provide the information that test users need to select appropriate tests.

Test Developers Should:

1. Define what each test measures and what the test should be used for. Describe the population(s) for which the test is appropriate.
2. Accurately represent the characteristics, usefulness, and limitations of tests for their intended purposes.
3. Explain relevant measurement concepts as necessary for clarity at the level of detail that is appropriate for the intended audience(s).
4. Describe the process of test development. Explain how the content and skills to be tested were selected.
5. Provide evidence that the test meets its intended purpose(s).
6. Provide either representative samples or complete copies of test questions, directions, answer sheets, manuals, and score reports to qualified users.
7. Indicate the nature of the evidence obtained concerning the appropriateness of each test for groups of different racial, ethnic, or linguistic backgrounds who are likely to be tested.
8. Identify and publish any specialized skills needed to administer each test and to interpret scores correctly.

Test users should select tests that meet the purpose for which they are to be used and that are appropriate for the intended test-taking populations.

Test Users Should:

1. First define the purpose for testing and the population to be tested. Then, select a test for that purpose and that population based on a thorough review of the available information.
2. Investigate potentially useful sources of information, in addition to test scores, to corroborate the information provided by tests.
3. Read the materials provided by test developers and avoid using tests for which unclear or incomplete information is provided.
4. Become familiar with how and when the test was developed and tried out.
5. Read independent evaluations of a test and of possible alternative measures. Look for evidence required to support the claims of test developers.
6. Examine specimen sets, disclosed tests or samples of questions, directions, answer sheets, manuals, and score reports before selecting a test.
7. Ascertain whether the test content and norms group(s) or comparison group(s) are appropriate for the intended test takers.
8. Select and use only those tests for which the skills needed to administer the test and interpret scores correctly are available.

*Many of the statements in the Code refer to the selection of existing tests. However, in customized testing programs test developers are engaged to construct new tests. In those situations, the test development process should be designed to help ensure that the completed tests will be in compliance with the Code.

Reprinted by permission. Copyright © 1988 by the Joint Committee on Testing Practices, c/o American Psychological Association, 1200 Seventeenth St., N.W., Washington, DC 20036

B Interpreting Scores

Test developers should help users interpret scores correctly.

Test Developers Should:

9. Provide timely and easily understood score reports that describe test performance clearly and accurately. Also explain the meaning and limitations of reported scores.
10. Describe the population(s) represented by any norms or comparison group(s), the dates the data were gathered, and the process used to select the samples of test takers.
11. Warn users to avoid specific, reasonably anticipated misuses of test scores.
12. Provide information that will help users follow reasonable procedures for setting passing scores when it is appropriate to use such scores with the test.
13. Provide information that will help users gather evidence to show that the test is meeting its intended purpose(s).

Test users should interpret scores correctly.

Test Users Should:

9. Obtain information about the scale used for reporting scores, the characteristics of any norms or comparison group(s), and the limitations of the scores.
10. Interpret scores taking into account any major differences between the norms or comparison groups and the actual test takers. Also take into account any differences in test administration practices or familiarity with the specific questions in the test.
11. Avoid using tests for purposes not specifically recommended by the test developer unless evidence is obtained to support the intended use.
12. Explain how any passing scores were set and gather evidence to support the appropriateness of the scores.
13. Obtain evidence to help show that the test is meeting its intended purpose(s).

C Striving for Fairness

Test developers should strive to make tests that are as fair as possible for test takers of different races, gender, ethnic backgrounds, or handicapping conditions.

Test Developers Should:

14. Review and revise test questions and related materials to avoid potentially insensitive content or language.
15. Investigate the performance of test takers of different races, gender, and ethnic backgrounds when samples of sufficient size are available. Enact procedures that help to ensure that differences in performance are related primarily to the skills under assessment rather than to irrelevant factors.
16. When feasible, make appropriately modified forms of tests or administration procedures available for test takers with handicapping conditions. Warn test users of potential problems in using standard norms with modified tests or administration procedures that result in non-comparable scores.

Test users should select tests that have been developed in ways that attempt to make them as fair as possible for test takers of different races, gender, ethnic backgrounds, or handicapping conditions.

Test Users Should:

14. Evaluate the procedures used by test developers to avoid potentially insensitive content or language.
15. Review the performance of test takers of different races, gender, and ethnic backgrounds when samples of sufficient size are available. Evaluate the extent to which performance differences may have been caused by inappropriate characteristics of the test.
16. When necessary and feasible, use appropriately modified forms of tests or administration procedures for test takers with handicapping conditions. Interpret standard norms with care in the light of the modifications that were made.

D Informing Test Takers

Under some circumstances, test developers have direct communication with test takers. Under other circumstances, test users communicate directly with test takers. Whichever group communicates directly with test takers should provide the information described below.

Test Developers or Test Users Should:

17. When a test is optional, provide test takers or their parents/guardians with information to help them judge whether the test should be taken, or if an available alternative to the test should be used.

18. Provide test takers the information they need to be familiar with the coverage of the test, the types of question formats, the directions, and appropriate test-taking strategies. Strive to make such information equally available to all test takers.

Under some circumstances, test developers have direct control of tests and test scores. Under other circumstances, test users have such control. Whichever group has direct control of tests and test scores should take the steps described below.

Test Developers or Test Users Should:

19. Provide test takers or their parents/guardians with information about rights test takers may have to obtain copies of tests and completed answer sheets, retake tests, have tests rescored, or cancel scores.

20. Tell test takers or their parents/guardians how long scores will be kept on file and indicate to whom and under what circumstances test scores will or will not be released.

21. Describe the procedures that test takers or their parents/guardians may use to register complaints and have problems resolved.

The concern for the development of competent training in construction and responsible use of tests is not new. The recommendations reinforce the need to maintain a vigil related to such problem areas as the abuse and misuse of tests, lack of criterion-related validity, bias, measurement fallibility, and lack of accountability. With regard to accountability it should be noted that if the profession doesn't take the responsibility and leadership, the public will. The cry for renewed energies and resources to be found on important testing issues should be heeded around the country.

Qualifications and Standards for Test Purchasers

Another effort to regulate test purchase and dissemination, and to some extent, test use has also been mounted by a subcommittee of the Joint Committee on Testing Practices (Eyde, Moreland, & Robertson, 1988). The Test User Qualification Working Group has undertaken three studies which (a) described the functions and activities of test users by undertaking a job analysis, (b) identified the elements of good test use and comprehensive requirements for engaging in good testing practices, and (c) developed model test purchaser forms and a model test qualification form. The focus of qualification was on knowledge and experience of test users, rather than relying solely on job titles, academic credentials, state licensure or certification, or professional association membership. Following are the seven general clusters of potential test misuse factors.

Test Use Factors	*Illustrative Subelements*
1. Comprehensive Assessment	Follow-up to get facts from psychosocial history to integrate with test scores, as part of interpretation.
2. Proper Test Use	Acceptance of responsibility of competent use of the test.
3. Psychometric Knowledge	Consideration of standard error of measurement.
4. Maintaining Integrity of Test Results	Making clear that cutoff scores imposed for placement in special programs for the gifted are questionable because they disregard measurement error.
5. Accuracy of Scoring	Using checks on scoring accuracy.
6. Appropriate Use of Norms	Not assuming that a norm for a given job (or group) applies to a different job (or group).
7. Interpretive Feedback	Willingness and ability to give interpretation and guidance to test takers, in counseling.

These factors were derived from an examination of 86 test misuse practices. These factors were in turn related to 50 commercial tests (e.g., group educational tests, individual intelligence tests, objective personality tests, readiness tests, etc.). All of the above information was integrated into a set of suggested qualifications to be used by test publishers to regulate the purchase of materials and services. The qualifications include:

1. Level of training
2. Professional credentials
3. Academic courses
4. Practicism/internship experience
5. Continuing education (workshops, seminars, conferences)
6. Reading of professional journals

Such a list would have to be modified by a publisher depending on the nature of the test in question and the consequences of its use.

It can be seen, then, that the profession is concerned about the many issues surrounding the development and use of tests in all areas of human endeavor. Despite the shortcomings of some tests and users, tests have proven to be valuable educational tools. As Angoff and Anderson (1963) have noted:

> For both human and practical reasons, the standardized test is a necessary outcome of the philosophy of a modern democratic society in which large masses of individuals, competing for educational awards or simply seeking better self-understanding, assemble for an objective, unbiased evaluation of their abilities. No other method that we know of today can provide measurement for the tremendous numbers of individuals who demand objective consideration of their talents. Certainly no other method that we know of today can accomplish this measurement as equitably as the standardized test.

Content Review Statements

1. The testing profession is continually subject to criticism, some of which is justified and most of which is not.
2. Many of the criticisms leveled at tests and testing would be more appropriate if aimed at the users of tests.
3. Criticisms of testing revolve around the issues of:
   a. Discrimination against minority and disadvantaged groups.
   b. Imperfect predictability.
   c. Inflexible classification of individuals.
   d. Implied measurement of innate characteristics.
   e. Potentially harmful social, educational, and psychological effects.
   f. Potential dangers in controlling curricula.
   g. Invasion of privacy.
4. The majority of the problems posed by the use of educational and psychological tests can be overcome with common sense, intelligent application, establishment of standards, and education.
5. Most of the criticisms of external tests can be stilled by the cooperative efforts of the testing profession, school administrators, college faculties, test publishers, and admissions officers.
6. Common misapprehensions about tests rest on the false beliefs that:
   a. Tests are perfectly reliable.
   b. Test norms constitute standards.
   c. Intelligence and achievement are separable.
   d. Tests measure only recall of specific facts.
7. College admission and scholarship testing programs have been criticized for their:
   a. Duplication.
   b. Lack of demonstrated relevance.
   c. Cost.
   d. Susceptibility to coaching.
   e. Susceptibility to invidious interschool comparisons.
   f. Possible adverse psychological effects on examinees.
8. Recent court decisions have required that educational and psychological tests, particularly those bearing on employment, be of proven validity.
9. Ideally, the use of validated tests should work to reduce discrimination in employment and educational situations.

10. Through the development of guidelines, codes, and ethical standards, professional organizations are making great strides toward eliminating the unethical practices associated with test use.
11. Documentation of test development procedures can help prepare for legal attacks.
12. Professional organizations have established important guidelines and standards for test developers to protect test users.
13. Individuals involved in test administration should maintain a respectful attitude toward test instruments, individuals, and the setting in which the tests are to be applied.
14. The intelligent use of tests constitutes one of the most powerful, fair, comprehensive, and democratic methods of improving the quality of life for individuals and society.

Speculations

1. What way could the *Code of Fair Testing Practices* have an impact on your professional life?
2. In what way have any of the legal challenges to testing had an impact on your professional life? Do you feel such challenges are justified?
3. Do you feel the testing profession is adequately monitoring itself? If yes, how; if not, how can it be improved?
4. Which criticisms of tests and testing are justified in your mind and which are not?
5. What are some ways tests and measurements can have positive influences in our schools?
6. What are some dangers that we have to be on the lookout for when using educational tests and measurements?
7. What are some consequences of *not* using tests and measurements in our schools?
8. What topics would you include in a speech to a group of parents on *The Importance of Tests and Measurements in Our Schools?* How would it be different for a group of students? A group of teachers? A group of community business leaders? The Board of Education?
9. What role, if any, should the Federal government have in controlling the testing industry?

Suggested Readings

Educational Testing Service. (1980). *An approach for identifying and minimizing bias in standardized tests: A set of guidelines.* Princeton, NJ: Educational Testing Service. This excellent set of "standards" deal with all aspects of test development from item writing to scoring. Language and cultural experience factors are of critical concern.

Kellaghan, T., Madaus, G. F., & Airasian, P. W. (1982). *The effects of standardized testing.* Boston: Klumer-Nijhoff.

Messick, S. (1981). Evidence and ethics in the evaluation of tests. *Educational Researcher, 10*(9), 9–20.

Robinson, C. M. (1988). Improving education through the application of measurement and research: A practitioner's perspective. *Applied Measurement in Education, 1*(1), 53–65. A representative of the public schools calls for collaboration to improve the nation's schools.

Chapter 3

Measurement and the Teaching-Learning Process

Teaching and Learning—Before Testing
A Model for Instructional Development
Measurement—Driven Instruction: Pros and Cons
Teaching Practices—Evaluation Practices
Measurement Competencies Needed by Teachers
Teaching and Testing: Some Pitfalls
Content Review Statements
Speculations
Suggested Readings

Teachers and educators are decision makers. Decisions are made about what and how to teach, when, and to whom. A teacher may make several hundred instructional decisions an hour in a typical classroom. Rational decisions are based on relevant data. Using an integrated educational assessment system can help provide that relevant data (Airasian & Madaus, 1983).

Teaching and Learning—Before Testing

In the beginning there were educational goals and objectives to be accomplished. Teacher and student work *together* to accomplish these objectives. Both need information on how well they are doing. They need to know if they have "arrived" or need to "change trains" to continue on toward the desired educational destinations. There are alternative modes of educational travel. After many decades of research on the teaching-learning process no universal and definitive answers to the question, "What is the most effective way to teach?" are available. Some guidelines for general approaches are available. Based on their review of the relevant research literature Brophy and Good (1986) concluded that student achievement is significantly enhanced if:

1. The teacher is actively involved in actual teaching or supervising learning.
2. There are frequent lessons (for total class or individuals).
3. The teacher (a) presents information, (b) develops concepts through lecture, (c) requires students to recite or respond to questions, (d) provides feedback, (e) manages and monitors limited seat work, and (f) provides feedback and reteaching as necessary.

Brophy and Good (1986) have found that this kind of direct instruction is particularly helpful in increasing the achievement of low ability-low achieving students.

A similar set of teaching activities that has been shown to be effective in enhancing learning has been described by Rosenshine (1985). They include the following six functions: (a) daily review of previous day's work, (b) presentation of new content/skills, (c) student practice on new materials, (d) feedback and corrections, (e) independent practice, and (f) weekly and monthly review with reteaching as necessary. A detailed list of instructional functions that research and practice support as having a positive impact on student learning is presented in Table 3-1. Some experts refer to this approach as *direct instruction.*

Whenever feedback is required measurement can make a contribution. It may be in the form of formal tests or informal assessments. The instructional situations just described basically relate to day-to-day activity. Periodically the teacher (principal, superintendent) will also want to step back and take snapshots of the larger picture of learning. This might be at the individual, classroom, school, or system level.

A Model for Instructional Development

One simply does not walk into a classroom and begin teaching. As with any complex process, planning must precede implementation. Instructional planning tasks can and should be approached systematically. Many theories of teaching (Joyce & Weil, 1986; Snelbecker, 1985) and models for the design of instruction (Bass & Dills, 1984; Gagné & Briggs 1979; Reigeluth, 1983) have been developed. Those readers who have gone through a teacher preparation program will undoubtedly recall course work related to instructional strategies. If they were lucky enough to be at an "enlightened" school or college of education, they also would have been exposed to coursework in educational measurement. A comprehensive model of the instructional development process should interrelate both the teaching process skills and measurement. Such a system has been created by Dick and Carey (1990). The basic components of their system are graphically presented in Figure 3-1. The solid lines represent direct sequence or action, and the dotted lines represent the feedback process: feedback in the sense that information (data, measurements) is used for decision making, that is, to revise an objective or learning experience.

It is interesting to note that the major concepts of assessment, measurement (tests), and evaluation discussed in Chapter 1 are prominently evident in the Dick-Carey model. Obviously measures of expected outcomes need to be developed—in

Table 3-1 Instructional Functions

1. Daily review, checking previous day's work, and reteaching (if necessary):
   Checking homework · feedbk
   Reteaching areas where there were student errors
2. Presenting new content/skills:
   Providing overview
   Proceeding in small steps (if necessary), but at a rapid pace
   If necessary, giving detailed or redundant instructions and explanations
   Phasing in new skills while old skills are being mastered
3. Initial student practice:
   High frequency of questions and overt student practice (from teacher and materials)
   Prompts are provided during initial learning (when appropriate)
   All students have a chance to respond and receive feedback
   Teacher checks for understanding by evaluating student responses
   Continue practice until students are firm
   Success rate of 80% or higher during initial learning
4. Feedback and correctives (and recycling of instruction, if necessary):
   Feedback to students, particularly when they are correct but hesitant
   Student errors provide feedback to the teacher that corrections and/or reteaching is necessary
   Corrections by simplifying question, giving clues, explaining or reviewing steps, or reteaching last steps
   When necessary, reteach using smaller steps
5. Independent practice so that students are firm and automatic:
   Seatwork
   Unitization and automaticity (practice to overlearning)
   Need for procedure to ensure student engagement during seatwork (i.e., teacher or aide monitoring)
   95% correct or higher
6. Weekly and monthly reviews:
   Reteaching, if necessary

Rosenshine, B. (1985). Teaching functions in instructional programs. *The Elementary School Journal, 83*(4), 335–351.

this case, criterion-referenced measures. In addition, a formative and summative evaluation of learning experience (unit or course) should be undertaken. Assessment is the integrating construct. Consideration is given to entry behaviors, together with measurement and evaluation of existing behaviors. Following are brief descriptions of the components of the Dick-Carey system.

Identifying Instructional Goals. The old adage "If you don't know where you're going, you may end up somewhere else," is as true in education as it is in vacationing. We need maps to guide us. Instructional goals can serve as desired locations on that map. Each

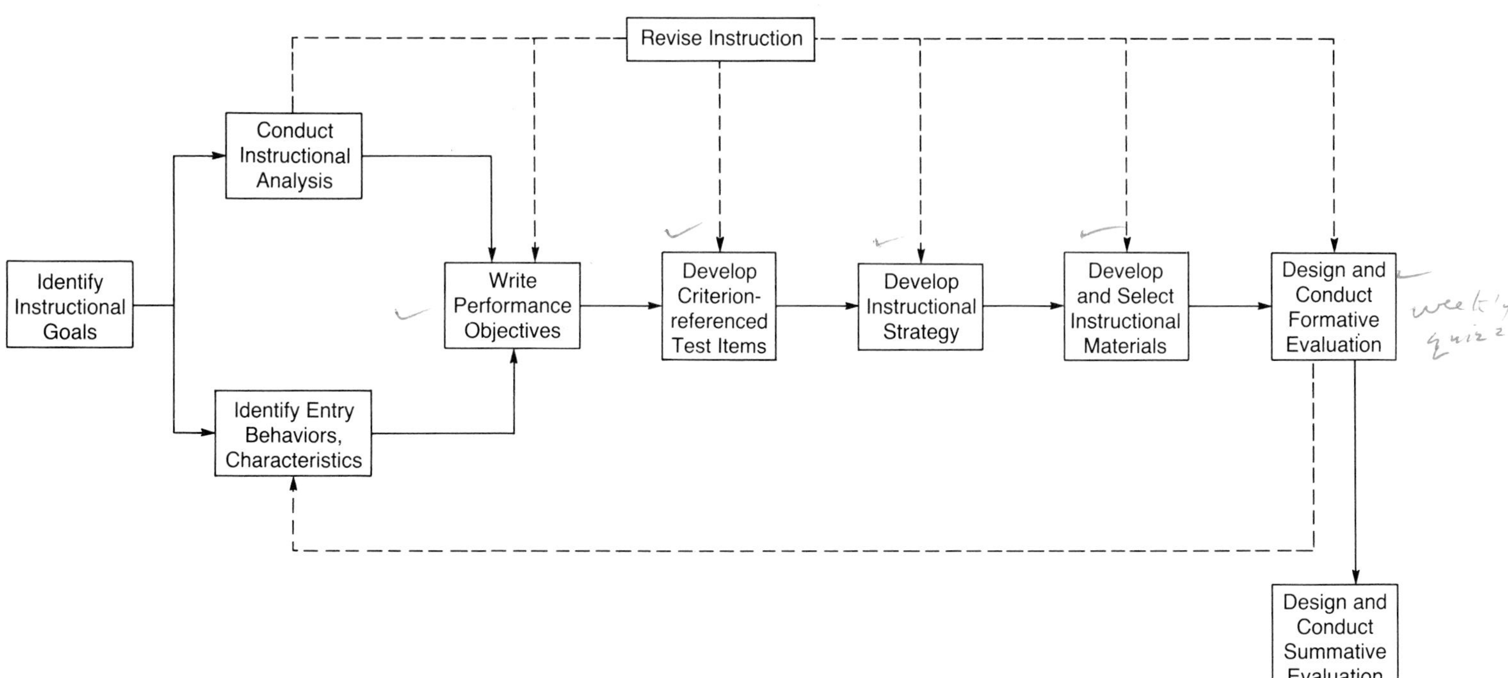

Figure 3-1

Instructional development model (Dick and Carey, 1990)

teacher must ask, "What do I want my students to be able to do at the end of this instructional experience?" It might be something so simple as being able to recognize and write the letters of the alphabet, or as complex as conducting a quantitative and qualitative analysis of an unknown chemical substance. A needs assessment may be undertaken, or goals may be "given" by the county or state curriculum guides. See Chapter 4 for an expanded discussion of this topic.

Conducting an Instructional Analysis. Once you know where you want to go, or where you and your students together will travel, you need to assess what it will take to get there. Each learning task needs to have the appropriate subordinate skills identified.

Identifying Entry Behavior and Characteristics. The subordinate skills may need to be developed or they already may be possessed in varying degrees by different students. This analysis is basically a "prerequisite" evaluation. Are there special needs of the learner that must be considered in designing the instructional activities?

Writing Performance Objectives. It's time to get truly operational. The old-fashioned term for a performance objective is "behavioral objective" (BO). BOs have been around for a long time and help us specify exactly what changes we wish to bring about in our students.

Developing Criterion-Referenced Test Items. The key criterion for any test item, as was noted in Chapter 1, is *relevance,* that is, the match between item (or task) and performance objective. Creating good measurements is a very difficult job!

Developing an Instructional Strategy. Given goals and objectives, and taking into account student entry level, a decision is made as to what would be the most effective media to be used. Consideration must be given to the optional conditions for learning (Gagné, 1985). These would include preinstruction activities, method of presentation, practice, feedback, and evaluation.

Developing and Selecting Instruction. One may develop or create a new instructional method or technique, select one from commercial sources, or borrow from colleagues. Such factors as time, cost, number of students to be served, and obviously nature of behavior to be shaped will influence development vs. selection decision.

Designing and Conducting a Formative Evaluation. The focus here is on how to improve the instruction. The "instruction" might be as small as a unit on fractions, or as large as a curriculum. A variety of data-types should be used so as to reflect different aspects of the instruction, for example, objectives (good–bad), instructional material (understandable–not understandable), instruction (effective–ineffective).

Revise Instruction. Here is the key to the process. Good instruction is iterative. Use data to make rational decisions about how to improve that which ye have wrought. Gather data on how effective the instruction was, yes, but also about how the students felt about the instruction. Did they like it in general, or what of it in particular was satisfying?

Revision could go all the way back to the objectives strategy selected, or focus only on the effectiveness of the materials.

Conduct a Summative Evaluation. After revisions are made and the instruction is implemented, another evaluation can be undertaken. Although the evaluation is summative the resulting data again could be used formatively, as to compare and contrast this final version with a competing approach. Critical at this stage, as at the previous one, are applications of standards and criteria. See Chapter 16 for examples.

Summative and Formative Evaluation

The focus on the relationship between instruction and evaluation, and on the potential contribution of evaluation to the improvement of quality and quantity in education as argued in the foregoing discussion, has been underscored by Scriven's (1967) distinction between "summative" and "formative" evaluation. He notes that the goal of evaluation is always the same, that is, to determine the worth and value of something. That "something" may be a microscope, a unit in biology, a science curriculum, or an entire educational system. Depending upon the role the value judgments are to play, evaluation data may be used developmentally or in a summary way. In the case of an overall decision, the role of evaluation is summative. An end-of-course assessment would be considered summative. Summative evaluation may employ absolute or comparative standards and judgments.

Formative evaluation, on the other hand, is almost exclusively aimed at improving the educational experience or product during its developmental phases. A key element in the formative technique is feedback. Information is gathered during the developmental phase with an eye to improving the total product. The evaluation activities associated with the development of *Science—A Process Approach*, the elementary science curriculum supported by the National Science Foundation and managed by the American Association for the Advancement of Science during the several years of the program's development, were used in centers throughout the country. Summer writing sessions were then held at which tryout data were fed back to the developers. A superior product resulted. The summative-formative distinction among kinds of evaluation reflects differences in intent, rather than different methodologies.

The use of evaluation in this formative way almost implies that evaluation may be viewed as a kind of research effort, which it is. The importance of the use of measurement data is evident in the Dick-Carey model outlined in Figure 3-1. There is, of course, a danger that the measurement data may play a too important role in determining the content and methods of instruction.

Measurement-Driven Instruction: Pros and Cons

Tests are being used extensively in society, particularly in education. Many say they are being used too extensively—that we have gone test-crazy in the schools. With any tool there is admittedly a danger of overuse or misuse. But the potential and actual benefits of using tests in education, particularly in competency-based instruction, outweigh the dangers, particularly if intelligent use is made of relevant data. Although all the answers are not in, Measurement-Driven Instruction (MDI) represents one viable approach to increasing achievement. Measurement-Driven Instruction occurs when "high-stakes tests," usually promotion, exit, or state instructional quality/accountability tests, are allowed to influence the instructional program that prepares students to take such tests. The approach shares major philosophies and methodologies with our old friend "mastery learning" (Kulik, Kulik, & Bangert-Downs, 1990).

One of the frequently voiced criticisms of commercial tests or tests other than classroom ones is that they exert an unwarranted, unwanted, and uneven influence on the curriculum. But as Popham, Cruse, Smart, Sandifer, & Williams (1985) have noted:

> [A] testing program if deliberately designed to do so, can become a major force in improving an instructional program. If the assessment devices used are criterion-referenced tests that have been deliberately constructed to illuminate instructional decision-making or if there are significant instructional consequences tied to pupils' test performances, then the testing program will drive the instructional program.

But some claim that it is not a good idea to allow tests to drive instruction (Bracey, 1987). Some of the criticisms of measurement-driven instruction (MDI), together with rebuttals are presented below (Popham, 1987a).

Criticism	*Issue*	*Rebuttal*
MDI will lead to narrow focus on little bits and pieces of content. Trivial outcomes will be taught as that's what tests test.	Curricular Fragmentation	High level outcomes can and are measured with objective tests. All tests, e.g., CRT do not just measure minimum competency. Control of what outcomes are measured is in the hands of educators not testers.
Tests cause important objectives to be eliminated from the curriculum.	Curricular Deflection	Tests are only "samples" of behavior. Value judgments must be made. Trying to measure all important outcomes would *increase* the amount of testing.

	Curricular Stagnation	
MDI tends to hold to the *status quo* as that's what is on the tests.		As the curriculum is revised so are the tests. Good tests can illuminate what is going on in the schools.
	Teacher Inflexibility	
Having a restricted curriculum causes teacher to only teach for the tests.		Teachers are likely to be forced to find new and creative ways to teach important outcomes.
	Reduced Student Aspiration	
Students will only study for the tests.		Education is more than what is on tests. Good teachers will not allow students to focus exclusively on test objectives.
	Role of Testing	
Tests should come after instruction for summative purposes.		Tests provide a valuable service by helping educators conceptualize what they are trying to accomplish. If a test is properly constructed and, in fact, is an operational definition of what is to be accomplished, then it can become a goal unto itself. Don't overlook the formative role of tests.

It is probably the case that MDI is best conceptualized at the school system level. This allows for sufficient abstraction of objectives so as not to particularize objectives. At this level there is still plenty of room for teacher creativity at the classroom level. Popham (1987a) suggests that a properly conceived MDI system will include (a) criterion-referenced measures, (b) defensible content, (c) an efficient number of objectives/goals, (d) guidelines for instructional development, and (e) institutional support (e.g., staff development activities). MDI helps drive out wasted time where classrooms are choked with wasted and irrelevant activities.

Does MDI work? Yes! Popham, Cruse, Rankin, Sandifer, and Williams (1985) report data at both local and state levels showing how performance with regard to in-class reading and math have dramatically increased since competency (high stakes) testing was introduced. Other indicators such as reduction of dropout rates and improved student and teacher attitudes toward school, in addition to overall improvement in achievement, suggest that increased scores can, in part, be traced to MDI. MDI has been particularly effective with minority students and weaker students (Kulik, Kulik, & Bangert-Downs, 1990).

Teaching Practices—Evaluation Practices

Most educators agree that measurement and evaluation are integral components of the instructional process. Progress toward the achievement of instructional goals must be periodically evaluated if effective teaching and learning are to be accomplished. It is widely recognized that educational objectives and learning experiences are intimately related. It is less apparent to many that objectives, learning experiences, *and* measurement-evaluation activities are also intimately related. It is the interaction of these three elements in a well-planned program of education that best promoted the desired changes in pupil behavior. The intimate relationship of instruction and assessment activities has been well defined by Dressel (1954, pp. 23–24). His listing of the parallel elements in these two activities illustrates their common objectives:

Instruction	*Evaluation*
1. Instruction is effective to the degree that it leads to desired changes in students.	1. Evaluation is effective to the degree that it provides evidence of the extent of changes in students
2. New behavior patterns are best learned by students when the inadequacy of present behavior is understood and the significance of the new behavior patterns thereby made clear.	2. Evaluation is most conducive to learning when it provides for and encourages self-evaluation.
3. New behavior patterns can be more efficiently promoted by teachers who recognize the existing behavior patterns of individual students and the reasons for them.	3. Evaluation is conducive to good instruction when it reveals major types of inadequate behavior and the contributory causes.
4. Learning is encouraged by problems and activities that require thought and/or action by each individual student.	4. Evaluation is most significant in learning when it permits and encourages the exercise of individual initiative.
5. Activities that provide the basis for the teaching and learning of specified behavior are also the most suitable for evoking and evaluating the adequacy of that behavior.	5. Activities or exercises developed for the purpose of evaluating specified behavior are also useful in the teaching and learning of the behavior.

After examining in detail the objectives of both activities, Dressel concludes that they do not really differ in methods or materials. They can be differentiated only when evaluating achievement at the close of a period of instruction.

These demands on the teacher to produce relevant and reliable measuring devices suggest the need for a variety of test construction competencies. Some of these are discussed in the next section.

Measurement Competencies Needed by Teachers

The roles played by teachers are varied and significant. Their instructional and interpersonal skills are vital to the educational development of today's youth. A great number of their instructional skills are related to assessing student progress, both formally and informally. These competencies are critical as they relate directly to the gathering of information needed to make rational instructional decisions.

A committee made up of representatives of four professional organizations (American Association of Colleges of Teacher Education, American Federation of Teachers, National Council on Measurement in Education, and the National Education Association) has recommended a set of seven general assessment competencies needed by an effective teacher (National Council on Measurement in Education, 1990). Below are descriptions of the preliminary *Standards for Teacher Competence in Educational Assessment of Students* and some comments:

Standard	*Comment*
Teachers Should Be Skilled in	
1. Choosing Assessment Methods Appropriate for Instructional Decisions.	1. Criteria which should be considered are technical adequacy, usefulness, convenience, and fairness. A variety of methods should be used and a teacher should know where to obtain information about them.
2. Developing Assessment Methods Appropriate for Instructional Decisions.	2. If high-quality commercial methods are not available, teachers must create them. Methods include: classroom tests, oral exams, rating scales, performance assessments, observation schedules, and questionnaires.
3. Administering, Scoring, and Interpreting the Results of Both Commercially Produced and Teacher Produced Assessment Methods.	3. Knowledge about the common methods of expressing assessments is essential. A large number of quantitative concepts need to be assimilated (e.g., descriptive statistical methods, reliability, validity, etc.).

4. Using Assessment Results in Making Decisions about Individual Students, Planning Instruction, in Developing Curriculum, and in School Improvement.	4. Assessments are valueless unless they are applied at both group and individual levels. Planning is a vital part of the educational process.
5. Developing Pupil Grading Procedures that use Pupil Assessments.	5. Grades and marks should be data-based. Grading, although subjective to a great extent, can be rational, justifiable, and fair. The rules must be the same for everyone.
6. Communicating Assessment Results to Students, Parents, Other Lay Audiences, and Educators.	6. An effective communication should include not only the facts but an indication of the limitations and implications as well. In addition everyone involved must use terminology in the same way.
7. Recognizing and Having Knowledge about Unethical, Illegal, and Inappropriate Assessment.	7. Potential dangers of invasion of privacy and discrimination exist, and these—together with legal and professional ethics—should always be in the forefront of a teacher's mind while planning and implementing assessment tasks.

As one approaches teaching and testing there are some common dangers that must be avoided. To be forewarned is to be forearmed.

Teaching and Testing: Some Pitfalls

There is no doubt that a student feels tension and anxiety before, during, and after a testing experience. This is particularly true if the test is of great consequence to the examinee, that is, in a high-stakes test. Midterms and finals, college entrance exams, and scholarship qualifying exams are examples of tests likely to evoke considerable test anxiety potentially harmful to the student. In the classroom situation, improper tests and use of tests can damage the teacher-student relationship. The misuse of tests stems primarily from two sources: (a) misunderstanding of the proper role of tests, and (b) failure to appreciate the emotional problems posed for some children by any ego-threatening evaluation procedure. Among the potential problems are the following dangers.

1. If a teacher looks upon the norm on a standardized test as a goal to be reached by all children, and criticizes those who fail to meet this rigid standard, the pupils will quite naturally come to think of tests as hurdles rather than as stepping stones to development.

2. If a teacher, in interpreting test results, fails to take into account other relevant information—ability differences, health status, home background, and the like—he or she is likely to render an unjust appraisal of a child's work, which may well have the effect of discouraging or antagonizing the child.

3. If teachers overemphasize tests in the evaluation program, and fail to realize that they cover only a part of the desired outcomes, they run the risk of placing undue emphasis on certain objectives and of confusing pupils as to what they are supposed to be learning.

4. If a teacher habitually uses test results as bases for invidious comparisons among pupils, not only is the pupil-teacher relationship damaged, but also the relationships among the pupils.

5. If a teacher berates or scolds a child because of poor performance on a test, the teacher may be building up unfavorable attitudes toward future testing and learning.

6. If teachers fail to let pupils know how they did on a test, or give any indication of how the testing is related to instructional purposes, it is hard for the pupil to make sense of the procedure.

7. If a teacher is insecure, and feels threatened by the tests, it is almost certain that this attitude will be communicated to the children. If a school or systemwide program is in operation, in the planning of which teachers have had no part, and the purposes of which they do not understand, they obviously will be in no position to make clear to the pupils how the testing is likely to do them any good. If the test results are used as a means of appraising teacher competence, the temptation becomes very strong for the teacher to teach for the tests.

8. If a teacher is unsympathetic to a testing program in which he or she must participate, and makes slighting or sarcastic reference to "these tests that we have to give again," he or she is certainly engendering a poor attitude on the pupil's part; even his or her pupils are shrewd enough to sense, however vaguely, that by such behavior the teacher is abdicating his or her rightful position.

Such common sense procedures as returning test papers as soon as possible, discussing test items with the entire class, and demonstrating to the class the uses of test information help to develop proper student attitudes and a healthy perspective on the place and value of testing in the instructional program. There is no substitute for respect of individual student needs and desires.

Enough philosophy, discussion, background, and theory; it's time to start planning for instrument development.

Content Review Statements

1. Direct instruction can significantly promote achievement, particularly of low-ability students.
2. The systematic development of instructional programs involves the:
   a. Identification of goals
   b. Identification of entry behavior and characteristics
   c. Conducting of an instructional analysis of performance requirements
   d. Writing of performance objectives
   e. Writing of criterion-referenced test items
   f. Development of an instructional strategy
   g. Development and/or selection of instructional materials
   h. Conducting of a formative evaluation
   i. Revision of instruction based on formative evaluation data
   j. Conducting of a summative evaluation
3. Summative evaluation refers to an end of experience assessment.
4. Formative evaluation refers to the use of data through feedback to improve a program during its development.
5. Measurement-driven instruction involves the use of high-stakes tests of educational achievement to highlight student progress and curricular effectiveness.
6. If not properly monitored, measurement-driven instruction can result in fragmentation and trivialization of educational outcomes.
7. Measurement-driven instruction can result in focused, efficient, and effective instruction.
8. The processes of teaching and testing are intimately related.
9. In interpreting test scores to students, the teacher should carefully consider the potential psychological impact of such scores and the many related factors that bear on the meaning of the scores.
10. Students have inalienable rights to an interpretation of their scores.
11. Teachers need to master measurement competencies related to the following skills:
    a. Selecting appropriate methods
    b. Developing appropriate instructional assessment methods
    c. Administering, scoring and interpreting assessment
    d. Applying measurement data in instructional decision making
    e. Establishing pupil grading procedures
    f. Communicating assessment results to relevant audiences
    g. Approaching assessment in legal and ethical manner

Speculations

1. How do tests help enhance learning?
2. How are formative and summative evaluations different? How are they alike?
3. What are the advantages and disadvantages of measurement-driven instruction? Does one outweigh the other?
4. What are the measurement and testing competencies needed by teachers?

5. A parent has challenged the time you spend giving your tests as well as those mandated by the state. How would you respond?

Suggested Readings

Cole, N. S., & Moss, P. A. (1989). Bias in test use. In R. L. Linn (Ed.), *Educational measurement* (3rd ed.). Washington, DC: American Council on Education and the Macmillan Company. Central to this essay is consideration of the impact of different types and sources of bias on test validity.

Crooks, T. J. (1988). The impact of classroom evaluation practices on students. *Review of Educational Research, 58*(4), 438–481. Research data from over 14 fields reflected in 242 references provide nine categories of recommendations.

Linn, R. L. (1983). Testing and instruction: Links and distinction. *Journal of Educational Measurement, 20*, 179–189.

Natriello, G. (1987). The impact of evaluation processes on students. *Educational Psychologist, 22*(2), 155–175. A conceptual framework is presented to view the influence a variety of elements have in the evaluation process.

Nitko, A. J. (1989). Designing tests that are integrated with instruction. In R. L. Linn (Ed.), *Educational measurement* (3rd ed., pp. 447–474). New York: Macmillan.

Bev's Diary

Beverly's stream of consciousness diary continues. . . .

Well, the first class wasn't bad at all. My classmates seem to really be interested in learning how to build and use tests. Dr. Sig Nificant may not look or sound like Richard Burton, but things moved along at a pretty good pace. I never realized how many aspects of our lives are influenced by tests. Almost from the cradle to the grave. It was interesting to learn about the German, French, and English influences on the testing movement here in America. In considering how tests are developed it struck me how similar the process was to our old friend the "Scientific Method"—shades of elementary science. The concept of "educational assessment" is a big and complex one, but seems to make sense relative to what the public schools are trying to accomplish. The tough part is evaluating, making those value judgments about what is good, effective, acceptable, and worthy of merit. I get tense when marking time rolls around.

The media seem to almost weekly carry somebody's criticism of tests and testing on reports of some legal action. I'm sure there's more to it than what meets the public eye. There's also probably some eye-wash as well. As long as we don't get the eyes infected, we'll do O.K.

I found the discussion about legal issues, particularly those surrounding the use of tests in selection as part of external testing programs, to be particularly interesting. It only seems logical that strong legal precedents are needed to protect not only the test user (the innocent?) but the producer as well. After all testing is an expensive activity, both in terms of test-taking time and costs of development—whether a classroom or standardized test. Like so many contemporary educational tools, tests can be abusive (and abused) if placed

Part Two

Planning for Instrument Development

in the hands of the untrained and/or unscrupulous. The fact that educational reform is at the forefront of society's concerns makes fair testing codes extremely important. Let's not use tests for purposes for which they were not created.

I've begun a unit on different forms of verse with my Third Period freshman English class. We got started on limericks (not the naughty kind). The kids love the playing with words and it's a super exercise on synonyms and rhyming. I thought I'd try my hand at some for my testing class.

A really good test needs a plan
The ingredients won't come from a pan
You have to hunt and to scratch
To find the right match
And make the best effort you can.

A pretty young teacher named Hortense
Found that giving tests made her tense
She read in a book
How to mix and to cook
Now all of her tests make good scents.

A bit amateurish, perhaps, but I shared them with some of my classmates and they laughed. I guess that's worth something. It helps reduce stress!

Chapter 4

Specifying Educational Outcomes

Educational achievement can be defined as the extent to which specified objectives are accomplished by individual students. Most classroom measurement is based on objectives-referenced or criterion-referenced approaches to testing, although norm-referenced measurement also has its place. All approaches require objectives. In developing methods to measure the extent of achievement, the test constructor for either classroom or standardized test must specify a detailed set of objectives to guide instrument development. A content domain must be specified. The statement of educational objectives (purposes or goals) in terms of expected pupil changes and outcomes constitutes one of the most important elements in the development of a sound classroom test. Objectives provide guidelines for both instruction and evaluation. Objectives serve as standards against which the final validity or relevance of the items and the test will be judged. The extent to which the test adequately samples from this domain of objectives is referred to as *content validity*.

The present chapter will deal primarily with cognitive (knowledge and thinking) outcomes. Brief consideration will be given psychomotor objectives. Those interested in affective educational outcomes are referred to an extended consideration of attitudes, interests, and values in Chapter 17. The terms *objective* and *outcome* will be used interchangeably throughout the text.

An educational objective may be broadly defined as *a statement of desired change in pupil behavior, knowledge, or affect.* Thus, an objective represents a value judgment, and reflects the purposefulness of education. In another sense it represents a normative concept, a standard to be sought by all students. Some teachers rebel at the notion of "setting standards," but who is in a better position than the teacher to make judgments about what students should learn? It is part of the responsibility of a teacher to delineate learning objectives and activities.

An acceptable objective has two components, a "content" element and a "behavioral" element. It is with respect to the behavioral element that most educational objectives are found wanting. As Mager (1962) points out, instructional objectives are frequently couched in such vague, ambiguous terms as "to know," "to appreciate," "to believe," "to have faith in," and the like, which have very little value in the processes determining units of instruction and directing evaluation. A useful set of objectives is couched in terms of expected changes in overt student behavior.

Types of Outcomes

Many systems are available for classifying educational objectives and outcomes. Dressel (1960), for example, has characterized objectives as (a) achievable or unachievable; (b) explicit or implicit; (c) intrinsic or transcendental; (d) individual or societal; (e) ultimate or immediate; and (f) general or specific. A detailed discussion of the last two types of objectives should help clarify the process of identifying and stating objectives and highlight the importance of objectives in test development.

Ultimate and Immediate Objectives

Ultimate objectives are behaviors ordinarily not observable under classroom conditions. They are important goals of education, but cannot, under normal circumstances, be directly evaluated. Ultimate objectives frequently refer to the projected adult behavior of children and adolescents. Examples of ultimate (broad goal) objectives are sound health habits, intelligent voting behavior, and critical attitudes about literature and the arts.

We must, therefore, approach the evaluation of ultimate objectives by way of immediate (intermediate, approximate) or short-range objectives. A teacher would specify a set of immediate objectives measurable under classroom conditions. It is assumed and inferred that accomplishment of the several short-range objectives is directly related to one or more ultimate objectives. Suppose, for example, that an instructor of a graduate-level course in educational tests and measurements adopted the following ultimate objective: "Upon completion of the course, the student will return to his classroom and write better tests." It is not feasible to gather data on the student's accomplishment of this objective. But data on such immediate objectives as recall of specific guidelines for constructing multiple-choice items, comprehension of the concept of reliability, and ability to apply methods of estimating validity can be used as approximate measures of the achievement of the ultimate objectives.

General and Specific Outcomes

General objectives are similar to ultimate objectives, but often have some comparability over wide grade ranges (e.g., development of reading skills). Specific objectives are usually unique to particular courses, and are stated in terms of expected student behavior. Differences in specific objectives can be traced not only to variations in content but also to relative emphasis on similar objectives across grades or classes. General objectives are useful in providing an overall framework within which the instructional program may be viewed. In addition, they serve as categories or rubrics under which specific objectives may be collected in efficient groupings, which in turn help in the direction of measurement and evaluation efforts.

There is a danger that general objectives may become too global and too influenced by Madison Avenue to be meaningful. Henry Dyer (1967, p. 9) cites the following paragraph from the 1947 report of the President's Commission on Higher Education as an example of "word magic":

> The first goal in education for democracy is the full, rounded, and continuing development of the person. The discovery, training, and utilization of individual talents is of fundamental importance in a free society. To liberate and perfect the intrinsic powers of every citizen is the central purpose of democracy, and its furtherance of individual self-realization is its greatest glory.

As Dyer notes, "it sings to our enthusiasms," but is not couched in terms that permit one to discern when educators have "liberated and perfected the intrinsic powers of a citizen." Nor does this kind of statement help to explain how to calibrate the roundness of his development. Some of us are easier to calibrate than others. But a statement at this level specifying, for instance, that "each student graduating from high school shall, if he desires it, be adequately prepared to enter a vocation" has very concrete implications for vocational education.

Some teachers argue that high-quality instruction can exist without explicit formal statements of the goals of education. This may be true, but assessment cannot be accomplished without a set of operational definitions of instruction. General objectives are usually dictated by community and societal needs, and the teacher is left the task of translating these goals into specific objectives.

It frequently happens that the list of specific objectives for a course of instruction becomes unmanageably long. The breakdown of the instructional program into small but intelligible units has the overriding advantage, however, of greatly facilitating test development. In practice, a compromise between an exhaustive list and a manageable one generally results.

An example of a general objective and related specific objectives will prove helpful at this point:

GENERAL OBJECTIVE: The student will be able to evaluate a test he or she has constructed and administered.

SPECIFIC OBJECTIVES: The student will be able to
a. Determine the difficulty level of test items.
b. Determine the discrimination power of items.
c. Relate test items to the educational objectives.
d. Estimate internal consistency reliability.

This list of specific objectives is obviously not exhaustive, but it should be obvious that it would make item writing (and instruction) a much easier task than would a single general objective.

Developmental and Mastery Objectives

Gronlund and Linn (1990) have proposed a somewhat different classification of objectives. They divide educational outcomes into *mastery* and *developmental* objectives. In a general sense these categories correspond to our immediate versus ultimate classification. At the mastery level are foundational or basic information and skill objectives. These objectives represent minimal essentials that must be mastered before moving to higher levels. The developmental objectives tend to be ones that are more complex and appear later in the study of a subject area or in life. In this regard they are ultimate, in that they tend not to be observed under classroom conditions. Both kinds of objectives are important as are the related instructional experiences. It is likely that criterion-referenced measurement approaches would be appropriate for mastery objectives and norm-referenced measurement for developmental objectives. A continuum is implied in the distinction. For example, at one end we have mastery of basic arithmetic operations and at the developmental level we require the solving of quadratic equations. In social studies we might be interested in:

MASTERY: The ability to recall major sources of income for selected African countries, and/or

DEVELOPMENTAL: Describe current world problems resulting from recent political changes in Africa.

The current minimum competency testing movement is based in part on a desire of legislators to hold students and schools accountable for mastery objectives.

All evaluation is not objectives-based. Scriven (1972) and Stake (1975), for example, have described general approaches to evaluation which use an inductive rather than the usual deductive approach. Qualitative methods and naturalistic observation are used in these "goal-free" approaches. Objectives (in a sense, hypotheses) are inferred from observational data. Rather than evaluate from a prescribed framework, a description of ongoing activities is used to identify which objectives are being addressed.

Levels of Specificity in Educational Outcomes

Educational objectives, like people, come in all shapes and sizes. There are big ones that at times are so ponderous that they don't say anything and can't move anywhere. There are others so small as to be almost microscopic. Many are so minuscule that you can't see them and are meaningless because they are so small, even nitpicky. "Truth," as so often is the case, is probably somewhere in the middle. Outcomes that are useful probably have enough bulk to make themselves visible and make a statement, but not be too small as to become intellectually invisible. One might conceive of outcomes as falling on a continuum of specificity. Figure 4-1 should help visualize the individual differences in specificity. It contains a variety of terms that are frequently used to help focus and direct educational efforts. At the very general end we have educational goals like, "Become a good citizen." In the middle (Taxonomy of Educational Objectives) we might have, "Applies Archimedes principles of specific gravity in problem solving." At the specific end we have test items: "What domestic animal is most closely related to the wolf?"

Note that the spacing of the outcome-related terms is not even, as objectives and categories of objectives are not all created equal. Figure 4-1 is not an equal interval scale. It can be seen that goals like those from national educational commissions would be left—the *far* left—on our continuum, and the ultimate in specificity is the test or performance item on the right. The test task is an actual sample of what we want the student to know or be able to do. If not an actual sample, it is as good an approximation as we can create.

The process of stating objectives is an iterative one; each level helps one understand the levels above and below it. There is lots of interaction. Developments at one level frequently have implications for other levels, and one obtains the most complete understanding—particularly once the major developmental lines have become clear—by working back and forth among the various levels. Thus it is clear that objectives can and must be stated at a variety of levels of specificity, for both testing and curriculum building.

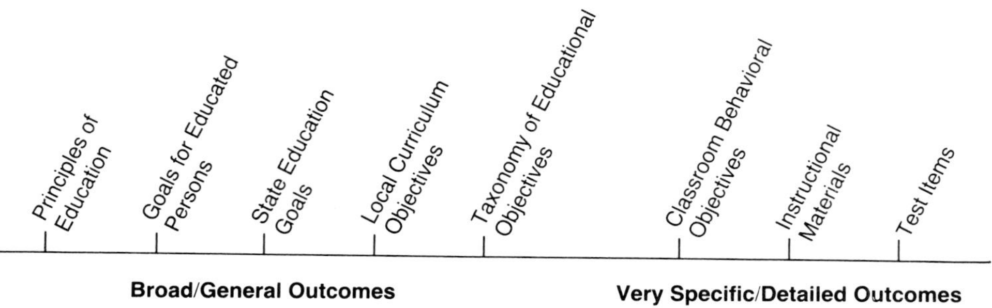

Figure 4-1

Degrees of specificity of educational outcomes

Illustration of Relationship Between General Objectives, Specific Objectives, and Test Items

The basis of validity for an achievement test rests, for the most part, on the match between intended outcomes and the measures of those outcomes. Stated another way the basis of validity (relevance) is the relationship of objective and item. The overall or sum total test validity (defined in terms of a content domain, see Chapter 13) is kind of an aggregate of the individual items. One approach to assessing test validity is to have experts make judgments about the number of items that match their respective objectives. All of this assumes that everything is in balance—in other words, there is symmetry and proportionality between instructional intent and actual instruction. See Chapter 5 for a discussion of the concept of "test blueprint" or "table of specification" which relates very directly to balance. Following are three sample objectives and items. It may seem that we are a little premature on item writing, but the idea of relevance is so important that an early introduction can't hurt.

The examples are taken from a science report card of the National Assessment of Educational Progress (Mullis & Jenkins, 1988). Three levels of specificity are represented. At the first level is the General Objective or goal. Goals are useful in that they help focus us on the appropriate instructional path to follow. Next come the Specific Objectives detailing the content and processes to be measured. Finally the test item itself represents an operational definition of our objective.

GENERAL OBJECTIVE: Knows everyday science facts

SPECIFIC OBJECTIVE: Can read and interpret simple graphs

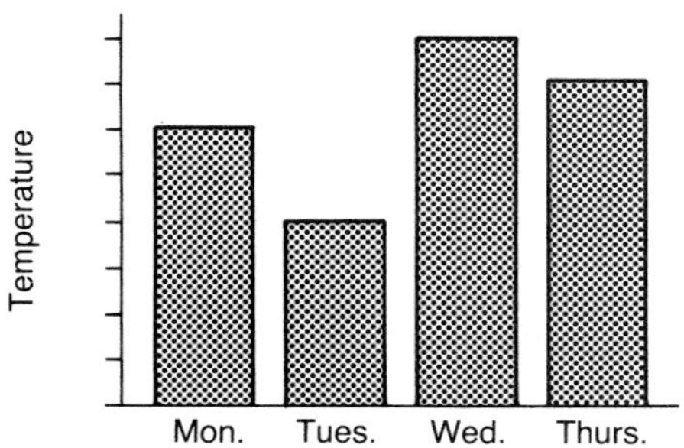

The graph above shows the high temperature on each day for four days. Which day was the hottest?

◦ Monday

◦ Tuesday

• Wednesday

◦ Thursday

GENERAL OBJECTIVE: Applies basic scientific information

SPECIFIC OBJECTIVE: Can make inferences about the outcomes of experimental procedures

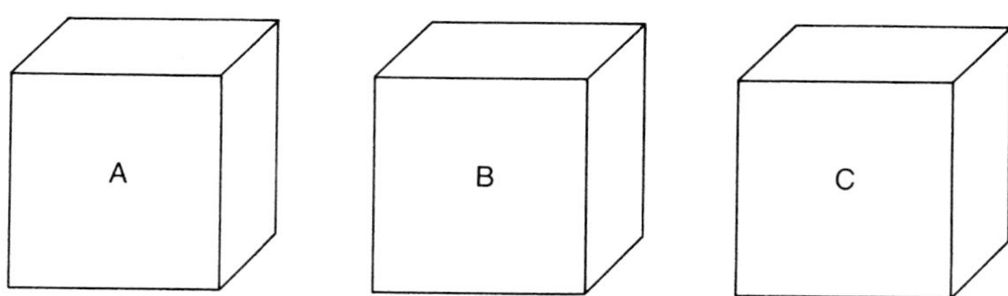

Blocks A, B, and C are the same size. Blocks B and C float on water. Block A sinks to the bottom. Which one of the following do you know is TRUE?

- • Block A weighs more than block B.
- ◦ Block B weighs more than block C.
- ◦ Block C weighs more than block A.
- ◦ Block B weighs more than block A.
- ◦ I don't know.

GENERAL OBJECTIVE: Integrates specialized scientific information

SPECIFIC OBJECTIVE: Can apply basic principles of genetics

A female white rabbit and a male black rabbit mate and have a large number of baby rabbits. About half of the baby rabbits are black, and the other half are white. If black fur is the dominant color in rabbits, how can the appearance of white baby rabbits best be explained?

- ◦ The female rabbit has one gene for black fur and one gene for white fur.
- • The male rabbit has one gene for black fur and one gene for white fur.
- ◦ The white baby rabbits received no genes for fur color from the father.
- ◦ The white baby rabbits are result of accidental mutations.

Choice of Outcomes

Usually many more objectives will be proposed than any student, teacher, or school can digest. The final selection of objectives will be dictated in part by the intended function of the school, the assigned role of the portion of the curriculum being developed, a realistic appraisal of what can be accomplished, and the degree of abstraction appropriate to the level of curriculum being developed. Tyler (1964) has discussed two criteria that embody the major considerations in the choice of objectives: (a) the educational philosophy of the person or institution making the selection, and (b) the extent to which the objectives are in keeping with pyschological realities affecting what can be taught at a given age in the light of the time available and previous learning. This is referred to as "developmentally appropriate."

Is the objective consistent with the school's philosophy of education? This criterion engages the values emphasized in a given school situation. Selection will involve such concerns as the school's view of the satisfying and effective life for an individual in our society. What are the most important values? What is the proper relation between the individual and society? What are the proper relations between individuals? Should different kinds of education be provided for different segments of society? Answers to these and similar questions relating to a school's philosophy clearly influence what is ruled out, what is chosen, and what is emphasized.

Is the objective consistent with accepted knowledge and theories about learning, instruction, and the discipline? Theories of learning and instruction assist in determining whether given objectives are applicable to particular grades or learning sequences. Theory can help keep one realistic about the choice of objectives for short- and long-term emphasis. It can help one to identify appropriate entry behaviors and follow-up behaviors, and to distinguish objectives that are not amenable to teaching from those that are suited to the instructional process.

The Taxonomy of Educational Objectives

One attempt to provide a framework for the entire panorama of educational objectives is the *Taxonomy of Educational Objectives*—so-called because it is a hierarchical classification scheme. Since the *Taxonomy*'s authors were much concerned with the holistic nature of learning, educational objectives are divided solely for purposes of convenience into three domains—cognitive, affective, and psychomotor. Most of the objectives for conventional courses are in the cognitive and affective domains, and a framework has been developed for each of these (Bloom, 1956; Krathwohl, Bloom, & Masia 1964). Tentative frameworks for the psychomotor domain also have been developed. These frameworks are hierarchical in nature, that is, the lowest level of behavior in the hierarchy is believed to be the least complex, and its achievement is presumed to be the key to successful achievement at the next higher level in the structure.

The structure proposed in the *Taxonomy* is educationally, logically, and psychologically consistent. The *Taxonomy* represents an educational system in that the categories correspond to a teacher's concerns in developing curricula and selecting learning experiences. It is logical because its categories are precisely defined and can be subdivided. It is psychological because it is consistent with current thought in the psychological sciences, although it is not dependent upon any particular theory.

The *Taxonomy* is not a traditional content classification scheme applicable in various subject-matter areas. It represents a set of behavioral goals per se, as well as a system for developing goals.

The major reason for developing the *Taxonomy* was to facilitate communication among educational researcher, curriculum developer, and evaluator. The *Taxonomy* has received its widest acceptance among educational testers and evaluators because of their need for explicit statements of objectives.

The Structure of the Cognitive Domain

The cognitive domain is composed of categories theoretically graded from simple to complex and from concrete to abstract. There is modest research evidence to support its organization (Cox & Wildemann, 1970). A synopsis of the *Taxonomy* is presented in Table 4-1.

A brief description of the major categories follows:

Knowledge: Recall or recognition in an appropriate context of specific facts, universal principles, methods, process patterns, structures, or settings. Little is required beyond bringing to mind the appropriate material.

Comprehension: The lowest level of what is commonly called "understanding," requiring that the individual be able to paraphrase knowledge accurately, explain or summarize it in his own words, or make logical extensions in terms of implications or corollaries.

Application: The ability to select a given abstraction (idea, rule, procedure, or generalized method) appropriate to a new situation and to apply it correctly.

Analysis: The ability to dissect a communication or concept into its constituent elements in order to illustrate the hierarchy or other internal relation of ideas, show the basis for its organization, and indicate how it conveys its effects.

Synthesis: The arrangement of units or elements of a whole in such a way as to create a new pattern or structure.

Evaluation: Qualitative and quantitative judgment about the extent to which material and methods satisfy criteria determined by the teacher or student.

There have been several attempts to validate the claim of the *Taxonomy* to hierarchical structure, which, if validated, would mean that achievement at a higher level of behavior is dependent upon achievement at a previous level. For relevant reviews of TOEO literature see Seddon (1978), Furst (1981), and Travers (1980). Kropp, Stoker, and Bashaw (1968), among others, have obtained empirical evidence

Table 4-1 Synopsis of the Taxonomy of Educational Objectives: Cognitive Domain

Knowledge

1.00 *Knowledge.* Recall of information
1.10 Knowledge of specifics. Emphasis is on symbols with concrete referents.
 1.11 Knowledge of terminology.
 1.12 Knowledge of specific facts.
1.20 Knowledge of ways and means of dealing with specifics. Includes methods of inquiry, chronological sequences, standards of judgment, patterns of organization within a field.
 1.21 Knowledge of conventions: accepted usage, correct style, etc.
 1.22 Knowledge of trends and sequences.
 1.23 Knowledge of classifications and categories.
 1.24 Knowledge of criteria.
 1.25 Knowledge of methodology for investigating particular problems.
1.30 Knowledge of the universals and abstractions in a field. Patterns and schemes by which phenomena and ideas are organized.
 1.31 Knowledge of principles and generalizations.
 1.32 Knowledge of theories and structures (as a connected body of principles, generalizations, and interrelations).

Intellectual Skills and Abilities

2.00 *Comprehension.* Understanding of material being communicated, without necessarily relating it to other material.
 2.10 Translation. From one set of symbols to another.
 2.20 Interpretation. Summarization or explanation of a communication.
 2.30 Extrapolation. Extension of trends beyond the given data.
3.00 *Application.* The use of abstractions, in particular, concrete situations.
4.00 *Analysis.* Breaking a communication into its parts so that organization of ideas is clear.
 4.10 Analysis of elements. E.g., recognizing assumptions.
 4.20 Analysis of relationships. Content or mechanical factors.
 4.30 Analysis of organizational principles. What holds the communication together?
5.00 *Synthesis.* Putting elements into a whole.
 5.10 Production of a unique communication.
 5.20 Production of a plan for operations.
 5.30 Derivation of a set of abstract relations.
6.00 *Evaluation.* Judging the value of material for a given purpose.
 6.10 Judgments in terms of internal evidence. E.g., logical consistency.
 6.20 Judgments in terms of external evidence. E.g., consistency with facts developed elsewhere.

that gives at least modest support to the order of the first three categories of the cognitive domain. The order of the more complex categories has largely failed to find support in these studies. All of the investigators encountered problems in developing measures, particularly objective ones, at the most complex end of the continuum. The difficulty of accurately classifying a higher-level item is compounded by the fact that the student's prior experience with the material on which the item is based may have resulted in his or her learning by rote a problem that would be complex if totally unfamiliar. Such a problem would belong in a lower category, such as Knowledge, for the student who learned it by rote, but would be a measure of more complex behavior for the student who met it afresh.

Illustrative Cognitive-Domain Objectives

The following list of objectives should illustrate the flavor of the *Taxonomy*.

Recall of major facts about particular cultures. (Knowledge)
Knowledge of scientific methods for evaluating health concepts. (Knowledge)
Skill in translating verbal mathematical material into symbolic statements, and vice versa. (Comprehension)
Ability to predict the probable effect of a change in a factor on a biological situation previously at equilibrium. (Application)
Ability to recognize form and pattern in literary and artistic works as a way of understanding their meaning. (Analysis)
Skill in distinguishing facts from hypotheses. (Analysis)
Ability to recount a personal experience effectively. (Synthesis)
Ability to plan a unit of instruction for a particular teaching situation. (Synthesis)
Ability to compare a work with the highest known standards in its field, especially other works of recognized excellence. (Evaluation)
Ability to recognize logical fallacies in arguments. (Evaluation)

Illustrative Taxonomy Objectives for Elementary Students

Higher-order outcomes can be stated and used with elementary students. To illustrate that point and provide an overview of the *Taxonomy* the following summary is provided (Reisman & Payne, 1987).

Knowledge: Recall or recognition in an appropriate context of specific facts, universal principles. methods, process patterns, structures, or settings. Little is required beyond bringing to mind previously learned information.
To say the letters of the alphabet in order.
To point to all of the e's in a word.
To state the definition of the word *mammal*.
Comprehension: The lowest level of what is commonly called "understanding," requiring that students be able to paraphrase knowledge accurately, explain

or summarize in their own words, or make logical extensions to implications or corollaries.

To translate a simple word sentence to a simple number sentence.
To summarize the main ideas of a paragraph.
To predict the ending of a story.

Application: The ability to use a given abstraction (idea, rule, procedure, or generalized method) appropriate to a new situation and apply it correctly.

To follow safety rule when the fire drill bell rings.
To make cookies using a recipe.
To compose a paragraph using proper usage and good sentence structure.

Analysis: The ability to break down a communication or concept into its constituent elements in order to illustrate the hierarchy or other internal relations of ideas, show the basis for its organization, and indicate how it conveys its effects.

To recognize statements of fact and opinion in a short story.
To underline the main ideas in a letter.
To identify the parts of a sentence.

Synthesis: The arrangement of units, parts, or elements in such a way as to create a new pattern or structure. To create geometric shapes using only circles, squares, and triangles.

To write a poem.
To construct a collage.

Evaluation: The making of judgments about the value, for some purpose, of ideas, works, solutions, methods, materials, etc. The criteria for evaluation may be determined by the student or the teacher, and the judgments may be qualitative or quantitative.

To write a critique of a short story.
To draw a conclusion based on data.

The Usefulness of the Cognitive-Domain Taxonomy

The comprehensiveness of the *Taxonomy* has made it useful in determining whether or not a formulated set of objectives includes objectives at all levels appropriate to the curriculum under consideration. The *Taxonomy,* like a periodic table of elements or a check-off shopping list, offers a panorama of possible objectives. In particular, it provides many examples of complex objectives, which are frequently omitted or given insufficient emphasis.

The *Taxonomy* has also been used in the analysis of examinations and teaching practices to compare the emphases in course objectives with those in test questions and instruction. As might be expected, the balance between factual knowledge and thinking called for in the statement of objectives frequently fails to be actualized in the examination items or materials of instruction. Heavy emphasis on memorization is indicated by the disproportionate use of the Knowledge category, often outweighing other categories combined. It is not unusual to find that 50 to 90 percent of the total time available is spent on knowledge instruction.

When searching for ideas for a new curriculum, the work of others is frequently most helpful. If one's own work and that of others are both formulated in terms of the *Taxonomy*, comparison is markedly facilitated. Translation of objectives into the *Taxonomy* framework can provide a basis for more precise comparison. Furthermore, where similarities exist, it becomes possible to treat experiences regarding the value of certain learning experiences with more confidence.

It is also important to note the implications of the hierarchical nature of the *Taxonomy* for curriculum building. If the foregoing analysis is correct, then a hierarchy of objectives in a given subject-matter area suggests a readiness relationship between those objectives lower and higher in the hierarchy. Thus, the *Taxonomy* may suggest the sequence in which objectives should be pursued in the curriculum.

The *Taxonomy* is intended to assist those operating at the unit and course level. Statements of objectives for smaller units of instruction, such as programmed books used with teaching machines or computers, require a finer category system, such as Gagné's (1985).

Considerations in Stating Specific Educational Objectives

Two major factors must be considered in constructing statements of educational objectives: content and form. Objectives should be evaluated not only in terms of subject matter (content), but also in terms of the way in which the subject matter is treated or expressed (form). These two dimensions are significantly related, and can influence the utility of objectives, and the quality of the resulting test and items. Desirable characteristics of objectives will be discussed in this section.

Content

1. Objectives should be appropriate in terms of level of difficulty and prior learning experiences. If the *Taxonomy* were used as a guide, objectives encompassing all six major levels might be stated for a college-level course, but the first three levels might be emphasized for a fifth-grade social studies unit. This is not to say that higher-order outcomes—that is, problem solving and logical thinking—should not be focused on in the early grades. They should! For a fifth-grade social studies unit:

UNACCEPTABLE: The student will trace the economic and philosophical origins of communism.

ACCEPTABLE: The student will identify three European countries where peaceful changes were brought about in communist political organizations.

2. Objectives should be "real," in the sense that they describe behaviors the teacher actually intends to act on in the classroom situation. Frequently a teacher

will state that he or she intends to bring about changes in the "attitudes" and "appreciations" of his students, but plans no specific learning experiences to achieve these kinds of objectives. This is not to say that they are not useful or desirable objectives, but that if one adopts an objective one must evaluate progress toward it. Conversely, if an objective is not part of the actual instructional program, one shouldn't evaluate it.

UNACCEPTABLE: Students will learn to love science.

ACCEPTABLE: After a visit to a local hospital, pharmacy students will better appreciate the importance of scientific experimentation.

3. A useful object will describe both the content and the mental process or behavior required for an appropriate response. A list of objectives should *not* become a "table of contents"—a list of topics to be covered in class. Such a list should describe the overt behavior expected and the content vehicle (e.g., instructional procedure) that will be used to bring about change.

UNACCEPTABLE: Students will know world capitals.

ACCEPTABLE: Students will be able to recall the capitals of the countries in the North Atlantic Treaty Organization.

4. The content of the objectives should be responsive to the needs of both the individual *and* society.

ACCEPTABLE: Students can describe the requirements for becoming registered voters in their state.

5. Generally, a variety of behaviors should be stated, since most courses attempt to develop skills other than "recall." Only recently, however, have we made a concerted effort to abandon the stultifying emphasis on the memorization of facts. This seems strange in light of the results of relevant research, which have been available for some time. Tyler (1933), for example, has shown that knowledge of specific information is not a lasting outcome of instruction. On the other hand, the higher-order mental abilities and skills (e.g., application and interpretation) show much greater stability.

Form

1. Objectives should be stated in the form of expected pupil changes. They should *not* describe teacher activities. If we are to measure and evaluate validly, we must articulate precisely what we expect students to be able to do at the end of a course or unit of instruction.

UNACCEPTABLE: The teacher will describe the major events in the United States Civil War.

ACCEPTABLE: The student will recall the military event that directly led to the outbreak of hostilities at the beginning of the United States Civil War.

2. Objectives should be stated in behavioral or performance terms. The terms used should have the same meaning for student and instructor. Mager (1962) points out that words such as "identify," "differentiate," "solve," "construct," "list," "compare," and "contrast" communicate more precisely and efficiently than do traditional educational terminology. In general, the broad class of words called "action verbs" is preferable. Objectives must be stated operationally if we are to evaluate them adequately. Following is an example.

UNACCEPTABLE: The student will see the importance of the Magna Carta.

ACCEPTABLE: The student will be able to identify three major provisions of the Magna Carta that relate directly to the Constitution of the United States of America.

Although wordier, the "Acceptable" objective better clarifies the task and surely is more informative to the instructor in terms of both content and behavior. See Table 4-2 for a useful list of "behaviors."

3. Objectives should be stated singly. Compound objectives are likely to lead to inconsistent measurement. At the beginning of a course, a teacher may have in mind a particular objective, say, "The student should be able to recall, comprehend, and apply the four major correction-for-guessing formulas." When it comes time to measure the achievement of this objective, any of the three behaviors might be measured. In addition, those selected may or may not be measured in proportion to the emphasis given them in class. If the resulting test is not responsive to the objectives of instruction, it is invalid for the purpose of determining whether these goals have been accomplished. Another shortcoming of compound objectives is that the easier portions of the objectives may be measured because it is easier to write recall (knowledge) items than application items. Again, the relevance of the test is destroyed.

4. Objectives should be parsimonious. Statements of instructional goals are easier to work with when trimmed of excess verbiage. Following is an example.

UNACCEPTABLE: The student will be capable of establishing a quantitative chemistry design with which, when presented with an unknown compound, the student will thereafter correctly identify its constituent elements.

ACCEPTABLE: The student will describe verbally a design for an experiment to test for a chemical unknown.

(Text continues on page 78)

Table 4-2 Instrumentation of the Taxonomy of Educational Objectives: Cognitive Domain

Taxonomy Classification	Key Words: Examples of Infinitives	Key Words: Examples of Direct Objects
1.00 Knowledge		
1.10 Knowledge of Specifics		
1.11 Knowledge of Terminology	to define, to distinguish, to acquire, to identify, to recall, to recognize	vocabulary terms, terminology, meaning(s), definitions, referents, elements
1.12 Knowledge of Specific Facts	to recall, to recognize, to acquire, to identify	facts, factual information, (sources), (names), (dates), (events), (persons), (places), (time periods), properties, examples, phenomena
1.20 Knowledge of Ways and Means of Dealing with Specifics		
1.21 Knowledge of Conventions	to recall, to identify, to recognize, to acquire	form(s), conventions, uses, usage, rules, ways, devices, symbols, representations, style(s), format(s)
1.22 Knowledge of Trends and Sequences	to recall, to recognize, to acquire, to identify	action(s), processes, movements(s), continuity, development(s), trend(s), sequence(s), causes, relationship(s), forces, influences
1.23 Knowledge of Classification and Categories	to recall, to recognize	area(s), type(s), feature(s), class(es), set(s), division(s), arrangement(s), classification(s), category/categories
1.24 Knowledge of Criteria	to recall, to recognize, to acquire, to identify	criteria, basics, elements
1.25 Knowledge of Methodology	to recall, to recognize, to acquire, to identify	methods, techniques, approaches, uses, procedures, treatments

(*continued*)

Source: W. S. Metfessel, W. B. Michael, and D. A. Kirsner, Instrumentation of Bloom's and Krathwohl's taxonomies for the writing of educational objectives. *Psychology in the Schools* 6 (1969): 227–231. Reprinted by permission of the publisher.

Table 4-2 *(Continued)*

Taxonomy Classification	Key Words: Examples of Infinitives	Key Words: Examples of Direct Objects
1.30 Knowledge of the Universals and Abstractions in a Field		
1.31 Knowledge of Principles and Generalizations	to recall, to recognize, to acquire, to identify	principle(s), generalizations(s), proposition(s), fundamentals, laws, principal elements, implication(s)
1.32 Knowledge of Theories and Structures	to recall, to recognize, to acquire, to identify	theories, bases, interrelations, structure(s), organization(s), formulation(s)
2.00 Comprehension		
2.10 Translation	to translate, to transform, to give in own words, to illustrate, to prepare, to read, to represent, to change, to rephrase, to restate	meaning(s), sample(s), definitions, abstractions, representations, words, phrases
2.20 Interpretation	to interpret, to reorder, to rearrange, to differentiate, to distinguish, to make, to draw, to explain, to demonstrate	relevancies, relationships, essentials, aspects, new view(s), qualifications, conclusions, methods, theories, abstractions
2.30 Extrapolation	to estimate, to infer, to conclude, to predict, to differentiate, to determine, to extend, to interpolate	consequences, implications, conclusions, factors, ramifications, meanings, corollaries, effects, probabilities
3.00 Application	to apply, to generalize, to relate, to choose, to develop, to organize, to use, to employ, to transfer, to restructure, to classify	principles, laws, conclusions, effects, methods, theories, abstractions, situations, generalizations, processes, phenomena, procedures
4.00 Analysis		
4.10 Analysis of Elements	to distinguish, to detect, to identify, to classify, to discriminate, to recognize, to categorize	elements, hypothesis/hypotheses, conclusions, assumptions, statements (of fact), statements (of intent), arguments, particulars

Table 4-2 *(Continued)*

Taxonomy Classification	Key Words: Examples of Infinitives	Key Words: Examples of Direct Objects
4.20 Analysis of Relationships	to analyze, to contrast, to compare, to distinguish, to deduce	relationships, interrelations, relevance, relevancies, themes, evidence, fallacies, arguments, cause-effect(s), consistency, consistencies, parts, ideas, assumptions
4.30 Analysis of Organizational Principles	to analyze, to distinguish, to detect, to deduce	form(s), pattern(s), purpose(s), point(s) of view(s), techniques, bias(es), structure(s), theme(s), arrangement(s), organization(s)
5.00 Synthesis		
5.10 Production of a Unique Communication	to write, to tell, to relate, to produce, to constitute, to transmit, to originate, to modify, to document	structure(s), pattern(s), product(s), performance(s), design(s), work(s), communications, effort(s), specifics, composition(s)
5.20 Production of a Plan or Proposed Set of Operations	to propose, to plan, to produce, to design, to modify, to specify	plan(s), objectives, specification(s), schematic(s), operation(s), way(s), solution(s), means.
5.30 Derivation of a Set of Abstract Relations	to produce, to derive, to develop, to combine, to organize, to synthesize, to classify, to deduce, to develop, to formulate, to modify	phenomena, taxonomies, concept(s), scheme(s), theories, relationships, abstractions, generalizations, hypothesis/hypotheses, perceptions, ways, discoveries
6.00 Evaluation		
6.10 Judgments in Terms of Internal Evidence	to judge, to argue, to validate, to assess, to decide	accuracy/accuracies, consistency/consistencies, fallacies, reliability, flaws, errors, precision, exactness
6.20 Judgments in Terms of External Criteria	to judge, to argue, to consider, to compare, to contrast, to standardize, to appraise	ends, means, efficiency, economy/economies, utility, alternatives, courses of action, standards, theories, generalizations

The streamlined version is clearer and communicates more effectively.

5. Objectives should be grouped logically, so they make sense in determining units of instruction and evaluation.

6. The conditions under which the expected pupil behavior will be observed should be specified. The objectives "to be able to solve problems in algebra," though useful, could be improved as follows: "Given a linear algebraic equation with one unknown, the learner must be able to solve for the unknown without the aid of references, tables, or calculating devices" (Mager, 1962). Although a little more wordy, the intent of the instructor and the expected student behavior are now clearly identifiable.

7. If possible, the objective should contain a statement indicating the criteria for acceptable performance. Criteria might involve time limits or a minimum number of correct responses. Following is an example.

UNACCEPTABLE: The student will be able to identify examples of each part of speech.

ACCEPTABLE: When presented with a grammatically correct paragraph of at least three sentences, the student will be able to identify examples of each part of speech.

Both student and instructor know what is expected of them.

How elaborately should objectives be specified? What degree of refinement is necessary? These questions do not have absolute answers, and they require decisions on the part of the teacher-evaluator. Suffice it to say that the more refined the objectives, the easier the task of measurement. Obviously, there is a point of diminishing returns. The list could become so lengthy and involved that it would be unwieldy, confusing, and perhaps negatively reinforcing to the writer. Instructors are encouraged to consider the guidelines listed above in developing a suitable style to express their objectives.

Following are several specific objectives from a course in educational tests and measurements that illustrate many of the points in the foregoing discussion.

The student should be able to:

1. Write a multiple-choice item free of grammatical errors.
2. Correctly classify a set of test items according to the six major categories of the *Taxonomy of Educational Objectives.*
3. Select the most important rule in constructing matching exercises from a list of positive suggestions.
4. Construct a scoring checklist for an essay item.

Figure 4-2 contains the "World's Worst Specific Objective" to illustrate in summary form the problems that might be encountered in writing a good instructional objective. As it stands the objective is beyond help. There are probably five or six

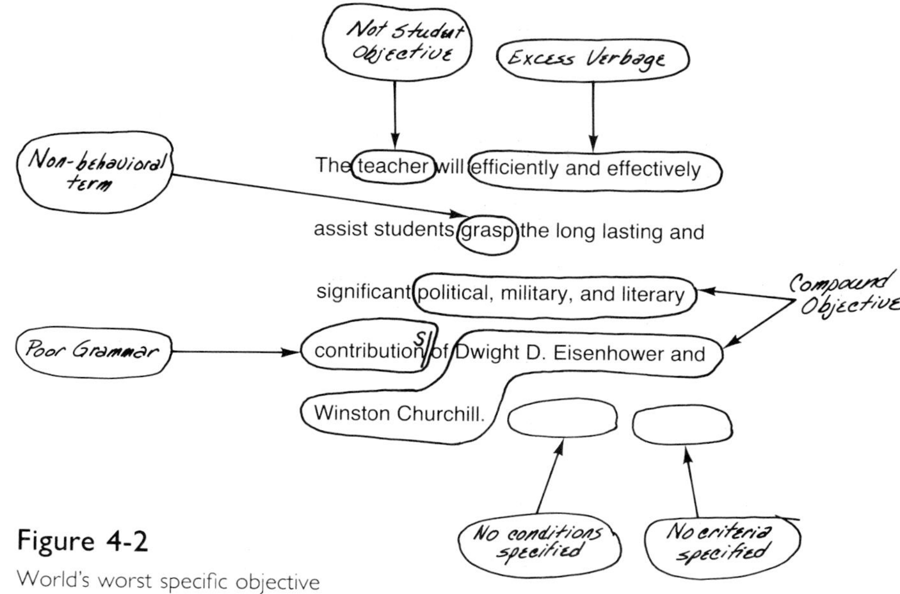

Figure 4-2

World's worst specific objective

objectives implied in this collection of words. It would be merciful to simply remove the life support system and begin anew.

Behavioral Cognitive Categories for the Taxonomy of Educational Objectives

Objectives may be stated, as we have seen, at a variety of levels of abstraction. The *Taxonomy* is not behavioral. To assist in application at a behavioral level, Metfessel, Michael, and Kirsner (1969) have provided a series of verbal guidelines useful in operationalizing specific levels of the *Taxonomy.* That portion of their guidelines dealing with the cognitive domain is summarized in Table 4-2. Their use of infinitives and direct objects should facilitate the writing of instructional objectives, which, although keyed to the *Taxonomy,* are closer to being behavioral statements.

Objections to Explicit Statements of Educational Objectives

While many consider the explicit formulation of behavioral objectives a very useful approach, that attitude is not universal. Atkin (1968), Eisner (1967), Macdonald and Walfron (1970), and Broudy (1970), among others, have voiced serious objections to the extensive use of behavioral objectives in teaching, evaluation, and curriculum development. A majority of the objections involve fear of creating a lockstep instructional setting and failing to provide for spontaneity and creativity. Admittedly, the possibility of a mechanical approach to instruction exists but the advantages attendant on the use of explicit statements of goals to clarify intent and assist in the selection of content, behavior to be changed, and instructional materials probably outweigh the disadvantages.

It is imperative that the teacher's instructional intent be communicated to the student. The following anecdote, reported by Yelon and Scott (1970, p. 5), illustrates a possible result of failure to communicate:

> At a parent-teacher conference the teacher complained to Mr. Bird about the foul language of his children. Mr. Bird decided to correct this behavior. At breakfast he asked his oldest son, "What will you have for breakfast?" The boy replied, "Gimme some of those damn cornflakes." Immediately Mr. Bird smashed the boy on the mouth. The boy's chair tumbled over and the boy rolled up against the wall. The father then turned to his second son and politely inquired, "What would you like for breakfast?" The boy hesitated, then said, "I don't know, but I sure as hell don't want any of those damn cornflakes!"

Moral: If you want someone to change his behavior, tell him your goals.

Popham (1969), has summarized 11 major objections to the use of behavioral objectives. He then proceeds to respond to each objection. The following parallel lists (adapted from Wynn, 1973) serve to summarize the advantages and disadvantages of behavioral objectives.

Objection to Behavioral Objectives	*Rebuttal to Objection*
1. Trivial behaviors are easiest to operationalize. Really important outcomes will be underemphasized.	1. Explicit objectives more readily focus attention on important goals.
2. Prespecification prevents the teacher from capitalizing on unexpected instructional opportunities.	2. Ends do not necessarily specify means. Serendipity is always welcome.
3. Other types of educational outcomes are also important, for example, for parents, staff, community.	3. Schools can't do everything. Their responsibility is to pupils.
4. Objectively, mechanistically measured behaviors are dehumanizing.	4. The broadened concept of evaluation includes "human" elements.
5. Precise, preplanned behavior is undemocratic.	5. Society knows what it wants. Instruction is naturally undemocratic.
6. Behaviorally described teaching is unnatural and makes unrealistic demands on teachers.	6. Identifying the status quo is different than applauding it.
7. In certain areas, for example, fine arts and humanities, it is more difficult to measure behaviors.	7. Sure it's tough, but it is still a responsibility.

8. General statements appear more worthwhile to outsiders. Precise goals appear innocuous.	8. We must abandon the ploy of "obfuscation by generality."
9. Measurability implies accountability. Teachers might be judged solely on their ability to produce particular results.	9. Teachers should be held accountable for producing changes.
10. It is more difficult to generate precise objectives than to talk about them in vague terms.	10. We should allocate the necessary resources to accomplish the task.
11. Unanticipated results are often most important. Prespecification may cause inattentiveness.	11. Dramatic unanticipated outcomes cannot be overlooked. Keep your eyes open!

Psychomotor Objectives

Several attempts have been made to specify the elements of a psychomotor taxonomy. Only the models proposed by Simpson (1966) and Harrow (1972) attempt to organize the behaviors into a sequential hierarchy.

Harrow's Taxonomy of the Psychomotor Domain

The most comprehensive system for classifying psychomotor behaviors developed to date is Harrow's (1972). This system assumes that psychomotor behaviors represent an operationalization of cognitive and affective intentions. The classifications are arranged along a continuum from a low level of observable movement to a highly integrated level of complex movement. Following is an outline of Harrow's (1972, pp. 96–98) psychomotor taxonomy:

- Reflex Movements
  - Segmental Reflexes
  - Intersegmental Reflexes
  - Suprasegmental Reflexes
- Basic-Fundamental Movements
  - Locomotor Movements
  - Nonlocomotor Movements
  - Manipulative Movements
- Perceptual Abilities
  - Kinesthetic Discrimination
  - Visual Discrimination (acuity, tracking, memory)
  - Auditory Discrimination (acuity, tracking, memory)
  - Tactile Discrimination
  - Coordinated Abilities (eye, hand, and foot)

Physical Abilities
- Endurance (muscular, cardiovascular)
- Strength
- Flexibility
- Agility

Skilled Movements
- Simple Adaptive Skill
- Compound Adaptive Skill
- Complex Adaptive Skill

Nondiscursive Communication
- Expressive Movement (posture, gestures, facial expression)
- Interpretive Movement (aesthetic, creative)

With regard to her psychomotor taxonomy classifications, Harrow states:

> Acting as a basis for all movement behavior is the first category, reflex movement (1.00), and the second category, basic of fundamental movement patterns (2.00), is actually the combining of reflex movements into inherent movement patterns. The learner responds involuntarily in the first category and, though the movement patterns in the second category are inherent within the learner, he utilizes these patterns during voluntary movement. It is upon these voluntary movement patterns that he builds his skilled movements. The next two categories, perceptual abilities (3.00) and physical abilities (4.00), are further developed through maturation and learning. The learner goes through many learning experiences that sharpen his perceptual abilities, and engages in many activities that increase the quality of his physical abilities. The efficiency and degree of skilled movement attained by any learner is based upon the learner's control of his basic or fundamental movements, the degree of efficiency with which he perceives stimuli, and the level of development he has attained in the fourth category of physical abilities. Once the learner has acquired a skilled movement vocabulary (5.00) he has the necessary tools (an efficient body—an accurate perceptual system—and skilled movement repertoire) for modifying and creating aesthetic movement patterns (6.00) (p. 33).

Illustrative Psychomotor Objectives

Following are selected objectives adapted from Harrow's (1972) psychomotor taxonomy. The reader should refer to the list of categories for specific classifications. Due to the autonomic nature of classification—Reflex Movements—no objectives need to be developed by teachers.

At the end of the school year, the preschool student will be able to accomplish a two-footed jump beginning with both feet parallel, using the arms for forward thrust and landing with both feet together. (Basic Fundamental Movement)

The student will be able to distinguish between a penny, a nickel, a dime, and a quarter solely by touch 100 percent of the time. (Perceptual Ability)

Upon completion of a six-week training session, the student will have improved his grip strength by at least five pounds as measured by a dynamometer. (Physical Ability)

A first-year typing student will be able to type at least 30 words per minute during a five-minute typing test with no more than five errors. (Skilled Movements)

The student will be able to produce a recognizable rhythmic pattern for at least 30 seconds. (Nondiscursive Communication)

The purposes of education are reflected in our goals and objectives. The more detailed they are the greater their usefulness for guiding instruction and evaluating the effectiveness of that instruction. Educators, for people other than teachers also use objectives, frequently adopt or adapt already existing objectives or sets of objectives for their own purposes. Whether creator or borrower, one must be sure that the objectives (a) are compatible with school and system goals, (b) are representative of best current pedagogical thought, (c) are compatible with student background, experience, and ability, (d) are reflective of the current state of knowledge, (e) are couched in terms of expected student performances, and (f) contain a description of the conditions under which that behavior is to be observed.

Case Study Application

Objectives for an Undergraduate Reading Education Course

Introduction. The development of reading skills is central to virtually all aspects of an individual's academic and vocational pursuits. If we are to do anything about the very significant national and international literacy problem it must be through the improvement of reading skills. Hopefully, each succeeding generation will be more literate than the last, or at least that would be a reasonable goal. We are called upon to read and understand large amounts of information every day. With the "knowledge explosion" the ability to input, comprehend, and integrate this information in an efficient and effective manner can often determine the difference between success and failure, passing or not passing, being promoted or not. The development of reading skills in students is very much contingent upon high quality instruction. High quality instruction in turn is dependent upon effective teacher training. We have now backtracked to the reason for offering a course in the teaching of reading for preservice juniors in an early childhood education or elementary education college curriculum.

Course and curriculum. This is the first required five-credit-hour quarter-long course for junior preservice students in early childhood or elementary education. Students generally spend six weeks in learning about methods and materials used in the teaching of reading. They then spend three weeks in elementary classrooms and they finish the quarter by spending the last week of the quarter on campus after their field experiences to share and seek solutions and resolutions. A typical text for this course might be: Burns, P. C., Roe, B. D., & Ross, E. P. (1984). *Teaching reading in today's elementary schools.* Boston: Houghton Mifflin.

The major aims (goals) of the course are to provide preservice teachers with declarative, procedural, and conditional knowledge in the following areas:

- reflection on the reading process and beliefs about teaching reading
- emerging literacy
- language experience activities
- decoding strategies
- comprehension strategies
- classroom discussion strategies
- basal reading lessons
- modifications of the reading program for bilingual learners
- modifications of the reading program for exceptional children
- evaluation for individual and group progress

Class activities include whole- and small-group discussions of assigned readings, teaching simulations by professors and students, minilectures, and audiovisual presentations.

The course grade is based on the midterm exam, final exam, and several other assignments: daily written journals, field-based teaching, written lesson plans, written assignments from course textbooks, and classroom observations. The present case study will focus on the midterm exam.

Following are 29 sample objectives for the first six weeks of the course. The original list contained 42 objectives. Six of these objectives (indicated with an asterisk*) would not become part of the midterm exam plan; they (a) related to activities that were part of later coursework, or (b) were performance objectives aimed at campus or field experience classroom activities.

Evaluate each objective in comparison to the guidelines presented in the chapter relative to content and form. Suggest improvements.

Reflection on the Reading Process and Beliefs about Teaching Reading

The Student Should Be Able to:

1. Associate different instructional practices with three conceptual frameworks (models) of the reading process.
2. Recognize the importance of automaticity in the reading process.

Emerging Literacy

The Student Should Be Able to:

3. Recognize instructional activities that emphasize the uses of language.
4. * Read two children's books aloud using appropriate voice inflections, introductory activities, and follow-up activities.

5. Identify ways to create a classroom environment where learning to read is supported.

Language Experience Activity (LEA)

The Student Should Be Able to:

6. Identify the purposes of Language Experience Activity.
7. Recognize the characteristics of a particular Language Experience Activity.

* 8. Plan and teach two language experience activities.

Decoding Strategies

The Student Should Be Able to:

9. Identify the goal of decoding strategies.
10. Recognize three types of decoding strategies.
11. Apply phonics generalizations to decode nonsense words.
12. Apply syllabication rules

Comprehension Strategies

The Student Should Be Able to:

13. Recognize the purpose of Informed Strategies for Learning.
14. Recognize the characteristics of Informed Strategies for Learning
15. Recognize the characteristics of Question-Answer-Relationships.

Discussion Strategies

The Student Should Be Able to:

16. Identify three different types of discussion activities.
17. Recognize characteristics of three different types of discussion activities.

* 18. Participate in classroom discussions that use various formats.

Basal Reading Lessons

The Student Should Be Able to:

19. Identify the basal reader's emphasis as skills instruction, vocabulary instruction, oral reading, silent reading, comprehension instruction, guided practice, evaluation and use of children's literature.
20. Recognize the purpose and function of a scope and sequence chart.
21. Identify alternatives to round robin reading.

* 22. Plan and teach several basal reading lessons.

The Reading Program and Exceptional Children

The Student Should Be Able to:

23. Recognize reading instructional activities that are appropriate for exceptional children (both hard-to-teach and the gifted).

* 24. Modify a basal lesson so that it is appropriate for an exceptional student.

The Reading Program and Bilingual Learners

The Student Should Be Able to:

25. Differentiate between the terms bilingual learner, multicultural education, first language and second language.
26. Recognize instructional activities that are appropriate for bilingual learners and will increase multicultural appreciation in the classroom.
27. * Modify a basal lesson so that it is appropriate for bilingual learners.

Evaluation

The Student Should Be Able to:

28. Recognize characteristics of norm-referenced and criterion-referenced tests.
29. Differentiate between characteristics of test reliability and validity.

Content Review Statements

1. The establishment of educational goals and instructional objectives is a time-consuming, important, and often frustrating task.
2. The specification of outcomes is probably the single most important step in educational assessment.
3. An educational objective is a statement of desired change in pupil behavior.
4. Objectives may be classified as:
   a. Ultimate or immediate
   b. General or specific
   c. Cognitive, affective, or psychomotor
   d. Mastery or developmental
5. Objectives may be classified at different levels of specificity, depending upon their origin and projected method of application.
6. Objectives are derived from:
   a. Analysis of the needs of individuals and society
   b. Subject-matter experts
   c. Professional societies and commissions
   d. Analyses of the learning process itself
7. In selecting an instructional objective, one must consider its consistency with the school's educational philosophy and with accepted knowledge and theories of learning and instruction.
8. Educators must accept that value judgments cannot be avoided in the selection or specification of educational objectives.
9. The *Taxonomy of Educational Objectives* is a nonsubject-matter hierarchical classification of educational outcomes related to each other and to the teaching-learning process.
10. The major categories of the Cognitive Domain in the *Taxonomy of Educational Objectives* are:
    a. Knowledge
    b. Comprehension
    c. Application

d. Analysis
e. Synthesis
f. Evaluation

11. A good educational objective should:
    a. Deal with actual relevant classroom behaviors.
    b. Be appropriate to the students involved.
    c. Be stated in the form of expected change in individual student behaviors.
    d. Have direct implications for the modification and assessment of behavior.
12. Objections to the explicit statement and prespecification of educational objectives focus on:
    a. The likelihood of emphasizing trivial and easily specified behaviors
    b. Reduced spontaneity and flexibility in the classroom
    c. The likelihood of overlooking other important outcomes
13. Harrow's *Taxonomy of Psychomotor Objectives* proposes the following six categories:
    a. Reflex movements
    b. Basic fundamental movements
    c. Perceptual abilities
    d. Physical abilities
    e. Skilled movements
    f. Nondiscursive communication
14. Providing students with a list of course objectives can enhance the learning experience.

Speculations

1. What are the characteristics of a good instructional objective?
2. Does the *Taxonomy of Educational Objectives: Cognitive Domain* make sense to you? Why or why not?
3. Can all educational outcomes be expressed as behavioral objectives?
4. What are the advantages and disadvantages of behavioral objectives?
5. Are goals or objectives more valuable from an educational standpoint?
6. Is form or content more important in an instructional objective?
7. Are taxonomies really helpful?
8. Is it always necessary to have instructional objectives?
9. Are developmental or minimum competency objectives more important? Why?

Suggested Readings

Davies, I. K. (1976). *Objectives in curriculum design.* New York: McGraw-Hill.

Fuchs, L. S., & Fuchs, D. (1986). Effects of systematic formative evaluation: A meta-analysis. *Exceptional Children, 53,* 199–208. A systematic review of 21 studies revealed that students of teachers who use objectives-based measurement performed better than those students of teachers who did not regularly use such procedures.

Gronlund, N. E. (1985). *Stating behavioral objectives for classroom instruction.* New York: Macmillan.

Hunkins, F. P. (1969). Effects of analysis and evaluation questions on various levels of achievement. *Journal of Experimental Education, 38*(2), 45–58. Teachers' questioning techniques can enhance student learning.

Kapfer, M. B. (Ed.) (1971). *Behavioral objectives in curriculum development.* Englewood Cliffs, NJ: Educational Technology Publications. This collection of 43 selected readings and bibliography from a variety of sources is an extremely valuable reference volume.

Mager, R. F. (1962). *Preparing objectives for programmed instruction.* San Francisco: Fearon Publishers. This brief (now classic) but excellent programmed text provides rationale and procedures for stating operational educational objectives.

Stake, R. E. (1970). Objectives, priorities, and other judgment data. *Review of Educational Research, 40,* 181–212.

Chapter 5

Planning for the Development, Administration, and Scoring of the Measuring Instrument

To insure the best possible test, one must plan for it. Appropriate planning involves consideration of a large number of factors, including (a) the type of measurement procedure to be used, (b) the length of the test, (c) the type of items, (d) the range and difficulty level of the items, (e) the arrangement of items, (f) the time limits, (g) the scoring system, (h) the manner of reporting results, (i) the method of recording responses, and, most important of all, (j) the subject matter, mental operation, or behavior to be sampled. Several of the more important decision points in test planning are discussed in this chapter (Embretson, 1985).

Overview of the Test Development Process

The test development process is a complex one, consisting of a variety of tasks and activities. A flow chart of the major activities is presented in Figure 5-1, which is based on an analysis of the test development process and a PERT (Program Evalua-

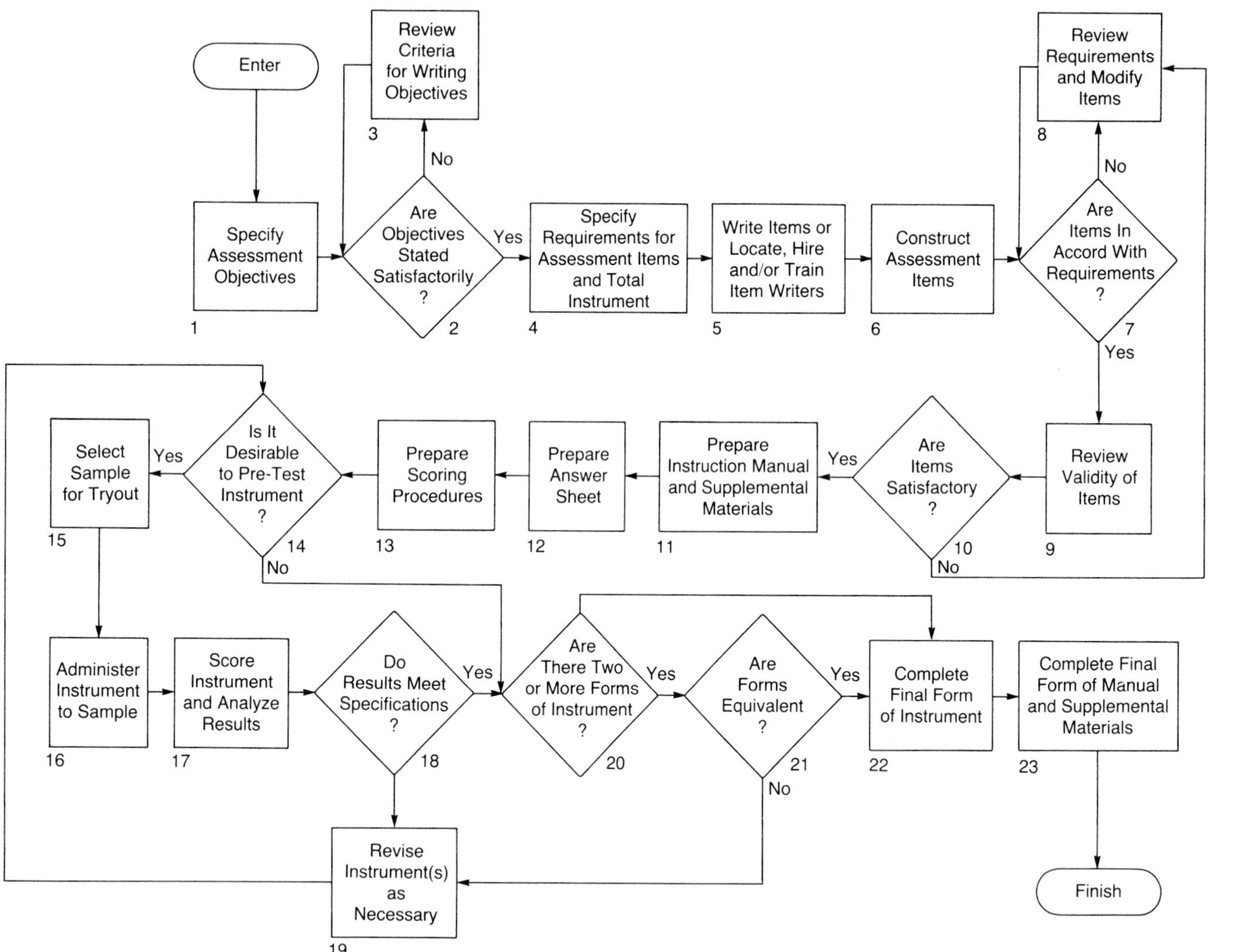

Figure 5-1

Flow chart describing process of constructing assessment devices

tion and Review Technique) chart. The system is virtually self-explanatory and should provide the reader with a good perspective on the entire process. Those activities and decisions related to the development of parallel forms are obviously of less relevance to the classroom teacher. The desirability of having available comparable forms of a classroom test (e.g., for purposes of pre- and post-testing, or to handle the problems of absentees, or for testing under crowded conditions in which cheating might be anticipated, or for research purposes) should not be overlooked. The specific form that each activity in the chart takes will, of course, depend on the assessment requirements. Of particular concern are those decisions related to activities 2, 7, 10, 18, 20, and 21. These decisions require skills and a knowledge of measurement, evaluation, testing, and assessment. With regard to Activity 3, the reader is referred to Chapter 4 which describes the development of instructional objectives. In Activity 4, consideration must be given to such factors as item format, time available, directions for administration, behavior measured, and language. This overview may appear a bit overwhelming. There is no doubt that it is a lot of work. Time and experience will make the task easier. In addition, some of the steps in the process may be taken at different times, and some decisions may be made at different times—depending on the intent in building the test.

Just as a competent contractor and architect must have blueprints in order to erect buildings with functional integrity and stability, so must the test developer have a similar set of specifications. The blueprint includes many important components.

Components of a Test Blueprint

Decisions must be made early on in the development of the blueprint about a number of components of the test. All of these decisions must flow from the purpose(s) of creating the instrument initially. It was noted in Chapter 1 that contemporary measurement practice tends to focus on two methodologies: criterion-referenced and norm-referenced. With these two general methods in mind let us overview some major decision points in the test development process.

1. *Test Development Should Flow Directly from Purpose.* All decisions about how the instrument is created and applied should flow directly from the intent in creating the device. Millman and Greene (1989) have concisely summarized categories of the kinds of inferences that a teacher is likely to make with tests. Figure 5-2 is an adaptation of that classification system.

The inferences described are for individuals. Data could be aggregated (e.g., across classes, grades, schools) for purposes of curriculum evaluation. *Tests are only as valid as the inferences we can make from their scores.* Either norm-referenced or criterion-referenced methods could be used with either type of application. The choice depends on whether the inference or decision is based on absolute (CRT) or relative (NRT) standards. The content basis of the inferences is the *curriculum.* The content domain might be expanded to include the development of intellectual skills

		TIME IN CURRICULUM		
		Before Instruction	During Instruction	After Instruction
APPLICATION	Description of Attainments	Placement	Diagnosis	Grading
	Mastery Decision	Selection	Instructional Guidance	Promotion

Figure 5-2

Kinds of classroom inferences made from tests (after Millman & Greene, 1989)

and abilities. If this content dimension is added to the curriculum, then our measurement intent would move from an achievement to an ability testing orientation.

The intimate relationship between test development and data collection can further be illustrated by a reference to the variety of decisions that educators must make. A variety of decisions requires a variety of data. A summary of data requirements relative to three general categories of decisions is provided in Table 5-1. The similarity to the decision types in Figure 5-2 (before, during, and after instruction) is evident. There are three important messages in Table 5-1. The first relates to the value of pretesting. The need, desire, and value of determining where a student "is"

Table 5-1 Outline for Obtaining Information Needed in an Evaluation Program Designed to Aid in Decision Making in All Phases of Instruction

	Phase I: Planning Instruction	**Phase II: Guiding Instruction**	**Phase III: Evaluating Results of Instruction**
Major questions or decisions	What is to be studied? (What are the needs of these pupils with respect to this content?) Where should instruction start?	How should intruction be carried out? When is the class (or a student) ready to move on?	Have pupils mastered and retained important learning outcomes?

Table 5-1 (*Continued*)

	Phase I: Planning Instruction	**Phase II: Guiding Instruction**	**Phase III: Evaluating Results of Instruction**
Basis for planning	Course outline. Specification of units and objectives. The textbook outline. Specification of prerequisite sequences.	Diagnostic outline of units or major topics. Identification of possible instructional alternatives. Specification of mastery criteria for objectives, units, topics.	Specification of essential content and skills (especially those needed as basis for subsequent courses).
Specific types of information needed	Do students already have mastery of any of course content? What have students studied before? Do students have prerequisites for course? What is present student status in mastery within sequence? Do certain topics have special interest and meaningfulness for students?	Do students have mastery or partial mastery of some topics within units? What type of instruction is most effective for this class (or for this student)? Have students mastered what they have been studying (objective, topic, unit)?	Have students retained the essential content and skills?
Possible sources of information	Course pretest. Standardized achievement tests. Student records. Placement test. Readiness tests. Aptitude tests.	Unit pretest. Interview with student. Student records. Personal knowledge of student. Aptitude tests. Quiz covering a given objective or topic (CET).* Unit posttest. Student work. Interview. Observation.	End-of-course exam. Standardized achievement test. Projects. Observation.

*Curriculum embedded test.

Source: From *Measuring Pupil Achievement and Aptitude,* Second Edition, p. 208, Table 10.1, by C. M. Lindvall and A. J. Nitko, © 1975 by Harcourt Brace Jovanovich, Inc. Reprinted by permission of the publisher.

in your instructional plan is critical. Such information provides for a more rational and helpful approach to teaching. Second, we need to know how we and the students are doing during instruction; relevant test results can help us monitor progress. Information on which students have not mastered projected objectives and where reteaching needs to take place would be illustrative decisions to be made during instruction. A final "big picture" of the effect and impact of the learning experience can be a third area where measurement can contribute to decision making in the classroom. A "terminal" end-of-experience measurement can help both student and instructor see how all the pieces fit together. It can also help teachers see areas where change in instruction might be needed next time. Another but more elaborate decision-measurement framework has been presented by Airasian and Madaus (1972). They use four decision categories: placement, formative, diagnostic, and summative.

2. *Areas and Proportions of Content in Test Should Be Specified.* Specification of content should reflect purpose of test, curriculum, and instruction. Any of the three major categories of school outcomes can be included—cognitive, affective, psychomotor (although the emphasis is usually on cognitive objectives). A listing of topics covered and the amount of time spent on each is a good start in clarifying the content dimension.

3. *The Categories and Nature of Process Objectives (Behaviors) in the Test Should Be Specified.* Content doesn't exist in and of itself; something must be done with it. Content must be recalled or manipulated in some way, for example, applied, used in problem solving, analyzed, and so forth. This dimension lends itself to classification according to the *Taxonomy of Educational Objectives* (Bloom, 1956). Again the nature of the instructional activities should be a helpful guide in describing the distribution of process outcomes. How much time did the teacher spend in developing student comprehension or application of a particular content area would be the typical kind of question asked. One device useful in bringing together the content and process dimensions is the *table of specifications.* The construction of this device is discussed in the next section.

4. *The Number and Type of Items Should Be Discussed.* The term "item" as used in this book will mean a test question or task, problem, or stimulus that requires a response from an individual, either from examinees themselves or from observers. In an achievement testing context, *item* usually translates into multiple-choice, true-false, completion, or essay. The number of items to be used will be a function of the objectives and time available, with higher-order problem solving and reasoning outcomes tending to require more time and to be more difficult than knowledge items. Mehrens and Lehmann (1984) have summarized research suggesting that examinees can, on the average

1. Answer one multiple-choice item each 75 seconds.
2. Answer a short-answer, completion, matching, or true-false item each 50 seconds.

3. Answer six restricted-response essay items (one-half page each) in one hour.
4. Respond to three extended-response essay items (two–three pages) per hour of testing time.

In most achievement testing situations we do not want speed to be a factor; therefore we use sufficient items to measure the intended objectives that can be answered in the available time. Everyone should have fair and equitable time to finish the test. Do not hesitate to spread the testing over several periods if the data are important to collect. The test will, in most cases, be timed but not speeded. A timed test is one for which a specified amount of time is allowed for completion. Usually 90 percent will finish. A speeded test is also timed, but speed influences scores because performance is based on number of completed tasks per unit of time. The number of items per objective used will be a function of the weight given that objective in the table of specifications. Popham (1990) has suggested that a minimum of 10 items should be used for each major behavior assessed. Stated another way each row or column in the table of specifications should start with 10 items. Depending on the importance of the behavior/test, this figure might drop down to 5 or increase to 15–20. The number of items on the test is also important because of its relationship to reliability. In general the greater the number of items the better the consistency of measurement.

5. *Directions for Administration Need to Be Written.* These directions would be both for the person administering the test and the person taking the test. The conditions under which the test is to be administered need to be specified along with the materials needed, for example, special answer sheets, and so on. Is the test group or individually administered? Is the test a preassessment, intermediate, or final exam? What are the time limits? Will a correction formula for guessing be applied? These are some important questions to be addressed with regard to administration.

6. *Scoring Criteria Should Be Specified.* Each item, task, or question should have performance criteria described. Measurement is, after all, the comparison of "something" against a standard. The prespecification of scoring criteria is particularly important for items requiring student-constructed responses. The responses may range from a numeral or word, to complex and extended answers to essay items.

There are additional components that could be addressed such as specifying the readability level of the items/test, how items should be grouped or sequenced, and the kind of reliability and/or item analysis to be conducted, if any.

Constructing a Table of Specifications

Ordinarily the first step to be taken in developing a measuring instrument would be to review the objectives of this instructional program, both those originally proposed and those actuallly attended to. A convenient way to conduct this review is through the use of a "table of specifications" (TOS). This table is simply a two-way grid or chart that relates the two major components of an educational objective: the "content" element and the "behavioral" or process outcome element. In addition, the table should contain percentages that reflect the relative emphases given each objective in the instructional situation. A sample table of specifications is presented in Table 5-2.

It should be noted that the Behavior Dimension uses the first four categories of the *Taxonomy of Educational Objectives.* There are, obviously, alternative ways of viewing this dimension. Some of these schemes have been summarized in Table 5-3. These alternative methods range from the very general (Smith and Tyler) to the specific (Walbesser). All deserve the reader's consideration. The behavior categories selected for use in a table of specifications are heavily influenced by the level of the student and the nature of the subject matter.

In practice the content categories are probably more detailed than those in Table 5-2. Let us repeat that the greater the detail in the test blueprint and table of

Table 5-2 Sample Abbreviated Table of Specifications for a Course in Educational Tests and Measurement Used in Developing Midsemester Exam

	Behavior Dimension								
	Recall (BD_1)		**Comprehension (BD_2)**		**Application (BD_3)**		**Analysis (BD_4)**		
Content Dimension	Cell #	%	Cell #	%	Cell #	%	Cell #	%	Total Content Dimension
History of Testing (C_1)	(1)	5	(8)		(15)		(22)		5
Uses of Tests (C_2)	(2)	3	(9)	4	(16)		(23)		7
Measurement Terminology (C_3)	(3)	3	(10)	2	(17)		(24)		5
Planning the Test (C_4)	(4)	1	(11)	6	(18)	3	(25)		10
Constructing Supply-Type Questions (C_5)	(5)	2	(12)	11	(19)	8	(26)	3	24
Constructing Selection-Type Items (C_6)	(6)	4	(13)	6	(20)	12	(27)	7	29
Constructing and Scoring Essay Tests (C_7)	(7)	4	(14)	8	(21)	5	(28)	3	20
Total Behavior Dimension		22		37		28		13	100%

Table 5-3 Alternative Ways of Conceptualizing the Behavior Dimensions of Tables of Specification

Smith and Tyler (1942)	Ebel and Frisbie (1991)
1. Development of effective thinking methods 2. Cultivation of useful work habits and study skills 3. Acquisition of wide range of significant interests 4. Appreciation of aesthetic experiences 5. Development of social sensitivity 6. Personal social adjustment 7. Acquisition of important information 8. Development of physical health 9. Development of consistent life philosophy	1. Understanding of terminology vocabulary 2. Understanding of fact, principles, or generalization 3. Ability to explain or illustrate (relationships) 4. Ability to calculate 5. Ability to predict under specified conditions 6. Ability to recommend appropriate action 7. Ability to make an evaluative judgment
Raths (1938)	**Walbesser (1965)**
1. Functional information 2. Various aspects of thinking 3. Attitudes 4. Interest, aims, purposes, appreciations 5. Study skills and work habits 6. Social adjustments and sensitivity 7. Creativeness 8. Functional social philosophy	1. Identifying 2. Distinguishing 3. Naming 4. Ordering 5. Describing 6. Applying rules 7. Stating rules 8. Demonstrating 9. Interpreting

specifications, the easier the item construction task. Some compromise between the extremes of objectives—highly specific and highly general—will result in a reasonably balanced test.

Having developed a table of specifications the teacher-evaluator will now write items corresponding to each cell in the table. He or she will write a number of independent items in proportion to the representation of each objective in the table. Again, with reference to Table 5-1 the test constructor would write 5 percent of the items (assuming the use of short-answer varieties) on the midsemester exam to measure the objectives of Cell 1, 3 percent of Cell 2, and so on. If an instructor is using essay items, the percentages might reflect the amount of time and scoring weight given to certain items. In this way the evaluator insures proportionality, or what was referred to in the next section as "balance" in the test. Balance is interpreted relative to the amount of time spent on certain topics and skills in class, which in turn reflects the importance of selected objectives.

One of the frequently encountered problems in constructing a table of specifications is knowing how to operationally allocate weights to the cells in the TOS. Two general approaches are possible. The first involves simply classifying each instructional objective into one of the cells of the TOS (using both dimensions) and then expressing that frequency as a percentage of the total number of objectives. One will have to spend more time on certain objectives than others, therefore some adjustment in the percent-weights will have to be made to reflect the varying instructional emphases. A second approach is simply to distribute the percentages for each new total, for example, 5, 7, 5, 10, 24, 29, and 20 over the columns using trial and error to get the correct totals for each column. For example in Table 5-2 all 5 percent for History of Testing went to the Recall cell, but only 3 percent of User of Tests went to Recall whereas 4 percent went to Comprehension.

Tables of specification should be shared with students, for what an instructor has done is to condense a unit or course into a simple two-way grid. The percentages allow students to apportion their study time not only in terms of content, but also in terms of what kinds of tasks they will be asked to perform. Some sample test items would also help the student prepare for the exam. The exam should have both a pretest or motivational effect, as well as posttest or instructional effect.

In summary, the use of a table of specifications in test development will help insure (a) that only those objectives actually pursued in instruction will be measured, (b) that each objective will receive the appropriate relative emphasis in the test, and (c) that by using subdivisions based on content and behavior, no important objectives will be overlooked or misrepresented.

What kinds of criteria will be used to evaluate the test we are planning? Following is a discussion of some characteristics of a high-quality measuring instrument that we will want to keep in mind before, during, and after test development to help insure validity.

Criteria for Evaluating Measuring Instruments

How does one judge the quality of a classroom test? This question frequently goes unanswered due to (a) lack of knowledge about standards and criteria for evaluation, or (b) lack of effort. If either of these conditions exists, the assessment activity cannot be a meaningful one for student or instructor, both of whom should profit from the experience. The student profits because the process of preparing for the test causes him or her to review and interrelate the material. We might call this learning experience a pretest or motivational effect. Upon completion of the test, assuming close proximity between the test and knowledge of the results, a posttest or learning effect should be also noted. The instructor should not only profit from the experience of reviewing his or her instruction, but also from the significant data about student learning he or she derives. In constructing a test, a teacher is asked to summarize the salient elements of instruction in terms of content, student behavior, and classroom activity. The instructor then summarizes these elements in the form of questions to be presented to students. Instructors are next, obviously, forced to "think through" their instruction and thus gain a perspective on their teaching and insight into the organization of the material that should prove beneficial to themselves and their students.

As the teacher constructs a test, what are some of the important factors that should be considered? Ebel (1965, pp. 281–307) has provided a very useful summary of qualities of a good test:

1. *Relevance.* Relevance is the correspondence between the behavior required to respond correctly to a test item and the purpose or objective in writing the item. The test item should be directly related to the course objectives and actual instruction. When used in conjunction with educational measurement, relevance must be considered the major contributor to validity.

2. *Balance.* Balance in a test is the degree to which the proportion of items testing particular outcomes corresponds to the "ideal" test. The framework of the test is outlined by a table of specifications.

3. *Efficiency.* Efficiency is defined in terms of the number of meaningful responses per unit of time. Some compromise must be made among available time for testing, scoring, and relevance.

4. *Objectivity.* For a test question to be considered objective, experts must agree on the "right" or "best" answer. Objectivity, then, is a characteristic of the scoring of the test, not of the form (e.g., multiple-choice, true-false) of the questions.

5. *Specificity.* If subject-matter experts should receive perfect scores, test-wise but course-naive students should receive near-chance scores, indicating that course-specific learnings are being measured.

6. *Difficulty.* The test items should be appropriate in difficulty level to the group being tested. In general for a norm-referenced test, a maximally reliable test is one in which each item is passed by half of the students. For a criterion-referenced test difficulty could be judged relative to the percentage passing before and after instruction. Difficulty will be dictated by skill and knowledge measured and ability of student (see Chapter 11).

7. *Discrimination.* For norm-referenced tests the ability of an item to discriminate is generally indexed by the difference between the proportion of good (or more knowledgeable) and poor (or less able) students who respond correctly. For a criterion-referenced test we tend to think of discrimination in terms of pre-post differences (see Chapter 11) or the ability of the test or item to differentiate competent (masters) from less competent (nonmasters) (see Chapter 12).

8. *Reliability.* Reliability is a complex characteristic, but generally involves consistency of measurement. Consistency of measurement might be judged in terms of time, items, scorers, examinees, examiners, or accuracy of classifications.

9. *Fairness.* To insure fairness, an instructor should construct and administer the test in a manner that allows students an equal chance to demonstrate their knowledge or skill.

10. *Speededness.* To what degree are scores on the test influenced by speed of response? For most achievement tests, speed should generally not be allowed to play a significant role in determining a score, and sufficient time should generally be allowed for all or most examinees to finish the test.

Taken together these characteristics spell "validity" as, in the aggregate, they determine what the test measures and how these scores should be interpreted.

For the most part, a test constructor or user may evaluate the instrument in light of the foregoing 10 factors by careful examination of the test and/or the data it yields. Obviously, consideration should be given to these factors before, during, and after test development and administration. The refinement of a test is a continuous and ongoing process.

The characteristics of difficulty and discrimination have greatest relevance if one's intent is to maximize the measurement of inter- or intra-individual differences. If the intent is to assess progress toward a specified set of objectives, they may have less applicability in instrument development. See Chapter 16 for a clarification of the issues involved in constructing and interpreting criterion-referenced and norm-referenced measures.

Wall and Summerlin (1972) have completed an interesting and useful comparative application of the characteristics of a good measuring instrument. They examine teacher-made and standardized tests in light of each of the 10 characteristics. The results of their analysis are shown in Table 5-4.

Test Administration

After deciding on the measurement procedures to be used, several important additional decisions must be made. The teacher-evaluator must decide on the administration procedures to be followed. If he or she has selected a standardized test, many of the decisions have already been made. The test manual will contain very detailed directions which must be followed precisely. If the scores are to be legitimately compared with those of the standardization group, an attempt to duplicate the standardization testing conditions must be made.

Rigidly controlled administration is just as important to a teacher-made test as to a standardized test. This is particularly true if a teacher anticipates combining the score distributions from a number of different tests or sections of the same course in order to arrive at evaluations.

Many factors are involved in test administration. The form in which the test is presented, the preparation of the students for the test, and the actual conditions of testing need to be considered. Obviously, each student should have a copy of the test. Films, oral presentations, and slides have been used to administer tests with

Table 5-4 Relative Merits of Teacher-Made and Standardized Tests

Characteristic	Teacher-Made	Standardized
Relevance	Measures objectives for the class	Measures achievement for typical classes
Balance	Measures objectives in same proportion as time spent on instruction	Measures a large variety of objectives
Difficulty	Is geared to the group being tested	May vary; usually averages around 50 percent passing for all items
Reliability	Usually not calculated; normally very low but can be as high as standardized tests if carefully planned	Usually high; normally .85 and above
Speededness	Sufficient time is usually given for completion of test	Strict time limits are typical
Discrimination	Each question helps to differentiate between high- and low-scoring students if differentiation is goal; if testing for mastery this characteristic is meaningless	Attempts to find individual differences between students, with each question contributing to differentiation of those scoring high and low
Specificity	Measures specific learnings	Attempts to measure specific learning
Objectivity	There is agreement among experts on answers to items chosen	Answers have usually been checked by subject-matter experts

some degree of success. The most noteworthy characteristic of these methods, which is at once an advantage and a drawback, is the control of presentation. The fixed rate, even if generous, does not allow all students to manifest their natural test-taking behavior or to review questions. The feeling of excessive pressure would not seem desirable, but concern and involvement in and focused attention on the test-taking task would be necessary.

Guidelines for Test Administration

If test scores are to have any meaning, they must be gathered under uniform and optimal conditions. This is particularly true if the intent is to make comparisons between individuals or against an absolute scoring standard. Anyone who ever has been involved in large-scale testing programs knows the importance of preparation. The administration of any group test, particularly a standardized test, is a complex task. To facilitate the process of test administration, Prescott (undated) has prepared a set of guidelines which, although most relevant to standardized tests, can be applied to classroom tests as well. Prescott's suggestion that the examiner take the test is a very good one. The guidelines are as follows:[1]

Before the Testing Date

1. Understand nature and purposes of the testing:
   a. Tests to be given.
   b. Reasons for giving tests.
2. Decide on number to be tested at one time.
3. Decide on seating arrangements.
4. Decide on exact time of testing.
   a. Avoid day before holiday.
   b. Avoid conflicts with recess of other groups.
   c. Make sure there is ample time.
5. Procure and check test materials:
   a. Directions for administering.
   b. Directions for scoring.
   c. Test booklets:
      (1) One for each pupil and examiner.
   d. Answer sheets:
      (1) One for each pupil and examiner.
   e. Pencils (regular or special).
   f. Stopwatch or other suitable timer.
   g. Scoring keys.
   h. "Testing—Do Not Disturb" sign.
   i. Other supplies (scratch paper, etc.).
6. Study test and directions carefully.
   a. Familiarize yourself with:
      (1) General make-up test.
      (2) Time limits.
      (3) Directions.
      (4) Method of indicating answers.
   b. Take the test yourself.
7. Arrange materials for distribution.
   a. Count number needed.
8. Decide on order in which materials are to be distributed and collected.
9. Decide what pupils who finish early are to do.

Just Before Testing

1. Make sure central loudspeaker is disconnected.
2. Put up "Testing—Do Not Disturb" sign.
3. See that desks are cleared.

[1]From George A. Prescott, *Test Service Bulletin 102, Test Administration Guide.* Formerly issued by the Test Department of Harcourt Brace Jovanovich, undated.

4. See that pupils have sharpened pencils.
5. Attend to toilet needs of pupils.
6. Check lighting.
7. Check ventilation.
8. Make seating arrangements.

During Testing

1. Distribute materials according to predetermined order.
2. Caution pupils not to begin until you tell them to do so.
3. Make sure that all identifying information is written on booklet or answer sheet.
4. Read directions exactly as given.
5. Give signal to start.
6. Write starting and finishing times on the chalkboard.
7. Move quickly about the room to:
   a. Make sure pupils are marking answers in the correct place.
   b. Make sure pupils are continuing to the next page after finishing the previous page.
   c. Make sure pupils stop at the end of the test.
   d. Replace broken pencils.
   e. Encourage pupils to keep working until time is called.
   f. Make sure there is no copying.
   g. Attend to pupils finishing early.
8. Permit no outside interruptions.
9. Stop at the proper time.

Just After Testing

1. Collect materials according to predetermined order.
2. Count booklets and answer sheets.
3. Make a record of any incidents observed that may tend to invalidate scores made by pupils.

The directions for taking the test should be as complete, clear, and concise as possible. The student must be made aware of what is expected of him or her. The method of responding should be kept as simple as possible. Reducing the possible mechanical complexities involved in responding is very important for younger students. Instead of using one of the many convenient National Computer Systems, Scantron, or other preprinted answer sheets, the student (up to Grade Four) might be allowed to respond on the test booklet. The directions should also contain instructions on guessing. This problem will be discussed in greater detail in a later section.

Criteria for Preparing Test Directions

Traxler (1951) has offered seven excellent common sense criteria that should be kept in mind when writing the directions for a test. These are:

1. Assume that the examinees and examiner know nothing at all about objective tests.
2. In writing the directions, use a clear, succinct style. Be as explicit as possible, but avoid long drawn-out explanations.
3. Emphasize the more important directions and key activities through the use of underlining, italics, or different type size or style.
4. Give the examiner and each proctor full instructions on what is to be done before, during, and after the administration.
5. Field or pretest the directions with a sample of both examinees and examiners to identify possible misunderstandings and inconsistencies and gather suggestions for improvement.
6. Keep the directions for different forms, subsections, or booklets as uniform as possible.
7. Where necessary or helpful, give practice items (or, if possible, tests) before each regular section. This is particularly important when testing the young or those unfamiliar with objective tests or separate answer sheets, for example, the educationally or culturally disadvantaged, foreign students, or special education students.

Any important test should be announced well in advance; do not dangle the threat of a surprise test over the students' heads. Such an "announced test" procedure is more likely to result in effective study.

If possible, practice should be given in taking tests. This is very important if unusual items or ways of asking questions (e.g., analogy items) are to be used. Again, the younger student would probably benefit most from this practice.

Obviously, the testing room should be as conducive as possible to concentration on the task at hand. Very little research has been done on the effect of distractions on test results. The results of the few investigations that have been undertaken seem to indicate that absolute quiet may not be as important as one might expect. The same general conclusion has been reached concerning the general physical health of a student at the time of testing. Nevertheless, freedom from distractions would seem desirable.

Unless an instructor considers time a major factor in learning, achievement tests should be administered in a way that allows all, or nearly all, students enough time to finish. In general, speed of response is not a relevant variable; allowing sufficient time for the test tends to reduce wild guessing and results in a more reliable measure, particularly if one's concern is with relative achievement performance. There are, of course, situations in which speed alone or a combination of speed of response and level of performance are significant.

It is probably a sound idea to arrange items on the basis of increasing difficulty (actual or estimated). Locating easy items at the beginning of the test, thereby providing success experiences, makes good psychological sense. It is also desirable to group together items requiring similar types of responses. Such a grouping tends to allow the development of a mental or mechanical set conducive to answering a particular type of item.

There is more to test administration than simple distribution and collection of the exam booklets and answer sheets. The "psychological state" of the examinee needs to be considered. Two dimensions of this state are test-wiseness and test anxiety.

Test Scoring

Common sense probably yields more helpful suggestions for test scoring than does prolonged discussion. Obviously, responses need to be recorded in a convenient form so that scoring can proceed efficiently. If scoring is to be done by hand, it should be checked. A number of devices and machines utilizing mark-sensing methods of a mechanical, electrical, or optical nature are available to assist in test scoring. Their cost, however, is still beyond the budgets of most schools. Answer keys and scoring rules should, of course, be prepared before actual scoring. This is very important if supply questions, particularly extended-response essay questions, are used. (See Chapter 8 for suggestions for scoring essay items.) In addition, it is an excellent idea to have a colleague check the content, phrasing, and keying of the items.

Optical Scanning

The development and application of optical scanning hard- and software, particularly desktop scanners, has greatly increased the efficiency of information processing. Increased efficiency not only with regard to the scoring of test answer sheets but also the creation of information on student schedules and registration, attendance, inventory control, personnel tracking and record keeping, health histories, food service reports, surveys, payroll preparations and financial accounting, and instructional management. A great variety of off-the-shelf forms (full- or half-sheet) are available. Response documents can also be created for a modest cost. Figure 5-3 contains a display of answer documents that are available from National Computer Systems.

Developing Hand-Scoring Answer Keys

If standard commercial or separate preprinted answer sheets are to be used, the punch-out overlay scoring template can be applied. These templates are available from most commercial test and answer sheet producers and service organizations. Many teachers, because of the peculiarities of the subject matter, behavior, or examinee involved must develop their own answer sheets. Three major types of hand-scoring answer keys: the fan (or accordion), strip, and cutout key, can be developed by teachers.

Fan key. This type of key (see Figures 5-4 and 5-5) consists of a series of columns, extending from the top to the bottom of the page, on which are

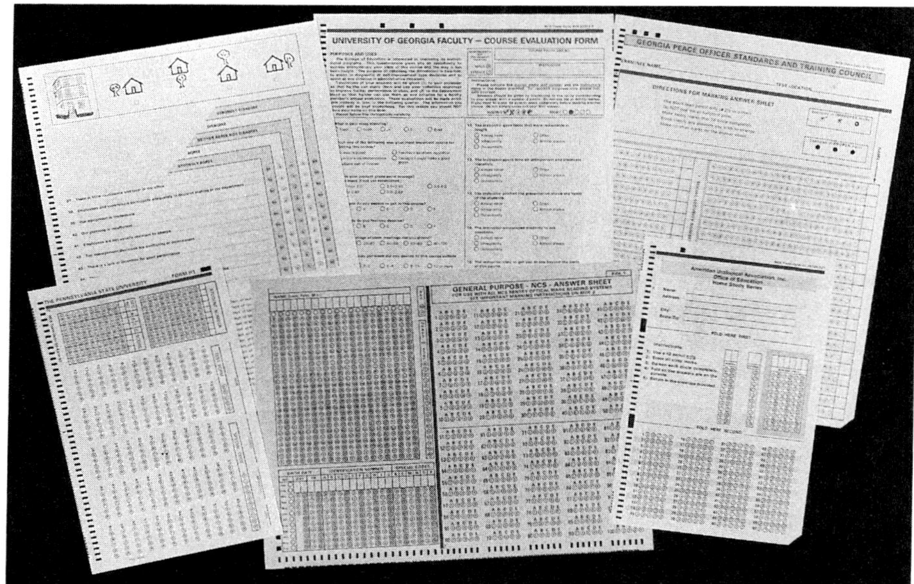

Figure 5-3

Sample general and custom NCS optical scanning forms (Photo Courtesy, Jim Morgenthalers, Instructional Resource Center, University of Georgia)

recorded acceptable answers or directions scored for the individual items. The key and answer sheet are the same size and identically spaced. Usually each column corresponds to a page of the test. The key is folded along vertical lines separating its columns and is superimposed on the appropriate page of the test or next to the appropriate column of the answer sheet and matched to the corresponding responses.

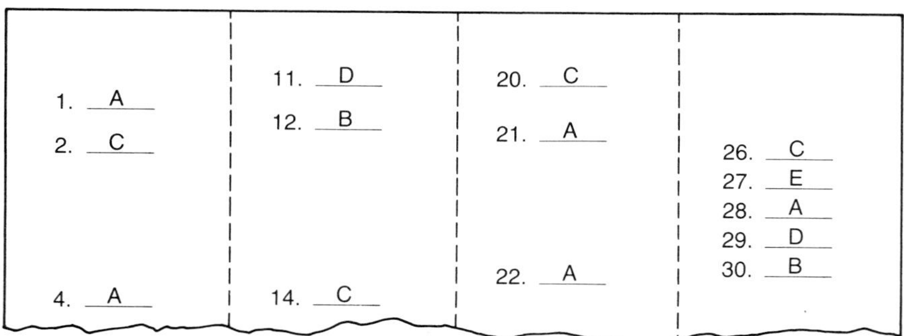

Figure 5-4

Fan key for scoring responses on the test sheets

1. B	16. B	31. D
2. B	17. C	32. D
3. B	18. C	33. B
4. C	19. A	34. A
5. A	20. D	35. D
6. B	21. A	36. C
7. A	22. B	37. B
8. D	23. C	38. B
9. D	24. C	39. A
10. B	25. D	40. C

Figure 5-5

Fan key for scoring responses recorded on separate answer sheet

Strip key. Similar to the fan key, this method employs the use of separate columns, usually on cardboard (see Figure 5-6).

Cutout key. Windows are cut to reveal letters, numbers, words, or phrases on the answer sheet. The key is superimposed on a page of the test or answer sheet (see Figure 5-7).

Two of the most common problems encountered in making decisions about test scoring involve the weighting of responses and corrections for guessing.

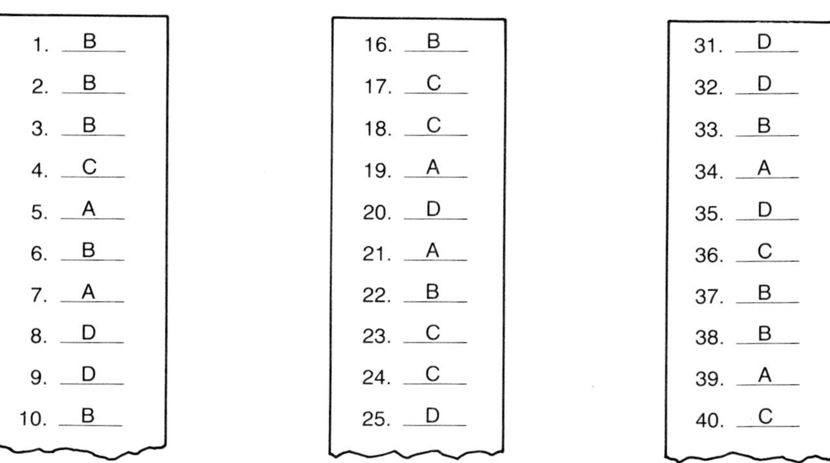

1. B	16. B	31. D
2. B	17. C	32. D
3. B	18. C	33. B
4. C	19. A	34. A
5. A	20. D	35. D
6. B	21. A	36. C
7. A	22. B	37. B
8. D	23. C	38. B
9. D	24. C	39. A
10. B	25. D	40. C

Figure 5-6

Strip key

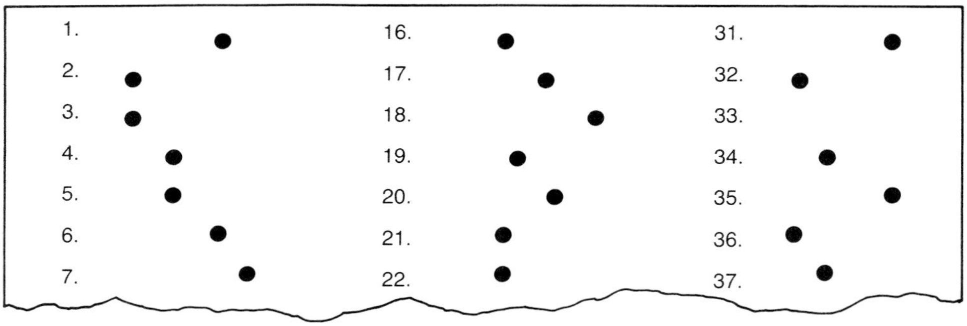

1.	16.	31.
2.	17.	32.
3.	18.	33.
4.	19.	34.
5.	20.	35.
6.	21.	36.
7.	22.	37.

Figure 5-7
Cutout key

Weighting Test Items and Alternatives

Teachers often believe and it seems intuitively reasonable that differential weighting of items or alternative answers provide more discriminating measures. To some extent this is true. If differential weights can be identified and applied on the basis of quality of response, difficulty level, or some other basis that is at least logically if not empirically justified, there is a tendency for the weighted items and tests to be more reliable. The difference in the reliabilities of weighted and unweighted items is generally quite small, especially if the test is reliable to begin with. If a test is of moderate reliability, differential weighting may slightly increase the consistency of measurement. The scoring task is, of course, thereby made more complex.

Confidence weighting procedures have also been developed to incorporate student assurance about answers to questions. This technique is not recommended as it introduces a personality variable into an already complex process.

In light of his own research and the results of other investigations Guilford (1954) concluded that "*differential weighting* of items is most effective in short tests and usually pays little dividends when there are more than 10 to 20 items" (p. 447). Weights of 1 or 0 (i.e., right or wrong) are appropriate for most achievement, aptitude, and general mental ability tests and, in general, differential weighting is not worth the trouble it entails.

Correction for Guessing

Researchers have for more than 30 years been investigating the problem of whether or not to correct for guessing. There is still no definite answer or agreement among the experts. The main purpose of applying corrections is to discourage dishonest or "wild" guessing by extracting a penalty for it. Guessing's most important effect is not on individual scores but on the reliability of the test. If the test is reliable to begin with, chance success is relatively unimportant and its effects are negligible.

If guessing is thought to be a problem on a particular test, two methods are available to control it. Some technicians favor the use of "instructions" against guessing, the rationale being that a request not to guess will in fact inhibit guessing, thereby decreasing the element of chance success. The problem with such instructions is that students do not know when they have complete knowledge, no knowledge, or partial knowledge. Therefore, they may make guesses that are not pure, while a pure guess is based on no knowledge. Instructions usually introduce personality variables and tempt students' gambling instincts. The bold take more chances than the timid and are, therefore, more likely to gain an advantage.

Some experts prefer to use correction formulas, usually in conjunction with but sometimes without "do not guess" directions. The most frequently used formula is:

$$\hat{S} = R - \left(\frac{W}{n - 1}\right), \tag{5.1}$$

where $\hat{S}$ = the corrected score;
R = the number of correct responses;
W = the number of wrong responses, not counting omitted items, and
n = the number of options for each item.

It is obvious that as the number of choices per item increases the likelihood of guessing correctly decreases. Such a formula is really a correction for the number of omitted responses. If no items are omitted, scores corrected for guessing, by subtracting a fraction of the wrong responses, correlate perfectly with uncorrected scores. In general, corrected and uncorrected scores rank students in about the same relative positions. This is particularly true if all students attempt all items and the test is reliable to begin with.

Traub, Hambleton, and Singh (1968) have demonstrated the effectiveness of what might be considered a "psychological" correction for guessing. The formula for the correction is as follows:

$$\hat{S} = R + \frac{O}{n} \tag{5.2}$$

The terms are defined as before, with the addition of the term

O = the number of omitted items.

The corrected score is considered to be a correction due to the fact that the student is given proportional credit for not guessing on items. Although Equation 5.2 correlates perfectly with Equation 5.1, it may have a different psychological impact on the examinee. It is, of course, necessary to alert students to the fact that this correction is to be applied and to explain the terms. If a teacher anticipates a test as being difficult (e.g., a pretest) then one might consider using a correction, but in general it is not worth the effort.

Generally, directions concerning guessing like the following are sufficient: "Answer every item without omissions. Select the alternative you feel is best even though you are not absolutely sure." These directions are preferred not only because the effect of guessing is spread throughout the group, but because then we have a "complete" picture of the performance of all students on all items.

Since we live in an age of technology it is not surprising that many of the mechanical tasks involved in test development, assembly, administration, scoring, and reporting can be handled very efficiently by computer.

Computer Applications in Test Development and Administration

Computers have changed the lives of professionals and laypersons alike. Massive amounts of data can be accessed and processed in support of development and decision making. Computer applications in educational measurement have the potential to drastically change the ways we create, assemble, administer, analyze, report, and interpret test results. It may be the case that just the availability of a personal computer and word processing and graphics software will turn out to be the greatest boon ever for the teacher-tester. Tests can be easily created, corrected, and printed. Computerized measurement systems can significantly facilitate the use of test data in the service of education.

Bunderson, Inouye, and Olsen (1989) have described four "generations" of applications of computer technology. These applications are summarized in Table 5-5. Computerized testing (CT) is today very prevalent, particularly with regard to test scoring. The collecting of large item pools (including the necessary supporting graphics) and item banks provides for the opportunity to create tests efficiently. It may be the case that eventually there will a computer on every teacher's desk to assist not only in test assembly but also with the paper blizzard that threatens to engulf us all. The use of computers in test scoring has been going on for several decades and has more than realized its potential. Test administration can be more uniformly controlled through computer technology, and testing time is in fact reduced.

Computerized adaptive testing (CAT) has also been described as tailored or customized testing as the examinee's path through a set of tasks is determined by performance and/or response time. In a real sense each test is individualized. CAT is based on a psychometric theory called *item response theory* which assumes that the likelihood of answering an item correctly is a function of examinee ability, guessing, item difficulty, and item discrimination. Testing time is significantly reduced through CAT.

The development of Continuous Measurement (CM) parallels that of computer-assisted instruction. The difference lies in the interaction of measurement and the treatment. Actual instructional decisions are assisted through the use of test data. To develop CM systems requires considerable expense and time to calibrate tests and instructional materials.

Intelligent Measurement (IM) captures the knowledge of experts to create interpretation or prescriptive advice. Combinations of scores and data about the examinee

Table 5-5 Applications of Computer Technology in Educational Measurement

Category	Measurement Applications
Computerized Testing (CT)	Assembly Administration Scoring Reporting
Computer Adaptive Testing (CAT)	Modification of Administration on Basis of Examinee Responses
Continuous Measurement (CM)	Measurements Embedded in Curriculum Dynamically Monitor Examinee Progress
Intelligent Measurement (IM)	Data Bases Are Used to Create Test Interpretations

Source: After Bunderson, Inouye, & Olsen, 1989.

are collected in an individualized but "standard" printout. Applications can be found in academic and vocational counseling, individually administered personality or intelligence tests, and tutoring. Theories of learning or personality can be incorporated into the development of IM systems.

Complex software and expensive computer hardware are not needed to achieve technological efficiency in measurement. For a few thousand dollars one can obtain a compact optical scanner, printer, and personal computer capable of computerized testing, and elementary applications of computer adaptive testing, continuous measurement, and intelligent measurement. Figure 5-8 contains a configuration such as that just described. Depicted is a Sentry 3000 optical scanner from National Computer Systems and an IBM microcomputer and a printer. The simple process of recording data for computer input with a pencil mark makes optical scanning a fast, accurate, and efficient means of data collection. The Sentry 3000 can scan up to 600 sheets per hour with an automatic feed mechanism. It can function as a "stand alone" or as an element in a network. Test analysis software (such as Microtest-II) is available to score, prepare descriptive summaries, and undertake test/item analyses. In addition, software such as MicroCAT support item banking and graphics for item creation. The systems will also allow for CAT applications.

The computer can but do our bidding. It is only as smart as we make it. In the final analysis test development is a human activity, and to attempt to remove the human element would detract from the meaningfulness of the results of the activity. It is hard work, but it can be rewarding to both test developer and test taker.

Figure 5-8

Configuration of Sentry 3000: Optical Mark Reading Scanner from National Computer Systems, an IBM microcomputer, and a printer

Getting ready to test takes almost as much time as building the test (almost). Good planning will make the task not only easier, but more meaningful to both teacher and student. A number of important measurement issues were touched upon in this chapter. Among these were: (a) How should I weigh and balance different content and process outcomes in my test blueprint? (b) How many items of what type can I use? (c) How should the directions for a test be stated? (d) What are alternate modes of test administration that are currently available? and (e) What should I do about the problem of guessing? If it's worth doing, it's worth doing right!

Case Study Application

The availability of objectives for the Reading Education exam now allows us to create a table of specifications (TOS) for the midterm exam. The central problem to be addressed is what weights should be assigned to the cells of the TOS. One starting point is the amount of instructional time devoted to topics. Following is a summary of these data.

Content Area (Goals)	*Class time*	*Expected Relative Weights for Each Content Area*	*Actual Weight*
Reflection on the reading process & beliefs about teaching reading	4.5 hrs.	13.00%	14.00%
Emerging Literacy	6 hrs.	17.00%	20.00%
Language Experience Activity (LEA)	3 hrs.	8.50%	6.00%
Decoding Strategies	6 hrs.	17.00%	19.00%
Comprehension Strategies	1.5 hrs.	4.30%	5.00%
Discussion Strategies	1.5 hrs.	4.30%	4.00%
Basal Reading Lessons	8 hrs.	23.00%	17.00%
Reading Program & Exceptional Children	1.5 hrs.	4.30%	5.00%
Reading Program & Bilingual Learners	1.5 hrs.	4.30%	4.00%
Evaluation	1.5 hrs.	4.30%	6.00%
TOTAL	35 hrs.		

After instruction took place the weights were adjusted to reflect the *actual* amount of time spent on each topic. The intended and actual weights are quite close.

The next decision relates to what kind and how much emphasis should be placed on the behaviors measured by the items. It was felt that 80 items would be sufficient for a 100-minute class period, and that the following weights should be placed on the respective behavioral outcomes:

Behavioral Outcome	*Weight*
Knowledge	65.00%
Comprehension	25.00%
Application	9.00%
Analysis	1.00%

The emphasis was on knowledge and comprehension outcomes because (a) the exam was a midterm and therefore heavily concerned with "foundation" information, and (b) application outcomes were dealt with in the field-setting classrooms during the second half of the course.

With this available information create a TOS indicating the number of items in each cell. In addition write a set of examinee directions for taking the test that would be on the test booklet.

Content Review Statements

1. In planning for the development of an assessment device, consideration needs to be given to:
   a. The type of measuring procedure used.
   b. Length of the instrument.
   c. The range of difficulty of items.
   d. Time limits.
   e. Objectives to be sampled.
   f. Arrangement of items.
   g. Scoring procedures.
   h. The method of recording and reporting results.
2. The most important decision to be made during test development is what to measure.
3. The development of a table of specifications (a two-way grid contrasting content and behavioral outcomes) can greatly facilitate both the instructional and the test development process.
4. The *Taxonomy of Educational Objectives* provides very useful categories to help develop a table of specifications.
5. A good measuring instrument should, as a rule, be:
   a. Relevant
   b. Balanced
   c. Efficient
   d. Objective
   e. Specific
   f. Appropriately difficult and discriminating
   g. Reliable
   h. Fair
   i. Unspeeded
6. A relevant measurement contains samples of behavior directly related to the objectives.
7. A balanced measurement must weigh test behaviors in proportion to their actual occurrence.
8. An efficient measurement provides the maximum number of relevant scorable responses per unit of time.
9. The extent to which experts agree on the scorability of a measurement is an indication of its degree of objectivity.
10. Item difficulty and discrimination in educational measurements should depend upon the projected use of the results, the level of student and subject matter, and the nature of students' prior instructional experience.
11. Each student should have a fair opportunity to demonstrate his or her knowledge or skill.
12. Most educational measurements should be unspeeded so that comparable behavior samples can be gathered from all students.
13. The types of outcomes measured are not readily apparent from the format of the measurement procedure used.

14. Carefuly controlled conditions should prevail when administering a test, particularly a standardized test.
15. The directions for taking a test should be as clear and concise as possible.
16. Great care needs to be taken in specifying test-scoring procedures.
17. Optical scanning is the most efficient method of collecting test responses in the public schools.
18. Teachers may profitably use fan, strip, or cutout keys in test scoring.
19. If all individuals attempt all items, a correction for guessing on objective tests is probably not needed.
20. The greater the variety of outcomes measured and the more frequent the measurement, the greater the reliability of the assessment.
21. The results of all tests should be discussed with individual students and/or the entire class.
22. The teacher should give students samples of the questions he or she will ask on tests and should allow practice on them to reduce test anxiety and make possible a fairer sampling of behavior.
23. The chances of achieving a passing score by chance on a reliable classroom test are extremely small.
24. The differential weighting of response alternatives on a multiple-choice exam rarely improves its measuring capacity.
25. Computer applications in test development include test:
    a. Assembly
    b. Administration
    c. Scoring
    d. Analysis
    e. Reporting/Interpreting

Speculations

1. "To correct-for-guessing or not correct-for-guessing, that is the question." What is the answer?
2. Why is a table of specifications important in test development?
3. Describe some applications of computers in testing.
4. What are some ways in which arranging items in different ways within a test could influence performance?
5. Describe the optimal conditions under which either standardized or nonstandardized tests should be administered.
6. What testing conditions are best for you?
7. Is the differential weighting of (a) item alternatives, or (b) items justified? Why?
8. In selecting a test what criteria should be considered and why?
9. Do you think the directions for taking a test are really all that important? In what way?
10. How would you rank-order the 10 criteria for a high-quality measuring instrument? Justify your ranking.

Suggested Readings

Antes, R. L. (1989). *Preparing students for taking tests.* Bloomington, IN: Phi Delta Kappa. Contains advice on test-taking strategies for both standardized and teacher-made tests, and ways of dealing with test anxiety.

Fuchs, D., & Fuchs, L. S. (1986). Test procedure bias: A meta-analysis of examiner familiarity effects. *Review of Educational Research, 56*(2), 243–262. An analysis of 22 studies involving 1,489 subjects revealed higher scores for students where the examiner was familiar and when subjects were of low socioeconomic status.

Lindquist, E. F. (Ed.). (1951). *Educational measurement.* Washington, DC: American Council on Education. The following chapters probably contain the most comprehensive treatment of the topics discussed in this chapter: Chapter 5, "Preliminary Considerations in Objective Test Construction," by E. F. Lindquist; Chapter 6, "Planning the Objective Test," by K. W. Vaughn; and Chapter 10, "Administering and Scoring the Objective Test," by Arthur E. Traxler.

Linn, R. L. (Ed.). (1989). *Educational measurement* (3rd ed.). Washington, DC: American Council on Education and the Macmillan Company. The following chapters are representative of current thought on the topics of this chapter: Chapter 8, "The Specifications and Development of Tests of Achievement and Ability," by Jason Millman and Jennifer Greene; Chapter 9, "The Four Generations of Computerized Educational Measurement," by C. Victor Bunderson, Dillon K. Inouye, and James B. Olsen; Chapter 10, "Computer Technology in Test Construction and Processing," by Frank B. Baker; and Chapter 12, "Designing Tests That are Integrated with Instruction," by Anthony J. Nitko.

Thorndike, R. L. (Ed.). (1971). *Educational measurement.* (2nd ed.). Washington, DC: American Council on Education. The following chapters are representative of the topics of this chapter: Chapter 3, "Planning the Objective Test," by Sherman N. Tinkelman; Chapter 6, "Reproducing the Test," by Robert L. Thorndike; Chapter 7, "Test Administration," by William V. Clemans; and Chapter 8, "Automation of Test Scoring, Reporting and Analysis," by Frank B. Baker.

Wodtke, K. H., Harper, F., Schommer, M., & Brunelli, P. (1989). How standardized is school testing? An exploratory observational study of standardized group testing in kindergarten. *Educational Evaluation and Policy Analysis, 11*(3), 223–235.

Bev's Diary

I'm getting philosophical! Life is like a big map with many routes and turns. It's kind of like that in building a test, but be careful you don't take a wrong turn. That's why I need a plan—but putting together a test blueprint is more work than I imagined.

Part of planning is not just about building the test itself, but how it will be administered. I talked with my friend Denise, a second-grade teacher at Glynn Elementary School this morning during our daily early morning walk, and she said that she had asked some of her kids to write out some instructions to a friend about how to take tests. She was surprised at the level of sophistication of second graders. She shared some of their comments with me. Among them were the following:

> "Don't get eney food on the test"
> "Don't get nervise"
> "Do good luck on it"
> "Get a good night sleep the night before the test"
> "You should practice doing your test"
> "Eat a good brekfes—eat eggs and orange jusic"
> "If you don't know one make a good guess"
> "Look at the ground and think when you don't know answer"
> "Good Georgia Bulldog luck"

So it would seem again that out of the mouths of babes oft times come gems.

Part Three

Constructing Measuring Instruments

Well, the honeymoon is over. It's time to start to build a test. I never knew so much work was involved in constructing a high-quality measuring instrument. Objectives to the left of me, items to the right, a blueprint up front, and who knows what's gaining on me from the back. One thing I must remember is to make sure and teach what I said I was going to in the manner in which I said I was going to, and evaluate only that which I taught. That's a big responsibility, but somebody once said no pain–no gain, or if you want to dance you have to pay the band. In any event a worthwhile product requires maximum effort.

Following are the limericks for this week. This is getting to be fun!

Sometimes when I give a big test
My students think it's a great pest
They fume and they snort
And then they retort
Help me, which answer is best?

Writing good items is most arduous
It takes lots of work and is tortuous
For phrasing is hard
None of us writes like the Bard
Be careful the results are not calamitous.

Chapter 6

An Introduction to Item Writing and Constructing Short Answer and True-False Items

Preliminary Considerations
General Guidelines for Item Writing
Writing Supply Items
Writing True-False Items
Content Review Statements
Speculations
Suggested Readings

Effective educational assessment will result from careful planning, imaginative and skillful question writing, careful formulation of questions into a total test, and fair proper administration and scoring. Effectiveness also depends on the quality of instruction preceding testing and on the intelligent subsequent interpretation and use of test scores. The author noted in the previous chapters that test planning, whose importance is often underestimated, involves decisions about learning outcomes, the contexts in which they are most likely to be demonstrated, and the kinds of stimuli necessary or likely to elicit them. Item writing would follow logically from the test development sequence outlined above, and—make no mistake—it is a difficult and time-consuming task. We do, however, make very important decisions about curricula, students, programs, and institutions on the basis of tests that we have prepared. Therefore maximum efforts are required. What follows are kind of idealized guidelines. Don't be intimidated by them. Use them as standards along with common sense in writing items.

Item writers need to keep one major principle in mind: The item needs to match the intent (objective). The previously discussed characteristic of *relevance* is of paramount concern. Do not forget that the kinds of tests we construct not only reflect on our teaching but can and do influence it. How we test, for example, will influence how students study.

The writing of test questions, items, or exercises basically involves finding the most suitable manner in which to pose problems to students. Sometimes this can result in some interesting challenges as seen in the examples contained in Table 6-1.

Table 6-1 Creative Measurement Approaches from America's Campuses

HISTORY: Describe the history of the papacy from its origins to the present day, concentrating especially, but not exclusively, on its social, political, economic, religious, and philosophical aspects and impact on Europe, Asia, America, and Africa. Be brief, concise, and specific.

MEDICINE: You have been provided with a razor blade, a piece of gauze, and a bottle of Scotch. Remove your appendix. Do not suture your work until it has been inspected. You have 15 minutes.

PUBLIC SPEAKING: 2,600 riot-crazed aborigines are storming the test room. Calm them. You may use any ancient language except Latin or Greek.

MUSIC: Write a piano concerto. Orchestrate and perform it with flute and drum. You will find a piano under your chair.

EDUCATION: Develop a foolproof and inexpensive system of education that will meet the needs of all segments of society. Convince both the faculty and rioting students outside to accept it. Limit yourself to the vocabulary found in the Dick and Jane Reading Series.

PSYCHOLOGY: Based on your knowledge of their works, evaluate the emotional stability, degree of adjustment, and repressed frustrations of the following: Alexander of Aphrodisias, Rameses II, Gregory of Nyssa, and Hammurabi. Support your evaluations with quotations from each man's works, making appropriate references. It is not necessary to translate.

SOCIOLOGY: Estimate the sociological problems that might accompany the end of the world. Construct an experiment to test your theory.

BIOLOGY: Create life. Estimate the differences in subsequent human culture if this form of life had been developed 500 million years ago, with special attention to the probable effect on the English parliamentary system. Prove your thesis.

ENGINEERING: The disassembled parts of a high-powered rifle have been placed in a box on your desk. You will also find an instruction manual printed in Swahili. In 10 minutes a hungry Bengal tiger will be admitted to the room. Take whatever action you feel appropriate. Be prepared to justify your decision.

POLITICAL SCIENCE: There is a red telephone on your desk. Start World War III. Report at length on its sociopolitical effects, if any.

EPISTEMOLOGY: Take a position for or against truth. Prove the validity of your position.

GENERAL KNOWLEDGE: Describe in detail your general knowledge. Be objective and specific.

Reprinted from "Capital M," a publication of MENSA.

Such problems may involve the recall of learned information or the use of some higher-order mental abilities. The next two chapters present guidelines and suggestions that have been found useful in constructing two of the major classes of "objective" short-answer items—supply and selection. The supply (student/respondent constructs response/answers) items examined will be simple direct questions and completion items. The selection items (choice among alternatives) discussed will be of the true-false, multiple-choice, and matching varieties. The essay question is considered by some experts to fall in the "supply" category, and a distinction is sometimes made between extended-response and restricted-response supply questions. We are here considering only the short-answer (e.g., a single word, phrase, or sentence) supply item. Essay or extended free-response items will be considered in Chapter 8.

Historically, supply items have been referred to as "recall" or short-answer items, and selection items as "recognition" items. The distinction may not be warranted, implying as it does that we are only measuring qualitative differences in memory.

We refer here only to the form in which the response to a test question is to be made. The student either constructs his own response or identifies the correct answer in a list of alternatives. The instructional objective being measured depends upon the content and structure of the item itself, rather than on the form of the response. There are some data in the literature of experimental psychology to suggest that tests of recognition yield higher scores than do tests of recall (Postman & Rau, 1957). If we can accept length of retention as a criterion of success, however, we also have evidence that recall and recognition activities are very highly correlated (Bahrick, 1964). Thus supply and selection items can measure related behavior, and the decision about the type to use will probably be arbitrary or dictated by such practical considerations as ease of scoring.

Preliminary Considerations

By way of preview, let us point out five principles that need to be considered as one prepares to construct items:

1. Adequate provision should be made for measuring all of the important outcomes of instruction.
2. The test and its items should reflect the approximate emphases given various objectives in the course.
3. The nature of the test and its items must take into account the nature of the group to be examined.
4. The nature of the test and its items must take into consideration the conditions under which the test is to be administered.
5. The nature of the test and its items must take into consideration the purpose it is to serve.

Implicit in these principles are several prerequisites for sound item construction. The first and probably most obvious prerequisite is competence in the subject matter to be examined. The test constructor should be a scholar in the broadest and finest sense of the word. The teacher/test constructor must have a grasp of the basic principles and knowledges, as well as the common fallacies.

But command of the subject matter is a necessary but not sufficient condition for writing effective items. The test constructor must also possess skill in item writing. The item writer must be aware of the various ways in which questions can be asked and the kinds of objectives for which each is best suited. Some of these knowledges may be acquired in courses in test construction or from the references listed at the end of this chapter. The best approach is, of course, a combination of formal study and experience. One must actually write many items of various types, and try them out with students, before one can develop skill and perspective on the relative advantages and disadvantages of the various question forms.

An integral aspect of item-writing skill is, of course, mastery of verbal and written communication skills. The item writer must be able to apply the rules of grammar and rhetoric. Test items are probably read more closely than any other type of nonlegal written communication.

If item construction and test development do not proceed from a rational and well-developed philosophy of education, the resulting items are likely to treat only superficial aspects of instruction. The resulting test would be of variable quality. The specification of defensible instructional objectives is of paramount importance in test construction.

And finally, the item writer must be a kind of educational and developmental psychologist. Test constructors must possess knowledge of how students learn and develop. Such knowledge of individual differences will allow them to accomplish an optimal matching of test questions and students. One would not, for example, use analogy items with third-grade students, because the mechanically contrived way of asking questions does not correspond to the usual instructional program at this level and students are unfamiliar with the form. We do not want the mechanics of a test question to interfere with measurement.

Let us now turn our attention to some guidelines for writing items. Many of the suggestions in the remainder of this chapter will be considered common sense. But, unfortunately, the application of common-sense principles in test development is often found wanting. If, in the following three sections, we can underscore the importance of common sense in item writing, we will have made a worthwhile contribution.

General Guidelines for Item Writing

Before considering specific item types, it would be profitable to consider some general principles for item writing. Remmers, Gage, and Rummel (1965) have summarized six principles applicable to all short-answer items:

1. *Avoid using items which, in terms of either content or structure, could be considered obvious, trivial, meaningless, or ambiguous.* If a test developer does not

rely heavily upon a table of specifications to guide item and test development, these types of unsatisfactory items may result.

2. *Follow the rules of punctuation, grammar, and rhetoric.* Again, the importance of command of language and expressive skills in item development is emphasized.

3. *Use items that have a "right" or "definitely correct" answer, or at least an answer upon which experts agree.* This item characteristic was described in Chapter 5 as "objectivity."

4. *Avoid items that rely on obscure or esoteric language.* Unless one's intent is to test vocabulary, it is not desirable to elicit responses whose correctness depends upon size of vocabulary or reading ability. If key words are obscure, even the better students will fail to give them sufficient attention, and the items may become "trick" or "catch" questions.

5. *Avoid interrelated items.* This situation arises when the content of one item (e.g., the stem or alternatives in a multiple-choice item) furnishes the answer to other items. Inasmuch as we frequently test the same content area a number of times, it is difficult to avoid interrelated items, and only very careful inspection of the test will reveal them.

6. *Avoid items containing "irrelevant cues."* Irrelevant cues probably constitute the chief fault of most classroom tests. Irrelevant cues are a class of defect that leads a student to the correct answer independent of his knowledge or skill. Such defects may take the form of grammatical clues, word associations or definitions, a systematic difference in the correct answer, or stereotyped language, to name only a few. The type of cue will vary with the type of item. A test that contains a large number of items with irrelevant cues is probably measuring nothing more than test-wiseness or intelligent test-taking behavior.

A general checklist of questions relating to the quality of item content and structure is presented in Table 6-2. It is based on material originally created by Dr. Harold Bligh, former managing editor of the Test Division of Harcourt, Brace, and World, Inc., 1962.

Let us now turn our attention to specific item types and guidelines for their construction. Many of the suggestions for certain item types are applicable to the other types as well, and the suggestions given here were selected on the basis of practical applicability.

Writing Supply Items

Supply items are generally of two types: simple direct questions (e.g., Who was the first American astronaut to fly in space?) and completion items (e.g., The name of

Table 6-2 Checklist of Achievement Item Writing Principles

Item Content	**Yes**	**No**
1. Does item deal with content of sufficient importance and significance?	_____	_____
2. Are variety of cognitive outcomes measured?	_____	_____
3. Is content too specific?	_____	_____
4. Is item content up-to-date?	_____	_____
5. Is content unambiguous so that student does not have to make unwarranted interpretations?	_____	_____
6. Are items grouped by content?	_____	_____
7. Is content appropriate for grade and ability level?	_____	_____
8. Are vocabulary and readability levels appropriate for examinees?	_____	_____
Item Structure		
9. Is problem statement clearly expressed?	_____	_____
10. Is test free from interrelated items (items give answer to other items)?	_____	_____
11. Is best question format used for given objective?	_____	_____
12. Is item free from ambiguous wording?	_____	_____
13. Is item free from irrelevant cues?	_____	_____
14. Can answers to questions be objectively scored?	_____	_____
15. Are multiple-choice answers mutually exclusive?	_____	_____
16. Are multiple-choice answers plausible?	_____	_____
17. Are multiple-choice answers grammatically parallel?	_____	_____
18. Are multiple-choice answers of comparable length?	_____	_____
19. Is test free from trick or catch questions?	_____	_____

the first American astronaut to fly in space was ________________.). The chief advantage of the supply item is that it minimizes the effect of guessing. Because the student is required to construct his or her own response, supply items constitute one of the best ways of measuring objectives associated with the first level (Knowledge) of the *Taxonomy of Educational Objectives.* Such an emphasis on memory, in moderation, is probably not unreasonable. Students must possess a certain amount of knowledge or factual information before they can do anything else. Thus an instructor's decision to check on specific facts, which are requisite to further work with supply items, is justified.

Another outstanding advantage of supply items, particularly for those teaching and testing in the early grades, is that they are "natural." Teaching in the elementary grades frequently employs the so-called Socratic question-and-answer format. In testing, then, the use of simple direct questions follows logically from the method of instruction. Supply items are also efficient from the instructor's standpoint, that is, they allow the student to summarize long and often complex problem-solving processes in a single brief statement, thereby facilitating scoring.

One of the disadvantages of supply items is that scoring is not always completely objective. It is surprising how often students come up with correct but unanticipated answers. Unless the scoring key is revised in light of alternative correct answers, serious injustices may be perpetrated on students. Lack of objectivity can frequently be traced to the use of ambiguous words in the item. Because they are easily prepared, supply items too frequently become *only* a matter of identification and/or naming. For example, it would be far more meaningful to know what proved to be the weaknesses of the Articles of Confederation than to know in what year they were signed. It is unlikely that a test composed primarily of recall kinds of items would reflect all relevant instructional objectives.

It should be noted that the following specific guidelines are not "rules" in the strict sense of the word, but ways of asking questions that have been found useful. In many instances the choice of style depends on the personal preferences of the item writer and the intent in writing the item.

1. *Require short, definite, clear-cut, and explicit answers.* An indefinite statement is likely to lead to scoring problems for instructors and response problems for students.

FAULTY: Ernest Hemingway wrote ______________.

IMPROVED: *The Old Man and the Sea* was written by ______________.
Who wrote *The Old Man and the Sea*?

A correlated problem relates to the context of the item. Since test items, but particularly completion/supply items, are dependent on context for meaning, they can be ambiguous. Context is used here in the sense that the examinee must have sufficient information to be able to respond intelligently to the questions. The previous faulty item about Ernest Hemingway does not give test takers sufficient clues as to what the questioner is asking.

2. *Avoid multimutilated statements.* Merely introducing blanks liberally into a statement—from a text, for example—can only lead to ambiguity. In addition, the instructor is not sure which portion of the statement the student is responding to and therefore which objective is being measured. One can end up with a nonsensical sequence of blanks.

FAULTY: ______________ pointed out in ______________ that freedom of thought in America was seriously hampered by ______________ ______________ ______________ ______________.

IMPROVED: That freedom of thought in America was seriously hampered by social pressures toward conformity was pointed out in 1830 by (*De Tocqueville*).

3. *If several correct answers* (e.g., synonyms) *are possible, equal credit should be given to each one.*

4. *Specify and announce in advance whether scoring will take spelling into account.*

5. *In testing for comprehension of terms and knowledge of definitions, it is often better to supply the term and require a definition than to provide a definition and require the term.* The student is less likely to benefit from verbal association cues if this procedure is followed. In addition, asking the student to supply the definition is a better measure of his knowledge.

FAULTY: What is the general measurement term describing the consistency with which items in a test measure the same thing?

IMPROVED: Define "internal consistency reliability." The item has been classified as "comprehension" as the examinee is required to state in his or her own words (paraphrase) the definition, and this equates to comprehension.

6. *It is generally recommended that in completion items the blanks come at the end of the statement.* Beginning an item with a blank is awkward for the student and may interfere with his comprehension of the question. In general, the best approach is a simple and direct one.

FAULTY: A (an) ______________ is the index obtained by dividing a mental age score by chronological age and multiplying by 100.

IMPROVED: The index obtained by dividing a mental age score by chronological age and multiplying by 100 is called a (an) ______________.

In this instance perhaps a direct question format might be preferred.

IMPROVED: What is the term used to describe the index obtained by dividing a mental age score by chronological age and multiplying by 100?

7. *Minimize the use of textbook expressions and stereotyped language.* When statements are taken out of context, they tend to become ambiguous. The use of paraphrased statements, however, will reduce the incidence of correct responses that represent meaningless verbal associations. In addition, it should reduce the temptation to memorize the exact wording of the text or lecture material.

FAULTY: The power to declare war is vested in ______________.

IMPROVED: Which national legislative body has the authority to declare war?

Or better yet, perhaps a true-false item could be used.

IMPROVED: Congress has the authority to declare war.
True False

8. *Specify the terms in which the response is to be given.*

FAULTY: Where does the Security Council of the United Nations hold its meetings?

IMPROVED: In what city of the United States does the Security Council of the United Nations hold its meetings?

A high degree of precision is particularly important in mathematics questions stated in free-response form. Otherwise, the student may be faced with the problem of trying to guess the degree of error to be tolerated. Is one decimal place accuracy sufficient? Two decimal place accuracy? Different students may come to different conclusions.

FAULTY: If a circle has a 4-inch diameter, its area is ____________.

IMPROVED: A circle has a 4-inch diameter. Its area in square inches correct to two decimal places, is ____________.

9. *In general, direct questions are preferable to incomplete declarative sentences.*

FAULTY: Gold was discovered in California in the year ____________.

IMPROVED: In what year was gold discovered in California? ____________.

10. *Avoid extraneous clues to the correct answer.* The grammatical structure of an item may lead a student to the correct answer, independent of his knowledge, particularly if the number of alternative answers is small.

FAULTY: A fraction whose denominator is greater than its numerator is a ____________.

IMPROVED: Fractions whose denominators are greater than their numerators are called ____________.

In the faulty item above, the article "a" functions as an irrelevant clue. Similarly, blanks should be of uniform length so as not to suggest the extensiveness of the expected response.

Writing True-False Items

In responding to constant-alternative items, the examinee chooses one of two alternatives that remains the same throughout a series of items. The alternatives are usually True and False. These are variations. Other forms might be: yes-no, right-wrong, true-false-depends, correct-incorrect, same-opposite, true-false and converse true or converse false, true-false with correction variety, and true-false-qualification. Because it is the most common representative constant-alternative type, the true-false item will be used as an example in this section.

Of all the types of items used in educational measurement, the true-false variety is probably the most controversial. At one extreme we have such statements as:

> True-false items undoubtedly have more popularity than merit. A true-false test tends to give inconsistent results. . . . The use of true-false items in classroom tests is not recommended. (Gorow, 1966)

At the other end of the opinion continuum, we have:

> Acquiring command of knowledge is . . . the central purpose of education. All knowledge is knowledge of propositions. . . . The essential purpose of logical reasoning is to test the truth or falsity of deductive propositions. Propositions are expressed in sentences which may be true or false. This is the stuff of which human knowledge (and true-false tests) are made. (Ebel, 1965)

It is the author's feeling that, despite some difficulties in constructing such items, the true-false question is a potentially valuable data-gathering procedure. There are a number of advantages to the use of true-false items. Most prominent among these is efficiency. An instructor can present a large number of such items per unit of testing time. This allows him to survey large content areas to obtain an estimate of students' knowledge. Scoring of true-false items and tests is, of course, rapid and easy. If great care is exercised in their construction, such items can be used to test understanding of principles and generalizations. In addition, they can profitably be used to assess persistence of popular misconceptions, fallacies, and superstitions (e.g., Swallowing watermelon seeds will result in appendicitis). As a footnote, it should be pointed out that the learning of significant amounts of misinformation from true-false items has *not* been demonstrated. What little mislearning does take place can be "washed out" if the test is reviewed by students and instructor. This is, of course, a recommended class activity no matter what type of item is used. Finally, true-false items are well adapted to testing situations in which only two responses are possible (e.g., School emergency exits should open inwardly).

The disadvantages and limitations of true-false items may outweigh their merits unless thoughtful judgment and intelligence are exercised. Some experts say that, although seemingly easy to construct, meaningful and error-free constant-alternative items are the most difficult of all "objective" questions to write. Quality and precision of language are crucial to these items. Ambiguous terminology and reading ability probably have the greatest effect on true-false items, since a student must respond, in most instances, to a single unqualified statement. Obviously, the smaller the stimulus, the greater the chance for misinterpretation. Guessing can also have a significant effect. On a 50-item true-false test "blind guessing" is likely to result in a score of 25. The result, of course, is to reduce the usable range of scores from 50 (zero to 50) to 25 (25 to 50). It would, however, be a rare event for a student to respond blindly. Almost all students will have some information about an item. In addition, although the odds of a chance score of 25 on a 50-item test are 1 in 2, those of a chance score of 35 are 1 in 350. Once the indifference point (50-50) is passed, chance responses through guessing will work *against* the student. The solution is to increase test reliability by using a fairly large number of items, thereby reducing the overall effect of guessing. One final limitation of the true-false variety of constant-alternative items involves their susceptibility to "response sets." Response sets are tendencies to respond to test items on the basis of form rather than content. A response set labeled "acquiescence"—the reliable tendency to respond "true" when in doubt about a particular item—has been identified. This behavior, although constant and reliable, is unrelated to the purpose of the item and test, and therefore confounds the meaning of the scores. The best way to overcome this problem is to construct a reliable test to begin with. In addition, balancing the number of true and false items might help. There is some evidence, however, that false items discriminate better; perhaps a 60-40 split in favor of the false statements is the best recommendation.

Despite the seemingly overwhelming evidence of the limitations of true-false items, they can prove useful in classroom tests if used in moderation with upper-level students. One would not recommend a test entirely composed of constant-alternative items. Specific suggestions for improving true-false items follow.

1. *Avoid the use of "specific determiners."* Specific determiners are a class of words that function as irrelevant cues. For example, it has been found that, on most classroom tests, items that include the words "only," "no," "none," "always," "never," and so forth, are generally false. On the other hand, items containing words like "could," "might," "can," "may," and "generally" will usually be true.

FAULTY: No picture–no sound in a television set may indicate a bad 5U4G tube.

IMPROVED: A bad 5U4G tube in a television set will result in no picture–no sound.

The use of the negatives no picture–no sound should not pose a problem here as it is simply a description of the condition of the television set. A test-wise but unknowledgeable student would be likely to decipher the correct answer in the imprecise wording of the item. If the number of true and false specific determiners is evenly balanced, their influence is reduced. There are, of course, situations in which an instructor may successfully use specific determiners in true-false items whose answers are the opposite of those suggested by the words in the question (e.g., The area of a rhombus is always equal to one half the product of its diagonals).

2. *Base true-false items upon statements that are absolutely true or false, without qualifications or exceptions.* This is a difficult requirement for the contents of some subject-matter areas (e.g., history, literature) where trends, generalizations, and principles are hard to demonstrate empirically. Statements that are not absolutely true or false are likely to perplex examinees, particularly the more knowledgeable, if an element of ambiguity can be introduced. Examinees may read different assumptions into the statement, and one can no longer be sure what the item is measuring.

FAULTY: World War II was fought in Europe and the Far East. This appears to be an excellent item, but appearances can be deceiving. Responses to the item will depend upon one's interpretation of the item's content span. Did the test constructor wish to consider the location of all of WWII, or to focus on selected theaters of combat?

IMPROVED: The primary combat locations in terms of military personnel during World War II were Europe and the Far East.

3. *Avoid negative stated items when possible and eliminate all double negatives.* Such phrasing may cause a student to miss an item because he does not comprehend the question. Double negatives are frequently interpreted as emphatically negative. Such items might be used to measure translating ability in an English course, but their general usefulness is negligible; they should be avoided.

FAULTY: It is not frequently observed that copper turns green as a result of oxidation.

IMPROVED: Copper will turn green upon oxidizing.

4. *Use quantitative and precise rather than qualitative language where possible.* Again, the specificity of word meanings comes into play in judging the effectiveness of an item. Such words as "few," "many," "young," "long," "short," "large," "small," and "important," unless accompanied by a standard of comparison, are open to interpretation and thus ambiguous.

FAULTY: Many people voted for Richard Nixon in the 1972 Presidential election.

IMPROVED: Richard Nixon received more than 60 percent of the popular votes cast in the Presidential election of 1972.

5. *Avoid stereotypic and textbook statements.* Such statements, when taken out of context, are ambiguous and frequently meaningless and trivial.

FAULTY: From time to time efforts have been made to explode the notion that there may be a cause-and-effect relationship between arboreal life and primate anatomy.

IMPROVED: There is a known relationship between primate anatomy and arboreal life.

A related problem arises when text material is quoted verbatim and turned into a true-false statement by inserting *no* or *not*. Such statements may appear ambiguous and place too great a premium on rote memorization, are awkward to read, and can be ambiguous.

FAULTY: An equilateral rectangle is not a square.

6. *Avoid making the true items consistently longer than the false items.* There is a tendency, particularly on the part of the beginning teacher and item writer, to write systematically longer true items. This phenomenon results from concern that all necessary qualifications be made, so that there can be no doubt that the item is, in fact, true.

7. *Avoid the use of unfamiliar or esoteric language.* Comprehension of an item is determined by its difficulty. It is always best to keep its language simple and straightforward and not to confound the student with five-dollar words when fifty-cent ones will do.

FAULTY: According to some peripatetic politicos, the *raison d'être* for capital punishment is retribution.

IMPROVED: According to some politicians, justification for the existence of capital punishment can be traced to the Biblical statement, "An eye for an eye."

8. *Avoid complex sentences with many dependent clauses.* Highly involved sentences and compound statements tend to distract the examinee from the central idea of the item. It is a poor practice to make one of the dependent clauses in a true-false item, false. It is likely that students will not focus on such seemingly unimportant parts of the statement, and the item becomes a "trick" or "catch" question. With compound statements, the student does not know which element is to be judged true or false.

FAULTY: Jane Austen, an American novelist born in 1790, was a prolific writer and is best known for her novel *Pride and Prejudice*, which was published in 1820. There are so many details in this item that the student does not know on which one to focus. The item is false for many reasons (Austen was a British novelist, 1775–1817, and the book was published in 1813), and different students will get credit for different amounts of knowledge.

IMPROVED: Jane Austen is best known for her novel *Pride and Prejudice.*

9. *It is suggested that the crucial elements of an item be placed at the end of the statement.* The function of the first part of a two-part statement is to "set the problem." To focus on the effect in a cause-and-effect relationship, for example, one should state the true cause in the first portion of the statement, and a false effect at the end. Conversely, to focus on the cause, one should state the true effect first, and a false cause at the end of the statement. This procedure is suggested because the student is likely to focus on the last portion of a statement he reads. Thus the instructor's objective and the student's attention will be synchronized. The following item is intended to focus on the effect.

FAULTY: Oxygen reduction occurs more readily because carbon monoxide combines with hemoglobin faster than oxygen does.

IMPROVED: Carbon monoxide poisoning occurs because carbon monoxide dissolves delicate lung tissue.

Obviously, "true" cause-and-effect items are also useful.

So often in education, and the behavioral sciences in general for that matter, there is a gap between theory and practice. Such may be the case in using short-answer and true-false items. These item types are frequently maligned as measuring nothing of importance. Sometimes in practice this happens, but it does not mean that significant educational outcomes cannot be measured. The method is there—use it intelligently.

Case Study Application exercises related to the content of our Reading Education Course and the measurement methods considered in this chapter will be included in the Case Study Application of Chapter 7.

Content Review Statements

1. The writing of test items, questions, or exercises basically involves finding the most suitable manner in which to pose problems to students.
2. A supply-type item requires the examinee to construct his own response to a direct question or incomplete statement.
3. A selection-type item requires the student to decide between two or more possible answers.
4. Common shortcomings of teacher-made tests include:
   a. Too great a reliance on subjective but presumably absolute standards.
   b. Hasty development and insufficient length.
   c. Focusing on trivia and easily measured outcomes to the exclusion of important achievements.
   d. Poor format, structure, and grammar.
5. Prerequisites for writing good achievement test items include:
   a. A rational philosophy of education.
   b. Command of verbal and written communication skills.
   c. Command of subject matter.

   d. Command of item-writing techniques.
   e. Knowledge about how students learn and develop.
6. General guidelines for writing "objective" items include:
   a. Avoiding obvious, trivial, meaningless, obscure, or ambiguous content.
   b. Following accepted rules of grammar.
   c. Avoiding irrelevant or unintended clues or cues to the correct answer.
   d. Avoiding interrelated items.
   e. Using items whose scoring would be agreed upon by experts.
   f. Stating questions in clear explicit terms.
   g. Providing equal credit for equally correct answers.
   h. Specifying the terms in which the answer is to be stated.
   i. Minimizing textbook expressions and stereotyped language.
   j. Stating items in the form of direct questions.
   k. Avoiding the use of "specific determiners" such as "only," "all," "none," "always," and "could," "might," "may," or "generally."
7. Supply items have the advantages of:
   a. Minimizing the effect of guessing.
   b. Being adaptable to actual classroom instructional practice, for example, the Socratic method.
   c. Providing good measures of knowledge.
8. The scoring of supply items is not always completely objective.
9. The use of true-false items is an objective and efficient method for surveying student knowledge.
10. False items tend to be more discriminating than true items and should probably constitute about 60 percent of the true-false items used.
11. There is no evidence that mislearning is stimulated by the use of true-false items, particularly if the test results are reviewed with students.
12. Although it influences scores to some extent, the effect of guessing on constant-alternative items is minor.

Speculations

1. What are the advantages and disadvantages of using the supply and completion item format?
2. What are the major faults in writing supply and completion items?
3. What are the advantages and disadvantages of using the true-false item format?
4. What are the major pitfalls in writing true-false kinds of items?
5. Are specific determiners always bad?
6. Have you ever met a true-false item you didn't like? Why?
7. Why is it sometimes hard to complete a completion item?

Suggested Readings

Cangelosi, J. S. (1990). *Designing tests for evaluating student achievement.* New York: Longman. This paperback is concerned exclusively with instrument development. Chapter 9, "True-False Items," and Chapter 11, "Short-Answer Matching and Other Objective-Test Items" are among the best available on item writing. Item writing is both art and science.

Ebel, R. L., & Frisbie, D. A. (1991). *Essentials of educational measurement* (5th ed.). Englewood Cliffs, NJ: Prentice Hall. See Chapter 8 for an excellent discussion of true-false item writing.

Gronlund, N. E., & Linn, R. L. (1990). *Measurement and evaluation in teaching* (6th ed.). New York: Macmillan. Chapter 6, "Constructing Objective Test Items: Simple Forms" contains good advice and examples.

Kubiszyn, T., & Bôrich, G. (1990). *Educational testing and measurement* (3rd ed.). Glenview, IL: Scott, Foresman. Chapter 6 is a good overview of item writing in general.

Chapter 7

Constructing Multiple-Choice and Matching Achievement Test Items

Multiple-choice items require the examinee to select an answer from among several alternatives (options, choices, foils) which change with each item. The selection may be made on any number of bases, for example, correct or best, most inclusive, cause or effect, most similar or dissimilar, and so on.

Each item is composed of a *stem* or *lead*, which sets the problem and alternative responses. The stem may be an incomplete statement (to be completed by the alternatives) or a direct question. Only one response is correct or best, and the others should be plausible but incorrect. Other formats may involve selecting the best from several correct answers, or a less desirable but sometimes used complex format where combinations may be correct (e.g., "a" and "c," but not "b" or "d"). For this reason the incorrect alternatives are sometimes referred to as "foils" or "distractors." They serve to distract the less kowledgeable and skillful student away from the correct answer.

The most common form of choice-type test item, and the one we concentrate on in this section, is the multiple-choice item. Probably the most flexible of all item types, it can be used to assess knowledge as well as such higher mental processes as application and analysis. Since alternative answers serve as a standard of comparison, these items are relatively free from ambiguity. This characteristic is one of their advantages over true-false items. Furthermore, the effect of guessing is markedly reduced, though not eliminated. In a 10-item four-alternative multiple-choice test, the probability of obtaining a score of seven or more by chance alone is 1 in 1000. To achieve freedom from guessing comparable to that of a four-alternative item multiple-choice test would require a true-false test of 200 items. The effectiveness of the multiple-choice item is, therefore, obvious. Multiple-choice items are generally preferable when the correct answer is long or can be expressed in a variety of ways. The use of plausible incorrect alternatives, therefore, can test fine discriminations and allow the test constructor easily to control the difficulty level of the items by varying the homogeneity of responses. The multiple-choice item is relatively free of "response sets" of the type described in connection with true-false items. As contrasted with true-false items, multiple-choice items can provide valuable diagnostic information if the alternatives are carefully constructed and if they represent different degrees of "correctness."

The primary limitation of multiple-choice items is that effective ones are difficult to construct. Plausible distractors are often difficult to find or construct (particularly that fourth or fifth incorrect option). One excellent source of alternatives is the pool of incorrect answers supplied when the stem of the multiple-choice item is administered as a free-response item. Multiple-choice items are subject to almost as many irrelevant cues as is any other type of short-answer question. The relatively greater amount of written stimulus material contributes to this situation, and also increases reading time and reduces the number of items (as compared with supply and selection items) than can be presented per unit of time. Their greater flexibility and reliability, however, more than compensate for this lessened efficiency. Some suggestions for writing multiple-choice items follow.

Suggestions for Writing Multiple-Choice Items

1. *It is recommended that the stem be a direct question.* Although there is no research evidence to support the preferability of the direct question lead ("Who invented the first artificial heart?") over the incomplete statement ("The first artificial heart was invented by"), it has been found in practice that the novice item writer will produce fewer weak and ambiguous items if the direct question lead is used. One of the problems is that the use of the incomplete stem requires the examinee to recreate the question that was in the item writer's mind which may be wasteful of the test taker's time and energy. There are many situations in which an incomplete statement stem would be acceptable or perhaps preferable. Just be sure that the incomplete statement stem unequivocally implies a single direct question.

2. *The stem should pose a clear, definite, explicit, and singular problem.* This suggestion follows from the preceding one. The major potential weakness of incomplete statements leads is that they are frequently too incomplete; in many instances the examinee must read the alternatives in order to determine what the question is.

The direct question stem is more likely to make explicit the basis on which the correct response is to be chosen. It is generally easier for an item writer to express complex ideas with the direct question format. If the incomplete statement lead is used, it should be meaningful in itself and imply a direct question rather than leading into a collection of unrelated true-false statements.

FAULTY: Salvador Dali is
a. a famous Indian statesman.
b. important in international law.
c. known for his surrealistic art.
d. the author of many avant-garde plays.

IMPROVED: With which one of the fine arts is Salvador Dali associated?
a. surrealistic painting
b. avant-garde theatre
c. polytonal symphonic music
d. impressionistic poetry

3. *Include in the stem any words that might otherwise be repeated in each response.* Streamlining an item in this way reduces reading time and makes for a more efficient question.

FAULTY: Milk can be pasteurized at home by
a. heating it to a temperature of 130°.
b. heating it to a temperature of 145°.
c. heating it to a temperature of 160°.
d. heating it to a temperature of 175°.

IMPROVED: The minimum temperature that can be used to pasteurize milk at home is:
a. 130°.
b. 145°.
c. 160°.
d. 175°.

4. *Items should be stated simply and understandably, excluding all nonfunctional words from the stem and alternatives.* The inclusion of extraneous words increases reading time and thereby reduces item efficiency. In addition, the central problem may become obscured, which leads to ambiguity.

FAULTY: Although the experimental research, particularly that by Hansmocker, must be considered equivocal and the assumptions viewed as too restrictive, most testing experts would recommend as the easiest method of significantly improving paper-and-pencil achievement test reliability to
a. increase the size of the group being tested.
b. increase the differential weighting of items.

c. increase the objectivity of scoring.
d. increase the number of items.
e. increase the amount of testing time.

IMPROVED: Assume a 10-item, 10-minute paper-and-pencil multiple-choice achievement test has a reliability of .40. The easiest way of increasing the reliability to .80 would be to increase
a. group size.
b. scoring objectivity.
c. differential item scoring weights.
d. the number of items.
e. testing time.

5. *Avoid interrelated items.* Instructors occasionally and unintentionally write items that overlap. That is, the stem or alternatives to one item give away the answer to other items. This is more likely to happen when the test is long. It may be necessary in some cases to index key words or concepts to check on overlap. Casual reading is rarely sufficient.

6. *Avoid negatively stated items.* Every attempt should be made to keep the use of such items to a minimum, as they are frequently awkward and difficult to comprehend. If "not," "no," "never," "none," "except," or a similar term is to be used, it should be highlighted for the student by underlining or capitalizing it. One is often better off rewriting the item positively.

FAULTY: None of the following cities is a state capital except
a. Bangor
b. Los Angeles
c. Denver
d. New Haven

IMPROVED: Which of the following cities is a state capital?
a. Bangor
b. Los Angeles
c. Denver
d. New Haven

7. *Avoid making the correct alternative systematically different from other options.* The usual example of a "systematically different correct alternative" is a correct answer that is obviously longer and more precisely stated than the distractors. There is an unconscious tendency to include *all* relevant information so that the correct alternative will be unequivocally correct. A related error is the attempt to make the correct alternatives more technical than the foils.

8. *If possible, the alternatives should be presented in some logical, numerical, or systematic order.* Again, our purpose is to so structure the question that responding

to it will be facilitated. Alphabetizing single-word, concept, or phrase alternatives has *not* been shown to bias responses.

9. *Response alternatives should be mutually exclusive.* Overlapping or synonymous responses should be eliminated because they reduce the discrimination value of an item and allow examinees to eliminate two or more alternatives for the price of one.

FAULTY: Who wrote *Penrod?*
  a. Lewis Carroll
  b. Samuel Clemens
  c. Booth Tarkington
  d. Mark Twain

IMPROVED: Who wrote *Penrod?*
  a. Lewis Carroll
  b. Bret Harte
  c. Booth Tarkington
  d. Mark Twain

FAULTY: If a test has a reliability of .78, what percentage of an observed score is attributable to errors of measurement?
  a. Over 5%
  b. Over 10%
  c. Over 20%
  d. Over 30%

The precise answer is 22%, but because of the way the alternatives are phrased, an examinee is likely to be unsure how to respond. The closest answer is "c," but alternatives "a" and "b" overlap "c" and must also be considered correct.

IMPROVED: If a test has a reliability of .50, what percentage of an observed score can be attributed to errors of measurement?
  a. 2.5%
  b. 5%
  c. 25%
  d. 50%

10. *Make all responses plausible and attractive to the less knowledgeable or skillful student.* The options to a multiple-choice item should include distractors that will attract the unprepared student. Foils should include the common misconceptions and/or errors. They should be familiar, natural, and reasonable.

FAULTY: Which of the following statements makes clear the meaning of the word "electron"?

a. An electronic tool
b. Neutral particles
c. Negative particles
d. A voting machine
e. The nuclei of atoms

IMPROVED: Which of the following phrases is a description of an "electron"?
a. Neutral particle
b. Negative particle
c. Neutralized proton
d. Radiated particle
e. Atom nucleus

11. *The response alternative "None of the above" should be used with caution, if at all.* Although some testing experts recommend the use of this alternative, particularly with mathematics items, the author generally does not recommend its use. When "None of the above" is the correct answer there is no assurance that the examinee does, in fact, know the answer. Consider the following elementary example:

FAULTY: What is the area of a right triangle whose sides adjacent to the right angle are 4 inches and 3 inches long respectively?
a. 7
b. 12
c. 25
d. None of the above

The answer is 6 square inches, and the knowledgeable student would select alternative "d." But a student who solved the problem incorrectly (e.g., solving for the hypotenuse, which is 5), and came up with an answer not found among the alternatives, would also select the correct answer, "d," thereby getting the item right for the wrong reason. The response "None of the above" may function very well as an alternative if the correct answer is included among the preceding alternatives. In such a situation, it would function as an all-inclusive incorrect alternative covering a multitude of sins.

IMPROVED: What is the area of a right triangle whose sides adjacent to the right angle are 4 inches and 3 inches respectively?
a. 6 sq. inches
b. 7 sq. inches.
c. 12 sq. inches
d. 25 sq. inches
e. None of the above

12. *Make options grammatically parallel to each other and consistent with the stem.* Lack of parallelism makes for an awkward item and may cause the examinee

difficulty in grasping the meaning of the question and of the relationships among the alternative answers.

FAULTY: As compared with the American factory worker in the early part of the 19th century, the American factory worker at the close of the century

a. was working long hours.
b. received greater social security benefits.
c. was to receive lower money wages.
d. was less likely to belong to a labor union.
e. became less likely to have personal contact with employers.

IMPROVED: As compared with the American factory worker in the early part of the 19th century, the American factory worker at the close of the century

a. worked longer hours.
b. had more social security.
c. received lower money wages.
d. was less likely to belong to a labor union.
e. had less personal contact with his employer.

Lack of parallelism between stem and alternatives may also lead to a "grammatical clue" to the correct answer.

FAULTY: A two-way grid summarizing the relationship between test scores and criterion scores is sometimes referred to as an

a. correlation coefficient.
b. expectancy table.
c. probability histogram.
d. bivariate frequency distribution.

The article *an* leads the student to the correct answer (b).

IMPROVED: Two-way grids summarizing test-criterion relationships are sometimes called

a. correlation coefficients.
b. expectancy tables.
c. bivariate frequency distributions.
d. probability histograms.

13. *Avoid such irrelevant cues as "common elements" and "pat verbal associations."* Because multiple-choice items require association between several options and a lead statement, any similarity between key words in the stem and alternatives may function as irrelevant cues. The term "irrelevant cue" describes an item fault that leads the examinee to the correct answer regardless of his knowledge of the topic under examination. Common elements in the stem and correct alternatives are the most obvious type of irrelevant cue.

FAULTY: The "standard error of estimate" refers to
a. the objectivity of scoring.
b. the percentage of reduced error variance.
c. an absolute amount of possible error.
d. the amount of error in estimating criterion scores.

The test-wise but unknowledgeable student, seeing the terms "estimate" in the stem and "estimating" in the fourth option, would be led to the correct answer.

FAULTY: The "standard error of estimate" refers to
a. scoring errors.
b. sampling errors.
c. standardization errors.
d. administration errors.
e. prediction errors.

Although we have made the alternative more homogeneous and eliminated the common elements, we are still left with a faulty item. The problem now is the verbal association between "estimate" and "prediction," which would again lead the student to the correct answer.

IMPROVED: The "standard error of estimate" is most directly related to which of the following test characteristics?
a. Objectivity
b. Reliability
c. Validity
d. Usability
e. Specificity

Here is another example.

FAULTY: What led to the formation of the States Rights Party?
a. The level of Federal taxation
b. The demand of states for the right to make their own laws
c. The industrialization of the South
d. The corruption of many city governments

IMPROVED: What led to the formation of the States Rights Party?
a. Increased levels of Federal taxation
b. The demand by voters to make their own laws
c. The industrialization of the South
d. The corruption of many city governments

14. *In testing for understanding of a term or concept, it is generally preferable to present the term in the stem and alternative definitions in the options.* The examinee is

less likely to benefit from pat verbal associations, particularly if the correct answer is a paraphrase, rather than a verbatim extract from the text.

FAULTY: What name is given to the group of complex organic compounds that occur in small quantities in natural foods that are essential to normal nutrition?
  a. Calories
  b. Minerals
  c. Nutrients
  d. Vitamins

IMPROVED: Which one of the following statements is the best description of a vitamin?
  a. A complex substance necessary for normal animal development, which is found in small quantities in certain foods
  b. A complex substance prepared in biological laboratories to improve the nutrient qualities of ordinary foods
  c. A substance extracted from ordinary foods, which is useful in destroying disease germs in the body
  d. A highly concentrated form of food energy, which should be used only on a doctor's prescription

The *improved* item better focuses the task on determining whether or not the examinee "knows" the general definition of vitamin.

15. *Use "objective" items.* In other words, use items on whose correct answers virtually all experts would agree. It is an interesting, humbling, and informative experience to have a colleague key one's tests. But it is perhaps of greater importance to go over each test with one's students, who are probably the best "test critics."

Illustrative Multiple-Choice Items for the Cognitive Domain of the Taxonomy of Educational Objectives[1]

The *Taxonomy of Educational Objectives,* as was noted in Chapter 4, is a highly valuable source of ideas for achievement test items. The following items are presented to illustrate the variety of outcomes that can be measured using the *Taxonomy* as a guide. (See pages 67–70 for an overview of the *Taxonomy.*)

Knowledge of Specific Facts

1. The Monroe Doctrine was announced about 10 years after the
   a. Revolutionary War

[1]From the book *Taxonomy of educational objectives, Handbook II: The cognitive domain,* edited by B. Bloom. New York: David McKay Company, Inc., 1956. Reprinted by permission of the publisher.

b. War of 1812
c. Civil War
d. Spanish-American War.

Knowledge of Principles and Generalizations

2. Which of the following statements of the relationship between market price and normal price is true?
   a. Over a short period of time, market price varies directly with changes in normal price.
   b. Over a long period of time, market price tends to equal normal price.
   c. Market price is usually lower than normal price.
   d. Over a long period of time, market price determines normal prices.

Translation from Symbolic Form to Another Form, or Vice Versa

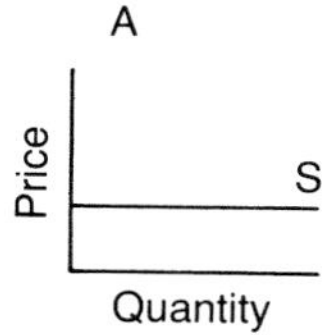

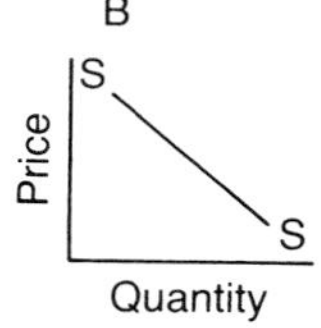

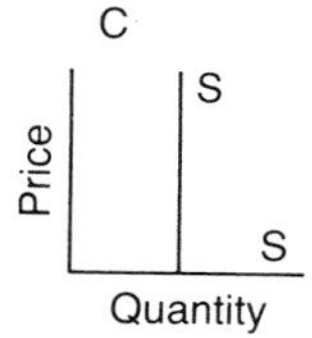

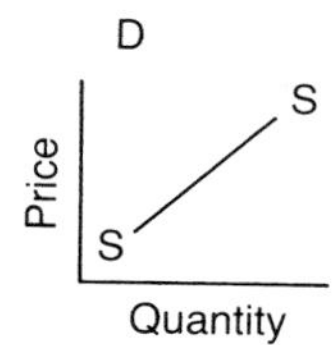

3. Which of the above graphs best represents the supply situation where a monopolist maintains a uniform price regardless of the amounts which people buy?
   a.
   b.
   c.
   d.

Application

In the following items (4–11) you are to judge the effects of a particular policy on the distribution of income. In each case assume that there are no other changes in policy that would counteract the effect of the policy described in the item. Mark the item:

A. if the policy described would tend to *reduce* the existing degree of inequality in the distribution of income,
B. if the policy described would tend to *increase* the existing degree of inequality in the distribution of income, or
C. if the policy described would have *no effect*, or an indeterminate effect, on the distribution of income.

Policy

____ 4. Increasingly progressive income taxes.
____ 5. Confiscation of rent on unimproved urban land.

_____ 6. Introduction of a national sales tax.
_____ 7. Increasing the personal exemptions from income taxes.
_____ 8. Distributing a subsidy to sharecroppers on Southern farms.
_____ 9. Provision of educational and medical services, and low-cost public housing.
_____ 10. Reduction in the degree of business monopoly.
_____ 11. Increasing taxes in periods of prosperity and decreasing them in periods when depressions threaten.

Analysis

12. An assumption basic to Lindsay's preference for voluntary associations rather than government orders . . . is a belief
    a. that government is not organized to make the best use of experts.
    b. that freedom of speech, freedom of meeting, freedom of association, are possible only under a system of voluntary associations.
    c. in the value of experiment and initiative as a means of attaining an ever-improving society.
    d. in the benefits of competition.

13. The relation between the definition of sovereignty given in Paragraph 2 and that given in Paragraph 9 is best expressed as follows:
    a. There is no fundamental difference between them, only a difference in formulation.
    b. The definition given in Paragraph 2 includes that given in Paragraph 9 but in addition includes situations which are excluded by that given in Paragraph 9.
    c. The two definitions are incompatible with each other; the conditions of sovereignty implied in each exclude the other.

Judgments in Terms of External Criteria: Given Possible Bases for Judgments about Accuracy, Recognize Criteria That Are Appropriate

For items 14–19, assume that in doing research for a paper about the English language you find a statement by Otto Jespersen that contradicts one point of view on language you have always accepted. Indicate which of the statements would be significant in determining the value of Jespersen's statement. For the purpose of these items, you may assume that these statements are accurate. Mark each item using the following key:

A. Significant positively—that is, might lead you to trust his statement and to revise your own opinion.
B. Significant negatively—that is, might lead you to distrust his statement.
C. Has no significance.

_____ 14. Mr. Jespersen was Professor of English at Copenhagen University.
_____ 15. The statement in question was taken from the very first article that Mr. Jespersen published.

_____ 16. Mr. Jespersen's books are frequently referred to in other works that you consult.

_____ 17. Mr. Jespersen's name is not included in the *Dictionary of American Scholars.*

_____ 18. So far as you can find, Jespersen never lived in England or the United States for any considerable length of time.

_____ 19. In your reading of other authors on the English language, you find that several of them went to Denmark to study under Jespersen.

Ilustrative Multiple-Choice Items Using Graphic Materials

Instructors in all subject areas encounter situations in which only pictorial, diagrammatic, or visual material is suitable for purposes of measurement. The use of such materials allows for great flexibility in the assessment of a variety of content areas and learning outcomes. Such stimuli can be used equally well to measure knowledge, comprehension, and application. Complex learning outcomes can be measured with items based on graphic materials. To illustrate this contention, the following items and explanations have been reproduced from *Multiple-choice Questions: A Close Look,* a pamphlet published by Educational Testing Service.[2] The items are intended for high-school and college students.

Question 1

The shading on map (in Figure 7-1) is used to indicate

* A. population density
B. percentage of total labor force in agriculture

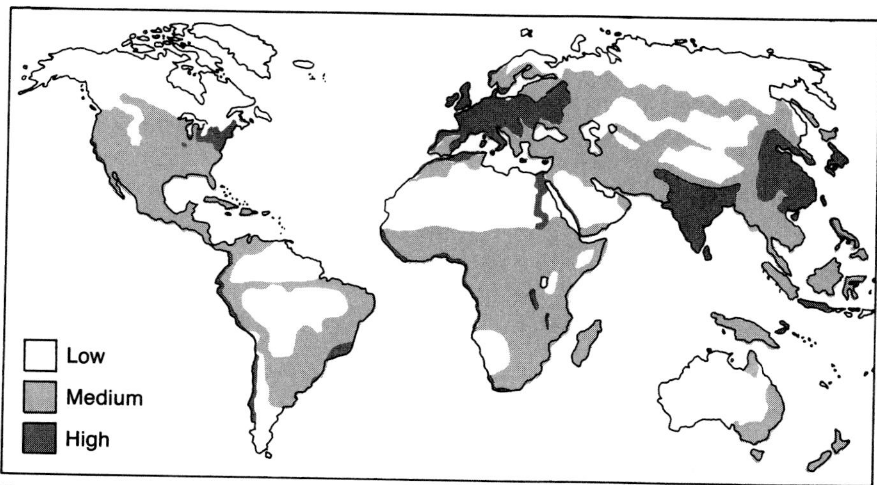

Figure 7-1

[2]From *Multiple-choice questions: A close look.* Copyright © 1963 by Educational Testing Service. All rights reserved. Reproduced by permission.

C. per capita income
D. death rate per thousand of population

Many of the multiple-choice questions included in tests in the social sciences require the student to make use of his general knowledge in the interpretation of materials. Thus, this question does not simply ask: What areas of the world have the highest population densities? Rather, it presents a novel situation in which the student must infer that only one of the choices offered provides a plausible explanation of the shadings on the map.

An examination of the map clearly shows that choice A, population density, is the proper response. The darkest shading, which according to the map's legend indicates the highest degree of whatever the shading represents, covers such high-density areas as the northeastern part of the United States, a large part of Europe, the Nile valley, India, Japan, and Eastern China. If this is not a sufficient clue, the areas with the lightest shading include such underpopulated areas as the Arctic regions, tropical South America, the Sahara and Arabian deserts, and most of Australia.

Choice B, the percentage of the total labor force in agriculture, though attractive if only India and China are examined, is clearly incorrect when applied to the northeastern United States.

Choice C, per capita income, is plausible only if the student's analysis of the map is limited to the dark shading in the United States and Western Europe (and even there it is not entirely correct); the dark shadings in China and India certainly indicate choice D, death rate per thousand of population, since the latter might be expected to be high for India and China, but low for the United States and Europe.

Question 2

The graph (in Figure 7-2) represents the political composition from 1922 to 1955 of which of the following?
A. German Bundestag
B. French National Assembly
C. Italian Chamber of Deputies
* D. British House of Commons

To answer this question correctly, the student must be able to do several things. First, he or she must be able to read the graph. Then, using the information he or she can infer from it, he or she must interpret it in the light of his or her knowledge of European history and government from 1922 to 1955 and conclude which legislative body may properly be so depicted. In such a process, it is possible for different students to make use of different information to arrive at the correct answer.

In examining the graph, the student should note that the party system shown is essentially a two-party one, although there is a third party that, for most of the period shown, decreased in representation. The student may also note the years in which elections were held, the years that Party A received majorities, the fact that Party B did not receive a majority until 1945, and the fact that in the elections of 1923 and 1929 neither party received a majority.

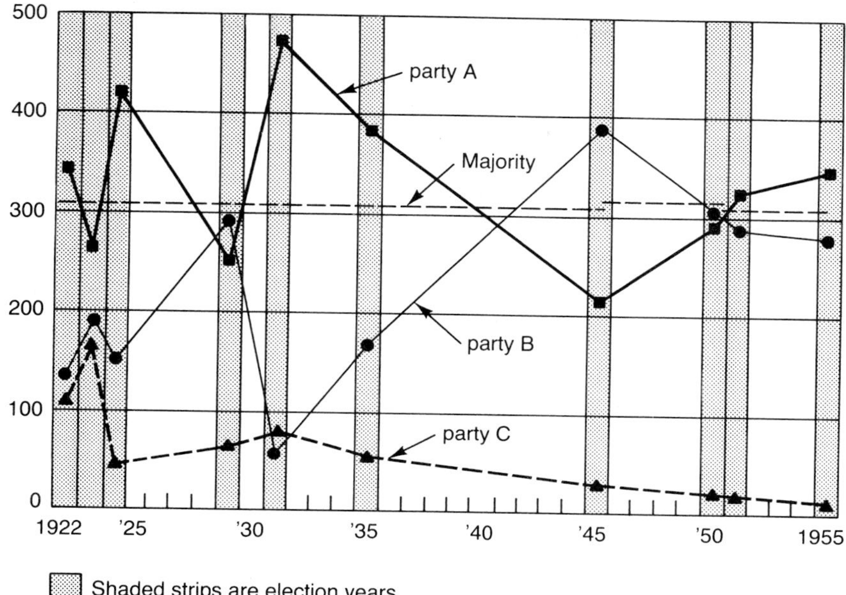

Figure 7-2

In considering the first of the four possible answers, the German Bundestag, the student should recognize that during the period through 1932—that of the Weimar Republic—no single party in Germany was able to attain a majority, partly because of the multiplicity of parties. After Hitler came to power in 1933, parties other than the Nazi Party were outlawed. These facts do not fit the graph.

The French National Assembly, the second possible answer, contained far more than three parties both before and after World War II. The Italian Chamber of Deputies should also be rejected as a possible answer because, after Mussolini came to power in 1924, it became less and less important until, in 1938, it was superseded by a Chamber of Fasci and Corporations and political parties were suppressed.

Question 3

In the following question you are asked to make inferences from the data given you in Figure 7-3, a map of the imaginary country Serendip. The answer must a probability rather than a certainty. The relative sizes of towns and cities are not shown. To assist you in the location of the places mentioned in the questions, the map is divided into squares lettered vertically from A to E and numbered horizontally from 1 to 5.

Which of the following cities (in Figure 7-3) would be the best location for a steel mill?

A. Li (3A)
* B. Um (3B)

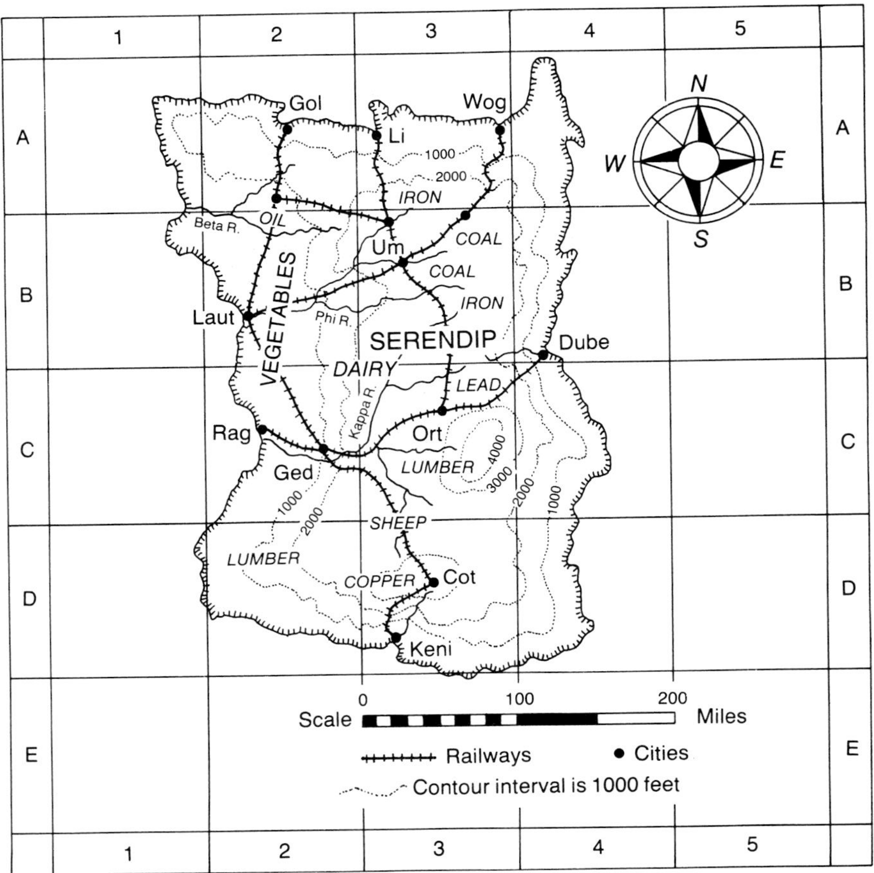

Figure 7-3

C. Cot (3D)
D. Dube (4B)

A map of an imaginary country such as this offers numerous possibilities for questions measuring important understandings. One could ask several questions requiring an understanding of the symbols used on the map. To measure student comprehension of the meaning of contour lines, for example, one might ask which railroad has the steepest grades to climb. Similar questions can be developed requiring knowledge of the factors influencing population distribution, economic activities, and the like.

The question referring to the map requires knowledge of the natural resources used in producing steel and an awareness of the importance of transportation facilities in bringing these resources together. It was part of a general achievement test given to high-school seniors.

The student who knows that iron is the basic raw material in steel and that coal commonly provides the necessary source of heat would proceed to locate deposits of these resources in relation to the cities listed in the question. He or she would be able to eliminate Cot immediately, since there is no iron or coal in its vicinity, although Cot might be an attractive choice to students who mistakenly think that copper is a basic ingredient of steel. Both Li and Dube are located reasonably near supplies of iron, and therefore might be attractive choices. Um, however, is the more clearly "correct" response, not only because there are deposits of iron and coal nearby, but also because they are more readily transportable by direct railroad routes.

Question 4

This question is based on the following situation:

A piece of mineral is placed in a bottle half-filled with a colorless liquid. A two-holed rubber stopper is placed in the bottle. The system is then sealed by inserting a thermometer and connecting a glass tube to the stoppered bottle and a beaker of limewater as shown in Figure 7-4.

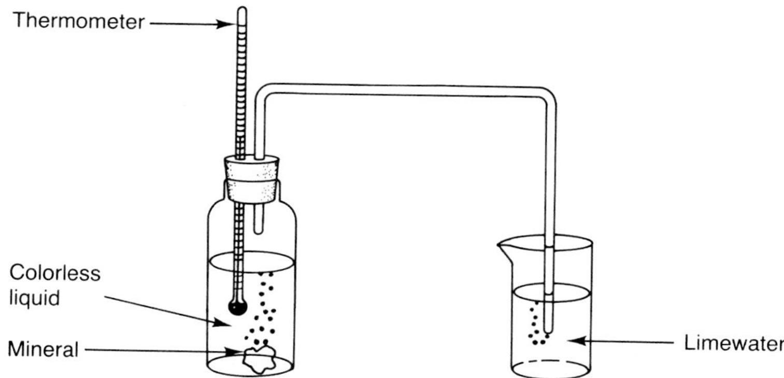

Figure 7-4

The following series of observations is recorded:

I. *Observations during the first few minutes:*
   1. Bubbles of a colorless gas rise to the top of the stoppered bottle from the mineral.
   2. Bubbles of colorless gas begin to come out of the glass tube and rise to the surface of the limewater.
   3. The limewater remains colorless throughout this period of time.
   4. The thermometer reads 20°C.

II. *Observations at the end of 30 minutes:*
   1. Bubbles of colorless gas continue to rise in the stoppered bottle.
   2. The piece of mineral has become noticeably smaller.

3. There is no apparent change in the level of the colorless liquid in the bottle.
4. The liquid in the bottle remains colorless.
5. The thermometer reads 24°C.
6. The limewater is cloudy.

Which of the following is the best explanation for the appearance of gas bubbles at the end of the tube in the beaker of limewater?

A. The pressure exerted by the colorless liquid is greater than that exerted by the limewater.

* B. The bubbles coming from the mineral cause an increased gas pressure in the stoppered bottle.

C. The temperature increase at the end of 30 minutes causes an expansion of gas in the stoppered bottle.

D. The decrease in the size of the piece of mineral causes reduced pressure in the stoppered bottle.

E. The glass tube serves as a siphon for the flow of gas from the bottle to the beaker.

This question is taken from a test designed to be used with a new curriculum in high-school chemistry. The question is only one of a series based on the experimental situation described. Questions in the series are grouped in sequence in order to permit the student to think intensively about one situation for an extended period of time. The student is asked to deal with a realistic laboratory situation—one he has not yet encountered in the course—and to employ scientific problem-solving ability in using the data given to answer the questions.

Choice A is both vague and irrelevant. It is unspecific about where the pressure is exerted and has nothing to do with the cause of the bubbles.

Choice C sounds plausible. In itself, the statement is not incorrect, since the temperature increase will cause an increase in gas pressure in the stoppered bottle. However, students who are in command of the subject will realize that the increase in gas pressure due to the rise in temperature is insignificant compared with that caused by the bubbles coming from the mineral.

Choice D is incorrect. Some students may not realize this, but even if the statement were correct, it would offer an incorrect explanation for the appearance of the bubbles in the beaker.

Many good students reject choice E, but many less able students choose it, probably because the arrangement looks somewhat like a siphon and they have heard of the use of siphons in transferring fluids.

Students who understand the forces at work in the situation described will know that bubbles would appear at the end of the tube in the beaker when the pressure exerted by the gas from the stoppered bottle exceeded the pressure exerted by the limewater at the end of the tube. They will also realize that the limewater pressure would remain essentially constant. Choice B, therefore, accounts best for the appearance of gas bubbles at the end of the tube in the beaker.

In addition to the kinds of items presented here, many other possibilities exist. Drawings, blueprints, paintings, photographs, and the like may also profitably be used as stimulus material. In addition to being efficient, the use of such materials can stimulate student interest. Test materials that use pictorial representation can be intrinsically interesting, succinct, understandable, and realistic. Two difficulties exist: It is sometimes difficult to locate appropriate material, and reproduction can be complicated. The availability of copying machines can make duplication of graphic test material practical.

Using Multiple-Choice Items to Measure Problem Solving and Logical Thinking

Public schools are placing greater emphasis on problem-solving skills, and society is demanding individuals with significant skills in this area. Various terms have been used to describe the basic operations of application. Terms like *critical thinking* and *logical reasoning* are used as rubrics under which the basic processes of problem identification, specification of alternative solutions, evaluation of consequences, and solution selection are grouped. The actual process may be cognitive, as in playing bridge, or a combination of cognitive and psychomotor skills, as in the case of automobile engine diagnostics. One of the distinct advantages of paper-and-pencil problem-solving measures is that they can be used to simulate complex, expensive, and infrequently occurring situations.

A step-by-step procedure for creating problem-solving measures has been described by Dunning, 1954, as cited in Adams, 1964.

Step 1. Decide on the principle or principles to be tested. Criteria to be considered

1. should be known principles but the situation in which the principles are to be applied should be new.
2. should involve significantly important principles.
3. should be pertinent to a problem or situation common to all students.
4. should be within the range of comprehension of all students.
5. should use only valid and reliable sources from which to draw data.
6. should be interesting to the students.

Step 2. Determine the phrasing of the problem situation so as to require the student in drawing his conclusion to do one of the following:

1. Make a prediction.
2. Choose a course of action.
3. Offer an explanation for an observed phenomenon.
4. Criticize a prediction or explanation made by others.

Step 3. Set up the problem situation in which the principle or principles selected operate. Present the problem to a class with directions to draw a conclusion or conclusions and give several supporting reasons for their answer.

Step 4. Edit the students' responses, selecting those that are most representative of their thinking. These will include conclusions and supporting reasons that are both acceptable and unacceptable.

Step 5. To the conclusions and reasons obtained from the students, the teacher now adds any others that he or she feels are necessary to cover the salient points. The total number of items should be at least 50 percent more than is desired in the final form to allow for elimination of poor items. The following list is a guide to the type of statements that can be used.

1. True statements of principles and facts
2. False statements of principles and facts
3. Acceptable and unacceptable analogies
4. Appeal to acceptable or unacceptable authority
5. Ridicule
6. Assumption of the conclusion
7. Teleological explanations

Step 6. Submit test to other judges for criticisms. Revise test in view of criticisms.

Step 7. Administer test. Follow with thorough class discussion.

Step 8. Conduct an item analysis.

Step 9. In the light of steps 7 and 8, revise the test.

Following are some sample problem-solving items. (Based in part on material developed by science educators at the University of Georgia: Drs. James R. O'Key, Russell Yeang, and Michael J. Podilla.) These kinds of items can frequently be difficult and complex, but the range of application is considerable relative to both content and grade level.

1. Frank wanted to go to California. But Frank's father, who is quite strict with Frank, stated emphatically that he could not go unless he earned a B average for the year. Frank's father always keeps his promises. When summer came, Frank went to California. If, from this information, you conclude that Frank earned a B average, you must be assuming that
   a. Frank had never made a B average before.
   b. Frank had no money of his own.
   c. Frank's father was justified in saying what he did.
   d. Frank went with his father's consent.
   e. Frank was sure he would be able to go.
2. Consider these facts about the coloring of animals:
   - Plant lice, which live on the stems of green plants, are green.
   - The greyish-mottled moth resembles the bark of the trees on which it lives.
   - Insects, birds, and mammals that live in the desert are usually sandy or grey in color.

- Polar bears and other animals living in the Arctic region are white.
- Jungle-dwelling tigers are yellowish in color and have parallel stripes which tend to camouflage them among the leaves and stems.

Which one of the following statements do these facts tend to support?

a. Animals that prey on others use color as a disguise.
b. Some animals imitate the color and shape of other natural objects for protection.
c. The coloration of animals has little to do with their surroundings.
d. Protective coloration is found more among insects and birds than among mammals.
e. Many insects and animals have protective coloring.

Read the following paragraphs and then answer Items 3 through 7.

> In an area that had been moderately grazed, a steel tube 18 inches in diameter and 12 inches long was driven 9 inches into the ground. The part of the tube that was above ground, 3 inches deep and 18 inches in diameter, was filled with water. It took eleven minutes for all the water to soak into the ground. Another tube of the same size was similarly placed in a nearby ungrazed area. In this location the water soaked into the ground in one and one-half minutes.
>
> When this experiment was reported to a high-school class, a student said it showed that *water soaks into ungrazed land faster than it soaks into grazed land.*

Items 3 through 7 are statements that might be made in a discussion of this student's conclusion. Assuming that the information given in the first paragraph is accurate, decide which of the following answers best describes each statement.

Answers:

A. This statement tends to *support* the conclusion.
B. This statement tends to make the conclusion *doubtful.*
C. This statement *neither* supports the conclusion nor conflicts with it.

3. If *all* the grass had been grazed off the first area, the water would have taken longer than 11 minutes to soak in.
4. Grazing should be restricted by state laws.
5. Conserving water in the soil is more important than feeding cattle.
6. The second tube might have been made of a porous material, which itself absorbed a large amount of water.
7. The composition of the soil in the two areas was approximately the same.

Simulated observations or experiments can form a good context within which to measure problem-solving and logical-thinking skills.

A farmer observed the mice that live in his field. He found that the mice were either fat or thin. Also, the mice had either black tails or white tails.

This made him wonder if there might be a relation between the size of a mouse and the color of its tail. So he decided to capture all of the mice in one part of his field and observe them. The mice that he captured are shown in Figure 7-5.

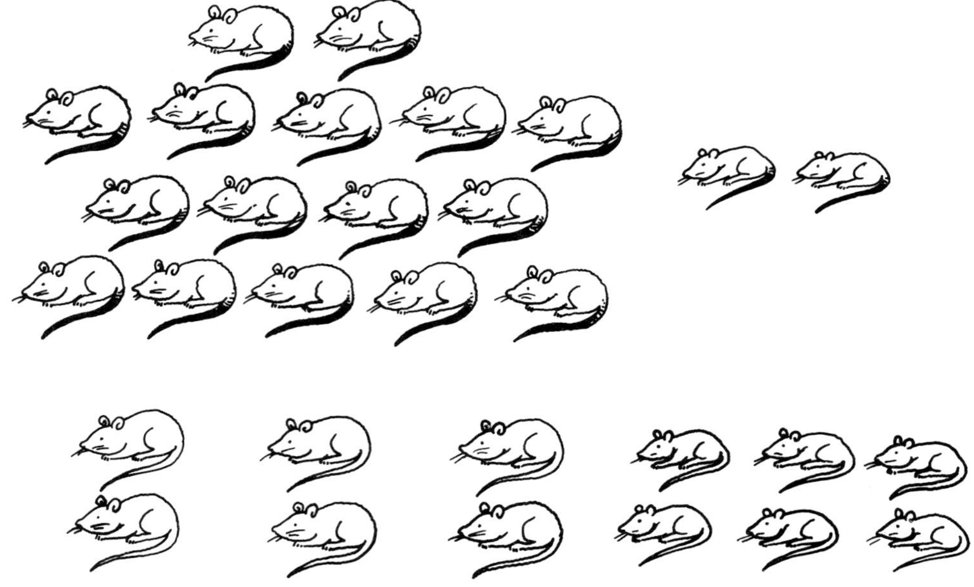

Figure 7-5

8. Do you think there is a relation between the size of the mice and the color of their tails (that is, is one size of mouse more likely to have a certain color tail and vice versa)?
   a. Yes
   b. No.
9. Reason
   a. 8/11 of the fat mice have black tails and 3/4 of the thin mice have white tails.
   b. Fat and thin mice can have either a black or a white tail.
   c. Not all fat mice have black tails. Not all thin mice have white tails.
   d. 18 mice have black tails and 12 have white tails.
   e. 22 mice are fat and 8 mice are thin.

Writing Matching Exercises

The matching exercise is a variation of the multiple-choice question. While the multiple-choice question usually presents a single problem and several solutions, the matching exercise presents several problems and several solutions. The list of alternative solutions is constant for each new problem or stimulus. It is because of this constancy of alternatives that the quality and homogeneity of options so significantly influence the effectiveness of the entire exercise. Matching exercises may concentrate on form or content. Pictorial material can be used with success in these types of exercises. Content might be related to events, inventions, results, definitions, quotations, dates, or locations. At a more sophisticated level, matching (classification or key-list) items may concern (a) cause-and-effect relationships, (b) theoretical statements and experimental bases, and (c) a phenomenon and its explanation in terms of principles, generalizations, or theories.

Most such exercises contain two columns, one on the left-hand side of the page containing the stimuli or premises, and one on the right side containing responses. Compound matching exercises (e.g., state-major industry-city or authors-novels-nationalities) are, of course, possible, but are used infrequently.

The matching exercise's chief advantage is efficiency in time and space. It uses the same set of response alternatives for a whole group of items. The matching exercise is, therefore, a compact and efficient method of rapidly surveying knowledges of the who, what, when, and where variety.

The matching exercise is not well adapted to the measurement of higher-order abilities. It is particularly susceptible to irrelevant cues, implausible alternatives, and the awkward arrangement of stimuli or responses; thus, great care is needed in development. Several suggestions for constructing or revising matching exercises follow:

1. *Matching exercises should be complete on a single page.* Splitting the exercise is confusing, distracting, and time consuming for the student.

2. *Use response categories that are related but mutually exclusive.* If this suggestion is not followed, ambiguous items or items requiring multikeying will result. Responses should be drawn from the same domain (e.g., do not mix dates and names of inventors in the same response list) but should not overlap. The degree of relatedness among stimuli and/or responses will, of course, dictate the degree of difficulty of the exercise.

3. *Keep the number of stimuli relatively small* (e.g., 10–15), *and let the number of possible responses exceed the number of stimuli by two or three.* This is, admittedly, an arbitrary suggestion but is related to a point well worth considering. If a matching exercise is too long, the task becomes tedious and the discrimination too fine. A related problem is the possibility that the use of matching items might "overweight" the test. Because of their compactness, their weight in the test relative to the objectives and other item types may become disproportionate. One should also avoid matching the numbers of stimuli and responses, as this increases the likelihood that a student will benefit from guessing or from the process of elimination. In this regard the cautious use of the response "None of the above" may be recommended. One might include a statement in the test directions to the effect that the responses may be used more than once.

4. *The directions should clearly specify the basis for matching stimuli and responses.* Although the basis for matching is usually obvious, sound testing practice dictates that the directions spell out the nature of the task. It is unreasonable that

the student should have to read through the stimulus and response lists in order to discern the intended basis for matching. It is also a good idea to include in the directions a statement to the effect that a response option may be used once, more than once, or not at all.

5. *Keep the statements in the response column short and list them in some logical order.* This suggestion is intended to facilitate response to the exercise. The responses should be so stated and arranged (e.g., alphabetically, chronologically, etc.) that the student can scan them quickly.

The following matching exercise does not embody the suggestions made above.

FAULTY: Directions—Match List A with List B. You will be given one point for each correct match.

List A	*List B*
a. cotton gin	a. Eli Whitney
b. reaper	b. Alexander Graham Bell
c. wheel	c. David Brinkley
d. TU54G tube	d. Louisa May Alcott
e. steamboat	e. None of these

The primary shortcomings of this matching exercise may be summarized as follows:

1. The directions fail to specify the basis for matching or mechanics for responding.
2. The two lists are enumerated identically.
3. The responses are not listed logically—in this case, alphabetically.
4. Both lists lack homogeneity.
5. There are equal numbers of elements in both lists.
6. The use of "None of these" is questionable in this exercise, serving as a giveaway to List A elements "c" and "d." Furthermore, if a student uses it for element "e" of List A, it is not clear that he knows who did, in fact, invent the steamboat.

An improved version of the exercise follows:

IMPROVED: Directions—Famous inventions are listed in the left-hand column, and inventors in the right-hand column below. Place the letter corresponding to the inventor in the space next to the invention for which he is famous. Each match is worth 1 point, and "*None of these*" may be the correct answer. Inventors may be used more than once.

Inventions	*Inventors*
_____ 1. steamboat	a. Alexander Graham Bell
_____ 2. cotton gin	b. Robert Fulton
_____ 3. sewing machine	c. Elias Howe
_____ 4. reaper	d. Cyrus McCormick
	e. Eli Whitney
	f. None of these

Many other types of short-answer items could be discussed. Such question forms as the rearrangement exercise (Cureton, 1960), interpretive exercise (Gronlund & Linn, 1990), analogies (Remmers, Gage, & Rummel, 1965, pp. 258–259), and problem-solving items (Adams, 1964, pp. 345–347) have been found useful in educational measurement. Space limitations will not allow us to consider these forms here, but the reader is referred to the above for additional treatments of item writing.

Writing Test Items for Elementary and Junior High-School Students

The development of test items for young students is a difficult task.[3] This is particularly true if the teacher has decided to use so-called "objective" or short-answer questions. Two of the main difficulties in writing items for the young involve (a) the development of comprehensible and appropriate stimulus materials, and (b) the development of a scheme for recording student responses efficiently.

At the kindergarten level, the best way to record answers is perhaps to have the youngsters draw an X on a picture. A series of pictures can be accompanied by a series of questions, as shown in Figures 7-6a, 7-6b, and 7-6c.

Figure 7-6a

[3]The material in this section is based on Dr. Clarence Nelson's monograph *Improving objective tests in science* (1967), pp. 18–21. Sample items reproduced by permission of the National Science Teachers Association.

1. Put an X on the picture of things that are alive.
2. Put a Y on the picture of each thing that is an animal.
3. Put a Z on the picture of each thing that is a mammal.
4. One of these three pictures is a kitty. Put an X on that picture.

Figure 7-6b

5. One of these three pictures shows what happens when something is heated or becomes warm. Put an X on that picture.

Figure 7-6c

To test for understanding of concepts, it is desirable to use a picture card illustrating objects similar but not identical to those discussed in class. If identical objects are used, one may be measuring recall rather than understanding.

A similar method of recording responses can be used at the first-grade level. Using pictorial material, the teacher may read the questions to the students. Two examples are seen in Figures 7-7a and 7-7b.

6. (The teacher demonstrates boiling, filtering, and straining of water, and then reads the text question.) Pure water can be taken out of salt water by:

Figure 7-7a

7. Salt has been mixed with chopped ice. If some of this chopped ice is packed around a container full of water, what will probably happen to the water in the container?

Figure 7-7b

Second- and third-graders can probably use a special answer sheet. The teacher may wish to make an answer sheet containing lettered or numbered squares as shown in Figure 7-8.

8.	a	b	c	10.	a	b	c
	□	□	□		□	□	□
9.	a	b	c	11.	a	b	c
	□	□	□		□	□	□

Figure 7-8

An alternative is to have the students circle the letters on an answer sheet. The questions could be handed out in duplicated form, and after the method for recording the answers is explained, the questions and answers could be read slowly to the students.

8. When a watch is laid flat on a table, if 12 on the dial represents north, then 9 on the dial represents
   a. south.
   b. east.
   * c. west.
9. If 12 on your watch dial represents north, which one of the following times represents southeast? (Use both the big and and the little hand of the watch.)
   * a. 4:30
   b. 7:30
   c. 10:30
10. On a clear day a person standing at the seashore looking at a ship several miles from the shore can see the
   a. entire ship.
   * b. upper part of the ship only.
   c. lower part of the ship only.
11. The horizon would be farthest away
   a. if you were standing on the seashore and looking out over the ocean.
   b. if you were on top of the Empire State Building or the Washington Monument and looking straight ahead.
   * c. if you were looking out of an airplane window while flying four miles above the earth.

Junior high-school students can use commercially available (e.g., NCS) answer sheets. Machine-scorable booklets can be successfully used with students beginning at the kindergarten level. A commercial scoring template may be used for hand scoring. If the answer sheet is teacher-made, a fan, strip, or cut-out key (see Chapter 5) may be used. Following is a series of test items aimed at measuring the junior high-school student's understanding of land-feature diagrams. The test item should not be one previously studied in class.

Items 12–16 are junior high-school science items and refer to the cross-sectioned land-feature diagram in Figure 7-9. Formations are indicated by Roman numerals.

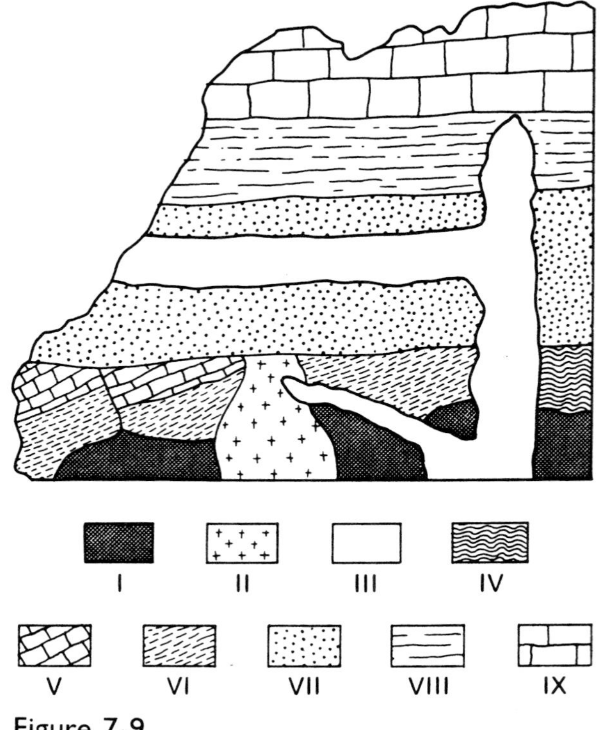

Figure 7-9

12. Fossils would be least likely to occur in
    * * a. III
    * b. V
    * c. VII
    * d. VIII
    * e. IX
13. An unconformity exists between
    * a. I and III
    * b. III and VI
    * * c. V and VII
    * d. VII and VIII
    * e. VIII and IX

14. The youngest formation is
    a. I
    b. II
    c. III
    d. V
    * e. IX
15. The oldest formation is
    * a. I
    b. II
    c. III
    d. V
    e. IX
16. Which formation is made up of igneous rock?
    * a. III
    b. V
    c. VII
    d. VIII
    e. IX

Similarly, the student's interpretation of a chemical formula not previously encountered can reveal whether or not he or she understands the symbols and conventions he or she has studied in class.

17. The number of atoms of oxygen in the formula $2A_2(SO_4)_3$ is
    a. 4
    b. 7
    c. 8
    d. 12
    * e. 24

Item writing is both art and science. Experience really helps improve the quality of your items. One of the most enlightening things you can do to help improve your items and tests is to sit and *listen* to a student work through, out loud, your questions. You would be surprised what good critics students can be, plus it makes them feel a part-ownership in the process. In architecture (for some), form follows function. This also may be the case in item writing. Some kinds of questions seem to lend themselves better to a direct question format—perhaps true-false, or when there are obviously a number of possible outcomes, multiple-choice. Sometimes extended samples of a student's own thinking are required; then we may move to the essay format (see Chapter 8). Trial and error, experience, and maybe a little formal study will help us make the best decisions.

Case Study Application

Below is an illustrative set of 24 items taken from the Reading Education midterm exam. Space does not permit reproduction of all 80 items from the exam. The items have been organized, for presentation purposes, by objectives. When administered, the test would have had items using the same format (e.g., supply, multiple-choice, true-false) grouped together for the convenience of student response. The intent here is to illustrate the item types discussed in Chapters 6 and 7, respectively. Readers are urged to try their own hands at creating items using a variety of formats with familiar content. One might write items about writing items—a good way to practice and study at the same time. Critique the following items from the standpoint of item-objective match and format. Do the items follow the guidelines? If not, then how could they be improved?

The items for this exam tend to cluster in three categories: Knowledge, Comprehension, and Application. Other and higher-order outcomes, for example, synthesis (of an instructional plan) and evaluation (of student performance) would come later and would probably require different approaches. For example a checklist might be used to evaluate the instructional plan, and an observation schedule might be developed to evaluate implementation of instructional lesson plans.

Each item is keyed to one of the objectives presented in the Case Study Application at the end of Chapter 4. The correct answers to each item are indicated with an asterisk (*).

OBJECTIVE: Associate different instructional practices with three conceptual frameworks (models) of the reading process (Objective 1).

LEVEL: Comprehension

1. Which of the following activities would you be *most* likely to observe in a classroom where the teacher had a *bottom-up orientation* to reading?
   a. Creative writing
   b. Story telling
   * c. Letter-naming drills
   d. Round-robin reading
2. A child substitutes the word "puppy" for the word "dog." If you were a teacher with a *top-down orientation* toward reading, what would you do?
   * a. Ignore the error.
   b. Ask the child to look at the word again and sound it out.
   c. Tell the child the word.
3. Mrs. Jones has a primarily *interactive orientation* toward the reading process. A student in her classroom comes to a word he or she cannot read. Which of the following suggestions would the teacher make to the child to help him or her decode the word?
   * a. Skip the word and try to figure out the word from the sentence meaning.
   b. Try to sound out the word by using the initial consonant and vowel sounds.
   c. Tell the child the word.

OBJECTIVE: Recognize the importance of automaticity in the reading process (Objective 2).

LEVEL: Knowledge

4. Why is it important that readers decode words automatically?
   * a. Readers need to direct their attention to the meaning of the text.
   b. Readers need to read fast enough so that they will not lose their place.
   c. Readers need to consciously attend to the mechanics of decoding.

OBJECTIVE: Recognize instructional activities that emphasize the uses of language (Objective 3).

LEVEL: Comprehension

5. Which of the following reading situations would *not* be recommended to enhance language meaning?
   a. Oral reading by the teacher
   b. Pretending to read a memorized story
   c. Rereading a favorite story
   * d. Reading a word list

OBJECTIVE: Identify ways to create a classroom environment where learning to read is supported (Objective 5).

LEVEL: Knowledge

6. Dramatic activities and role play help children develop social skills and aid language development.
   * a. True
   b. False

OBJECTIVE: Recognize the characteristics of a particular language experience activity (Objective 7).

LEVEL: Analysis

7. What is the *major* difference between a basal approach to reading instruction and a language experience approach to reading instruction?
   a. The language experience approach uses controlled vocabulary and the basal reader approach uses the children's natural language.
   b. The language experience approach uses more good literature than the basal reader approach.
   * c. The language experience approach uses stories dictated by the children and the basal reader approach uses "ready-made" stories.
   d. The language experience approach is more teacher-directed and the basal reader approach is more child-centered.

OBJECTIVE: Identify the goal of teaching students decoding strategies (Objective 9).

LEVEL: Comprehension

8. Which of the following statements expresses the *primary* goal of decoding instruction?
   a. To provide students with various ways to figure out new words
   b. To help students identify individual words which results in comprehension
   * c. To enhance independent usage of phonics skills, structural analysis, and context clue skills
   d. To enable students to read more quickly

OBJECTIVE: Recognize three types of decoding strategies (Objective 10).

LEVEL: Knowledge

9. What kind of decoding strategy would a student be using if he/she used words, phrases, and sentences surrounding an unknown word to decode the word?
   * a. Context clues
   b. Phonic principles
   c. Structural analysis
   d. Dictionary aids

OBJECTIVE: Apply phonics generalizations to decode nonsense words (Objective 11).

LEVEL: Application

10. Which of the following words contains a consonant digraph?
    a. Strip
    b. Swipe
    * c. Shell
    d. Blimp
11. Which of the following words contains a vowel digraph?
    a. Robe
    * b. Bail
    c. Stem
    d. Stork

OBJECTIVE: Apply syllabication rules (Objective 12).

LEVEL: Application

12. If "tiskal" were a word and "i" was short, where would it most likely be divided into syllables?
    * a. tis kal
    b. tisk al
    c. ti skal
    d. Not enough information

OBJECTIVE: Recognize the purpose of Informed Strategies for Learning (Objective 13).

LEVEL: Knowledge

13. Informed Strategies for Learning (ISL) focused on how to get information from a text rather than on learning the content of the text.
   * a. True
   b. False

OBJECTIVE: Recognize the characteristics of Informed Strategies for Learning (Objective 14).

LEVEL: Knowledge

14. Students learn to use Informed Strategies for Learning without direct instruction because the strategies are automatic.
   a. True
   * b. False

OBJECTIVE: Identify three different kinds of discussion and recognize their characteristics (Objective 16).

LEVEL: Application

15. Which of the following discussions would be appropriate if you needed to determine an instructional approach to use with a child who was experiencing little success with basal instruction?
   a. Subject-mastery discussion
   b. Issue-oriented discussion
   * c. Problem-solving discussion
16. What is the *major* purpose of an *issue-oriented discussion?*
   a. To identify the major points of a textbook chapter
   * b. To identify student's beliefs/feelings about a particular topic
   c. To identify information students know about a subject before they read a textbook chapter

OBJECTIVE: Identify alternatives to round-robin reading (Objective 21).

LEVEL: Knowledge

17. What is one way to overcome some of the negative aspects of "round-robin" reading?
   * a. Ask students to close their books if they are not reading.
   b. Have students take turns reading paragraphs.
   c. Ask students to follow along and assist each other with difficult words.
   d. Have students volunteer to read aloud and ask other students to follow along.

OBJECTIVE: Recognize reading instructional activities that are appropriate for exceptional children (both hard-to-teach and gifted) (Objective 23).

LEVEL: Knowledge

18. Even though gifted readers generally have a high level of fluency, they still need reading instruction and guidance.
  * a. True
    b. False
19. The language experience approach is not an acceptable alternative to basal instruction for the "hard-to-teach" child.
    a. True
  * b. False

OBJECTIVE: Differentiate between characteristics of reliable versus valid tests (Objective 29).

LEVEL: Comprehension

20. A reading test that assesses a child's use of phonics generalizations to decode words would be a valid measure of vocabulary meaning.
    a. True
  * b. False

OBJECTIVE: Recognize the purpose of Question-Answer-Relationships (Objective 15).

LEVEL: Comprehension

21. What is the *primary* purpose of Question-Answer-Relationships?
  * a. Teach children how to find information when they have to answer questions
    b. Help teachers develop different types of questions.
    c. Help children relate information they read about in the text with their personal information.

OBJECTIVE: Recognize the place of alphabet instruction in early reading instruction.

LEVEL: Application

22. What activity would have the most impact on developing early reading skills in very young children? (Answer: Reading aloud frequently to the child)

OBJECTIVE: Identify activities that foster early literacy development before formal reading instruction begins.

LEVEL: Knowledge

23. What characteristic is most important in selecting reading material for early reading experience? (Answer: Realism)

OBJECTIVE: Associate different instructional practices with three conceptual frameworks (models) of the reading process.

LEVEL: Comprehension

24. The unit of instruction emphasized in the top-down model of reading is ______________ . (Answer: A sentence)

Content Review Statements

1. Multiple-choice or changing-alternative items provide a flexible method of measuring a great variety of outcomes, particularly at the higher levels of mental ability.
2. Multiple-choice items should include logically related and arranged alternatives, provide a correct or preferable answer, and list plausible, grammatically parallel, but incorrect answers.
3. The use of a "None of the Above" or an "All of the Above" alternative should be cautious, particularly when it is keyed as the correct answer.
4. The more similar (homogeneous) the alternatives in a multiple-choice item, the higher the likelihood of good discrimination between high- and low-achieving students.
5. Many useful ideas for achievement test items can be found in the *Taxonomy of Educational Objectives, Handbook I: The Cognitive Domain.*
6. Graphic materials can provide a basis for measuring outcomes in a variety of subject-matter fields.
7. Selection items can be used effectively to measure problem solving and logical reasoning.
8. The matching item is a variation on the multiple-choice item and is useful in surveying knowledge of the who, what, when, and where variety.
9. Matching items should:
   a. Include very detailed directions for responding.
   b. Be limited to a single page.
   c. Be limited to about 10–15 pairs.
   d. Use mutually exclusive categories.
   e. Present stimuli and responses in some logical order.
10. Great care must be taken in developing test materials for young children.
11. The stem or lead to a multiple-choice item should pose a clear, definite, explicit, and singular problem to be solved or questions to be answered.
12. Items where the stem(s) or alternative(s) of one question may give the answer to another question should be avoided.
13. Avoid making the correct alternative systematically different from the incorrect alternatives (e.g., longer).
14. Where relevant, present multiple-choice alternatives in some logical or systematic order (e.g., numerical).

15. Response alternatives should be mutually exclusive (e.g., nonoverlapping numerical answers).
16. Avoid using common language or terms in the stem of a multiple-choice item and the correct answer.
17. Require the examinee to select among alternative definitions if the objective is to measure comprehension of terms.
18. Measurements used with the very young should:
    a. Have explicit directions, preferably read to the examinee.
    b. Have practice exercises.
    c. Be examined closely relative to the language used.
    d. Use separate answer sheets only sparingly.

Speculations

1. What are the advantages and disadvantages of using the multiple-choice test item format? What are the major guidelines in writing these kinds of items?
2. What are the major faults to be avoided in constructing matching exercises?
3. What are the major advantages and disadvantages in using the matching exercise?
4. In what way are true-false and multiple-choice items alike?
5. What is it that you don't like about multiple-choice items?
6. Is it possible to consistently measure higher-order educational outcomes with objective items?
7. What are some good sources of distractors for multiple-choice items?

Suggested Readings

Cangelosi, J. S. (1990). *Designing tests for evaluating student achievement.* New York: Longman. This paperback is concerned exclusively with instrument development. Chapter 10, "Multiple-Choice Items," and Chapter 11, "Short-Answer Matching and Other Objective-Test Items" are comprehensive and instructive.

Ebel, R. L., & Frisbie, D. A. (1991). *Essentials of educational measurement* (5th ed.). Englewood Cliffs, NJ: Prentice Hall. See Chapters 9 and 10, respectively, for good discussions of item writing.

Haladyna, T. M., & Downing, S. M. (1989). A taxonomy of multiple-choice item-writing rules, and validity of a taxonomy of multiple-choice item-writing rules. *Applied Measurement in Education,* 2(1), 37–50, 51–78.

Roid, G. H., & Haladyna, T. M. (1982). *A technology for test-item writing.* New York: Academic Press.

Chapter 8

Constructing and Scoring Essay Items and Tests

Many instructors, particularly neophytes, believe that essay tests are the easiest type of measuring instrument to construct and score. Nothing could be further from the truth. The expenditure of considerable time and effort is necessary if essay items and tests are to yield meaningful information. Essay tests allow for direct assessment of the attainment of a variety of objectives and goals. In contrast to traditional "objective" item types, they demand less construction time per fixed unit of student time but a significant increase in labor and time for scoring. According to some investigators the use of essay testing encourages more appropriate study habits. See Crooks (1988) for a review of the relevant literature.

Problems and procedures involved in constructing and administering essay items and tests, as well as scoring procedures, are discussed in this chapter.

General Types of Essay Items

Essay items may be classified according to a number of different but relevant criteria. Two categories that have been found particularly useful are discussed in the following section. There are, however, no hard and fast rules for determining when a "restricted response" essay becomes "extended." Three paragraphs? Five hundred words? The terms describe relative ends of a continuum.

Extended versus Restricted Response

One can differentiate the many types of essay items on the basis of the extensiveness of the student's response. The relative freedom of response has obvious practical implications for both instructor and student. From the instructor's standpoint, an extensive response to a few broadly based questions allows for an in-depth sampling of a student's knowledge, thinking processes, and problem-solving behavior relative to a particular topic. The open-ended nature of the task posed by an instruction such as "Discuss essay and objective type tests" is challenging to a student. In order to respond correctly, the student must recall specific information and organize, evaluate, and write an intelligible composition. On the other hand, because it is poorly structured, such free-response essay items would tend to yield a variety of responses from examinees, both with respect to content and organization, and thus to inhibit reliable grading. The potential ambiguity of an essay task is probably the single most important contributor to unreliability. In addition, the more extensive the responses elicited, the fewer questions an instructor may ask—which, in turn, may lower the content validity of the test.

It follows, therefore, that a more restricted-response essay item and/or test is, in general, preferable. An instruction such as "Discuss the relative advantages and disadvantages of essay and short-answer tests with respect to (1) reliability, (2) objectivity, (3) content validity, and (4) usability" presents a better defined task more likely to lend itself to reliable scoring and yet allow students sufficient latitude to organize and express their thoughts creatively.

Gronlund and Linn (1990) have identified 12 complex learning outcomes that can be measured effectively with essay items. These are the abilities to:

Explain cause-effect relationships.
Describe applications of principles.
Present relevant arguments.
Formulate tenable hypotheses.
Formulate valid conclusions.
State necessary assumptions.
Describe the limitations of data.
Explain methods and procedures.
Produce, organize, and express ideas.
Integrate learnings in different areas.
Create original forms (e.g., designing an experiment).
Evaluate the worth of ideas.

This list is not exhaustive but should highlight some of the potential learning outcomes that may be assessed by essay items and tests. In addition, some advocates of the essay item claim that it can be used to elicit creative behavior. Attempts to assess creativity through such methods, however, are still in the early stages of development.

Content versus Expression

It is frequently claimed that the essay item or test allows the student to present his or her knowledge and understanding and to organize the material in a unique form and style. More often than not, such factors as expression, grammar, spelling, and the like are evaluated in conjunction with content. If the instructor has attempted to develop students' expressive skills, and if this learning outcome is included in his or her table of specifications, the evaluation of such skills is legitimate. If expressive skills are not part of the instructional program, it is not ethical to evaluate them. If the score of each essay item includes an evaluation of the mechanics of English, this should, obviously, be brought to the attention of the student. If possible, separate scores should be computed for content and expression.

The decision to include either or both of these elements in a score, and the relative weighting of each, should be dictated by the table of specifications.

Specific Types of Essay Questions

The following set of essay questions[1] is presented to illustrate how the phrasing of an essay item can be framed to elicit particular behaviors and levels of response.

I. **Recall**
   A. Simple recall
      1. What is the chemical formula for hydrogen peroxide?
      2. Who wrote "The Emergence of Lincoln"?
   B. Selective recall in which a basis for evaluation or judgment is suggested
      1. Which three individuals in the nineteenth century had the most profound effect on contemporary life?

II. **Understanding**
   A. Comparison of two phenomena on a single designated basis
      1. Compare the writers of the English Renaissance to those of the nineteenth century with respect to their ability to describe nature.
   B. Comparison of two phenomena in general
      1. Compare the French and Russian Revolutions.
   C. Explanation of the use or exact meaning of a phrase or statement
      1. The Book of John begins "In the beginning was the word . . ." From what philosophical system does this statement derive?
   D. Summary of a text or some portion of it
      1. State the central thesis of the Communist Manifesto.
   E. Statement of an artist's purpose in the selection or organization of material
      1. Why did Hemingway describe in detail the episode in which Gordon, lying wounded, engages the oncoming enemy?

[1]Reprinted and modified with permission from *Testing Bulletin No. 2*, "The Writing of Essay Questions," published by the Office of Evaluation Services, Michigan State University, September 1967.

2. What was Beethoven's purpose in deviating from the orthodox form of a symphony in Symphony No. 6?

III. **Application.** It should be clearly understood that whether or not a question elicits application depends on the preliminary educational experience. If an analysis has been taught explicitly, a question involving that analysis is a matter of simple recall.

A. Causes or effects

1. Why may too frequent reliance on penicillin for the treatment of minor ailments eventually result in its diminished effectiveness against major invasion of body tissues by infectious bacteria?
2. Why did fascism flourish in Italy and Germany but not in England and the United States?

B. Analysis (It is advisable not to use the word *analysis* in the question itself)

1. Why was Hamlet torn by conflicting desires?
2. Why is the simple existence of slavery an insufficient explanation for the outbreak of the American Civil War?

C. Statement of relationship

1. It is said that intelligence correlates with school achievement at about .65. Explain this relationship.

D. Illustrations or examples of principles

1. Name three examples of uses of the lever in typical American homes.

E. Application of rules or principles in specified situations

1. Would you weigh more or less on the moon? On the sun? Explain.

F. Reorganization of facts

1. Some writers have said that the American Revolution was not merely a political revolution against England but also a social revolution, within the colonies, of the poor against the wealthy. Using the same evidence, what other conclusion is possible?

IV. **Judgment**

A. Decision for or against

1. Should members of the Communist Party be allowed to teach in American colleges? Why or why not?
2. Is nature or nurture more influential in determining human behavior? Why?

B. Discussion

1. Discuss the likelihood that four-year private liberal arts colleges will gradually be replaced by junior colleges and state universities.

C. Criticism of the adequacy, correctness, or relevance of a statement

1. The discovery of penicillin has often been called an accident. Comment on the adequacy of this explanation.

D. Formulation of new questions

1. What should one find out in order to explain why some students of high intelligence fail in school?
2. What questions should a scientist ask in order to determine why more smokers than nonsmokers develop lung cancer?

Special Problem Areas

Four specific sources of difficulty likely to be encountered in the use of essay tests, and ways to minimize them, are in need of elaboration.

Question Construction

The preparation of the essay question is perhaps the most important step in the developmental process. Language usage and word choice are particularly important during task construction. The language dimension is very critical not only because it controls the comprehension level of the item for the examinee, but also because it specifies the parameters of the task. You need to narrowly specify, explicate, define, and otherwise clarify what it is that you want from the respondent. Take, for example, the silly item, "Describe the origins of World War I." This recall knowledge item related to the complex events contributing to the outbreak of hostilities in 1914 would really leave the examinee in a quandary. Did the author wish to focus on the multinational forces of nationalism, imperialism or communism, political events, military events, or the assassination of Archduke Ferdinand of Austria? A more meaningful rephrasing of our WWI question might be: "What were the principal diplomatic events in Europe between 1890 and 1913 that contributed directly to the outbreak of World War I?" This task is better defined and unequivocally calls for the recall of specific selected information. What, if anything, is done with this information will depend on how the material was handled in the classroom. But sometimes definiteness is not enough, as illustrated by the author's favorite essay item: "Describe the world and give two examples." The question must also have an answer that "experts" could agree upon, thereby rendering it *objective.* Here is another item that allows too much latitude in interpretation: "Comment on the significance of Darwin's *Origin of Species.*" The intent is to provide sufficient range to meet student need to display his or her mastery of the material. Unfortunately, one could write for hours on the question and never address the intent of the instructor. An improved version follows: "Darwin, in his *Origin of Species*, emphasized that natural selection resulted in the survival of the fittest. To what extent has this been supported or refuted by subsequent biological research?" Limits have now been placed on the problematic situation.

Essay items are frequently disdained because it is claimed that they do not measure higher-order outcomes. This is perhaps a problem with how they are, in fact, used and not a legitimate comment on how they can be used. Following are two sample essay items taken from the *Taxonomy of Educational Objectives.* Depending on instructional background and level of student, this task to produce a plan or set of operations measures at least at the Analysis level.

Several authorities were asked to participate in a round-table discussion of juvenile delinquency. They were given the following data about City X and communities A, B, and C within City X.

	For City X as a Whole	*For Community A*	*For Community B*	*For Community C*
Juvenile Delinquency Rate (annual arrests per 100 persons ages 5–19)	4.24	18.1	1.3	4.1
Average Monthly Rental	$60.00	$42.00	$100.00	$72.00
Infant Death Rate (per 1000 births)	52.3	76.0	32.1	56.7
Birth Rate (per 1000 inhabitants)	15.5	16.7	10.1	15.4

In addition, they were told that in Community A the crimes against property (burglary, etc.) constituted a relatively higher proportion of the total juvenile offenses than in Communities B and C, where crimes against persons (assasult, etc.) were relatively greater.

How would *you* explain the differences in these juvenile delinquency rates in light of the above data? (You may make use of any theory or material presented in the course.)

In light of your explanation of the data, what proposals would you make for reducing juvenile delinquency rate in each of the three communities?

Reader Reliability

The classic studies of the reliability of grading free-response test items were undertaken in 1912 and 1913 by Starch and Elliott (1912, 1913a, 1913b). In three studies focusing on high-school English, history, and mathematics, Starch and Elliott found tremendous variation in the independent gradings of a standard set of papers. They found discrepancies of up to 48 points in English, 49 points in geometry, and 70 points in history. Even recent research, employing highly sophisticated designs and analysis procedures, has failed to demonstrate consistently satisfactory agreement among essay graders. A study by Myers, McConville, and Coffman (1966) involving 145 readers, 80,000 essays, and a five-day reading period found average single-reader reliabilities of .41. When the number of readers was increased to four, the average reliability rose to .73. This significant increase in reliability was obtained under controlled conditions, with trained graders who read "holistically" and used a four-point scale. The implication of this research is clear: Several readers should participate in the grading of essay exams. The fallibility of human judgment cannot be underestimated as a source of unreliability in the scoring of essay examinations.

Research has shed light on some of the specific contributory factors in lack of reader reliability. Marshall and Powers (1969), for example, have experimentally demonstrated that preservice teachers are influenced by such factors as quality of composition and penmanship, even when they are explicitly instructed to grade on content alone. In addition Chase (1986, 1983) has illustrated the effect of item readability, gender, and race on essay scoring.

Instrument Reliability

Even if an acceptable level of scoring reliability is attained, there is no guarantee that we are measuring consistently (see Chapter 12). There remains the issue of the sampling of objectives or behaviors represented by the test. Traxler and Anderson (1935), for example, found that although experienced readers could agree on the scoring of two different forms of an essay test, the correlation between the forms was only .60. Thus it is possible for the reliability of scoring to exceed the reliability of the instrument itself.

It has been suggested by some experts that the essay test is less susceptible than the objective test to the effect of guessing. This may not be the case. If the examinee is torn between two or more responses to an open-ended question, he or she still must guess between them. Such guessing, if widespread, can contribute to increased error and decreased reliability. The only difference between guessing on essay and objective tests is that the essay writer devises his own alternatives, while the alternatives are provided on an objective test.

One way to increase the reliability of an essay test is to increase the number of questions and restrict the length of the answers. The more specific and narrowly defined the questions, the less likely they are to be ambiguous to the examinee. This procedure should result in more uniform comprehension and performance of the assigned task, and hence in the increased reliability of the instrument and scoring. It also helps insure better coverage of the domain of objectives.

Instrument Validity

The number of questions on the test influences validity as well as reliability. It has been suggested that the first step in developing an achievement test is to summarize the instructional objectives in the form of a table of specifications. As commonly constructed, an essay test contains a small number of items; thus, the sampling of desired behaviors represented in the table of specifications will be limited, and the test will suffer from lowered validity—specifically, decreassed content validity. The limited sampling affects not only the behavior measured, but also coverage of subject matter. Hopkins, Stanley, and Hopkins (1990) have summarized studies showing that an essay exam elicits about half the knowledge an individual possesses about a particular topic, but requires twice as much time as a short-answer test.

There is another sense in which the validity of an essay test may be questioned. Theoretically, the essay allows examinees to construct a creative, organized, unique, and integrated communication. Very frequently, however, they spend most of their time simply recalling and assembling information, rather than integrating it. The behavior elicited by the test, then, is not that hoped for by the instructor or dictated by the table of specifications. Obviously, validity suffers in a situation such as this. Again, one way to handle the problem is to increase the number of items on the test.

Scoring Essay Tests

Most instructors would agree that the scoring of essay items and tests is among the most time-consuming and frustrating tasks associated with conscientious classroom measurement. Instructors are frequently unwilling to set aside the large chunks of time necessary to score a stack of "blue books" carefully. It almost goes without saying that if reliable scoring is to be accomplished an instructor must expend considerable time and effort.

Before turning to specific methods of scoring, several general comments are in order. First, it is critical that the instructor prepare in advance a detailed "ideal" answer. This answer will serve as the criterion by which each student's answer will be judged. If this is not done, the results could be disastrous. The subjectivity of the instructor could seriously inhibit consistent scoring, and it is also possible that student responses might dictate correct answers. Second, it is generally recommended that student papers be scored anonymously, and that all the answers to a given item be scored at one time, rather than grading each student's total test separately.

The mechanics of scoring generally take different forms, depending on whether the focus of the essay task is content or subject matter, or whether the focus is on assessing an individual's ability to create a unique communication that is consistent with accepted standards and guidelines for expression, style, and grammar.

Table 8-1 contains an outline of possible approaches to essay scoring as a function of the intent of using this measurement item type. The two foci are content (or subject matter), such as the Civil War or the anatomy of the human heart, and composition. Three approaches to scoring are generally acknowledged (Odell, 1981). Following is a brief description and discussion of these approaches.

Holistic Scoring for Content Knowledge or Communication Effectiveness

Experienced readers make gross judgments about the quality of a given paper. The judgments are simply reported in terms of two or more evaluation categories (e.g., acceptable/unacceptable; A/B/C/D/F; inadequate/minimal/good/very good). As many as eight categories may be used. Comments sometimes accompany the feedback to writers. Such a procedure, if not done anonymously, can be very susceptible to "halo" rating errors. As described here the holistic scoring (HS) approach is usually focused on assessing writing effectiveness. The method also could be applied in evaluating content achievement, but probably with considerably less reliability. The holistic approach also lacks detailed diagnostic value unless it contains extensive comments, in which case it almost becomes analytic.

Table 8-1 Combinations of Essay Scoring Methods and Focus Dimensions

Scoring Method	Focus Dimension: Content (Subject Matter)	Communication
Holistic	Gross overall evaluation	Gross overall evaluation
Modified Holistic	Limited number of objectives	Limited number of dimensions
Analytic	Checklist point scoring of content	Detailed critique of essay

Modified Holistic Scoring for Communication Effectiveness

This procedure, sometimes referred to as "primary trait," basically involves the making of gross judgments of worth—as is the case with total holistic scoring—but the reporting of the communication value of the essay is done through the application of categories and scales like those included in Figure 8-1. Benchmark or "range finder" illustrative essays are usually identified. The holistic dimension is reflected in the fact that each "domain" (see Figure 8-1) is holistically scored. The modified holistic scoring approach (MHS) is considered to be a very efficient method for gaining a comprehensive picture of student writing ability. In addition, it is reliable and can be used by knowledgeable raters after approximately 20–24 hours of training. In most applications the MHS approach is used: two readers for each paper, with the results being combined. Sometimes weights reflecting differential importance are applied to the scores.

The selection of questions or prompts is crucial. You don't want content to influence the ratings; keep it neutral so that the paper will only reflect true writing ability. A prompt such as "Describe your knowledge" won't get it done. In addition to the usual "contentless" prompt, the essay may be formulated as an autobiographical incident, memoir, business letter, story, problem solution, evaluation, or a simple reporting of information.

Modified Holistic Scoring for Content Knowledge

In reality there is probably very little use of the modified holistic approach to scoring essays for content knowledge. If applied in its fullest form it would involve a rater making judgments about the adequacy of knowledge a student exhibited about a limited number of objectives. For example, the teacher of a human anatomy and physiology class might present the student with an essay task requiring students to describe the following major systems: skeletal, reproductive, digestive, circulatory, and urinary. Judgments would be made about the adequacy of student descriptions.

GEORGIA BASIC SKILLS WRITING TEST

Scoring Dimensions, Definitions, and Components

CONTENT/ORGANIZATION: The writer establishes the controlling idea through examples, illustrations, and facts or details. There is evidence of a sense of order that is clear and relevant.

- Clearly established controlling idea
- Clearly developed supporting ideas
- Sufficiently relevant supporting ideas
- Clearly discernible order of presentation
- Logical transitions and flow of ideas
- Sense of completeness

STYLE: The writer controls language to establish his/her individuality.

- Concrete images and descriptive language
- Easily readable
- Varied sentence patterns
- Appropriate tone for topic, audience, and purpose

SENTENCE FORMATION: The writer forms effective sentences.

- Appropriate end punctuation
- Complete sentences or functional fragments
- Appropriate coordination and/or subordination

USAGE: The writer uses standard American English.

- Clear pronoun references
- Correct subject-verb agreement
- Standard form of verbs and nouns
- Correct word choice

MECHANICS: The writer employs devices necessary in standard written American English.

- Appropriate capitalization
- Appropriate internal punctuation
- Appropriate formatting
- Correct spelling

Score Point 1: The writing is **Inadequate.** Very few if any of the components for the dimension are demonstrated.

Score Point 2: The writing is **Minimal.** Some of the components for the dimension are demonstrated.

Score Point 3: The writing is **Good,** yet, not exceptional. Many of the components are demonstrated, and these are demonstrated successfully.

Score Point 4: The writing is **Very Good.** Most of the components are demonstrated, and these are demonstrated consistently.

Figure 8-1

Georgia modified holistic scoring guide

The analysis of responses would be more detailed than holistic, but less than analytic scorings.

Analytic Scoring for Communication Effectiveness

This method involves evaluating a number of specific categories, generally fewer than 10. Qualitative judgments are then made within categories. In general, this method emphasizes the totality or "wholeness" of the response and is used when the instructor is focusing on expression rather than content. Rating methods are generally efficient, but their reliabilities are very much tied to the number of categories and subdivisions within categories. The categories chosen are usually determined by the "ideal" answer constructed by the instructor. Another useful approach is to use a standard set of categories, particularly if one's primary interest is in evaluating English composition. A rating method found useful by Paul Deiderich in his research on writing ability, and by many classroom teachers, is presented in Table 8-2. This scale weighs organization 50 percent, style 30 percent, and mechanics 20 percent. By using appropriate, if arbitrary, multiplications, the 40-point scale translates into a 100-point scale. Such a translation is useful if an instructor is disposed or required to report percentage grades.

The ultimate critique of an essay, however, is the detailed analysis paragraph by paragraph, line by line, and word by word. This type of analysis has the maximum benefit to the student. It obviously takes a great deal of time and effort, but such detailed analyses are impractical when composition is included as part of large scale assessment, that is, on a statewide basis.

Table 8-2 Diederich's Scale for Grading English Composition

Quality and development of ideas	1 2 3 4 5			
Organization, relevance, movement	1 2 3 4 5	______	× 5 =	______
		Subtotal		
Style, flavor, individuality	1 2 3 4 5			
Wording and phrasing	1 2 3 4 5	______	× 3 =	______
		Subtotal		
Grammar, sentence structure	1 2 3 4 5			
Punctuation	1 2 3 4 5			
Spelling	1 2 3 4 5			
Manuscript form, legibility	1 2 3 4 5	______	× 1 =	______
		Subtotal		
		Total grade		______%

1 = Poor *2 = Weak* *3 = Average* *4 = Good* *5 = Excellent*

Source: Adapted from A. Jewett and C. E. Bish, eds., *Improving English composition.* Washington: National Education Association, 1965. Reprinted by permission of the National Education Association.

Analytic Scoring for Content Achievement

The analytic—or the Checklist Point Score—method involves partitioning the "ideal" response into a series of points or features, each of which is specifically defined. It is a scoring technique particularly useful if the content is to be emphasized over expression. Each element in the answer is identified and a credit value attached to it. If possible, the instructor's table of specifications should be used as a guide for determining credits.

As an illustration of this method, consider the following restricted-response question: "What are the principal reasons that research in the social sciences has not progressed as far as has that in the biological and physical sciences?" The instructor's ideal answer might be: "Since the social scientist is himself part of what he is attempting to study, he cannot achieve the objectivity possible in the more precise sciences. Further, the conclusions he reaches frequently run counter to deeply held prejudices and are therefore unacceptable. Feeling that many of the social affairs of men are not susceptible to scientific study, people have been less willing to subsidize social research than medicine, for example. Finally, the scientific study of nature has a much longer history than the scientific study of man. This history has provided a much larger body of data and theory from which to progress."

The essential elements in this ideal answer are identified and quantitative weights are assigned to each. The checklist point score sheet might look something like this:

Element of Answer	*Possible Points*
1. Scientist part of his subject	2
2. Prejudice	3
3. Lack of financial support	2
4. Short history	1
5. Small body of facts and theory	1
6. Organization	1
7. Language usage	1

This approach to scoring has several advantages. An analysis of the instructor's ideal response quite frequently reveals that the original question needs to be recast in order to elicit the desired response, which may result in a readjustment of time limits. A final advantage of the checklist point score method is its reliability. If used conscientiously, the analytic method can yield consistent scores on restricted-response essay items for different graders.

The difference between analytic and modified holistic is perhaps more a matter of degree than kind as both involve making general judgments. Many of the suggestions for using essay items discussed in this chapter, as well as other recommendations by measurement authorities, are summarized in Table 8-3. All are self-explanatory with the exception of the eighth. Testing experts generally recommend against the use of optional questions. Their use results in essay tests that measure what the student knows, rather than what he doesn't know. If a test is to provide useful information about learning outcomes, negative as well as positive evidence

Table 8-3 Suggestions for Constructing, Evaluating, and Using Essay Exams

Limit the problem that the question poses so that it will have an unequivocal meaning to most students.
Use words which will convey clear meaning to the student.
Prepare enough questions to sample the material of the course broadly, within a reasonable time limit.
Use an essay question for the purposes it best serves, i.e., organization, handling complicated ideas, and writing.
Prepare questions which require considerable thought, but which can be answered in relatively few words.
Determine in advance how much weight will be accorded each of the various elements expected in a complete answer.
Without knowledge of students' names, score each question for all students. Use several scores and scorers if possible.
Require all students to answer all questions on the test.
Write questions about materials immediately germane to the course.
Study past questions to determine how students performed.
Make gross judgments of the relative excellence of answers as a first step in grading.
Word a question as simply as possible in order to make the task clear.
Do *not* judge papers on the basis of external factors unless they have been clearly stipulated.
Do *not* make a generalized estimate of an entire paper's worth.
Do *not* construct a test consisting of only one question.

Source: Adapted with permission from *Testing Bulletin No. 1,* Essay tests: General considerations. Published by the Office of Evaluation Services, Michigan State University, 1971.

should be gathered. We are emphasizing here the diagnostic use of essay tests. There may be situations in which it is legitimate to allow a student to select the questions he will answer. Such a situation might be a statewide testing program with little control of the curriculum, in which an optional choice would probably constitute a fairer testing practice. But in a classroom testing situation, allowing a choice of questions is generally not recommended.

Scoring Essay Items for Affective Outcomes

The extended-response essay item may be used to examine a variety of affective outcomes. The wealth of material provided by responses to problematic situations may be subjected to a content analysis. Recurring themes in the essays of individuals or whole classes may be related to attitudes toward subject matter or the learning environment. Whether or not a given teacher wishes to investigate changes in attitudes will, of course, depend on his particular instructional objectives. A student's interests and values may more strongly influence his response to an essay question than does the question itself. Clinical psychologists have, of course, long used the "free-response mode" to gain insights into personality dynamics. The main difficulty in using the essay in this fashion is the enormous amount of effort required to standardize procedures. As an exploratory technique, it has a great deal to recommend it.

Large-Scale Assessment of Writing Performance

One of the most significant movements in public education is the large-scale assessment of writing performance at selected grades. This is being done both informally at the local level and formally at the state level. State-level data gathered for accountability purposes can be very valuable. Such data give classroom teachers, schools, and systems valuable information regarding the progress of students in developing written communication skills. Each year brings an increase in the number of states implementing mass writing assessment programs. Public education is being increasingly criticized by national commissions, reports, and surveys for its lack of attention to concerns of literacy and particularly to the development of writing skills. It is suggested that teachers are lax in their attention to the cultivation of such skills. From an instructional standpoint the teaching of writing skills is very time consuming and must compete with other important objectives. The big problem in the evaluation of student essays requires considerable time and effort. But feedback is a critical element in the instructional process. The data needed are more than judgments of "acceptable" or "unacceptable," and should help direct the student toward areas requiring improvements.

In doing large-scale writing assessments the modified holistic scoring (MHS) method previously described can be used effectively. Figure 8-1 contains a description of the MHS method used in the state of Georgia to score papers at grades 6, 8, and 10. Papers are read by a minimum of two readers; if there is a significant lack of agreement the paper is rated by another independent pair of raters. "Model" papers are periodically inserted into the system to monitor reliability and accuracy. A reader can, on the average, score a paper in two minutes. Average agreement within one rating scale point within each of the five domains (see Figure 8-1) can be achieved in 90 percent of the cases.

Figure 8-2 contains a sample essay from the Georgia Basic Skills Writing Test Scoring Manual (1987). The prompt for this essay was: "What would you change in your school if you could be principal for a day?" The scoring by one rater and the attendant annotation is as follows:

Content/Organization (Score 1)

The writer does not demonstrate competence in any of the components. A controlling idea ("I finally have the power to change things in my school") is apparent, but the single supporting idea (changing the schedule) is not sufficient to establish a controlling idea. The gap in information between the first and second paragraphs results in a confusing organization. The paper reads as if an entire paragraph had been left out.

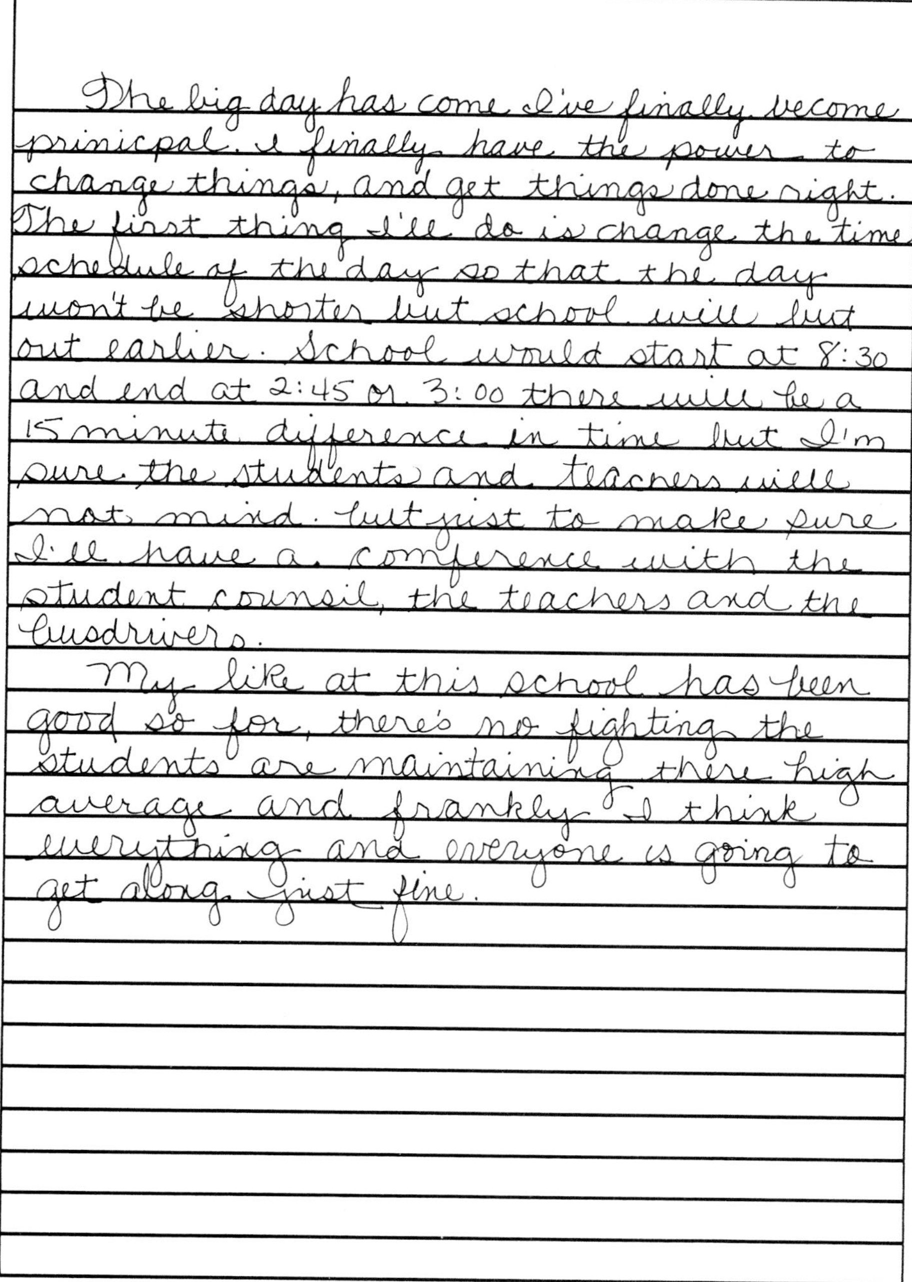

The big day has come I've finally become prinicpal. I finally have the power to change things, and get things done right. The first thing I'll do is change the time schedule of the day so that the day won't be shorter but school will let out earlier. School would start at 8:30 and end at 2:45 or 3:00 there will be a 15 minute difference in time but I'm sure the students and teachers will not mind. but just to make sure I'll have a conference with the student counsil, the teachers and the busdrivers.

My like at this school has been good so for, there's no fighting the students are maintaining there high average and frankly I think everything and everyone is going to get along just fine.

Figure 8-2

Unacceptable writing assessment sample

Style (Score 2)

The language is mechanical, with very little description. However, there is some evidence of sentence variety and the paper is easily readable. The tone of the final paragraph almost succeeds in getting the reader into the writer's fantasy of being principal. The creative present-tense immediacy establishes a believable tone. Competence in some of the components is demonstrated.

Sentence Formation (Score 2)

Sentence level competence is mixed at best. Overall, there are few sentences in the paper, with frequent errors in end punctuation. Some of the sentences are either run-ons or contain ideas that run together (". . . there will be a 15 minute difference but I'm sure the students . . ."). The writer does demonstrate, however, a minimal if inconsistent competence in coordination and subordination.

Usage (Score 3)

The writer does demonstrate control of many usage concepts. Subject-verb agreement is correct, and there are no incorrect word choices. There is a single instance of a shift in verb tense from the conditional "would start" to the future "will be." No judgment can be made about competence in pronoun reference, as the writer uses only the first person pronoun. Instances of usage are correct but not varied. The brevity of the paper limits the demonstration of competence to a low "3."

Mechanics (Score 2)

The demonstration of competence in format is limited. Several simple words are misspelled, including "there" for "their" and "averge" for "average." While some introductory commas are missing, in some instances they are present. Capitalization is correct, but instances are limited to the first word of sentences and the first person singular pronoun. The witer does not often err, but neither does he or she shine.

The scoring for two raters after applying importance weights is as follows:

	Rater 1	*Rater 2*	*Sum*	*Weight*	*Total*
Content/ Organization	1	2	3	3	9
Style	2	2	4	2	8
Sentence Formation	2	2	4	1	4
Usage	3	2	5	1	5
Mechanics	2	1	3	1	3
GRAND TOTAL					28

This total score of 28 is out of a maximum possible 64 points. The criteria for passing had been set at 34, so this student would not have passed, but could retake the test. Figure 8-3 contains an essay that received a score of 37 in response to the same prompt and passed.

Obviously not all papers are scorable. Papers may be rejected if they are too short (e.g., four lines), non-English, off-topic, illegible, or incomprehensible; or if "white-out" correction fluid has been used.

The essay form is one of the most flexible measurement methods available. It can be used to assess knowledge, the results of problem solving, and the ability of students to communicate and express themselves. Despite common misconceptions, creating essay items and tests is a time-consuming task. The phrasing of the question is critical. The poser of the questions must tread the line between *excessive generality,* where adequate answers cannot be compared in the available time, and *excessive specificity,* where all the examinee has time to do is recall and recount information. All of these factors reflect on the major problem of essay items and that is the reliability and validity of scoring. Sometimes we must make the effort and expend the time because this is the only way in which we can get the information we need.

Case Study Application

Following is a brief short essay exercise aimed at measuring student knowledge about the use of the Language Experience Approach to the teaching of reading. The LEA sometimes uses group-composed stories or compositions based on field trips, school activities, or personal experiences. Sometimes the chart summaries of these stimulus topics must include special words, observations, job assignments, questions to be answered, imaginative stories or poems, or class rules. In situations where the child's own language experiences are unique, that is, a ghetto child, the LEA may have some real benefits. A lot of the ideas contained in LEA served as a foundation for the development of the currently popular whole-language or integrated approaches to reading instruction and as an alternative to the basal-reader technique. The essay is aimed at achievement, and is *not* intended to measure the student's ability to communicate in the sense that a creative essay assignment might attempt to do. It is assumed that reasonable standards of grammar would, however, apply.

ESSAY: The Language Experience Approach is one of the most popular and serviceable approaches to the teaching of reading. Briefly describe in grammatically correct form three advantages and three disadvantages of this approach. Allow about 6 minutes for your response. This exercise is worth 20 points.

RESPONSE: "The Language Experience Approach is one of the better approaches to use because teachers and kids like it. It lets them tell you what they know based on their life. Kids can use their motor and thinking skills. Learning makes them feel good because they can read and write about things they know.

If I became principal today, I would change the rule of having to keep your shirt-tail packed in. The three reasons why I believe it should be changed are that it only pertains to boys, it usually carries a harsh punishment, and it is not a very good rule. For these three reasons the rule of having to keep your shirt-tail packed in should be changed.

~~It~~ The rule of having to keep your shirt-tail packed in only pertains to boys. Yes, only boys have to pack their shirt-tails in and them some are proctically ignored by the faculty. Girls don't have to pack their shirt-tails in. They get to wear them out, some down past their knees. The faculty says their is a difference if you can't recoznize it. If so, what is the difference?

In many ways harsh punishment is ~~given~~ given in the rule of having to keep your shirt-tails packed in. Usually if you are caught with your shirt-tail out, you may receive more licks, and possibly face suspension.

In two ways it is not a good rule of having to keep your shirt-tail packed in. The first reason is that the rule is not common among ther schools. This is probably the only school in our district which the school has no exceptable explaration for having this rule. The students have done nothing for this.

If I were principal, I would change the rule of having to keep your shirt-tail ~~to~~ packed in because of the three reasons that it only pertains to boys, it may result in harsh punishment, and it is not a very good rule.

Figure 8-3

Acceptable writing assessment sample

On the other side of the coin is the fact that making the charts of experiences can be boring and take a lot of class time. But anything worthwhile is going to take time."

Criteria

The respondent could have selected from the following ideas in creating his or her answer. Each correctly identified element is worth two points, and eight total points were allowed for grammar and spelling.

Pro

1. Every child has some experience he/she can talk, read, or write about.
2. A variety of modalities are used.
3. Teacher and student work together.
4. Students' self-concept is enhanced.

Con

1. Lack of sequential development
2. Language experience charts can be boring
3. Making charts is time consuming.
4. May lead to memorization.
5. Lack of vocabulary control.

With this information, assign a total score to the sample essay.

Content Review Statements

1. Essay items and tests can be used to assess a variety of learning outcomes, particularly those related to an individual's ability to organize, analyze, synthesize, and express evaluations of material, ideas, facts, and concepts.
2. The use of extended-response essay items allows examinees to express themselves freely and the instructor to explore in depth a sampling of student knowledge and skills.
3. The use of restricted-response essay items provides for an efficient survey of a moderately large content area.
4. The answer to an essay item may be strictly evaluated in terms either of accuracy of content or clarity of expression (including organization).
5. Reliability of grading is one of the major obstacles to the effective use of essay items and tests.
6. Reliability of the sampling of student knowledge and skills is another potential problem area in essay testing.
7. The validity of essay items and tests in terms of objectives must be a matter of great concern to the examiner.
8. An instructor should almost never rely exclusively on essay items to assess the total learning outcomes of a unit or course of study.
9. The global or holistic rating of the components of an essay item—such as organization, style, and mechanics of expression—is one approach to scoring essays for communication effectiveness.

10. Modified holistic scoring procedures can be efficiently and effectively used to assess large numbers of papers.
11. It is recommended that an analytic method be applied in scoring essay items for content.
12. An instructor should write an "ideal" answer to a given essay question for use as a guide in evaluating individual student answers.
13. Use of the Checklist Point Score method allows each element of an essay answer to be objectively assessed when both content and expression are to be assessed.
14. Essay items may be used to explore various affective learning outcomes.
15. Essay items should:
    a. Be relevant and limited in scope.
    b. Contain clearly defined tasks.
    c. Be scored anonymously.
    d. Be scored using the Checklist Point Score method.
    e. Be the same for all students.

Speculations

1. Why are the following bad essay items? "Describe the world and give two examples," and "Is it true what they say about Dixie?"
2. What are some procedures that can be used to help improve the scoring/grading of essay items and tests?
3. What does it mean to score an essay using the "modified holistic method"?
4. When should the "Checklist Point Score method" of evaluating essay items be used?
5. What are the advantages and disadvantages of allowing students to choose which essay items to answer?
6. Which is more important in an essay—content or grammar?
7. Are there meaningful differences between extended and restricted essay items?

Suggested Readings

Breland, H. E., Camp, R., Jones, R. J., Morris, M. M., & Rock, D. A. (1987). *Assessing writing skill* (Research Monograph No. 11). New York: College Entrance Examination Board.

Coffman, W. E. (1971). Essay examinations. In R. L. Thorndike (Ed.), *Educational measurement* (2nd ed., pp. 271–302). Washington, DC: American Council on Education. This 32-page chapter contains a comprehensive and integrated survey of the research and practice of essay testing.

Greenberg, K. L., Wiener, H. S., & Donovan, R. A. (1986). *Writing assessment issues and strategies.* New York: Longman.

Gronlund, N. E., & Linn, R. L. (1990). *Measurement and evaluation in teaching* (5th ed.). New York: Macmillan. Chapter 9, "Measuring Complex Achievement: The Essay Test," contains many excellent suggestions on how to phrase questions to elicit the desired student behavior.

Hopkins, K. D., Stanley, J. C., & Hopkins, B. R. (1990). *Educational and psychological measurement and evaluation* (7th ed.). Englewood Cliffs, NJ: Prentice Hall. Chapter 8, "Constructing and Using Essay Tests" begins with a very interesting historical overview (from before biblical times) which leads to a detailed consideration of modern-day practices.

Ruth, L., & Murphy, S. (1988). *Designing writing tasks for the assessment of writing.* Norwood, NJ: Ablex.

White, E. M. (1985). *Teaching and assessing writing.* San Francisco: Jossey-Bass.

Chapter 9

Using Observation and Simulation with Rating Scales to Assess Process, Performance, and Product Outcomes

Most of the myriad of possible achievement outcomes in our schools and classrooms can be assessed with formal paper-and-pencil devices. This is particularly true of learning outcomes that involve knowledge, verbal and thinking skill development, comprehension, and intellectual problem solving. In addition, it is becoming increasingly apparent that many affective outcomes can be assessed with paper-and-pencil measures, providing data useful for both student and teacher. But this is not the whole story. It is difficult at best to approach the assessment of proficiency in many skill areas and in situations in which personal-social development is emphasized. The best approach to assessing behavioral changes is direct observation of those behaviors. We need to know not only whether a student *knows* what to do, but also whether he or she *can* do it, and finally we would like to know if he or she *will* do it. The assessment of behaviors and outcomes in lifelike and realistic (as opposed to the classroom atmosphere) situations can supply us with some of the most valid data for decision making.

Advantages of Observational Methods

The use of observational methods has been slighted in most school assessment situations, probably because of the difficulty of developing and applying the techniques. There are, however, many advantages to observation (Evertson & Green, 1986; Medley, 1982).

1. Observational and qualitative evaluation methods allow us to gather data, particularly about social-emotional-personal adjustment, in valid and reliable and precise ways not possible with more traditional methods.
2. Observational methods allow us to test an individual's ability to apply information in lifelike situations.
3. Because of the similarity between the testing situations and the setting in which the skills and knowledge are likely to be used, we find that observational measures tend to have higher predictive validity than do many other methods of predicting successful job performance.
4. Observational methods are easily adapted to a variety of settings, tasks, and kinds of individuals, at all age and educational levels.
5. Observational data can serve as an invaluable supplement to achievement and ability data available from other sources.
6. Observation provides both qualitative and quantitative data.
7. The use of data from a variety of sources results in a more reliable overall assessment.
8. The fact that observations take place in natural settings enhances their integration into the total instructional program and allows the instructor to use observation as part of the teaching process.

Disadvantages and Difficulties in Using Observational Methods

Observing students is a difficult task. Many factors influence what a teacher perceives and how his or her observations are reported. Training and experience are the prime contributors to the development of effective observational skills. There are a number of pitfalls that both experienced and inexperienced observers need to avoid (Prescott, 1957, p. 100; Cronbach, 1963a).

1. *Faulty knowledge.* Armed with misinformation and mistaken ideas about human development and behavior, a teacher can distort observational records and the resulting interpretations.

2. *Uncritical acceptance of data.* Failure to distinguish between fact and opinion and the acceptance of rumors can lead to distortion of facts.

3. *Failure to prespecify objectives.* Obviously, if we don't know what we are looking for, we may observe irrelevant behavior.

4. *Conclusion leaping.* Drawing inferences from a single incident and failing to consider contradictory data can lead to faulty conclusions.

5. *Failure to consider situational modifiers.* Behaviors result from many influences, and observations must take context into account. A single behavior may have two or more antecedents.

6. *Making false inferences from unreliable data.* The tendency to generalize from too limited a sampling of behaviors, and to make judgments on the basis of a few incidents, is a common pitfall.

7. *Failure to distinguish behaviors.* In most modern classrooms many activities take place simultaneously. It is difficult to distinguish relevant from irrelevant behavior.

8. *Failure to recognize personal expectations.* Teachers must realize that their observations will be colored by their own expectations, preferences, biases, and psychological needs.

9. *Failure to record observations accurately.* Observations should be recorded when they occur, or immediately afterward. Otherwise, selective forgetting may operate to reduce the validity of the report. There is a tendency to forget things that conflict with our own beliefs and expectations more readily than those that coincide with them.

10. *Excessive certainty.* Inferences from observations should be considered tentative and hypothetical until corroborative evidence is obtained.

11. *Oversimplification.* One should guard against assigning a single cause to a single behavior; behavior has multiple determinants.

12. *Emotional thinking.* We tend to give disproportionate weight to incidents that have had a disturbing effect on us.

13. *Substitution fallacy.* There is a tendency to substitute an observed behavior for a desired objective—for example, substituting teacher behavior (process) for the criterion of pupil performance. Observing shop work or physical education, one may tend to substitute "how students do something" for the quality of the product. This pitfall suggests the danger of giving such variables as "student-teacher interaction" or "group participation" the status of ultimate criteria.

Applications of Observational Data

Despite the pitfalls to be avoided in collecting observational data, such data can make a number of very valuable contributions to the improvement of the teaching-learning situation (Galton, 1987). Observational data may be used to study:

1. Group responsibility.
2. Group participation.
3. Attitudes toward subject matter.
4. Individual student interaction with the group.
5. Individual student and teacher interaction.
6. Teacher and class interaction.
7. Individual student achievement.
8. Class achievement.
9. Unanticipated but related outcomes.
10. Individual students in light of instructional hypotheses.
11. Teaching techniques.
12. Personal and academic problem areas.

Observational methods are particularly useful in studying an individual's manipulative and psychomotor skills. In addition, opportunities to gather data in naturally occurring or contrived situations are limited only by teacher creativity. Interpersonal relationships can be observed and objectively summarized. Observation is a means of monitoring important outcomes, particularly those dealing with application skills, without encroaching on instructional time or disrupting the class. The presence of an outside observer may, however, inhibit the "naturalness" of the situation.

The application of observation data in assessing interpersonal relationships and performance skills will be treated in detail later in this chapter.

Using Rating Scales to Record Observational Data

Rating scales are frequently used to record the results of observations. They may be easily applied in collecting self-observation of self-report data. The three scales most frequently used in educational settings are numerical, graphic, and checklist. These types of scales are efficient with respect both to the amount of time required to complete them and to the number of individuals who can be rated. Moreover, they do not require sophisticated raters and are relatively easily constructed. On the other hand, rating scales are all too often based on undifferentiated gross impressions and susceptible to conscious or unintentional distortion. The use of "anchored points" using descriptions, behaviors, products, illustrations, or samples can enhance the usefulness of rating scales (Berk, 1986b; Borman, 1986).

Numerical Scales

Numerical scales generally take the form of a sequence of defined numbers. The definitions of the numbers might be in terms of degree of favorableness, frequency, pleasantness, or agreement with a statement. Color or odor, for example, might be rated as:

5 = Most pleasant
4 = Moderately pleasant
3 = Neutral
2 = Moderately unpleasant
1 = Most unpleasant

Guilford (1954) cautions against using negative numbers or defining the end categories so extremely that no one will select them. It is probably a good idea to create more categories than one actually intends to use so as to maximize discrimination. One might, for example, use a scale like the following to gather the data:

4 = Always
3 = Usually
2 = Sometimes
1 = Never

Then combine categories 1 and 2, and 3 and 4 for analysis purposes. Research seems to indicate that, depending upon the nature of the task and the sophistication of the rater, from 7 to about 20 categories at the outside may be used. With checklists, as few as two categories (e.g., present-absent) can be used reliably.

The verbal definitions of the rating or numbers on a numerical scale may lead to semantic confusion. This problem is well illustrated by a study by Simpson (1944), who asked a population of high-school and college students to indicate what

Table 9-1 Meanings Assigned to Selected Frequency Terms Used in Rating Scales

Term	Average of Midpoint Ranges Assigned	Range of Middle 50% of Assignments
Always	99	98–100
Very Often	88	80–93
Usually	85	70–90
Often	78	65–85
Generally	78	63–85
Frequently	73	40–80
Rather Often	65	45–80
Sometimes	20	13–35
Occasionally	20	10–33
Seldom	10	6–18
Rarely	5	3–10

Source: Adapted from Simpson (1944).

certain terms connoted for them. For example, does the term "often" mean: 65 times in 100 (or even less) or 85 times in 100? A selected sample of Simpson's results is presented in Table 9-1. It is obvious that individuals define terms very differently. It is the overlap in the range of the middle 50 percent for adjacent terms that really introduces the ambiguity in measurement. Such differences undoubtedly serve to lower both the validity and the reliability of ratings. Simpson did find, however, that there were no appreciable differences between the sexes in the intepretation of frequency terms. One possible method of overcoming the problem of variable definitions is to specify the frequency to be assigned to each rating term. The following scheme might be used:

5 = Almost always (86 to 100 percent of time)
4 = Generally (66 to 85 percent of time)
3 = Frequently (36 to 65 percent of time)
2 = Sometimes (16 to 35 percent of time)
1 = Rarely (0 to 15 percent of time)

Although this procedure allows for some latitude in interpretation, it provides raters with a common frame of reference.

Graphic Scales

Another popular rating format is the graphic scale, which is ordinarily a straight line—sometimes vertical but usually horizontal—adorned with various verbal cues to the rater. Guilford (1954) presents the following example of a graphic scale:

Is the student a slow or quick thinker?

Extremely Slow	Sluggish Plodding	Thinks with Ordinary Speed	Agile-Minded	Exceedingly Rapid

The rater is free to place a checkmark anywhere along the scale. In scoring, we might superimpose equal-interval categories (perhaps using a ruler) and assign numerical weights, for example, the midpoint between Agile-Minded and Exceedingly Rapid might be weighted 5, and so on. This procedure is similar to the scoring method suggested for the semantic differential technique described in Chapter 18. Another scoring approach involves the use of a ruler to measure the distance between one of the end categories and the checkmark. The suggestion of precision in such a procedure is probably not justified. One should avoid using extremely long lines, which tend to produce a clustering of ratings; the resulting increase in reliability is so slight that the extra work involved is unjustified. It is probably also a good idea to determine the location of the "high" or "good" end of the scale randomly, for example, it might be on the right for one characteristic and on the left for another.

Graphic rating scales are simple and easy to administer and can be intrinsically interesting, although scoring can be time consuming relative to other methods.

An illustration of some of the many forms that a graphic rating scale may take has been presented by Guion (1965), and reproduced in Figure 9-1. The form of such a scale may range from simple (A and B) to fairly structured (I). Increased structuring better defines the task for the rater. The optimal number of rating points is probably seven to nine. Generally, one should provide more rating categories than one intends to measure to help spread ratings out, get more discrimination, and avoid "clumping" around a particular value. It is not unusual to select an odd number of points (E) so that the "average" will have a central position on the scale, yielding maximum discrimination. An even number of points can sometimes be used profitably, particularly if they are collapsed for scoring, for example, using a four-point scale (Never, Sometimes, Usually, and Always) to gather data, but scoring dichotomously. Some raters find it easier to make judgments when numerical point scales (B) are converted to verbal scales (C). However, an additional interpretation problem is thus introduced: the possibility that raters will read different meanings into the verbal cues. In any event, rating scales used with care and intelligence can yield very meaningful data. They are particularly adaptable to assessing products and performances.

Checklists

Another popular method of recording the results of observations is the checklist. Even though the observer is checking categories, "checklists" are still considered ratings as we sum the number of or frequency with which behaviors occurred or characteristics were noted. Checklists can be used by relatively naive raters and tend to make complex judgments unnecessary. It is imperative, however, that the categories be as clear and precise as possible. The developer of a checklist would be well advised to use behavioral terms if at all possible. Checklists may be used to assess:

1. Which instructional objectives or skills have been met or mastered.
2. Student interests, hobbies, problems, preferred reading matter, radio or television programs, and the like.
3. Student behavior in a variety of settings, especially behavior problems in elementary school.
4. Conformity to prescribed sequences of steps in task performance.
5. Student products.

Bonney and Hampleman (1962) cite the following example of a checklist used by an industrial arts teacher to identify the unsatisfactory items in a woodwork product before it goes to the finishing room.

Unsatisfactory Items in Woodwork Product

_____ 1. Knots	_____ 4. Joint Shrinkage
_____ 2. Lack of Filling	_____ 5. Veneer Sand-through
_____ 3. Core or Glue	_____ 6. Glaze or Burnish

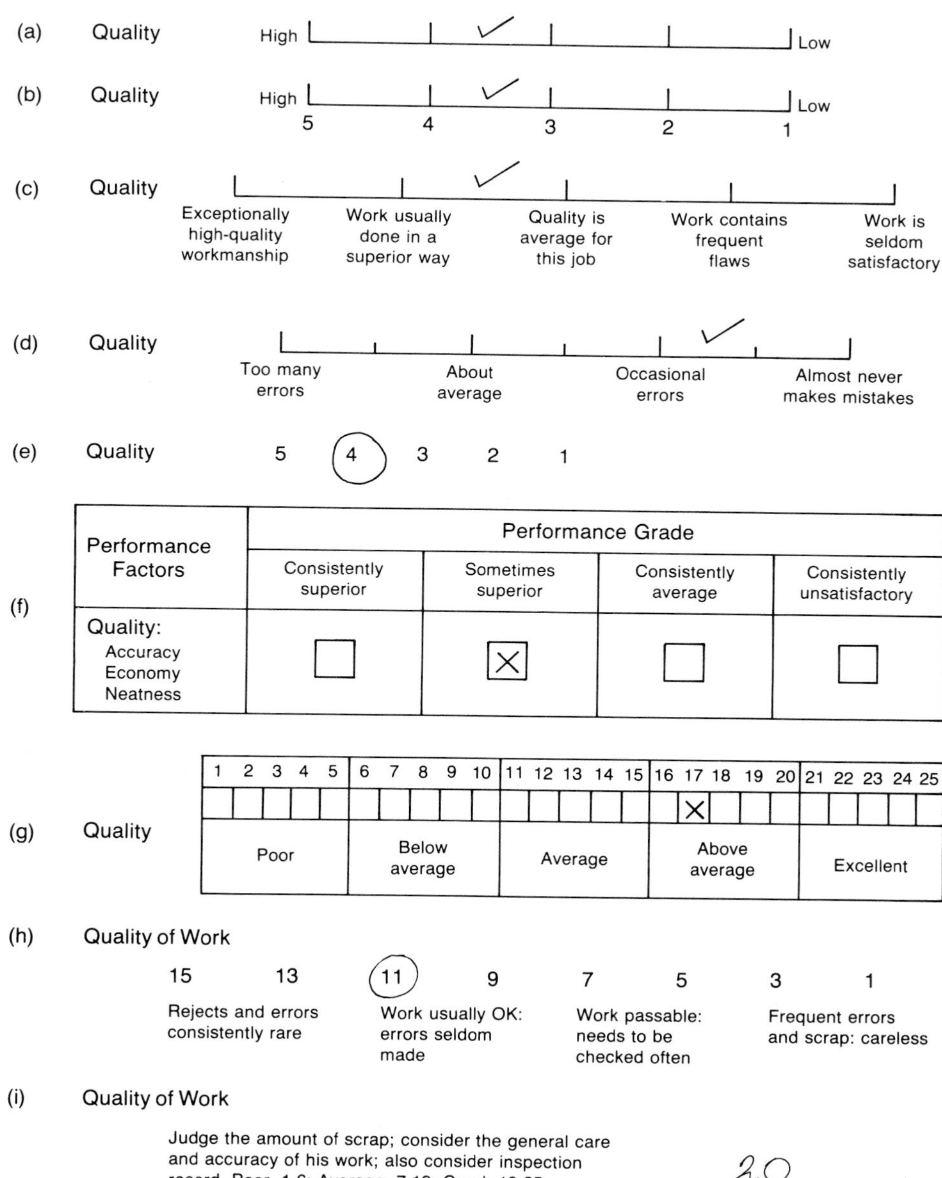

Figure 9-1

Variations of a graphic rating scale. *Source:* From *Personnel Testing* by R. M. Guion. Copyright © 1965 by McGraw-Hill. Used with permission of McGraw-Hill Book Company.

_____ 7. Loose Veneer
_____ 8. Tear-outs
_____ 9. Rough Machinery
_____ 10. Warpage
_____ 11. Dimensions
_____ 12. Operation Missing
_____ 13. Veneer Discolored
_____ 14. Veneer Split
_____ 15. Rounded Edges
_____ 16. Exposed Glue
_____ 17. Coarse Sanding
_____ 18. Grain and Color of Veneer
_____ 19. Damage
_____ 20. Open Joints

An individual's "score" on the checklist may simply be the number of items checked or not checked, or a standard for an acceptable product may be established. If some elements of the checklist are more important than others from an instructional standpoint, differential weights might be applied. A range of three possible values would probably suffice.

There is a tendency on the part of some raters to use too many or too few items in a checklist. This response set can be combatted by requiring a fixed number of checks by the rater. Whether or not to use this technique will, of course, depend upon the nature and intended use of the checklist.

Rating Errors

Despite the many advantages of using rating scales there are several kinds of errors associated with their application. Among these errors are:

Ambiguity—The tendency to have different raters interpret rating terms in different ways. This is well illustrated with the previously summarized data of Simpson (1944) in Table 9-1.

Leniency—The tendency to rate or evaluate favorably those whom they know well higher than they should. This kind of "generosity" can be offset somewhat by adjusting the scale to include a greater proportion of more positive points. For example:

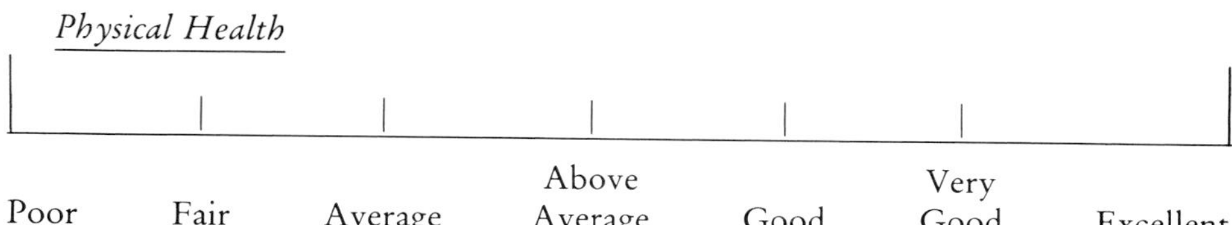

This kind of error is greatest, as one might expect when the rater must face the ratee with the results.

Central Tendency—The reluctance to give extreme ratings. Sometimes raters are reluctant to take extreme positions, either positive or negative. This tends to cause ratings to clump up in middle of scale. Sometimes can counteract by spacing descriptive phrases physically further apart on scale.

Halo—A gross undifferentiated rating on a specific trait or behavior which is biased because it is based on an overall or total general attitude. "Larry

Bird is a great basketball player, therefore everything he does on the court is excellent—pass, shoot, play defense, etc." Halo can be either positive or negative and can generalize across domains, for example, obnoxious personality = intellectual deficits.

Logical—The tendency to give similar ratings to traits that seem to be logically related in the mind of the rater. If one views "self-confidence" and "aggressiveness" to be part of the same personality dimension then they might rate an individual similarly just on that basis rather than the behavior being observed.

Contrast—Some raters will evaluate or describe ratees in a direction opposite of themselves. "I am an extremely well-organized person; therefore, no one can be as organized as I am."

Proximity—Nearness in time or location on a rating form. Traits to be rated on the same page tend to correlate higher than if they were rated on different pages.

Probably the best approach to reducing rating errors is through training and practice. Intelligence is only very modestly correlated with rating reliability. The dictum, "know thyself" is good preparation for an observer/rater.

The Development and Use of Anecdotal Records

An anecdotal record is a description of what an individual does or says. It describes in concrete detail the situation in which the action or comment occurs, and what others present do or say. Randall (1936), who is credited with the development of the anecdotal record concept, defines it as a

> . . . record of some significant item of conduct, a record of an episode in the life of the student, a word picture of the student in action; the teacher's best effort at taking a word snapshot at the moment of the incident; any narrative of events in which the student takes such part as to reveal something which may be significant about his personality.

The main thrust of the anecdotal record is to record social and emotional facets of a pupil's growth and adjustment. Records can also be made of other dimensions of relevant classroom or extra classroom standing of individual students. Collected over a period of time, anecdotal material can provide a longitudinal view of a student's growth and patterns of change.

A sample anecdotal record is presented in Table 9-2. The kinds of information summarized in the anecdotal record could probably not be gathered in any other way.

Possible Uses of Anecdotal Material

The rich behavioral information collected in anecdotal form can be used in many ways, some of which are listed below:

Table 9-2 Illustrative Anecdotal Record

Date: 9/17/92 **Student's Name:** Susan

Observer: Chelsea (Student Teacher)

Description of Incident:

The fifth grade class was working on a social studies display that involved the construction of models of many different kinds of homes common to different nationalities and countries. Susan was asked to work with Towana, a black girl, to build, study, and make a class report on a typical South American home. At first Susan refused the assignment and asked to be allowed to work with one of her friends, another white girl. When the teacher insisted that she carry out the first assignment she began her project quite reluctantly. As her work progressed, her interest in the country and in working with Towana became overtly enthusiastic.

Comment:

It appears that Susan has gained more than a knowledge of other lands and customs from this project. Susan has begun to work through some of her feelings regarding other races, and apparently may become more accepting and less fearful as a result of her experience.

1. Anecdotal records may supplement data gathered in other ways to assess progress toward a set of objectives.
2. Anecdotal records may suggest aspects of the curriculum that need to be reviewed or revised for particular students, or may suggest beneficial remedial activities.
3. Such data are useful in parent-teacher conferences to pinpoint specific areas of concern.
4. Anecdotal data can increase the teacher's insight into new students' strengths and weaknesses.
5. Many of the incidents reported in anecdotal form could be useful to school counselors, and teachers should make every effort to share them with counselors and other teachers to whom they are relevant.
6. Certain anecdotal records may have implications for vocational guidance and communication with educational and business personnel outside the school. Care should be taken to respect the security of such material and release it only in confidence.

Suggestions for Generating and Improving Anecdotal Records

1. Determining in advance what is to be observed and being alert to unusual behavior.
2. Reporting only the "what" and "how" of the subject's actions and interactions with others.
3. Describing in detail the scene at the beginning of each period of observation.
4. Reporting in sequence each step in the course of every action by the subject.

5. Allowing no overlap between factual description and interpretation of the incident(s).
6. Observing and recording sufficient material to make the report meaningful and reliable.
7. Recording the incident during or as soon after the observation as possible.
8. Restricting a given record to a single incident.
9. Recording both positive and negative incidents.
10. Collecting a number of anecdotes on a given student before attempting to make inferences.
11. Gaining practice in writing anecdotal records.
12. Establishing a plan for obtaining periodic systematic anecdotal samples.

Simulation: Observing and Recording Learning Performances, Procedures, Processes, and Skills

A great deal of instructional time, particularly in the early grades, is devoted to the development of specific performance skills. Examples are laboratory work, handwriting, physical skills, speaking, social skills, music, artistic and dramatic skills, essay writing, and a variety of vocational skills. We are, of course, interested in the products of learning, but are also concerned with *how* the student arrives at his or her product. Often the development of a technique or skill can be considered an end in itself or so intimately tied to the product as to be inseparable (Berk, 1986b; Priestly, 1982).

The key to performance measurement is simulation; most paper-and-pencil devices suffer from artificiality. Developmental situations in which an individual can exhibit real-life behaviors generally increase the relevance and accuracy of the assessment.

The advantage to simulation is that it can be both a teaching and testing method. When presented in a game-like form, particularly to young children, simulations also have the motivational value of being fun. Simulation allows for the collection of data for events or situations that only occur rarely. Think, for example, of flight simulation used to train jet pilots. The simulation of an emergency such as the loss of an engine can then be used to train the test pilot's skills. The dynamic functions of the human body and disease processes can be simulated to again train and test. Role playing is an effective and inexpensive method to examine interpersonal communication and counseling skills. The building of a "city" in an elementary classroom (with post office, supermarket, bank, etc.) is another practical kind of simulation.

In educational settings, one must consider practical limitations, and the development of a simulation test therefore involves compromises. Fitzpatrick and Morrison (1971) note that in making these compromises one must:

1. Determine through careful analysis the critical aspects of the criterion situation it is desired to simulate in view of the purpose of the simulation.

2. Determine the minimum fidelity needed for each aspect and estimate the worth of increasing fidelity beyond the minimum.
3. Develop a scheme for representing a reasonably comprehensive set of aspects, within the limits of available resources.
4. Adjust comprehensiveness and fidelity, compromising as necessary to achieve a balancing of considerations but with primary attention to the aspects shown by analysis to be most critical for the purpose at hand.

The most important step in developing a simulation exercise is identifying the criterion, which usually involves a task analysis. Some major aspects of a task analysis are:

1. Developing a simulation that represents the entire performance as accurately as possible.
2. Specifying those elements in the task that are of greatest relevance to the quality of performance. Some of these elements might be:
   a. Speed of performance.
   b. Accuracy of performance.
   c. Number and seriousness of procedural errors.
   d. Errors in following instructions.
   e. Discrimination in selecting appropriate tools or equipment.
   f. Economy of effort (amount of "lost motion").
   g. Timing (in the use of machinery or physical performances such as gymnastics).
   h. Intensity or force (in sports).
   i. Coherence and appropriateness of the sequence of steps followed.
3. Selecting elements for observation in proportion to their emphasis in instruction or training.
4. Evaluating these elements in light of the conditions necessary for accurate measurability.
5. Selecting those elements that require minimal time and expense.

The task analysis, then, basically involves identifying those elements that are to be measured and scored.

There are many types of simulation tests. Fitzpatrick and Morrison (1971) have identified four major types:

Type	*Characteristics*
Situation Tests	Examinee role-plays in lifelike setting, which may be social or involve apparatus.
In-Basket Tests	Examinee is presented data, for example, letters, records, or memoranda, and asked to simulate decision-making or administrative behavior. Simulates on-the-job performance.

Work-Sample Tests	A standardized job-relevant task is presented, and performance is observed. Task is usually a duplicate of actual criterion performance, for example, operating a key punch or typing.
Problem-Solving Games	Such games are frequently used in business, industry, and the military to assess problem-solving skills. Competition with a standard is usually involved.

In summary, the development of a performance simulation test is similar to that of any test, and includes the following steps:

1. Analysis of the desired performance.
2. Identification of crucial and representative elements for observation.
3. Selection of an appropriate simulation situation.
4. Specification of the sequence of tasks that incorporate these crucial elements.
5. Specification of the materials needed by the examinee to accomplish the tasks.
6. Preparation of directions for examinee.
7. Development of methods for recording results of simulation.

Following are examples of performance tests in a variety of subject areas.

Skill in Using a Microscope

In this classic performance test, developed many years ago by Ralph Tyler, the instructor uses a checklist (see Table 9-3) to observe the sequence of actions required for proper identification of a specimen. The teacher is able to note not only what the student does correctly, but also the kinds of errors he or she makes. Such data have diagnostic implications, and can be used to correct the student's actions.

Skill in Driving an Automobile

It is one thing to be able to answer a series of paper-and-pencil questions about the operation of an automobile, and quite another to accomplish the task. Many psychomotor behaviors and skills require actual demonstration. The checklist in Table 9-4 is one approach to the description of driving performance.

Skill in Softball Batting

Many skills developed in physical education classes lend themselves to direct observation. A method of evaluating one of these skills is presented in Table 9-5. The

Table 9-3 Checklist of Student Reactions to an Object Under the Microscope

Student's Actions	Sequence of Actions	Student's Actions	Sequence of Actions
a. Takes slide	1	w. Adjusts concave mirror	
b. Wipes slide with lens paper	2	x. Adjusts plane mirror	
c. Wipes slide with cloth		y. Adjusts diaphragm	
d. Wipes slide with finger		z. Does not touch diaphragm	10
e. Moves bottle of culture along the table		aa. With eye at eyepiece turns down coarse adjustment	11
f. Places drop or two of culture on slide	3	ab. Breaks cover glass	12
g. Adds more culture		ac. Breaks slide	
h. Adds few drops of water		ad. With eye away from eyepiece turns down coarse adjustment	
i. Hunts for cover glasses	4	ae. Turns up coarse adjustment a great distance	13, 22
j. Wipes cover glass with lens paper	5	af. With eye at eyepiece turns down fine adjustment a great distance	14, 23
k. Wipes cover with cloth		ag. With eye away from eyepiece turns down fine adjustment a great distance	15
l. Wipes cover with finger		ah. Turns up fine adjustment screw a great distance	
m. Adjusts cover with finger		ai. Turns fine adjustment screw a few turns	
n. Wipes off surplus fluid		aj. Removes slide from stage	16
o. Places slide on stage	6	ak. Wipes objective with lens paper	
p. Looks through eyepiece with right eye		al. Wipes objective with cloth	
q. Looks through eyepiece with left eye	7	am. Wipes objective with finger	17
r. Turns to objective of lowest power	9		
s. Turns to low-power objective	21		
t. Turns to high-power objective			
u. Holds one eye closed	8		
v. Looks for light			

Source: R. W. Tyler, A test of skill in using a microscope. *Educational Research Bulletin 9* (1930): 493–496. Reprinted by permission of the author.

Table 9-3. Checklist of Student Reactions to an Object Under the Microscope (*continued*)

Student's Actions	Sequence of Actions
an. Wipes eyepiece with lens paper	____
ao. Wipes eyepiece with cloth	____
ap. Wipes eyepiece with finger	18
aq. Makes another mount	____
ar. Takes another microscope	____
as. Finds object	____
at. Pauses for an interval	____
au. Asks, "What do you want me to do?"	____
av. Asks whether to use high power	____
aw. Says, "I'm satisfied"	____
ax. Says that the mount is all right for his eye	____
ay. Says he cannot do it	19, 24
az. Told to start new mount	____
aaa. Directed to find object under low power	20
aab. Directed to find object under high power	____

Noticeable Characteristics of Student's Behavior	Sequence of Actions
a. Awkward in movements	____
b. Obviously dexterous in movements	____
c. Slow and deliberate	X
d. Very rapid	____
e. Fingers tremble	____
f. Obviously perturbed	____
g. Obviously angry	____
h. Does not take work seriously	____
i. Unable to work without specific directions	X
j. Obviously satisfied with his unsuccessful efforts	X

Skills in Which Student Needs Further Training	Sequence of Actions
a. In cleaning objective	X
b. In cleaning eyepiece	X
c. In focusing low power	X
d. In focusing high power	X
e. In adjusting mirror	X
f. In using diaphragm	X
g. In keeping both eyes open	X
h. In protecting slide and objective from breaking by careless focusing	X

Characterization of the Student's Mount	Sequence of Actions
a. Poor light	X
b. Poor focus	____
c. Excellent mount	____
d. Good mount	____
e. Fair mount	____
f. Poor mount	____
g. Very poor mount	____
h. Nothing in view but a thread in his eyepiece	____
i. Something on objective	____
j. Smeared lens	X
k. Unable to find object	X

Table 9-4 Checklist for Driving Performance

Aspect Observed	Classifications of Effectiveness		
Student posture			
Seat adjustment made	Yes	Questionable	No
Mirror adjustment made	Yes	Questionable	No
Foot position (dimmer switch and accelerator)	Correct	Par. Correct	Incorrect
Hand position (10 and 12 o'clock)	Correct	Par. Correct	Incorrect
Posture (erect and behind wheel)	Correct	Par. Correct	Incorrect
Putting automobile in motion			
Releases handbrake	Yes	Questionable	No
Starts auto forward	Smoothly	Unevenly	Jerkily
Shifts gears (low to second)	Quietly	Some Noise	Grinding
Shifts gears (second to high)	Quietly	Some Noise	Grinding
Steering in road	Direct	Weaving	Assistance Required
Bringing automobile to a stop			
Puts hand out and down	Precise	Understandable	Unidenti-fiable
Slows car down	Smoothly	Unevenly	Jerkily
Brakes to a stop	Smoothly	Unevenly	Jerkily
Sets hand brake	Yes	Questionable	No
Parks car off pavement	Yes	Questionable	No
Showing consideration for others			
When pulling out from curb	Yes	Questionable	No
When stopping	Yes	Questionable	No
Shows respect for rights of others	Yes	Questionable	No
When in question as to others' rights, relinquishes his	Yes	Questionable	No
Response to other drivers' signals and tolerant of their errors	Yes	Questionable	No

Source: J. M. Bradfield and H. S. Moredock, *Measurement and evaluation in education* (New York: Macmillan, 1957), p. 346. Reprinted by permission of J. M. Bradfield.

use of such a checklist by an experienced observer can yield efficient and accurate results.

Assessing Products

Many of the difficulties encountered in assessing interpersonal relationships and performances are also met when we attempt to measure the quality of student products. Such factors as the physical effort required to construct measures, complexity,

Table 9-5 Sample Checklist for Softball Batting Form

Date **Rater's initials** **Player's name** __________

__________ **Captain's name** __________

Instructions: Rate the player each time he bats. Place a tally mark in the space which precedes the best description of player's form in each of six categories. Indicate your observation of errors in the right-hand half of the page, again with a tally mark. Write in any additional errors and add comments below.

	Errors
1. Grip	
___ good	___ Hands too far apart
___ fair	___ Wrong hand on top
___ poor	___ Hands too far from end of bat
2. Preliminary stance	
___ good	___ Stands too near plate
___ fair	___ Stands too far away
___ poor	___ Rear foot closer to plate than forward foot
	___ Stands too far forward
	___ Stands too far backward
	___ Bat not in readiness position
3. Stride or footwork	
___ good	___ Fails to step forward
___ fair	___ Fails to transfer weight
___ poor	___ Lifts back foot from ground
4. Pivot or body twist	
___ good	___ Fails to twist body
___ fair	___ Fails to wind up
___ poor	___ Has less than 90° of pivot
5. Arm movement or swing	
___ good	___ Arms held too close to body
___ fair	___ Rear elbow held too far up
___ poor	___ Bat not held parallel to ground
6. General (Eyes on ball, judgment of pitcher, etc.)	
___ good	___ Jerky action
___ fair	___ Tries too hard
___ poor	___ Poor selection of bat
	___ Lacks confidence

Source: M. G. Scott and E. French, *Better teaching through testing* (New York: A. S. Barnes, 1945). Reprinted by permission of the publisher.

administrative difficulties, and questions of validity and scoring are among the more prominent considerations. Although many products have physical dimensions that may be measured (e.g., size, weight, number of errors, color), a number of more qualitative dimensions also need to be assessed. Such dimensions might be the flavor of a cake, the composition of a painting, or the neatness of handwriting. There is no doubt that aesthetic properties are more difficult to assess than physical attributes.

Process and product are intimately related, as was noted previously. The decision to focus on product or process, or a combination of both, rests on the answers to the following questions:

1. Are the steps involved in arriving at the product either indeterminate or covert?
2. Are the important characteristics of the product apparent, and can they be measured objectively and accurately?
3. Is the effectiveness of the performance to be discerned in the product itself?
4. Is there a sample product available to use as a scale?
5. Is evaluation of the procedures leading to the product impractical?

If the answer to each of these five questions is "yes," the teacher may wish to focus his or her assessment efforts on product evaluation.

Products can be readily assessed by the careful application of rating scales and checklists. (The reader is urged to review pages on the development of these recording methods.) The usefulness of any product assessment will depend on the accuracy with which its distinctive features have been delineated and defined. Assuming that the critical elements have been identified and appropriately weighted, observational scales like the ones in Tables 9-6, 9-7, and 9-8 may be used to collect data.

Assessing the Quality of an Artistic Product

Assessment in the artistic and aesthetic areas of human activity is difficult at best and nonexistent at worst. The problem posed by the wide variety of relevant variables is compounded by the basically subjective nature of aesthetic standards. The assessment task can, however, be approached systematically and directly. One direct approach is illustrated by the rating chart in Table 9-6.

This chart might be used to assess a high-school freehand drawing using pencil and charcoal. The number of elements and the number and specificity of the quality categories might be expanded, but an excellent start has been made.

Assessing Woodshop Products

A variety of mechanical devices is available for measuring the quality of shop products, including gauges, rulers, T-squares, and calipers. However, mechanical devices alone cannot measure all significant product characteristics. Almost any metal, plastic, or wood product has many qualitative dimensions. A rating scale useful in assessing the adequacy of nail fastenings has been developed by Dorothy C. Adkins and is presented in Table 9-7. The use of 10 categories may require overly fine

Table 9-6 Rating Scale for Evaluating Freehand Art Drawing

	D	C	B	A
1. Drawing				
a. Accuracy of proportion *or* Suitability of distortion				
b. Relationship of proportions				
c. Stability of subjects				
d. Ease of interpretation				
2. Composition				
a. Balance				
b. Rhythm				
c. Spatial relations				
d. Textural interest				
3. Feel for Medium				
a. Line quality				
b. Tone quality				
4. Subject Matter				
a. Interest				
b. Arrangement				

Key to Variations

D—Drawing shows no regard for aspect being judged.
C—Aspect not well utilized.
B—Aspect noteworthy, but room for improvement at this grade level.
A—Aspects adds materially to the excellence of the picture.

Source: J. M. Bradfield and H. S. Moredock, *Measurement and evaluation in education* (New York: Macmillan, 1957), p. 345. Reprinted by permission of J. M. Bradfield.

discriminations, but the general analytic approach to rating this fairly simple skill has much to recommend it.

Assessing Food Products

An efficient scale for evaluating a specific food product, namely waffles, is presented in Table 9-8. Note that both physical and aesthetic qualities are rated. The systematic summary of such data should be useful both for assessment and for teaching purposes.

One of the trends in educational measurement is to use more observational or qualitative information. Such data can be used to confirm more traditional kinds of information such as that derived from test scores. Looking at the same student or

Table 9-7 Sample Rating Scales for Nail-Fastening

1. Straightness	1 2 3 4 5 6 7 8 9 10
	Are nails driven straight, heads square with wood, no evidence of bending?
2. Hammer marks	1 2 3 4 5 6 7 8 9 10
	Is wood free of hammer marks around nails?
3. Splitting	1 2 3 4 5 6 7 8 9 10
	Is wood free of splits radiating from nail holes?
4. Depth	1 2 3 4 5 6 7 8 9 10
	Are depths of nails uniform and of pleasing appearance?
5. Spacing	1 2 3 4 5 6 7 8 9 10
	Are nails spaced too close or too far apart?
6. Utility	1 2 3 4 5 6 7 8 9 10
	Will the nails hold?

Source: Dorothy C. Adkins, *Construction and analysis of achievement tests* (Washington: Government Printing Office, 1947), p. 231. Reprinted by permission of the author.

Table 9-8 Food Score Card for Waffles*

			Score
1. Appearance	Irregular shape	Regular shape	1. ____
2. Color	Dark brown or pale	Uniform, golden brown	2. ____
3. Moisture Content	Soggy interior or too dry	Slightly moist interior	3. ____
4. Lightness	Heavy	Light	4. ____
5. Tenderness	Tough or hard	Tender; crisp crust	5. ____
6. Taste and Flavor	Too sweet or flat or taste of leavening agent or fat	Pleasing flavor	6. ____
		Total Score	____

*Rate on a scale from 1 to 3.

Source: Clara M. Brown, *Food score cards: Waffles,* no. 53 (Minneapolis: University of Minnesota Press, 1940).

performance from different perspectives can be most revealing and hopefully confirm our evaluations. Confirmation should lead to greater confidence in the validity of our information, and better data should result in better educational decisions. Rating scales help us summarize these observations and are particularly valuable if the "points" are described or illustrated.

Oral Exams

Oral exams are kind of like oral supply or completion items where the examinee completes or supplies an answer for a question or series of questions posed by an examiner. The oral exam is commonly used with (a) elementary-school children, (b) graduate students, and (c) students physically unable to take written tests. Although not used systematically in American education, the oral exam is a potentially useful technique. Certain measurement purposes can be better achieved with this technique than any other.

The value of oral exams is readily apparent. While written exams assume that the examinee understands the questions, the oral examiner can see if his question is understood. Further, the examiner can probe the depth of a student's understanding of a topic. Such probing also gives some indication of the thought processes used by the student. Not to be overlooked is the advantage of flexibility, that is, the variety of behaviors that can be sampled. The technique of oral examination allows for the testing of both generalization and specific fact. In addition, the examiner(s) can observe a wide range of reactions to different stimulus questions. If a student hesitates in responding, fumbles for appropriate words, and manifests signs of stress, these reactions may be taken into account in appraising his degree of competence. It is with these types of behavior that examiners of doctoral candidates are frequently concerned. They are interested not only in how much the candidate knows, but also in how he expresses and handles himself in front of a group. In this respect the oral examination is realistically related to contemporary life. Prospective teachers, for example, must be able to use their knowledge in speaking. In many other vocational activities the spoken use of knowledge far exceeds its application in other ways.

Despite their potential advantages, several serious weaknesses of oral exams inhibit their use. Probably the most thoroughly documented weakness of the oral examination is its unreliability. The difficulty of maintaining comparable standards of judgment, selective perceptions, and interpretation on the part of different examiners, and the limited sampling of the breadth of the student's knowledge, potentially contribute to both unreliability and invalidity. Such factors as (a) lack of precision in the conduct of an oral exam, (b) failure to preplan the questions, and (c) the relative inefficiency of the oral exam in terms of faculty time serve to detract from its usefulness. The oral exam, nevertheless, has a great deal to offer as an assessment procedure. The use of the technique requires careful planning. Another important disadvantage is the amount of time necessary to conduct a thorough oral exam. It is difficult, also, to know how to prepare for an oral exam. It is good to know that you will have an opportunity to exhibit your knowledge and reasoning ability. But how do you prepare for that? Probing questions can reveal a great deal, but there is always the danger that they may also sidetrack or confuse the central issue(s). It is both an advantage and a disadvantage for this method that the response to questions will be spontaneous. The examiner likes this, but it may threaten the examinee. Extraneous factors such as the physical appearance and attractiveness of both parties can unfortunately influence the effectiveness of the oral exam. An overview of some of the factors that should be considered in the planning and use of oral exams is summarized in Table 9-9. The following exhibit contains a bit of humor related to

Table 9-9 Principles of Oral Examinations

1. Use oral examinations only for the purposes for which they are best suited, i.e., to obtain information as to the depth of student's knowledge, where oral presentation is clearly a purpose of the course or program, or where other means are simply inappropriate.
2. Prepare in advance a detailed outline of materials to be sampled in the examination even to the extent of writing questions which will be asked.
3. Determine in advance how records of student performance will be kept and what weights will be assigned various factors.
4. Keep the questioning relevant to the purposes of the course or program.
5. Word questions in such a way that the students can see the point of the question with minimum difficulty.
6. Where several examiners are involved, make each one responsible for questions on a specified part of the full examination.
7. Judge students on the basis of their performance precisely defined—not in terms of a generalized impression of their total appearance.
8. Pose questions which students with the training which has preceded a particular examination can reasonably be expected to know. An examination is not the place for an instructor to demonstrate his own erudition.
9. Use both general and specific questions but do so in some logical order.
10. Do not spend a disproportionate time probing for the answer to one question. If the first several questions do not elicit the desired response, move on to some other matter.
11. Develop some facility with several basic techniques for successful oral examining, such as (a) creating a friendly atmosphere, (b) asking questions, and (c) recording responses.
12. Make a written record of the student's performance at the time it is given. However, do so without disturbing the student or disrupting the flow of the examination.
13. In most situations allow students ample time to think through and make responses to questions.
14. Avoid arguing with the student. It is his show—let him make the most of it.

Source: Reprinted and abridged with permission from *Testing bulletin no. 7*, published by the Office of Evaluation Services, Michigan State University, 1967.

how *not* to use oral exams. The piece, of unknown origin, implies many things to be avoided when oral questioning procedures are used. Graduate students in particular will appreciate the satirized guidelines.

In summary there are two requisites if an examiner is interested in measuring and evaluating products or performances (behaviors). There are (a) a sample of the product or performance and (b) a systematic guide for evaluating and recording the

WHAT NOT TO DO IN AN ORAL EXAM UNLESS YOU WANT TO SCARE THE EXAMINEE TO DEATH

1. Before beginning the examination, make it clear to the examinee that his whole professional career may turn on his performance. Stress the importance and formality of the occasion. Put him in his proper place at the outset.
2. Throw out your hardest question first. (This is very important. If your first question is sufficiently difficult or involved, he will be too rattled to answer subsequent questions, no matter how simple they may be.)
3. Be reserved and stern in addressing the examinee. For contrast, be very jolly with the other examiners. A very effective device is to make humorous comments to the other examiners about the examinee's performance, comments which tend to exclude him and set him apart, as though he were not present in the room.
4. Make him answer each problem your way, especially if your way is esoteric. Constrain him. Impose many limitations and qualifications in each question. The idea is to complicate an otherwise simple problem.
5. Force him into a trivial error and then let him puzzle over it for as long as possible. Just after he sees his mistake but just before he has a chance to explain it, correct him yourself, disdainfully. This takes real perception and timing, which can only be acquired with some practice.
6. When he finds himself deep in a hole, never lead him out. Instead, sigh and shift to a new subject.
7. Ask him snide questions, such as "Didn't you learn that in Freshman Calculus?"
8. Do not permit him to ask you clarifying questions. Never repeat or clarify your own statement of the problem. Tell him not to think out loud, that what you want is the answer.
9. Every few miniutes, ask him if he is nervous.
10. Station yourself and the other examiners so that the examinee can not really face all of you at once. This enables you to bracket him with a sort of binaural crossfire. Wait until he turns away from you toward someone else, and then ask him a short direct question. With proper coordination among the examiners it is possible under favorable conditions to spin the examinee through several complete revolutions. This has the same general effect as item 2.
11. Wear dark glasses. Inscrutability is unnerving.
12. Terminate the examination by telling the examinee, "Don't call us; we will call you."

evaluation of that product or performance. The combination of observational data collection methods and rating scales can provide a useful approach to gathering data that cannot be gathered practically any other way.

Case Study Application

It is a rewarding and exciting experience to teach a skill or concept and then evaluate the hoped-for instructional effectiveness in a classroom setting. To assess whether or not that skill or concept transfers to an external performance situation can frequently be stressful for both student and instructor. Knowing what is expected and how it will be evaluated helps reduce the inherent ambiguity in the situation, which in turn hopefully reduces anxiety.

The present chapter has dealt with approaches to measuring academic skill and knowledge applications and performances in the sense that many kinds of educational outcomes need to be observed, reviewed, and/or rated. You now will have an opportunity to demonstrate your grasp of these methods by creating two measurement tools: (a) an evaluation form for a sample Reading Education Lesson Plan, and (b) a brief observational schedule to be used during prepractice teaching. First, evaluating a lesson plan.

Following is a description of the requirements for a teaching lesson plan. Use it as a basis for developing some systematic procedure that could be applied in evaluating a set of such plans. The form should be as clear and precise as possible as it will be shared with the students as they prepare their plans. The procedure could take many forms. It might be a simple checklist with an indication of satisfactory or unsatisfactory. That's probably not very discriminating. Perhaps a rating scale would be better. In any event let your imagination run wild.

Another interesting experience would be to try your hand at an observational tool for describing and evaluating teaching performance (not effectiveness). Again perhaps a checklist might be appropriate, or maybe a rating scale could be used to specify behaviors to be observed. Common sense and experience can suggest many more.

Reading Education Lesson Plan Format

Topic: Brief description of topic.

Grade: The level for which you think the lesson is appropriate.

Instructional Goal: General statement concerning what you expect your students to gain from participating in lesson.

Purpose (Rationale): Purpose includes general statement of *why* you are teaching this topic. This statement should be written and orally communicated to the students.

Introduction (Focusing Event): The introduction describes the way you will start the lesson. You should plan a stimulating, motivating introduction to help insure students' attention to the lesson.

Content (Curriculum): List the specific facts and concepts you expect children to grasp after this lesson. Use this section to clarify your thinking about what is appropriate for the students to study. Think about whether you are planning to teach material that is too easy or too hard.

Objectives: Be sure they are stated in behavioral terms. When possible include a description of the conditions under which the behavior is to be observed and the criteria for evaluating performance. Objectives should reflect depth of content and both higher and lower level thinking skills.

Activities (Procedures): Activities must match objectives. Include at least one teacher-centered activity and one learner-centered activity. Label both activities. Be sure to include enough activities per objective to improve likelihood of mastery of objective. In addition give consideration to the scheduling of activities/events.

Materials: List materials you will need for each activity. Be sure to plan interesting materials and media to illustrate concepts you are teaching. Materials must be referenced to each corresponding activity.

Closure: How will you summarize the lesson? Write this important step down and remember to *do* it. The teacher and/or the students can summarize the day's lesson. Sometimes closure can be done at the end of group work before the children go to work on individual projects.

Enrichment/Remedial: Plan as you would regular objectives. Specify who you are planning to use activities with.

Evaluation: Match evaluation procedures to the objectives they check. How will you know if your students have mastered the objectives? Evaluation is written in terms of what the teacher will do, while objectives are written about what the students will do. If your evaluation is teacher observation you need to explain what you will be looking for.

Content Review Statements

1. Observational and simulation techniques may be used to assess a variety of learning outcomes expressed as feelings, performances, or products.
2. The potential advantages of observational methods over paper-and-pencil measures are that they:
   a. Are uniquely adaptable to certain learning outcomes.
   b. Are useful in assessing applications in real-life activities.
   c. Supplement other data sources.
   d. Can provide both quantitative and qualitative information.
3. The difficulties of making valid and reliable observations derive from:
   a. Preobservation knowledge and psychological set on the part of the instructor.
   b. Failure to see isolated bits of behavior in the total context of the setting.
   c. Confusion of description and interpretation.
4. Observational methods may be used to study:
   a. Individual and/or group behavior.
   b. Instructional procedures and their influences.

   c. Student products and procedures.
   d. A variety of psychomotor and interpersonal behaviors.
5. Considerable care must be exercised in developing the wide variety of instruments, such as numerical and graphic rating scales and checklists, used to record the results of observations.
6. Rating scales should probably be limited to 10 points or less of gradation for each characteristic.
7. Rating errors include:
   a. ambiguity
   b. leniency
   c. central tendency
   d. halo
   e. logical
   f. contrast
   g. proximity
8. Anecdotal records of significant behavioral incidents can greatly enhance teacher understanding of student behavior and achievement, and thus increase the relevance of parent conferences and instructional planning.
9. Anecdotal records should:
   a. Be brief but complete.
   b. Be limited to single behavioral incidents.
   c. Describe "what happened."
10. The key to the assessment of student performances and skills is the simulation of the criterion behavior.
11. The four major types of simulation tasks are situation tests, in-basket tests, work-sample tests, and problem-solving games.
12. The development of simulation performance tasks involves:
    a. Analysis of the desired or criterion behavior.
    b. Identifying and selecting for study the most crucial elements to be observed.
    c. Providing directions and materials for the student.
    d. Recording the results of the simulation.
13. Performance, process, and procedure objectives may be considered ends in themselves.
14. The performances of students in such subject fields as music, vocational education, physical education, art, drama, public speaking, and science can be effectively studied through the use of rating scales and checklists.
15. Student products may also be validly assessed through the use of rating scales and checklists.
16. The key to the valid and reliable assessment of both performances and products is the specification of the expected criterion behavior.
17. Oral exams have the advantages of:
    a. allowing for the determination of examinee comprehension of the task.
    b. exploring examinee strengths and weaknesses.
    c. being used with examinees who cannot respond in writing.
    d. providing an opportunity to observe examinees to "think on their feet."
    e. testing for both generalization and fact.

18. Oral exams have the potential disadvantages of:
    a. unreliability of evaluation.
    b. susceptibility to anxiety and stress.
    c. lack of guidelines for examinee preparations.

Speculations

1. What dimensions do observational methods contribute to educational measurement and evaluation?
2. What are the difficulties and problems in using observational methods?
3. Is it acceptable to observe a student without his or her knowledge?
4. What kinds of errors are there in using rating scales and what can be done to control them?
5. Is the use of anecdotal material really worth the effort?
6. What are some ways that *simulations* can better be utilized as approaches in measurement and evaluation?

Suggested Readings

Amidon, E. J., & Hough, J. B. (1967). *Interaction analysis: Theory, research and application.* Reading, MA: Addison-Wesley. This collection of 30 articles deals with one of the most significant methodological breakthroughs to occur in educational research and evaluation.

Evertson, C. M., & Green, J. L. (1986). Observations as inquiry and method. In M. C. Wittrock (Ed.), *Handbook of research on teaching* (3rd ed., pp. 162–213). New York: Macmillan.

Fitzpatrick, R., & Morrison, E. J. (1971). Performance and product evaluation. In R. L. Thorndike (Ed.), *Educational measurement* (2nd ed., pp. 237–270). Washington, DC: American Council on Education. Chapter 9 presents illustrations of methods that can be employed in measuring achievement performance tests. Suggestions for the development and scoring of such tests are also summarized.

Gronlund, N. E. (1959). *Sociometry in the classroom.* New York: Harper and Row. This book, a comprehensive integration and interpretation of the sociometric literature and its meaning for education, has a definite how-to-do-it flavor. Some things, like some people, just get better with age.

Gronlund, N. E., & Linn, R. L. (1990). *Measurement and evaluation in teaching* (5th ed.). New York: Macmillan. Chapters 15 and 16, "Evaluating Learning and Development: Observational Techniques," and "Evaluating Learning and Development Peer Appraisal and Self-Report," of this excellent text contain some very useful suggestions and summaries of guidelines and principles. The section of Chapter 15 on anecdotal records is particularly informative.

Guilford, J. P. (1954). *Psychometric methods* (2nd ed.). New York: McGraw-Hill. Chapter 11 is one of the most comprehensive descriptions of rating methods available. In addition, the chapter surveys the relevant research findings.

Hoge, R. D. (1985). The validity of direct observations measures of pupil classroom behavior. *Review of Educational Research, 55*(4), 469–483. Data supported the validity of broad measures of classroom behavior (e.g., on-task vs. off-task).

Moos, R. H. (1979). *Evaluating educational environments: Procedures, measures, findings, and policy implications.* San Francisco: Jossey-Bass. The climate is a very important moderator of the teaching-learning-testing process.

Stiggins, R. J. (1987). Design and development of performance assessments. *Educational Measurement: Issues and Practice,* 6(3), 33–42. An instructional module demonstrating how planned systematic observations can be used to measure communication skills. Generalized step-by-step guidelines are presented. (*See also* Stiggins, R. J. *Evaluating students by classroom observation: Watching student effort.* Washington, DC: NEA, 1986.)

Webb, E. J. *et al.* (1981). *Unobtrusive measures: Nonreactive research in the social sciences* (2nd ed.). Chicago: Rand McNally. This fascinating collection of methods is presented in a most appealing and understandable form.

Wortham, S. C. (1990). *Tests and measurement in early childhood education.* Columbus, OH: Merrill. Chapter 5, "Informal Evaluation Measures: Observations" and Chapter 6, "Informal Measures: Checklists and Rating Scales" are particularly useful for the primary and elementary school teacher.

Bev's Diary

After our last two weeks of tests and measurements class, I'm tempted to copyright all of my test items. A good well-written functional test item is a very valuable commodity. And wow! Was I naive about essay items. I thought you could walk up to the board and create a winner—no way! I'm getting nosy about what my fellow teachers are doing about their in-class testing, how they use the results, and what the kids think about it. I really must be more systematic about the way in which I gather data. Since I'm an English teacher, that business about the importance of language comes through loud and clear. Words are fun to play with but in constructing exams remember to "KISS" them: Keep it Simple and Straighforward. I shudder when I think back to some of the tests I have given (and taken, for that matter). Another eye-opener was all the possible things that can and will go wrong with rating scales. Like essay items, you can't simply sit down and construct one. Why is it that everything worthwhile takes effort?

Next up is a unit on quantitative methods; therefore in honor of the occasion a poem is offered on the facing page.

Part Four

Summarizing Data and Instrument Refinement

When faced with an equation to solve
I think my mind will dissolve
For I just get the shakes
When I recall what it takes
To make a mathematical resolve

An aspiring young scholar named Clarence
Pursued his research with endurance
But while running his analyses
Developed some paralyses
In places not covered by insurance

There once was a man from Lavidity
Who was forever in search of validity
But when gathering his stats
He confused his this with his thats
So all he could get was reliability

Chapter 10

Describing Measurement Data

It is not the author's intent, nor is it possible to develop the reader's statistical competencies to a high degree in this brief chapter. An effort is made, however, to provide sufficient knowledge of and skill in elementary statistical procedures to facilitate the development, refinement, and interpretation of a variety of measuring devices. The statistical procedures to be described are applicable to such questions as "What is the typical score on this test?" "What is the average score?" "How variable or 'spread out' are the scores on this test?" "What are some methods useful in summarizing individual student scores?" and "How can I describe the relationship of scores on my test to scores on a criterion measure that purports to measure the same variable?" In most instances, such topics as central tendency, variability, and correlation are presented by describing and illustrating the commonly used indices. Short-cut procedures, subject to some error but useful in analyzing classroom tests, are described.

The techniques and methods described in this chapter probably have greatest application to norm-referenced measures but they can also be used profitably with criterion-referenced measures. The material on "relative position" relates directly to test interpretation as it is described in Chapter 15.

Why Study Statistics?

Five of the many reasons the study of statistical methods is important to the student of measurement are briefly discussed.

First, and probably most important, the use of statistics greatly facilitates summarizing and describing large amounts of data about an individual student or group of students. Questions relating to average class performance and the spread of scores can be answered by application of appropriate statistical techniques.

Second, intelligent use of certain statistical procedures can be very helpful in interpreting test scores. Raw scores, for example, scores indicating the number of correct responses on a test, are relatively meaningless in and of themselves. Raw scores need to be summarized and related to some meaningful reference point, for example, the average score on a particular test for a local or nationally representative group, to have meaning for student, school administrator, or parent. Certain kinds of "derived scores," some of which are described in this chapter, can profitably be used to communicate information about educational achievement.

Third, knowledge and comprehension of, and skill in using, certain statistical techniques are necessary for adequate analysis and evaluation of measuring instruments. Such test characteristics as reliability and validity can only be precisely assessed through the use of statistical methods.

Fourth, certain numerical facts, summarized in the form of statistical indices, aid in making decisions about, and evaluating, student achievement. The assignment, of course, marks an example of an area in which knowledge of typical or average performance and the variability of scores can significantly influence judgments about, and the system used to report, individual student performances.

Last, as a kind of "extra added attraction," the study of statistics allows really serious students to read with greater understanding research in their discipline, research on testing and measurement, and test manuals.

Tabulating Data and Frequency Distributions

The first step a test user ordinarily takes in analyzing the results of a test that has been administered is to create a *frequency distribution* of the scores. Such a distribution is obtained by relating each test score to a number that indicates the frequency with which it occurs. In an ordinary classroom situation this can probably best be accomplished by listing the scores from high to low and tallying the number of times each occurs. It is sometimes desirable, when the class is very large and the range of scores great, to group the scores into intervals of predetermined and uniform size. To determine the size interval to be used, it is suggested that the range of scores be determined (range = highest score minus lowest score plus one) and divided by some number between 10 and 20. This procedure is recommended because most experts feel that 10 to 20 class intervals are sufficient to summarize the data efficiently and yet neither grossly misrepresents the actual nature of the underlying distribution nor introduces excessive grouping errors in the statistics to be computed. For most applications, particularly with classroom-size data sets, it is not necessary to group scores. Simply set the interval size equal to one. A set of 30 hypothetical scores on a seventh-grade American History test with a maximum of 50 points has been summarized in Table 10-1. The interval size used was one. This distribution of scores would be described as slightly *negatively skewed,* that is, there is a relatively high frequency of high scores, and the scores decrease in frequency toward the low or negative end of the score scale. Conversely, if one found a relatively high frequency of low scores, with the frequencies trailing off at the high or positive end of the score scale, the frequency distribution would be described as *positively skewed.* See Figure 10-1—(a) and (b)—for examples of both negatively and positively skewed distributions. Skewness, at a general level, is described in terms of the "tail" of the distribution.

The frequency distribution provides a teacher with a graphic picture of the performance of the group as a whole on a given test. The degree of skewness, in turn, *may* indicate something about the general difficulty level of the test for a particular group of students. If the test is very easy scores might clump up at the high (or right) end of the scale and fall off to the left (negative skewness), or bunch up at the low (left) end of the scale and trail off to the high score side if the test were very difficult (positive skewness).

It should be noted that for most classroom tests and small data sets ($N < 100$) it is usually *not* necessary to group the scores, that is, use an internal size greater than one.

Data Display

Data come to us in all shapes and sizes. They come in batches, bunches, clumps, groups, collections, and piles. We need some methods to help us sort out the data and begin to make some sense of them. One useful method is that of using a *stem and leaf plot.* It's easy and quick, and helps us "see" the picture the data presented to our statistical eye. A stem and leaf plot is formed by creating a stem and putting leaves on it. We will use the 25 hypothetical Verbal scores from the *Dean Aptitude Test* in Table 10-2 to illustrate. The numbers have no more or less than two digits. The first digits will be the stem and the second digits are the leaves. A vertical line is drawn with the stem on the left side (by row) and the leaves on the right side. Figure 10-2 contains the completed display in three steps. Note how the entire original set of scores is captured in plot (c). Basically a picture of a slightly negatively skewed distribution is seen.

If one were to rotate our data tree 90° counterclockwise we would have the beginnings of a *histogram.* A histogram is a graphic display of data with observations located on the horizontal axis (sometimes grouped intervals) and the frequency of

Table 10-1 Illustration of Determination of Frequency Distribution and Calculation of Percentile Ranks for 30 Hypothetical Scores on American History Test

Raw Scores on American History Test

49	33	25	37	41	39	44	21	37	35
35	42	33	38	36	36	36	28	34	31
38	29	24	37	40	31	38	38	27	38

(1) Scores (X)	**(2) Tally**	**(3) Frequency (f)**	**(4) Frequency X Score (f X)**	**(5) Cummulative Frequency (Cf)**	**(6) Percentile Rank (PR_x)**	**(7) Score Squared (X^2)**	**(8) Frequency X Score Squared (f X^2)**
49	1	1	49	30	100	2401	2401
.	.	.	.	.	.	.	.
44	1	1	44	29	97	1936	1936
43							
42	1	1	42	28	93	1764	1764
41	1	1	41	27	90	1681	1681
40	1	1	40	26	87	1600	1600
39	1	1	39	25	83	1521	1521
38	~~1111~~	5	190	24	80	1444	7220
37	111	3	111	19	63	1369	4107
36	111	3	108	16	53	1296	3888
35	11	2	70	13	43	1225	2450
34	1	1	34	11	37	1156	1156
33	11	2	66	10	33	1089	2178
32							
31	11	2	62	8	27	961	1922
30							
29	1	1	29	6	20	841	841
28	1	1	28	5	17	784	784
27	1	1	27	4	13	729	729
26							
25	1	1	25	3	10	625	625
24	1	1	24	2	7	576	576
23							
22							
21	1	1	21	1	3	441	441
SUM		30	1050				37820

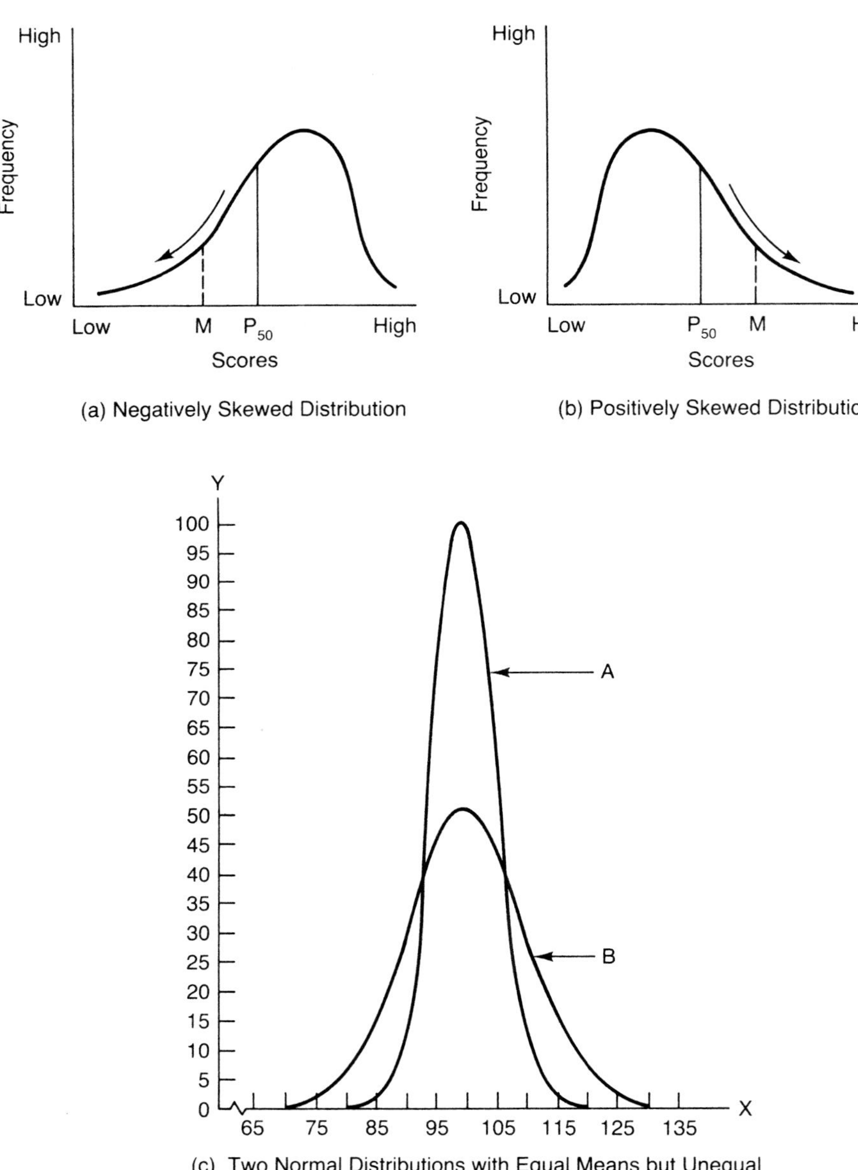

Figure 10-1

Illustrative frequency distributions

Table 10-2 Twenty-five Hypothetical Verbal Scores from the *Dean Aptitude Test*

23	42	53	60	70
87	61	65	43	81
74	74	59	62	56
54	63	67	68	62
69	83	71	85	72

those observations represented along the vertical axis. See Figure 10-3 for a kind of building block histogram. Again we can "see" the slight negative skew in the display. We're not done yet. One more to go. If we join the midpoints of the boxes at the top of each column we will have an unsmoothed *polygon* (or *frequency polygon*). See Figure 10-4 for just such a polygon.

A stem-and-leaf display is useful in examining smaller data sets, say of 100 observations or less (some say 50 or less), whereas the histogram is well adapted to large data sets. The data sets from most classroom tests would be found to be the "small" side.

Relative Position—Percentile Ranks

Raw test scores, as has been said, have relatively little meaning in and of themselves. It is not generally recommended that an instructor interpret an individual student's

Stems (a) TENS		Stems with Unordered Leaves (b) TENS		Stems with Ordered Leaves (c) TENS	
2		2	3	2	3
3		3			
4		4	32	4	23
5		5	6943	5	3469
6		6	128720395	6	012235789
7		7	42014	7	01244
8		8	7135	8	1357

Figure 10-2

Stem and leaf plot of raw data from Table 10-1

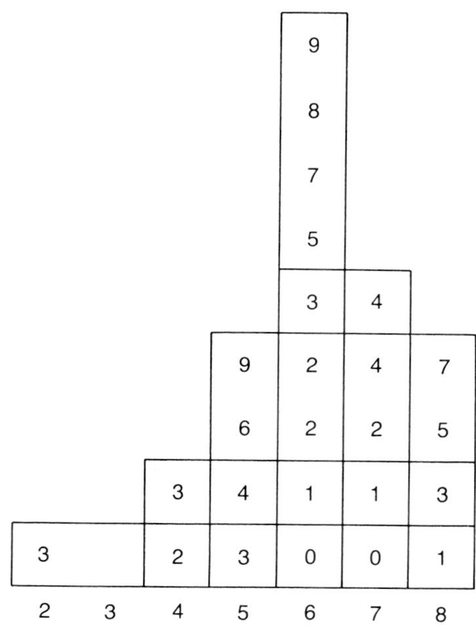

Figure 10-3

Histogram from stem and leaf plot of Figure 10-2

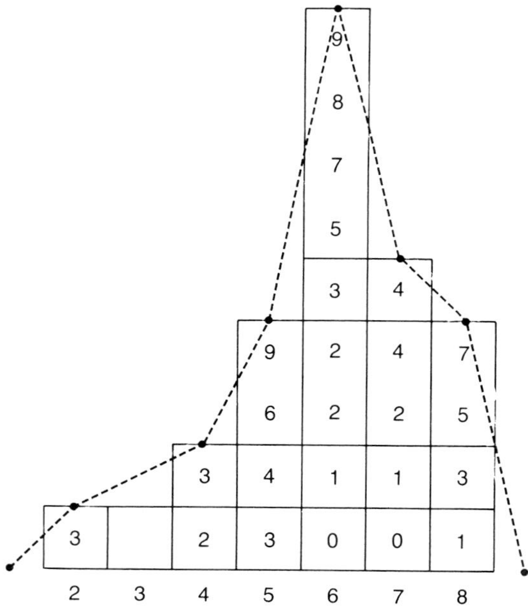

Figure 10-4

Polygon (dotted lines) from histogram of Figure 10-3

performance in terms of the proportion of the total number of test questions (items, points) answered correctly unless one is using criterion-referenced measures. The primary difficulty here is that a test, being only a sample of behavior, could yield misleading interpretations if the "percent correct of total possible points" procedure was employed, because other test samples might result in markedly different results and interpretations. Knowledge about the universe of behavior being sampled, the reliability of the test, and the difficulty levels of the items would need to be considered in making such an "absolute" type of test interpretation. We need, then, some method of deriving a score or number that will have meaning for an individual student particularly if we are using norm-referenced measures. At the crudest level, rank in the group might be used, but the size of the group will obviously play a significant role in determining the meaning assigned to a particular rank (e.g., a rank of 3 in a group of 10 vs. a rank of 3 in a group of 1000). A derived score that has been found useful in describing individual student performance is the percentile rank (PR). *A percentile rank is the percentage of scores at and below the given score point.* To calculate a percentile rank, one merely counts the number of scores at or below the given score (the cumulative frequency, Cf_i), divided by the total number of students (N), and multiplied by 100. With reference to the data in Table 10-1, one could determine the PR for a score of 33 as follows:

$$\text{Percentile Rank} = \frac{Cf_i}{N} \times 100, \qquad (10\text{-}1)$$

where Cf_i = the number of cases at and below the interval containing the given score of interest (used when interval size is one). With reference to the data in Table 10-1, the percentile rank for a score of 33 is

$$PR_{33} = \frac{10}{30} \times 100 = 33$$

To facilitate the computation of percentile ranks, it is suggested that a *cumulative frequency* column be included in a summary data table. Such a column is derived simply by adding successively the frequencies associated with each interval beginning with the bottom score and working up. Using the procedure just described, percentile ranks have been calculated for the hypothetical American History data in Table 10-1, and are listed in Column 6. Interpretive problems sometimes arise because the highest score always gets a percentile rank of 100. The mistake is sometimes made that the person with a percentile rank of 100 got all the items correct. Two procedures are sometimes followed to help with this potential problem. One is to calculate percentile ranks from the midpoints; therefore there will be no 100. The other is simply to assign a percentile rank of "99" to the highest score and a "1" to the lowest score.

What does our percentile rank of 33 mean? It means that if you got a score of 10 on this test in comparison with your classmates, you did as well as or better than 33 percent of the people in your group.

A Graphic Aid for Calculating Percentile Ranks

Calculating all those percentile ranks can be a lot of work. Sometimes selected percentile ranks are calculated and plotted against the raw scores. One might calculate 25 percent to 33 percent of the values, plot them, then "smooth" the curve. Such a curve is called an *ogive*. Beginning with a raw score of 21 every other percentile rank-raw score pairs of Table 10-1 have been plotted and smoothed in Figure 10-5. The advantage to this curve is that you can use it with a relatively high degree of accuracy to estimate any percentile rank, even those for which the raw score has not been observed or achieved. If you gave the American History test again, and were able to assume that the original and new groups were comparable in major respects, then you could use the ogive to get a percentile rank for a score not observed in the original group, for example, a raw score of 32. Using a straightedge and going up from the raw score scale at 32 until we hit the curve, and then left over to the percentile rank scale leads to an estimate of around 30 for the percentile rank for a raw score of 32. Accuracy is a function of the number of data points (the more the better), and the precision of the graphing.

Another method for describing relative position in terms of standard deviation units will be described later in this chapter in the section on "Standard Scores."

The Total Distribution—Percentiles

If we are interested in describing how an individual student performed, percentile ranks are useful derived scores. But how can we describe the overall performance of the group? If our focus is on the total distribution, percentiles (P_x) constitute useful descriptive reference points. A percentile is a score point below which a given percent (x) of scores fall. The 50th percentile (usually referred to as the median and denoted P_{50}), for example, is that score point above which 50 percent of the scores fall and below which 50 percent of the scores fall. Although related to each other (for example, the percentile rank of a score of 29 is 20, and the 20th percentile is 29) PRs and P_xs summarize different characteristics of a distribution of scores and the methods of calculation differ; more importantly they are used for different purposes. With PRs one begins with a score point and ends with a percent; with P_xs one begins with a percent and ends with a score point.

There are fancy formulas that can be used to calculate percentiles but for most purposes simple counting will suffice. For example that very popular percentile, the median (P_{50}), can be approximated by simply counting one-half the scores (frequencies) and looking to see what the raw score is that divides the distribution in half. Looking at the frequency distribution in Table 10-1, our best guesstimate of the median (P_{50}) would be around 35.5. That's close enough. We would estimate the P_{25} to be about 30 (25 percent of the scores are below this point) and P_{75} to be about 37.5 (75 percent of the scores are below this point). We have 50 percent of the scores within 7.5 points of each other. This suggests that the scores are scrunched up.

Our ogive (Figure 10-5) can come in handy in estimating percentiles just as it

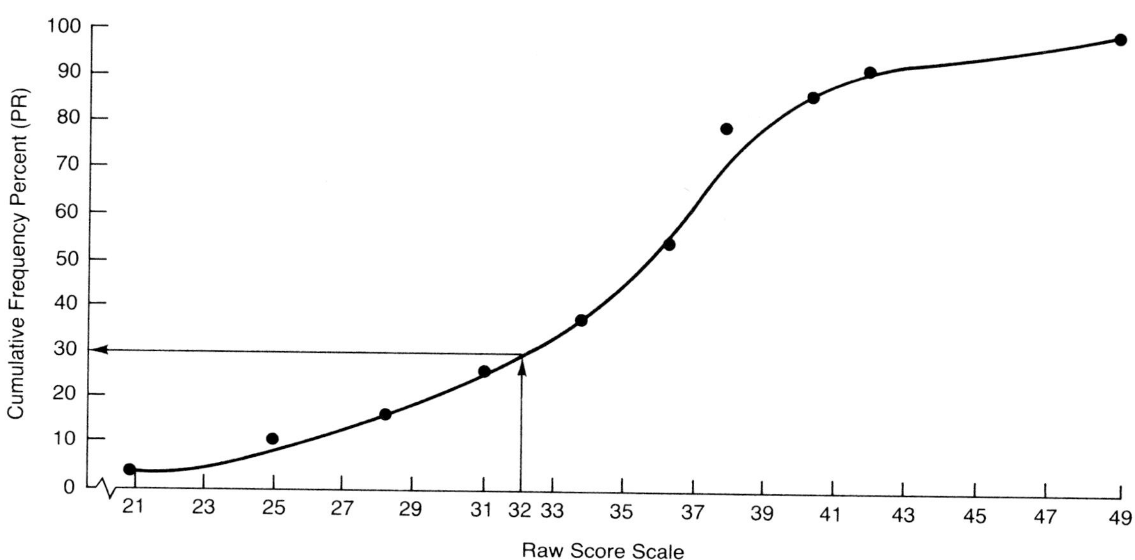

Figure 10-5

Ogive of raw scores and percentile ranks (estimating percentile ranks)

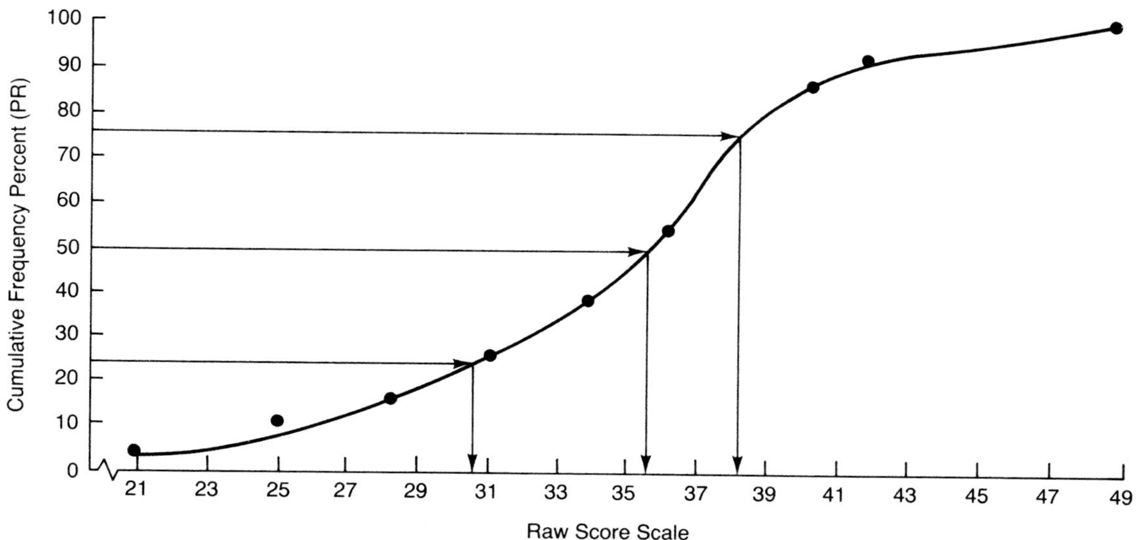

Figure 10-6

Ogive of raw scores and percentile ranks (estimating percentiles)

did in estimating percentile ranks. Let's confirm our estimates of P_{25}, P_{50} and P_{75} by going from the percent scale (percentile rank) to the score scale (see Figure 10-6. As you can see they are a pretty good match!)

One should become familiar with the procedure for obtaining percentiles, not only because they are useful in describing one's own score distribution, but also because the norms of most standardized educational and psychological tests are reported in the form of percentiles.

Selected percentile points are worthy of special mention, because they are frequently referred to in test manuals and the measurement literature:

1. The nine percentile points that divide a distribution into 10 equal parts are called deciles, and are symbolized as follows: D_1, D_2, D_3, etc.
2. The three percentile points that divide the distribution into four equal parts are called quartiles, and are symbolized as follows: Q_1, Q_2, and Q_3.

Identities such as the following should also be kept in mind:

$$\text{Median} = P_{50} = D_5 = Q_2$$
$$P_{25} = Q_1$$
$$P_{75} = Q_3$$

Average or Typical Performance

We have already described one index of average performance, the median. The median is a useful statistic because it is relatively unaffected by extreme scores and therefore useful with skewed distributions which are frequently encountered with classroom data. In many cases the best measure of "averageness" is the arithmetic mean, which is indexed by adding all scores and dividing the sum by the number of scores. Expressed as a formula:

$$M = \frac{\Sigma X}{N} \quad \text{or} \quad \frac{\Sigma fX}{N} \tag{10-2}$$

where

M = the symbol for the arithmetic mean
X = one observed score
f = frequency of an observed score
Σ = "the sum of"
N = the total number of scores in the distribution

The resulting mean (see Table 10-1) would be:

$$M = \frac{\Sigma fX}{N} = \frac{1050}{30} = 35$$

It is interesting to note the discrepancy between the mean ($M = 35$) and the estimated median ($P_{50} = 35.5$) of the distribution of hypothetical test scores. It will be recalled that we had described this frequency distribution as slightly negatively skewed. Since the mean is sensitive to every score in a distribution, and since the median is essentially based on frequencies, one would expect a discrepancy between these two measures when the underlying distribution is skewed. Referring back to Figure 10-1, we find the general expected trend, with the mean just a tiny bit smaller than the median for our negatively skewed distribution. The more extreme the skewness the greater the discrepancy between these two measures of central tendency.

The Variability of Performances

It should be apparent at this point that measures of central tendency (e.g., the mean and median) describe only one important characteristic of a distribution of scores. It is often highly desirable to describe how "spread out" or variable the scores in a distribution are. Whereas the mean and median are points on the score scale, a measure of variability must of necessity represent a distance among the score scale. Two reasonable reference points that describe distance along the score scale are the First Quartile (Q_1, or P_{25}) and the Third Quartile (Q_3, or P_{75}). The difference between these two score points, which describe the middle 50 percent of the scores, the Interquartile Range (IQR) can be used as a measure of variability (IQR).

$$IQR = Q_3 - Q_1 \tag{10-3}$$

If we take the interquartile range and divide by 2 we have a frequently referred to statistic called, cleverly, the semi-interquartile range (Q):

$$Q = \frac{Q_3 - Q_1}{2} \tag{10-4}$$

In the previous section on percentiles we had already identified Q_1 and Q_3 as P_{25} and P_{75}. The values we obtained were 30 and 37.5 respectively. Q would therefore be:

$$Q = \frac{37.5 - 30}{2} = 3.75$$

In a symmetrical distribution tending toward normality one would usually find 25 percent of the score between $Q_2 + 1Q$ and 25 percent between $Q_2 - 1Q$.

A more informative, refined, and sensitive statistic, useful in describing the variability of distributions of scores, is the standard deviation (S). The square of the standard deviation is called the variance (S^2). The standard deviation, in essence, represents the "average amount of variability" in a set of measures, using the mean as a reference point. Strictly speaking, the standard deviation is the positive square root of the average of the squared deviations about the mean. The most elementary form of the standard deviation formula is:

$$S = \sqrt{\frac{\Sigma f(X - M)^2}{N}} \tag{10-5}$$

It can be seen that the deviations about the mean $(X - M)$ are the basic unit used to describe variability, and that the greater the variability the greater the standard deviation. Part c of Figure 10-1 shows two distributions in which the scores exhibit different degrees of variability. The value of S will be larger for distribution B. Getting all these deviation $(X - M)$ scores is a lot of work, and you really have to watch your decimals, so we better stay with the raw scores. Probably the easiest raw score formula for standard deviation is:

$$S = \sqrt{\frac{\Sigma fX^2 - NM^2}{N}} \tag{10-6}$$

This is a good formula to use with a calculator. Note that we are using the raw scores squared and the mean squared. In this case the standard deviation using Equation 10-6 and the 30 raw scores of Table 10-1 would be:

$$S = \sqrt{\frac{37820 - 30(1225)}{30}} = \sqrt{\frac{1070}{30}} = \sqrt{35.67} = 5.97 \text{ or } 6$$

Why is the variability of a set of scores, and particularly the standard deviation of such scores, of interest? First, a measure of variability is descriptive. It reflects the degree of similarity in performances within groups of students. It can also be used to describe the variability between groups of students. Variability will influence the interpretation of the scores both of individual students and the total group. Second, variability and the standard deviation are tied very closely to the concepts of reliability and validity. In general, the greater the variability of scores, the greater the reliability at least for norm-referenced measures. And again, in general, the greater the reliability the greater the possibility that an acceptable level of validity can be obtained. Third, the standard deviation is used to derive standard scores, which are in turn useful in both interpreting scores of individual examinees and combining data for decision-making purposes, for example, assigning marks.

A frequently asked question is: "Is my standard deviation the right size, or is it too large or too small?" Standard deviations don't need to undergo reduction or enhancements. They are what they are, that is, they are descriptive of the data. Now it might be an expected size or an unexpected size depending somewhat on the number of cases. For large data sets ($N > 400$) one would probably expect a range of about 6 standard deviations; for small groups ($N < 15$ or 20), we would probably only expect a range of about 3.5 standard deviations.

A short-cut method for estimating the standard deviation was originally suggested by W. L. Jenkins of Lehigh University and presented by Diederich (1964). This estimated standard deviation involves summing the raw scores in the upper one-sixth of the distribution, subtracting the sum of the raw scores for the lower one-sixth of the distribution, and dividing the result by half the total number of scores. Symbolically, the estimated standard deviation ($\hat{S}$) may be represented as follows:

$$\hat{S} = \frac{\Sigma X_U 1/6 - \Sigma X_L 1/6}{N/2} \qquad (10\text{-}7)$$

This formula has some intrinsic appeal for many because, of course, it does not involve extracting a square root. It should be noted, however, that the use of this approximation formula theoretically assumes a normal distribution and is therefore subject to additional errors when the curve is nonnormal. On the basis of extensive use of this estimate, informally reported by teachers and instructors, and brief research reports by Lathrop (1961) and McMorris (1972), it can be concluded that it is a robust statistic, that is, violations of the assumptions underlying its use do not seriously affect its accuracy. Lathrop found, for example, that even when used with small and nonnormal distributions, $\hat{S}$ was a good approximation of S, with something like a 3–5 percent error.

When we apply this formula to the data in Table 10-1 (where one-sixth of $N = 5$) we find $\hat{S}$ to be 6.07, which corresponds very favorably with the actual standard deviation of 5.97. For all practical purposes we can simply round our standard deviation value to an even 6. At this point one might ask what to do if one-sixth turns out to be part of a person. If, for example, we have 40 scores, a sixth of 40 (or 40/6) is about 6.7. To be accurate we should multiply .7 times the seventh score from the top and bottom and add it into the respective sum. In practice, since this procedure is an approximation, we can usually round to the next highest integer.

Relative Position—Standard Scores

Standard scores are really nothing more than scores derived from the raw distribution and expressed as deviations from the mean in terms of standard deviation units. They are preferred by many as measures of relative position. As opposed to percentile ranks, they indicate an individual's position in a collection of scores with reference to the mean of the original group. Both methods of reporting are important. Percentile ranks are sensitive to the shape of the distribution; standard scores are not. It might be argued that standard scores contain more information than PRs. The mean, however, describes just one important characteristic of a distribution, and we need also take into account the variability of scores, which will significantly influence score interpretation. If, for example, a distribution of scores is quite homogeneous, the scores being very closely clustered about the hypothetical mean of 80, a score of 70 may represent an extremely low level of relative performance. On the other hand, if there is a great deal of variability it is likely that quite a few scores will be found to fall below 70, which now represents fairly typical performance. Scores, then, whose distributions have standard deviations and means of some standard value are known as standard scores. The operations by which raw scores are converted into standard scores are called transformations. We shall now discuss two kinds of standard score transformations that are frequently used in reporting test data.

Linear Transformations

The simplest type of standard score transformation is a linear one. A frequently used standard score system referred to in statistics is the z score system. This type of score can be represented as follows:

$$z = \frac{X - M}{S} \tag{10-8}$$

Again referring to the American History data in Table 10-1, we can see that a score of 42 would have a z score of $+1.17$.

$$z = \frac{42 - 35}{6} = +1.17$$

What does this mean? Telling an individual that his z score was $+1.17$ would indicate that his performance was above average—in fact, more than one standard deviation above the mean—which may be more meaningful and informative than telling him that he had a PR of 86. It is obvious from Equation 10-8 that if a student had a score equal to the mean his z score would be zero; if it is one standard deviation above or below, his z score would be $+1.00$ or -1.00. Generally, plus and minus three z-score units (a range of six standard deviation units) will describe the full range of scores in any distribution. For a distribution of scores for a classroom test, the range may be considerably less.

Some individuals have trouble keeping track of the "sign" of z scores and working with decimals. The former problem, and to some extent the latter also, can be overcome by using the following standard score conversion:

$$Z = 10\left(\frac{X - M}{S}\right) + 50 \tag{10-9}$$

or

$$Z = 10(z) + 50$$

We now have a new system of standard scores, where the "standard" mean is

50 and the "standard" standard deviation is 10. Our raw score of 42 would now have a Z value of

$$Z = 10(+1.17) + 50 = 61.7 \text{ or } 62$$

Both z scores and Z scores represent linear transformations. In other words, if the standard scores and corresponding raw scores were plotted as points with reference to a set of coordinate axes, the points would fall in a straight line. We have not changed the relationship of the scores or the shape of the underlying distribution. We have, in fact, subtracted a constant from each score and divided each difference by a constant.

Nonlinear Transformations

Classroom tests seldom yield so-called normal distributions. A normal distribution or curve, as illustrated in Figure 10-7, is a graphic plot of a particular mathematical function. One cannot tell just by "looking at" a distribution whether or not it is normal. The normal curve, however, has certain characteristics that have proven useful in working with test data, for example, selected z score values define fixed percentages of scores. A system of standard scores has therefore been derived from the normal curve. These scores are called T scores. This system of standard scores is similar to Z scores in that the mean is 50 and the standard deviation is 10. We would find that the PRs for Z and T scores are the same only in the case of a "normal distribution." The term "normal distribution" is in quotation marks because there is no single normal curve, but a family or class of normal curves depending upon the mean and standard deviation of the underlying raw scores. Part c of Figure 10-1 shows two different normal curves. T scores can be derived for nonnormal distributions to allow us to project certain score interpretations based on assumption of normality, for example, if we had 12,000 students instead of 120. One procedure involves actually changing the shape of the original raw-score distribution by an area transformation with the use of a table of the normal curve. One would look up the normal distribution z score for given percentile rank values, and then use the transformation $T = 10(z) + 50$. Normalizing scores may be a reasonable thing to do if certain assumptions can be met. Many of the variables of education and psychology are normally distributed when based on large samples of individuals. Therefore, the normal curve may be a reasonable model for some kinds of measurements. In addition, since the normal curve has certain characteristics that facilitate test interpretation, the use of a normal score transformation may be helpful. It should be noted that an individual with a T score of 50 will not have a raw score equal to the mean if the underlying distribution is not normally distributed.

Figure 10-7 describes the relationship among many systems of standard scores and a normal curve. Note particularly the percentile equivalents for various standard deviation points along the score scale.

Appendix B contains a table showing the relationship between T and z scores and percentile ranks when the original distribution of scores is "normal."

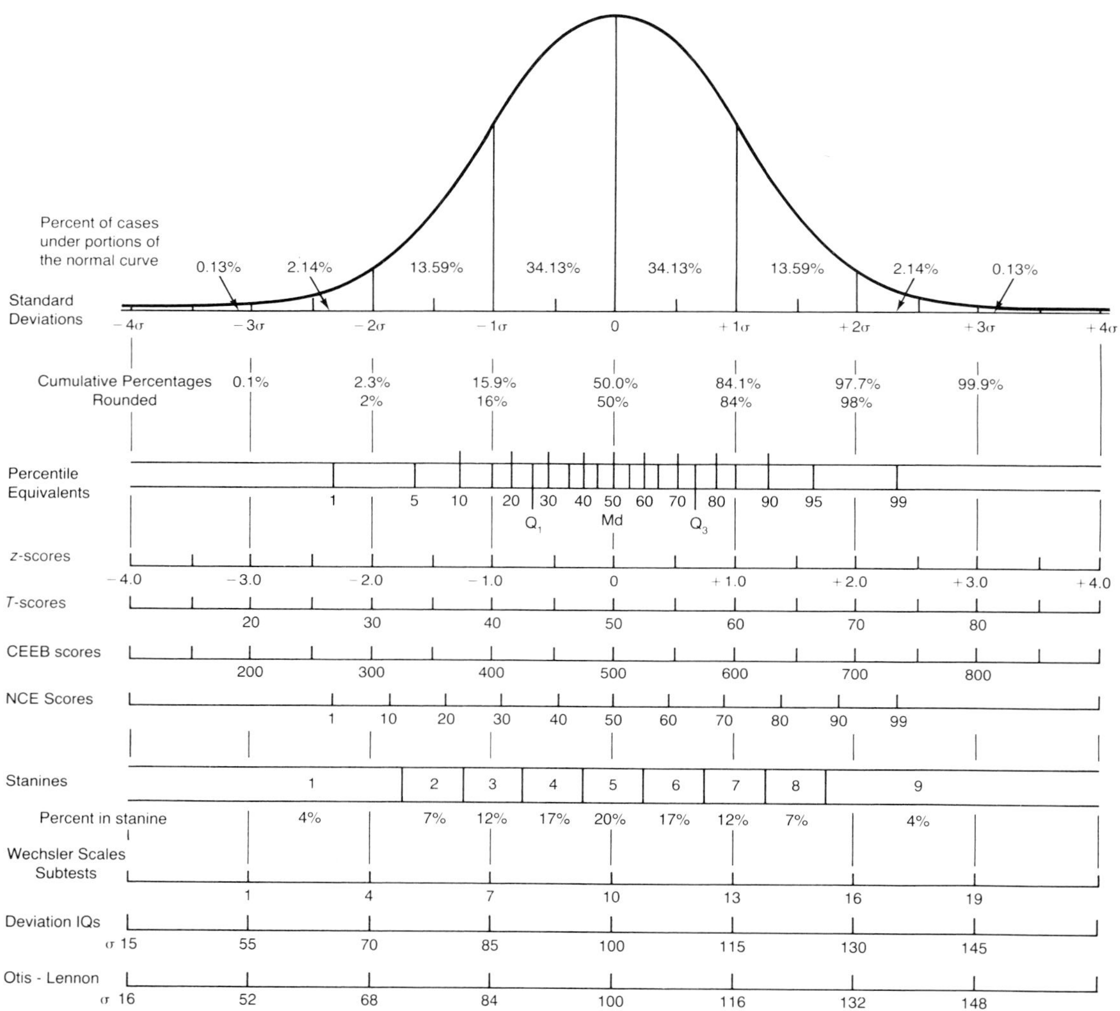

Figure 10-7

Relationships between the normal curve, percentiles, and various systems of standard scores. (*Source:* Test Service Bulletin *48 (January 1980). Published by the Psychological Corporation, San Antonio, TX*)

Two standard-score systems in Figure 10-7 are worthy of brief mention. The "standard nine" or stanine system of scores is increasing in popularity, particularly with publishers of standardized tests. It yields only nine possible values, which facilitates comprehension and interpretation, and is a normalized standard score. Its one drawback is that it groups together scores that might be quite different, assigning them the same stanine score, and therefore tends to mask individual differences. Stanines are actually defined in terms of standard deviation units. For example, a stanine of 5 includes those individuals who are within plus and minus .25 standard deviations of the mean, which in a normal distribution includes the middle 20 percent of the observations.

College Entrance Examination Board or CEEB scores are also a frequently used and encountered type of standard score. This system, used with the widely known Scholastic Aptitude Test and Graduate Record Exam, uses a score reporting system that avoids both negative numbers and decimals by arbitrarily setting the mean equal to 500 and the standard deviation to 100.

$$\text{CEEB Scores} = 100(z) + 500 \tag{10-10}$$

Another type of normalized standard score is the normal curve equivalent. Normal curve equivalents (NCE) were developed in response to a demand for a standard score system where the unit of measurement approximated an equal interval scale. If the assumption holds, differences between pairs of consecutive scores would be equal. Some psychometricians further argue that NCE scores can be used to compare scores on different tests. This is obviously a more refined method of reporting scores than percentile ranks.

The normal curve equivalent scale is a "normalized" scale, that is, it employs the normal curve as a mathematical model for its structure. To derive a NCE one (a) calculates percentile ranks for the scores in the distribution, (b) refers to a table of normal curve and identifies the normal deviate z score which corresponds to particular percentile ranks, and (c) multiplies each z by 21.06 and adds 50. Using Appendix B (Relationships Among T scores, z scores, and Percentile Ranks When Raw Scores Are Normally Distributed) will allow us to illustrate the conversion.

Assume a percentile rank of 62, the normal z score for which is 1.2. Multiplying by 21.06 and adding 50 gives us an NCE of 75.27 or 75 rounded. NCE conversion yields values from 1 to 99 and in that regard is similar to percentile ranks. Percentile ranks are based on an ordinal (or rank-ordered) scale whereas NCE values are based on an interval scale. This is an area transformation like those discussed earlier in the chapter, and in fact results in a change in the shape of original distribution.

Describing Relationships

In testing we are frequently called upon to describe the relationship between two sets of measures. The two measures might be scores by the same set of students on two different forms of the same test, thereby allowing us to describe reliability. Or they might be scores on a test, for example, the College Board Achievement Test in French, and a criterion measure such as final exam score in a first-year college French course, allowing us to describe the validity of the test.

Ideally, the first step in examining the relationship between two measures is to display the relationship or correlation graphically in the form of a scatter diagram. The procedure merely involves plotting the pairs of scores as dots on coordinate axes. Figure 10-8 is composed of six scatter diagrams showing varying degrees of

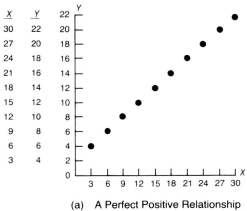

X	Y
30	22
27	20
24	18
21	16
18	14
15	12
12	10
9	8
6	6
3	4

(a) A Perfect Positive Relationship
($r = +1.00$)

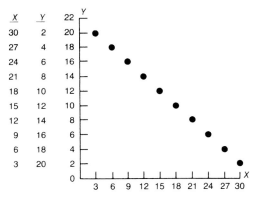

X	Y
30	2
27	4
24	6
21	8
18	10
15	12
12	14
9	16
6	18
3	20

(b) A Perfect Negative Relationship
($r = -1.00$)

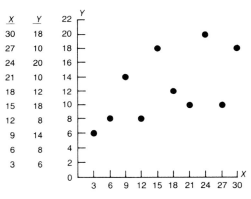

X	Y
30	18
27	10
24	20
21	10
18	12
15	18
12	8
9	14
6	8
3	6

(c) A Moderate Positive Relationship
($r = +.57$)

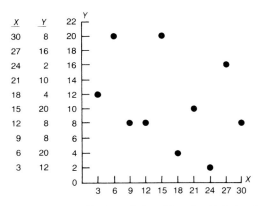

X	Y
30	8
27	16
24	2
21	10
18	4
15	20
12	8
9	8
6	20
3	12

(d) A Moderately Low Negative Relationship
($r = -.31$)

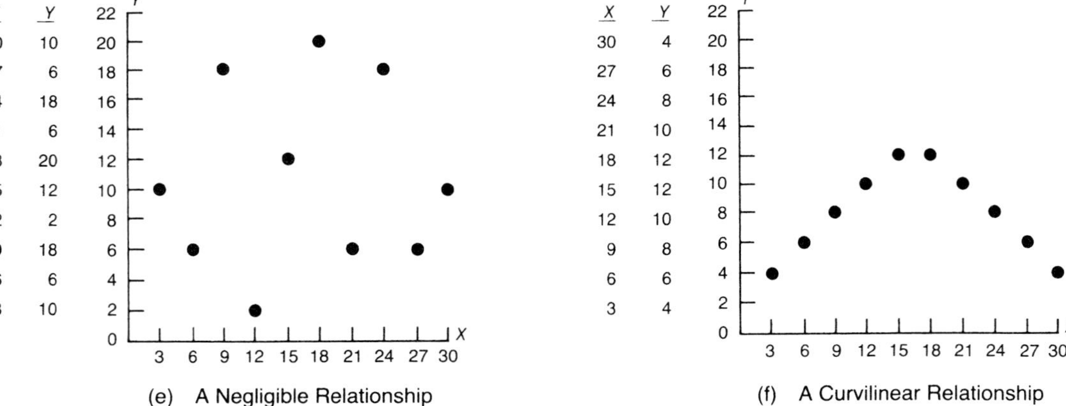

X	Y
30	10
27	6
24	18
21	6
18	20
15	12
12	2
9	18
6	6
3	10

(e) A Negligible Relationship
($r = +.007$)

X	Y
30	4
27	6
24	8
21	10
18	12
15	12
12	10
9	8
6	6
3	4

(f) A Curvilinear Relationship

Figure 10-8

Scatter diagrams showing various degrees of correlation

relationship. Diagram (a) shows a perfect positive correlation where the highest X value (30) is associated with the highest Y value (22), the second highest X value (27) is associated with the second highest Y value (20), and so on down to the lowest X value (3) and the lowest Y value (4). Conversely, in diagram (b) we see a perfect inverse relationship between the scores, with the highest X score (30) associated with the lowest Y score (2) and so on. Both (a) and (b) represent perfect correlations; only the direction of the relationship is different, (a) being positive and (b) negative. Diagram (e) shows no consistent pattern between the measures. Two factors, then, are associated in correlation, magnitude (high to low) and direction (positive and negative), with the former generally the more important. Scatter diagrams (a)–(d) presented in Figure 10-8 represent linear relationships, that is, have a tendency to follow a straight-line pattern. Curved-line relationships are, of course, possible (see diagram (f) in Figure 10-8). If one were examining the relationship between test anxiety and achievement-test performance, he might find that anxiety tended to be associated with increased performance up to a certain point, at which an increase in anxiety would be associated with decreased performance. One of the reasons for plotting scatter diagrams is to determine whether the relationship is linear or curvilinear and to get a "feel" for the data. The indices of correlation to be discussed in the remainder of this chapter are appropriate for linear relationships only, and the reader interested in curvilinear correlation procedures is referred to any number of standard texts (e.g., Guilford & Fruchter, 1978).

After graphically examining a relationship, we come to the problem of describing it quantitatively. The most frequently used index of linear relationship is the Pearson product-moment correlation coefficient (r) which, in its simplest form, may be presented as follows:

$$r = \frac{\Sigma z_x z_y}{N} \qquad (10\text{-}11)$$

where

z_y and z_y = standard scores of the form $(X - M)/S$
$\Sigma z_x z_y$ = the sum of the product of the z scores
N = the total number of pairs of observations

Using Equation 10-11, then, requires converting each X and Y score to a standard score, specifically a z score, multiplying the pairs of corresponding z scores, summing the products, and dividing by N. An illustration of the calculation of a product-moment correlation in this manner is presented in Table 10-3. Ordinarily the first step we would take in evaluating this relationship would be to look at a scatter diagram of the pairs of measures. This scatter diagram is presented in Figure 10-9. It might be a good exercise to use the sample reference scatter diagrams in Figure 10-8 to guesstimate the range where we are likely to find our numerical value for the rank difference correlation coefficient. The correlation of .89 is quite strong

Table 10-3 Illustration of Calculation of Product-Moment Correlation Between College Board French Test (X) and Final Exam Scores (Y) Using Standard Scores (z)

Student	**College Board Test (X)**	**Final Exam Score (Y)**	z_x	z_y	$z_x z_y$
A	448	70	−.67	−1.0	.67
B	572	80	.26	.0	.0
C	763	98	1.70	1.80	3.06
D	502	75	−.26	−.50	.13
E	629	86	.69	.60	.41
F	345	72	−1.44	−.80	1.15
G	525	68	−.09	−1.20	.11
H	417	70	−.90	−1.00	.90
I	327	66	−1.58	−1.40	2.21
J	518	84	−.14	.40	−.06
K	654	94	.88	1.40	1.23
L	780	97	1.83	1.70	3.11
M	528	85	−.07	.50	−.03
N	409	78	−.96	−.20	.19
O	644	83	.80	.30	.24
Σ	8061	1206			13.32
M	537	80			
S	133	10			

Correlation Using z Scores

$$r = \frac{\Sigma z_y z_y}{N}$$

$$r = \frac{13.32}{15} = \underline{\underline{.89}}$$

indicating that the CEEB test would have good validity. If the French test were given in high school and the course exam were for a freshman year course, we would be looking at the predictive validity of the French test. If the test and exam data were gathered at approximately the same time we would be investigating concurrent validity. In any event we would be examining criterion-related validity. At no time is there any inference of cause or effect. Many factors can influence the magnitude of the relationship between sets of measures or scores. Among these are (a) the nature of the variables being measured, (b) the size and variability of the sets of

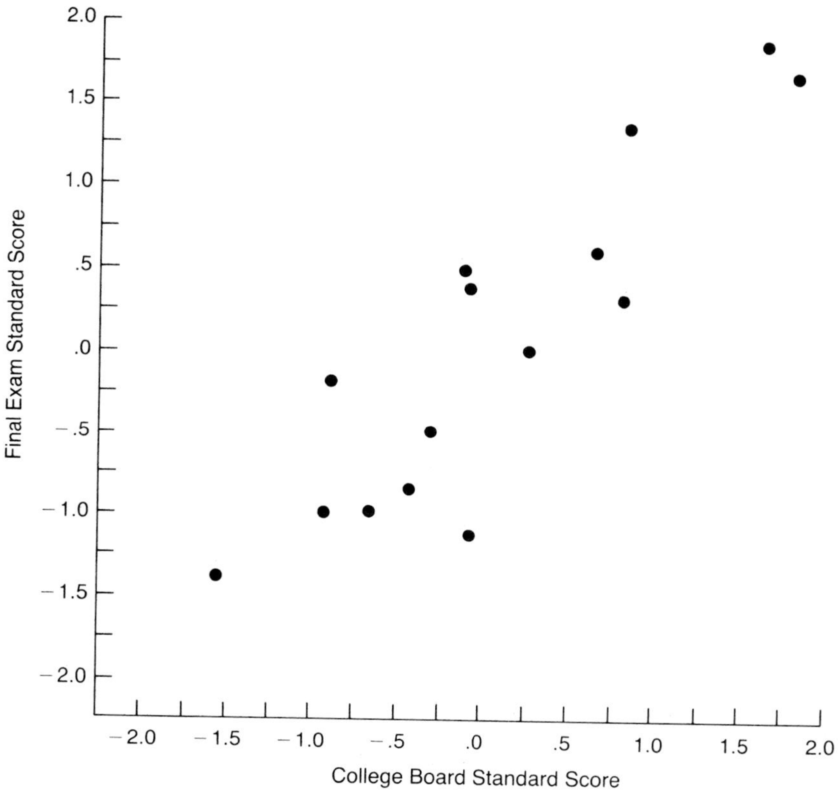

Figure 10-9

Scatter diagram for data of Table 10-3

scores, (c) the amount of time between the measurements, and (d) the reliability of either or both measurements.

There is a special case of the Pearson product moment correlation called biseral. It is used frequently in doing item analysis. It would be applied when one variable is continuous (e.g., the total score on the test) and the other is dichotomous (e.g., getting an item right or wrong).

The rationale for the method of calculating correlation coefficients is hopefully clear. If scores (people, products, objects, etc.) tend to rank themselves similarly on two different scales the rankings must be related, or correlated, or the numbers are said to co-vary together. It also may be the case that a third variable is pulling the two scores together. For example, let's say that scores on the Glynn Test of Cognitive Reasoning Ability correlates .77 with grades in an introductory educational psychology course. It may be the case that reading ability is influencing the two measures to be highly correlated because reading is important both in the course and on the test. We could confirm this by administering the Muth Reading Test and looking at the correlation between the scores on it, and our reasoning test and grades. Raw score formulas are also available and any reasonably comprehensive hand calculator will allow you to go directly from raw scores to the correlation. Following is the raw score formula for the Pearson product-moment correlation:

$$r = \frac{N\Sigma XY - (\Sigma X)(\Sigma Y)}{\sqrt{N\Sigma X^2 - (\Sigma X)^2}\sqrt{N\Sigma Y^2 - (\Sigma Y)^2}} \tag{10-12}$$

Direct, inverse, and curvilinear (Equation 10-12) (see diagram f in Figure 10-8) relationships are all possible. For linearly related variables correlation of +1.00 represents a perfect positive relationship between two variables, and one of −1.00 a perfect inverse or negative relationship. A correlaton of .00 indicates the total absence of linear relationship between the scores. It should be emphasized that a correlation of −.68 indicates the same magnitude of relationship as does a correlation of +.68, and that they would be equally useful in making predictions. It is not true, however, that a correlation of .60 indicates twice as strong a relationship as does a correlation of .30, that is, r is not directly proportional to the degree of correlation.

In calculating a correlation using Equation 10-11 or 10-12, we were essentially describing the relationship between X and Y in terms of an individual student's relative position on the two measures, expressed in standard score form. Correlation is invariant regardless of the linear units of measurement used. Earlier in this chapter we saw how ranks could also be used to represent relative position. There is an efficient procedure for correlating two sets of scores that uses only ranks. It is called the Spearman Rank Difference or Rank Order Correlation (r_s):

$$r_s = 1 - \left(\frac{6(\Sigma D^2)}{N(N^2 - 1)}\right) \tag{10-13}$$

where

ΣD^2 = the sum of the squared differences in ranks (the number 6 is a constant value)
N = the number of ranked pairs of scores

The procedure merely involves assigning a rank of "1" to the highest score on each variable, "2" to the next highest, and so on. Rankings are completed separately for the two variables being correlated. In the case of tied scores, averaged ranks are assigned. For example, if four examinees all had scores of 25 on the same test, and were tied for the ranks of 8, 9, 10, and 11, an average rank would be assigned—in this situation, 9.5 (8 + 9 + 10 + 11)/4. After the ranking has been completed (note that we cannot have more ranks than people and that the algebraic sum of the differences in ranks is zero), the differences in ranks are squared, summed, multiplied by 6, and substituted in Equation 10-13. This was accomplished on the same College Board and Exam scores of Table 10-3, and the calculations are summarized in Table 10-4. The rank difference correlation of .83 compares favorably with the product-moment correlation of .89. The rank difference tends to be a more conservative (lower) estimate of relationship than the product-moment, unless a large number of ties tend to inflate the obtained coefficient. The Spearman correlation, because of its relative accuracy and computational ease, is recommended for use by classroom teachers as an adequate correlational index in analyzing their tests. How correlational procedures can be applied in evaluating test reliability and validity is described in Chapters 12 and 13 respectively.

The description of scores in terms of central tendency and variability, and in terms of relationship with other scores can be somewhat time consuming and might be viewed as an arduous task. But they are necessary tasks; being able to describe allows us to begin to draw inferences and make interpretations of very important data. A wise man once said that only after data have been summarized and communi-

Table 10-4 Illustration of Calculation of Spearman's Rank Order Correlation with Hypothetical College Board (X) and French Final Exam (Y) Scores from Table 10-3

Student	College Board Test (X)	Final Exam Score (Y)	Rank of x	Rank of y	D $R_x - R_y$	D^2 $(R_x - R_y)^2$
A	448	70	11	12.5	−1.5	2.25
B	572	80	6	8	−2.0	4.0
C	763	98	2	1	1.0	1.0
D	502	75	10	10	0.0	0.0
E	629	86	5	4	1.0	1.0
F	345	72	14	11	3.0	9.0
G	525	68	8	14	−6.0	36.0
H	417	70	12	12.5	−0.5	0.25
I	327	66	15	15	0.0	0.0
J	518	84	9	6	3.0	9.0
K	654	94	3	3	0.0	0.0
L	780	97	1	2	−1.0	1.0
M	528	85	7	5	2.0	4.0
N	409	78	13	9	4.0	16.0
O	644	83	4	7	−3.0	9.0
				SUM	0.0	92.5

$$r_s = 1 - \left(\frac{6\,(\Sigma D^2)}{N\,(N^2 - 1)}\right) = 1 - \left(\frac{6\,(92.5)}{15\,(15^2 - 1)}\right) = 1 - \frac{555}{3360} = \underline{\underline{.83}}$$

cated do they become information, and rational decision-making is based on information. Hopefully that information will be as descriptive and accurate as possible.

Case Study Application

The 80-item Reading Education midterm exam was administered to a class of 18 students approximately five weeks into the quarter, and a final exam (80 items) was administered one week before the end of the quarter. Following is a list of their raw scores:

Midterm Exam						*Final Exam*					
S_1	58	S_7	58	S_{13}	62	S_1	65	S_7	63	S_{13}	67
S_2	47	S_8	58	S_{14}	51	S_2	51	S_8	59	S_{14}	52
S_3	58	S_9	55	S_{15}	65	S_3	61	S_9	57	S_{15}	69
S_4	59	S_{10}	52	S_{16}	57	S_4	67	S_{10}	57	S_{16}	56
S_5	68	S_{11}	62	S_{17}	62	S_5	74	S_{11}	71	S_{17}	67
S_6	55	S_{12}	57	S_{18}	52	S_6	53	S_{12}	53	S_{18}	63

In summarizing the performances of this group there are probably five activities that are important. They are (a) displaying the data in a meaningful way, (b) calculating indices of central tendency, (c) calculating indices of variability, (d) expressing individual performances, and (e) describing relationships. Complete these activities for the following statistics or diagrams on the *midterm* exam. Construct or calculate using the midterm data:

Data Display	*Central Tendency*	*Variability*	*Relative Position for a Score of 57*
(1) Frequency distribution	(1) Mean	(1) Range	(1) Percentile rank
(2) Frequency polygon	(2) Median	(2) Standard deviation	(2) Standard scores (z, Z, CEEB, and NCE)
		(3) Estimated standard deviation (Lathrop)	
		(4) Inter-quartile range	
		(5) Semi-interquartile range	

Describing Relationships

(1) Prepare a scatter diagram for the pairs of Midterm and Final Exam scores
(2) "Guesstimate" the correlation using Figure 10-8 as a guide.
(3) Calculate the Spearman Rank Order Correlation (Equation 10-13).

Content Review Statements

1. The study of statistics is important because of the use of statistical methods.
   a. Facilitates the summarization and description of data.
   b. Assists in the interpretation of test scores.
   c. Is necessary for an adequate analysis of measuring instruments.
   d. Facilitates the decision-making use of test data.
2. A frequency distribution of test scores reveals the number of scores in each category along the score scale.
3. The frequency distribution facilitates examination of the shape of the distribution and, in particular, recognition of skewness or the tendency of scores to bunch up at the extremes of a distribution.
4. Stem and leaf plots are efficient and picturesque methods of summarizing data which are alternatives to frequency distributions for small data sets.
5. A percentile rank, which describes the percentage of scores at or below a given score (or the midpoint of a set of scores), is useful in interpreting individual performances.
6. A percentile rank is calculated by dividing the total number of scores (N) into the cumulative frequency at and below a given score (or midpoint), and multiplying the result by 100.
7. A percentile is a score point that divides a score distribution into specified percentages or areas of the total distribution.
8. The graph of cumulation frequency percent against scores (and ogive) facilitates obtaining percentile ranks and percentiles.
9. The median is that percentile (score point) that divides the total score distribution into four equal areas.
10. The First (Q_1), Second (Q_2), and Third (Q_3) Quartiles divide the distribution into four equal areas.
11. A distribution of scores that is asymmetrical may be characterized as skewed.
12. A positively skewed distribution has a high frequency of low scores and trails off to a low frequency of high scores.
13. A negatively skewed distribution has a high frequency of high scores and trails off to a low frequency of low scores. Many achievement measures yield negatively skewed distributions.
14. The mean, or arithmetic average, is obtained by adding all the scores and dividing the sum by the total number of scores.
15. If the mean is larger than the median, it is likely that the distribution is positively skewed. Conversely, if it is less than the median the distribution is likely to be negatively skewed.
16. The variability (or spread) of a distribution of measures may be described by the standard deviation, the interquartile or semi-interquartile range, or the range.
17. The variances of a set of scores is calculated by adding the squared deviations of the scores (from the mean of all the scores) and then dividing the total by the number of scores.
18. The standard deviation is the positive square root of the variance.
19. The standard deviation can be estimated by dividing half the number of scores into the difference between the sums of the upper and lower one-sixths of the distribution of the scores.

20. In general, the greater the total number of scores, the greater the range of scores in standard deviation units.
21. The variability of scores is likely to be positively related to total test reliability, and to some extent to validity.
22. Standard scores represent methods of expressing test scores that have fixed means and standard deviations.
23. The basic standard score is the *z* score, which is calculated by dividing the standard deviation into the difference between a given raw score and the mean of all the scores.
24. A *Z* score is obtained by multiplying a *z* score by 10 and adding 50.
25. A *T* score is the same as a *Z* score when the scores are normally distributed.
26. The normal curve is an idealized theoretical (mathematical) bell-shaped curve that represents the distributions of some kinds of educational and psychological data, particularly when a large number of observations is involved.
27. The distribution of scores from classroom tests is rarely normal.
28. A College Board or CEEB standard score is obtained by multiplying the *z* score by 100 and adding 500.
29. Nonnormal distributions can be converted to normal distributions by transforming all raw scores to percentile ranks and then entering a normal curve table, which gives *z*-score equivalents of the percentile ranks (see Appendix C).
30 Stanine standard scores are usually normally distributed single-digit scores having a mean of approximately 5 and a standard deviation of approximately 2.
31. Normal curve equivalents are normalized standard scores arrayed across an equal interval scale.
32. A correlation coefficient represents the degree of relation between a series of paired scores.
33. Correlation coefficients range from -1.00, indicating a perfect negative or inverse relationship, through .00, indicating the absence of relationship, to $+1.00$, indicating a perfect positive direct relationship.
34. When pairs of scores are expressed as z scores, the correlation coefficient is the average of the *z*-score products.
35. A correlation can be assessed using differences between ranks of paired scores (the Spearman Rank Difference method).
36. Examination of the degree and direction of relationship in a set of paired scores is facilitated by the plotting of the pairs on a two-way grid (scatter diagram).
37. The more closely the plots of pairs of scores fall on a diagonal, the higher the correlation; the diagonal running from the lower left to upper right corners is positive, and that running from the upper left to lower right corners is negative, assuming the scores have been plotted low to high, left to right, and bottom to top of the scatter diagram.
38. Correlation methods are useful in studying test reliability and validity.

Speculations

1. What are the alternatives to using quantitative methods in testing? What would be the consequences of using them?
2. Why is "variability" such an important concept in tests and measurement?

3. How does the phrase "A Picture is Worth a Thousand Words" apply to statistical methods?
4. Try to orally describe to a friend the concepts of (a) relative position, (b) central tendency, (c) variability, and (d) relationship.
5. Why are there so many different ways to express test scores?
6. What is standard about a standard score?
7. Discuss how the concept of "averageness" makes (a) logical sense, (b) statistical sense, and (c) educational sense.
8. What would a horticulturalist say about a stem and leaf plot?

Suggested Readings

The following are pretty much standard textbooks in quantitative methods. It is suggested that the interested reader examine primarily descriptive methods, with particular attention being paid to data display.

Guilford, J. P., & Fruchter, B. (1978). *Fundamental statistics in psychology and education* (6th ed.). New York: McGraw-Hill.

Moore, D. S. (1985). *Statistics: Concepts and controversies* (2nd ed.). New York: Freeman.

Mosteller, F., Fienberg, S. E., & Rourke, R. E. K. (1983). *Beginning statistics with data analysis.* Reading, MA: Addison-Wesley.

Chapter 11

Analyzing and Using Test Item Data

Item-analysis techniques are among the most valuable tools classroom teachers or any test developer can apply in attempting to improve the quality of their tests. The techniques are valuable for all types of tests including achievement, aptitude, and personality. The use of even the most elementary item-analysis procedures can bring about a remarkable improvement of classroom instruments. In addition, item data have very valuable instructional applications. The methods discussed in this chapter are aimed primarily at improving measures of the norm-referenced variety. Further consideration is given to item-selection techniques relevant to criterion-referenced tests and items in Chapter 16.

Item analyses are conducted for four general purposes: (a) to select the best available items for the final form of a test; (b) to identify structural or content defects in the items; (c) to detect learning difficulties of the class as a whole, identifying general content areas or skills that need to be reviewed by the instructor; and (d) to identify for individual students areas of weakness in need of remediation.

There are three main elements in an item analysis. One is examination of the *difficulty* level of the items, that is, the percentage of students responding correctly to each item in the test. Another is determination of the *discriminating* power of each item. Item discrimination in its simplest form usually, but not always, refers to the relation of performance on each item to performance on the total test. For a classroom test, item discrimination is generally indexed by the number or percentage of high-scoring individuals (based on total score) responding correctly versus the number of low-scoring individuals responding correctly.

A third element in item analyses, if multiple-choice or matching items are used in the test, is examination of the effectiveness of the distractors (foils, or alternative answers). Again, data derived from the high and low scorers are used. But now the complete response patterns associated with all the alternatives in each item are studied, rather than just the correct answer.

Many sophisticated item-analysis procedures are available. The more mathematically complicated and rigorous techniques are beyond the scope of this book, and the reader is referred to the presentations by Wainer (1989) and Guilford (1954) for expanded treatments of the topic, particularly with regard to useful correlational procedures.

Preparing Data for Item Analysis

Preparing data for the item analysis of a classroom test generally involves counting the number of individuals in high- and low-scoring groups who answer each item correctly. This count can be accomplished by a show of hands in class or by examination of the answer sheets. An efficient show of hands approach has been outlined by Diederich (1964) and is recommended if the class is relatively small and sufficient time is available. In general, the following steps are followed in gathering and recording data for an item analysis:

1. *Arrange the answer sheets in order from high to low.* This ranking is usually based on the individual's total score on the test. An item analysis of data derived from high and low scorers (based on total score) is referred to as an internal item analysis. If an external criterion is used (e.g., another test that is supposed to measure the same thing as the one under analysis), the item analysis is referred to as an external item analysis. The total score on the test is the most satisfactory criterion on which to base a ranking of individuals for an analysis of a classroom test.

2. *High- and low-scoring groups are identified.* For purposes of item analysis, these two extreme sets of examination papers are called criterion groups. Each subgroup will generally contain from 25 to 50 percent of the total number of people who took the test. The goal is to include enough people in the criterion groups to justify confidence in the results, and yet keep the criterion groups distinct enough to insure that they represent different levels of ability. Kelley (1939) has shown that maximally reliable item discrimination results will be obtained when each criterion group contains 27 percent of the total. Thus, in undertaking an item analysis on a classroom test, between 25 and 33 percent represents a reasonable size for the crite-

rion groups. *The high and low groups, however, must contain the same number of individuals.*

3. *Record separately the number of times each alternative was selected by individuals in the high and low groups.*

4. *Add the number of correct answers to each item made by the combined high and low groups.*

5. *Divide the total number of correct responses by the maximum possible, that is, the total number of students in the combined high and low groups, and multiply the result by 100.* This percentage is an estimate of the *difficulty index*. Some test constructors allow items to be omitted, and students inadvertently omit items. If all individuals have not attempted all items, item-difficulty indices should be obtained by dividing the total number of correct responses by the number of individuals who attempted the item. On speeded tests, omitted items in the middle of the test should probably be considered wrong, but those at the end should be considered omitted.

6. *Subtract the number of correct answers made by the low group from the number of correct answers by the high group.*

7. *Divide this number (the difference, H-L) by the number of individuals contained in the subgroup (i.e., the number in the high [or low] group).*

This decimal number is the *discrimination index*.

Sample item data and the resulting indices derived from the procedures described above are presented in Table 11-1. These data refer to four hypothetical multiple-choice items answered by different classes (thus producing fluctuating numbers of cases in the high and low groups). The procedure for deriving indices of difficulty and discrimination can, of course, be used profitably with two-choice (e.g., true-false), matching, or any number of multiple-choice objective item types. Further, the concepts of difficulty and discrimination may be applied in evaluating more subjective item types, for example, completion and, with some difficulty, essay items.

The reader may now legitimately ask how these data can be used to improve his test. The following three sections will consider the use of item-analysis data in improving the quality of a classroom test.

Using Information About Item Difficulty

An item's difficulty level is important because it tells the instructor something meaningful about the comprehension of, or performance on, material or tasks contained in the item. Referring to Item 1 in Table 11-1, one can see that the item is easy (estimated difficulty index = 83 percent). Note here an apparent paradox, namely,

Table 11-1 Sample Item-Analysis Data Derived from Four Hypothetical Multiple-Choice Items

	Group	Group Size	Response Alternatives[1] 1	2	3	4	5	Total No. Correct (H and L)	Difficulty Index	(H-L)	Discrimination Index
Item 1	High	12	0	11	0	1	0	20	83%	2	+.17
	Low	12	2	9	1	0	0				
Item 2	High	25	2	2	20	1	0	26	52%	14	+.56
	Low	25	5	8	6	2	4				
Item 3	High	16	2	2	8	2	2	6	19%	−2	−.13
	Low	16	4	3	4	1	4				
Item 4	High	30	20	3	2	1	4	28	47%	12	+.40
	Low	30	8	1	8	9	2				

[1]Underlined numbers indicate correct answers.

that the higher the value of the difficulty index the easier the item. This paradox is comprehensible when we recall that the difficulty index represents the percentage of the total number of respondents answering the item correctly. In other words, there is an inverse relationship between the magnitude of the index and what it purports to represent. In any event, an instructor might be justified in concluding that with respect to Item 1, nearly everyone had command of the material. Extremely high difficulty indices, however, may indicate a structural defect in the item. The data for Item 1 may have been obtained from the following item:

Item 1. Among the major contributors to low reliability are:

1. an appropriate time limit.
2. inadequate samplings of content and individuals. *
3. lack of content heterogeneity in the test.
4. differential weighting of alternatives in scoring each item.
5. poor lighting in the testing room.

Upon examination of the content and structure of the test, it is obvious that a grammatical clue exists. The stem calls for a plural response, and the only plural response is "2"—which in this case happens to be the correct answer. A student who noticed this clue could respond correctly to the item without knowing the

* Keyed as correct.

answer. This irrelevant clue could alone account for the high difficulty index, particularly where the low group is concerned. The lesson here is obvious. In selecting items for a test, consideration of content alone or item analysis data alone can be very misleading. Both factors need to be considered in accepting items for the final form of the test.

The difficulty index described in this chapter is only an estimate of the "real" difficulty level of an item. It is based on the responses of only the high- and low-scoring groups. The middle groups, usually from 50 to 33 percent of the total, have been eliminated. It is assumed, and has been found true in practice, that approximately half of the middle group will score like the high group and half like the low group. The index is only an estimate from another standpoint. Guessing may be a factor on any test item, particularly if the item is quite difficult. Each item should theoretically be corrected for guessing. For a classroom test, however, this scoring refinement is probably unnecessary.

A number of authorities have shown that if a test is composed entirely of items at the 50 percent difficulty level, it is possible for it to be maximally reliable or, more precisely, to evidence maximum internal consistency. In other words, items at the 50 percent level allow for item-discrimination indices to obtain their maximum possible value: unity. In a sense median difficulty may be viewed as a necessity but not a sufficient condition for acceptable discrimination. It may be desirable, however, to include in the test items that are fairly easy (those at the beginning of the test for psychological reasons) or fairly difficult (those measuring highly complex learning outcomes). When these types of items are included in the test, generally lowered (internal consistency) reliability estimates will be obtained. Cureton (1966) has shown this to be particularly crucial if Kuder-Richardson Formula 20 is used. (See Chapter 12 for a discussion of this approach to test reliability.) A paradox is evident. If an instructor uses the *Taxonomy of Educational Objectives* as a framework for instruction and measurement, the resulting test will of necessity reflect a range of item-difficulty indices. This will result in lower Kuder-Richardson reliabilities, despite the fact that it represents a desired state of affairs. Two recommendations should help ameliorate the problem. First, limit the range of item difficulties, for example, between 30 and 70 percent. Second, interpret the Kuder-Richardson reliabilities derived from classroom tests with caution. Whereas we generally desire Kuder-Richardson values above .85 for published tests of achievement, aptitude, and intelligence, on a single classroom test .70 might be considered acceptable. In addition, it is assumed that other data will be gathered, so that the reliability of the composite score used to make a final decision will reach a higher and more acceptable level.

Another paradox exists with regard to the measuring of the item difficulty indices. If a teacher has done a good job in teaching a particular concept skill or fact students will perform well on items related to that topic. Item difficulty values will be high in numerical value, for example, 85, meaning that a large percentage of the students did well. If most everyone did well then there is no room for the item(s) to discriminate. We don't like items that don't discriminate, right? An item is being penalized (persecuted) for doing a good job. The topic might be thrown out. Better we should look at discrimination in terms of percentage passing prior to instruction relative to after instruction. See sections on criterion-referenced measures later in this chapter for further discussion.

A useful application of item-analysis data is to develop a chart that relates student performance on each item (correct = +, incorrect = 0) and the content of the item. A sample chart for five students and four items is presented below. It is apparent that the concept of reliability could be profitably reviewed.

	Student				
Item Content	S_1	S_2	S_3	S_4	S_5
Use of table of specifications	+	+	0	0	+
Computing mean	+	0	0	+	+
Definition of reliability	+	0	+	0	0
Intrepreting correlation coefficient	+	+	0	+	+

In addition, several areas in need of review for individual students have been highlighted by reproducing the responses of each examinee to each item. When the class and number of items are large, the sheer mechanics of recording responses can be quite laborious. The benefits that accrue to both student and instructor can, however, be substantial. In such cases, items with similar content could be grouped together. Another interesting variation is to refer back to the original table of specifications, particularly if the *Taxonomy of Educational Objectives* was used to develop it, and use the corresponding behavior categories instead of content categories.

Using Information about Item Discrimination

Item discrimination has been defined as the degree to which an item differentiates the high achievers from the low achievers. A perfect positively discriminating item would be answered correctly by all of the high group and none of the low group; the discrimination index would then be +1.00. If all of the low group and none of the high group responded correctly, the index would be −1.00. In a sense, we might interpret the discrimination index as the correlation of the item with the total test score. Extreme values are almost never observed on a classroom test. Items in the middle range of positive discrimination are usually found in practice.

The data reported in Table 11-1 for Item 2 were obtained from the following item:

Item 2. A teacher proposes the following objective for a course in Fine Arts: "The pupils should be able to understand and appreciate good music." The principal drawback to this objective, from a measurement standpoint, is that it is a

1. general objective.
2. student objective.

* 3. nonbehavioral objective.
4. teacher objective.
5. compound objective.

This item is "sound" from a number of standpoints. The "middle difficulty level" criterion has been met, with an index of 52 percent. In addition, it discriminates between the high and low groups, as indicated by the index of +.56. The item is structurally sound and measures a desirable outcome, namely, the ability to apply knowledge about objectives in a new situation. Another possible explanation for the good discrimination is that the alternatives contain plausible but incorrect answers.

In general, all items in a test of relative achievement should discriminate positively. This assumes that we are striving for an additive scale, in which item scores are summed, and that we want each item to make a positive contribution. It is also assumed that we are interested in developing a test of relative achievement, as opposed to a mastery test, in which all items do not necessarily need to meet an internal-discrimination criterion. It is usually assumed in developing a classroom test that high positive total scores will be correlated with more knowledge and skill.

An instructor will occasionally find a negatively discriminating item such as the following (refer to Table 11-1 for appropriate item-analysis data):

Item 3. Which of the following alternatives best summarizes the limitations of the *Taxonomy of Educational Objectives*?

1. For the most part it is written in nonbehavioral terms.
2. It deals with "inferred" rather than "real" behavior.
3. It may restrict our thinking only to the categories of the *Taxonomy.*
4. The categories of the *Taxonomy* are not mutually exclusive.

* 5. All of the above are limitations of the *Taxonomy.*

This item, answered correctly by more of the low group than the high group, is apparently ambiguous. One possible source of ambiguity is the nature of the task. In essence, the student is required to make a value judgment. Most students apparently do not possess enough information to make an appropriate judgment. The use of "all of the above," though correct in the instructor's eyes, may have contributed to the difficulty of the task (difficulty index = 19 percent) and made responding to the item easier for the low than the high group. Students in the low group may have been able to identify correctly two of the "limitations" and therefore been drawn to answer 5. It is difficult to speculate about the line of thinking followed by the high group. The item obviously does not work well and should be rewritten or discarded.

Another point is raised by the data on Item 3. It was found that discrimination for this item was low, as was the difficulty index. In general, extremely difficult or extremely easy items will show very little discrimination.

An instructor will select items for the final or a future form of his test that have the highest discrimination indices and measure the desired outcomes of instruction.

Ebel (1965) suggests that items with discrimination indices below +.40 could benefit from rewriting, and that those below +.20 should be improved or discarded.

Examining Distractor Effectiveness

An *ideal* item, at least from a statistical item-analysis standpoint, is one that all students in the high group answer correctly and all students in the low group miss. In addition, the responses of the low group should be evenly distributed among the incorrect alternatives. Again, however, this rarely happens in practice. The situation illustrated by Item 4 is frequently encountered.

Item 4. The primary purpose of using a "table of specifications" in achievement test development is to:

* 1. help insure that each objective will be given the desired relative emphasis on the test.
2. show the students the content to be covered by the test.
3. translate statements of objectives from nonbehavioral, to behavioral terms.
4. translate ultimate into immediate objectives.
5. show the students what to study for.

Again referring to the item-analysis data in Table 11-1, it can be seen that, despite appropriate levels of difficulty and discrimination, the item can be improved. First, the responses of the low group are not evenly distributed among the incorrect alternatives. Also, answers 2 and 5 have a particularly low frequency of selection, and are therefore not contributing much to the item. In fact, they are making a negative contribution, because more members of the high group than the low group are selecting them. The low frequency of selection of 2 and 5 might be accounted for by their content. They are similar, and relative to the stem are implausible. They should be replaced or eliminated because they just take up reading time. Incidentally, there is nothing sacred about the practice of providing four or five alternative answers for all multiple-choice items. Tversky (1964), as we have noted previously, has shown mathematically that the use of three alternatives per item will maximize the discriminability, power, and information yielded per unit of time. This makes intuitive sense; we all know how hard it is to invent consistently "good" fourth and fifth distractors. They frequently turn out to be merely space fillers.

Limitations of Item Analysis

In addition to the limitations of small sample size and the possibility of reduced content validity, several other cautions should be noted.

Some experts suggest that internal item analyses should be completed only on tests that measure essentially the same mental functions. For a classroom achievement test, which generally deals with heterogeneous learning outcomes, item-analysis techniques like those described in this chapter should be considered crude devices for refining the test. If for no other reason, instructors should conduct an item analysis to force themselves to look critically at the measurements they are using to make important decisions about students.

The type of item, format, and reading level are among the many factors which can influence test and item difficulty. One should also be cautious about what damage may be due to the table of specifications when items not meeting minimum criteria are eliminated from the test. They must be replaced or rewritten.

Item-analysis techniques are less directly applicable to essay tests, although information related to mean performance on each item might have diagnostic significance for an instructor. In addition one could contrast the mean performance on an essay item for a "high achieving or scoring" group with that of a "low achieving or scoring" group to see if the item differentiates levels of performance.

The items on rating scales—either self-rating or observational—can also be subjected to item analysis procedures. Chapter 18 contains a description of how Likert summated rating items can be item-analyzed.

Another limitation of item-analysis data relates to its use in a diagnostic manner. It has been suggested that, by building a chart relating each student's response to each item, evaluations could be made of either individual or class strengths and weaknesses. One must be cautioned that such evaluations are based on limited information that may call into question the reliability of judgments. Even when items are grouped on the basis of content or outcome (comprehension, recall of knowledge, application, and the like), only a few samples of behavior are available for analysis. Chance could therefore play an important role, at least for individual analyses, in determining the consistency and validity of a performance on a given item. As we increase the number of samples of behavior, we also increase the likelihood that we can have confidence in the results. The problem of attempting to base diagnoses on limited item information is not peculiar to classroom tests and practices. Many commercial test publishers erroneously encourage their clientele to make specific subject-matter judgments on the basis of item data. Decisions like these should be based on many sources of data, which may include the results of a diagnostic test (see Chapter 14) developed specifically to aid in guiding remediation.

Selecting Items for Criterion-Referenced Measures

It will be noted in Chapter 16 that, since most criterion-referenced measures are used in conjunction with mastery learning and individualized instruction programs, difficulty is encountered in selecting the "best" items for a test. If everyone masters the material and the test items are tied very closely to specific objectives, nearly everyone should do well on all the items. Therefore, it might be reasonable to expect and select items at about the 80 percent level of item difficulty, if instruction has been effective. It is imperative that students who participate in the item analysis of measures for use in criterion-referenced situations *have already worked through the material* being tested. It might be advisable for the reader to refer to the suggestions by Cox and Vargas (1966) and Popham (1990) concerning some approaches to item selection for criterion-referenced measures. These approaches tend to rest on data derived from performances at different times (pre- to post-) or between groups (masters vs. nonmasters).

Finally, the instructor should be warned about being blinded by statistics. Item-analysis data suggest the kinds of learning that have taken place and the items that are in need of repair. The final decision about an item must be made by considering not only item-analysis data but also the content and structure of the item and the nature of the group being tested.

Developing an Item Data File

Teachers are encouraged to develop a file of test items. Recording items on 3″ × 5″ or 5″ × 8″ cards and accumulating data on their difficulty and discrimination over several administrators allows for the refinement and improvement of classroom tests. Such a file has the advantages of:

1. Encouraging the teacher to undertake an item analysis as often as is practical.
2. Allowing for accumulated data to be used to make item analyses more reliable.
3. Providing for a wider choice of item format and objectives—in other words, greater flexibility in test construction.
4. Facilitating the revision of items and suggesting ideas for new items.
5. Facilitating the relation of the test item and its objective to the table of specifications.
6. Facilitating the physical construction and reproduction of the test, because each item is on a separate card.
7. Accumulating a large enough pool of items to allow for some items to be shared with students for study purposes.

A test item file has the disadvantages of:

1. Requiring a great deal of clerical time.
2. Inhibiting creative test-construction efforts on the part of the teacher by allowing for access to ready-made items.
3. Providing the opportunity for the file of items to dictate the content of instruction.

These negative factors can influence a teacher's measurement practices, but the overall advantages on an item file certainly outweigh them.

A sample item-analysis data card suitable for objective items from classroom tests is presented in Table 11-2. Table 11-3 contains an item analysis card used in the 1988 standardization of the Eighth Edition of the *Stanford Achievement Test.* The item analyzed in Table 11-3 was considered a good one and was included in the final version of the test. The item meets an acceptable discrimination criterion

Table 11-2 Sample Item-Analysis Data Card

(Front)

Item No.: 37
Topic: Trade barriers
Level: Comprehension—Middle School
Cell: 14 **Objective:** 14

Reference: Klein's *Introduction to Economics,* rev. ed., 1992, pp. 201–214.

Item 3. A tariff may be defined as a tax on
1. imported goods.
2. money brought into the country.
3. exported goods.
4. imported cats and dogs.

(Back)

Item No.: 37

Test: Midterm
Class: 7th

	First Use		Second Use		Third Use	
Options	Upper Third	Lower Third	Upper Third	Lower Third	Upper Third	Lower Third
*1	15	8				
2	0	3				
3	3	3				
4	2	1				
5						
Omits	0	0				
Difficulty	58%					
Discrimination	.35					
Date	2/14/93					
Class Size	60					

Comments: Item discrimination and difficulty are good. Important objective is measured.

(in the form of biserial correlations). In addition the item shows an appropriate grade progression in the percentage of pupils answering it correctly (alternative "3").

This chapter has only hinted at the many potential uses of item-analysis data. Such data are particularly useful to a teacher in identifying instructional deficiencies in programs, for individual students, and for entire classes. Keep in mind, however, that a single test item in and of itself is quite unreliable and should be combined with other information.

Table 11-3 Sample Item Card for the National Item Tryout Program of the Eighth Edition of the *Stanford Achievement Test Series*

Item Code Number: J05121
Level: Primary 3
Subtest: Computation
Objective: Multiply a two digit number by a number less than 10, product less than 1000, presented in vertical form.
Item:

```
 64  o 364
×6   o 382
     o 384
     o 402
     o NH
```

Key: 3
Booklet Number: 44
Item Number: 34

Grade 3 $N = 747$
biserial correlation coefficient = .64

	Option Number					
	1	2	3*	4	5	Omit
Total	12	6	26*	9	43	5
Upper 23%	7	4	60*	4	24	1
Middle 54%	13	5	19*	10	48	5
Lower 23%	15	9	6*	10	50	9

Grade 4 $N = 736$
biserial correlation coefficient = .77

	Option Number					
	1	2	3*	4	5	Omit
Total	5	1	76*	2	12	3
Upper 23%	0	1	97*	1	2	1
Middle 54%	3	2	83*	1	9	1
Lower 23%	16	2	35*	5	31	10

Source: Reproduced from Preliminary Technical Report, *Stanford Achievement Test Series* (Eighth Edition), 1988. Reprinted by permission.

Computer/School-Based Item and Test Analysis

The availability of inexpensive software for personal, mini, and mainframe computers significantly facilitates the task of conducting an item analysis. Classroom teachers, schools, or systems can now conduct not only their own test administration programs but can score tests and complete test analyses (Nitko & Hsu, 1984). A teacher can efficiently create a test, gather responses on optical scanning forms, create class rosters with scores and summary statistics, and complete item test analyses. A comprehensive microcomputer system should have the capability to create a student data base, complete test and item analyses useful in making instructional decisions, and store items and assemble tests. Roid (1989) has reviewed 14 comprehensive systems currently commercially available.

There are obvious advantages and disadvantages to local test scoring and analysis. Thomas (1987) has identified some of these.

Advantages of Local Test/Item Processing

1. Quicker turnaround time
2. Reduced costs
3. Opportunity to create better match with curriculum
4. More up-to-date information for school or system evaluations
5. Flexibility in types of tests used
6. Easier to handle makeups
7. Adds another use for multipurpose micros
8. May facilitate sharing of information within and between schools, as well as with central office
9. Assists in development of local norms
10. Better control, therefore probably better accuracy
11. Provides opportunity for staff development with regard to measurement and testing issues and procedures

Disadvantages of Local Test/Item Processing

1. Staff training
2. Accountability for quality control
3. Maintenance of systems now rests on local personnel
4. Greater chance for test security problems
5. Need for some specialized personnel to deal with software and hardware problems

The advantages outweigh the fewer but important disadvantages. With proper hardware and software, school systems can duplicate the basic scoring services offered by commercial test publishers. It is even possible to use selected commercial tests under licensure agreements. To implement such a system requires leadership, and a motivated and committed staff.

Doing an item analysis of one's own tests can be a very revealing experience. Better to be revealed and improved than covered up and forgotten!

Case Study Application

The item data for the *first 21* items of the Reading Education midterm exam were summarized for the class of 18 students in Table 11-4. An analysis of item difficulty,

Table 11-4 Summary of Responses of 18 Students to 21 Items of Reading Education Midterm Test

Student	Total Score on 80 Item Midterm Exam	Item																				
		1	**2**	**3**	**4**	**5**	**6**	**7**	**8**	**9**	**10**	**11**	**12**	**13**	**14**	**15**	**16**	**17**	**18**	**19**	**20**	**21**
S_1	58	a	c	b	c	d	b	b	a	b	c	b	c	b	a	c	b	c	a	a	a	b
S_2	47	c	a	c	c	b	a	b	a	a	b	b	a	a	b	a	a	a	a	b	b	c
S_3	58	d	b	b	b	c	b	c	b	a	b	a	a	a	b	b	a	b	a	b	b	c
S_4	59	c	a	a	a	d	a	c	c	a	c	b	a	a	b	a	b	a	a	b	b	a
S_5	68	c	a	a	a	d	a	b	c	a	c	b	b	b	b	b	b	a	a	b	b	c
S_6	55	a	b	c	a	b	a	b	c	a	c	b	c	a	a	c	b	c	a	a	b	a
S_7	58	a	c	c	a	b	b	a	c	b	b	a	b	a	b	a	a	c	b	b	b	c
S_8	58	a	b	c	c	b	c	a	a	a	b	b	b	b	b	a	b	c	a	b	a	c
S_9	55	a	c	a	a	d	a	b	c	a	c	b	b	b	b	a	b	c	a	b	b	a
S_{10}	52	c	a	c	a	b	a	c	a	a	c	b	b	a	b	b	c	c	a	b	b	c
S_{11}	62	c	a	a	a	d	a	c	a	a	c	c	a	a	b	a	b	c	a	b	b	c
S_{12}	57	c	c	a	c	a	c	b	a	a	c	a	a	b	a	b	b	a	b	a	b	a
S_{13}	62	c	c	a	a	d	a	b	c	a	c	b	a	b	b	c	b	c	a	b	b	a
S_{14}	51	c	c	a	a	b	a	b	a	a	c	b	b	a	a	a	c	c	a	b	b	a
S_{15}	65	c	a	c	a	d	a	c	c	a	c	b	a	a	b	b	b	a	a	b	b	c
S_{16}	57	b	a	b	b	d	b	c	b	b	c	b	b	a	a	c	c	a	b	b	a	b
S_{17}	62	c	a	a	a	d	a	c	c	a	c	b	b	b	b	b	b	c	a	b	b	c
S_{18}	52	a	c	c	a	d	a	b	a	a	c	b	a	a	b	a	a	c	a	b	b	c

item discrimination (the relationship of each item with the total score on the test), and distractor effectiveness of the multiple-choice items should be undertaken. Table 11-4 is a summary of (a) the total scores of each student on the total 80-item test, and (b) responses to the first 21 sample items presented at the end of Chapter 7. These are real data. Your task, if you agree to do it, is to complete an item analysis of the sample 21 items using the High-Low method with one-third of the scores in each group. Following is the scoring key for the 21 items:

1. c	8. c	15. c
2. a	9. a	16. b
3. a	10. c	17. a
4. a	11. b	18. a
5. d	12. a	19. b
6. a	13. a	20. b
7. c	14. b	21. a

In determining which students are in the *high* and *low* groups the reader should refer back to the frequency distribution created at the end of Chapter 10. Be sure to review the item-analysis method and format described in this chapter.

Content Review Statements

1. Item-analysis techniques are among the most powerful tools a teacher can use to improve the quality of classroom tests.
2. Item analyses are undertaken to select the best items, identify faulty items, and detect individual or class learning difficulties.
3. Item analysis generally involves an examination of item difficulty, item discrimination, and, if multiple-choice items are used, distractor effectiveness.
4. Item difficulty (p) can be indexed by the proportion of examinees who respond correctly or in a particular direction.
5. Item difficulty can be estimated from the proportion (or percentage) of the combined high-scoring and low-scoring thirds of the total distribution of scorers responding correctly to the item.
6. Item difficulties will range from 0 to 100 percent.
7. Item discrimination (D) can be indexed by subtracting the number of low-scoring students (the lower one-third of the total score distribution) from the number of high-scoring students (the upper one-third), and dividing the difference by the number that represents one-third of the total group.
8. The range of D is from -1.00 to .00 to $+1.00$.
9. To examine distractor effectiveness for multiple-choice items, the responses to each alternative for the high and low groups are inspected separately.
10. Item-difficulty values should generally fall in the range from 30 percent to 70 percent if the intent is to maximize the measured differences between individuals.
11. Item-discrimination values should be as large as possible if the intent is to maximize the measured differences between individuals.
12. In general, the greater the number of items with high discrimination values the higher the internal-consistency reliability of the test.
13. Items with extremely high or low difficulty indices should be examined closely for possible structural or content defects or ambiguity.
14. Examining the mean scores on individual essay items separately for high- and low-scoring students can provide useful information on discrimination.
15. Plotting the responses of each student to each item in terms of correctness (+ = right, − = wrong) can help identify individual student or class strengths and weaknesses.
16. If criterion-referenced measures are used, items with higher difficulty values are likely to be found.
17. The concept of within-group item discrimination has less value in the criterion-referenced use of tests.
18. If items are eliminated from a test because of poor difficulty or discrimination indices, they should be replaced with other items measuring the same objectives.
19. Developing an item file will assist the teacher in refining test items and provide considerable flexibility in test development.

20. Items in the middle range of difficulty tend to yield better discrimination indices.
21. The best criterion-referenced items tend to be those that show an increase in percentage passing as a function of instruction (pre- to post-) as those that discriminate proficient students from less proficient students.

Speculations

1. What are the purposes for doing an item analysis?
2. Discuss the concepts of test and item difficulty and discrimination.
3. How are the methods for selecting items for criterion-referenced tests different from those used to select items for norm-referenced tests?
4. What are the characteristics of good alternative answers on a multiple-choice test item?
5. How are "discrimination" and "bias" different?

Suggested Readings

Carey, L. M. (1988). *Measuring and evaluating school learning*. Boston: Allyn and Bacon. Chapter 10 of this well-written text, "Performing a Test Item Analysis," emphasizes instructional improvement through item analysis.

Henryssen, S. (1970). Gathering, analyzing, and using data on test items. In R. L. Thorndike (Ed.), *Educational measurement* (2nd Edition). Washington, DC: American Council on Education. Chapter 5 is a comprehensive overview of practical and technical issues for the intermediate student.

Katz, M. (1961). Improving classroom tests by means of item analysis. *Clearing House, 35*, 265–269. Presents detailed instructions for a useful method of analyzing classroom achievement test items.

Lange, A., Lehmann, I. J., and Mehrens, W. A. (1967). Using item analysis to improve tests. *Journal of Educational Measurement, 4*, 65–68. The procedures outlined in this chapter are illustrated in this brief article.

Sax, G. (1989). *Principles of educational psychological measurement and evaluation* (3rd Edition). Belmont, CA: Wadsworth. Chapter 8 relates item data to norm- and criterion-referenced measures, item response theory, and the purposes of testing.

Chapter 12

Defining and Assessing Reliability

The Concepts of Errors in Measurement
Defining Reliability
Classical Reliability Test Theory
Methods of Assessing Reliability
Factors Influencing the Interpretation of Reliability
Reliability of Criterion-Referenced Mastery Tests
Case Study Application
Content Review Statements
Speculations
Suggested Readings

We have thus far considered some of the basic steps in developing a test. The learning outcomes to be measured have been identified, data-gathering procedures specified, items written and analyzed, the instrument administered, and scores summarized. It is time now to step back and examine how well the job has been accomplished. We must seek answers to the questions "Does the test measure what I want it to measure?" and "Does the test measure consistently?" The former question relates to *validity* and the latter to *reliability*. Most test experts consider reliability an aspect of validity. They also say you cannot have validity without reliability. Problems relating to (a) the definitions, (b) the methods of estimating, and (c) the factors influencing reliability are considered in this chapter, and those related to questions of validity are addressed in Chapter 13. Although our discussion of these two highly important test characteristics will be aimed at the individual who is actually engaged in test development, any individual involved in selecting, administering, and interpreting tests must be thoroughly familiar with these concepts in order to make intelligent and meaningful use of test results.

The Concepts of Errors in Measurement

Most tests developed by behavioral scientists yield quantitative descriptions of individuals. In general, we are less concerned with the scores themselves than with what they represent and the characterizations they provide.

Our testing hopes, however, are rarely completely realized. For example, if we administer a test today, wait three weeks, and administer it again, it is highly unlikely that an individual would obtain the same score on both occasions. Another example is a situation in which we are interested in predicting how well a particular high-school student will perform in college. We have results from a scholastic aptitude test and we know how scores on it relate to grades during the first semester of the freshman year. On the basis of a test score we predict a C average, only to find that our student achieves a B average. Errors are obviously involved in both situations—errors in measuring and errors in estimating (or predicting).

It is noted in Chapter 10 that two statistical indices useful in describing the variability of a set of scores are the standard deviation and the square of the standard deviation, the variance. What contributes to these indices of variation? Obviously, and hopefully, the primary contributors are true individual differences in the trait or skill measured by the test. Such factors as reading ability, memory, the physical condition of the examinee or testing room, and the form of the item may also differentially affect the individuals taking the test, causing their scores to be higher or lower than they should be. These factors, since they do not represent what we want to measure, must be considered as errors. Some kinds of errors are more important than others. Guessing on a difficult test and the subjectivity sometimes encountered in evaluating essay questions can be the source of very significant errors. The physical condition of the examinee and testing environment (within reasonable limits) do not represent sources of error that are likely to seriously distort the meaning of the scores. Whether a factor is a serious or less serious error will depend on the intent in developing and using the test. For example, psychological change in an individual over time is not likely to be a serious error in assessing the equivalence of two forms of the same test; however, changes from the junior year in high school until the end of the freshman year in college could prove to be a serious source of error in predicting achievement from an academic ability test.

Errors may be meaningfully categorized as *unsystematic* or *systematic*. Unsystematic sources of variation are those factors whose effects are orderless, show no consistent pattern, and fluctuate from one testing occasion to the next. Perhaps the purest form of unsystematic error would be guessing or inconsistent ratings of essays. It changes from item to item, test to test, and examinee to examinee. Motivation to perform well on an achievement test, for example, could differentially influence individuals on the same or different occasions. In addition, such factors as variation in attention to the test task and guessing could act as unsystematic sources of error. Systematic effects are those whose influences are the same for an individual on different testing occasions, or for all examinees on the same occasion. If, for example, the test administrator does not rigidly adhere to the time limits specified in the directions for a speeded test and allows every examinee an extra five minutes, scores would be spuriously inflated. The extra time influences the scores in a way that, although constant in the situation, changes the meaning of the scores. Such factors as learning, training, forgetting, fatigue, and growth can function as systematic sources of errors, in some cases increasing and in others decreasing the scores that would have resulted under error-free conditions. One of the limitations of the systematic vs. unsystematic classification is that it is not mutually exclusive. In other words, a given factor, for example, the physical condition of the testing room or anxiety, may be systematic in one situation (e.g., the exposure of all examinees to the same poor lighting conditions) and unsystematic in another (e.g., different testing room in a test-retest situation).

On the one hand, the problems associated with controlling and assessing the effects of unsystematic errors are problems of determining reliability. On the other hand, the use of a variety of experimental procedures to determine the extent to which a test is affected by constant errors reflects on the validity of a test (see Chapter 13).

Defining Reliability

We have noted that the influence of unsystematic errors in measurement is the problem with which the determination of reliability is concerned. In fact, we will define the reliability of a test as the degree to which the test and its scores reflect true or nonerror variance. In other words, we may define the reliability of a test and its scores as the degree to which they are influenced by unsystematic factors. That's kind of a fancy way of saying that if a test has reliability it should produce *consistent* results. Reliability will be represented symbolically as r_{tt}. In a real sense this symbolizes the correlation of the test with itself.

One need only reflect briefly on possible sources of variability to realize the tremendous variety of factors that may influence test scores. It's sometimes scary to think about all the things that can go wrong. Some sense of this variety can be gained from a brief examination of Table 12-1. Part of the variance within a set of scores can be attributed to lasting and general traits (Category I of Table 12-1). Almost any test performance will depend on such general characteristics, which are persistent for most individuals. They are clearly systematic, and should be treated as such in any sequence of operations designed to estimate reliability. Classical test theorists consider systematic factors as being "true" characteristics of the individual. Categories II, III, and IV may be considered true or error variance, depending upon the reliability-estimating technique. Category V will always be considered as error variance.

It is interesting to note that a national committee of testing experts has concluded that "the estimation of clearly labeled components of error variance is the most informative outcome of a reliability study, both for the test developer wishing to improve the reliability of his instrument and for the user desiring to interpret test scores with maximum understanding. The analysis of error variance calls for the use

Table 12-1 Possible Sources of Variance in Performance on a Particular Test

I. *Lasting and general characteristics of the individual*
   A. Level of ability on one or more general traits, which operate in a number of tests
   B. General skills and techniques of taking tests
   C. General ability to comprehend instructions

II. *Lasting but specific characteristics of the individual*
   A. Specific to the test as a whole (and to parallel forms of it)
      1. Individual level of ability on traits required in this test but not in others
      2. Knowledges and skills specific to particular form of test items
   B. Specific to particular test items
      1. The "chance" element determining whether the individual does or does not know a particular fact (sampling variance in a finite number of items)

III. *Temporary but general characteristics of the individual* (factors affecting performance on many or all tests at a particular time)
   A. Health
   B. Fatigue
   C. Motivation
   D. Emotional strain
   E. General test-wiseness (partly lasting)
   F. Understanding of mechanics of testing
   G. External conditions of heat, light, ventilation, etc.

IV. *Temporary and specific characteristics of the individual*
   A. Specific to a test as a whole
      1. Comprehension of the specific test task (insofar as this is distinct from IB)
      2. Specific tricks or techniques of dealing with the particular test materials (insofar as this is distinct from IIA 2)
      3. Level of practice on the specific skills involved (especially in psychomotor tests)
      4. Momentary "set" for a particular test
   B. Specific to particular test items
      1. Fluctuations and idiosyncrasies of human memory
      2. Unpredictable fluctuations in attention or accuracy, superimposed upon the general level of performance characteristic of the individual

V. *Variance not otherwise accounted for (chance)*
   A. "Luck" in the selection of answers by "guessing"

Source: R. L. Thorndike, *Personnel selection.* New York: John Wiley and Sons, 1949, p. 73. Reprinted by permission of the publisher.

of appropriate experimental design" (American Psychological Association, American Educational Research Association, and National Council on Measurement in Education, 1985). Cronbach, Gleser, Nanda, and Rajaratnan (1972) and Brennan (1983) have explicated a theory labeled "generalizability" that adheres very closely to this conception of reliability.

Classical Reliability Test Theory

What follows is an attempt at an intuitive explanation of classical reliability theory. It was clarified and summarized by Gulliksen (1950) and has been augmented by many over the past several decades. Among the current theories are item-response or latent-trait theory which is based on a mathematical model of how test takers of differing ability respond to items, and generalizability theory which views examinee scores as samples from a universe of possible observations (Crocker & Algina, 1986). The logic of classical test theory, although not completely unambiguous, helps us to conceptualize the inferential process we call educational measurement.

We begin with the idea of a "true" score, that is, a score or observation which is free from error, particularly random error. When applying classical true score theory to the assessment of reliability, that error is of the unsystematic variety. The hypothetical true score for an individual might be conceived of as the mean of an infinite number of parallel forms of the same test or simply as the score on a random sample of items from a universe of items for a given individual. Hopefully, individual scores on a test contain a lot of that "true" score, that portion of the score that is unaffected by error. Therefore we can think of the score on a test in the following manner:

$$\text{Observed Score} = \text{True Score} + \text{Error}$$

or

$$X = T + E \quad \text{and} \quad T = X - E$$

The error component of our expression is sometimes positive and sometimes negative. It averages out to zero. We know that people differ from one another with regard to almost all characteristics be they cognitive, affective, or psychomotor. Therefore, we can conceive of a distribution of observed, true, and error scores for a group of examinees. Associated with that distribution then would be a certain amount of variability, such that

$$\text{Variance of Observed Scores} = \text{Variance of True Scores} + \text{Error Variance},$$

or

$$S_X^2 = S_T^2 + S_E^2 \quad \text{and} \quad S_T^2 = S_X^2 - S_E^2$$

Reliability (r_{tt}) is theoretically defined as the ratio of true and observed score variances

$$r_{tt} = \frac{S_T^2}{S_X^2}$$

Stated another way, reliability is that part of observed score variance which is true variance. In the foregoing formula if the ratio resulted in a .80, we could say that 80 percent of each observed score, on the average, was composed of true knowledge, ability, or whatever. But we don't know what the true component really is, so we have to estimate it. We can rewrite our reliability ratio subtracting for S_T^2 as follows

$$r_{tt} = \frac{S_X^2 - S_E^2}{S_X^2} \quad \text{or} \quad r_{tt} = 1 - \frac{S_E^2}{S_X^2}$$

We can estimate S_E^2 with a number of methods, for example, test-retest, equivalent forms, and so forth.

We might even try to describe reliability directly by simply computing it from scores. For example if we gave parallel forms of a test on two different occasions to the same group of examinees we could derive a difference score from the pairs of scores: d = (Time 1 score) − (Time 2 score). The standard deviation of these differences is sometimes referred to as the standard error of measurement. More about the standard error of measurement later in this chapter, but for now suffice it to say that the smaller it is the more consistent is the measurement.

By using different methodologies we can assess different contributors to or components of the observed and error scores.

Methods of Assessing Reliability

The two basic methodological considerations in assessing reliability are *time* and *content.* We can take samplings of test performance over time to check on stability reliability and over content by using different forms of the test to check on equivalence. The relationship between these two dimensions is seen in Figure 12-1. Because it is obviously more economical to estimate reliability from a single administration of a test there are a lot of formulas and "quickie" methods. Equivalence reliability is particularly important when we are making inferences about a student's performance on a "domain" of tasks.

Building two forms of a test also can be a revealing experience for test constructor/item writers as the process allows them to check on themselves as architects and builders. Stability reliability is important in examining criterion-related validity, particularly when we are concerned with predicting future performance criteria or behavior with the test. For some kinds of tests, for example, intelligence and personality, we are concerned with both equivalence and stability. Suffice it to say that reliability does limit validity sometimes mathematically, and sometimes conceptu-

TIME (Administration) \ CONTENT (Form)	Same	Different
One Administration	Internal Consistency (Split-Test, Kuder-Richardson)	Equivalence
Two Administrations	Stability	Equivalence and Stability

Figure 12-1

Relationship of time and content in assessing reliability

ally. We always consider the reliability of our primary measure, for example, the achievement test, but when we use it to predict future behavior or a score on another test or criterion, we also need to consider the reliability of the criterion. For example, it doesn't make much sense to try to predict success in first year college French if we don't have a reliable (or valid for that matter) measure of that language competency.

Let's use this information about test theory and type of application in outlining some specific procedures that can be applied in estimating reliability. Reliability changes every time a test is used whether with the same or different examinees. But we can make some very good estimates of what the reliability will be based on what it was.

Reliability Determined from Repetition of the Same Test

This technique simply involves administering the same form of a test to the same examinees on two or more occasions and correlating the scores. There is usually a significant delay between administrations. Since the same form of the test is used on both occasions, lasting-general and lasting-specific factors are considered true variance, and temporary-general and temporary-specific are considered error. This method has the advantage of requiring only one form of a test, and the distinct disadvantage of being significantly influenced by practice and memory. In addition, the test-retest method may cause an interaction between the test and examinee, particularly when used with personality inventories. Having taken the inventory once may have caused him to introspect, which might result in significant score changes the second time the inventory is administered. Some testing experts claim that the test-retest method is an estimate of the reliability *not* of the instrument but of the examinee. It must nevertheless be conceded that such information is useful within a specific testing situation. One could not expect, for example, to estimate future behavior if scores on the prediction test did not hold up over time.

Reliability Determined from Equivalent Forms of a Test

In order to determine reliability in this way one must, of course, have two forms of the test. The items on each form must be parallel in terms of the content and the mental operation required to respond to the items. In developing equivalent forms, the test developer must begin with a complete and detailed set of specifications. Such a blueprint would ideally specify item type, difficulty level, content coverage, and the like. In a real sense the correlation of equivalent forms serves to monitor the consistency and ability of the item writer. More important, however, this correlation serves as a check on the sampling from the universe of behaviors in question. There is no particular reason to believe that any given set of 35 vocabulary items is superior or inferior to any other set. If we find a high degree of response consistency over forms of the test, however, we will have greater confidence in the sampling of items, that is, greater confidence that the samples of items accurately represent the universe from which they were drawn.

Application of this reliability-estimating procedure merely involves administering two forms of the same test to the same group, and correlating the scores. Referring to Table 12-1, we can see that the variances considered true or error depend upon the interval between testings. Categories I and IIA will be treated as systematic (or true) variation. Categories IIB and IVB, in addition to V, will be treated as unsystematic or error. Categories III and IVA will be treated as true if the retesting is immediate, for example, same day, and as error if there is a delay of several weeks or more between testings. The latter procedure is generally recommended.

Reliability Determined from Comparable Parts of a Test

Both reliability-estimating techniques described above require two test administrations of the measuring device. This can take considerable time and effort. Several methods have been devised to estimate reliability from a single administration of a test. Although practical, single-administration estimating procedures have the disadvantage of designating and treating the sources of variance in Categories III and IV of Table 12-1 as systematic, and therefore probably yield an inflated estimate of reliability as compared with equivalent forms. The procedures usually involve splitting a test in half and using information derived from the half-tests, in terms of either a correlation or variance, to estimate the reliability of the full-length test. The four bases used most frequently for splitting a test in half are (a) random halves, (b) top and bottom halves, (c) "equivalent" halves, and (d) odd and even halves. The last two methods are worthy of special consideration. The "equivalent halves" approach is probably the most desirable of the split-test procedures for estimating reliability. In a sense, it parallels the equivalent-forms method. The determination of equivalence requires that a matching of pairs of items be undertaken, guided by the original test blueprints or table of specifications. After the test is administered, a score for each of the equivalent halves is derived. A more efficient procedure that yields very similar results, at least for a teacher-made test, is the odd-even method. Here again, two scores are derived for each examinee, one from the odd-numbered

Table 12-2 Hypothetical Data Used in Estimating Reliability from the Single Administration of a Test

Student	Odd Items					Even Items					Odd Score	Even Score	Total Score
	1	3	5	7	9	2	4	6	8	10			
A	+	0	+	0	+	+	0	+	+	0	3	3	6
B	+	0	0	0	0	+	0	+	0	0	1	2	3
C	+	+	+	+	0	+	+	+	+	+	4	5	9
D	0	+	+	0	0	0	+	0	+	0	2	2	4
E	0	+	+	+	0	+	+	0	0	0	3	2	5
F	+	0	0	0	0	0	0	0	0	0	1	0	1
G	+	+	+	+	0	+	+	0	+	0	4	3	7
H	+	0	+	+	0	0	+	+	0	0	3	2	5
I	+	0	0	0	0	0	+	0	0	0	1	1	2
J	+	+	+	+	+	+	+	+	+	+	5	5	10
K	+	0	+	0	0	+	+	0	+	+	2	4	6
L	+	+	+	0	+	+	+	+	0	+	4	4	8
M	0	0	0	0	0	0	0	0	0	0	0	0	0
N	+	+	0	+	0	0	+	+	+	+	3	4	7
O	+	+	+	+	+	+	+	+	+	0	5	4	9
P	+	+	0	0	0	+	+	+	+	+	2	5	7
Q	+	+	+	0	0	+	+	0	0	0	3	2	5
R	+	0	0	+	0	+	0	+	0	0	2	2	4
S	+	0	0	0	+	+	0	0	0	0	2	1	3
T	0	0	0	0	0	+	0	0	0	0	0	1	1
U	+	+	0	+	+	+	+	+	0	0	4	3	7
V	+	+	0	0	0	+	+	+	0	0	2	3	5
W	0	+	0	0	0	+	0	0	0	0	1	1	2
X	+	+	0	0	+	+	0	+	0	+	3	3	6
Y	0	+	0	+	0	0	+	0	0	+	2	2	4
Nc	19	15	11	10	7	13	16	13	9	8			
p	.76	.60	.44	.40	.28	.72	.64	.52	.36	.32			
q	.24	.40	.56	.60	.72	.28	.36	.48	.64	.68			
pq	.18	.24	.25	.24	.20	.20	.23	.25	.23	.22			

$M_o = 2.48$ $\quad M_e = 2.56$ $\quad M_x = 5.04$ $\quad \Sigma pq = 2.24$

$S_o^2 = 1.85$ $\quad S_e^2 = 2.09$ $\quad S_x^2 = 6.84$

$S_o = 1.36$ $\quad S_e = 1.45$ $\quad S_x = 2.62$

items and one from the even. This procedure has been followed with sample data from a 10-item test administered to 25 students whose results are summarized in Table 12-2.

At this point the determination of reliability may take either of two directions. Let us look first at a correlational procedure for estimating reliability from half-test scores. We would first determine the Pearson product-movement or Spearman rank-order correlation between the scores on the odd and even halves of the test. (Readers may wish to refresh their memories about rank-order correlation by referring to Table 10-4.) For our example, the rank-order correlation was found to be .752. This correlation describes the relationship between scores on the halves of the test, but we are interested in the full-test reliability. We must, therefore, put the test like Humpty Dumpty back together again. Application of the Spearman-Brown formula allows us to estimate the full-length test reliability. The Spearman-Brown formula is a succint summary of the relationship of the number of items as a test and reliability. One can see that relationship in Figure 12-2. It can be seen that as the test is lengthened the reliability increases. The lower the initial reliability the greater the effect of lengthening the test. If the beginning reliability is good, for example, around .80, increasing length would not be necessary or probably practical. Other means to increase reliability are also available, for example, removing "bad" items (refer back to Chapter 11).

The general form of the Spearman-Brown formula is as follows:

$$r_u = \frac{nr}{1 + (n - 1)r} \qquad (12\text{-}1)$$

where

n = the number of times the test is to be lengthened,
r = the original test reliability or correlation

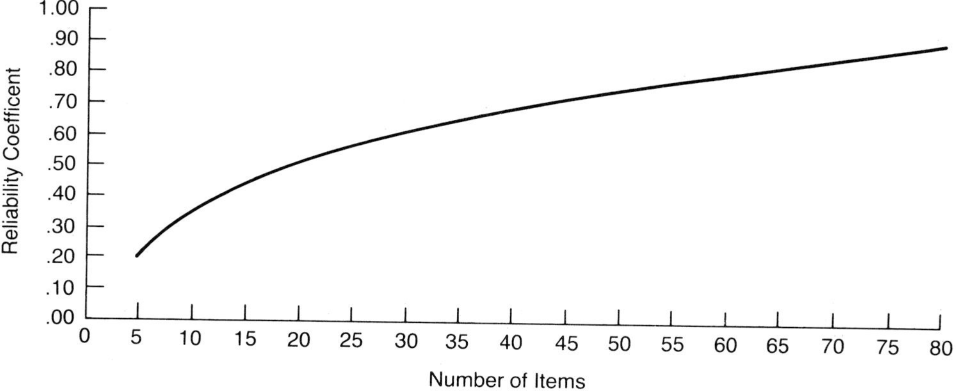

Figure 12-2

Relationship between test length and reliability

In our example, we are trying to determine the full-test reliability if the length of the test were doubled. Equation 12-1 could be written as follows:

$$r_{tt} = \frac{2r_{oe}}{1 + r_{oe}} \tag{12-2}$$

where

r_{oe} = the correlation between the odd and even halves of the test,
r_{oe} = .752

with

$$r_{tt} = \frac{2(.752)}{1 + (.752)} = \frac{1.504}{1.752} = .86$$

Obviously .86 is larger than .75. What does this tell us about what variable has a great influence on test reliability? Yes, the length or number of items on the test is a very important factor. Assuming that most reliability coefficients over .70 are within an acceptable range, our obtained estimate of .86 would allow us to use this hypothetical test with a relatively high degree of confidence. The Spearman-Brown formula could also be used to estimate the effect of reducing the length of the test—for example, if we had a 100-item test with a reliability of .90. Responding to a 100-item test takes a long time. What would be our best estimate of the reliability if we dropped back to 50 items? The symbol "n" in Equation 12.1 now becomes a decimal, in this case .50 as we are reducing the length of the test by 50 percent. Substituting in Equation 12-1 we would find that eliminating 50 items (being careful not to distort the content coverage) would yield a new reliability estimate of .82. Quite a saving in student testing time. The Spearman-Brown is only an estimate of what is likely to happen, but empirical research strongly supports its usefulness and accuracy.

As was noted, the Spearman-Brown formula—as expressed in Equations 12-1 and 12-2—really describes the effect of lengthening the test on reliability. Generally, as we increase the number of items we increase reliability. This assumes that the items added are equivalent to the original items in terms of functions measured, difficulty level, and the like. One additional assumption of Equation 12-2 is that the standard deviations of the two halves of the test are equal. Cronbach (1951) has shown that violation of this assumption will lead to an overestimate of reliability. Although the overestimation is not extremely large—not more than 5 percent when one variance is 50 percent as large as the other—some error is introduced. Because of this tendency to overestimate, the relative inefficiency of rank-order correlation procedures with large groups, and the need to use the Spearman-Brown formula, a more direct method of estimating reliability from the halves of a test is suggested.

The following calculating formula, first described by Flanagan (1937) should be used:

$$r_{tt} = 2\left(1 - \frac{S_o^2 + S_e^2}{S_x^2}\right) \tag{12-3}$$

where

S_o^2 and S_e^2 = the raw score variance on the odd and even halves of the test respectively,

and

S_x^2 = the variance of total test raw scores

Application of this formula to the data in Table 12-2 yields the following results:

$$r_{tt} = 2\left(1 - \frac{1.85 + 2.09}{6.84}\right) = .85$$

Our reliability estimate is almost identical to that derived by Equation 12-2, because the variances are not very discrepant. Equation 12-3 is really an estimate of the degree of equivalence between the two full-length tests, which are as similar as are the two halves of one test. It therefore represents for some test experts a very reasonable estimate of reliability. Equation 12-3 is useful not only because of the less restrictive assumptions underlying its use, but also because the variances involved in the formula may be estimated using the approximation formula of a standard deviation presented in Chapter 10 (see Equation 10-9 and Table 10-2). Another plus for this method is that it can be used with two test halves that have a mix of item types. For example, we might have taken our hypothetical final exam test and randomly divided it into two halves *each* of which contained a 15-point essay question, four 3-point problems, 20 multiple-choice, 10 true-false, and five completion items. We could calculate two half-test scores and use Equation 12-3.

Reliability Determined from Item Data

Intuition suggests that if one wants to determine whether or not the items in a test measure the same thing, one should examine item scores as well as examinee scores. A reliability-estimating procedure developed a long time ago by Kuder and Richardson (1937) does just this. The usual formula assumes, however, that the items in the test (a) are scored right or wrong, (b) are not significantly influenced by speed, and (c) measure a common factor. The last assumption is of critical importance when estimating the reliability of a classroom test. In many instances, such tests are not homogeneous with respect to content and/or learning outcome measured. Therefore, caution must be exercised in applying either of the two Kuder-Richardson formulas described below. The most frequently used Kuder-Richardson formula, number 20 (this is the same as Cronbach's Alpha, 1951, when items are scored dichotomously), can be expressed as follows:

$$r_{tt} = \left(\frac{k}{k-1}\right)\left(\frac{S_x^2 - \sum pq}{S_x^2}\right) \tag{12-4}$$

where

k = the number of items in the test
p = proportion of examinees answering item correctly (or the proportion responding in a specified direction)
q = $1 - p$
S_x^2 = the variance of the total test raw scores

Calculation of the term pq can be facilitated through the use of columns 1 and 3 of the table in Appendix A. The term p or q can be entered in column 1 and the term pq read directly from column 3. The term pq represents the variance of an item. It is assumed that items that measure the same thing will have fairly homogeneous difficulty levels and, therefore, variances. If items on a norm-referenced test all have difficulty levels of about 50 percent a test will tend to be maximally reliable. The use of the correction factor $(k/k - 1)$ we ask the reader to accept on faith. Note, however, that if we have a small number of items, say 10, the correction can be relatively large as compared to a situation in which we have 80 items. Applying Equation 12-4 to the hypothetical data in Table 12-2, we find that:

$$r_{tt} = \left(\frac{10}{10-1}\right)\left(\frac{6.84 - 2.24}{6.84}\right) = (1.11)(.67) = .74$$

This value is noticeably lower than any other we have seen thus far. The discrepancy might be attributed to overestimation by the other methods or underestimation by KR_{20} because of failure to meet assumptions. Inasmuch as KR_{20} is a very precise method, that is, it considers actual item variances, it will be the accepted value. Since the item variances of classroom tests tend to be relatively similar, we may be able to shortcut the actual calculation of the item variances. This can be done by using Kuder-Richardson formula Number 21. The use of this formula assumes that the items all have the same difficulty level. KR_{21} is written:

$$r_{tt} = \left(\frac{k}{k-1}\right)\left(1 - \frac{M(k-M)}{kS_x^2}\right) \tag{12-5}$$

where

k = the number of items on the test
M = the mean of the total test raw scores
S_x^2 = the variance of the total test raw scores.

Knowing only the number of items, mean, and variance (which can be approximated from Equation 10-9), we can calculate a reasonably precise estimate of reliability. Again using the data in Table 10-2 we find that:

$$r_{tt} = \left(\frac{10}{10 - 1}\right)\left(1 - \frac{5.04(10 - 5.04)}{10(6.84)}\right) = .70$$

This reliability estimate, although close, is less than that derived from Equation 12-4 (KR_{20}). Such will be the case unless all of the items in the test are of the same difficulty level.

Saupe (1951) has derived some very efficient estimates of KR_{20} reliability. One of these, which he labels R_{20}', can be expressed as follows:

$$R_{20}' = \left(\frac{k}{k - 1}\right)\left(1 - \frac{.20k}{S_x^2}\right) = .79 \qquad (12\text{-}6)$$

Now all we need to know is the number of items and variance and we can estimate reliability with a high degree of efficiency and accuracy—if the number of items and the variance are reasonably large. This brief formula yields an estimate of reliability very close to those made above:

$$R_{20}' = \left(\frac{10}{10 - 1}\right)\left(1 - \frac{.20(10)}{6.84}\right) = .79$$

Cureton, Cook, Fischer, Laser, Rockwell, and Simmons (1973) have provided another method of estimating internal consistency reliability that is useful to the classroom teacher. Their formula reads as follows:

$$r_{tt} = 1 - .043k\left(\frac{N}{\sum X_{U1/6} - \sum X_{L1/6}}\right)^2 \qquad (12\text{-}7)$$

where

k = total number of dichotomously scored items on test
N = total number of subjects about whom we have data

$\Sigma X_{U1/6}$ = the sum of the total scores for individuals in the upper one-sixth of the distribution

$\Sigma X_{L1/6}$ = the sum of the total scores for individuals in the lower one-sixth of the distribution.

The reader will recall that use was made of the terms $\Sigma X_{U1/6}$ and $\Sigma X_{L1/6}$ in estimating standard deviation in Chapter 10.

Using the data in Table 12-2, we find that Equation 12-7 gives us an estimate close to the others we have calculated:

$$r_{tt} = 1 - .043(10)\left(\frac{20}{36 - 6}\right)^2 = .81$$

One-sixth of N is 3.3, but because this is too few individuals upon which to base an estimate we rounded to 4.

Faced with all these formulas, which one should a teacher select to analyze his or her tests? Since most of the formulas presented in this section on reliability have been shown by the author (Payne, 1963) to yield highly similar results, the decision will probably be based on familiarity with the formulas, computational ease, form of the data, or nature of the test. Taking all these factors into account, we recommend Flanagan's formula (Equation 12-3). It has the advantages of relative ease of calculation and the fact that items need *not* be scored right or wrong to justify its use, that is, you can use it with rating scales and essay items, or combinations of items with different point values.

Factors Influencing the Interpretation of Reliability

Actually we can interpret a reliability coefficient at face value. We could get fancy and go back to Table 12-1 and use a variance components analysis, but that's a little heavy for classroom application. Using our true and error ratio model we might say that a reliability coefficient of .80 can be loosely interpreted as meaning that 80 percent of a given score represents true "something," that "something" is a question of validity. The other 20 percent is error. What kind of error depends on the method of reliability estimation? If a teacher creates a test with reliability of .45 should it be thrown out? No! It can be added to other measures, thereby probably making the total quite reliable. We can also throw out some of the bad items on the basis of item analysis (Chapter 11) and improve reliability.

In addition to the intrinsic factors already identified as influencing test or criterion reliability, especially test length, two additional factors need to be considered: group heterogeneity and speededness.

The Influence of Variability on Reliability

Heterogeneity refers to the range of talent or individual differences represented in the group with which reliability study is undertaken. It is logical that if a standard deviation is small we will not be able to discriminate reliably among members of a homogeneous group. We have described reliability in terms of the influence of error. Assume a specified amount of unsystematic error, and assume further that with error constant we find that Group A has a large standard deviation and Group B a small standard deviation. If we estimate reliability by correlating two forms of a test, we would find that Group A has the larger reliability coefficient, while the amount of error is the same for both groups. Another example would be the selection for a job of only the top 20 percent of applicants based on a test score and the correlation of these scores with some job proficiency criterion (e.g., supervisor's ratings). The resulting validity coefficient would, of necessity, be low because of the restricted range of individual differences represented in the group. We need a method for expressing the reliability of a test independent of variability. This can be accomplished by using the *standard error of measurement* (S_{em}):

$$S_{em} = S_x \sqrt{1 - r_{tt}} \qquad (12\text{-}8)$$

The standard error of measurement theoretically represents an estimate of the standard deviation of the (unsystematic) errors obtained in repeated sampling with parallel forms of a test with the same subjects. In addition to serving as an index of reliability independent of group variability, the S_{em} may be used to assist in interpreting test scores. The individual's score may then be conceived of as a band or interval rather than a point. A frequently used procedure is to establish "reasonable limits" (plus and minus), corresponding to two or three times the S_{em}, around an observed score. Let us consider a practical situation in which the use of the standard error of measurement can facilitate decision making with a test. As a college admissions officer, you have required all applicants to take the Great Aptitude Test. You intend to select the freshman class, other things being equal, from the top half of the ability distribution. The "cutoff score" corresponds to a score of 70. Karen has a score of 65. On the basis of her academic record and recommendations, she appears to be someone who could greatly benefit from a college education. Because her test score did not equal or exceed the cutoff score, should she be rejected? No! We know that tests are fallible, that is, not perfectly accurate. Some errors of measurement are always present, and these errors sometimes cause scores to be higher or lower than they should be. We need to take into consideration, then, the error of measurement in interpreting Karen's score. We might ask, "Is it possible that Karen's *true* score is higher than the cutoff point on the admissions test?" Such a question assumes that an observed test score is composed of some true ability plus some error. Our task is to specify and evaluate the error component of the test score. Let us assume that our Great Aptitude Test has a standard deviation of 20 and a reliability of .75. Using Equation 12-8, we find that S_{em} is equal to 10. If we establish reasonable

Table 12-3 Standard Errors of Measurement for Given Values of Reliability Coefficient and Standard Deviation

	Reliability Coefficient					
SD	.95	.90	.85	.80	.75	.70
30	6.7	9.5	11.6	13.4	15.0	16.4
28	6.3	8.9	10.8	12.5	14.0	15.3
26	5.8	8.2	10.1	11.6	13.0	14.2
24	5.4	7.6	9.3	10.7	12.0	13.1
22	4.9	7.0	8.5	9.8	11.0	12.0
20	4.5	6.3	7.7	8.9	10.0	11.0
18	4.0	5.7	7.0	8.0	9.0	9.9
16	3.6	5.1	6.2	7.2	8.0	8.8
14	3.1	4.4	5.4	6.3	7.0	7.7
12	2.7	3.8	4.6	5.4	6.0	6.6
10	2.2	3.2	3.9	4.5	5.0	5.6
8	1.8	2.5	3.1	3.6	4.0	4.4
6	1.3	1.9	2.3	2.7	3.0	3.3
4	.9	1.3	1.5	1.8	2.0	2.2
2	.4	.6	.8	.9	1.0	1.1

Source: *Test Service Bulletin* 50 (1956). Published by the Psychological Corporation, San Antonio, TX.

limits of $1S_{em}$ around her observed score (65 plus and minus 10), we note that it would be quite possible for Karen to obtain a score above the cutoff score if tested again. We are, therefore, justified in including Karen in the pool of applicants from which we wish to select the freshman class. A useful reference is presented in Table 12-3. This table, from an article by Ricks (1956), presents the standard errors of measurement (Equation 12-8) for selected combinations of standard deviation values and reliability coefficients. For most purposes it will be sufficiently accurate if the table is entered with values nearest the actual ones.

The standard error of measurement is useful not only in describing measurement consistency, but also in interpreting different scores for the same individual or different tests, or for different individuals on the same test (see the section in Chapter 15 on profile interpretation).

The Effect of Speededness on Reliability

It was noted that one of the bases that might be used to classify a test is the extent to which speed influences scores. At one extreme are pure speed tests, whose items are easy and all of approximately equal difficulty. At the other extreme are power tests. The items in a power test are generally arranged in increasing order of difficulty. Perfect scores on power tests are unlikely even with the most generous time limits. The selection of a reliability-estimating technique will be influenced by the extent to which speed affects the scores. A test user or developer must first decide whether he wants speed of response to have a significant influence on the scores, and then select an appropriate reliability-estimating technique with a pure speed test. The maximum difference between the odd and even scores would be one, assuming that if an item is attempted it will be answered correctly. The half-test scores would obviously be highly correlated and an overestimated reliability would result. The appropriate procedure would be to use equivalent forms, or perhaps separately timed halves.

Reliability of Criterion-Referenced Mastery Tests

Criterion-referenced or mastery tests (see Chapter 16) are different than the usual objectives-based test in that success is usually defined in terms of whether or not a student met a particular performance standard (or criterion) or not. The decision is usually absolute, pass/fail, graduate/not graduate, promoted/not promoted, or simply met cutoff score or did not meet cutoff score.

The methods available to assess the reliability of such tests are cumbersome and require computer hardware and complex software. Subkoviak (1988) has created an efficient method of estimating the classification consistency (master or nonmaster) based on a single test administration. He uses coefficient *Kappa* (K) to represent this index of consistency (Cohen, 1960).

Consider the data in the following 2 × 2 table:

		Administration Two or Half Two (Even): Master	Administration Two or Half Two (Even): Nonmaster	
Administration One or Half One (Odd)	Master	a	b	$(a + b)$
	Nonmaster	c	d	$(c + d)$
		$(a + c)$	$(b + d)$	N

The letters in the cells represent the frequency of people so classified.

The consistency of classification (A) is simply the proportion of examinees classified the same way on two administrations (see Equation 12-9).

$$A = a + d/N \tag{12-9}$$

It was noted earlier that reliability based on two administrations or forms could be approximated by two halves of the test. If we look back at our table we can think of it now not as administration one and two, but as Half One and Half Two. To be classified as a master or nonmaster there has to be a criterion, for example, must get 80 percent correct. In our half-test example to be consistently classified as a master a student would have had to gather 80 percent on Half One and 80 percent on Half Two. The halves could be equivalent or odd-even splits. The proportion $A = a + d/N$ is descriptively useful, but in order to interpret it we would need to know how many agreements might have arisen by chance. Chance agreements could be determined as follows:

$$A_{\text{chance}} = [(a+b)(a+c) + (c+d)(b+d)]/N^2 \tag{12-10}$$

Combining the two ideas, proportion of agreements and chance gives us coefficient Kappa (Cohen, 1960):

$$K = (A - A_{\text{chance}})(1 - A_{\text{chance}}) \tag{12-11}$$

What does Kappa tell us? It describes the gain in classification consistency we have realized by using the test. It is a ratio of the actual gain to the maximum gain, or the gain in consistency yielded by using the test expressed as a percentage of the maximum possible.

Let's look at an example. But first we have to have a criterion. Using the data of Table 12-2 we will be generous and say that mastery equates to 60 percent (3 of 5 correct). A student must get 60 percent on *both* halves of the test to get into cell "a," and less than 60 percent on *both* halves to get into cell "d." Classifying all 25 students in Table 12-2 yields the following results:

	Mastery Classification				*Mastery Classification*		
Student	*Odd*	*Even*	*Cell*	*Student*	*Odd*	*Even*	*Cell*
A	Y	Y	a	N	Y	Y	a
B	N	N	d	O	Y	Y	a
C	Y	Y	a	P	N	Y	c
D	N	N	d	Q	Y	N	b
E	Y	N	b	R	N	N	d
F	N	N	d	S	N	N	d
G	Y	Y	a	T	N	N	d
H	Y	N	b	U	Y	Y	a
I	N	N	d	V	N	Y	c
J	Y	Y	a	W	N	N	d
K	N	Y	c	X	Y	Y	a
L	Y	Y	a	Y	N	N	d
M	N	N	d				

Summarizing our classifications we find

		Even Half: Master	Even Half: Nonmaster	
Odd Half	Master	9	3	12
	Nonmaster	3	10	13
		12	13	25

The proportion of agreements (Equation 12-9) A = 19/25 = .76. That's not too bad, but how does it compare with what we would expect on the basis of chance? The proportion of chance agreement classifications (Equation 12-10) would be:

$$A_{\text{chance}} = [(12)(12) + (13)(13)]/N^2 = 306/625 = .49$$

Therefore Kappa would be:

$$K = (.76 - .49)/(1 - .49) = .27/.51 = .53$$

Is that good, bad, or neutral? Subkoviak notes that Kappa ranges from 1.00 to .00. We have a 53 percent gain in classification consistency by using the test. Subkoviak suggests that for classroom measurement application, for example, the use of a single full period test of minimal reliability (r_{tt} = .70), one can reasonably expect Kappas in the range .35–.50. The higher the better. All other things being equal, the more restrictive (the fewer masters) the cutoff score, and the higher the reliability of the test, the better gain in using the test for classification purposes. Tests being used to make important decisions (e.g., promotion) should yield Kappas above .70.

This is a lot of work. Fortunately there are tables that allow us to approximate (again thanks to Subkoviak, 1988) Kappa based only on knowledge about (a) the cutoff score in raw numbers, (b) the test mean, (c) the test standard deviation, and (d) the reliability of the test. We would ordinarily calculate all of the statistics b–d for each test we give anyway. Right? The approximations (really no need to interpolate, round to nearest tabled entry value) are contained in Table 12-4. Note we need a reliability estimate. We could use Equations 12-1, 12-3, 12-5 and 12-6 or 12-7 if we are in a hurry. Equation 12-4 gave us a value of .74 for the data of Table 12-2. Next we need a standard score (z) which reflects the mastery/nonmastery cutoff score. Equation 12-12 will give us that standard score.

$$z = \frac{(X_c - .5 - M_x)}{S_x} \tag{12-12}$$

where

X_c = is the raw cutoff score
.5 = a constant used because a discrete distribution

has been approximated from a continuum. Get it? You had to know!

M_x = raw score mean (total test)

S_x = raw score standard deviation/which can be approximated with Equation 10-9

For the data of Table 12-2, z works out to be

$$z = \frac{(6 - .5 - 5.04)}{2.62} = .18$$

Using Table 12-4, we find Kappa to be .49 which is very close to our calculated value of .53.

The concept of reliability is of paramount importance in educational and psychological measurement. If the analysis of a test does not reveal an acceptable amount, we cannot have confidence in the use of the test to evaluate and make decisions about students.

Table 12-4 Approximate Values of the Kappa Coefficient

z	.10*	.20	.30	.40	.50	.60	.70	.80	.90
.00	.06	.13	.19	.26	.33	.41	.49	.59.	.71
.10	.06	.13	.19	.26	.33	.41	.49	.59	.71
.20	.06	.13	.19	.26	.33	.41	.49	.59	.71
.30	.06	.12	.19	.26	.33	.40	.49	.59	.71
.40	.06	.12	.19	.25	.32	.40	.48	.58	.71
.50	.06	.12	.18	.25	.32	.40	.48	.58	.70
.60	.06	.12	.18	.24	.31	.39	.47	.57	.70
.70	.05	.11	.17	.24	.31	.38	.47	.57	.70
.80	.05	.11	.17	.23	.30	.37	.46	.56	.69
.90	.05	.10	.16	.22	.29	.36	.45	.55	.68
1.00	.05	.10	.15	.21	.28	.35	.44	.54	.68
1.10	.04	.09	.14	.20	.27	.34	.43	.53	.67
1.20	.04	.08	.14	.19	.26	.33	.42	.52	.66
1.30	.04	.08	.13	.18	.25	.32	.41	.51	.65
1.40	.03	.07	.12	.17	.23	.31	.39	.50	.64
1.50	.03	.07	.11	.16	.22	.29	.38	.49	.63
1.60	.03	.06	.10	.15	.21	.28	.37	.47	.62
1.70	.02	.05	.09	.14	.20	.27	.35	.46	.61
1.80	.02	.05	.08	.13	.18	.25	.34	.45	.60
1.90	.02	.04	.08	.12	.17	.24	.32	.43	.59
2.00	.02	.04	.07	.11	.16	.22	.31	.42	.58

*Estimated reliabilities (.10 – .90)

Case Study Application

We have now progressed from objectives to a table of specifications to item construction to administration and data summary, and finally through item analysis. We next need to assess the reliability of the Reading Education Midterm Exam before we can have any confidence in using the results. Since a reliability estimate based on multiple administrations of our midterm is not practical, the focus must be on one of the single administration internal consistency estimating methods. Kuder-Richardson formula 20 is the most accurate and frequently reported index of internal consistency. It will be used in this exercise. Refer back to the item data contained in Table 11-4 in the Case Study Application of Chapter 11. Let us assume that these 21 items represent an intact test. Use the data from *all* 18 examinees for these 21 items to calculate KR_{20} (Equation 12-4). In addition, for fun and comparative purposes, also calculate KR_{21} (Equation 12-5). Hint: You will obviously have to score the 21-item test for each student; therefore, refer back to the beginning of the Chapter 11 Case Study Application for the scoring key. In that same regard you also will need the p (difficulty) values generated for those items 21 in the Case Study for Chapter 11.

To make life a little more interesting and challenging calculate Kappa (Equation 12-11). And if you're really motivated try the Kappa approximation using Table 12-4. For both of these we must treat the test as a criterion-referenced measure. Use the arbitrary criterion of 65 percent correct for each half of the test. This should round to seven items correct for each half.

Now for the ultimate measure of total commitment to the exploration of single administration test reliability alternatives. Use the split-test data just identified for the Kappa analysis and apply Equations 12-2, 12-3, 12-6, and 12-7. When all the data have been collected try your hand at an interpretive synthesis of these coefficients.

Content Review Statements

1. Educational and psychological tests must always be considered fallible measuring instruments due to the influence of many kinds of errors, primarily involving sampling of behaviors, examinee instability, and scoring.
2. Unsystematic errors, for example, guessing, fluctuate both within and between testing situations and primarily tend to reduce test reliability.
3. Systematic errors—for example, the extension of test administration time, yielding inflated scores—are consistent and primarily tend to affect test validity.
4. Test reliability generally involves consistency in measurement with different sets of items, examinees, examiners, occasions, or scorers.
5. In general, if a test is valid it is also reliable; however, the converse is not always true.
6. Test-retest reliability requires administering the same test on two different occasions and correlating the results.
7. Equivalent-forms reliability is established by correlating scores on two forms of a test constructed from the same table of specifications.
8. Internal-consistency reliability can be estimated by correlating the scores on two halves

of a test and applying the Spearman-Brown formula, one of the Kuder-Richardson formulas, or one of a number of other estimating formulas.

9. Length, objectivity, and the mental functions measured are three factors that significantly influence test reliability.
10. Kuder-Richardson reliability coefficients estimated from speeded tests tend to be spuriously inflated.
11. Estimating internal-consistency reliability with Kuder-Richardson formula 21 requires only knowledge of the mean, variance, and number of items, if the items are dichotomously scored.
12. If the range of item difficulties on a test is large, Kuder-Richardson formula 21 may yield a low reliability estimate reflecting lack of item homogeneity.
13. The standard error of measurement is a general estimate of the magnitude of unsystematic errors expressed in actual test-score units.
14. Multiplying the standard deviation of the test scores by the square root of the difference between the reliability coefficient and unity will provide an estimate of the standard error of measurement.
15. In general, tests composed of items that measure similar content or mental functions tend to have higher reliabilities than those that measure dissimilar functions.
16. Coefficient Kappa can be used to describe the gain in classification agreement by using criterion-referenced or mastery tests.

Speculations

1. Why are there so many different ways to estimate test reliability?
2. What are the factors that can influence measurement reliability?
3. How would you demonstrate the reliability of a test you had developed?
4. Describe the many different ways the concept of "error" influences tests and measurements.
5. Do the reliability coefficient and standard error of measurement tell us different things about a test? If yes, what? If no, why?
6. Why can humans not live by reliability alone?
7. What do Humpty Dumpty and uncorrected split-half reliability coefficients have in common?
8. How does item analysis influence reliability?
9. Why is it difficult to assess the reliability of criterion-referenced measures?
10. What are some possible interpretations of the statement, "My mother-in-law is 90 percent reliable"?

Suggested Readings

American Educational Research Association, American Psychological Association, and National Council on Measurement in Education. (1985). *Standards for educational and psychological testing.* Washington, DC: American Psychological Association. Chapter 2, "Reliability and Errors of Measurement," contains a discussion of the primary and secondary standards for test reliability.

Crocker, L., & Algina, J. (1986). *Introduction to classical and modern test theory.* New York: Holt, Rinehart & Winston.

Mehrens, W. A., & Lehmann, I. J. (1987). *Using standardized tests in education.* New York: Longman. Chapter 3, "Reliability," introduces us to a little elementary classical test theory.

Sax, G. (1989). *Principles of educational psychological measurement and evaluation* (3rd Edition). Belmont, CA: Wadsworth. Chapter 9, "The Reliability of Measurements," is both current, comprehensive, and readable.

Symonds, P. M. (1928). Factors influencing test reliability. *Journal of Educational Measurement, 19,* 73–87. It is absolutely amazing how accurate this classic survey is today. Old is not necessarily out-of-date.

Chapter 13

Defining and Assessing Validity

Defining and Assessing Validity
Content Validity
Criterion-Related Validity
Construct Validity
Curricular and Instructional Validity
Common-Sense Approaches to Establishing Achievement Test Validity
Effects of Item Analysis on Reliability and Validity
Validating Affective Measures
Case Study Application
Content Review Statements
Speculations
Suggested Readings

Following are some credible definitions of validity.

> Validity is an integrated evaluative judgment of the degree to which empirical evidence and theoretical rationales support the adequacy and appropriateness of inferences and actions based on test scores or other modes of assessment. (Messick, 1989)

> Validity . . . refers to the appropriateness, meaningfulness, and usefulness of the specific inferences made from test scores. (APA, 1985)

> Test validity involves three concerns: first, one wants to know that a test is measuring what it is supposed to measure; second, one wants to know as fully as possible what the score obtained from the use of the test means; and third, one wants to know how an individual's score on a test relates to other observable facts about the individual. (Wolf, 1982)

Nice words, but can they all be right? Yes! Why? Because validity is a very particularistic, specific, and individualistic concept. A test is not valid in general, but for a particular interpretation in a specific application. One needs, therefore, to test the test's validity before one can accept the inferences to be drawn from the test results.

This chapter describes various approaches to establishing the validity of measures commonly used in education and psychology.

Defining and Assessing Validity

The concept of constant or systematic error was described in the previous chapter. The relationship of error to test validity implies that there exists some standard or standards for evaluating the presence or absence of such errors. Criteria must be identified, constructed, or collected by the test developer, or sometimes by the user, in order that judgments about validity may be made. The nature of the criteria used to evaluate the validity of a test will in turn be dictated by the purposes of developing and using the test. Three rather broad aims or purposes of testing have been identified (American Psychological Association 1985):

1. *The test user wishes to determine how an individual performs at present in a universe of situations that the test situation is claimed to represent.* For example, most achievement tests used in schools measure the student's performance on a sample of questions intended to represent a certain phase of educational achievement or certain educational objectives. The type of validity described here is generally referred to as *content validity.*

2. *The test user wishes to forecast an individual's future standing or to estimate an individual's present standing on some variable of particular significance that is different from the test.* For example, an academic aptitude test may forecast grades, or a brief adjustment inventory may estimate what the outcome would be of a careful psychological examination. Validity defined in this way is called *criterion-related validity.*

3. *The test user wishes to infer the degree to which the individual possesses some hypothetical trait or quality (construct) presumed to be reflected in the test performance.* For example, he wants to know whether the individual stands high on some proposed abstract trait such as "intelligence" or "creativity" that cannot be observed directly. This may be done to learn something about the individual, or it may be done to study the test itself, to study its relationship to other tests, or to develop psychological theory. We are here concerned with the *construct validity* of a test.

The type of validity information gathered will, of course, depend upon the use to be made of the test results. Using the broadly defined test-use categories, three types of validity have been defined. However, the method employed to determine validity could form the basis for an alternative classification. It is useful to distinguish between types of validity that (a) are primarily dependent upon a rational analysis of the test and its items, and those that (b) rely on empirical and statistical evidence.

Content Validity

In general, content validity is evaluated on the basis of a rational analysis of the item content. Take, for example, an educational achievement test. Validity would be assessed by the professional judgments of an instructor in light of the instructional objectives of a particular class or school. The instructor would seek an answer to this question: How adequately do the items of this test measure the objectives, in terms of both subject matter and cognitive skills, that I want them to measure? Content validity rests on the specification of the universe of behavior to be sampled. For a standardized achievement test, this specification might take the form of a statement in the test manual summarizing the textbooks or subject-matter experts consulted or the course syllabi reviewed. For an informal classroom test, the universe might be defined in terms of a table of specifications developed by the teacher. In either case, content validity is the match between a test item and the objective it is supposed to measure—also sometimes referred to as relevance.

With increasing frequency commercial test publishers are providing extensive listings of the objectives upon which their items were based. Descriptions would include content specifications, and may also specify the mental operation necessary to perform successfully on the test, for example, application, analysis, and so forth.

Criterion-Related Validity

To establish a claim for criterion-related validity, however, one must draw upon statistical or experimental data. These data are usually presented in the form of correlation coefficients. Means, standard deviations, or other descriptive indices derived from groups known to differ on the variable being measured are occasionally brought to bear on validity claims. The chief problem in using correlational techniques to establish validity involves the identification of an acceptable criterion. The criterion must be external to the test and provide a direct measure of the variable in question. If one were interested in the variable "academic success during the freshman year in college," a criterion measure might be a grade-point average or score on a comprehensive examination. A test estimating either of these criteria might then be developed and experimentally administered to a group of high-school seniors. Later their scores would be correlated with grade-point averages or exam scores obtained at the end of their freshman year in college. If the correlation is high (e.g., +.80), we would conclude that the test has a high degree of criterion-related validity and could be used confidently to make predictions.

Following are some "typical"—if anything, nowadays, is typical—criterion-related validity coefficients.

1. Total score on fall *Metropolitan Readiness Test* and end of first-grade scores on Metropolitan Achievement Test: Word Knowledge (.81), Word Analysis (.75), and Reading (.61). (Swanson, Payne, & Jackson, 1981)
2. Correlation between Graduate Record Exam-Verbal and master's degree grade-point average (.36). (Payne, Wells, & Clarke 1971)
3. Correlation between self-expressed sense of competence for security police and job performance: Quality (.34), Efficiency (.34), and Adaptability (.30). (Steel, Mento, Davis, & Wilson, 1989)

In addition to correlation indices, a useful way of summarizing criterion-related validity data is in an *expectancy table.* An expectancy table is a two-way grid that relates test and criterion scores. A simple expectancy table relating scores on the Sentences subtest of the Differential Aptitude Test and grades in a Rhetoric course for 100 freshman females is presented in Table 13-1. The left-hand portion of the table summarizes the entries from a bivariate frequency distribution or scatter diagram similar to those described in Chapter 9. In the right-hand portion of the table, each cell frequency has been converted to a percentage based on the total number of tallies in its row. These data might be interpreted as follows: of the 23 freshman women who took the course in Rhetoric and had test scores between 50 and 59, 39 percent (or 9 individuals) received a grade of C, 35 percent (or 8) received Bs, and 26 percent (or 6) received a grade of A. Not one of the students with a score of 50 or more obtained a grade lower than C, but since only three women scored this low,

Table 13-1 Expectancy Table Relating DAT Sentences Scores to Grades in Rhetoric for 100 College Freshman Females*

Total No.	Number Receiving Each Grade					Test Scores	Percent Receiving Each Grade					Total Percent
	F	D	C	B	A		F	D	C	B	A	
1					1	80–89					100	100
5				1	4	70–79				20	80	100
22			3	14	5	60–69			14	63	23	100
23			9	8	6	50–59			39	35	26	100
22		3	13	6		40–49		14	59	27		100
16	1	3	9	3		30–39	6	19	56	19		100
8	1	4	3			20–29	13	50	37			100
2		2				10–19		100				100
1		1				0–9		100				100
100	2	13	37	32	16	M = 48.58						
						S = 15.20						

*Correlation = .71

Source: Reprinted from A.G. Wesman, Expectancy tables: A way of interpreting test validity. *Test Service Bulletin, 38* (1949): 12. Published by the Psychological Corporation. San Antonio, TX.

this generalization is somewhat risky. We might, then, use this expectancy-table information to predict the performance of women who take this course in the future.

The situation is applicable to either the predictive or concurrent use of tests, depending on the amount of elapsed time between the collection of test scores and criterion data and the purpose for which the scores are intended. With regard to the concurrent use of criterion-related validity data, one might be interested in answering a general question such as: "Can I substitute this test score for a more elaborate and expensive criterion measure?" Here the test scores and criterion data would be gathered at the same time and correlated.

Construct Validity

Construct validity is investigated through the use of rational analytic, statistical, and experimental procedures. If a researcher is developing a measure of test anxiety, he or she would want to be confident that the items in his or her instrument represent a reasonable sample of the kinds of anxiety responses that a student might make in a testing situation and that the scores on his or her instrument change when anxiety is experimentally manipulated. Experimental manipulation might be accomplished by administering the instrument under stressful and nonstressful conditions using different instructions. An analysis of the scores would ideally reveal differences in the expected direction, as a function of the two types of experimental instructions.

Construct validity involves the "psychological meaningfulness" of a test score, that is, the degree to which certain theoretical or explanatory constructs can account for item responses and test performances. It is generally relevant where no single criterion is available or acceptable in defining the variable or trait of interest.

The specific techniques employed to provide evidence of construct validity are varied, and in many instances are limited only by the creativity and ingenuity of the investigator. The logic of construct validity parallels the application of the scientific method. The development or use of theory (or a nomological net) that interrelates various elements of the construct under investigation is central (Cronbach & Meehl, 1955). Hypotheses based on a theory are derived and predictions are made about how the experimental test scores should relate to specified variables. These predictions may involve hypothesizing a positive or negative relationship. For example, we would want our measure of test anxiety to correlate positively with a second measure of test anxiety, but not with intelligence. The hypotheses are now subjected to experimental verification. Cronbach and Meehl (1955) suggest five types of evidence that might be assembled in support of construct validity. These have been succinctly stated by Helmstadter (1964) as follows:

Group differences. Samples of individuals assumed or demonstrated to differ on the variable under investigation would be predicted to exhibit differential performance. Data gathered in this way are essentially cross-sectional.

Changes in performance. Longitudinal studies might be undertaken to show changes over time or occasions for the same group. One would expect, for example, that scores on an achievement test would rise as students progress through a course.

Correlations. Obviously, a test should be positively correlated with another test that purports to measure the same variable, and show no correlation with measures of entirely different variables. The convergent-discriminant validity notion of Campbell and Fiske (1959) follows logically here from the experimental methods of similarities and differences suggested by Cronbach and Meehl (1955) in their classic discussion of construct validity.

Internal consistency. Internal consistency involves interitem correlations, that is, the degree to which items measure the same thing. Whether internal consistency should be high or low depends on one's theory and predictions about it.

Studies of the test-taking process. What does the examinee do when he takes a test? What mental processes are involved in responding to the items? Does the form of the test and its items seem to make a difference? These are some of the questions that should be investigated.

Table 13-2 contains a brief outline of what a construct validation study might look like. Our hypothetical measure of motivation for academic achievement would have to be based on some theory, for example, McClelland's *n*-achievement (Atkinson, 1958). Items would have to be based on the theory and then data gathered. It requires a great deal of work, but consider what we are trying to do—confirm that the interpretation of the scores say something meaningful about the examinee.

It should be obvious that the three types of validity discussed above are not

Table 13-2 Hypothetical Construct Validation of a Measure of Motivation for Academic Achievement

Type of Validity Evidence	**Example**
Group Differences	Ability of items to discriminate between under- and overachieving students.
Changes in Performance	Study of scores on motivation instrument over time to see if fluctuations are related to academic performance differences or score sensitivity by instructional intervention.
Correlations	Correlations with other motivation measures, teacher estimates of effort, grades, and achievement test scores.
Internal Consistency	Calculation of Kuder-Richardson formula 20, and factor analyses.
Studies of Test-Taking Process	What is motivation *not* correlated with, for example, socially desirable responses, aptitude, anxiety. Relate scores to original theory.

independent. Content validity, for example, must usually be present before criterion-related validity can be demonstrated. Establishing construct validity requires data derived and used in establishing both content and criterion-related validity. Also, we have implied that the demonstration of content validity is primarily a subjective process. But if we consider the content validity of a classroom test, for example, to be defined in terms of instructional objectives and curriculum, we should be able to demonstrate validity empirically by contrasting the performances of subjects who are course-sophisticated and those who are course-naive. Such a procedure would surely indicate whether or not exposure to the content and instruction of a particular course makes any difference in test performance. This procedure has been advocated by Ebel (1956) and applied successfully by Krouskopf (1964). Cronbach (1971) has also suggested that one examine content validity empirically by correlating scores from two forms of the same test, both developed from the same content domain. A combination construct validity-reliability procedure, then, can help us understand and demonstrate content validity. Suffice it to say that there is no single way to estimate validity, because the kind of evidence desired depends on the projected use of the results. A test, then, is not valid or invalid in general, but in relation to the purposes for developing and using it.

It is a law of measurement that test scores must be reliable before they can be valid. In a very real sense, however, validity is not strictly a characteristic of the instrument but of the *inference* that is to be made from the test scores derived from the instrument. We need primarily to be concerned with the validity of the interpretation we make from test results (Cronbach, 1971).

Face Validity

The term *face validity* is sometimes used to describe the appearance of the test and/or items relative to what the examinee was told to expect: for example, "Do these items look like they measure mathematical problem solving?" Obviously the test should have credibility as it will influence how seriously the test taker approaches the tasks, and in a sense how the public will accept the results. Basically face validity is a judgment call, and perhaps a question of marketing, but it is not a technical dimension of validity.

Curricular and Instructional Validity

The real demands and limitations of a classroom situation do not allow the luxury of exploring all types of validity. Probably the best that classroom teachers can do is to examine their teaching situation and instruction and decide which validity needs should be assessed. All instructional programs involve three things: objectives, a curriculum, and an instructional process. When assessment time comes, the teacher must consider the relation each of these three elements bears to the measure of student progress being used. The diagram in Figure 13-1 represents the three elements in the instructional process and a summative or formative achievement test.

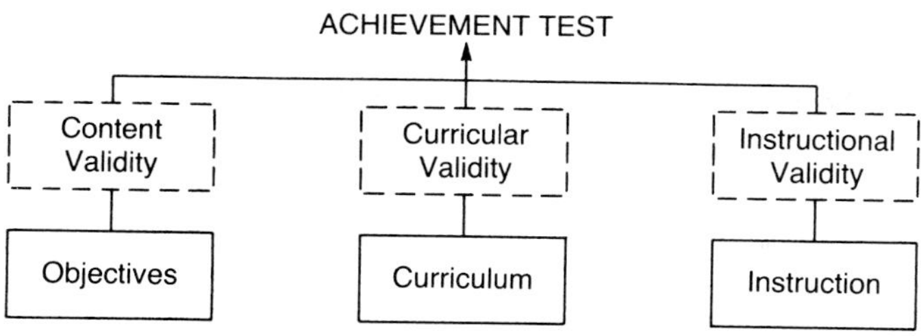

Figure 13-1

Factors influencing achievement test validity

Content validity is used here as it was previously defined, that is, the extent to which the test adequately samples from domain of relevant and intended outcomes.

Curricular Validity

As stated previously, the validity of a test or item depends on its matching the objective. Objectives are operationalized in many different ways. In other words, a variety of instructional materials could be used to address a particular objective. To tell if a test or item matches the curriculum materials, you should map the relations of these two elements. For example, use a table of specifications (a two-way grid with content along one dimension and expected behavior along the other) to cross-reference the test and materials (Schmidt, 1983). Curricular validity relates directly to the issue of the extent to which the test content is addressed in the curriculum materials.

Instructional Validity

The ultimate test of a test or item is whether or not it represents a reasonable sample of what actually went on in the classroom. The test must measure what was taught. Theoretically, objectives, curriculum, and instruction correspond almost perfectly. But many factors can disturb this perfection. Students don't always behave in predicted ways and therefore we must sometimes adjust or modify our instruction. For the test to be instructionally valid, the test must sample relevant instructional outcomes. Ideally evaluation of instructional validity should come from an independent observer. Usually instructional validity, however, rests on a subjective judgment of the teacher. Legal challenges have confirmed the legitimacy of this type of validity.

There is some support in the testing profession for the positions taken by Yalow and Popham (1983) regarding curricular and instructional validity. They claim that these are really not kinds of *test* validity but that, rather, they reflect on the opportunities that students have had to become prepared to perform on the test. But correct interpretation of test scores should take account of as many factors as possible that may affect scores. Therefore, we should accept curricular and instructional validity as components in assessing the overall "validity" of the intended purpose in gathering and interpreting the scores.

Common-Sense Approaches to Establishing Achievement Test Validity

Validity is not something added on at the end of test development but should be built into the instrument while it is being created and assembled. After it has been developed we can check how good a job we did by examining the test results against accepted criteria. We wish to answer in the affirmative to the question, "Are the scores on this test telling us what we want to know about this student?"

There are some steps—some formative, some summative—that can be taken to help build in validity. Most of these apply to achievement tests, but many of the procedures would generalize to any educational or psychological measuring instrument. Among the steps are:

1. *Use objectives as a basis for item construction.* This strikes at the heart of content validity, namely the *relevance* of the items in comparison with *intent.* Value judgments are involved, but hopefully those are based on experience and knowledge.

2. *Use accepted item-writing principles.* Make sure that the items, tasks, and questions are free from cues and ambiguity and meet the highest communicative standards.

3. *If multiple behaviors are being sampled they should be in proper proportion.* For an achievement test this means using a table of specifications or test blueprint.

4. *Extraneous sources of influence on test responses need to be eliminated or controlled.* Possible bias (e.g., gender, racial, commonality of experience) should be investigated empirically and eliminated or adjusted (e.g., use separate norms by sex). Such response tendencies as social desirability and test anxiety are some of many that need to be controlled.

5. *Extraneous sources of distraction during test administration need to be controlled.* Every examinee is entitled to demonstrate his or her maximum performance or respond in a quiet and disturbance-free environment.

6. *Verify correctness, appropriateness, and accuracy of answers to items and scoring of tasks.* Objectivity is a major contributor to validity.

7. *Test materials must be appropriate to the level of functioning and experience.* One example of this common-sense guideline is that the readability of verbal items must be within the comprehension range of the examinee.

8. *Check the reliability of the measures used.* The old adage that a test cannot be valid without being reliable is true.

9. *Where possible check test scores against external criteria.* It would seem logical that achievement test scores should relate to such external measures as teachers' grades, performance during future educational experiences, and scores on other relevant informal or standardized measures.

10. *Test items that are related to change during instruction should be retained for future use.* Training or instruction should have an impact on test scores or task performance.

Effects of Item Analysis on Reliability and Validity

It has been suggested that items in the middle range of difficulty that show a high degree of discrimination should be selected for the final form of a test. Such a procedure helps insure that the test has a high degree of internal-consistency reliability because items that are highly correlated with the total score are likely to be highly correlated with each other. This procedure assumes that an instructor has the opportunity to pretest the items. Very frequently, however, this opportunity does not present itself. Two alternatives are available.

The first requires rescoring of the test *after* the item analysis has been completed. Although bad items cannot be rewritten, poor items can be eliminated. The analyzed and rescored test should be more reliable than the original. A large number of items cannot, of course, be eliminated. If this were allowed to happen, many of the important learning outcomes would not be measured, and the content validity of the test would be lowered. The rescoring procedure must be used with caution. Informal studies by the author have indicated, in addition, that the correlations between original and rescored tests run in the high +.90s, suggesting essentially unchanged ranking.

The second and more desirable alternative to pretesting is to select items from a file set up over a period of time. When a particular item is used, the resulting item-analysis data are recorded on a card. Such data are accumulated until the instructor has weeded out most of the poor items, and can select items with a greater degree of confidence. The availability of an item file provides a great deal of flexibility for an instructor. It allows, for example, parallel forms of a test to be assembled with comparative ease. Another justification for developing an item file is that a teacher usually has small samples of students on whom to try out the items. This limitation can be overcome by accumulating information on each item. The comparability of the groups and testing conditions is important in accumulating data. Such a subtle factor as the position of an item on a test may also be of significance. Item-analysis data, then, must be considered "relative," meaning that an instructor cannot expect an item to function in exactly the same way on two or more occasions.

Validating Affective Measures

The following five methods may be employed in validating affective measures. The similarity with the Cronbach and Meehl (1955) categories used with construct validity is intentional.

1. *Content validation.* The usual procedure for validating affective measures is to "build in validity." It is assumed that the domain or area to be assessed has been well described, ideally in behavioral terms. If scale items are tied very closely to behavioral objectives, some measure of validity can be assured.

2. *Contrasted groups.* Groups known or assumed to differ with regard to the affective variable are used to examine item responses or total scores on the instrument. Thurstone and Chave (1929), for example, contrasted churchgoers and non-churchgoers in validating their scale measuring attitudes toward the church. A more contemporary example can be found in the work of Moore and Sutman (1970), who have reported the development and validation of an instrument to assess high-school students' attitudes toward science. The instrument was composed of 60 items and used a 4-point rating scale (1 = agree strongly—4 = disagree strongly). Following are four sample items:

> Anything we need to know can be found out through science.
> Science is so difficult that only highly trained scientists can understand it.
> Scientists discover laws which tell us exactly what is going on in nature.
> The products of scientific work are mainly useful to scientists; they are not useful to the average person.

To validate the scale, the researchers developed instructional lessons aimed at *changing the attitudes of the students.* Experimental and control (regular science instruction) groups were shown to differ in the expected direction after treatment.

3. *Correlations with self-reported behaviors.* The investigator gathers attitude scores and then surveys the respondents' past behavior verifying these attitudes. Differing descriptions of behavior should correspond to differing scores if the instrument has validity.

4. *Expert judgments.* A group of experts could be polled regarding which responses indicate which attitudes. A high index of agreement would be required.

5. *Correlations with actual behavior.* It is possible, particularly through observation, to discern how different students react in different situations. One then needs to determine whether this behavior is in line with the students' expressed attitudes or preferences. One educational researcher, for example, has demonstrated the feasibility of using empirical keying and validation procedures traditionally associated with aptitude tests to develop a predictive academic interest inventory for use with college freshmen. The procedure involves administering a pool of items theoretically

related to a variable of concern—in this case, academic field of interest upon entering school. After the passage of considerable time (e.g., two years), a student's major field of study is correlated with his responses to the inventory items previously administered. This approach to interest inventory development has the distinct advantage of increasing, and to some extent assuring, validity. The inventory items are correlated with actual behavior. This approach is much more likely to yield a valid instrument than is merely asking a student to respond to such a statement as "I think teaching would appeal to me" and assuming validity.

This chapter was probably perceived as a bit overwhelming. But give it a chance. Read and study it a couple more times. Outline the major points. The content is *that* important, just as the content of any test is *that* important.

Case Study Application

The items of a test must measure the intended instructional objectives. We call this test characteristic *relevance* and it is directly related to test validity. It is also hoped that the intended objectives are, in fact, the ones implemented in the classroom. Test constructors must use their best professional judgment in evaluating the match between item and objective. For a classroom test the teacher is by far the most credible judge. Other teachers who are responsible for a particular course could serve as "expert witnesses" relative to *relevance.*

Another important dimension of content validity relates to the sampling of outcomes or behaviors for a unit or course. To a great extent the parameters of these outcomes are described by the test blueprint or table of specifications.

Having another teacher try to classify your items into your table of specifications can be a most enlightening and humbling experience. As an exercise in investigating content validity, figure out some way to compare the classifications of our sample 21 Reading Education midterm exam questions contained in Table 13-3, and those by a colleague-expert judge. The original items were presented in Chapter 7. Colleague classifications were in terms of one of the 40 cells ($C_1 - C_{40}$) in the table of specifications. The colleague classifications were as follows:

Item	*Cell*	*Item*	*Cell*
1	1	12	24
2	1	13	5
3	11	14	5
4	4	15	26
5	12	16	16
6	2	17	7
7	23	18	8
8	14	19	8
9	4	20	20
10	24	21	13
11	24		

Table 13-3 Original Classification of 21 Reading Education Midterm Exam Questions

	Behavioral Outcome				
Content	Knowledge	Comprehension	Application	Analysis	Total
Reflection	4 C^{1}	1 2 3 C^{11}	C^{21}	C^{31}	4
Emerging Literacy	6 C^{2}	5 C^{12}	C^{22}	C^{32}	2
LEA	C^{3}	C^{13}	C^{23}	7 C^{33}	1
Decoding Strategies	9 C^{4}	8 C^{14}	10 11 12 C^{24}	C^{34}	5
Comprehension Strategies	13 14 C^{5}	21 C^{15}	C^{25}	C^{35}	3
Discussion Strategies	C^{6}	C^{16}	15 16 C^{26}	C^{36}	2
Basal Reader	17 C^{7}	C^{17}	C^{27}	C^{37}	1
Exceptional Children	18 19 C^{8}	C^{18}	C^{28}	C^{38}	2
Bilingual Learners	C^{9}	C^{19}	C^{29}	C^{39}	0
Evaluation	C^{10}	20 C^{20}	C^{30}	C^{40}	1
Total	8	7	5	1	21

Note: See Case Study Application for Chapter 7 for original items and Chapter 4 for the original objectives.

Table 13-4 Assessment of Teaching Performance

	Evaluation			
Task	Unacceptable	Needs Improvement	Acceptable	Excellent
1. Specifies or selects learner objectives for lessons	U	NI	A	E
2. Creates or selects learner activities.	U	NI	A	E
3. Creates or selects material and/or media.	U	NI	A	E
4. Plans activities and/or assignments which take into account learner differences.	U	NI	A	E
5. Creates or selects procedures or materials for assessing learner performance on objectives.	U	NI	A	E
6. Uses instructional time effectively.	U	NI	A	E
7. Provides a physical environment that is conducive to learning.	U	NI	A	E

Table 13-4 *(Continued)*

Task	Evaluation			
	Unacceptable	Needs Improvement	Acceptable	Excellent
8. Uses acceptable written expression with learners.	U	NI	A	E
9. Uses acceptable oral expression.	U	NI	A	E
10. Demonstrates command of subject matter on reading education.	U	NI	A	E
11. Uses instructional methods acceptably.	U	NI	A	E
12. Matches instruction to learners.	U	NI	A	E
13. Uses instructional aids and materials during the lesson observed.	U	NI	A	E
14. Implements activities in a logical sequence.	U	NI	A	E
15. Gives or clarifies explanations related to lesson content.	U	NI	A	E
16. Uses learner responses or questions regarding lesson content.	U	NI	A	E
17. Provides information to learners about their progress throughout the lesson.	U	NI	A	E
18. Communicates personal enthusiasm.	U	NI	A	E
19. Stimulates learner interest.	U	NI	A	E
20. Demonstrates warmth and friendliness.	U	NI	A	E
21. Helps learners develop positive self-concepts.	U	NI	A	E
22. Maintains learner involvement in instruction.	U	NI	A	E
23. Redirects learners who are off-task.	U	NI	A	E
24. Communicates clear expectations about behavior.	U	NI	A	E
25. Manages disruptive behavior.	U	NI	A	E

One of the methods mentioned in the chapter for assessing test validity required correlating test scores with some relevant external criterion. It would be hoped that scores on our Reading Education midterm exam (and final exam and lesson plan evaluation as well) would be related to classroom teaching performance. The form in Table 13-4 was completed by a trained student teaching supervisor for each of our 18 reading education students midway through their student teaching experience. The form is an adaptation of the *Teacher Performance Assessment Instrument* used with beginning teachers in the state of Georgia. There was approximately 18 months between when the midterm exam was administered and the teaching performance assessments were made. To check on criterion-related validity correlate the following pairs of scores. Use the rank-order correlation method. The Assessment of Teaching Performance (ATP) total scores were derived using the following scheme: Unacceptable = 0 points, Needs Improvement = 1 point, Acceptable = 2 points, and Excellent = 3 points. See Millman and Darling-Hammond (1990) for an excellent collection of readings about teacher evaluation.

Student	*Midterm Exam*	*ATP*
1	47	30
2	58	48
3	58	51
4	52	28
5	51	53
6	55	49
7	58	45
8	58	57
9	55	52
10	59	54
11	57	54
12	62	55
13	68	71
14	52	46
15	57	61
16	62	52
17	65	65
18	62	59

Content Review Statements

1. Test validity should be viewed in terms of the intent of testing and the use(s) to which the data are to be put.
2. A test is not valid or invalid in general, but with respect to a particular criterion in a particular situation with a particular group.
3. Content validity involves how well the items on a test sample a defined universe of tasks.
4. The chief problem in establishing criterion-related validity is defining and securing a reliable measure of the criterion.
5. Criterion-related validity involves the ability of a test to estimate, usually through the use of correlational procedures, an individual's status in relation to some relevant criterion.
6. Correlations between test and criterion data which were gathered at about the same time are called concurrent validity coefficients.

7. Correlations between test and criterion data that gathered at quite different times are called predictive validity coefficients.
8. Construct validity involves the degree to which we are able to infer from a test score whether or not an individual possesses some hypothetical trait or characteristic.
9. Content validity relies on the proper delineation of the behaviors to be assessed and can be judged in light of the table of specifications.
10. Expectancy tables are useful in the interpretation of criterion-related validity.
11. Construct validity can be examined, usually on intelligence and personality measures, by noting:
    a. Differences between groups assumed or known to differ in relation to the construct or trait in question.
    b. Changes in performances as a result of treatment related to the construct.
    c. Correlations with other reliable and valid measures of the construct.
    d. The degree to which the items on the test tend to measure the same thing.
    e. The factors that influence the test-taking performance itself.
12. Curricular validity can be established by correlating the instructional objectives and instructional materials.
13. Instructional validity of a test must rest on the demonstrated implementation of objectives-based teaching.
14. Construct validation procedures are very useful in validating affective measures.

Speculations

1. Why are there so many different ways to estimate test validity?
2. Is one kind of validity more important than another?
3. How would you demonstrate the validity of a test you had developed?
4. What are some reasons why a test and a criterion may *not* be related?
5. Describe ways in which the idea of an "expectancy table" could be used in this class.
6. Why is it logical that a test can be reliable without being valid, but not vice versa?
7. What is the relationship of item analysis to reliability?
8. Under what conditions can you justify *face validity?*
9. Would you use different procedures to determine the validity of a criterion-referenced test versus a norm-referenced test? If yes, how would the methods be different?
10. Are the phrases "valid test" and "valid interpretation" equivalent? Why?
11. If a commercial test publisher said his scholastic ability test had high validity, what kinds of questions would you ask? What questions would you ask in response to the same claim for an achievement battery?

Suggested Readings

American Educational Research Association, American Psychological Association, and National Council on Measurement in Education. (1985). *Standards for educational and psychological testing.* Washington, DC: American Psychological Association, Chapter 1, "Validity," provides an overview of the primary and secondary technical validity standards for published tests.

Cronbach, L. J. (1971). Test validation. In R. L. Thorndike (Ed.), *Educational measurement,* (2nd Edition). Washington, DC: American Council on Education, See Chapter 14. Intended for the intermediate and advanced student, this chapter contains the latest thinking on the topic of one of the nation's foremost experts. Rather than approaching the validation of the test per se, Cronbach describes methods useful in validating interpretations of data arising from specified procedures.

Helmstadter, G. C. (1964). *Principles of psychological measurement.* New York: Appleton-Century-Crofts. Chapters 4, 5, and 6 contain some of the most readable discussions of content, criterion-related, and construct validity available. The presentations are simultaneously brief and technically correct.

Mehrens, W. A., & Lehmann, I. J. (1987). *Using standardized tests in education.* New York: Longman. Of particular value is the section of Chapter 4 ("Validity") on validity and decision making.

Messick, S. (1989). Validity. In R. L. Linn (Ed.), *Educational measurement* (3rd Edition). New York: Macmillan. Lots of philosophy and theory. Excellent for the advanced student in search of an understanding of construct validity.

Bev's Diary

I'm getting tired! Thirteen chapters finished and what seems like a million words. Being a student is hard work. How does Sigi expect us to remember all this stuff? Reading some of the journal articles was tedious, particularly those from the *Journal of Obscure Statistics* and *Psychotika*. But actually the "number" stuff wasn't so bad. As long as you can add, multiply, subtract, and divide you can survive.

I ran a reliability analysis of my last exam—not very good results, I'm afraid. I did an item analysis, threw out a bunch of bad items, and recalculated the reliability—it went up significantly. I must remember to replace those "bad" items when I use that test or one like it again. I also asked a fellow English teacher to "key" my test and match my objectives to the items. Results were better here, but we still had to discuss a number of questions.

Our coordinator of testing says that there isn't a week that goes by where she doesn't

Part Five

Standardized Measures

receive a flier from some company pushing an all-purpose test that can measure everything for everyman. Everything from a tickle to an itch can be measured if the price is right. I guess that's maybe even a bit too cynical, even for me. I'm sure there are lots of ways to separate psychometric wheat from measurement chaff.

The SAT, the MAT, the CAT and the WRAT
So many names I don't know where I'm at
I studied the ads
And eliminated the fads
Now I've got it all down pat.

Chapter 14

Standardized Scholastic Achievement and Aptitude Tests and Testing Programs

Standardized tests have maintained their popularity over many decades because of their convenience and generally high technical quality. Standardized tests are constructed by measurement and content experts. These kinds of measurements provide methods for obtaining samples of behaviors under uniform conditions, that is, a fixed set of questions is administered with the same set of directions and timing constraints. In addition, the scoring procedure is carefully delineated, monitored, and controlled. A standardized test usually has been administered to a norm or standardization group so that a person's performance can be interpreted by comparing it to the performance of others. The test then is considered norm-referenced. Criterion-referenced tests can also be standardized.

Classification of Standardized Tests

Standardized tests can be classified in many ways. It was noted in Chapter 5 that we might use the method of administration as a basis for classifying tests. Tests, therefore, might be considered oral, written, or behavioral. Tests might be administered to large groups by a single administrator or on a one-examinee/one-examiner basis. Educational measures can also be used to gather data on an individual's maximum performance or typical performance—maximum efforts being expected on achievement and aptitude tests, and typical responses on personality measures. It perhaps makes more sense to think about the purposes or uses to which the information is to be put than to cogitate about the methods of classifying tests.

A typical set of "use categories" has been presented by Mehrens and Lehmann (1987). They describe how tests can be used to assist in making *instructional, guidance, administrative, and research* decisions.

Different kinds of tests can be used to provide relevant information for the making of these four kinds of decisions. Achievement tests or assessments of an individual's status with regard to a particular set of instructional, training, or educational objectives may be relevant with regard to all four purposes. Achievement tests may be classified as diagnostic, single-subject, or battery. A diagnostic test is administered to isolate specific weaknesses in a restricted range of achievement and skill development in a subject area. Single-subject tests measure specialized areas included in the curriculum, and separate tests are available in nearly every subject at appropriate grade levels. In some respects a battery is a collection of single-subject tests. Achievement tests measure the effects of formal educational experiences.

A clear distinction between aptitude (especially academic aptitude) and achievement tests is sometimes difficult to see as both can be influenced by formal educational experience, but aptitude measures (including readiness tests) are administered before the learning program, and achievement tests are administered after the fact. However, there are differences in what each type of test asks students to do on the test. According to Hopkins and Antes (1990), achievement tests measure (a) the effects of special programs, (b) the effects of a relatively standardized set of experiences, (c) the effects of learning that occur under partially known and controlled conditions, and (d) what the individual student can do at a given point in time. Aptitude tests on the other hand tend to measure or predict (a) the effects of the cumulative influence of experiences, (b) the effects of learning under relatively uncontrolled and unknown conditions, and (c) the future behavior, achievements, or performance of individuals as groups. *Aptitude* tests include scholastic aptitude tests, general mental ability tests, intelligence tests, multiaptitude tests, or specific aptitude tests used to predict success in general academics, a subject, or a special occupational area. They measure students' out-of-school abilities and problem-solving skills as well as abilities developed as a result of general experience. Aptitude batteries sometimes include combinations and paper-and-pencil cognitive items along with psychomotor tasks such as assessments of finger dexterity and hand-eye coordination. Scholastic aptitude tests are often contrasted with group or individual intelligence tests (e.g., *Wechsler Intelligence Scale for Children—Revised*), (Wechsler, 1974). There are similarities, in form and content, but the major difference between these tests rests on the greater variety of abilities sampled by intelligence tests.

Affective interest, personality, and attitude inventories generally survey affective variables related to mental health, self-esteem, life adjustment, and career, vocational, and academic interests and orientations.

Types of Tests and Decision Making

The relationship between type of test and decision-making purpose is summarized in Table 14-1. It is taken from a book on standardized testing authored by Mehrens and Lehmann (1987). One of the first things you will note is that in many instances the jury is still out regarding the applicability of certain kinds of tests in certain situations. Information requirements must be based on the requirements of the decision to be made. The interest, personality, and attitude measures could logically be combined into an "affective" category (see Chapters 17 and 18). The greatest

Table 14-1 Purposes of Standardized Tests*

	Kinds of Tests				
Purposes	Aptitude	Achievement	Interest	Personality	Attitude
Instructional					
Evaluation of learning outcomes	×	×	?	?	
Evaluation of teaching	×	×			
Evaluation of curriculum	×	×	?		?
Learning diagnosis	×	×			
Differential assignments within class	×	×	?	?	?
Grading	?	?			
Motivation		?			×
Guidance					
Occupational	×	×	×	×	×
Educational	×	×	?	?	×
Personal	?	?	×	×	×
Administrative					
Selection	×	×	?		
Classification	×	×	×		
Placement	×	×	?		
Public relations (information)	×	×	?		
Curriculum planning and evaluation	×	×			
Evaluating teachers	?	?		?	
Providing information for outside agencies	×	×			
Grading	?	?			
Research	×	×	×	×	×

*"×" indicates that a test can and should be used for that purpose. "?" indicates that there is some debate about whether or not a test can serve that purpose.

From: *Standardized Tests in Education* by William A. Mehrens & Irvin J. Lehmann. Copyright © 1987 by Longman Publishing Group.

proportion of test uses relate to individual student evaluation, the diagnosis of strengths and weaknesses, instructional program planning, and the measurement of growth.

The remainder of this chapter focuses on achievement and scholastic aptitude tests as these represent the major kinds of tests that local school personnel are most likely to use. Those readers interested in a more comprehensive overview of standardized tests are referred to Cronbach (1990) and Anastasi (1988).

Contrasting Standardized and Nonstandardized Achievement Tests

A perspective on the nature of standardized achievement tests can be gained by contrasting standardized and nonstandardized (teacher-made) tests with regard to validity, reliability, and usability. Stanley (1964) has provided informative contrasts of relative strengths and weaknesses. These contrasts are summarized in Table 14-2. In matching measurement procedures to instructional objective, such factors as flexibility of technique, nature of the objective (with respect to both content and behavior), level of student, and time available for test administration and scoring need to be considered. It is unlikely that any single procedure will be used exclusively. A combination of methods generally provides the most comprehensive valid measurement.

Uses of Standardized Achievement Tests

Achievement has been defined as the extent to which specified instructional objectives are attained. Achievement tests, then, provide evidence about a student's status or level of learning. They may deal with knowledge of facts and principles as well as the ability to apply them in complex and usually lifelike situations.

Achievement tests hold a relatively unique position among the many types of educational and psychological tests. Measures of intelligence, personality, and the like deal with "constructs." We hypothesize and infer the presence of the construct from the responses to the instrument. Thus we have only indirect evidence of its nature. In assessing an achievement behavior, we attempt to measure a sample of the behavior itself; the evidence is therefore more direct.

Achievement-test data may be applied in a variety of ways by teachers, principals, and other administrative and supervisory personnel. Walter W. Cook has identified 15 major functions served by achievement tests (Cook, 1951, p. 36). According to Cook, achievement tests direct curriculum emphasis by:

1. Focusing attention on as many of the important ultimate objectives of education as possible.
2. Clarifying educational objectives to teachers and pupils.
3. Determining elements of strength and weakness in the instructional program of the school.
4. Discovering inadequacies in curriculum content and organization.

Achievement tests also, according to Cook, provide for educational guidance of pupils by:

5. Providing a basis for predicting individual pupil achievement in each learning area.
6. Serving as a basis for the preliminary grouping of all pupils in each learning area.
7. Discovering special aptitudes and disabilities.

Table 14-2 Advantages and Limitations of Standardized and Nonstandardized Tests with Respect to the Criteria of Validity, Reliability, and Usability

	Standardized	
Criterion	Advantages	Limitations
1. Validity		
a. Curricular	Careful selection by competent persons. Fits typical situations.	Inflexible. Too general in scope to meet local requirement fully, especially in unusual situations.
b. Statistical	With best tests, high.	Criteria often inappropriate or unreliable. Size of coefficients dependent upon range of ability in group tested.
2. Reliability	For best tests, fairly high—often .85 or more for comparable forms.	High reliability is no guarantee of validity. Also, reliability depends upon range of ability in group tested.
3. Usability		
a. Ease of Administration	Definite procedure, time limits, etc. Economy of time.	Manuals require careful study and are sometimes inadequate.
b. Ease of Scoring	Definite rules, keys, etc. Largely routine.	Scoring by hand may take considerable time and may be monotonous. Machine scoring preferable.
c. Ease of Interpretation	Better tests have adequate norms. Useful basis of comparison. Equivalent forms.	Norms often confused with standards. Some norms defective. Norms for various types of schools and levels of ability are often lacking.
Summary	Convenience, comparability, objectivity. Equivalent forms may be available.	Inflexibility. May be only slightly applicable to a particular situation.

Table 14-2 (*Continued*)

Criterion	**Nonstandardized** Advantages	**Nonstandardized** Limitations
Essay		
1. Validity		
a. Curricular	Useful for English, advanced classes; affords language training. May encourage sound study habits.	Limited sampling. Bluffing is possible. Mixes language factor in all scores.
b. Statistical		Usually not known.
2. Reliability		Reliability usually quite low.
3. Usability		
a. Ease of Administration	Easy to prepare. Easy to give.	Lack of uniformity.
b. Ease of Scoring		Slow, uncertain, and subjective.
c. Ease of Interpretation		No norms. Meaning doubtful.
Summary	Useful for part of many tests and in a few special fields.	Limited sampling. Subjective scoring. Time consuming.
Objective		
1. Validity		
a. Curricular	Extensive sampling of subject matter. Flexible in use. Discourages bluffing. Compares favorably with standard tests.	Narrow sampling of functions tested. Negative learning possible. May encourage piecemeal study.
b. Statistical		Adequate criteria usually lacking.
2. Reliability	Sometimes approaches that of standard tests.	No guarantee of validity.
3. Usability		
a. Ease of Administration	Directions rather uniform. Economy of time.	Time, effort, and skill required to prepare well.
b. Ease of Scoring	Definite rules, keys, etc. Largely routine. Can be done by clerks or machine.	Monotonous.
c. Ease of Interpretation	Local norms can be derived.	No norms available at beginning.
Summary	Extensive sampling. Objective scoring. Flexibility.	Preparation requires skill and time.

Julian C. Stanley, *Measurement in Today's Schools* (4th edition), 1964. Reprinted by permission of Prentice Hall. Englewood Cliffs, New Jersey.

8. Determining the difficulty of material a pupil can read with profit.
9. Determining the level of problem-solving ability in various areas.
10. Enabling pupils to think of their achievements in objective terms.
11. Giving pupils satisfaction for the progress they make, rather than for the relative level of achievement they attain.
12. Enabling pupils to compete with their past performance record.
13. Measuring achievement objectively in terms of accepted educational standards, rather than by the subjective appraisal of teachers.
14. Enabling teachers to discover the areas in which they need supervisory aid.
15. Affording the administrative and supervisory staff an overall measure of the effectiveness of the school organization and of the prevailing administrative and supervisory policies.

The foregoing functions are those primarily served by comprehensive batteries. Such batteries have limited value in planning the instructional programs of individual students or identifying individual strengths and weaknesses. They are useful in making intraindividual and interindividual comparisons across broad subject-matter areas and identifying areas in which more focused testing would prove informative. Although the lack of curriculum detail is a drawback, norm-referenced interpretations of strengths and weaknesses are a potential positive contribution of batteries.

With increasing frequency, test publishers are offering custom-made tests created to the specifications of a local or state school system. Often, however, they tend to be reconfigurations of the company's already existing tests or a selection of questions from their item banks.

Types of Standardized Achievement Tests

There are three general types of standardized achievement tests. The first is the *survey battery,* which consists of a group of individual subject-matter tests designated for use at particular levels. The second category is the *specific subject* or area test. The third category is the *diagnostic* test, which is usually administered when a survey battery or specific subject test indicates a substandard performance. Its purpose is to diagnose the area or areas of weakness so that remedial instruction may be instituted. Following are brief discussions of these three categories of standardized achievement tests, accompanied by descriptions of representative tests of each type.

Survey Batteries

Comprehensive survey achievement batteries are the mainstay of school testing programs, providing valuable information about the effectiveness of various instructional programs. The last two or three decades have seen a significant improvement in the quality of achievement batteries, particularly in regard to the learning outcomes measured and the quality of normative data made available to facilitate interpretation.

The content of a battery will, of course, vary according to the level of student achievement being measured. Despite being fairly broad in coverage, they are still significantly narrower than most school curricula. We teach many more things than the tests test. In addition commercial test publishers are in the business of making money and they must therefore market instruments that share the greatest appeal to potential purchasers. One way of increasing that general appeal is to include items that tap objectives that are common to a large number of curricula. Using a "common denominator" guideline for objectives tested would obviously have the effect of narrowing the range of outcomes assessed. Let the potential user be aware of tests claiming to measure every relevant educational outcome. This is a very serious limitation when such measures are used to evaluate schools, teaching, or teachers. Relevance is the construct in test validity. The "breadth"-of-curriculum problem is probably greater at the secondary school level than at the elementary school level. Table 14-3 suggests the range and variety of educational achievements that can be measured with the six batteries of the *Stanford Achievement Test Series* (SATS) (Kelley et al., 1988). There is a general trend toward an increase in the range of content coverage as one moves up the grade scale, and a tendency throughout to measure comprehension rather than recall of specific facts. Also evident is extensive and comprehensive coverage of a variety of abilities. The articulation over grade levels provides a basis for tracking student progress which also reflects on school effectiveness. The term *articulation* as used here refers to the development of a score-reporting scale which has comparable meaning over different levels of a test. Some school systems are opting to build their *own* system-level tests and testing programs. This is an expensive proposition but has the advantage of having maximally relevant tests in consideration of the curriculum. Such system testing programs tend to be criterion-referenced in nature and cover fewer content areas at fewer grade levels.

A distinct advantage of the survey battery over a series of individual subject-matter tests from different publishers is its simultaneous standardization of all subtests. Scores on individual subtests can thus be considered comparable, since the normative data were derived from the same population.

The *Stanford Achievement Test Series* is an illustrative survey battery. Many other high-quality batteries are also commercially available, for example, the *Iowa Tests of Basic Skills, Comprehensive Tests of Basic Skills, Metropolitan Achievement Tests,* and the *Science Research Associates Achievement Series.* The *Stanford* is selected only for illustrative purposes. The *Stanford* is made up of three components: the *Stanford Early School Achievement Test* (grades K–1.5), the Primary, Intermediate, and Advanced batteries (grades 1.5–9.9), and the *Stanford Test of Academic Skills* (grades 9.0–12.9). The *Stanford* was originally published in 1923 and is now in its eighth edition. Changes in school curricula and the need to update normative data make periodic revision and restandardization necessary. Double the needed number of items were created and field-tested. Normative data were gathered from all 50 states using a sampling plan that took into account such demographic variables as size of school district, ethnicity, region of the country, and density of student population. The total standardization and research sample consisted of 600,000 students. That's a lot! Items were revised by content experts, copy editors, measurement specialists, teachers, and an independent panel of educators whose job it was to control for potential racial, gender, or ethnic bias. One of the valuable features

Table 14-3 Condensed Outline of the Content and Instruction of the Eighth Edition of the *Stanford Achievement Test Series*

Subtest	**SESAT 1**	**SESAT 2**	**Primary 1**	**Primary 2**	**Primary 3**	**Intermediate 1–3**	**Advanced 1–2**	**Task 1–3**
Grade (Content)	1st half K	2nd half K 1st half 1	1	2	3	4–6	7–8	9–12
Recommended Administration Points	K.0–K.5	K.5–1.5	1.5–2.5	2.5–3.5	3.5–4.5	4.5–7.5	7.5–9.9	9.0–12.9
Sounds and Letters	×	×						
Word Study Skills			×	×	×			
Word Reading/	×	×	×					
Reading Vocabulary				×	×	×	×	×
Sentence Reading		×						
Reading Comprehension			×	×	×	×	×	×
Language Mechanics					×	×	×	
Language Expression					×	×	×	
Language/English			×	×				×
Study Skills					×	×	×	×
Spelling			×	×	×	×	×	×
Listening	×	×	×	×	×	×	×	
Concepts of Number			×	×	×	×	×	
Computation			×	×	×	×	×	
Applications			×	×	×	×	×	
Mathematics	×							×
Environment	×	×	×	×				
Science					×	×	×	×
Social Science					×	×	×	×
Using Information					×	×	×	×
Thinking Skills					×	×	×	×

of the '88 *Stanford* is the dual standardization of the batteries together with the *Otis-Lennon School Ability Test.* This dual standardization of achievement and ability measures allowed for an enhancement called Achievement/Ability Comparisons (AAC) which allow a user to interpret *Stanford* performances in light of students' expected ability. Most major publishers of survey batteries now provide dual standardization with a school or mental ability test.

Technical characteristics of the *Stanford* are quite reasonable. At the Intermediate 1 level (grades 4–5, Form J), for example, spring standardization data yielded internal consistency reliability estimates ranging from .81 (Listening) to .99 for the complete battery of scores, and form-to-form reliabilities ranging from .76 (Listening) to .90 (Total Mathematics). One index of comparability of a test is the relationship between editions of the test. In the case of the *Stanford* the following correlations between the seventh and eighth editions were observed for fourth graders: Total Reading .83, Total Mathematics .89, Total Language .88, and Listening .80. Such data support school system confidence in the use of scores over time.

Following are sample items from Form J of the Intermediate 1 level of the *Stanford.*

READING VOCABULARY

Directions

Choose the word or group of words that means the same, or about the same, as the underlined word. Then mark the space for the answer you have chosen.

Sample A

Something that is huge is very—

A. damp
B. big
C. pretty
D. bright

Directions

Read the sentence in the box. Then choose the answer in which the underlined word is used in the same way. Mark the space for the answer you have chosen.

Sample B

He had a ring on his finger.

In which sentence does the word ring mean the same thing as in the sentence above?

A. He lost his new key ring.
B. The teacher will ring the bell.
C. The children held hands to form a ring.
D. She was wearing a gold ring.

CONCEPTS OF NUMBER

Directions

Read each question and choose the best answer. Then mark the space for the answer you have chosen.

Sample

Which is the numeral for twenty-three?

A. 23
B. 203
C. 230
D. 2003

MATHEMATICS APPLICATIONS

Directions

Read each question and choose the best answer. Then mark the space for the answer you have chosen. If a correct answer is *not here*, mark the space for NH.

Sample

Jane had 7 posters. Then she gave 3 to Dan. How many posters does Jane have left?

A. 10
B. 9
C. 5
D. 4
E. NH

SPELLING

Directions

Read each group of phrases. Look at the underlined word in each phrase. One of the underlined words is not spelled correctly for the way it is used in the phrase. Find the word that is *not* spelled correctly. Then mark the space for the answer you have chosen.

Sample A

A. a ship at sea
B. over his eye
C. buy a ticket
D. one the game

LANGUAGE MECHANICS

Directions

Read each sentence. Decide which word or group of words belongs in the blank. Then mark the space for the answer you have chosen.

Sample B

The bank will open at nine __________.

F. oclock'
G. o'clock
H. oc'lock
J. oclock

LANGUAGE EXPRESSION

Directions

For each question, read all four groups of words. One group of words forms a correct sentence. Each of the other choices is wrong because it does not form a complete sentence, or because it forms more than one sentence. Decide which group of words forms a correct sentence. Then mark the space for the answer you have chosen.

Sample A

A. Since early this morning.
B. Brian opened the package.
C. Coming down the street.
D. Somewhere in the house.

Directions

For each of the following questions, first read the sentences that are in the box. Then choose the answer that *best* joins the sentences in the box into one clear sentence without changing their meaning. Mark the space for the answer you have chosen.

Sample B

He is my friend.
He won the race.

A. My friend, he won the race.
B. My friend won the race.
C. He won the race, my friend.
D. By my friend, the race was won.

SCIENCE

Directions

Read each question and choose the best answer. Then mark the space for the answer you have chosen.

Sample

Which of these is most like the butterfly above?

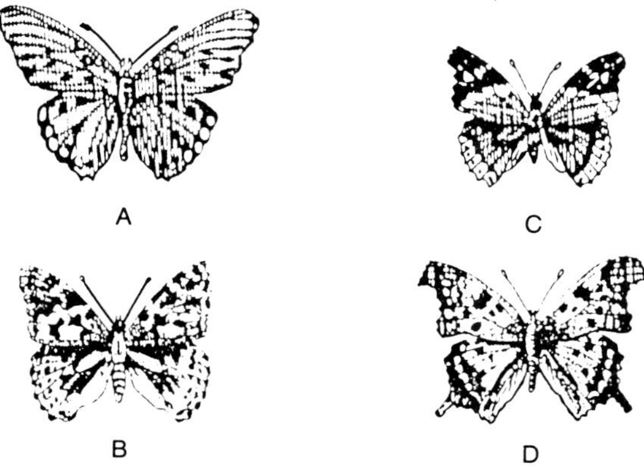

SOCIAL SCIENCE

Directions

Read each question and choose the best answer. Then mark the space for the answer you have chosen.

Sample

SOCIAL SCIENCE

The picture shows a—

A. village
B. city
C. state
D. country

The variety of educational outcomes that can be measured using the multiple choice format is amazing. It takes time to gather good information. The complete battery of Form J of the *Stanford* Intermediate 1 level survey requires 12 sittings which work out to a total of six hours and forty-five minutes. The cost averages between $5.00 and $6.00 depending on the services and reports that are requested.

Specific Subject Tests

Individual tests on special topics do not differ significantly from the kinds of subtests found in most survey batteries. They do differ in depth of coverage. The specific subject test contains more items and covers more aspects of a topic than does a subtest from a battery purporting to measure the same material. There are, in addition, many specialized tests on topics not commonly covered by batteries, for example, economics, trigonometry, physics, chemistry, and computer programming.

The primary reason for using individual tests, as opposed to battery subtests, is that they provide detailed accounting. In some cases single-subject tests may be individually administered—for example, the *Woodcock Reading Mastery Tests—Revised* (Woodcock, 1987)—thereby allowing for flexibility in administration and observation of test performance in a face-to-face situation. Specific tests are generally administered after an unusual student performance is noted on one or more subtests of a survey battery or to explore a subject area in depth. Such tests are being used with less frequency due to already crowded testing schedules. In any event, test batteries generally cover the desired topics. Currently available single-subject tests tend to be in mathematics and reading.

A typical comprehensive system is the *Gates-MacGinitie Reading Test* (G-MRT) (MacGinitie & MacGinitie, 1989). *The Gates-MacGinitie* is a group-administered measure of beginning reading skills and language concepts for grade one. In grades two through twelve it includes vocabulary and comprehension. The G-MRT has normative data available for fall, winter, spring, or out-of-level testing. *Out-of-level testing* takes place when students are tested at their functional level, rather than at their grade or age placement. This practice is sometimes followed when the test content is too difficult or inappropriate. An examinee is then assessed with a "lower" level test. There is no reason out-of-level testing cannot be undertaken at the high end of the ability scale, for example, with academically gifted students. Vocabulary reference lists, for example, Dale's List of 3000 Words Known by Students in Grade Four were used to balance nouns, verbs, adjectives, and other parts of speech. Comprehension subject matter focused on fictional story material in the early grades, poetry, natural and social sciences, and the arts at the upper grades. An innovation in reporting G-MRT performances is the use of *Extended Score Scales* (ESS). The ESS were developed so that student progress could be continuously monitored over time. It is assumed that the standard score ESS allow for equivalent interpretations of score differences at different levels. For example, a difference of 25 ESS units anywhere on the scales represents the difference between the achievement of beginning Grade 5 and beginning Grade 6 students (at time of standardization). Aaron and Gillespie (1990) have noted that, "The tests are an excellent first screening for large groups of students and can also be used to identify pupils at the beginning reading stage who need additional specific skill evaluation. The discussion of evaluation procedures and recommendations for mediation are excellent and are a strong feature of the testing program."

Diagnostic Tests

Diagnostic tests are usually administered after an extended period of instruction, sometimes to a group but usually to individuals, to identify learning weaknesses in a detailed and analytical way, with a view to remediation. The initial use of an achievement battery to identify students who demonstrate inadequate learning is generally recommended. Diagnostic tests are intended for use with students who are observed or known to be having problems. The diagnostic process might involve the following sequence: (a) informal assessment by teacher, (b) survey battery, (c) group diagnostic test, and (d) individual diagnostic test. Individual diagnostic tests are usually administered by testing experts. A standardized diagnostic test can be used to (a) identify for the student and instructor the types of errors being made, (b) make the instructor aware of the important elements, difficulties, and subject and skill sequences in the learning process, and (c) suggest remedial procedures. A substantial amount of diagnostic testing to obtain even more detailed information about pupil difficulties makes use of informal teacher-made devices and direct observation of behavior.

In addition to exhibiting the usual characteristics required of a test (e.g., high reliability, validity, and objectivity), diagnostic tests should (a) be tied to specific curricular objectives and expected learning outcomes, (b) include items that directly measure and analyze specific functions or emphasize selected mechanical aspects of learning, (c) suggest specific remedial procedures for the errors indicated by responses to specific items, and (d) cover reasonably broad integrated learning sequences. Hayward (1968) has suggested three critical questions that need to be asked when selecting a diagnostic reading test. These questions are generalizable to any diagnostic test:

1. Does the test measure the necessary component skills, and do the subscores represent meaningful areas for providing remedial instruction?
2. Are the subscore reliabilities sufficiently high (above .90) for individual application?
3. Are the intercorrelations among the subscores sufficiently low (below .65) to warrant differential diagnosis?

Unfortunately, most of the diagnostic tests available do not meet even minimal criteria. There is a lack of efficient high-quality instruments that may be used diagnostically in program planning. Many achievement batteries attempt to serve as *both* survey instruments and diagnostic tests. The general procedure is to provide between five and ten subject scores and an item-by-item or objective-by-objective breakdown of the individual student scores. Such a breakdown is too general and based on too few items to be considered a reliable procedure. It is difficult to state just how many items are necessary. This should be determined empirically. Studies have shown that one can get acceptable reliability with as few as six to ten items. The procedure may be of some value when used as an initial screening, but such an analysis should not form the basis for instruction. It might be fairer to say that diagnostic tests differ from survey and specific subject-matter tests in the degree of refinement with which they measure achievement than to say that they measure different kinds of achievement. Another way of viewing the distinction between survey and single-subject tests, on the one hand, and diagnostic tests, on the other, is that the former tend to focus on and sample common curricular content, whereas the latter tests sample typical errors or mistakes.

Diagnostic tests usually cover either arithmetic skills or reading. A brief description of two representative diagnostic tests should illustrate the general approach to developing diagnostic tests and the kinds of information they yield.

The *Stanford Diagnostic Mathematics Test* (SDMT) (Beatty, Madden, Gardner, & Karlsen, 1984) is one of the best available diagnostic mathematics tests. The SDMT's two equivalent forms can be used with students in grades 1.5 through 12. The fall/spring standardization has normative data reported in five forms: percentile ranks, stanines, scaled scores, grade equivalents, and normal curve equivalents. The number of items range from 90 to 117; administration time is from 85 to 100 minutes, depending on level; and tests can be hand- or machine-scored. Reports are available for individual students and at the class, building, and system level. Following is a list of the separate reliable scores available with Form G at the tenth grade level.

1.0 Number System and Numeration
    1.1 Whole Number and Decimal Place Value
    1.2 Rational Numbers and Numeration
    1.3 Operations and Properties
2.0 Computation
    2.1 Addition with Whole Numbers
    2.2 Subtraction with Whole Numbers
    2.3 Multiplication with Whole Numbers

- 2.4 Division with Whole Numbers
- 2.5 Fractions
- 2.6 Decimals
- 2.7 Percent
- 2.8 Equations

3.0 Applications

- 3.1 Problem Solving
- 3.2 Read and Interpret Tables and Graphs
- 3.3 Geometry and Measurement

SDMT items are keyed to Content/Skill Progress Indicators which focus on starting points for instruction.

Another representative diagnostic test is the *California Diagnostic Reading Test* (CTB/McGraw-Hill, 1988). This instrument provides information in six overlapping level batteries for students in grades 1.1 through high school. It can be hand- or machine-scored and can be used with the publisher's TESTMATE, a microcomputer software system that enables users to report both norm-referenced and objectives-mastery information. The test is also linked with the extensive *Comprehensive Tests of Basic Skills* (CTB/McGraw-Hill, 1987).

Following is a list of the domains sampled.

1.0 Word Attack

- 1.1 Visual Discrimination
- 1.2 Auditory Discrimination
- 1.3 Word Analysis

2.0 Vocabulary

3.0 Reading Comprehension

4.0 Reading Applications

- 4.1 Skimming and Scanning
- 4.2 Reading Rate
- 4.3 Reference Skills
- 4.4 Life Skills

As was the case with the *Stanford*, an attempt was made to control for possible bias by content examination and empirical means.

These tests are typical and representative of their type. Adoption of one or the other would depend on a detailed analysis of the skills measured, type of information likely to result, and ease of administration in addition to technical information on reliability, validity and adequacy of normative data.

Early Childhood and Readiness Testing

It is difficult to decide if early childhood tests and readiness tests like those used at kindergarten and first grade levels are achievement or ability tests. Perhaps the search for the "correct" classification is nothing more than an academic exercise. We generally think of an achievement test as being a device to assess the impact of a specified curriculum, whereas a readiness test is used to measure if a child has acquired the basic knowledge and skills necessary to move into more formal and structured learning experiences. Readiness tests typically include measures of auditory memory, beginning consonants, letter and visual matching, and basic number concepts. With increasing frequency kindergarten programs are using structured curricula aimed at testing these basic skills and knowledge. Given this typical application we should probably think of the readiness test as an ability test—at least ability as influenced by preschool, kindergarten, and home experiences. It is unacceptable to make a decision about placement or promotion on the basis of a single test score. Therefore, if standardized tests are used at the kindergarten level, they should be used along with teachers' assessments and observations. One must consider the developmental level and needs of the child.

There appears to be a movement toward the use of structured formal assessments as well as informal assessments in the early grades, particularly at the end of kindergarten. The potential user must be alerted to the fact that assessment (group or individual) with any device at these early age levels may be unreliable. Abilities are not yet fully developed and there is great variability among children in the developmental processes. Typical of a new approach is that reflected in the California Test Bureau/McGraw-Hill *Early Childhood System* (CTB/McGraw-Hill, 1990). The comprehensive system includes a developmental checklist for use by teachers, a group paper-pencil assessment test, a group paper-pencil ability test, and extensive instructional activities materials keyed to the assessment materials. The teacher-administered individual checklist (*Developing Skills Checklist*) covers the following areas:

Area	*Sample Tasks*
Mathematical Concepts and Operations	Identifying Numerals Joining and Separating Sets
Language	Naming Body Parts Labeling Objects
Memory	Naming Letters Blending C-V-C Words
Writing and Drawing	Printing First Name Left-Right Progression
Visual	Matching Same/Different Identifying Colors
Motor	Gross Motor Fine Motor
Print Concepts	Differentiating Words/Numerals Identifying People Reading
Auditory	Identifying Same/Different Rhyming

Even a quick glance over the sample tasks suggests that they represent fundamental academic survival skills which must be mastered if progress in school is to be achieved. The tie between checklist tasks and very specific instructional materials is a big plus for this package. The instructional materials include manipulatives. Data are reported as national and/or local percentile ranks, national and/or local stanines, and normal curve equivalents. Internal consistency estimates range from .67 (visual discrimination) to .96 for the total checklist (160 items). The materials also include a parent inventory and socio-emotional observational scales.

Scholastic Ability Tests

Scholastic ability (sometimes referred to as school ability or scholastic aptitude) measures are useful in (a) assessing students' potential to cope with school learning tasks, (b) suggesting possible student placement for school learning functions, and (c) helping evaluate school learning in relation to the academic talents that students bring with them to school learning situations. Processes typically measured by school ability tests include but are not limited to: following directions, detecting similarities and differences, classifying, completing analogies and matrices, and specifying sequences. In addition such measures incorporate measures of the examinees' ability to see relationships, apply generalizations in new and different contexts, think logically, reason, and think critically.

Scores on mental ability tests tend to be fairly stable even over several years, but the interpretation can be influenced by many different factors. Of particular importance is socio-economic class. For an extended discussion of the development and measurement of mental ability measures the reader is referred to Cronbach (1990).

The Spectrum of Scholastic Performance Tests

Cronbach (1990) has noted that ability measures can be distributed along a continuum defined at one end by a high loading of specific or formal school learning experiences and at the other end by minimal influence of formal schooling. These two poles reflect differences between aptitude and achievement tests, with aptitude at the less specific pole and achievement at the more specific pole. Figure 14-1 represents this spectrum. The "loadings" on various types of tests account for the arrangement of the measures. There are no pure forms of these measures to define the ends of or points along the continuum, but classroom knowledge tests and a matrix test come very close to purity at the respective extremes. Most measures used in the public schools fall in the middle of the spectrum or toward the "maximum" end. Even after adjusting for errors of measurement, aptitude and achievement scores correlate very highly. All this means is that they tend to rank people in the same way. It may also imply the influence of a third variable resulting in the two measures to be related. Since there is a difference in content and ability needed to perform on a test, each type of test still yields separate, different, and somewhat

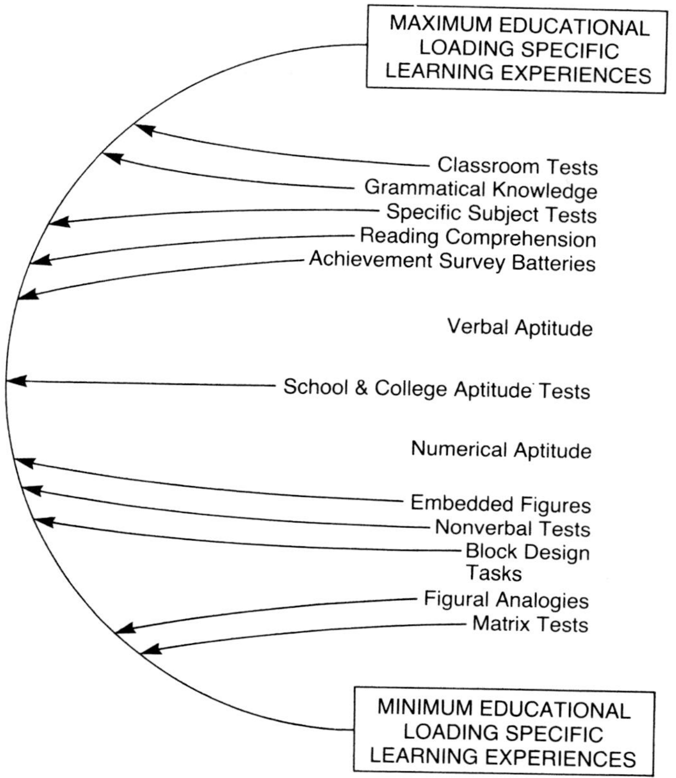

Figure 14-1

Spectrum of ability tests

unique information. If aptitude and achievement tests are used for similar purposes, do we need both kinds of tests? Yes, for several reasons. Use of aptitude tests saves time as the administration time tends to be considerably shorter than that required by an achievement battery. Obviously the information yielded by the two types of tests is different because the tasks and content are different. In some respects aptitude tests are "fairer" (in the sense of having an equitable opportunity to perform) as they are less influenced by school-learned abilities; a person is less apt to be penalized or discriminated against with an aptitude as opposed to an achievement test. We need both kinds of tests!

Applications of Scholastic Aptitude Test Data

There are a variety of areas in which scholastic aptitude test data can assist decision makers. The decision to be made may revolve around classroom instruction, guidance, or administrative uses.

Instructional decisions might focus on the individualization of instruction. If a teacher has some knowledge about the general ability level about his or her students individually or collectively, better informed choices of instructional methods and materials are possible. The general understanding of how an individual is performing is enhanced if we are aware of student ability level. The identification of the so-called under- and overachiever could result from contrasting aptitude and achievement data. In this regard aptitude test data help teachers develop realistic expectations of students. Aptitude data can be used to identify exceptionality. Individual differences in the ability to benefit from instruction vary considerably within and between classes. A group scholastic aptitude test could be used to identify (a) those students in need of diagnostic testing, and (b) those likely to benefit from enrichment experiences. Although the research results are mixed, aptitude data can be used effectively to form ability groups. Such groups significantly facilitate a teacher's ability to focus instruction.

Guidance decisions with regard to educational programs or occupational choice rely on various types of aptitude measures, particularly if these decisions require extensive post-high school education or training. Specialized aptitude batteries are especially helpful in vocational guidance. A kind of hidden plus in using a multifactor battery is that almost everyone does well on some tasks, thereby leading to positive feelings of accomplishment.

Administrative decisions with regard to selection, classification, and placement can be made with ability test data in conjunction with other information. The common basis for admission decisions provided by scholastic aptitude tests has been well documented. With increasing costs in higher education, for example, some selectivity is necessary. Aptitude test scores are useful in making predictions of success. Thorndike and Hagen (1986) have synthesized the research with regard to scholastic, school, or mental ability test scores and school success. They note that:

1. Aptitude test scores are substantially related to school marks.
2. High correlations between school ability measures and achievement have been found in elementary school, but tend to decrease as one goes up the educational ladder through college—but relationships are still considerably greater than chance.
3. Previous school achievement correlates as high or higher with later school success, as do aptitude scores.
4. Measures of aptitude and current or past achievement combined give the best prediction of future achievement.
5. Aptitude tests correlate higher with standardized measures of achievement than with school marks.
6. Aptitude and academic success vary in their degree of relationship according to subject matter.

To a lesser degree aptitude scores have only very modest relationships with success in occupational training programs.

A generally acknowledged problem in using and reporting aptitude scores (particularly single-score tests) is that there is a danger of "labeling" a student. This is always a problem when categories or classifications are used. Test scores should be viewed and used as descriptions, not as explanations.

A Representative Scholastic Aptitude Test

Illustrative of scholastic aptitude tests is the *Otis-Lennon School Ability Test* (Otis & Lennon, 1988). Many other high-quality school or mental ability tests are available from commercial publishers, for example, *Test of Cognitive Skills* and *Cognitive Abilities Test.* The OLSAT is presented here only for illustrative purposes. The OLSAT comprises several levels for use with students in grades from kindergarten to Grade 12. Table 14-4 contains an overview of the content structure of the OLSAT.

A variety of outcomes is measured. The classification of a test item as verbal or nonverbal hinges upon whether knowledge of language is requisite to answering the item. Dual standardization with the *Stanford Achievement Test Series* makes for a particularly valuable combination.

Technical characteristics of the OLSAT are comparable to those of most of the group school ability tests available from major test publishers. The item arrangement, for example, within Level E which is appropriate for Grades 4 and 5 is *spiral omnibus.* This arrangement requires items to be rotated throughout the test according to item type and difficulty. A periodic change from easy to difficult helps insure that students will not become discouraged by encountering increasingly more difficult items. Difficulty level of vocabulary was controlled throughout the test.

Spring and fall standardizations were undertaken with four major demographic categories being used to match against national school data: region, socioeconomic status, urbanity, and ethnicity. Standardization samples were large. In Grade 4, for example, 16,229 students were involved in the standardization, and in Grade 5, 17,000 students. Size is important but *representativeness* is more important.

Internal consistency reliability coefficients ranged from .85 to .93, and criterion-related validity correlations with *Stanford Achievement Test* ranged from .69 to .85. These validity coefficients are quite high, but perhaps not unexpected as both measures were standardized on the same population of students. The data do suggest that a strong common factor runs through both the ability and achievement measures. It is probably best to describe this general factor as a combination of ability and amount and quality of formal educational experiences. This is confirmed by the correlation of .79 between the Verbal and Nonverbal scores of the OLSAT. A correlation that high suggests the presence of a common factor between two apparently different kinds of measures.

It was noted in Chapter 13 on test validity that for tests in which a universally accepted criterion does not exist, a theoretical base that would aid in score interpretation is necessary. The OLSAT has adopted the framework of Vernon and Burt (referred to in the literature as the Hierarchical Theory of Human Abilities) (Vernon, 1961). Spearman's *g* factor is at the top of the hierarchy (see Figure 14-2). Just below *g* are two broad major group factors corresponding to "verbal-educational" and "practical-mechanical" abilities. These are followed by minor group and specific factors. The OLSAT focuses on the shaded area in Figure 14-1. As was noted

Table 14-4 Content and Structure of the *Otis-Lennon School Ability Test*

Cluster/Item Type	Test Level A (Kindergarten)	B (Grade 1)	C (Grade 2)	D (Grade 3)	E (Grades 4–5)	F (Grades 6–8)	G (Grades 9–12)
Verbal							
Verbal Comprehension							
Following Directions	×	×	×				
Antonyms				×	×	×	×
Sentence Completion				×	×	×	×
Sentence Arrangement				×	×	×	×
Verbal Reasoning							
Aural Reasoning	×	×	×				
Arithmetic Reasoning	×	×	×	×	×	×	×
Logical Selection				×	×	×	×
Word/Letter Matrix				×	×	×	×
Verbal Analogies				×	×	×	×
Verbal Classification				×	×	×	×
Inference					×	×	×
Nonverbal							
Pictorial Reasoning							
Picture Classification	×	×	×				
Picture Analogies	×	×	×				
Picture Series	×						
Figural Reasoning							
Figural Classification	×	×	×	×			
Figural Analogies	×	×	×	×	×	×	×
Pattern Matrix	×	×	×	×	×	×	×
Figural Series	×	×	×	×	×	×	×
Quantitative Reasoning				×			
Number Series					×	×	×
Numeric Inference					×	×	×
Number Matrix					×	×	×

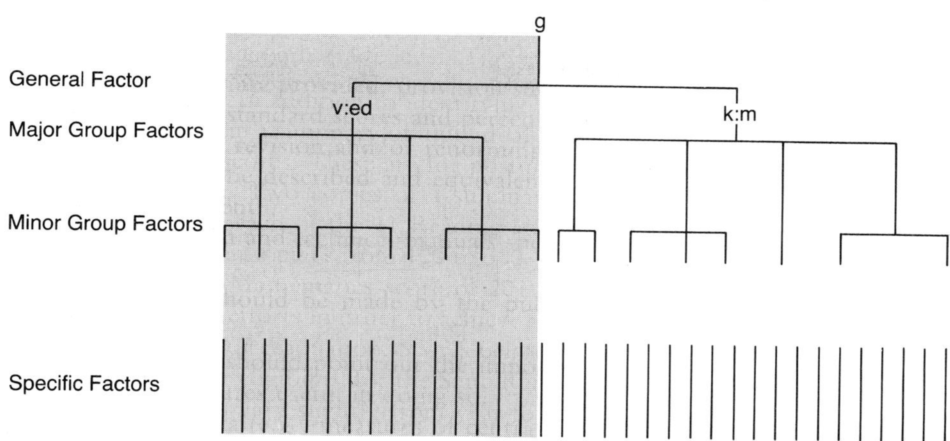

Figure 14-2

Schematic representation of the hierarchical theory of human abilities

previously the correlation among items and scores of the OLSAT confirm the presence of the *g* factor as well as some relatively independent skills.

In addition to the usual kinds of normative indices such as percentile ranks, scaled scores, normal curve equivalents, and stanines, OLSAT performances also can be reported in terms of a School Ability Index (SAI $= 16 \times z$-score $+ 100$). This score looks kind of like an old-fashioned deviation intelligence quotient. The SAI is basically a normalized standard score which is useful in describing performance by age.

Following on pages 336 and 337 are sample items from the OLSAT Practice Test that was prepared to help students become familiar with the types of questions on the regular form of the test. It is suggested that the Practice Test be used approximately one week before the administration of the full OLSAT. Use of the Practice Test is, in fact, a full-blown simulation that includes not only practice items but practice in how to use the answer sheets. There is a significant question as to what extent having practice on items just like those on the test invalidates interpretation about performance on the actual test.

Examination of the OLSAT and *Stanford Achievement Test* items obviously reveals different content. The emphasis on the OLSAT is definitely on reasoning and the ability to see relationships, whereas SAT items are very fact-, subject-, and basic operations-oriented.

VERBAL SCALE ITEMS

Antonyms

1. The opposite of success is—
   A. difficulty B. betrayal C. ignorance D. failure
   E. exhaustion

Word Matrix

2. The words in the box go together in a certain way. Choose the word that goes where you see the question mark.

paint	pain	pan
paste	past	?

F. tap G. tan H. pan J. pat K. pin

Verbal Inference

3. Bill and Kim are taller than James, who is shorter than Mark. We know that—
   A. Bill and Kim are the same height
   B. Kim is older than James
   C. Mark is taller than Bill
   D. Bill and Kim are brothers
   E. James is the shortest

NONVERBAL SCALE ITEMS

Figural Analogies

4.

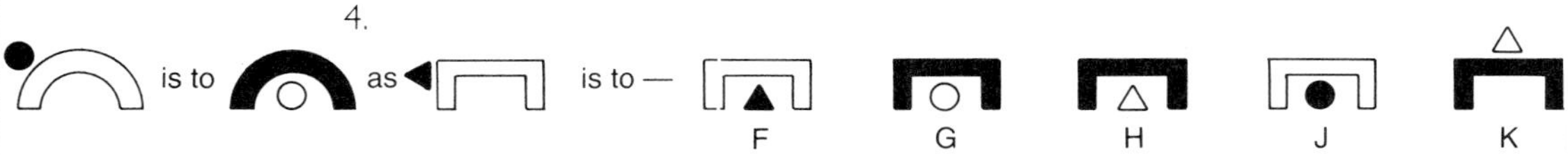

is to as is to —

F G H J K

Series Completion

5. The drawings in the first part of the row go together to form a series. In the next part of the row, choose the drawing that goes where you see the question mark.

?

F G H J K

NONVERBAL SCALE ITEMS

Numeric Inference

6. What number is ten more than the difference between eight and ten?

   A. 8 B. 10 C. 12 D. 18 E. 20

Number Matrix

7. The numbers in the box go together in a certain way. Choose the number that goes where you see the question mark.

2	4	6
4	6	8
6	8	?

   A. 4 B. 10 C. 12 D. 14 E. 16

*Items on Practice Test reprinted from Practice Test for *Otis-Lennon School Ability Test*, 1988 by permission of copyright holder, Harcourt Brace Jovanovich, Inc.

Scholastic aptitude tests are used extensively in higher education to assist in making admissions decisions. Data from such tests as the *Scholastic Aptitude Tests* and the American College Testing Assessment Program provide baseline data that are at least on a common scale and yield score which have comparable meaning as opposed to high-school grades where standards tend to vary dramatically.

Multiple Aptitude Tests

Tests like the OLSAT tend to focus on abilities and aptitudes that are likely to have the greatest "payoff" in academic settings. The development and refinement of statistical techniques such as factor analysis (a search for commonalities among intertest correlations) has led to the refinement of test packages or batteries useful in academic, employment, and military settings. As the term implies, multifactor batteries contain assessments of a variety of differential abilities, usually covering the cognitive (verbal and numerical), perceptual (spacial and form), and psychomotor (manual dexterity and fine motor coordination) domains.

At the secondary school level the *Differential Aptitude Tests* (DAT) have been found useful in educational counseling and career guidance and exploration. The DAT contains eight tests requiring two hours and 45 minutes of testing time. The undivided tests are: Verbal Reasoning, Numerical Ability, Abstract Reasoning, Mechanical Reasoning, Space Relations, Spelling, Language Usage, and Clerical Speed and Accuracy. The combination of verbal and numerical aptitude scores is considered a measure of general scholastic aptitude. One of the positive characteristics of the DAT is that examinees are provided a profile of different skills and abilities, and almost everybody has some assets.

The United States Employment Service uses the General Aptitude Test Battery (GATB). Twelve tests yield nine scores: intelligence, verbal aptitude, numerical aptitude, spatial aptitude, form perception, clerical perception, motor coordination, finger dexterity, and manual dexterity. The public schools have access to the use of the GATB and have found it very useful in vocational counseling. This is because specific occupations have been grouped into job families with multiple-score cutoffs established. An adolescent interested in exploring the world of work would find the two-and-a-half hours required for testing to be a good investment.

The composition of the Armed Services Vocational Aptitude Battery (ASVAB) is similar to the GATB. The "occupational" patterns to be matched are quite different. The ASVAB (Form 14 for high school students) yields three academic composites and four occupational composite scores. The occupational composites are: Mechanical and Crafts, Business and Clerical, Electronics and Electrical, and Health, Social, and Technology. Those individuals considering military service would find the ASVAB a useful tool.

The National Assessment of Educational Progress

The kinds of external tests and testing systems described to this point have for the most part originated from local or state requirements. The federal government is also involved in testing via the National Assessment of Educational Progress (NAEP).

The ever-increasing cost of public education is a matter of growing concern to professional educators, laypersons, and government personnel. The concept of accountability is being implemented in a variety of ways to make the educational process more effective and efficient. Efficiency, of course, influences cost. Billions of dollars are spent in the United States each year on buildings, salaries, and curricula, with minimal attention to the effectiveness of these expenditures. The purpose of the National Assessment of Educational Progress is to collect information that can be used in rational decision making about our schools. The resulting data would have implications both for curricula and for the allocation of funds.

The NAEP (currently administered by Educational Testing Service) is a censuslike survey of the knowledge, skills, understanding, and attitudes of certain groups of young Americans. It focuses on growth and decline in selected educational attainments of young Americans. Subject areas such as citizenship, science, writing, music, mathematics, literature, social studies, reading, art, and career and occupational development are examined cyclically. The first assessment cycle began in 1969, with coverage of science, writing, and citizenship. Repeated assessments reveal whether change has occurred. Since the initial assessment, data have been gathered on over 1.4 million students. Extreme care is exercised to avoid identifying any individual, student, school, city, or state. A given student will respond to only a portion of the exercises.

Approximately half of the exercises administered during any given year are reported. Results in the form of Report Cards are reported as percentages of various groups that respond correctly (and incorrectly) to the exercises. The groups are made up of individuals representing various combinations of the following categories:

1. Ages 9, 13, and 17, and young adults (ages 26–35).
2. Geographic region—Northeast, Southeast, Central, and West.
3. Size of community—big cities, urban fringes, medium-size cities, and less populated places.
4. Type of community—impoverished inner cities, affluent suburbs, and rural areas.
5. Sex.
6. Color—black, nonblack, and total.
7. Socioeducational background.

Extensive effort was expended by scholars, school personnel, and representatives of the public to identify the most relevant objectives of American education. The resulting objectives were then translated, mostly under contract with commercial test developers, into a variety of tasks—some paper-and-pencil, some group activities, and a variety of other formats.

Currently available NAEP data suggest that American education is at a crossroads (Applebee, Langer, & Mullis, 1989). Although long-term gains are reflected in the major subject areas of reading, mathematics, and science, and the gap between white and nonwhite students is decreasing, desired absolute levels of performance are still not being approached. In particular there is a deficiency with regard to the development of higher-level cognitive problem-solving skills. Major changes in curriculum and instruction may be needed in order to bring about substantive changes. Data from NAEP suggest the likelihood that success can result if changes are made. It was found, for example, that students who reported participatory and varied instructional practices in science and literature classes tended to have higher performance than those students who were exposed to traditional approaches such as textbook reading, completion of individual exercises in workbooks or on the board, and teacher "explanations." The interplay of instruction and testing is obvious. Test data can help us see what we are doing in the schools and with our students.

To facilitate interpretation of results and comparisons across assessment years for age groups and subpopulations, a five-level proficiency scale was devised. The NAEP mathematics scale was computed as a weighted composite over five content areas. These were (a) knowledge and skills, (b) higher level applications, (c) measurement, (d) geometry, and (e) algebra. Following is a set of definitions and items illustrating the levels of proficiency concept.

Level 150—Simple Arithmetic Facts

Learners at this level know some basic additional and subtraction facts, and most can add two-digit numbers without regrouping. They recognize situations in which addition and subtraction apply. They also are developing rudimentary classification skills.

Which of these numbers is closest to 30?

◦ 20

• 28

◦ 34

◦ 40

Level 200—Beginning Skills and Understanding

Learners at this level have considerable understanding of two-digit numbers. They can add two-digit numbers, but are still developing an ability to regroup in subtraction. They know some basic multiplication and division facts, recognize relations among coins, can read information from charts and graphs, and use simple measurement instruments. They are developing some reasoning skills.

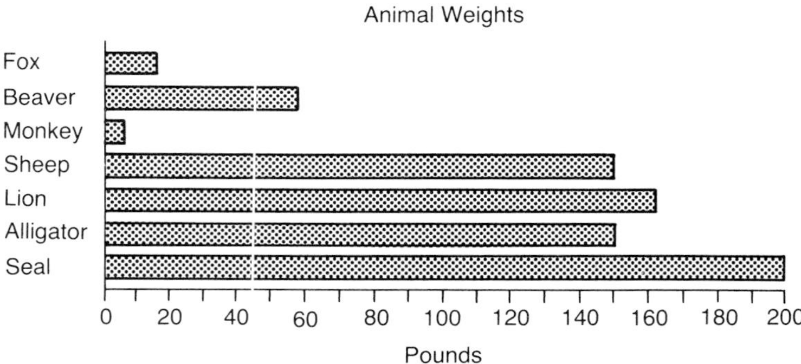

The animals that weigh less than 100 pounds are

◦ alligator, sheep, lion

◦ monkey, sheep, lion

• fox, beaver, monkey

◦ fox, lion, seal

Level 250—Basic Operations and Beginning Problem Solving

Learners at this level have an initial understanding of the four basic operations. They are able to apply whole number addition and subtraction skills to one-step word problems and money situations. In multiplication, they can find the product of a two-digit and a one-digit number. They can also compare information from graphs and charts, and are developing an ability to analyze simple logical relations.

Sam has 68 baseball cards. Juanita has 127. Which number sentence could be used to find how many more cards Juanita has than Sam?

- • 127 − 68 = □
- ○ 127 + □ = 68
- ○ 68 − □ = 127
- ○ 68 + 127 = □
- ○ I don't know

Level 300—Moderately Complex Procedures and Reasoning

Learners at this level are developing an understanding of number systems. They can compute with decimals, simple fractions, and commonly encountered percents. They can identify geometric figures, measure lengths and angles, and calculate areas of rectangles. These students are also able to interpret simple inequalities, evaluate formulas, and solve simple linear equations. They can find averages, make decisions on information drawn from graphs, and use logical reasoning to solve problems. They are developing the skills to operate with signed numbers, exponents, and square roots.

Refer to the following graph. This graph shows how far a typical car travels after the brakes are applied.

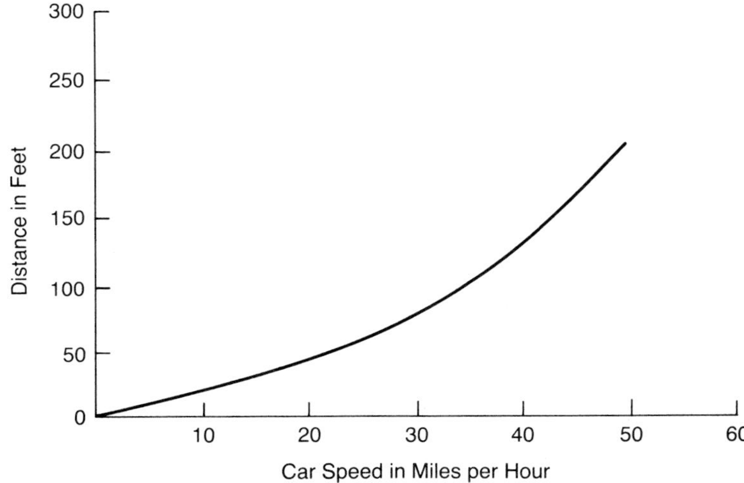

A car is traveling 55 miles per hour. About how far will it travel after applying the brakes?

- ◦ 25 feet
- ◦ 200 feet
- • 240 feet
- ◦ 350 feet
- ◦ I don't know.

Level 350—Multistep Problem Solving and Algebra

Learners at this level can apply a range of reasoning skills to solve multistep problems. They can solve routine problems involving fractions and percents, recognize properties of basic geometric figures, and work with exponents and square roots. They can solve a variety of two-step problems using variables, identify equivalent algebraic expressions, and solve linear equations and inequalities. They are developing an understanding of functions and coordinate systems.

Christine borrowed $850 for one year from the Friendly Finance Company. If she paid 12% simple interest on the loan, what was the total amount she repaid?

ANSWER $952

A typical report of mathematics achievement might look like the data display in Table 14-5.

It is distressing to note that over a quarter of middle school students (representing more than three-quarters of a million students) had not mastered skills in whole-number addition, subtraction, multiplication, and division necessary to perform everyday tasks. One might have expected higher percentages of students at age 13 and 14 demonstrating success in dealing with decimals, fractions, percents, and basic geometry and algebra, given the emphasis on those topics in middle/junior high school. The fact that nearly 50 percent of 17-year-olds do not possess these skills has serious implications for these individuals as they approach graduation and the world of work or, for some, higher education. These are "life support" mathematical skills.

Establishing a Schoolwide Assessment System

If educators are truly concerned with the "total student," it is imperative that a comprehensive assessment system be established. The term *assessment* is used intentionally, in preference to *testing* because most schools have testing programs to meet accreditation requirements. The data from such programs are usually filed away and never benefit student, teacher, or administration. The backbone of an assessment system can, however, be the testing program. It needs to be supplemented with

Table 14-5 Percentages of Students at or Above Proficiency Levels on NAEP Scales—1986: Ages 9, 13, and 17

Level/Description		Elementary School (Age 9)	Middle School (Age 13)	High School (Age 17)
350	Can solve multi-step problems and use basic algebra	0	0	6
300	Can compute with decimals, fractions, and percents; recognizes geometric figures, and solves problems	1	16	51
250	Can add, subtract, multiply, and divide using whole numbers	21	73	96
200	Can add and subtract two-digit numbers and recognize relationships among coins	74	99	100
150	Knows some basic addition and subtraction facts	98	100	100

From Applebee, Langer, and Mullis (1989).

periodic assessments of such nontraditional variables as student attitudes toward school and learning, classroom environment, parental attitudes, and teacher values. The cost of a schoolwide program is not inconsequential, and may be many dollars per student per year. The potential benefit to the student, school, and society justifies the cost. Data from a comprehensive program can be used to (a) improve the instructional program, (b) facilitate curriculum revision, (c) assist in educational vocational counseling, (d) help the administrative staff appraise the overall impact and effectiveness of the educational program, and, most importantly, (e) help the individual examine his progress and strengths.

Designing a Program

The design of a schoolwide program has at least nine major phases:

1. Examination of the school's educational philosophy and purpose in establishing the system. Answers are sought to the question, "What information is desired and why?"

2. Solicitation of staff cooperation and involvement in program development.
3. Communication to all faculty of the nature, extent, and purpose of the assessment.
4. Designation of those who will use and have access to the information.
5. Determination of the manner in which information will be used.
6. Designation of responsibilities for the execution of the program.
7. Stimulation of financial and moral support for the program.
8. Provision for the administrative machinery for reevaluation of the program.
9. Interpretation of the program to the community. The last phase is particularly critical as the general public becomes increasingly involved in setting school policies and monitoring the educational process.

Criteria for an Effective Program

Traxler (1950) has presented a set of 15 criteria that can be employed in examining the effectiveness of an assessment system. These criteria, in the form of "critical questions," are as follows:

1. Is the program comprehensive?
2. Does the program include all the students in the school?
3. Are the tests given at regular intervals?
4. Are the tests administered at times of the year that maximize their usefulness?
5. Are the tests in the school's testing program comparable?
6. Do the tests used agree with the objectives and the curriculum of the school?
7. Are the specific tests carefully chosen?
8. Are the tests carefully administered to each group?
9. Are the tests scored accurately?
10. Are the test results interpreted in terms of appropriate norms?
11. Are the test results quickly disseminated to teachers and counselors in understandable terms?
12. Are the test results recorded on individual cumulative record forms?
13. Is a definite attempt made to relate the test scores to other kinds of information?
14. In addition to the regular testing program, is there provision for special testing as needed?
15. Does the school have an in-service program for educating teachers in the use of test results?

This list of criteria suggests some very important requirements for an effective assessment system. Among the most important is, of course, the match between the school curricular objectives and the test items and information available relative to their interpretation. Technical adequacy and security are also major considerations. The final criterion worth commenting on is the need to see that all users of the test data, decision makers and audiences, receive the information when it is needed in a timely and understandable form.

A Hypothetical Testing Program

The following testing program is considered "hypothetical" as each school system (and, to some extent, school) has unique curricular and instructional requirements for the nature and timing of information needed for a variety of decision-making applications. Table 14-6 contains an outline of a possible K–12 student assessment system.

The criterion-referenced measures are usually of basic reading and math skills. The criterion-referenced measure might be from a commercial publisher or locally developed by the school system or a state agency. At the tenth grade level reading and math skills are assessed together with writing. The assessment of writing is increasingly becoming a major event in all testing programs. The ability to communicate in written form reflects on the application of these very important language skills.

Tests useful for guidance purposes may be employed at almost any point during the schooling process. Data from scholastic aptitude or school ability tests, multiple-aptitude batteries, and interest inventories can provide an extremely valuable starting point for educational and vocational counseling. Personality inventories also might be used as part of the guidance and counseling program.

When to schedule nonclassroom testing during the school year represents a dilemma. Data derived from a fall test administration should have maximum usefulness throughout the school year, if for no other reason than that it is recent relative to the start of school. Such data are less likely to be used for teacher evaluation or student promotion decisions. Fall data would have maximum value in planning instructional programs. The results of spring testing are likely to have their maximum value in program evaluation and in assessing school effectiveness.

Table 14-6 Hypothetical School Testing Program

Grade	Kind of Test
Kindergarten	Readiness
One	Achievement (usually criterion-referenced)
Two	Norm-Referenced Achievement Battery/School Ability Test
Three	Achievement (usually criterion-referenced)
Four	Norm-Referenced Achievement Battery/School Ability Test
Five	Optional (Achievement or Ability)
Six	Achievement (usually criterion-referenced), Writing sample
Seven	Norm-Referenced Achievement Battery
Eight	Achievement (usually criterion-referenced), Writing sample
Nine	Norm-Referenced Achievement Battery
Ten	Survey of basic skills (usually criterion-referenced)
Eleven	Scholastic Aptitude (optional)
Nine-Twelve	Vocational Aptitude/Interest Inventories

Locating Information About Tests

It would be impossible to list, let alone critically evaluate, all those tests that might be of interest to a particular instructor or administrator. A potential user needs information bearing on such questions as: (a) What types of tests are available that will yield the kinds of information I am interested in? (b) What do the "experts" say about the tests I am interested in? (c) What research has been undertaken on this test? (d) What statistical data relating to validity and reliability are available for examination? and (e) With what groups may I legitimately use this test? Answers to these and many other relevant questions may be found in one or more of the following resources:

1. *Mental Measurements Yearbooks.*
2. Test reviews in professional journals.
3. Test manuals and specimen sets.
4. Text and reference books on testing.
5. Bibliographies of tests and testing literature.
6. Educational and psychological abstract indexes.
7. Publishers' test catalogs.

Six additional sources should be mentioned.

8. *Test Critiques.* Seven volumes of in-depth evaluative studies of over 600 psychological, educational, and business tests (Keyser & Sweetland, 1980). Test Corporation of America also publishes compendia of reviews for testing children, young children, adolescents, adults, and older adults.

9. *Tests in Print* (Mitchell, 1991). Published by the Buros Institute of Mental Measurements this is a comprehensive listing of commercially available tests. It is cross-referenced to test reviews in the *Mental Measurements Yearbooks.* This is a very valuable reference.

10. *Directory of Selected National Testing Programs* (1987). A detailed listing of over 200 academic selection and certification tests.

11. *Educational Testing Service Test Collection Catalogs* (1989). A four-volume guide to thousands of tests in such areas as school and reading readiness, screening tests, vocational areas (clerical, mechanical), learning-disabled, cognitive ability and style, creative and divergent thinking, and intelligence.

12. *Index to Tests Used in Educational Dissertations* (Fabiano, 1989). An index to over 40,000 tests used in educational dissertations covering 1938–1980. Cross-referenced to the *Thesaurus of ERIC Descriptors* users can identify tests (and the population with which they were used) in such areas as achievement, personality, aptitude, physical fitness, and vocations.

13. *Directory of Unpublished Experimental Measures* (Goldman, Saunders, & Busch, 1974–1982). A reference list of tests identified from journal articles and organized into 23 content categories.

Any competent librarian can assist the reader in accessing other sources of information such as *Education Index, Dissertation Abstracts International, Psychological Abstracts, Educational Resources Information Center* (especially the one in Tests and Measurements), which publishes *Resources in Education* and *Current Index to Journals in Education.* Computer searches of these and other databases (DIALOG) can greatly facilitate information gathering.

Of the 13 resources listed above, the first three are probably the most immediately informative. These three sources will be discussed in turn, highlighting the types of information that each will provide.

The Mental Measurements Yearbooks

Probably the most useful sources of evaluative information about commercial tests are the *Mental Measurements Yearbooks.* Originated by the late Dr. Oscar K. Buros they are now the provence of the Buros Institute of Mental Measurements at the University of Nebraska. Up-to-date and comprehensive bibliographies, test reviews, and book reviews are published in the *Yearbooks,* 10 of which have been published to date. Buros' goal was to develop in the potential user and publisher a critical attitude toward tests and testing, to facilitate communication, and in general to bring about a significant increase in the quality of published tests. Specifically, Buros wanted the *Yearbooks* "(a) to provide information about tests published as separates throughout the English-speaking world; (b) to present frankly critical test reviews written by testing and subject specialists representing various viewpoints; (c) to provide extensive bibliographies of verified references on the construction, use, and validity of specific tests; (d) to make readily available the critical portions of test reviews appearing in professional journals; and (e) to present fairly exhaustive listings of new and revised books on testing, along with evaluative excerpts from representative reviews which these books receive in professional journals." The *Yearbooks* have made a significant and lasting contribution toward these ends.

Some sense of the extensiveness of the *Yearbooks* can be gained from a brief look at the contents of the 1,014-page *Tenth Yearbook* (Conoley & Kramer, 1989). The *Tenth* contains a bibliography of 396 commercially available tests and 569 critical reviews by measurement experts. In addition there are 1,153 references to the professional literature with an additional 727 from the reviewers. A breakdown of tests by type is contained in Table 14-7. In addition to data from the *Tenth Yearbook* Table 14-5 also includes percentages from the *Ninth Yearbook* which carries a 1985 copyright. It can be seen that the percentages are quite comparable which perhaps reflects on the stability of the commercial test market. The 1989 list does not contain, however, reviews of new or revised science tests or multiaptitude batteries. The 1985 list, on the other hand, does not contain English or Education

Table 14-7 Tests by Major Classification in the *Ninth* and *Tenth Mental Measurements Yearbooks*

Classification	Number 1989	Percentage 1989	Percentage 1985
Vocations	100	25.3	20.9
Personality	72	18.2	24.8
Miscellaneous	73	10.9	9.9
Developmental	31	7.8	4.0
Intelligence and Scholastic Aptitude	28	7.1	7.1
English	24	6.1	
Reading	24	6.1	6.9
Speech and Hearing	22	5.6	2.8
Education	20	5.1	
Achievement	12	3.0	4.8
Mathematics	9	2.2	3.3
Science			1.8
Social Studies	3	.8	.4
Fine Arts	2	.5	.6
Foreign Languages	2	.5	9.5
Sensory-Motor	2	.5	1.6
Neuropsychological	2	.5	1.0
Multiaptitude			.6
TOTAL	396	100.0	100.0

reviews which undoubtedly reflects the contemporary concern about both these areas. The Vocation Category contains both proficiency measures and interest inventories.

Due to the need for the most current information available there also exists an easily computer-searchable database for the MMY. Based on the MMY classification schemes a user can access the MMYD with a variety of algorithms to isolate tests for specific variables, populations, price, publication date, and so forth. Between *Yearbooks* the Buros Institute publishes a softback *MMY Supplement* with the most recent test reviews.

Test Reviews in Journals

Despite the fact that such authoritative comprehensive sources as the *Yearbooks* are available, it is often difficult to locate recent data on either new or old tests. Research data or questions related to reliability, validity, and usability, and occasional test reviews are periodically carried in the following journals: the *Journal of Educational Measurement, Applied Measurement in Education, Measurement and Evaluation in Guidance, Applied Psychological Measurement,* and the *Journal of Psychological Assessment.* In addition an excellent source of validity studies is the quarterly publication *Educational and Psychological Measurement.*

Test Manuals and Specimen Sets

After preliminary decisions have narrowed the field, a potential user should probably obtain specimen sets from publishers. Such a set usually contains a copy of the test questions, scoring key, answer sheets, examiner's manual, and occasionally a technical manual. The sets, available at a nominal cost, should be ordered on official school or institution letterhead stationery, because most publishers attempt to insure that their materials are distributed to qualified individuals only, in order to maintain security. If there is any question about the qualifications required for the purchase of a particular test, one should consult the publisher's catalog. Following are some excerpts from the *1989 Catalog for Tests, Products and Services for Education* for the Psychological Corporation with regard to qualifications for test purchases.

> The tests listed in this catalog are carefully developed assessment devices that require specialized training to ensure their appropriate professional use. Eligibility to purchase these tests is therefore restricted to individuals with specific training and experience in a relevant area of assessment. These standards are consistent with the *1985 Standards for Educational and Psychological Testing* and with the professional and ethical standards of a variety of professional organizations.

Tests are categorized as being:

> *Level A:* Purchase orders will be filled promptly. Registration is *not* required. [An illustrative Level A instrument would be an occupational interest inventory called the *Self-Directed Search.*—added by author]
>
> *Level B:* These tests are available to firms having a staff member who has completed an advanced level course in testing from an accredited college or university, or equivalent training under the direction of a qualified supervisor or consultant. Registration *is* required. [Examples of tests at this level would be the *Watson-Galser Critical Thinking Appraisal* and the *Metropolitan Achievement Tests (Sixth Edition).*—added by author]
>
> *Level C:* These tests are available only to firms for use under the supervision of qualified professionals, defined as persons with at least a master's degree in psychology or a related discipline and appropriate training in the field of personnel testing. The qualified person may be either a staff member or a consultant. Registration *is* required. [An example of a Level C test would be the *Wechsler Intelligence Scale for Children—Revised.*—added by author]

Once a user has been granted access to a particular test there are additional guidelines which must be followed. These relate to test security. Following is an excerpt of such test security precautions.

Purchaser agrees to comply with these basic principles of test security:

1. Test taker must not receive test answers before beginning the test.
2. Test questions are not to be reproduced or paraphrased in any way by a school, college, or any organization or person.
3. Access to test materials is limited to persons with a responsible, professional interest who will safeguard their use.
4. Test materials and scores are to be released only to persons qualified to interpret and use them properly.
5. If a test taker or the parent of a child who has taken a test wishes to examine responses or results, the parent or test taker is permitted to read a copy of the test and the test answers of the test taker in the presence of a representative of the school, college, or institution that administered the test.

The test manual is the most informative and readily accessible source of information about a specific test. Directions for administering and scoring the test, brief statistical information about validity, reliability, and norms, a description of the test's development, and suggestions for interpreting and using the test results constitute the usual content of the manual. The reviewer should remember, however, that the publisher has a vested interest, and all tests should be evaluated critically. Most Level B and C tests also have Technical Manuals available that contain extensive data on the development of the tests.

Selecting an Achievement Test

After informally reviewing several tests in a particular area and making a preliminary decision about the purpose of testing and the projected uses of the test data, the instructor would profit from a detailed examination of two or three tests. A set of evaluative questions that have been found useful in judging a test for possible use in schools is reprinted below. The first eight categories are essentially descriptive, but nevertheless important. For example, such factors as the affiliation of the author and the copyright data bear on such significant criteria as credibility, authenticity, and recency. The outline presented here is an adaptation and expansion of an outline originally developed by Cronbach (1960, pp. 147–153).

In undertaking a "critical analysis," one will consult many sources. The reader is referred to earlier pages in this chapter for information on identifying references. In addition, it would be well worthwhile for the test evaluator to refer to *Standards for Educational and Psychological Tests and Manuals* (American Psychological Association, 1985) for assistance in identifying minimally acceptable criteria for many of the variables described in this outline. It is usually a good idea to record the comments, evaluations, and sources consulted during the review process.

Outline for Critical Analysis of a Standardized Achievement Test

1. Title—Note complete and exact title of test.
2. Author—A brief summary of professional affiliations and credentials would be informative.
3. Publisher—Some publishers are more reputable than others. Check with experts in testing.
4. Copyright Date—Note dates of first publication and each revision.
5. Level or Group for Whom Test Is Intended—Such factors as age, grade, and ability level need to be considered. What background does the author presuppose for examinees? Is the test available at different levels? If so, which ones?
6. Forms of the Test—What forms of the test are available? If the forms are not essentially the same, major differences should be mentioned and evaluated. What evidence is presented on equivalence of forms?
7. Purpose and Recommended Use—Summarize the use of the test recommended by the author.
8. Dimensions of Areas that the Test Purports to Measure—Give a brief definition of description of the variables involved. If the test has a great number of scales (or scores) it may be necessary simply to mention the subscores and highlight only the group or distinctive scores. If at this point there is no match with local objectives or intents, one would probably terminate the review of this particular instrument.
9. Administration—Describe briefly. The median time required to complete the test should be indicated. If parts of the test are timed separately, note how many starting points are necessary. Are the directions easy for the test administrator to follow and the test takers to comprehend? Is special training required for valid administration? Is the test largely self-administering? Are there objectionable features?
10. Scoring—Scoring procedures should be described very briefly. Is the test planned and organized so that machine-scored answer sheets can or must be used? Is a correction for guessing justified and/or applied? (Refer to the discussion of guessing in Chapter 5.)
11. Source of Items—Where did the author get the items? What criteria were used in item selection? Are some items taken from other tests? If so, which ones?
12. Description of Items (Format and Content)—Briefly describe the major types of items used. Attention should be given to *item form* (e.g., multiple-choice, analogy, forced-choice) and *item content* (e.g., culture-free symbols, nonsense syllables, food preferences, occupational titles). How many response categories are there? Note a typical example of the major type(s) of items used. It is imperative that the actual items be evaluated in light of the questions a teacher would ask of the data.
13. Statistical Item Analysis—Was an item analysis made to determine item discrimination and difficulty? What were the results? What criteria were used to select items for the final form(s) of the instrument? What analytic techniques were used?

14. Method and Results of Validation Reported by Publisher and Author—For most tests this topic is related to categories 11, 12, and 13. One must ask, "What was done to make the test valid and useful?" Some tests are validated by expert judgment, some by an external criterion, and so on. What has the author done to demonstrate the validity of the test? What correlations with other tests are presented? Has an external criterion been used to evaluate the usefulness of the scores? This section should deal with data other than those obtained in the construction of the test. What specific "predictions" could one make from an individual's test score on the basis of the validity data presented?
15. Validity as Determined by Others—This is in many respects *the* crucial evaluative criterion. The recent literature should be consulted, and studies briefly summarized.
16. Reliability—State briefly how reliability was determined. Report interesting or unusual data on reliability. Was reliability computed separately for each subgroup or part of the test?
17. Norm Group(s)—How many were involved? How were they selected? Are separate norms available for each group with whom one might wish to compare an individual's score, that is, norms for each sex, age level, curriculum major, occupation?
18. Interpretation of Scores—How are scores expressed? (Percentile ranks, standard scores, grades scores?) What is considered a "high" score? A "low" score? How are these scores interpreted?
19. Major Evaluations by Experts—What assumptions are examined and what questions are raised in the *Mental Measurements Yearbooks?* What do measurement experts and the journals say about the test?
20. Cost Factors—The initial cost of booklets and answer sheets should be considered, as well as such factors as cost scoring, reusability of booklets, and availability of summary and research services.
21. Distinguishing Characteristics—What are the outstanding features of this test, its construction, and its use? Note both desirable and undesirable features.
22. Overall Evaluation—How well do such factors as validity, reliability, standardization, and item content coincide with the intended use of the test?

How should the information in these 22 categories be weighted? No universal answer can be given, since the selection of a particular test or battery depends upon the individual needs of specific instructors or schools. The purpose of testing must be foremost in the mind of the test evaluator. Such questions as "What specific information is needed?" and "How will the test data be interpreted and used?" are highly significant. Questions relating to validity, reliability, and the representativeness of the normative data should be critically reviewed and heavily weighted in the final decisions if the test is to be used in a norm-referenced way.

The critical evaluation of any standardized test is a time-consuming and involved process. But considering the kinds of decisions that will be made about students and programs as a result of such tests, the expenditure of effort is more than justified.

Standardized tests, particularly achievement and ability tests, represent valuable tools to be used to help realize human potential. They are sources of information, but they are not the *only* source of information. Legal and professional efforts are being made to insure fair and equitable use of tests, but we should not ascribe any shortcomings of use to the tool but to the user. Education and training are the major avenues to more informed test use and decision making.

Let us not forget the admonition of Walter S. Monroe who wrote in his 1917 text, *Educational Tests and Measurements,* "Standardized tests and scales are not 'playthings.' "

Content Review Statements

1. Standardized tests used in the schools are classified on the basis of the domain sampled: aptitude, achievement, or affective.
2. Standardized tests are carefully developed and tested on usually large and representative populations.
3. The term *standardization* refers to the uniform and controlled conditions required for administration and scoring, and sometimes to the availability of normative data.
4. Standardized achievement tests are usually based on extensive analyses of common educational outcomes.
5. Refined item-selection procedures and test analyses characterize standardized measures.
6. Standardized achievement tests are used to:
   a. Direct curricular emphases.
   b. Provide educational guidance.
   c. Stimulate learning activities.
   d. Direct and motivate administrative and supervisory efforts.
7. Achievement survey batteries provide an overview of the major instructional thrusts in primary, elementary, and secondary schools and colleges in such areas as language arts, mathematics, social studies, science, reading, and study skills.
8. Survey battery subtests have the advantage of being standardized on the same populations.
9. Specific subject or area tests provide detailed coverage of limited topics in such areas as chemistry, history, economics, foreign languages, and the like.
10. The diagnostic achievement tests usually applied in the fields of elementary reading and arithmetic:
    a. Provide very detailed analyses of student strengths and weaknesses.
    b. Have items that are tied to specific instructional objectives.
    c. Have scores with direct implications for actual remedial procedures.
11. Readiness tests sample fundamental skills such as auditory memory, visual memory, and letter and number concepts.
12. Scholastic aptitude tests as opposed to achievement tests tend to measure factors less influenced by formal educational experiences.

13. Ability measures can be used to assist in making instructional, educational, vocational, and administrative decisions.
14. Scholastic aptitude tests yield meaningful concurrent and predictive relationships with school success.
15. Information about standardized tests can be secured primarily from:
    a. Buros' *Mental Measurements Yearbooks*.
    b. Test reviews in professional journals.
    c. Test manuals, specimen sets, and publishers' catalogs.
16. In establishing a schoolwide assessment system, one must consider the following factors:
    a. School educational philosophy and objectives.
    b. The uses to which the data are to be put.
    c. Communication and security of results.
    d. Scheduling of tests.
    e. Evaluation of the testing program.
    f. Achievement of cooperation from teachers, administrators, students, and members of the community.
17. Schoolwide assessment systems must be responsive to the needs of students, teachers, and society.
18. Among the factors that must be considered in selecting a standardized achievement test for possible use are:
    a. Level and appropriateness of content.
    b. Cost.
    c. Copyright date.
    d. Adequacy of administration and scoring directions.
    e. Adequacy of reliability and validity data.
    f. Adequacy of suggested interpretive guides and normative data.
19. The National Assessment of Educational Progress (NAEP) is an attempt to provide censuslike survey data on the growth of knowledge, skills, understanding, and attitudes among educational subgroups.
20. NAEP is concerned with performance differences in a variety of subject areas, four age groups, various geographic regions, and community sizes and types, but not individual students, schools, systems, or states.
21. Multiple aptitude test batteries are useful in academic and vocational counseling, and career exploration.

Speculations

1. What kinds of information are you likely to obtain from the *Mental Measurements Yearbooks?*
2. On what basis is the use of comprehensive achievement test batteries justified or not justified in the schools?
3. Are measures of academic achievement and academic aptitude really different? If so, in what way?
4. What are the contributions of the National Assessment of Educational Process?

5. Why should or should not standardized achievement test results be used to assess teaching effectiveness?
6. Compare and contrast standardized and nonstandardized achievement tests.
7. What is "diagnostic" about a diagnostic achievement test?

Suggested Readings

Bauernfeind, R. H. (1963). *Building a school testing program.* Boston: Houghton Mifflin. This book provides an overall picture of the processes involved in developing a comprehensive and integrated testing program and presents informative discussions of basic measurement principles and factors in test interpretation.

Findley, W. G. (Ed.). (1963). *The impact and improvement of school testing programs* (62nd Yearbook of the National Society for the Study of Education). Chicago: University of Chicago Press. This high-quality reference work contains 12 chapters contributed by the country's leading testing experts.

Mehrens, W. A., & Lehmann, I. J. (1987). *Using standardized tests in education* (4th ed.). New York: Holt, Rinehart and Winston. This excellent reference book contains a comprehensive survey of aptitude, achievement, interest, personality, and attitude measures. The coverage of achievement tests is particularly informative and valuable.

Wilson, S. M., & Hiscox, M. D. (1984). Using standardized tests for assessing local learning objectives. *Educational Measurement: Issues and Practice, 3*(3), 19–22. A step-by-step procedure is described.

The following books have both educational and psychological orientation and are primarily concerned with commercially available standardized tests.

Aiken, L. R. (1988). *Psychological testing and assessment* (6th ed.). Boston: Allyn and Bacon.

Anastasi, A. (1988). *Psychological testing* (6th ed.). New York: Macmillan.

Cronbach, L. J. (1990). *Essentials of psychological testing* (5th ed.). New York: Harper & Row.

Cunningham, G. K. (1986). *Educational and psychological measurement.* New York: Macmillan.

Sax, G. (1989). *Principles of educational and psychological measurement and evaluation* (3rd ed.). Belmont, CA: Wadsworth Publishing Company.

Walsh, W. B., & Betz, N. E. (1985). *Tests and assessment.* Englewood Cliffs, NJ: Prentice Hall.

Chapter 15

Interpreting the Meaning of Standardized Norm-Referenced Test Scores

This chapter focuses on the problem of deriving meanings from scores on standardized tests. Many of the ideas and suggestions it offers can, however, be applied by classroom teachers to their own tests.

Methods of Expressing Test Scores

In the beginning there was a test score. This raw score from a measurement, be it the total number of correct answers, the ratings of some attitude items, or the amount of time needed to complete a task didn't know what it meant to those who received it. It needed some referent to help with interpretation. Scores that are modifications or transformations of the raw scores are called *derived* scores. There are generally two classes of referents—*absolute* and *relative*. One might use a procedure described in Chapter 16 where a score is expressed in terms of a maximum possible, for example, score of 75 correct answers on a 90-item test where each item is worth one point would receive a score, a *percent* score of 83. We might also talk of the percentage of objectives mastered. These kinds of derived scores are generally associated with criterion-referenced and mastery tests. It is easy to confuse percentage scores and percentile ranks. Parents in particular are likely to erroneously equate a percentile rank of 82 with getting 82 percent of the items correct or getting 82 percent of the possible points. Everybody can think in terms of 100 units. But where do the units come from? The key is the denominator. With regard to a *percent* score the denominator is the number of items or number of points. When calculating a *percentile rank* the denominator is the number of students below the one for which we were calculating the percentile rank.

Relative derived scores use a group or groups of test takers as a basis for scaling. Such data, when collected over large groups of test takers, are called *norms.* Hoover (1984) distinguishes between two types of score scales: status and developmental. The notion of status and developmental scales follows logically from the discussion of mastery and developmental objectives presented in Chapter 4. Status scales describe performance of individual students relative to a single comparison group. This group may simply be an individual teacher's class, school, system, or a national sample. The scales used to express performance under these conditions simply reflect a simple rank-ordering of individuals, with respect to other individuals, whereas percent scores provide a rank-ordering of scores with respect to a standard. Developmental scale scores describe performances with that of a series of different comparison groups such as grade level or age groups. As was noted in Chapter 10, sometimes scores are simply expressed as linear or one-to-one transformation or, in the case of percentile ranks, as *z* scores. Other times, depending on the intended use and the audience for the score, an area transformation is undertaken. The model frequently used for the area transformation is the normal curve. Users of standardized tests need to examine very carefully the technical description of the derivation of the score scales used with their measures.

The combination of the status and developmental scale categories, and linear and area transformation derivation categories yields four different families of score scales. These are summarized in Figure 15-1. The methods used to derive most of these scores have been described in Chapter 10. The only new score is the expanded standard score which employs sophisticated statistical techniques and usually requires the within-group (usually grade) distribution to be normal. It is assumed by some testing people that "normalizing" a distribution makes it into an equal interval scale. It does not!

There are other kinds of status standard scores—such as the College Entrance Examination Board Scores—that are used to report performance on the Scholastic Aptitude Test and the American College Testing program tests. There is also a variety of developmental scores that are created and used by different test publishers for different kinds of tests.

Kinds of Norms

The collections of derived scores that are formed into distributions for specified groups are referred to as norms. Norms are used for making relative interpretations

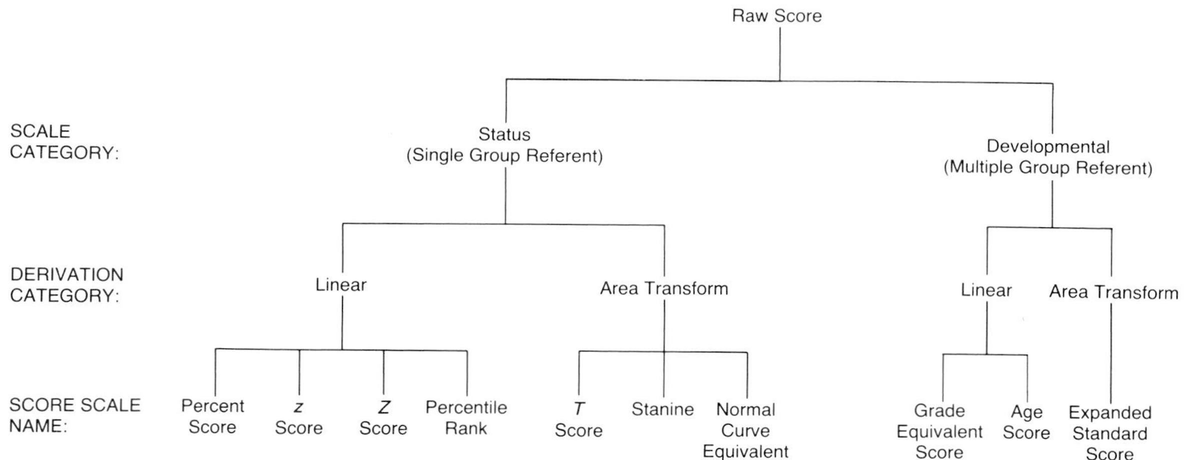

Figure 15-1

Types of derived score scales

of scores. In the following section we describe the major kinds of norms and comment on some of their strengths and weaknesses.

Percentile Rank Norms

Percentile ranks can be used to express local or national normative data, and are also particularly useful with classroom tests. The process merely requires developing a frequency distribution and calculating a percentile rank for each raw score according to the procedures outlined in Chapter 10. Given that an individual has a raw score equivalent to a percentile rank of 64, we can say that a performance is as good as or better than 64 percent of the people with whom we are contrasting it. The use of percentile ranks is recommended because they are readily understood by almost everyone and can be used with many types of tests and distributions of scores. The fact that percentile ranks depend on the frequency distribution creates a potential danger in interpretation. This danger involves the fact that the units used to express percentile ranks are not equal to raw-score units (except in the unlikely occurrence of a rectangular distribution, i.e., a distribution in which each observed score has the same frequency of occurrence). The difference in raw score units between percentile ranks of 84 and 88 is *not* equal to the differences between the percentile ranks of 50 and 54. We have, then, an interpretation based only on a ranking of individuals, without regard to differences between ranks. Because of the unequal units, percentile ranks should not be averaged (unless one wishes to describe average percentile ranks). The point is that the mean percentile rank is not equal to the percentile rank of the mean.

An illustration of the method used to determine percentile ranks from norm tables for a hypothetical mathematics test is presented in Figure 15-2. The procedure

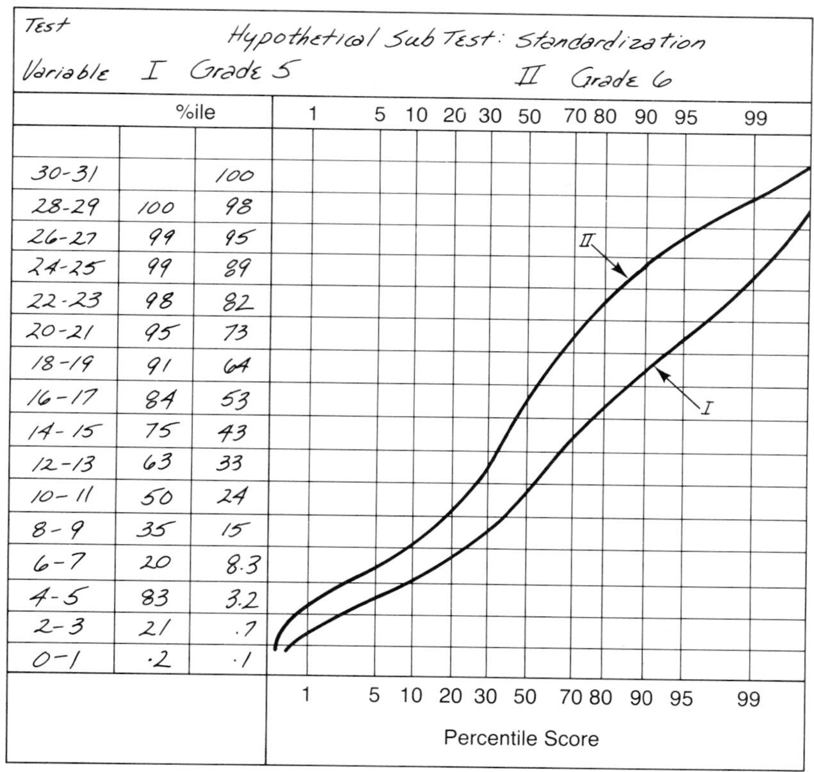

Test Variable	I Grade 5 %ile	II Grade 6 %ile
30-31		100
28-29	100	98
26-27	99	95
24-25	99	89
22-23	98	82
20-21	95	73
18-19	91	64
16-17	84	53
14-15	75	43
12-13	63	33
10-11	50	24
8-9	35	15
6-7	20	8.3
4-5	83	3.2
2-3	21	.7
0-1	.2	.1

Figure 15-2

Schematic illustration of determination of percentile rank norm lines for grades 5 and 6 on hypothetical mathematics test

is relatively straightforward. Each raw-score distribution (for Grade 5 and Grade 6 separately) was plotted on normal percentile paper, a smooth curve fitted to the points, and the percentile rank corresponding to each score was read. For Grade 5 a raw score of about 11 would have a percentile rank of 50, but for Grade 6 a raw score of about 17 would be needed for the same percentile rank. In other words, the 50th percentile for Grade 5 is 11, and for Grade 6 it is 17.

Standard Score Norms

As was the case with percentile ranks, standard scores can be used to express either local or national normative data. They are very effective with classroom tests. Standard scores have an advantage over percentile ranks in that they are a direct reflection of the raw score with regard to the size of the measurement unit. In addition, they are on a "standard scale" with fixed mean and standard deviation, which allows us to manipulate them mathematically with greater confidence. The reader is referred to Appendix C for a table showing the relationship between T and z scores, and percentile ranks when the underlying distribution is normally distributed. Another frequently used type of standard score is the normal curve equivalent (see Chapter 10).

There are some disadvantages in using standard scores. Standard scores are insensitive to the shape of the distribution. This fact relates to a problem of interpretation. Suppose an individual student had taken two tests, say a math and a science test. He achieved a standard score of +1.2 on each test. Could we conclude that his performance was *equivalent* on both tests? No! His performance might correspond to quite different percentile ranks depending on the shape of the individual distributions, and of course the fact that the tests measured different variables, had different number of items, means, and standard deviations. Equivalent standard scores do not mean equivalent interpretation on different measures or at different grade levels.

Grade-Equivalent Norms

A grade equivalent for a given raw score is the grade level of those students whose median (or mean) is the same as that particular raw score. If the median score of a group of seventh graders at the beginning of the school year is 54, all raw scores of 54 would have grade equivalents of 7.0. Decimal numbers are usually used, the first digit representing the school year and the second month in a 10-month school year.

A sample of grade equivalent norms from the *Stanford Achievement Test* is presented in Table 15-1. These norms are for the Social Science subtest (Grade 5, Form 1, Intermediate 1 level). Scores are expressed as raw scores, percentile ranks, stanines, grade equivalents, and scaled scores. To arrive at a grade equivalent, one need only determine a total raw score and read across to the grade equivalent. The reader will note the symbols "PHS" for raw scores of 46 or greater. This translates to "post high school." It should be noted at this point that normative data are frequently expressed for levels beyond those where standardized data were gathered. These norms and data-points are called "extrapolated" and are based on an assumed uniform learning curve. This assumption is frequently invalid. The norms of Table 15-1 were based on actual data gathered for students in Grades 4.8 to 5.8.

Again referring to Table 15-1 it can be seen that a raw score of 21 on the Social Studies subtest translates to a percentile rank of 10, a stanine of 2, and a grade equivalent of 3.5. Such a performance for a fifth grader would be considered subpar as evidenced by the GE of 3.5 and a performance that is interpreted to suggest this student did as well as or better than only 10 percent of the fifth graders on whom the test was standardized. It was in fact similar to the performance of a typical third grader in the fifth month of the school year.

It should also be noted that although a raw score of 21 yielded a percentile rank of 10 for social studies, the percentile rank equivalent might be quite different on another test in the battery, for example, spelling, math computation, and so forth. The caution must again be noted about the interpretation of the percentile rank of 10. It does not mean that the student got 10 percent of the items correct. In fact

Table 15-1 Sample Grade Norms for Intermediate I Form J for Students Tested in Grade 5 in the Spring on the *Stanford Achievement Test* (Eighth Edition)

Social Science

Raw Score	Percentile Rank	Stanine	Grade Equivalent	Scaled Score
50	99	9	PHS	765
49	99	9	PHS	742
48	98	9	PHS	717
47	97	9	PHS	702
46	95	8	PHS	691
45	92	8	12.5	682
44	88	7	10.5	674
43	85	7	9.3	668
42	80	7	8.5	662
41	76	6	8.0	656
40	72	6	7.6	652
39	67	6	7.2	647
38	63	6	6.8	643
37	59	5	6.5	639
.	.	.	.	.
.	.	.	.	.
.	.	.	.	.
21	10	2	3.5	585
20	9	2	3.4	582
19	7	2	3.2	578
18	6	2	3.1	575
17	4	2	2.9	571
16	3	1	2.8	568
15	3	1	2.5	564
14	2	1	2.3	560
13	1	1	2.0	556
12	1	1	1.8	552
11	1	1	1.6	548
10	1	1	1.4	543
9	1	1	1.2	538
8	1	1	1.0	533
7	1	1	K.8	527
6	1	1	K.5	520
5	1	1	K.2	512
4	1	1	PK	503
3	1	1	PK	492
2	1	1	PK	476
1	1	1	PK	450

Source: Reproduced from National Spring Norms Booklet of Stanford Achievement Test, Copyright © 1989 by the Psychological Corporation, San Antonio, TX. Reproduced by permission. All rights reserved.

assuming a 50-item test, the student got 42 percent correct. But getting 42 percent correct equated (in the norms table) to a percentile rank of 10, that is, the student did as well as or better than 10 percent of the people included in the norm.

Because they are expressed in terms of the units around which schools are organized, grade equivalents are assumed to be easily understood. In addition, they lend themselves to the plotting of achievement profiles in various subject areas, thus allowing for examination of a given pupil's strengths and weaknesses.

Flanagan (1951), however, has noted a number of the problems encountered in interpreting grade equivalents:

1. It is incorrect to say, for example, that a sixth grader who achieves a grade equivalent of 8 on a test is performing at an eighth-grade level. He has been taught and tested on sixth-grade material, not eighth-grade material. Rather, he performs as would the typical eighth-grader taking *his* test.

2. Grade equivalent norms assume uniform growth throughout the year, which is not the case within or across subject areas or grades. A grade score of 3.0 might yield a percentile rank of 40 on a reading subtest and a percentile rank of 20 on a math subtest of a survey achievement battery. The units of measurement are ambiguous. This lack of uniformity in scaling is illustrated in Figure 15-3. The curve represents a plot of grade equivalent scores and test raw scores, which obviously departs

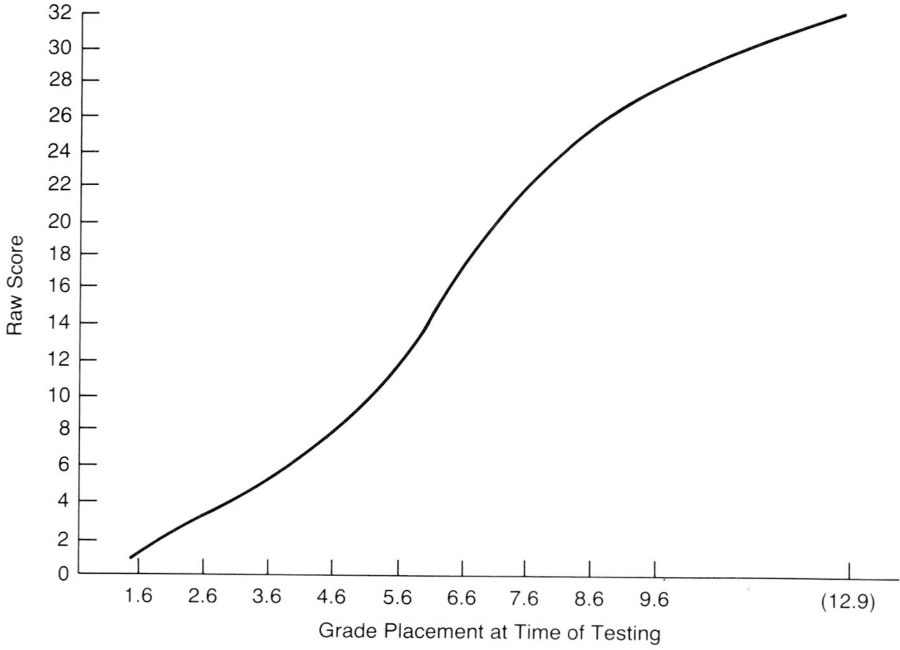

Figure 15-3

Hypothetical relationship between raw score and grade placement used to establish grade equivalents

from a straight-line relationship. Caution, then, must be used in interpreting a given individual's score on different subtests and on assessing growth. In other words, a change of three score points may result in a variable change in grade scores, depending on raw scores involved. *Students learn different subjects at different rates.*

3. It is impossible to test all grade levels. Therefore, a great many grade equivalents are based on extrapolated or interpolated values, which tend to be nothing more than statistical guesses. Extrapolated grade equivalents are estimates *beyond* the actual data base, and interpolated values are *between* actual data points.

4. The procedures used to determine grade equivalents tend to exaggerate the significance of small differences in raw scores because of customarily large within-grade variability.

5. There is a danger that, because of the correspondence between the label *grade equivalent* and the way the schools are organized, teachers will come to consider the grade equivalent a *standard* for performance. Such a misinterpretation attests to lack of knowledge of local objectives and individual differences.

6. A score on any achievement test is a function of the treatment of the subject matter in the curriculum. An assumption of uniformity for test standardization is unwarranted.

7. Extremely high or low grade equivalents are difficult to interpret due to the lack of reliable measurement at the extremes of any score scale.

8. Most norms tables are based on a 10-month school year and thus ignore the gains or losses of proficiency that occur during the summer months.

Because of these shortcomings, grade equivalents are frequently and ferociously attacked by members of the testing profession and the general public. Hoover (1984), however, suggests that as so often is the case, it is not an inherent weakness of the grade equivalent concept that is the problem, but it is the user who faults the interpretation. He also presents strong evidence that grade equivalents can be averaged and the grade equivalents below grade placement are fairly accurate indicators of level performance.

Suffice to say that grade equivalent scores should not be interpreted literally. They are useful, particularly for interpreting elementary-school performances and in areas characterized by continual development, but should only be used as rough guides to level of performance.

Age Norms

Similar to grade norms, age norms are based on average test performances at various age levels. The units are also unequal, that is, equal age units do not correspond to equal score units. They are useful for expressing growth in mental ability, reading ability, and other phenomena characterized by fairly consistent growth patterns and treatment in the instructional program. Age norms are probably underused. They can be useful in monitoring development and growth.

Local Norms

Local norms are valuable for many purposes besides those stated by test publishers. Due to the idiosyncrasies of the local curriculum, student body, community needs, and teacher characteristics, national norms may not be representative of the local instructional situation. Local school personnel must then develop their own reference data. Generating test data and summarizing them in the form of percentile ranks and standard scores would be most helpful, particularly for achievement test results. Some test manuals provide guidelines for the development of local norms. In addition, many test publishers will provide a norming service for a nominal fee.

Expectancy Norms

It is unreasonable to interpret performance on a test without reference to other relevant variables. For an achievement test, one relevant variable is student ability. Many test publishers therefore provide for the dual standardization of achievement and scholastic aptitude (or intelligence) tests. The correlation between achievement and aptitude measures is determined and, using the aptitude score, an expected achievement performance can be predicted. In this manner a student may be judged to be under- or overachieving in a particular subject. The expectancy table is one form in which these data are expressed (see Chapter 13 for a description of expectancy tables).

"User" Norms

In an effort to keep their norms as current as possible, test publishers occasionally accumulate data from systems who buy their tests and services. These current files of scores can be used to build tables of norms. Obvious bias exists in such so-called normative data as only the self-selected users of that particular test or battery are included in the database. Perhaps such data can be used to gauge fluctuations in performance over the life of the current edition. An enlightened system test coordinator can, in fact, accumulate or have the publisher accumulate data so that local norms can be established.

Developmental Standard Score Norms

It was noted earlier that a continuous developmental scale is desirable if we are to describe developmental level and measure growth. Expanded standard score scale norms are used for that purpose. Instruction is usually organized around grade groupings. Most developmental scales are therefore derived from grade-referenced groups. The intended use of a developmental or standard score system is to facilitate comparison of performances for the same individual on different forms or at different levels of the test, thereby allowing for the study of change in performance over time. The Eighth Edition of the *Stanford Achievement Test*, for example, reports its normative scores in the form of: raw scores, scaled scores (ranging from the 300s to 800s depending on level and form of the battery), individual percentile ranks, stanines, normal curve equivalents and grade equivalents, achievement/ability comparisons, small ($N < 50$) and large ($N > 50$) group percentile ranks and stanines, content cluster performance categories, skill groups, and item difficulty (p) values. Relationships among the stanines, percentile ranks, normal curve equivalents, and performance classifications are described in Figure 15-4.

The large and small group data are based on averages and are therefore less variable. The broad performance categories that might be used for instructional grouping are Below Average (stanines 1, 2, and 3); Average (stanines 4, 5, and 6), and Above Average (stanines 7, 8, and 9). Table 15-2 contains scaled scores for selected percentile ranks across grades K–12 for a hypothetical reading comprehension test. Note the proportional increase in standard score as one moves from the kindergarten to tenth percentile rank (402) to the ninetieth (469), and from the ninetieth of kindergarten (469) to the ninetieth level at twelfth (739). The continuous nature of the scaling is graphically reflected in Figure 15-5.

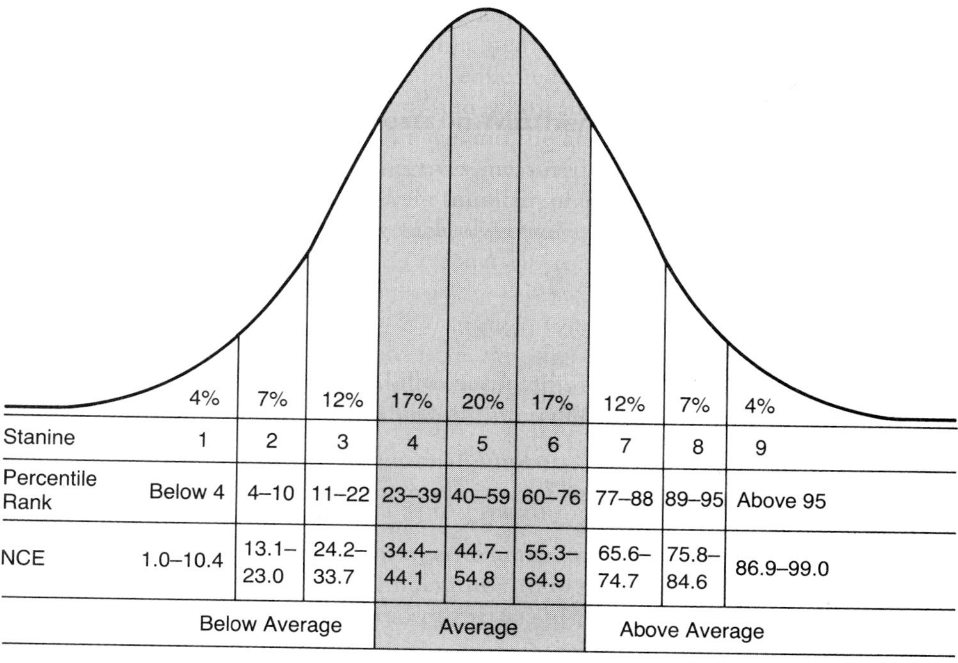

4% 7% 12% 17% 20% 17% 12% 7% 4%
Stanine 1 2 3 4 5 6 7 8 9
Percentile Rank Below 4 4–10 11–22 23–39 40–59 60–76 77–88 89–95 Above 95
NCE 1.0–10.4 13.1–23.0 24.2–33.7 34.4–44.1 44.7–54.8 55.3–64.9 65.6–74.7 75.8–84.6 86.9–99.0
Below Average
Average
Above Average

Figure 15-4

A normal distribution of stanines, percentile ranks, normal curve equivalents, and performance classifications

Table 15-2 Scaled Scores for Selected Percentile Ranks Across Grades for Hypothetical Reading Comprehension Test

Percentile Ranks	Grade K	1	2	3	4	5	6	7	8	9	10	11	12
90	469	608	643	667	679	695	704	711	720	726	732	735	739
75	445	563	617	640	656	672	681	688	697	703	709	712	715
50	427	516	584	609	626	646	653	663	672	678	682	686	688
25	415	482	550	579	595	616	625	636	646	652	655	659	661
10	402	463	523	555	569	591	601	613	623	628	631	634	637

Criteria for Published Norms and Manuals

A test manual should provide a comprehensive description of the procedures used in collecting normative data. Among the essential and desirable characteristics of normative data are the following (American Psychological Association *et al.*, 1985):

1. The nature, rationale, and derivation for the scales used to report scores should be spelled out early in test publications.
2. Normative data should be described so clearly that a potential user can readily judge the relevance of the norms for particular testing purposes.

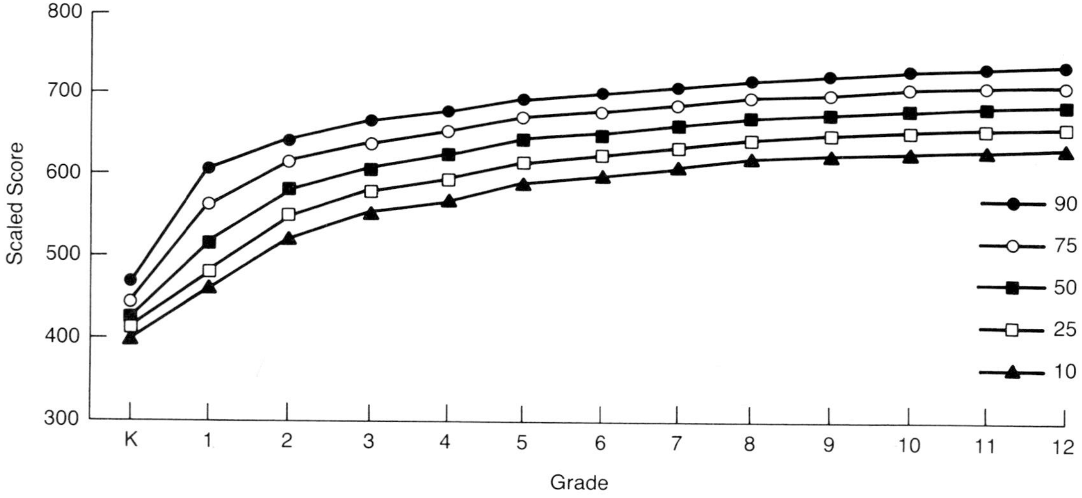

Figure 15-5

Plot of scaled scores for selected percentile ranks across grades for hypothetical reading comprehension test (data from Table 15-2)

3. Normative data should be reported in the form of standard scores and percentile ranks.
4. If grade norms are provided, provision should be made for conversion of grade equivalents to standard scores and percentile ranks.
5. With each test revision and/or renorming, relationships between new and old norms should be described and equivalency tables provided, particularly with regard to content.
6. Normative data and technical manuals should be published at the same time as the test.
7. Every effort should be made by the publisher to keep norms as current as possible.
8. The publisher should point out the importance of establishing local norms as well as procedures useful in doing so.
9. Descriptive data (e.g., measures of central tendency and variability) should be reported for the normative sample(s).
10. In addition to norms, tables should be provided showing the expectation a person who achieves a given test score has of attaining or exceeding some relevant criterion score.
11. Sufficient information should be provided on such variables as number of schools, sex, number of cases, geographic location, age, educational level, and the like, so that it can be determined whether a set of norms are in fact representative of the population they claim to represent.
12. Sampling procedures should be spelled out in detail.
13. Normative data should be reported only if the associated reliability and validity data are also available, and they should be related to score interpretation.
14. The testing conditions under which the normative data were obtained should be specified.
15. If profiling of different subtests is suggested, the relevant normative data should be comparable, that is, gathered on the same population(s).
16. If an anchor test was used to equate test forms its parameters should be described in detail.
17. Equivalence of alternative test administration modes should be documented (for example, computer administration).
18. Test manuals should (a) describe rationale for uses of test, (b) summarize relevant research, (c) list qualifications needed by users, (d) describe alternate response recording modes, and (e) explain interpretation guidelines in detail.
19. Promotional material should be accurate and honest.

Interpreting Profiles

Some publishers of multiscore instruments suggest that the scores be profiled to aid in interpretation. Such a graphic representation facilitates the examination of relative highs and lows, strengths and weaknesses, and positive and negative tendencies. For technical reasons differences between scores, particularly in batteries whose subtests focus on similar outcomes, are unreliable. Therefore, great caution must be exercised in interpretation. Treating small differences (which are likely to be chance differences) as significant can only lead to erroneous decisions.

One way to overcome the problem of interpreting differences in scores on the same profile is to rely on *percentile bands.* These bands are illustrated by the shaded areas in Figure 15-6 (pp. 370–371), which is a sample student profile for the *Sequential Tests of Educational Progress.* It can be seen that the scores are plotted not as points but as bands. Percentile bands correspond to the obtained score plus and minus one standard error of measurement (a measure of reliability—see Chapter 12 for a discussion of the standard error of measurement). These bands represent the ranges within which we can be reasonably sure of finding the student's "true" performance. If the bands for two different tests do *not* overlap, we can feel reasonably confident that the performances are different enough to warrant further consideration. Sometimes publishers will use larger bands. Instead of 68 percent, perhaps an 80 percent width will be used.

Three major types of information in score profiles need to be taken into account during interpretation. The *level* or *elevation* of the profile, which may be thought of as an individual's average score on all tests represented in the profile, must be considered. Second, *scatter* or *dispersion* should be examined. Scatter involves the extent to which an individual varies throughout the subtest. One measure of scatter is the standard deviation of scores for an individual on the different tests. A third characteristic of a score profile is the *shape,* which reveals the particular points at which the individual has high or low scores. A simple ranking of subtests from high to low on the profile should provide the necessary information. It should be noted that we are basically considering ways of "looking at" a profile. Obviously, some subtests are more important than others for any given purpose.

Teacher Responsibilities

There is no doubt that examinees feel tension and anxiety before, during, and after a testing experience. This is particularly true if the test is of great consequence to the examinee. Midterms and finals, college entrance exams, and scholarship qualifying exams are examples of tests likely to evoke considerable test anxiety potentially harmful to student performance. In the classroom situation, improper uses of tests can damage the teacher-student relationship. The misuse of tests stems primarily from two sources (Lennon, 1954): (a) misunderstanding of the proper role of tests, and (b) failure to appreciate the emotional problems posed for some children by any ego-threatening evaluation procedure. Specifically, Lennon notes eight kinds of problems:

1. If teachers look upon the norm on a standardized test as a goal to be reached by all children and if they criticize those who fail to meet this rigid standard, the pupils will quite naturally come to think of tests as hurdles rather than as stepping stones to development.

2. If teachers in interpreting test results fail to take into account other relevant information—ability differences, health status, home background, and the like—they are likely to render an unjust appraisal of a child's work, which may well have the effect of discouraging or antagonizing the child.

3. If teachers overemphasize tests in the evaluation program, and fail to realize that they cover only a part of the desired outcomes, they run the risk of placing undue emphasis on certain objectives and confusing pupils as to what they are supposed to be learning.

4. If teachers habitually use test results as bases for invidious comparisons among pupils, not only is the pupil-teacher relationship damaged, but also the relationships among the pupils.

5. If teachers berate or scold children because of poor performance on a test, they may be building up unfavorable attitudes toward future testing and learning.

6. If teachers fail to let pupils know how they did on a test, or give any indication of how the testing is related to educational purposes, it is hard for the pupil to make sense of the procedure.

7. If a teacher is insecure, and feels threatened by the tests, it is almost certain that this attitude will be communicated to the children. If a school- or systemwide testing program is in operation, in the planning of which the teachers have had no part, and the purposes of which they do not understand, they are obviously in no position to make clear to the pupils how the testing is likely to do them any good. If the test results are used as a means of appraising teacher competence, the temptation becomes very strong for the teacher to teach for the tests.

8. If teachers are unsympathetic to a testing program in which they must participate, and make slighting or sarcastic reference to "these tests that we have to give again," they are certainly engendering a poor attitude on the pupil's part; even young pupils are shrewd enough to sense, however vaguely, that by such behavior the teacher is abdicating this rightful position.

Such common-sense procedures as returning test papers as soon as possible, discussing test items with the entire class, and demonstrating to the class the uses of test information will help to develop proper student attitudes and a healthy perspective on the place and value of testing in the instructional program. There is no substitute for respect for individual students and their needs and desires.

Interpreting and Reporting Test Results to the Public

Because of their considerable interest and investment in education, members of the general public need to be apprised of student progress and achievement. One of the

Name *Lawrence* (Last) *Albert* (First) *E.* (Middle)

School *Midtown H.S. (1)* Grade or Class *11*

Age *16* (Years) *2* (Months) Date of Testing *Fall* (Fall or Spring) *1957-58* (Year)

Norms Used

- [x] Publisher's
- [x] Fall
- [ ] Local
- [ ] Spring

Grade or Class *11*

Other ______

© Copyright 1957, All rights reserved

Cooperative Test Division ETS Educational Testing Service · Princeton, N.J. · Los Angeles 27, Calif.

Here you can profile a student's percentile ranks on as many as six tests in the STEP series. In order for your comparisons between the areas to be valid, all tests included should be administered within a period of 4 or 5 months.

Recording. Directions for recording information and drawing percentile bands on the PROFILE form are included in each STEP MANUAL FOR INTERPRETING SCORES. Consult the manuals for the tests used.

Interpreting. To compare a student's performance on one of the tests in the STEP series with that of students in the norms group used, note the unshaded parts of the column above and below the percentile band. For example, if the Listening percentile band is 24-36, you know that 24 per cent of students in the norms group score lower than this student and 64 per cent score higher. In other words, this student's Listening performance is below average with respect to the norms group.

To compare a student's standings on any two tests in the STEP series, the following rules apply:

1. If the percentile bands for any two tests overlap, there is no important difference between the student's standings on those two tests.
2. If the percentile bands for any two tests do *not* overlap, standing represented by the higher band is really better than standing represented by the lower band.

Examples: According to local norms, a student's percentile bands for three tests are

Mathematics (2A)	50-62
Social Studies (2A)	60-71
Science (2B)	41-52

Bands for Mathematics and Social Studies overlap; there is no important difference between the student's standings in these two areas. The same is true of Mathematics and Science. However, bands for Science and Social Studies do not overlap; the student's standing in Social Studies is higher than his standing in Science.

More detailed discussions of interpretations are contained in each STEP MANUAL FOR INTERPRETING SCORES.

Figure 15-6

Sample student profile *Source: From STEP/SCAT Student Bulletin. Copyright © 1970 by Educational Testing Service. All rights reserved. Reproduced by permission.*

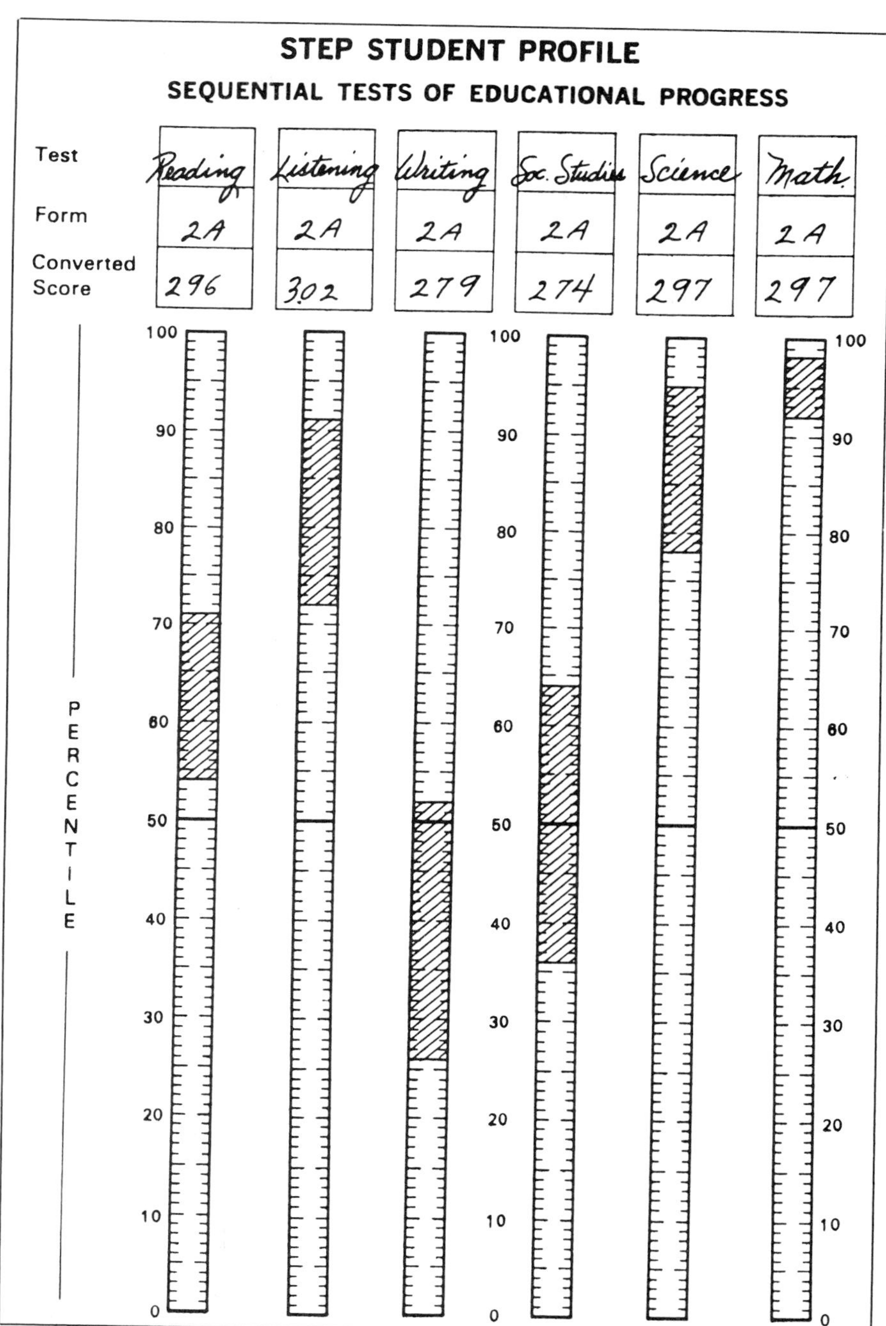

Figure 15-6

(Continued)

most efficient ways of communicating information on performance is probably the use of standardized tests scores. Despite their shortcomings, the results derived from standardized tests constitute an immediately understandable summary of student performances. It is imperative that public reports of test scores be carefully presented and explained. Hawes (1972) has summarized several guidelines for reporting test results to the public:

1. *Prepare the public and press for the impending report.* A briefing session should be held to discuss the intent of administering the tests and their use.

2. *Introduce the results with an explanation of test content.* A series of scores is in and of itself relatively meaningless. A description of the content of the tests will help communicate their value to individual students, the schools, and the public.

3. *Prepare a tabular summary of the results for general release.* Breakdowns accompanied by descriptions of such factors as full score ranges, medians, socioeconomic background of the school population, and sex differences will help convey a clearer picture of the results. Consideration might be given to ways of reporting results for special samples and comparative and growth data.

4. *Avoid the use of composite scores for each school.* Composite scores invite invidious comparisons between schools, and are open to misinterpretation and misuse. The use of composite scores in-house is, however, defensible.

5. *Avoid reporting grade equivalents.* The danger of using grade equivalents has been discussed. If possible, report percentiles by grade.

6. *Avoid implying that norms are standards.* One should emphasize that normative data are references and benchmarks. A more informative approach is to cite growth data over time (assuming the same tests are involved).

7. *For school-by-school release, report factors influencing test score meaning.* There are many relevant "input factors." Ability level of the student body, teacher turnover rate, per-pupil cost factors, socioeconomic base of the school population, average class size, pupil-teacher ratios, teacher salaries, minority enrollment, pupil mobility, average daily attendance, average years teaching experience, and educational level of the teachers are some of the variables that help to account for a school's test results. Any innovative approach—a large number of open classrooms, for example—should be acknowledged, because it influences curriculum and in turn affects test results.

8. *Provide an overall summary of the results.* It is better for the local educational agency to prepare the summary than to allow those less informed about tests to make possibly damaging interpretations. Emphasis should be on the broad significance of the results for the community, particularly regarding planning and the need for innovative programs.

There is more to test interpretation than simple reporting of scores. The cognitive (preparation) and affective (anticipation) "psychological state" of the examinee need to be considered.

Test-wiseness, Coaching, and Test Anxiety

We have become a test-oriented society! We test for entry into first grade, college, and most professions. We certify for the possession of semitechnical and technical skills and all sorts of competencies. Medicine, law enforcement, teaching, and many other careers are influenced by test scores. It is no wonder then that an examination of skills needed to take a test has come under the researchers' psychometric microscope. Hopefully, the major contribution to the score on any test or assessment is the required knowledge or skill being measured. But other factors, many of which were discussed in Chapter 5 on test preparation and administration, may also influence test scores. Among these are just plain experience in taking tests, how to use special answer sheets, the physical testing environment, and the psychological state of the test taker (Sarnacki, 1979).

Test-wiseness is a term sometimes used to describe a whole range of test-taking skills. Table 15-3 contains a summary (based on the analyses of Millman, Bishop, & Ebel, 1965) of two major contributors to test-wiseness. The first of these are basically examinee-controlled, for example, guessing strategy used, use of testing time, and so on. A second set of elements is under control of the test constructor, for example, grammatical consistency in items, number of interrelated items, and so on. Both of these categories of test-wiseness are independent of the examinee's knowledge or academic ability. It, test-wiseness, is nevertheless a cognitive skill that an examinee can apply to a variety of tests, and in fact can be taught. With the increased emphasis on test results, many schools are instituting programs aimed at enhancing student test-taking skills. Coaching, usually through the examination of old tests and items, is a frequently used method to try to improve student test scores. Some research supports the benefits of coaching. Bangert-Drowns, Kulik, and Kulik (1983) found that for 25 of the 30 studies they reviewed, coaching showed a positive effect on test performance. In the typical study, coaching would raise students' scores by .25 standard deviations. This effect would increase an average student's score from the 50th to 60th percentile, or by about 2.5 months on a grade equivalent scale. The more elaborate and broadly based the educational experience—whereby academic skills and knowledge are, in fact, taught, not just test-taking skills—the greater the likelihood of score improvement.

Test-taking training programs sometimes address specific test-taking techniques such as guessing and answer changing. Research suggests that contrary to folklore, if students have some information about what is being tested and can eliminate at least one alternative on a multiple-choice test they will benefit from guessing as they have ameliorated the probability estimates that were used to establish the correction-for-guessing formulas (Cross & Frary, 1977). Not to be overlooked is test anxiety. Payne (1984), for example, found significantly greater answer-changing behavior for black middle school students. In addition, black and female eighth

Table 15-3 An Outline of Test-wiseness Principles

I. Elements independent of test constructor or test purpose.
  A. Time-using strategy.
    1. Begin to work as rapidly as possible with reasonable assurance of accuracy.
    2. Set up a schedule for progress through the test.
    3. Omit or guess at items (see I.C. and II.B.) which resist a quick response.
    4. Mark omitted items, or items which could use further consideration, to assure easy relocation.
    5. Use time remaining after completion of the test to reconsider answers.
  B. Error-avoidance strategy.
    1. Pay careful attention to directions, determining clearly the nature of the task and the intended basis for response.
    2. Pay careful attention to the items, determining clearly the nature of the question.
    3. Ask examiner for clarification when necessary, if it is permitted.
    4. Check all answers.
  C. Guessing strategy.
    1. Always guess if right answers only are scored.
    2. Always guess if the correction for guessing is less severe than a "correction for guessing" formula that gives an expected score of zero for random responding.
    3. Always guess even if the usual correction or a more severe penalty for guessing is employed, whenever elimination of options provides sufficient chance of profiting.
  D. Deductive reasoning strategy.
    1. Eliminate options which are known to be incorrect and choose from among the remaining options.
    2. Choose neither or both of two options which imply the correctness of each other.
    3. Choose neither or one (but not both) of two statements, one of which, if correct, would imply the incorrectness of the other.
    4. Restrict choice to those options which encompass all of two or more given statements known to be correct.
    5. Utilize relevant content information in other test items and options.

II. Elements dependent upon the test constructor or purpose.
  A. Intent consideration strategy.
    1. Interpret and answer questions in view of previous idiosyncratic emphases of the best constructor or in view of the test purpose.
    2. Answer items as the test constructor intended.
    3. Adopt the level of sophistication that is expected.
    4. Consider the relevance of specific detail.
  B. Cue-using strategy.
    1. Recognize and make use of any consistent idiosyncrasies of the test constructor which distinguishes the correct answer from incorrect options.
      a. He makes it longer (shorter) than the incorrect options.
      b. He qualifies it more carefully, or makes it represent a higher degree of generalization.

Table 15-3 *(Continued)*

c. He includes more false (true) statements.
d. He places it in certain physical positions among the options (such as in the middle).
e. He places it in a certain logical position among an ordered set of options (such as the middle of the sequence).
f. He includes (does not include) it among similar statements, or makes (does not make) it one of a pair of diametrically opposite statements.
g. He composes (does not compose) it of familiar or stereotyped phraseology.
h. He does not make it grammatically inconsistent with the stem.

2. Consider the relevancy of specific detail when answering a given item.
3. Recognize and make use of specific determiners.
4. Recognize and make use of resemblances between the options and an aspect of the stem.
5. Consider the subject matter and difficulty of neighboring items when interpreting and answering a given item.

From "An Analysis of Test-Wiseness" by J. Millman, C.H. Bishop, and R. Ebel, *Educational and Psychological Measurement,* 1965, *25,* 707–726. Copyright 1965 by *Educational and Psychological Measurement.* Reprinted by permission.

grade students had significantly higher test anxiety scores than their counterparts. If the coaching and the teaching of test-taking skills only raise scores and do not improve the overall capacity of the student to perform better, then the validity of the test will have been violated.

Effects of Coaching on College Admissions Tests

In and above the technical and legal issues involved in the application of tests for making decisions, there exists an additional problem. That problem is concerned with the effect of public, private, and commercial coaching and training programs that have been developed to assist students to prepare for college admissions tests. It is very difficult to prepare a student for a particular secure test if training involves primarily the examination of old test items. If, however, coaching involves a more elaborate and broadly based educational experience whereby academic skills and knowledge are in fact taught, the likelihood of increasing test scores is improved. Such improvement is, however, very modest. A review of the literature by Pike (1978) revealed inconsistent results with respect to the effect of coaching on both verbal and math tests, specifically the *Scholastic Aptitude Test—Verbal* and *Math.* Simply retaking the test, will of course, in and of itself result in some score gain, so that intentional gains or gains derived from coaching should be judged against these kinds of *practice* change scores. A reasonable estimate of overall math gain resulting from a short-term instructional program (e.g., one to six hours), has found to be around ten CEEB score units, and for intermediate-term instruction (e.g., 50 hours) gains to be between 20 and 25 CEEB units (where the mean is 500 and the standard deviation is 100). Comparable results were found for SAT-V coaching programs. Two confounding factors in coaching studies would be the initial ability level of the subjects being coached and the similarity of the coaching materials to the criterion measure. It would appear that the greater this similarity and the longer the period of instruction the greater the positive impact. This impact, numerically, however, is quite small. Confirmatory evidence has been reported by Alderman and Powers (1979). These investigators found, after about 13 hours of instruction, a difference of eight CEEB units between the means of coached versus uncoached groups for the SAT-V. The crucial question here is not whether or not one can increase the scores but whether the increase (a) is worth the time and financial investment, and (b) helps the student perform better in college. The response to both questions is negative. Students might better spend their time being educated rather than coached. As a matter of fact Messick and Jungeblut (1981) have interpreted their extensive review data as suggesting that the student contact time necessary to achieve average score increases much greater than 20 or 30 points rapidly approaches that of full-time schooling. If significant gains had been observed, then a real question of test validity might have been raised. If coaching raised only the scores and did not improve the overall capacity of the student to perform better, then the validity of the test would have been destroyed. Since the score increases are small, the validity question is a moot one.

Test Anxiety

Every time we are evaluated there is some degree of anxiety present whether it is for a driving license or college admission. It is natural to be self-protective and want to have positive assessments of us by others. Sometimes, especially in educational settings, anxiety can inhibit performance. Test anxiety is generally described as an uncomfortable feeling before, during, and/or after an examination or evaluation (Sarason, 1980). It has cognitive, affective, and physiological components. In general the greater the significance of the test results or the greater the importance of the decision to be made on the basis of the test results, the greater the test anxiety. There are real and meaningful individual differences in test anxiety. Some respond with memory blocks; others with increased heart rate or sweating. Sometimes the anxiety may always be present during any test (trait) or it may be specific to a particular situation (state) (Spielberger, Gorsuch, & Lushene, 1970). The etiology of test anxiety has not been researched extensively (Allen, Elias, & Zlotlow, 1980). Dusek (1980) suggests, however, that it is probably associated with an aggregate of child-rearing techniques which do not provide the child with emotional support during problem-solving experiences. Whatever the origin, the teacher/test administrator must deal with the possible presence and effects of test anxiety.

After lamenting the fact that grandmothers either become ill or expire at astronomical rates around exam time, Chivdo (1987) suggests 20 activities that can significantly help to reduce test anxiety. These are:

1. Review the scope of the exam with the students.
2. If practical, use practice tests, and definitely use practice items.
3. Emphasize time limits.

4. Specify what may and may not be brought to the exam.
5. Review grading procedures and point values.
6. Review policies or make-up tests and retakes.
7. Provide study help with instructor or form study groups.
8. Allow for and encourage last-minute questions just before the exam.
9. Allow for breaks as appropriate for long exams or very young examinees.
10. Coach students on test-testing techniques.

This last item, coaching on test-taking skills, is very important particularly for young test takers. Practice really helps the potential examinee to become familiar with the usual testing procedures. Both examinee and examiner must keep in mind the concept that a test is only one sample of behavior and does not represent a microcosm of one's life. Some good suggestions for approaching the test are contained in Table 15-3 previously discussed in connection with test-wiseness. Common sense on the part of a test taker can make as important a contribution to preparing a class for testing and reducing test anxiety as any extended technical treatment; answer easy questions first, watch the clock, ask for clarification of questions, get rest before the test, eat a good meal (but not too much), practice filling in answer bubbles on machine-scored tests, and review to make sure you have answered each question.

Contemporary Test Interpretation Issues

Technological innovations and public and private demand for knowledge about school effectiveness have resulted in many changes in what type of data are collected, and how those data are transmitted and interpreted. Following is a discussion of three of the major issues that have arisen in this decade.

Computer-Generated Interpretations

With increasing frequency test publishers and computer software vendors are making available programs which will "create" interpretations of test scores. Programs may be purchased separately or as part of the reporting service packages offered by the publisher. In Chapter 5 this activity was referred to as "intelligent measurement" where extensive data bases are combined with expert judgment to describe representative printed narratives for different levels of performance and combinations of scores. These computer-generated narratives are available for measures in affective domain (personality and interests) as well as in the cognitive domain (achievement, aptitude, and intelligence). The diagnostic use of the computer interpretations of such personality inventories such as the *Minnesota Multiphasic Personality Inventory* is prevalent with clinicians. Figure 15-7 contains a sample individual student analysis of a hypothetical performance on Form J of the Intermediate 1 level of the *Stanford Achievement Test.* In addition to raw and standard scores, national grade percentile bands reflecting the "confidence range" for scores are presented (plus and minus one standard error of measurement). Also of interest is the AAC (Achievement/

STANFORD

ACHIEVEMENT TEST SERIES

TEACHER: JOHN WILLIAMS
SCHOOL: (B) LAKESIDE ELEMENTARY   GRADE: 4
DISTRICT: NEWTOWN   TEST DATE: 4/88

(C)	STANFORD	OLSAT
NORMS: NATIONAL	GRADE 4 SPRING	GRADE 4 SPRING
LEVEL:	INTER 1	E
FORM:	J	1

STUDENT SKILLS ANALYSIS FOR (A) BRIAN ELLIOTT

TESTS	NO. OF ITEMS	RAW SCORE	SCALED SCORE	NATL PR-S	LOC PR-S	GRADE EQUIV	AAC RANGE
Total Reading	94	70	143	50-5	45-5	4.8	LOW
Vocabulary	40	27	148	52-5	46-5	5.1	LOW
Reading Comp.	54	43	143	50-5	44-5	4.8	LOW
Total Math	118	58	143	44-5	45-5	4.6	LOW
Concepts of No.	34	14	137	32-4	26-4	3.8	LOW
Computation	44	22	145	50-5	56-5	4.8	MIDDLE
Applications	40	22	145	50-5	53-5	4.8	LOW
Total Language	60	47	149	61-6	56-5	5.4	MIDDLE
Lang Mechanics (D)	30	21	148	60-6	54-5	5.4	MIDDLE
Lang Expression	30	26	150	62-6	58-5	5.4	MIDDLE
Spelling	40	22	143	40-5	34-4	4.0	LOW
Study Skills	30	21	142	50-5	44-5	4.8	LOW
Science	50	31	139	44-5	38-4	4.6	LOW
Social Science	50	42	161	82-7	76-6	6.2	MIDDLE
Listening	45	25	130	49-5	45-5	4.7	LOW
Using Information	70	35	152	59-5	55-5	5.2	MIDDLE
Thinking Skills	101	45	146	52-5	53-5	4.9	LOW
Basic Battery	387	243	143	50-5	45-5	4.8	LOW
Complete Battery	487	316	145	52-5	47-5	4.9	LOW

OTIS-LENNON SCHOOL ABILITY TEST		RAW SCORE	SAI	AGE PR-S	AGE NCE	SCALED SCORE	GRADE PR-S	GRADE NCE
Total (F)	72	53	116	84-7	70.9	290	82-7	69.3
Verbal	36	27	117	85-7	71.8	295	83-7	70.1
Nonverbal	36	26	115	82-7	69.3	285	80-7	67.7

NATIONAL GRADE PERCENTILE BANDS

1 10 30 50 70 90 99 (E)

(G) AGE 10 YRS 2 MOS   READING GROUP GROUP 3   MATHEMATICS GROUP GROUP 2   COMMUNICATIONS GROUP GROUP 1   LANGUAGE GROUP GROUP 2

(H)

Recently this student took the Stanford Achievement Test. The tests in the Stanford series are described on the back of this report. This brief description of the scores presented above tells how the student did on the tests, compared to other students in the same grade from across the country. The Complete Battery score is a global indication of how well the student performed on all of the tests. The score for this student is well within the average range, which means that the student has performed about as well on all tests combined as the typical student in this grade.

In reading, the Vocabulary and Reading Comprehension test scores are in the average range for the grade. The student appears to be making reasonable progress in this area.

Overall performance in mathematics is also in the average range. However, performance on the Mathematics Computation and Mathematics Applications tests is somewhat better than performance on the Concepts of Number test. Additional experience in working with the properties of the number system could be helpful to future learning in mathematics.

Scores on the Language Mechanics and Language Expression tests are in the middle range for this grade. Practice in applying the skills measured by these tests to free writing tasks could be helpful. Scores on the Spelling and Study Skills tests are also in the middle range.

Performance on the Social Science test is in the above-average range for the grade, while the Science test score is in the average range. The student's understanding of the concepts in these two areas should continue to develop with further instruction.

Performance on the Listening test is in the middle range for this grade, indicating that the student can process information that is heard about as well as the typical student in the grade.

It is important to keep in mind that achievement test scores give only one picture of how a student is doing in school and that many things can affect a student's test scores. Therefore, it is important to consider other kinds of information as well. The school has more detailed information about how the student is doing.

Copyright © 1988 by Harcourt Brace Jovanovich, Inc.
All rights reserved. Printed in the United States of America.

Actual Size: $8\frac{1}{2}$" x $11\frac{3}{16}$"

THE PSYCHOLOGICAL CORPORATION
HARCOURT BRACE JOVANOVICH, INC

Figure 15-7

Computer-generated test interpretation for *Stanford Achievement Test*

Ability Comparison) ranges. The AAC shows how well, within limits, a student has performed on a particular subtest or total score as predicted by the student's total score on the *Otis-Lennon School Ability Test.* Our hypothetical student is apparently not performing up to expectations, as 13 of 19 SAT performances were below that which would have been projected on the basis of the OLSAT. The narrative is based on accumulated experience with the test and student performances.

The Wall Chart

In 1984 the then-Secretary of Education, Terrell Bell proposed that in the interest of accountability states would be listed on a "wall chart" ranked according to their mean *Scholastic Aptitude Test* scores. Such a procedure invites invidious comparisons. The totality of state education efforts cannot be encapsulated in a test score. There is no consideration of state history or circumstance, ever-changing economic conditions, or most importantly, the self-selection of test takers. The fewer students who take the test the higher the scores. The correlation in 1986 between SAT mean total score and proportion of graduating class who took the test was −.86. It has been proposed that assumed relevant variables could be used to adjust SAT scores to give a more valid picture of the rankings. Such variables as dropout rate, per-pupil expenditures, and racial, sex, and age proportions have been used. Unfortunately, the data were derived from total state statistics rather than from the test takers' data sets. Wainer (1986) has explicated five important pitfalls in the creation of the wall charts. Despite pitfalls the procedure will be continued, but proponents (Ginsburg, Noell, & Plisko, 1988) have called for many desirable changes, plus the possible use of data from the National Assessment of Educational Progress to assist in describing state educational effectiveness.

The Lake Wobegon Effect

The ever-present influence of the "accountability" movement in education usually has a positive impact, but perverse responses can also result. The improvement of the quality of curriculum, instruction, and school administrative practices is the most frequent outcome of demands for reform. Occasionally teachers will teach test material or deviate from proper test-taking procedures in an effort to inflate outcome measures. This reaction may be one of the underlying causes of Cannell's description of the so-called Lake Wobegon Effect, so named because of National Public Radio's Garrison Keillor's characterization of fantasized Lake Wobegon, Minnesota, children as all being above average (Cannell, 1988). His survey of 50 states revealed that no state had a mean which was below the 50th percentile for national elementary school norm groups. His data were derived from six different commercially available standardized tests. One must be cautious in interpreting the 100 percent above-median finding, as within each state there is only a *sample* of the elementary students. In addition to teaching for or to the test, probably the major source of the normal problems is the likelihood of bias or lack of representativeness in the original standardizations. Despite the extreme care that test publishers take in collecting data from representative school systems, schools, and classes, bias does creep in. Participation in the norming process is voluntary. Publishers do provide "free" goods and services to participating schools. If a school has a restricted budget these services might look very appealing. In addition, due to the phenomenal costs, test publishers only renorm their large batteries every six to nine years. This also means that norms are "time-bound," that is, the lag between revision and restandardization is behind current use. The implication of this is that current performances are probably better than the norms. Research also shows that the students in systems using a particular test service do better than nonusers, including those in the standardization.

> [I]f a state's average score in reading is at the 54th percentile, the proper interpretation of this score is that the average or typical *student* in the state performed better than 54% of the norming sample. It is not appropriate to conclude that all students in the state are above average in reading, that the state as a whole is above average in reading relative to other states, or that the state as a whole is above average in reading relative to the national norm. (Lenke & Keene, 1988)

This caution again underscores the potential danger of viewing norms on standardized tests as "standards" to be achieved by all students.

Following are some measures that are being taken to guard against distortion in norms' relevant interpretation: (a) better test security, (b) more frequent renorming, (c) less frequent testing which might also employ some matrix sampling scheme, (d) improved information for test users on interpretation of the meaning of scores, and (e) possible use of National Assessment of Educational Progress data to make normative interpretations. Based on his in-depth analysis of the problems (Mehrens & Kaminski, 1989) and remarks made before the Georgia Educational Research Association and School Test Coordinators in Atlanta on October 13, 1989, Dr. William A. Mehrens has noted that

1. The desire for accountability and test-curriculum match increases the tendency to teach toward specific objectives, skills, subskills, and maybe even items.
2. Teaching toward the test can be either helpful or harmful.
3. Inferences to a domain only sampled by the objectives will necessarily be incorrect if the preceding instruction was limited to only the objectives sampled.
4. Inferences from tests used to (a) inform the public about educational quality, or (b) inform parents and students about how the education of the student is progressing will almost always be to a domain that is greater than the objectives tested.
5. We are misleading the public, students, and perhaps ourselves when we limit instruction to the objectives tested.
6. It is inappropriate to use study guides or practice tests that encourage such limited instruction.
7. School districts and states must give serious attention to, and establish policies regarding:

a. What is appropriate test/curriculum match and what is inappropriate teaching to the test, and
b. What are legitimate and illegitimate study guides.

8. Test security must be maintained.

What the examination of this phenomena really means is that the testing industry must redouble its efforts to evaluate and inform the test-using community not only about the advantages of standardized testing, but about the potential negatives as well.

The interpretation of test scores—whether to individual students, colleagues, parents, or members of the community in general—requires careful preparation and a thorough understanding of what test scores mean, what influences them, and how they can be used. It is a demanding task.

Case Study Application

Our Reading Education midterm exam was administered to the class of Ms. F. Fraddle with the following results.

Mean = 57.56	Standard Deviation = 5.1
Reliability = .79	Number of Items = 80

Using these data, write out interpretations for the following scores. Readers may wish to refer back to the test in Chapter 10 to refresh their memories about the meaning of basic formulas. Basic data on the class performance are also contained in the Case Study Application associated with Chapter 10.

1. Red got a raw score of 64 on the test. What would be an (a) absolute and a (b) relative interpretation of his performance?
2. Chelsea got a raw score of 69 on the test. Is it likely that her score is meaningfully different from that of Red?
3. Assume that Chelsea's score translates to a grade equivalent of 13.3. What interpretation could be made of that performance?
4. Red's score is equivalent to a percentile rank of ? What does that mean?

Content Review Statements

1. Test performances may be interpreted in light of absolute standards, relative averages, or test content.
2. Norms will generally reference performances to a single group (status) or multiple groups (developmental).
3. Normative scores will either be linear (take the shape of the underlying raw score distribution) or reflect area transformation (usually to a normal distribution).
4. Normative data may be expressed in the form of raw scores, standard scores (z, Z, T, CEEB score, or stanines), percentile ranks, age scores, or grade scores.

5. The value of any set of normative data rests primarily on the nature, representatives, and number of students and schools included.
6. Percentile rank and standard score norms have direct interpretability if the national sample matches the local group in terms of relevant demographic and educational characteristics.
7. A grade equivalent is the average raw test score for a particular grade.
8. Among other problems, grade-equivalent norms suffer from the following shortcomings:
   a. A given grade equivalent does not mean the same thing for each student who receives it, whether the student is in the same class or grade, or is above or below it.
   b. Most grade norms are based on the untenable assumption of uniform growth throughout the year, and therefore use ambiguous units of measurement.
   c. Most grade norms discount the learning or loss of learning that occurs over the summer months.
   d. Extrapolated (estimated) grade norms are open to many misinterpretations.
   e. Grade norms should not be considered standards.
   f. The value of grade norms depends on the match between curriculum and test content.
   g. Extreme grade equivalents are difficult to interpret.
9. Age norms are based on average test scores at various age levels.
10. It is highly desirable to develop local test norms.
11. Expectancy norms for achievement tests can be developed by relating test scores to ability measures or other relevant external criteria.
12. Developmental standard score norms allow for the tracking of growth.
13. Published test norms should be:
    a. Clearly described.
    b. Expressed as standard scores and percentile ranks.
    c. As up-to-date as possible.
14. Profiling achievement test scores in various subject areas from the same battery allows for the identification of individual student and class strengths and weaknesses.
15. Percentile bands corresponding to the standard error of measurement should be used when profiling test scores.
16. In interpreting profiles, consideration should be given to the elevation, scatter, and shape of the profile.
17. In interpreting test scores to students, consideration should be given the potential psychological impact of such scores and the many related factors that bear on meaning.
18. A student has a right to an interpretation of his or her score on any test.
19. In interpreting and reporting scores to the public, care should be taken to:
    a. Explain the purpose of the tests.
    b. Avoid the use of composite scores for each school.
    c. Prepare a tabular and narrative summary.
    d. Avoid implying that norms are standards.
    e. Take into account the many economic and demographic variables that influence test scores.
20. Test-wiseness may interfere with what is being measured.

21. The effects of the coaching on college admissions tests are probably not worth the effort or expense.
22. Test anxiety can be decreased by working with the examinee on the purposes and procedures of test taking.
23. The Lake Wobegon Effect describes the phenomena of being at or above the 50th percentile.
24. Invidious comparisons are invited when states are ranked according to their means on the *Scholastic Aptitude Test.*
25. Computer-generated test interpretations need to be considered with caution.

Speculations

1. How can a teacher deal with test anxiety?
2. What does research say about the effects of coaching?
3. What are the most important characteristics of test norms?
4. What are "local norms"?
5. What are the advantages and disadvantages of grade equivalent scores used as norms?
6. Are there any conditions under which it is acceptable to "teach for the test"?
7. Is it likely that a test-wise student can successfully guess his or her way through a test?
8. What are the pros and cons of having separate norms tables for subsamples of school populations (e.g., ethnic or gender groups)?

Suggested Readings

Carey, L. M. (1988). *Measuring and evaluating school learning.* Boston: Allyn and Bacon. Chapter 14 is a very readable summary of approaches to interpreting standardized test results.

Gronlund, N. (1985). *Measurement and evaluation in teaching* (5th ed.). New York: Macmillan. Chapter 14 contains an educationally oriented discussion of the interpretation of test scores and use of norms.

Hopkins, K. D., Stanley, J. C., & Hopkins, B. R. (1990). *Educational and psychological measurement and evaluation.* Englewood Cliffs, NJ: Prentice Hall. Chapter 3 focuses on the types of and interpretation of normative scores.

Lyman, H. B. (1978). *Test scores and what they mean* (3rd ed.). Englewood Cliffs, NJ: Prentice Hall. An excellent overview of the many ways in which test scores may be reported. The emphasis on the interpretation of scores is a strong point of the book.

Miller, D. M. (1972). *Interpreting test scores.* New York: John Wiley & Sons. This self-study programmed book contains most of the basic information necessary for initial approaches to test interpretation.

Chapter 16

The Development and Application of Criterion-Referenced Competency Measures

One of the recent trends in educational assessment is the rebirth of, perhaps more correctly, rekindled interest in criterion-referenced measures. The evolution of the pass/fail marking system, with its emphasis on absolute standards, has also contributed to this approach to student assessment. Criterion-referenced tests are also sometimes referred to as minimum competency tests, competency tests, or mastery tests. Although the idea of basing a series of test items on specific performance criteria has existed since the turn of the century, not until the advent of mastery learning and individualized curricula was proper attention paid to this use of test scores. A criterion-referenced measure is one that is used to identify an individual's status with respect to a criterion or an established standard of performance (Popham & Husek, 1969). The standard of performance is usually a highly refined behavioral objective describing expected pupil changes and the conditions and criteria under which these changes can be exhibited.

Recent application of criterion-referenced measures (CRM) has included higher-order cognitive outcomes such as critical thinking and problem solving. The key to a CRM definition is a clear description of the topic or domain that is being sampled. Generally that domain is relatively homogeneous such as division of two-digit numbers, definition of key terms in a science unit, or contributions of 19th-century American writers. The better the definition, the better the measurement and interpretation of the score. It is not possible to distinguish a criterion-referenced measure from a norm-referenced measure or its resulting scores merely by looking at it; the differences show up in the use made of the scores. A CRM will usually yield percent scores (percent of maximum possible) whereas an NRM will express performance as percentile ranks or standard scores. The interpretation of scores—relative for norm-referenced and absolute for criterion-referenced—is the major difference between these two approaches to assessment.

One must be cautious in making decisions with scores that are made up of a limited number of items. Since CRM scores are usually tied to a limited but homogeneous set of objectives, and inferences are frequently made about performance relative to individual objectives, it is important to have sufficient items, perhaps as many as 10–20 per objective.

The two kinds of measures, CRM and NRM, could be envisioned on a continuum whose poles might be characterized as "Interpretation Tied to Specific Objectives" at one end and "Interpretation Tied to Relative Performances" at the other. It is quite possible for a criterion-referenced measure to be used in a norm-referenced way, but is less likely for the converse to be true. If scores are expressed in an absolute way (percent of maximum possible) one not only has an indication of performance against a standard, but we also have a relative ordering of students on the absolute scale.

Figure 16-1 shows a set of criterion-referenced items (Cox & Graham, 1966). This set of test items is interesting because it illustrates a potentially valuable application of criterion-referenced measures. These ten objective-item pairs are sequenced—that is, item 8 builds upon the knowledge and skills elicited by items 1 through 7. The total score on such an instrument has direct interpretability. Given a total score on a scaled measure, the instructor can discern which items an individual answered wrong. On a norm-referenced test, this is usually impossible. The application of the idea of analyzing learning sequences and hierarchies has been well illustrated by Gagné (1985).

Developing Criterion-Referenced Measures

Mayo (1970) has noted that the development of criterion-referenced measures closely parallels that of a traditional achievement test. In the development of the usual classroom test—or standardized test, for that matter—four general steps are followed (see Chapters 1 and 5 for a more complete overview):

1. Specification of expected student performance outcomes.
2. Construction, identification, collection, or adaptation of measuring methods appropriate to each outcome.

Objective	*Sample Test Items*
The student is able to:	
1. Recognize numerals from 1 to 10.	1. 1 2 3 4 "Draw a circle around the 2."
2. a. Determine which numeral comes before or after another numeral.	2. a. 10 8 5 2 "Draw a circle around the number that comes just after 7."
b. Determine which of two numerals is the larger or smaller.	b. 7 5 "Draw a circle around the larger numeral."
3. Discriminate between $+$, $-$, $=$, $\neq$.	3. $+$ $-$ $=$ $\neq$ "Draw a circle around the sign which means to add."
4. a. Add two single-digit numerals with sums to 10, vertically.	4. a. $\begin{array}{r} 5 \\ +\ 4 \\ \hline \end{array}$
b. Add two single-digit numerals with sums to 10, horizontally.	b. $3 + 1 =$
5. a. Add two single-digit numerals involving carrying, horizontally.	5. a. $8 + 3 =$
b. Add two single-digit numerals involving carrying, vertically.	b. $\begin{array}{r} 7 \\ +\ 8 \\ \hline \end{array}$
6. a. Add three single-digit numerals involving carrying, vertically.	6. a. $\begin{array}{r} 1 \\ 8 \\ +\ 4 \\ \hline \end{array}$
b. Add three single-digit numerals involving carrying, horizontally.	b. $7 + 3 + 2 =$
7. a. Place one- and two-digit numerals in a column so they could be added.	7. a. 15 16 2 "Place these numerals in a column so they could be added."
b. Determine which column of numerals is written so it could be added.	b. $\begin{array}{l} 15 \\ \ \ 16 \\ 2 \\ \hline \end{array}$ $\begin{array}{r} 15 \\ 16 \\ 2 \\ \hline \end{array}$ $\begin{array}{l} 15 \\ 16 \\ 2 \\ \hline \end{array}$ "Draw a circle around the column which is written so it could be added."

Figure 16-1

Criterion-referenced items

8. Add two two-digit numerals without carrying.	8.	20 + 11
9. Add two three-digit numerals without carrying.	9.	215 + 723
10. Add two two-digit numerals with carrying.	10.	58 + 36

Reprinted from the Summer 1966 issue of the *Journal of Educational Measurement*, Vol. 3, No. 2. Copyright 1966 by the National Council on Measurement in Education. Reprinted by permission of the author and publisher.

Figure 16-1
(Continued)

3. Selection of those post-tryout items that yield maximum discrimination against an internal criterion and are answered correctly by an average of about 50–60 percent of the students.
4. Establishment of guidelines for interpreting the scores against normative standards.

The first two steps are applicable to the development of criterion-referenced measures. Adjustments are, however, required in the final two steps. Inasmuch as criterion-referenced measures focus on an individual's performance on a set of tasks, discrimination—defined as the capacity of an item to distinguish between groups of more and less knowledgeable individuals—is a less applicable concept. We do hope, however, that an individual will learn as he progresses through the educational experience. Therefore, Cox (1971) has suggested an index of discrimination based on the relative proportions of students passing an item at the beginning and at the conclusion of a unit or course as the best indication of its effectiveness. One might expect an item on a mastery test to have a difficulty level as high as 85 percent or higher at the conclusion of instruction. With regard to interpretation of the resulting scores, it is sufficient to note that the meaning of an individual's score is derived from an examination of his or her skills or knowledge relative to his or her deficiencies. What is proposed is a kind of diagnostic interpretation tied to performance standards. The usual interpretation of scores on a criterion-referenced test is in terms of the percentage correct (score ÷ maximum number of points possible). Traditional indices are also used, such as standard scores. Assuming no deficiencies in the items, a criterion-referenced measure can be used to obtain a directly relevant sample of student behavior.

Differences Between Criterion-Referenced and Norm-Referenced Measures

Several of the differences between criterion-referenced and norm-referenced measures are briefly summarized below. The differences are in most cases matters of degree rather than kind.

Dimension	*Criterion-Referenced Measures*	*Norm-Referenced Measures*
1. Intent	Information on degree to which absolute external performance standards have been met	Information for relative internal comparisons
	Description of maximum performance by individuals, groups, and treatment	Comparisons of individuals, particularly when high degree of selectivity is required
2. Directness of measurement	Great emphasis	Lesser emphasis
3. Variability among scores	Relatively low	Relatively high
4. Difficulty of items	Items tend to be easy, but with some range	Item difficulty localized around 50 percent
5. Item type	Great variety, but less reliance on selection-type items	Variety, but emphasis on selection-type items
6. Item discrimination	Not emphasized	Greatly emphasized
7. Methods of establishing validity	Reliance on content validity	Emphasis on criterion-related validity
8. Emphasis on reliability	Focus on reliability of domain sampling; therefore internal consistency of some interest	Greater concern with parallel form and test-retest estimates of performance stability
9. Influence of guessing	Can be of consequence	Generally not a problem
10. Importance of which items are missed	High	Emphasis on number of missed items

Dimension	*Criterion-Referenced Measures*	*Norm-Referenced Measures*
11. Necessity for maintaining security of test items	Relatively low	Relatively high
12. Area of education best served	Instruction	Guidance Selection Grading

Several of these distinctions need further explanation. The single most important characteristic that distinguishes criterion-referenced measures (CRT) from norm-referenced measures (NRT) is the basis for interpretability. A CRT measure is focused on an *absolute* interpretation, for example, did Fred get the required 80 percent correct? A different approach is taken with an NRT measure where the basis for interpretation is *relative*, for example, how did students rank themselves on the test? Both are legitimate, but reflect different purposes in testing, that is, how much vs. where.

The variability of the scores is probably the second most important technical difference between the two approaches to measurement. Since criterion-referenced measures are most frequently used in mastery-testing situations, students who attempt items representing objectives they have seriously worked toward are highly likely to answer them correctly. Total scores are likely to be high. Therefore, variability among scores is likely to be low. Unfortunately, variability is a characteristic of scores that is highly related to the traditional indices of instrument quality and accuracy (e.g., measures of internal consistency reliability). These indices are, therefore, considerably less relevant to criterion-referenced measures than to norm-referenced measures.

One of the chief objectives in writing items for norm-referenced measures is to make them as discriminating as possible. By controlling for such factors as discriminability among alternative answers and vocabulary, one attempts to maximize discrimination and thereby increase variability. By contrast, the writer of criterion-referenced items is interested solely in making the item measure the objective in the most direct way. Questions, tasks, or exercises need not be limited to paper-and-pencil items, but could be orally presented situations or be behaviorally-based performance measures.

Since the items in a criterion-referenced measure represent a set of related objectives, they should be correlated. A measure of internal consistency (see Chapter 12) would be appropriate. The old problem of variability, however, presents itself. We should probably reduce our standards of acceptable reliability to about .50 to accommodate lowered variability.

Items that do not discriminate between more and less knowledgeable or skillful students need not be eliminated from a criterion-referenced test if they reflect an important learning outcome (see Chapter 11). Cox (1971) has reported the results of a study he conducted with Vargas demonstrating that, in a pre-post-test situation, an index based on subtraction of the percentage who passed the item on a post-test provided information useful in identifying pretest items of diagnostic significance. Some of these items would have been overlooked if traditional item-analysis methods had been used.

Following are some possible pre-post instruction percentage scores that might arise under CRM testing conditions for five items. The question might be, which items should be retained.

Item	*Percent Passing (Pre)*	*Percent Passing (Post)*	*Decision Retain for CRM*
13	55	81	Yes
23	15	19	No
41	86	91	Yes
57	73	47	No
69	21	36	Yes

Item 13 is obviously the "best" as it shows sensitivity to instruction moving from 55 percent passing to 81 percent passing. Item 23 is insensitive and needs to be examined and faults of the instruction and objective associated with it need to be revised. Even though Item 41 was easy pre- *and* post-instruction we would keep it if it measures an important outcome. Item 57 is obviously bad as it reflects negative change, and the data should serve to alert the teachers that something is wrong. Finally, although the change is small, 21 percent to 36 percent, we would keep Item 69 because we can tolerate a lower level of sensitivity in a criterion-referenced measurement.

Since we hope that individuals will achieve instructional objectives as a result of their educational experiences, we might expect an item on a criterion-referenced test to be answered correctly by a greater proportion of them after instruction than before it; if the instruction is successful, the proportion answering correctly should be high. Such indices of change in difficulty and absolute level of difficulty can be useful in assessing instructional effectiveness but should not be used to judge the adequacy of the item itself, as would be the case with norm-referenced tests. The quality of an item on a criterion-referenced test is a function of the degree to which it matches the objective and is directly interpretable with reference to it. Panels of expert judges could be employed to help make these item-objective evaluations.

Methods of assessing validity that employ correlation are generally less applicable to criterion-referenced measures due to lack of score variability. Instead, the test developer must rely on logical but subjective analysis of the match between item and objective (see the discussion of content validity in Chapter 13). Methods employing contrasted groups and mean scores can also be used. For example comparing the mean score on a writing competency exam for students in average versus advanced English class would help establish criterion-related validity. The reader should also be alerted to its fact that interpretation of CRM scores should be approached cautiously due to the limited number of items used to measure each objective. In this regard, perhaps the CRM falls between an NRM and a diagnostic test relative to the amount of detailed information derived from the test. The smaller the domain being sampled and the more homogeneous that domain, the fewer the number of items needed.

Creating Criterion-Referenced Items

One of the keys to valid interpretation of scores from criterion-referenced items and tests is the definition of the domain. Remember from Chapter 1 that criterion-referenced measures are created to yield scores that are directly interpretable in terms of specified performance standards. The standards are specified by describing systematically in detail a class or domain of tasks. The better the definition the more valid the interpretation (Nitko, 1980). How can we insure the closeness of relationship between domain and items? One step is to use structured item specifications. Item specifications are as important in CRM as in NRM (perhaps more so). Popham (1990) has described a five-part method that is helpful in creating a general framework that can be used to create multiple items. Basically the procedure requires the item writer to elaborate and amplify the objective to be measured. One begins with an objective, then adds information to reduce ambiguity in constructing the test tasks. The approach, although useful to the classroom teacher, is more likely to be used by organizations or systems where a large number of items of a similar type and intent must be produced.

The five elements in Popham's approach are as follows:

1. *General Description.* A brief description of the objective (outcome, behaviors) to be assessed is presented. The intent of creating the item is clarified.
2. *Illustrative Item.* Every item writer needs a model, therefore the sample item can be very helpful in "operationalizing" the objective. One must be careful that the sample item is not simply an item that gets cloned.
3. *Stimulus Attributes.* A set of descriptions are used to communicate the task(s) to be undertaken by the examinee. The descriptions serve to delimit the test-taking process.
4. *Response Attributes.* A set of descriptions of the response options from which the examinee either selects or will be used to create scoring criteria if the task calls for a constructed response.
5. *Specification Supplement.* Occasionally further elaboration is needed regards the stimulus task or response options, or dimensions of the administrative procedure needs to be explained (e.g., group vs. individual test administration).

The item specifications can be quite lengthy perhaps even a page or more. But remember that what we are doing is setting the parameters for a whole series of hopefully homogeneous test tasks. We want our description to be so explicit that multiple item writers will produce parallel items.

Following is a sample set of specifications created by Price, Martuza, and Crouse (1974) and illustrated by Martuza (1977).

GENERAL DESCRIPTION: The intent is to assess an individual's ability to apply selected rules in reading line graphs. Categorical information of two types is combined to create a graph which forms the basis of a series of items. The two categories of information are type (point or line), and trend in unit (random, increase, decrease).

SAMPLE ITEMS

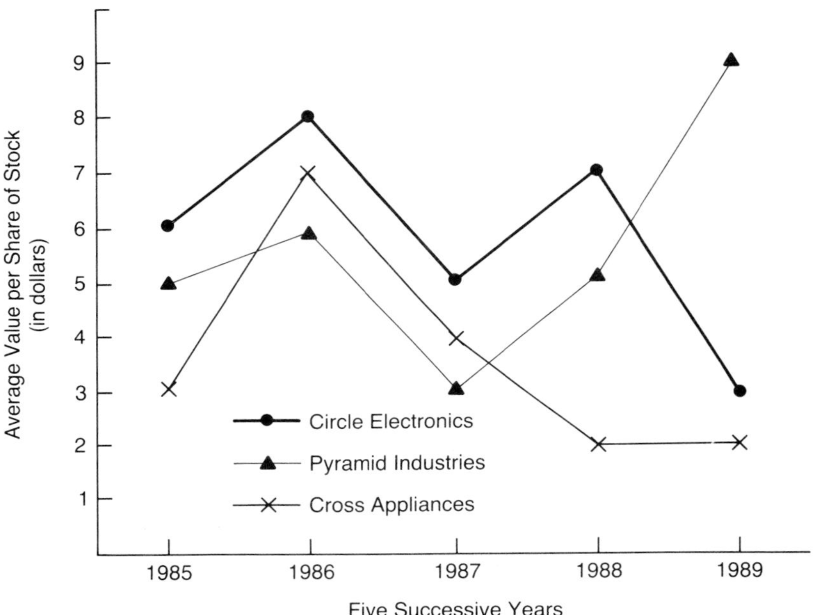

True False 1. The average value per share of Circle Electronics stock was greater than five dollars during the year 1986.

True False 2. The average value per share of Cross Appliances stock was less than five dollars during the year 1988.

STIMULUS AND RESPONSE ATTRIBUTES: The basic frame for the items was as follows: "The average value per share of (*company name*) stock was (+ or − *comparative*) than (*value*) during the year (*year*).

1. Company names for the eight items were selected randomly with the restriction that each company name was used at least twice and no more than three times.
2. The year values for the eight items were chosen randomly with the restriction that each year value was used at least once and no more than twice.
3. The comparative (greater than-less than) was assigned randomly to the items so that each appeared in four items of the subtest.

4. Within the four items containing the "greater than" comparative, the truth value was randomly assigned such that two propositions would be true and two would be false. The same procedure was used for the four "less than" comparative items.
5. For each item, the set of stock values that would satisfy the truth value for that item was determined, and one element of the set was randomly selected for inclusion in the item.

Obviously this approach would work best with highly structured content domain. The value of the specifications is not just for the creators of the items, but also for the users of the test information because the descriptions illustrate exactly what is being measured.

Standard Setting

Evaluation is just that—the making of a value judgment. The use of criteria and standards in evaluating outcomes of an evaluation study sets it apart from most other scientific activities. As most experts note, there must be "worth determination." Historically "worth" has been defined in statistical terms, for example, whether data fit a particular mathematical model. Recent trends focus on involving the stakeholder and/or evaluators in the process of setting outcome-based standards, for example, 50 percent of the students must master 75 percent of the outcomes.

There are vocal opponents and proponents of standard setting, particularly as regards the determination of student competence. Opponents argue that virtually all methods of establishing standards are arbitrary and it is difficult, if not impossible, to get judges to agree on applicable standards. Proponents cite research supporting good consistency in specifying standards, particularly when there is training involved and pilot test data are available to help guide decisions. For an extensive overview of issues and research results the reader is referred to Jaeger (1989).

A useful classification scheme for organizing some 38 different standard setting methods has been proposed by Berk (1986a) and modified by Jaeger (1989). An initial dichotomy is proposed: state vs. continuum. A state model assumes that competency is an all-or-nothing state, and therefore to be categorized as a master a perfect test performance is called for from the examinee. The procedure calls for adjusting backwards from 100 percent (e.g., to 90 percent) to set the standard. The continuum models assume that mastery or competence is continuously distributed. The standard-setting task is to search for all meaningful boundaries to establish categories. Continuum models can be test-centered or examinee-centered. All standard setting methods involve making judgments. This activity is implicit in all standard setting procedures.

Table 16-1 contains a summary of three approaches to standard setting.

An example of the test-centered approach should help illustrate the approach. In this case it will be Angoff's modified procedure (Angoff, 1971). Assume an instructor wishes to set a basic passing score for a midterm exam in an introductory statistics course. The exam is composed of 40 items such as on page 394.

Table 16-1 Summary of Categories of Standard-Setting Methods

Category	Description	Example
State	Adjustments down from 100 percent performance criterion are made based on judgments about fallibility of test and characteristics of examinees.	Child will have demonstrated mastery of specified knowledge, ability, or skill when he performs correctly 85 percent of time (Tyler, 1973).
Test-Centered Continuum	Population of judges make probability estimates about item performances of borderline or minimally competent examinees.	Minimum standards were researched based on the National Teacher Examination (Cross, Impara, Frary, Jaeger, 1984).
Examinee-Centered Continuum	Judges familiar with examinees categorize them (e.g., master, borderline, nonmaster), test is administered, overlap in distributions is assessed.	Second-grade basic skills tests (language arts, mathematics) were used to compare teacher judgments and examinee performance (Mills, 1983).

Source: After Jaeger (1989).

SAMPLE ITEM: A student obtains a raw score of 23 in a unimodel, moderately skewed distribution of test scores with a median of 23. What would be the student's *z* score?

(a) Exactly zero
(b) Greater or less than zero depending on value of the standard deviation
(c) Greater or less than zero depending on the direction of the skewness (answer)

A group of experts (instructors and advanced doctoral students) were asked to make judgments about each item. The judging directions were as follows:

> What percentage of minimally competent introductory statistics students will correctly respond to this item?

Judges (experts) were to select from one of the following percentages:

5%, 20%, 40%, 60%, 75%, 90%, 95%.

Each judge's estimates were summed thus yielding an "expected score" for a hypothetical minimally competent student. The expected scores were then averaged across judges. One can readily see some interesting variations on this approach. Data on previous students' performance on the item could be provided to the judges. Instead of a dichotomous decision data about multiple-competency categories could be gathered. Groups of students who had been previously classified on bases other than the test could have been administered the test and actual and expected results compared.

Training for Setting Standards

It was noted previously that in order for the collective judgment approach to work effectively some preparation and training must occur. This is particularly crucial when high-stakes standards are involved (e.g., setting grade promotion score standards). Popham (1987b) suggests several guidelines for preparing judges. Among the information necessary for *informed judgment* is:

1. Delineation of consequences of decision—what are potential effects on the individual and society?
2. Description of examination—if possible have decision makers take exams to assess difficulty level.
3. Provisions of information on reliability and validity of exam—in particular, questions of bias need to be addressed.
4. Overview of phase-in time for exam and system—shorter time perhaps calls for more relaxed standards.
5. Description of examinee instructional preparation for exam—was it adequate and sufficiently comprehensive?
6. Overview of audiences with interest in results of application of standard—an examination of possible vested interests in higher or lower standards.
7. Description of experts' recommendations—formal review of test by expert groups should be part of process.
8. Overview of field-test results and actual data on subgroups should be examined.
9. Assess standard-setting time-line alternatives—standards can be elevated or lowered depending on phase-in and preparation time.
10. Inform interested audiences about the process and products of standard setting—in particular, media representatives need to be prepared.

Standard setting is a very important, if complex and sensitive, task which needs to be taken seriously by policy makers and testing experts alike. If taken seriously it will require a great deal of preparation, planning, organization of data, and—above all—patience.

Minimum Competency Testing

The minimum competency testing movement, an outgrowth of criterion-referenced measurement, is a 20th-century educational phenomenon. For some it represents the beneficial application of a developing technology to help reform education, rectify social ills, and respond to the outcry of society that our public school graduates can't read, write, spell, count, or calculate as well as "we" think they should. Economic pressures and the need for accountability have helped push educators into a position where they must justify their expenditures and programs.

A minimum competency testing program typically involves the development, modification, and selection of a set of basic skill measures of computational and communication objectives. Such tests are usually criterion-referenced and with increasing frequency are tailor-made by the local school system or state education departments. Commercial test publishers now have programs for creating CRM for state and local systems. In addition, many standardized achievement batteries provide both CRM and NRM data. Many programs also include measures of so-called life survival skills, or real life or basic life skills such as career exploration, consumer evaluation skills, citizenship, and basic physical and mental health maintenance skills. Although primarily used as exit exams from high school, test data are also used to help make grade-to-grade promotion decisions.

Much controversy (McClung, 1978; Jaeger & Tittle, 1979) and several significant legal battles (Fisher, 1980) have been joined over installation of minimum competency testing programs. The chief claims for such programs are the establishment of egalitarian and uniform standards, minimum competencies being seen to represent realistic goals for educational programs, and local control. On the negative side are such factors as long-term start-up and phase-in time, the possible discriminatory use of the tests, the control and setting of standards, overemphasis on minimums with a corresponding deemphasis on maximums, and curricular concerns surrounding what should be the treatment for those who fail, that is, when and how should remediation take place.

Many test development issues present during the design and construction stage of any test are amplified for a minimum competency test. Chief among these is the match between test items and curriculum *and* instructional objectives, that is, do the test items measure not only the professed educational goals of the system, but also what was actually taught? The demonstration of acceptable types and levels of reliability is also important. It is particularly crucial that the developer of a minimum competency test be able to demonstrate that the test is measuring lasting general characteristics of the examinee. Test security may also be an issue as many public agencies, the local Board of Education, special interest groups, and/or the media may exert political pressure on the local systems or State Board of Education to release the test items for examination. The Freedom of Information Act and "sunshine" laws can also be invoked. The adverse effect on the usefulness of post-release data is obvious. Needless to say it would behoove anyone involved in developing or implementing a minimum competency testing program to work closely with an attorney at all times, document all steps used in the development of the instrumentation, and make sure that sound and acceptable professionally approved practices were used at all stages of instrument development and application.

Illustration of a State Competency Testing Program

Many states employ criterion-referenced tests to measure basic skills that educators have identified as being essential for all students to acquire in order to make academic progress. In addition information is provided to teachers and administrators to identify learners who may be in need of remediation. The data hopefully will be used by educational policy and decision makers, teachers, students, parents, and concerned citizens.

A representative student assessment program is outlined here to illustrate the process of development and reporting of CRM scores. The reader will hopefully appreciate the (a) detail in domain objectives specification, (b) close tie between objectives and items, (c) effort to communicate relevant information to audiences, stakeholders, and decision makers, and (d) the direct implication of performance for instruction.

Criterion-referenced measures are administered at state expense during the spring in Grades 1, 3, 6, and 8. In addition, systems have an option at their own expense to administer equivalent measures at Grades 2 and 4. At the tenth grade level there is the Basic Skills Test, the successful passing of which is required before graduation. A student may take this test as many times as necessary to achieve an acceptable passing score.

In addition to reading and mathematics every student in the state must demonstrate the ability to create a composition of no more than two pages on an assigned topic. The writing samples are scored by two raters according to (a) content and organization, (b) style, (c) sentence formation, (d) language usage, and (e) mechanics of English (see Chapter 8). The writing sample is collected in Grades 6, 8, and 10. Competence must be demonstrated at tenth grade level or beyond and is also required for graduation. Data at eighth grade are used to identify students who may be at risk with regard to writing skills

Objectives for Criterion-Referenced Tests in Mathematics and Reading

Listed below are each of the objectives measured by the criterion-referenced tests for grade eight. The criterion levels (number of items necessary for mastery) and total number of items measuring each objective are found in parentheses following each objective statement.

Mathematics

Concept identification. This skill area contains the basic vocabulary of mathematics and the interrelationships of different kinds of numbers. The student:

1. translates forms of rational numbers. (7 of 11 items)
2. identifies relations or properties of sets of numbers and operations. (9 of 13 items)
3. selects customary or metric units to measure length, area, volume, weight, time, and temperature. (6 of 9 items)
4. identifies relations and properties of sets of points. (9 of 13 items)

Component operations. This skill area involves actions on numbers and focuses on addition, subtraction, multiplication, and division, as well as using units of measurement. The student:

5. determines probabilities. (3 of 4 items)
6. computes with whole numbers, fractions, decimals, integers, and percents. (14 of 19 items)
7. applies formulas or units of measure to determine length, area, volume, weight, time, temperature, and amounts of money. (13 of 21 items)

Problem solving. This skill area requires the student to select or apply the appropriate concepts and/or operations necessary to solve problems. The student:

8. selects the appropriate operation for a given problem situation and the reverse. (4 of 6 items)
9. solves word problems. (6 of 9 items)
10. organizes data. (3 of 6 items)
11. interprets data that have been organized. (6 of 10 items)
12. estimates results. (3 of 4 items)

Reading

Literal comprehension. This area involves understanding information that is explicitly stated in written material. The student:

1. distinguishes between fact and opinion. (5 of 7 items)
2. recognizes explicitly stated main ideas, details, sequences of events, and cause-and-effect relationships. (12 of 17 items)
3. interprets instructions. (7 of 11 items)

Inferential comprehension. This area involves understanding information that can be determined from written material even though it is not directly stated. The student:

4. recognizes implicitly stated main ideas, details, sequences of events, and cause-and effect relationships. (14 of 23 items)
5. interprets word meanings and patterns of language. (5 of 9 items)
6. interprets figurative language. (4 of 6 items)
7. recognizes propaganda techniques. (4 of 6 items)

Problem solving. This skill area involves locating, recognizing, interpreting, or evaluating information needed to make decisions or solve problems. The student:

8. uses reference sources. (6 of 10 items)
9. makes generalizations and draws conclusions. (6 of 10 items)
10. makes predictions and comparisons. (9 of 13 items)
11. recognizes relevance of data. (4 of 6 items)

Standard-setting procedures similar to those described earlier in this chapter are applied each year in establishing passing scores.

Reports. Five major kinds of summary reports are produced from the student assessment system at the eighth grade level. They are:

Student labels. In addition to identifying information (e.g., grade, school, etc.) they contain a summary of individual student performance on each objective and scale scores. These are for posting in the student's cumulative folder.

Student report. Two copies of a summary of individual student performance relative to each of the 11 Reading and 12 Mathematics objectives. A scale score system ranges from 100 to 300. Total Reading scores of 193 or below or a total Mathematics score of 201 or below generally indicate need for additional efforts in order to achieve mastery on the Basic Skills Test which is needed for graduation. Scores below 202 in Reading or 201 in Mathematics indicate eligibility for the State Remedial Education Program. The criterion scores vary slightly from year to year. A copy of this report is shared with parent or guardian, and teacher.

School reports. A student achievement roster describes which objectives each student achieved and total scale scores. It is shared with school administrators and teachers.

Administrative reports. In addition to reports to teacher and local school personnel, grade level reports are prepared for individual school systems, as well as statewide summaries. Historical reports are prepared that allow schools and systems to monitor their progress over several years.

Technical reports. Among the technical reports are (a) item analyses detailing answer choices and difficulty level and (b) frequency distributions and percentile ranks for scaled scores.

Sample Items and Feedback from Criterion-Referenced Tests

Following are sample items and information from computer-generated printouts of student performance results for eighth grade mathematics and reading tests. The total test is divided into six sections, three for each skill area. Each of the two three-section units is preceded by a practice test. Administration directions are clear and standardized. The tests are not rigidly timed, but approximately 45 minutes is allowed for each of the six sections. Test administrators are allowed some discretion in timing, allowing an extra 5–10 minutes if it appears needed. The goal is for each student to complete as much of the test as possible without being constrained by time limits. It is suggested that testing take place on Tuesday, Wednesday, and Thursday in the morning. Usually two sittings are sufficient.

Mathematics. Following are three sample items (from 9) that relate to Math Objective 9: Solves Word Problems. A student would need to get 6 of the 9 items correct to have demonstrated mastery of the objective.

1. Sam wrote a computer program that divides each number entered by 8 and then adds 16. If 56 is entered, which answer appears?
   1. 8

2. 9
* 3. 23
4. 24

2. Two pencils cost 25 cents. If each student receives one pencil, which is the cost of pencils for a class of 30?
   1. $ .55
   * 2. $ 3.75
   3. $ 7.50
   4. $15.00
3. If all felines are mammals, all cats are felines, and all tigers are cats, which statement is true?
   1. All mammals are felines.
   2. All felines are tigers.
   * 3. All cats are mammals.
   4. All mammals are cats.

Based on a summary analysis of a recent spring administration the following results were observed:

58 percent of eighth graders in the *state* mastered the objective.
49 percent of eighth graders in the *county* mastered the objective.
59 percent of eighth graders in the *school* mastered the objective.

In addition, the following diagnostic information is provided to each teacher in summary form (below) as well as for each individual student. For Teacher A of 102 students tested in mathematics

1. 46 may need additional instruction in solving word problems involving money.
2. 1 may need additional instruction in solving simple logic problems.
3. 34 may need additional instruction in solving word problems.

These students are identified for the teacher. The first diagnostic is related to the foregoing item number 2, the second to item number 3, and the third to item number 1. This is extremely valuable information for the teacher.

Let's look at some sample items in Reading.

Reading. The following four items are for the Objective 8: Uses Reference Sources. This objective was tested with a total of 10 items, 6 of which had to be correct in order for the student to have mastered the objective.

4. In which card catalog drawer would one find the title card for *No Time for Lunch?*
   1. Foo-For
   2. Lom-Lyn
   * 3. Nap-No
   4. Tam-Tre

Use the dictionary entry to answer question 5.

neutral (noo-trel) adj. (1) not taking sides in a contest; (2) without color; (3) neither positive nor negative charge; (4) having no definite character. n. (5) a mechanical gear position.

As Robert watched the ball game, he remained *neutral.*

5. Which meaning is used?
   * * 1. 1
   * 2. 3
   * 3. 4
   * 5. 5

Use the Table of Contents to answer question 6.

Chapter	*Page*
Preface	1
Introduction	8
Wolves	16
Wild Dogs and Jackals	34
Hyenas	51
Coyotes	75
Foxes	93
Weasels, Mink, and Ermine	119
Bibliography	136
Index	142

6. On which page does the list of reference sources used in writing this book begin?
   * 1. 1
   * 2. 8
   * * 3. 136
   * 4. 142
7. Which source is most appropriate for locating the major rivers and lakes in the United States?
   * 1. almanac
   * * 2. atlas
   * 3. dictionary
   * 4. thesaurus

Performance on this objective was very good as:

93 percent of eighth graders in the *state* mastered the objective.
94 percent of eighth graders in the *county* mastered the objective.
94 percent of eighth graders in the *school* mastered the objective.

The diagnostics for this item were as follows:
Of your 102 students tested in Reading

1. 19 may need additional instruction in using a card catalog.
2. 3 may need additional instruction in using a dictionary or glossary to identify the meaning of words.

3. 3 may need additional instruction using reference parts of a book.
4. 2 may need additional instruction identifying appropriate persons, documents, or organizations as reference sources.

The diagnostics are in the same order as the items 4–7. The only potential problem was with the task of using a card catalog, item 1 where almost 19 percent of the students did not respond correctly.

Possible Applications of Criterion-Referenced Measures

As has been noted, the rekindled interest in criterion-referenced measurement is partially a response to the evolution of mastery learning and individualized instruction. It is not surprising, then, to find the major applications of criterion-referenced measures in these areas. At least eight general uses for criterion-referenced measures can be identified:

Placement in a Learning Program

The major function of a criterion-referenced measure used as a placement test is to provide a general profile of an individual's performance on a variety of work units. A mathematics placement test, for example, can be used to locate individuals differentially within a series of mathematics units variously labeled Numeration, Place Value, Addition, Subtraction, and so on. The challenge to the test constructor is to gather as much relevant information as possible in the most efficient manner. Placement tests should probably be administered at the beginning of the school year or at the outset of a new extended learning sequence.

Diagnosis of Individual Student Achievement

Perhaps the best use of a criterion-referenced measure is as a diagnostic tool. Used in this way, it should allow a student to "test out" of a particular unit. If this performance does not merit this, the resulting information will allow him and the instructor to identify areas in need of further study. Tests of this type can be teacher-made or with increasing frequency are available from commercial publishers.

Monitoring of Individual Student Progress

The periodic administration of a criterion-referenced test similar in comprehensiveness to the previously described placement tests should facilitate monitoring of student progress. Such a periodic check may also have a motivational function of the student. These measures might serve as the basis for end-of-unit examinations.

Both monitoring and placement measures are broader in coverage and objectives than are specific diagnostic measures.

Diagnosis of Class Achievement

Diagnostic tests may be applied on a classwide basis in the same way in which they are employed with individual students. Areas in which a majority of the students appear to be encountering problems might serve as focal points for remediation and for the planning and development of special remedial units.

Monitoring Class Progress

Again, individual student data could be aggregated for an entire class to provide the teacher and administration with a picture of group progress.

Evaluation of Curricula

Criterion-referenced measures might profitably be used to evaluate a limited-scope curriculum, unit, or skill-building activity. Accumulated data could be used to assess the progress of students toward a specified set of objectives. Competing programs utilizing comparable objectives but different instructional approaches could be compared. By comparing growth data, for example, for a series of objectives and items on a year-to-year basis, or comparing the growth rates of different groups in a given year, important evaluative data could result.

A relatively recent methodological innovation called item-person sampling might be employed in such studies of program (rather than student) performance. If, for example, a limited amount of examination time is available and a considerable number of objectives need to be assessed, item-person sampling or matrix sampling could be employed. Rather than requiring all individuals to respond to all items, subsets of items could be answered by subsets of individuals. Since the focus is on the program, rather than on individual student performance, all students need not answer all questions. Assume, for example, a 40-item criterion-referenced test covering an entire unit, and 80 students. We can randomly divide the 40 items into five eight-item tests, and the 80 students into five 16-person groups. Each group of 16 students takes a different eight-item test. All objectives are covered, and when the data are aggregated we have a comprehensive picture of the effectiveness of the entire program. For more information on the subject of item-person sampling, see Shoemaker (1973) and Sirotnik (1974).

Project and Program Evaluation

It may well be that the most significant application of criterion-referenced measures is the evaluation of innovative educational programs and projects. The use of criterion-referenced tests in the National Assessment of Educational Progress represents an application on a national scale. Programs built on the "accountability concept," for example, performance-contracting projects, represent another area in which criterion-referenced items and instruments can provide informative data.

Grouping on the Basis of Content Achievement

Some schools may wish to group or track students on the basis of ability in particular subject-matter areas. Criterion-referenced measures might be an excellent basis for such grouping.

A Minor Controversy

Criterion-referenced measures are intended to measure what, not how much, the student has or has not learned. Although originally limited to relatively simple learning outcomes, criterion-referenced measures are now beginning to be applied to complex objectives.

A minor controversy surrounds the use of criterion-referenced measures. It has been argued that criterion-referenced measures have limited applicability to the day-to-day classroom setting because (a) such measures do not tell us all we need to know, or perhaps the most important things we need to know, about student learning; (b) it is difficult to base criterion-referenced measurement on meaningful criteria of achievement; and (c) the mastery learning on which criterion-referenced measures focus represents only one classroom methodology used a small percentage of the time. One might add, however, that this percentage is increasing every year.

In response to these alleged limitations, it has been suggested that (a) criterion-referenced measures, although they do not "tell all," provide relevant information on the excellence or deficiency of an individual's performance; (b) the cost of development in teacher time and effort is not as great as suggested by detractors, particularly in regard to the generation of objectives; and (c) considerable time spent on developing skills in the schools and criterion-referenced measures are particularly well suited to assessment in these areas. It should be noted that the application of computer technology to the assembly of tests has been refined and that a lot of the technical problems have been worked out.

Suffice it to say that criterion-referenced measures are different, at least their uses are relatively individualistic. They should take their rightful place in the educational assessor's library. They can provide information not readily available from other sources and can be used to supplement but not supplant existing methodology. This approach to measurement makes a great deal of sense from an instructional standpoint and the techniques of developing CRMs are easily grasped by educators.

Content Review Statements

1. Criterion referencing focuses primarily on the use to which a test is to be put.
2. Each item or set of items in a test used in a criterion-referenced way represents a performance objective stated in behavioral terms.

3. Criterion-referenced measures are primarily used to assess individuals and the effectiveness of treatments.
4. Scores from criterion-referenced measures are directly interpretable in light of the objectives they measure, and ideally have immediate implications for the instructional program and quality of student progress.
5. It would be unusual for an assessment program to be devoted exclusively to the use of criterion-referenced measures or norm-referenced measures.
6. As opposed to *norm-referenced* measures, which assess interindividual differences and uses in selection situations, *criterion-referenced* measures are frequently characterized by:
   a. Low variability of total test scores across individuals.
   b. A large proportion of items that are relatively easy if the material has been mastered.
   c. Relatively low item discrimination.
   d. High reliance on a wide variety of item types, particularly performance measures.
   e. High reliance on content-validity methods to establish claims that the items and test measure what we want them to measure.
   f. Relatively low reliability.
7. Criterion-referenced measures rest primarily on *absolute* interpretations of performance.
8. Norm-referenced measures rest primarily on *relative* interpretations of performance.
9. Minimum competency testing programs are now a mainstay of most public school educational systems.
10. The diagnostic information yielded by criterion-referenced measures can have extremely valuable instructional implication for teacher and student.
11. Criterion-referenced measures can be used to:
    a. Place an individual within a learning sequence.
    b. Diagnose individual student and class achievement.
    c. Monitor individual and class progress.
    d. Evaluate curricula.
    e. Group students for instructional purposes on the basis of content achievement.
12. Standard-setting methods include approaches which are based on:
    a. Absolute criteria
    b. Criterion derived from idealized test/item performance
    c. Criterion derived from idealized examinees
13. Standard setting requires extensive preparation and training.

Speculations

1. What are the basic steps involved in developing criterion-referenced measures?
2. Is minimum competency testing justified in our schools? Why or why not?
3. How would you describe to a new teacher the ways in which criterion-referenced and norm-referenced measures are different?
4. What would you tell tomorrow's audience of the *Good Morning America* television program about the value of (a) criterion-referenced, and (b) high school exit certification exams?

Suggested Readings

Berk, R. A. (Ed.) (1984). *A guide to criterion-referenced test construction.* Baltimore: Johns Hopkins University Press. Eleven chapters by the leading experts in the field.

Block, J. H. (Ed.) (1971). *Mastery learning: Theory and practice.* New York: Holt, Rinehart and Winston. A useful little paperback summarizing major issues. The papers by Airasian (on evaluation), Bloom (on affective outcomes), and Carroll (on measurement problems) are well worth reading.

Glaser, R. (1963). Instructional technology and the measurement of learning outcomes: Some questions. *American Psychologist, 18,* 519–521. This classic paper started it all.

Haertel, E. (1985). Construct validity and criterion-referenced testing. *Review of Educational Research, 55,* 23–46.

Osterlind, S. J. (1988). Using CRTs in program curriculum evaluation. *Educational Measurement: Issues and Practice, 7*(3), 23–30. This instructional module, with end of unit self-test, guides the reader through a series of decision-making steps.

Popham, W. J. (Ed.) (1971). *Criterion-referenced measurement.* Englewood Cliffs, NJ: Educational Technology Publications. A collection of highly relevant and readable papers. One of the best single sources available.

Tittle, C. K. (1982). Competency testing. In H. E. Mitzel (Ed.), *Encyclopedia of educational research* (5th Edition), pp. 333–352. New York: Free Press. A variety of issues are addressed including legal problems.

Bev's Diary

One of the messages this month was, "Things aren't always what they appear." We looked at some standardized tests of ability and achievement in class. It's tough to tell what some of the items are measuring just by looking at the questions. You really need correlated objectives to help you evaluate the questions and tasks. But the best way is to try out the test and compare it with some meaningful criterion.

Speaking of criterion, Diary, I think we have to look very closely at those criterion-referenced tests that are used by all the states now that measure something called minimum competency. There are some very tricky issues related to both interpretation and application of results. One of the dangerous areas is using such tests to evaluate teacher effectiveness, as if teachers have control over the ability level of students who are assigned to their classes.

When you think of all the things that can influence a test score it's almost a wonder

Part Six

Measuring Affective Educational Outcomes

that we do as good a job as we do. In terms of interpretation I think factors outside the classroom are taking on more and more importance—not only the family, but the meaning of test scores relative to future employers and any future schooling.

I'm ready for something less technical. Look ahead and see several chapters dealing with affective outcomes. Which reminds me:

When asked to seek a new attitude
My students now ask for more latitude
To decide what to say
And what rules to go by
For this I should feel increased gratitude?

Chapter 17

The Nature, Importance, and Uses of Affective Outcomes and Measures

---

A definite and pervasive evolutionary change is taking place in education. This trend involves the nurture and naturalization of affective learning outcomes. The impact of affective outcomes is evident in the type and extent of research on affective outcomes published in the professional journals, the papers presented and discussed at professional, educational, and research meetings, the sensitizing experiences being introduced into teacher training programs, and the books published on humanizing the school curriculum. Nearly all teachers are aware that, no matter what they do, affective learning takes place. Gagné (1985), for example, has noted that

> [T]here are many aspects of the personal interaction between a teacher and his students that do not pertain, in a strict sense, to the acquisition of skills and knowledges that typically form the content of a curriculum. These varieties of interaction include those of motivating, persuading, and the establishment of attitudes and values. The development of such human dispositions as these is of tremendous importance to education as a system of modern society. In the most comprehensive sense of the word "learning," motivations and attitudes must surely be considered to be learned.

Affective and cognitive phenomena are not separate. They develop together and influence one another. Concern with both kinds of outcomes, then, is evidence of concern for the "whole person."

The Need to Assess Affective Outcomes

There are four primary reasons affective outcomes need to be assessed.

Affective variables influence an individual's ability to participate effectively in a democratic society. Attitudes toward institutions, practices, social groups, and the like affect and are affected by the efforts of society to maintain itself and meet the needs of its members. If for no other reason than this, affective objectives must be considered legitimate outcomes of concern to educators.

The development of skills and abilities related to the acquisition and growth of attitudes and values is necessary for a healthy and effective life. The development of rational attitudes and values is the result of intelligent examination of society's needs and those of the individual. Affective skills are necessary to the overall effective functioning of the individual in society. This observation has many implications for mental health. The development of attitudes and values can be a rational process and is therefore amenable to modification. That affective variables can be manipulated and changed has been repeatedly demonstrated. It has been shown that the kinds of experiences an individual has with a variety of tasks will influence the kinds of attitudes he develops. It has been shown experimentally, for example, that the experience of failure or success at a task is causally related to a variety of beliefs and values associated with the concept of achievement. There is also evidence that tasks that are either too easy or too hard are less motivating than those of moderate difficulty.

Affective outcomes interact with occupational and vocational satisfaction. In maintaining themselves economically, individuals must (a) relate effectively with their associates, (b) enjoy their work, (c) believe it possible to make maximal use of their abilities, and (d) feel that they are making a contribution to society. Kahl (1965) reasons that the values of mastery, activism, trust of others, and independence of family should be considered legitimate educational objectives, since they have been empirically related to socioeconomic achievement and upward mobility in our heavily industrialized society.

Affective variables influence learning. The interaction of teachers' and students' affective characteristics influences progress toward the attainment of classroom goals. Ripple (1965), in summarizing research on the affective characteristics of the learning situation, concluded that the attainment of classroom objectives is facilitated by (a) a generalized feeling of warmth in the learning environment, (b) tolerance of emotional and feeling expressions on the part of students, (c) democratic group decision making leading to stimulating activities, (d) the use of nonpunitive control techniques of considerable clarity and firmness, (e) reduced frustration and anxiety in learning tasks, and (f) shifting states of order based on the organization of emotions toward the achievement of goals. More specifically, Domino (1971) has experimentally demonstrated interaction between a student's achievement values, the instructor's teaching style, and the amount of—and the satisfaction with—learning. If students are learning material that interests them, they are likely to develop positive attitudes toward it. Attitudes have also been shown to be related to achievement. Bassham, Murphy, and Murphy (1964) have demonstrated with a sample of sixth grade students a relationship between positive attitudes and achievement in arithmetic.

A cautionary note needs to be added. The desire to improve, modify, adjust, expand, or in some way influence and alter attitudes and values should not obscure our primary concern with learning, not just making students feel better. Heath suggests that "we need to educate youth, not just his head nor his heart. The promise of affective education is that it will stimulate us to recover the person lost among our abstractions; its danger is that it may devalue man's most promising adaptive and educable skill: a disciplined intellect" (1972, p. 371).

Characteristics of Affective Variables

There are a number of levels of affective variables. Many terms have been used to describe these variables, including attitude, value, interest, opinion, appreciation, and motive. Because the concept of "attitude" holds a central position in research and literature on curriculum and instruction it will be the focus for discussion of affective variables. The observations in this chapter draw primarily upon material on attitudes, but these implications are germane to the entire affective domain.

Relationships between some of the terms used to describe affective outcomes and the various levels of the *Taxonomy of Educational Objectives* are illustrated in Figure 17-1.

The degree to which a feeling concept has been internalized is the factor that unifies the Affective Domain of the *Taxonomy.* Interests are considered more transitory and therefore less fully internalized. The development of a value system that strongly controls one's behavior is a relatively lasting general characteristic of the individual and is highly internalized. In the middle range of internalization we find attitudes that are somewhat internalized, and therefore influence behavior, but are not so rigidly set that they cannot be changed. Aiken (1988) has combined several definitions of attitude as follows:

> An attitude is a learned predisposition to respond positively or negatively to a certain object, situation, or person. As such, it consists of cognitive (knowledge or intellective), affective (emotional and motivational), and performance (behavioral or action) components. (p. 303)

Obviously the total individual is involved—the total student, his or her learning, action, and feelings. An earlier and more traditional explanation of attitude has been provided by Rokeach (1968). Rokeach has defined an attitude as a "relatively enduring organization of beliefs around an object or situation predisposing one to respond in some preferential manner" (p. 112). The key phrases in this definition are *relatively enduring* and *organization of beliefs.* The fact that attitudes are relatively

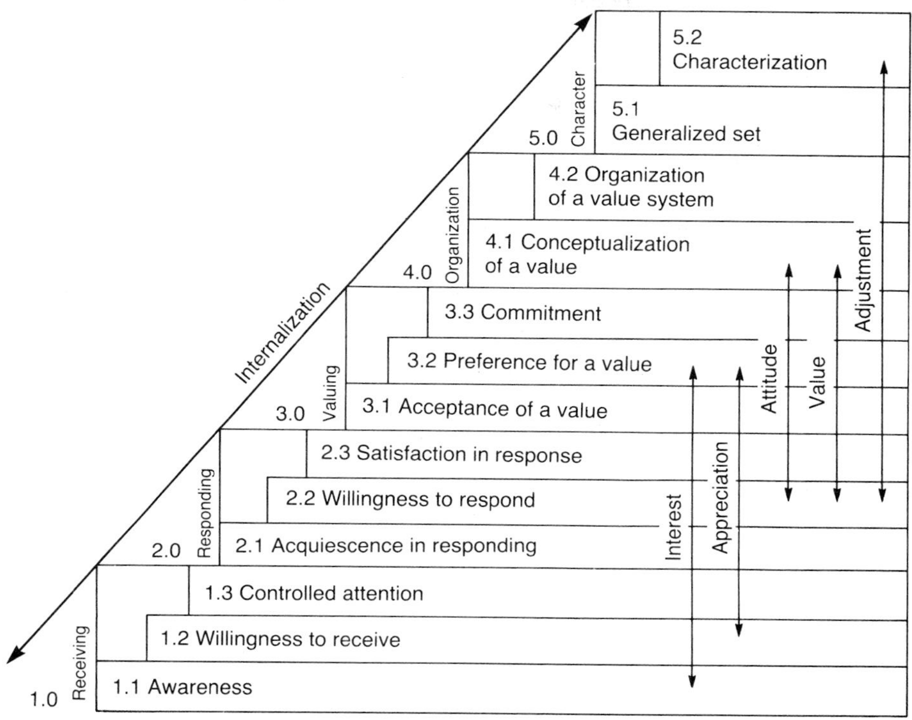

Figure 17-1

Range of meanings associated with common affective terms as defined by the *Taxonomy of Educational Objectives. Source: From Julian C. Stanley and Kenneth D. Hopkins,* Educational and psychological measurement and evaluation, *Copyright 1972. Reprinted by permission of Prentice Hall, Englewood Cliffs, NJ. Adapted from the book* Taxonomy of educational objectives, *edited by B. Bloom, D. Krathwohl, and B. Masia (New York: David McKay, 1956), by permission of the publisher.*

lasting suggests their potency in influencing behavior over fairly long periods of time. For example, an unfavorable attitude toward school, whether held by student or parent, has many potentially significant implications. Considering the total amount of time spent in formal educational settings, an unfavorable attitude could have serious inhibitory effects on learning. Most authorities agree that an attitude is not an irreducible element within personality, but represents a cluster of two or more interrelated elements. A belief is a single proposition, conscious or unconscious, inferred from what a person says or does. The content of a belief may characterize the object of belief as true or false, correct or incorrect, good or bad, or it may advocate a course of action. Following are three kinds of beliefs (Rokeach 1968):

> I believe that the sun rises in the east (Descriptive).
> I believe this ice cream is good (Evaluative).
> I believe it is desirable that children should obey their parents (Prescriptive).

It's one thing to talk about the theory of affect; it's quite another to try to specify relevant outcomes in an educational setting that have potential classroom implications.

Specifying Affective Outcomes with the Taxonomy of Educational Objectives

Although the authors of the *Taxonomy of Educational Objectives* (Bloom *et al.*, 1956) found it possible to structure the cognitive domain on simple-complex and concrete-abstract axes, the authors of the affective domain taxonomy (Krathwohl, Bloom, & Masia, 1964) found it necessary to add the dimension of *internalization* to provide a meaningful hierarchical structure. Internalization is the process by which an individual makes "positive values" part of his or her own personality. At first, this incorporation of new values, or adoption of new behavior, may have only isolated effects, but it gradually comes to dominate one's thinking and motivation until one's actions are consistent with his professed value orientation. Inner growth occurs as the individual becomes aware of and then adopts attitudes, principles, codes, and actions that are basic to his value judgments and that guide his conduct. Internalization has many elements in common with *socialization,* and is best understood by examining the categories in the affective domain of the *Taxonomy* structure. Stripped of their definitions, the sequence of categories and subcategories is as follows (Krathwohl *et al.* 1964, pp. 34–35):

1.0 Receiving (attending)
  1.1 Awareness
  1.2 Willingness to receive
  1.3 Controlled or selected attention
2.0 Responding
  2.1 Acquiescence in responding
  2.2 Willingness to respond
  2.3 Satisfaction in response
3.0 Valuing
  3.1 Acceptance of a value
  3.2 Preference for a value
  3.3 Commitment (conviction)
4.0 Organization
  4.1 Conceptualization of a value
  4.2 Organization of a value system
5.0 Characterization by a value or a value complex
  5.1 Generalized set
  5.2 Characterization

The lowest level of behavior in the structure is the individual's awareness of the elements in the environment that initiate the affective behavior and form the condition in which the affective behavior develops and occurs. Thus, the lowest category is 1.0 *Receiving*. It is subdivided into three categories. At the 1.1 *Awareness* level, the students' attention is attracted to the stimulus, for example, they develop some consciousness of the use of shading to convey depth and lighting in a picture. The second subcategory, 1.2 *Willingness to receive*, describes the state of having differentiated the stimulus from others and being willing to give it attention, for example, they develop a tolerance for bizarre uses of shading in modern art. At 1.3 *Controlled or selected attention*, the students look for the stimulus, for example, they are on the alert for uses of shading to create a sense of three-dimensional depth and to indicate the nature of lighting.

At the next level, 2.0 *Responding*, individuals respond regularly to the affective stimuli. At the lowest level of responding, 2.1 *Acquiescence in responding*, they merely comply with expectations, for example, at the request of a teacher, reproductions of famous paintings are hung in a dormitory room. They are obedient to traffic rules. At the next level, 2.2 *Willingness to respond*, they respond increasingly to an inner compulsion, for example, they voluntarily look for instances of good art in which shading, perspective color, and design have been well used. They have an interest in social problems broader than those of the local community. At 2.3 *Satisfaction in response*, they respond emotionally as well, for example, they work with clay to make pottery for personal pleasure. Up to this point, they have differentiated the affective stimuli, but they have not begun to seek them out and to attach emotional significance and value to them.

The next level, 3.0 *Valuing*, describes increasing internalization as behavior becomes sufficiently consistent to desire and hold a value. More specifically, Valuing is subdivided into: 3.1 *Acceptance of a value*, for example, there is a continuing desire to develop the ability to write effectively; 3.2 *Preference for a value*, for example, they actively seek out examples of good art for enjoyment to the level where they behave so as to further the impression actively; and 3.3 *Commitment*, for example, they have faith in the power of reason and the method of experimentation.

As the learners successfully internalize values, they encounter situations in which more than one value is relevant. This necessitates organizing values into a system, 4.0 *Organization*. And since interrelating values requires conceptualizing them in a form that permits organization, this level is subdivided into: 4.1 *Conceptualization of a value*, for example, desire to evaluate works of art they appreciate or to find out and crystallize the basic assumptions that underlie codes of ethics; and 4.2 *Organization of a value system*, for example, acceptance of the place of art in their lives as one of dominant value, or the weighing of alternative social policies and practices against the standards of public welfare as to value the importance of getting homework finished rather than watching wrestling on television.

Finally, the internalization and organization processes reach a point at which the individual responds very consistently to value-laden situations with an interrelated set of values and a structured view of the world. The *Taxonomy* category that describes this behavior is 5.0 *Characterization by a value or value complex*. This includes the subcategories 5.1 *Generalized set*, for example, they view all problems in terms of their aesthetic aspects, or they are ready to revise judgments and to change behavior in the light of evidence, and 5.2 *Characterization*, for example, they develop a consistent philosophy of life.

It is obvious that the behaviors suggested by affective objectives are much more difficult to define than those associated with cognitive learning outcomes. Nevertheless, affective objectives are important and should be systematically promoted by instructors. As long as an instructor can logically or empirically defend a behavior as representing a particular value, and can communicate that thinking to students, affective objectives can be considered as legitimate goals. One instructor might define "appreciation of art" in terms of the number of times a student visits an art museum during the semester; another instructor might specify other behaviors to fulfill this objective. But visits would represent a desired behavior and it would be observable. The need for behavioral description of affective objectives is as important, if not more so, than that required by cognitive objectives.

Difficulty may arise if students are aware of the affective objectives held for them by teachers. They may attempt to "please" the teacher by making the desired responses or by voluntarily engaging in the expected behavior. Some methods of handling this problem when using questionnaires and inventories will be dealt with in Chapter 18. Suffice it to say, however, that the advantages and value of considering affective outcomes, even with their attendant measurement problems, far outweigh the disadvantages. The importance of affect, not just in educational and occupational settings, but as part of "life" cannot be overemphasized as pollution, drugs, and overpopulation represent many areas where we need to educate attitudes.

In summary, the major characteristics of the affective domain continuum are: (a) increasing emotional quality of responses, (b) responses increasingly automatic as one progresses up the continuum, (c) increasing willingness to attend to a specific stimulus and (d) developing integration of a value pattern at the upper levels of the continuum.

Illustrative Affective Domain Objectives

Following are some sample objectives for the affective domain.

- Listens to music with some discrimination of mood and meaning and some recognition of the contribution of various musical instruments to the total effect.
- Contributes to group discussions by asking thought-provoking questions.
- Is willing to work for improvement of health regulations.
- Weighs alternative social policies and practices against the standards of the public welfare rather than the advantage of specialized and narrow interest groups.
- Is ready to revise judgments and change behavior in the light of evidence.
- Decides to avoid trying new drug as encouraged by peers.
- Does not drive car after two beers.
- Recycles aluminum cans and newspapers.

Behavioral Affective Categories for the Taxonomy of Educational Objectives

One of the criticisms frequently leveled at the *Taxonomy*, particularly by evaluators, is that it is not couched in behavioral terms. The possibility of some latitude in interpreting the various categories of the *Taxonomy* frequently makes the tasks of curriculum evaluation and test construction difficult. Metfessel, Michael, and Kirsner (1969) have made a very practical contribution by listing infinitives and direct objects that can be used to operationalize the *Taxonomy*. Table 17-1 may suggest many important objectives and assist in "behavioralizing" the *Taxonomy*.

Table 17-1 Instrumentation of the *Taxonomy of Educational Objectives:* Affective Domain

	Key Words	
Taxonomy Classification	Examples of Infinitives	Examples of Direct Objects
1.0 Receiving		
1.1 Awareness	to differentiate, to separate, to set apart, to share	sights, sounds, events, designs, arrangements
1.2 Willingness to Receive	to accumulate, to select, to combine, to accept	models, examples, shapes, sizes, meters, cadences
1.3 Controlled or Selected Attention	to select, to posturally respond to, to listen (for), to control	alternatives, answers, rhythms, nuances
2.0 Responding		
2.1 Acquiescence in Responding	to comply (with), to follow, to commend, to approve	directions, instructions, laws, policies, demonstrations
2.2 Willingness to Respond	to volunteer, to discuss, to practice, to play	instruments, games, dramatic works, charades, burlesques
2.3 Satisfaction in Response	to applaud, to acclaim, to spend leisure time in, to augment	speeches, plays, presentations, writings
3.0 Valuing		
3.1 Acceptance of a Value	to increase measured proficiency in, to increase numbers of, to relinquish, to specify	group membership(s), artistic production(s), musical productions, personal friendships

(continued)

Table 17-1 Instrumentation of the *Taxonomy of Educational Objectives:* Affective Domain (*continued*)

Taxonomy Classification	Key Words: Examples of Infinitives	Key Words: Examples of Direct Objects
3.2 Preference for a Value	to assist, to subsidize, to help, to support	artists, projects, viewpoints, arguments
3.3 Commitment	to deny, to protest, to debate, to argue	deceptions, irrelevancies, abdications, irrationalities
4.0 Organization		
4.1 Conceptualization of a Value	to discuss, to theorize (on), to abstract, to compare	parameters, codes, standards, goals
4.2 Organization of a Value System	to balance, to organize, to define, to formulate	systems, approaches, criteria, limits
5.0 Characterization by Value of Value Complex		
5.1 Generalized Set	to revise, to change, to complete, to require	plans, behavior, methods, effort(s)
5.2 Characterization	to be rated high by peers in, to be rated high by superiors in, and to be rated high by subordinates in	humanitarianism, ethics, integrity, maturity
	and	
	to avoid, to manage, to resolve, to resist	extravagance(s), excesses, conflicts, exorbitancy/exorbitancies

Source: W. S. Metfessel, W. B. Michael, and D. A. Kirsner, Instrumentation of Bloom's and Krathwohl's taxonomies for the writing of educational objectives. *Psychology in the Schools* 6 (1969): 227–231. Reprinted by permission of the publisher.

Popham's Strategy for Specifying Affective Objectives

In addition to Metfessel, Michael, and Kirsner's list of behavioral terms, the interested teacher may find Popham's relatively simple strategy useful in identifying and specifying affective learning outcomes. Its basic intent is to describe observable student behaviors that reflect attainment or nonattainment of these affective objectives. There are five general steps in the procedure (Popham, undated filmstrip):

1. Begin with a general statement of the broad affective objective.

Example: At the end of this course, students will have more favorable attitudes toward science.

2. Next, imagine a hypothetical student who personifies the objective. The intent is to describe the behavior likely to be exhibited by a possessor of this positive attitude.

Example: A student who has a positive attitude toward science is more likely to read scientific articles in popular magazines, attend science-fiction movies, and select science book titles.

3. Third, imagine a student who is a nonpossessor of the attitude or has a negative attitude toward the objective or stimulus.

Example: A student who has a negative attitude toward science would not choose magazine articles dealing with science, would not enjoy courses in science, and would not enjoy or choose to visit a science museum.

4. Describe a situation in which the attribute possessor and nonpossessor would respond differently. Define difference-producing situations in which the hypothetical individuals would behave differently. The situations might be contrived or occur naturally.

Example: When put in a forced-choice situation, students majoring in science will select more hypothetical book titles dealing with scientific topics than will individuals not majoring in science.

It is of great importance that the situations chosen be free of behavior-inducing cues. There should be no external pressure to respond in a particular way. Do not ask for a show of hands to indicate interest or request that students sign a survey of attitudes toward a course. The teacher may, however, wish to work out a code with students so that he can keep track of individual progress toward selected affective objectives.

The use of what Webb, Campbell, Schwartz, Sechrest, and Grove (1981) call unobtrusive measures is particularly well suited to many kinds of affective outcomes. Such measures are considerably less influenced by the desire of a student to please the teacher, unless they know they are observed and for what purpose. Observation during recess, free play, group activities, physical education activities, homeroom, on the bus, and in the school yard before and after school can provide valuable insights into affective behavior.

5. Select those difference-producing situations that most effectively, efficiently, and practically define the intended outcomes.

Some of the many methods that can be used to measure affective learning outcomes are described in Chapter 18.

Suggested Uses of Affective Measures

Applications of affective tests, particularly standardized measures, fall into five general categories: (a) classroom application, (b) screening and selection, (c) counseling, (d) research, and (e) program evaluation.

Classroom Applications

The imaginative classroom teacher can create many situations in which the use of affective measures makes a real contribution to the instructional program. The *Work Values Inventory* (Super, 1970), for example, could be used on a pre- or post-basis to assess changes in work values associated with a unit on the "world of work," or the WVI itself could be used as a starting point in exploring various occupations. It might be helpful to have students estimate their scores before taking the test, and then compare these estimates with the test results. Individual student scores or class means could then be compared with selected normative data. The study of vocations could be stimulated by this method; discussion might revolve around known differences between occupational groups. It could be noted, for example, that on the WVI psychiatrists score significantly higher than lawyers, CPAs, and engineers on Altruism; and that teachers score higher than psychologists on Security. The entire class or small groups could examine in detail how various occupations relate to scores on the WVI.

If teachers are particularly concerned about the school work habits of their students, a study habits inventory might be used to explore possible difficulties.

Inasmuch as the personnel offices of businesses and industries frequently administer tests of various dimensions of personality to prospective employees, classroom experience with an inventory should help students prepare for this experience. Practice on similar tests usually results in reduced anxiety in a formal assessment setting.

Screening and Selection

The *School Interest Inventory* (Cottle, 1966) is an instrument that illustrates well the sensible use of an affective measure. It is suggested that the SII be used on an intrainstitutional basis, so that a student's scores are compared only to those of other individuals in the same school. The SII is used to identify potential dropouts. Students in the seventh or eighth grade could be administered the SII, and their scores ranked from highest to lowest within grade and sex. (Higher scores indicate a greater probability of the student's dropping out of school.) Using any number of criteria, for example, a cutoff score of 25 or above or selection of the top 20 percent, one could identify students who might benefit from counseling. Counselees could consider the possibility of continuing in the same or another course of study, or explore vocational and social adjustments that do not require a high-school diploma. The counselor or teacher may also wish to set up "rap groups" in which personal, social, or vocational problems could be explored. Obviously, the use of a test as a screening instrument should be undertaken in conjunction with other relevant data. School achievement records, attendance, teachers' opinions, and age relative to school grade need to be considered.

Personnel managers frequently find that affective measures are useful in the hiring and placement of special classes of employees, and that scores may be related to job success. It is imperative when an affective measure is used in this manner that its relevance be demonstrable.

Counseling

Perhaps the major use of standardized affective measures involves counseling, guidance, and psychotherapy. The value of such measures is to stimulate individuals to "look at themselves" and in some cases identify a variety of types of psychopathology. The usual application is in personal development and career exploration. Such self-report devices can be used effectively as starting points or springboards to help establish rapport in an interview situation. Asking respondents to first predict their scores and then comparing predictions with actual results can be a very valuable experience for both students and counselors. This is particularly true when vocational interest inventories are used.

An example of a frequently used standardized affective measure is the *Study Attitude and Methods Survey* (Michael, Michael, & Zimmerman, 1988). In its current form the SAMS is a 90-item survey which requires one of four responses from Not At All Like Me to Almost Always, or Very Much Like Me. It is machine- or hand-scored for two purposes: (a) to identify students likely to have school difficulties due to poor study habits, and (b) to identify areas where counseling and guidance might help. Following are the six dimensions of the SAMS, together with a sample item.

Dimensions	*Interpretation*	*Sample Item*
Academic Interest—Love of Learning	School "turns you on," high scores likely to get good grades.	Many courses are so interesting that I find myself doing more work than assigned.
Academic Drive	Determined to do well in school by doing what is expected	I make every effort to do what the teacher expects of me.
Study Methods	Efficient use of time, review outline, budget effort	I classify and organize facts and points as I am reading, studying, or rewriting notes.
Study Anxiety	Below T-50 score indicates concern about assignments and exams. Goal clarifications needed.	Examinations make me so nervous that I do not do nearly so well on them as I should.

Dimensions	*Interpretation*	*Sample Item*
Lack of Manipulation	Low scores indicate tendency to "play" up to teacher to gain favor.	I am convinced that one of the best ways to get ahead in school is to flatter and play up to the teacher.
Alienation Toward Authority	High score 70–80 indicates comfort with rules, regulations, and requirements. Not trying to "beat the system."	It is my observation that teachers tend to require too much homework and other unimportant work.

Reliability data consist primarily of internal consistency coefficients (all .80 or above), and validity data were expressed as correlations with course grades and with other affective measures. Normative data are available for both high school and college populations.

A sample profile for a college student is presented in Figure 17-2. Note that raw scores are plotted on the profile sheet and can then be read as either normalized *T*-scores (with a mean of 50 and a standard deviation of 10) or percentile ranks. The reader may wish to refer back to Chapter 10 for a discussion of these two ways of expressing scores. Our hypothetical student scored high on Academic Interest (Love of Learning), Academic Drive, Lack of Manipulation, and Lack of Alienation Toward Authority. "High" in this case means a *T*-score of 50 or higher. There is a drive and desire to do well in school, and this student takes responsibility for his own behavior. It is not surprising that this student is not doing well in school when we see the low scores on Study Methods and Lack of Study Anxiety. Both these factors can have a very detrimental effect on performance. The student may wish to confer with a counselor or with teachers about ways to gain feelings of self-confidence and reduce feelings of tension and worry. Perhaps there is lack of communication between student and teacher. Study habits also need attention and, again, perhaps the teacher can provide suggestions on how to approach tasks. Commercial programs aimed at enhancing test-taking skills are available, for example, Improving Test-Taking Skills (Riverside, 1983). The use of a standardized measure in this way is relatively nonthreatening, can be accomplished by any of a number of professional staff, and can yield quite valuable benefits for the student. It should also be noted that being a multiscore instrument some considerations should have been given to the standard error of measurement and the basic concepts of reliability as discussed in Chapter 12.

Readers interested in the use of test scores in counseling are referred to books by Shertzer & Linden (1979), Anastasi, (1988), Aiken (1988), or the classic by Goldman (1961), and a recent summary of research and practice by Harmon (1989).

PROFILE SHEET FOR THE

STUDY ATTITUDES AND METHODS SURVEY

SHORT FORM – 1985

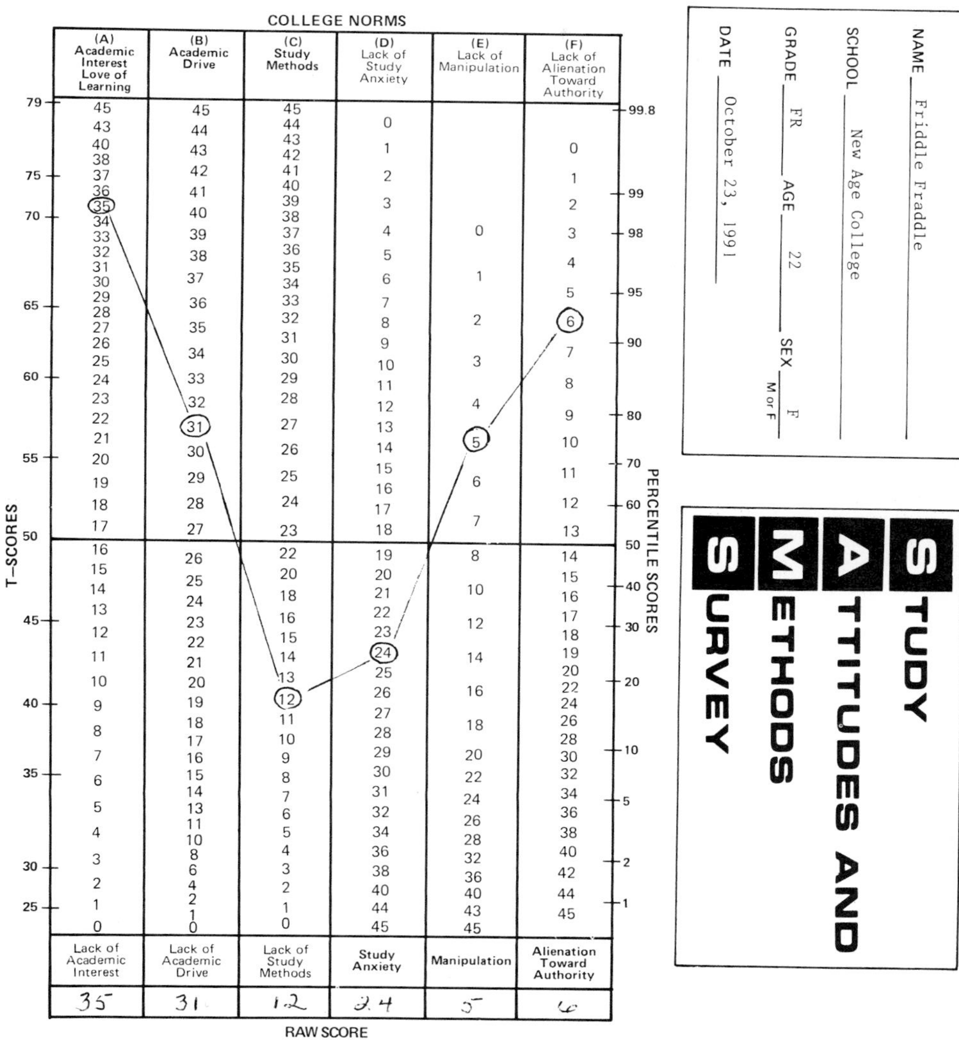

SAM 042

COPYRIGHT © 1976/1985 BY EdITS, SAN DIEGO, CALIFORNIA 92107

Figure 17-2

Study attitudes and methods survey. *Copyright © 1976/1985 by EDITS, San Diego, CA 92107*

Research

There are numerous fields of research using affective measures that might prove of interest to the educator. The authors of the *Study of Values* (Allport, Vernon, & Lindzey, 1970) for example, note that it has been used to research the following topics:

1. Differences in the scores of those in different college majors and occupational, religious, ethnic, and nationality groups.
2. Changes in values over time, and as functions of specific training and educational experiences.
3. Relationships with other attitude-, interest-, and cognitive-style measures.
4. Relationships between friendship choice and sociometric status.

Program Evaluation

Another area in which affective measures are achieving great popularity is program evaluation. Curriculum evaluation is receiving increased attention from educational measurement and assessment experts and consultants. Most state and federal educational programs require the assessment of affective variables, and local school systems are also becoming conscious of these important outcomes. Measures of such variables as attitude toward school, respect for self, and appreciation of artistic efforts are illustrative of educational product and process outcomes in a comprehensive evaluation system.

Issues in Developing and Using Affective Measures

A number of factors—both characteristics of teachers and technical problems—have inhibited the development and use of affective measures in the classroom.

Reluctance to Consider Affective Variables

Many educators are reluctant to become involved in teaching and evaluating affective objectives. Some feel that these learning outcomes are of minor importance or that this is an area in which education has no business. Admittedly, affective objectives can prove to be a source of controversy, particularly in this age of parental involvement and concern with school programs. But the conscious refusal to address affective objectives directly represents an affective stance in itself. It is becoming increasingly difficult to maintain a value-free posture in contemporary society. By now, hopefully, the reader must agree that affective and cognitive outcomes are very important and deserve fair treatment and time.

Lack of Time

The harried classroom teacher frequently complains that he or she has insufficient time to develop and apply adequate assessment procedures. Affective assessment is invariably the first type to be shortchanged. It is a matter of priorities. Time must be found to consider these important variables. Some time may justifiably be stolen from instructional activities because of the particularly intimate association between teaching for values and testing for them.

Lack of Faith

Disbelief that paper-and-pencil inventories and scales can measure variables related to meaningful behaviors is difficult to overcome. Evidence supports the contention that measured attitudes do relate to important school outcomes. In addition there are many techniques in addition to paper-and-pencil methods that can be used to measure affective outcomes.

Artificiality of the Situation

The problem of artificiality relates to the larger problem of validity. To ask individuals what they would do in a given situation and then assume that they would, in fact, do so if the opportunity presented itself is somewhat artificial. The fact that considerable reliance is often placed on *inference* in assessing affective outcomes must be accepted, but there remains the question of the relation of verbalized and actual behavior. All possible efforts must be made to insure that the relationship is as strong as possible.

It might be worthwhile to note two of the classic studies cited in support of the conclusion that the artificiality of attitude measures precludes valid assessment. Corey (1937) found a near-zero correlation between professed attitudes toward cheating and actual cheating on a series of classroom examinations. By allowing students to correct their own papers after the teacher had secretly copied and scored them, a cheating behavior measure was obtained. It was noted, however, that positive attitudes toward cheating were more prevalent on unsigned than signed questionnaires. LaPiere (1934) traveled around the United States with two well-dressed Oriental companions and visited several hundred hotels and restaurants. Only once were they refused service. When a mail survey was conducted several months later, over 90 percent of the respondents stated categorically that they would not serve Chinese. The authors concluded that general appearance, neatness, cleanliness, and quality of clothing and luggage were more influential than physical characteristics. Does the foregoing suggest that we should discount attitudes and values? No indeed! It does mean that great care needs to be exercised in assessing such variables. That an individual is willing to respond to an inventory has some meaning. The less personally controversial or threatening the attitude assessed, the greater the likelihood of a valid response.

Public versus Private Attitudes

The soundest approach to the interpretation of self-report statements on affective measures is to accept them as public declarations, rather than reflections of typical or private characteristics. Content plays an important part in determining the validity of self-reports. The nature of a favorite television program, auto styles, men's clothing, and political affairs are relatively nonthreatening general topics. But when individuals are pressed to make specific revelations about attitudes toward religion, relations with minority-group members, or candidates voted for in the last election, they are more likely to attempt to conceal their true feelings. Many of the affective variables dealt with in the classroom setting, however, are of the less personally threatening variety, and therefore lend themselves more readily to assessment.

Stability of Affective Outcomes

Affective characteristics generally maintain themselves over a long period of time. Research has shown that test-retest reliabilities of economic and political values are as high as .50 over a 20-year period. Stability decreases as the referent becomes more and more specific. It has been found, for example, that attitudes toward marriage, perhaps not unsurprising, were quite unstable.

Lack of Knowledge of Techniques

Lack of familiarity with methods that can be employed to measure affective outcomes obviously inhibits any assessment program. Most teacher-training programs fail to devote any systematic attention to the specification or measurement of affective outcomes. Even test and measurement classes devote only minimal time to the topic. Little wonder, then, that teachers in the field pay slight attention to formal measurement of affective variables. Perhaps they are adequately aware of the affective information they are collecting informally.

Problems of Semantics

The specification of objectives and the development of items for instruments require careful consideration of the meanings of words. Reading level, for example, needs to be considered.

Fakeability

Depending upon the way in which the data are to be used, given respondents may desire to distort inventory results and present an image of themselves that they believe will be to their advantage. Unconscious distortion also may take place, of course. Faking is most likely to occur on personality and interest inventories that are being used for employee selection or is in some other way of great consequence. That an inventory *can* be faked does not, however, imply that it will be faked, but it probably does mean that you can't completely trust the data as you really don't know if faking has occurred or not. Technical controls need to be built into the instrument (lie scales, consistency scales, adjustments for social desirability) before it is used. But faked information is in itself revealing in that it communicates how a person thinks it most desirable to appear.

Social Desirability

One type of faking involves the attempt of examinees to present a socially acceptable image of themselves. This type of distortion might be fairly prevalent in a classroom situation, due to a student's desire to please teachers or tell them what the student thinks they want to hear. Edwards (1957b) and Crowne and Marlowe (1960, 1964) have conducted considerable research on the influence of social desirability on self-report inventory scores. They have developed scales that can be used to assess the general tendency of an individual to present a socially desirable picture of him- or herself. These scales may be used during the development of an affective inventory to control for social desirability. By eliminating those items that correlate with the social desirability measure, some degree of control can be exercised. It might also be possible to obtain from a group of judges indications of the social desirability of the items or choices being presented, and to select all the items that fall within a relatively narrow range of social desirability or to match alternatives for equal social desirability. Or one may simply get "popularity" judgments of the statements used in an inventory and eliminate the "highs" and "lows," or match items.

Response Sets and Styles

The use of certain fixed categories of responses, for example, "yes," "agree," and "like," may introduce the possibility of response biases. Certain individuals, when in doubt, tend to choose the *agree* category irrespective of the content of the items. This phenomenon obviously distorts the meaning of the scores. Reviews of the relevant research by Cronbach (1946, 1950) and Block (1965) suggest that the forced-choice format can be employed to reduce response sets when fixed-response items or instruments are used.

Some Concerns and Cautions in Using Standardized Affective Measures

Although limited in quantity and quality standardized measures of affective learning outcomes are available for school and classroom use. The available measures tend to be in the areas of (a) academic interests, (b) motivation, (c) attitudes, and (d) values. One can find inventories of study habits and attitudes, work values, motivation for achievement, and general personality surveys. In addition to Buros' *Mental Measurements Yearbooks* one can find very useful reference to affective measures in compendia edited by Chunn, Cobb, and French (1975), Shaw and Wright (1967), and Sweetland and Keyser (1983).

There are many potential problems in using these kinds of measuring instruments. Cottle (1968) has identified the following 16 cautions and concerns.

1. As is the case with standardized achievement and aptitude tests, one must be sure that the objectives, item content, and scores of the instrument are consistent with those of the user. Otherwise, gross misassessment may result.

2. The administration, scoring, and interpretation of such measures should be handled directly by, or under the guidance of, a trained and competent professional.

3. Respect for the privacy and integrity of the examinee is imperative. *Affective inventories should be voluntary.* The right of an individual to refuse should be honored.

4. It is imperative that the intent of administering a particular test be explained in full to the student. The projected use of the results should also be described. Such a description and the attendant discussion should help to promote rapport, insure seriousness of intent, and arouse examinee motivation.

5. It is generally advisable to encourage an examinee to record his initial response to an item. Such a procedure will tend to elicit "typical" reactions. Extended deliberations tend to create confusion in the mind of the respondent.

6. If possible, a graphic procedure (e.g., a profile) should be used to report the scores. This is a particularly informative approach if a multiscore instrument is being used.

7. Inspection of single items should be discouraged because they tend to lack reliability.

8. During interpretation, the respondent should be provided a copy of the description of the results from scoring the instrument.

9. Scoring services should return answer sheets with the reported scores and/or profiles. Spot-checking for scoring errors is always desirable.

10. The private nature of an affective inventory precludes discussion of a particular score or set of scores with anyone but the examinee. However, summary statistics based on group data, in the form of means or standard deviations, are legitimate material for open discussion.

11. Profiles on scores should be regarded as held in trust for the individual or the institution. They should be released only to professionally competent persons with a legitimate right to access.

12. The reading level of the inventory must be appropriate to the individual or group being tested. Oral administration might be considered.

13. If norms tables are to be used to assist score interpretation, it is imperative that they be appropriate to the group tested and the administration procedure used.

14. If possible, any unusual reaction to the testing situation or to a specific item by an examinee should be recorded at the time of testing.

15. Because of the variability of affective behaviors, caution should be exercised in accepting and/or interpreting scores on inventories administered more than three to six months previous.

16. Probably most important of all, an interpretation should never be based solely on a single test score or set of scores from the same instrument. Nontest data must be used to put the scores in perspective and assist in the confirmation or contravention of an interpretation.

Some of these cautions are not unique to the use of affective measures. For example, numbers 7, 8, and 9 would apply to any measuring instrument, cognitive or affective, achievement or aptitude. The same could be said for the concerns highlighted in numbers 11, 13, 14, and 16.

Is it worth the effort to address affective outcomes? If you value the developing student as a total person and want him or her to experience a quality life, then educators must deal with affective issues.

Case Study Application

Cognitive outcomes have dominated the curricula of our schools since their inception. Hopefully, this chapter has highlighted the important role that affective outcomes can play in developing a totally educated person—a person who is academically and occupationally competent, and who can function effectively in society; a person possessed of positive self-image and the ability to appreciate our many and varied environments.

Take a few minutes and try your hand at creating some affective objectives for our reading education course. These would be objectives that our reading instructor would hold for our undergraduate teachers-in-training. The instructor would like to see movement toward the objectives. Try two types of objectives. One type would be tied to the *Taxonomy of Educational Objectives,* perhaps using the behavioral infinitives contained in Table 17-1. Another route would be the use of Popham's five-step strategy useful in identifying difference-producing situations where people holding different attitudes and beliefs would act or react differentially.

Another source of ideas is the section of the next chapter entitled "Approaches to the Assessment of Affective Outcomes." Implied in every useful affective objective would be the germ of an idea as to how to measure it.

Content Review Statements

1. Attitudes, values, interests, and other affective characteristics are learned in the classroom.
2. It is important for teachers to be concerned with affective learning outcomes, which influence the student's:
   a. Eventual ability to participate effectively in society.
   b. Development of a healthy personality.

c. Occupational and vocational satisfaction.
d. Learning.

3. Specifying affective outcomes (e.g., attitudes, interests, values, and the like) may be as important, or more important, than specifying cognitive or psychomotor outcomes.
4. Cognitive and affective outcomes interact to the degree that they are virtually inseparable.
5. Affective outcomes directly influence learning and also constitute legitimate educational outcomes in themselves.
6. How an individual feels about subject matter, school, and learning may be as important as how much he achieves.
7. The major categories of the Affective Domain of the *Taxonomy of Educational Objectives* are:
   a. Receiving (attending and awareness)
   b. Responding
   c. Valuing
   d. Organization
   e. Characterization by a value or value complex
8. The organizing principle in the Affective Domain of the *Taxonomy of Educational Objectives* is "internalization."
9. Internalization is the inner growth that occurs as the individual becomes aware of and then adopts attitudes, principles, codes, and sanctions that are basic to his value judgments and that guide his behavior.
10. The hierarchical continua of the Affective Domain have the following characteristics:
    a. Increasing emotionality of responses.
    b. Increasingly automatic responses.
    c. Increasing willingness to attend to particular stimuli.
    d. Increasing integration of diverse values.
11. Popham has developed a method for specifying affective objectives that involves:
    a. Generating a general affective statement.
    b. Imagining a hypothetical student who positively typifies the objective.
    c. Imagining a hypothetical student who negatively typifies the objective.
    d. Describing a situation in which these two individuals would respond differentially.
12. Affective measures can be used:
    a. In the classroom as stimuli for learning units.
    b. For research purposes.
    c. Screening and selection.
    d. Counseling
    e. Program evaluation.
13. The major standardized measures of affective learning outcomes useful to the classroom teacher focus on academic interests, motivation, attitudes, and values.
14. In using measures of affective learning outcomes, one should be careful to:
    a. Insure that the instrument and instructional objectives are in harmony.
    b. Have a qualified professional direct the administration, scoring, and interpretation.
    c. Respect the privacy of individual students.
    d. Explain to the students the reason for using a particular measure.

e. Insure that all students receive an interpretation of their scores.
f. Respect the security and confidentiality of student scores.
g. Draw upon all relevant nontest information in interpreting a test score.
h. Exercise caution in interpreting out-of-date test scores.
i. Examine carefully the characteristics of any norm group selected for reference purposes.
j. Select a measure at an appropriate reading and experience level.

15. Profiling scores on multiscore affective inventories is a useful aid to interpretation.
16. The critical reviews of standardized measures in Buros' *Mental Measurements Yearbooks* should be consulted when selecting a particular test.
17. Affective outcomes are hard to specify because it is difficult to identify appropriate overt behavioral evidence of the covert affect, and because they are ever-changing.
18. Lack of attention to affective outcomes tends to result in their erosion in the classroom.
19. A teacher will probably need to specify fewer affective than cognitive outcomes.
20. Among the many problems associated with assessing affective learning outcomes are:
    a. Teachers' and administrators' reluctance to consider affective variables.
    b. Lack of teacher time to develop measures.
    c. Lack of faith that we can measure affective outcomes.
    d. The artificiality of the measures of affective variables.
    e. Students' reluctance to reveal their true feelings.
    f. The instability of some affective outcomes.
    g. The influence of "social desirability" on responses to inventories.
    h. The fakeability of many instruments.
    i. Semantic difficulties in communicating about affective variables.
    j. Lack of knowledge about available measures and techniques.
    k. Distortion of responses to certain kinds of instruments due to the influence of response sets and styles.
    l. Difficulties in establishing the validity of affective measures.

Speculations

1. Close your eyes and just reminisce about the chapter you have just read. Now try to express your feelings in terms of the *Taxonomy of Educational Objectives-Affective Domain.*
2. Are we justified in including affective outcomes in our schools? Which ones?
3. How can we overcome some of the obstacles to the increased considerations of affective outcomes in our schools?
4. Why is it so difficult to express affective outcomes in behavioral terms?
5. What are some ways in which cognitive outcomes influence affective outcomes? And vice versa?
6. Using Popham's strategy, conceive of an attribute possessor and nonpossessor relative to an attitude toward educational measurement. In what kinds of situations would they respond differentially?
7. Can we, in fact, get students to respond meaningfully to instruments measuring affective outcomes? How?
8. Get three friends to write definitions for the following terms: neuroticism, depression,

happiness, and rage. Describe the results in light of how one might go about trying to measure these characteristics.

Suggested Readings

Anderson, L. W. (1981). *Assessing affective characteristics in the schools.* Boston: Allyn and Bacon. An easy-to-use reference with theory and method (and good examples).

Bills, R. E. (1975). *A system for assessing affectivity.* University, AL: The University of Alabama Press. Description of the development of a comprehensive system from planning through instrumentation.

Harmon, L. W. (1989). Counseling. In R. L. Linn (Ed.), *Educational measurement* (3rd ed.). New York: American Council on Education/Macmillan.

Lee, B. N., & Merrill, M. D. (1972). *Writing complete affective objectives: A short course.* Belmont, CA: Wadsworth. This brief field-tested self-instructional paperback will assist teachers, particularly those at the elementary and secondary level, in developing affective objectives and analyzing student behavior.

Mager, R. F. (1968). *Developing attitude toward learning.* Palo Alto, CA: Fearon. Describes three principles that teachers can apply in nurturing favorable attitudes toward subjects of study. Some consideration is also given to measurement.

Payne, D. A. (Ed.). (1980). *Recent developments in affective measurement.* San Francisco: Jossey-Bass.

Chapter 18

Methods of Measuring Affective Outcomes

Approaches to the assessment of affective variables are limited only by the creativity and motivation of the developer. Many methods have been developed by psychologists and sociologists in their studies of human behavior, but all too few have been communicated to, or translated for use by, educators. One of the attendant problems, in addition to those described in the following section, involves the difference between scaling an attitude dimension and using an instrument developed in the process of scaling research to measure individual differences in attitudes. Some of the methods described in this chapter were developed to investigate or scale an attitude domain; others are designed as direct measures of attitudes for application to human subjects (Payne, 1980).

Approaches to the Assessment of Affective Outcomes

Cattell, Heist, and Stewart (1950), after extensive review of the literature and personal research, have identified numerous methods that can be applied in the assessment of attitudes and sentiments, or, as they refer to them, "dynamic traits." Some of these methods are more useful in a classroom than others, but any of the techniques can be adapted for use in a variety of educational ways. Selections from their list and some additional methods follow:

1. *Money.* The amount of money an individual spends on certain activities and courses of action is a direct reflection of his attitude and interest. In elementary school simulation exercises involving purchases can be very revealing.

2. *Time.* The amount of time an individual devotes to certain activities is, to some extent, a reflection of his attitude toward them. A survey of time spent by students in various activities can be most revealing of their relative interests.

3. *Verbal expressions.* A host of assessment methods use verbal expressions of attitudes. The Likert, Semantic, Differential, and Opinionnaire methods decribed later in this chapter, are illustrative. Deri *et al.* (1948) have identified six types of questionnaires commonly used in attitude measurement: preference, stereotype, situational, social distance, opinions, and self-rating. The interview, either free-response or structured, might also be placed in this category.

4. *Measures of attention/distraction.* Records of the length of time an individual attends to a stimulus, or a ranking of stimuli (e.g., pictorial) according to responsiveness to them, could profitably be used as measures of attitudes. Failure to respond to certain stimuli is also meaningful behavior. We know about the attention time of students, particularly very young ones. If we can capture that attention and hold it we at least have a chance to teach.

5. *Fund of information.* The amount or type of information an individual possesses about a certain object, individual, or issue is to some extent a reflection of his attitude. As noted in the previous chapter there is a relationship between the cognitive and affective domains.

6. *Speed of decision (reaction time).* It may be that decisions are made more quickly about questions on which the subject has the strongest convictions.

7. *Written expressions (personal documents).* Analysis of such documents as biographies, diaries, records, letters, autobiographies, journals, and compositions can be very revealing of an individual's attitudes. A personal document has been defined by Allport (1942) as any self-revealing record that intentionally or unintentionally yields information about the structure, dynamics, and functioning of the author's

mental life. Student autobiographies are both revealing of important facets of an individual's life and representative of an opportunity to practice writing skills.

8. *Sociometric measures.* Analysis of friendship choices, social distances, preferences, and the general social structure of a classroom can be very informative about attitudes.

9. *Misperception/apperception methods.* Provided with ambiguous stimuli, an individual may be tempted to perceive them in accordance with his own interests, attitudes, and wishes. A great many projective techniques (e.g., ink blots) have been based on this assumption.

10. *Activity level methods.* There are a number of measures of the individual's general excitement level in response to a stimulus, among them (a) fluency (amount written), (b) speed of reading, and (c) work endurance.

11. *Observations.* The use of standardized reports systematically gathered by trained recorders operating within the limits of an explicitly stated frame of reference has provided extremely valuable data on attitudes per se and on the operation of these attitudes within the individual. The use of categorical observational systems was considered in Chapter 9 (see also Amidon & Hough, 1967).

12. *Specific performances and behaviors.* An individual's behavior can illustrate his or her attitudes and their influences. It is argued by some that behavioral measures are by far the most valid. The indirect methods we commonly use, however, can provide valid data if reasonable precautions are taken and stringent criteria are employed during the developmental stages. Webb *et al.* (1981) have written an extremely valuable reference work with examples of unobtrusive behavioral measures and observational methods.

13. *Physiological measures.* The use of autonomic and metabolic measures can provide useful data in controlled situations. Psychogalvanic response, pulse rate, muscle tension and pressure, and metabolic rate are some of the procedures employed.

14. *Memory measures.* Instructing an individual to learn given material, varying the controversial nature of the content, introducing an unrelated activity to distract the subject, and then asking him to recall all or part of the original material is one approach to the use of memory as an instrument of attitude assessment. The selective operation of memory in reminiscence, dream, or fantasy may also be analyzed.

15. *Simulations.* Contrived structured or unstructured activities can be used to stimulate and simulate affective responses. The use of role playing, for example, is useful both as an assessment as well as an instructional technique. Gamelike activities

provide particularly good opportunities to observe students under a variety of conditions, particularly with regard to interpersonal relations.

Writing Items for Self-Report Affective Measures

General guidelines and criteria are crucial to the development of statements for affective measures. Obviously, the statements themselves are of critical importance. All the sophisticated analytic techniques in the world will not overcome an inferior item that does not communicate. Edwards (1957a, 1957b) has provided a list of informal criteria for development and editing activities. **Avoid** statements that

1. refer to the past or future rather than to the present.
2. are factual or capable of being interpreted as factual.
3. may be interpreted in more than one way.
4. are irrelevant to the psychological object under consideration.
5. are likely to be endorsed by almost everyone or by almost no one.
6. do not reflect the entire range of the affectivity.
7. use language that is complex, ambiguous, or indirect.
8. are too long (more than 20 words).
9. contain more than one complete thought.
10. contain universals such as *all, always, none,* and *never* because they often introduce ambiguity.
11. contain words such as *only, just, merely,* and others of similar nature.
12. are formed with compound or complex sentences.
13. use words that may not be understood by those who are to be given the completed scale.
14. use double negatives.

Most of these suggestions are common sense and are based on the need to communicate. Some of the suggestions, for example, numbers 3, 7, 9, 11, and 14 are in common with the suggestions for writing cognitive test questions, particularly true-false items.

Corey's Simplified Scale Construction Technique

Corey (1943) has described a relatively efficient method for constructing an attitude scale. The test development process itself can serve as a learning experience for the students and teachers. Its steps are as follows:

1. *Collect a pool of statements.* Each student, for example, might be asked to write three or four statements representing various attitudes toward cheating. Illustrative statements might be:

Cheating is as bad as stealing.
If a test isn't fair, cheating is all right.
I won't copy, but I often let someone else look at my paper.
A little cheating on daily tests doesn't hurt.

2. *Select the best statements.* Using the criteria for constructing attitude statements described in the previous section, about 50 items might be culled from the initial pool of 100 or 150 statements. Duplicates are eliminated, as are statements that are obviously ambiguous to the teacher or students. The students, for example, might be asked to indicate all those statements on the master list that represent opinions favoring cheating (with a plus sign) and those representing negative opinions about cheating (with a minus sign). An agreement criterion of 80 percent is suggested; a show of hands is an efficient way to gather these data.

3. *Administer the inventory.* The following directions might be used:

> *Directions:* This is not a test in the sense that any particular statement is right or wrong. All these sentences represent opinions that some people hold about cheating on tests. Indicate whether you agree or disagree with the statements by putting a plus sign before all those with which you agree and a minus sign before those with which you disagree. If you are uncertain, use a question mark. After you have gone through the entire list, go back and draw a circle around the plus signs next to the statements with which you agree very strongly, and a circle around the minus signs if you disagree very strongly.

The inventory may be duplicated and distributed or administered orally. Discussion should be discouraged. Anonymous administration is preferable.

4. *Score the inventory.* Scoring may be accomplished by either teacher or student. The first step involves identifying those statements that were judged by the entire group (in Step 2) as *favoring classroom cheating.* Next, the following score values are applied: a plus sign with a circle receives five points, a plus sign alone four points, a question mark three points, a minus sign two points, and a minus sign with a circle one point. Thus, when a person disagrees very strongly with a statement that favors classroom cheating, he earns one point; if he agrees very strongly with the same statement, he gets five points.

Those statements that express *opposition to cheating* are scored in the opposite fashion: a plus sign with a circle receives one point, a plus sign alone two points, a question mark three points, a minus sign four points, and minus sign with a circle five points. In other words, a student who disagrees very strongly with a statement that opposes cheating actually has a very favorable attitude toward such a practice.

If the inventory contains 50 items, the maximum score possible is 250, which indicates a favorable attitude. The minimum score possible is 50, and an indifference score is in the neighborhood of 150.

Forced-Choice Selection Methods

A forced-choice item requires the respondent to select among choices that differ in content, rather than degree of favorableness or intensity. The examinee is directed to indicate which of several actions, contents, or objects is most characteristic of him. The number of choices usually ranges from two to four. The format may resemble that of a multiple-choice item—a stem and several alternatives—or it may be a description of a situation with associated questions, or a pair of choice-statements. When used in a two-choice situation with systematically varying content, the forced-choice technique is similar to the paired-comparison method. The score is simply the number of times a particular choice is made from a large number of possible choices. One or more of the choices may be scored on a particular scale. The primary advantages of the forced-choice pattern are that it

1. minimizes the subjective element in judgment.
2. reduces the respondent's ability to produce a desired outcome and is therefore less fakeable.
3. produces a better distribution and spread of scores with less piling up and skewness.
4. is quick, efficient, objective, and lends itself to machine-scoring.
5. produces scores easily analyzed with respect to reliability and validity.

The forced-choice format has been widely adopted in the construction of personality inventories. The *Kuder Preference Record Personal, Strong Vocational Interest Blank*, and *Edwards Personal Preference Schedule* are representative applications of the method.

This method has many possibilities for use in classroom measurement. Two examples will illustrate possible applications. The first is from a scale, the *Personal VEMS* test (VEMS stands for Values: Ethical, Moral, and Social), developed by Gardner and Thompson (1963) in their investigation of social values governing interpersonal relations among adolescent youth and their teachers. The VEMS requires a verbal response indicating the action that ought to be taken when confronting certain problem situations. Each decision implies the selection of one value over another. The values in question are loyalty, honesty, truthfulness, kindness, generosity, conformity, and impunitiveness. In an effort to encourage the respondent to become ego-involved in the situation, the respondent is asked in some items to supply the name of his best friend as a participant in the problem situation. Following are two sample items:

> You have just taken an important true-false examination in English. Your teacher has asked you to exchange papers so that you can grade each other's papers as she reads the answers aloud. You exchange papers with your best friend ______________ who is seated near you. He slips you a note which reads, "Please change a few of my answers when they are incorrect. I *have* to get a passing mark on this test!"

What Do You Think You *Ought* to Do?

_____ A. Help your friend so that he will get a passing mark on the test.
_____ B. Mark his paper in the same way you would grade the paper of any other classmate.

In this item, alternative A is scored on the Loyalty scale, and B on the Honesty scale.

> You and your classmate play a clarinet duet for the school assembly. There was much applause. Feeling rather pleased with her performance, your classmate says to a group of people you are standing with, "I guess I played it just about perfectly, didn't I?" You know that she squeaked a little on some of the high notes and that her timing was faulty in a number of instances.

What Do You Think You *Ought* to Do?

_____ A. Be generous and say to the person next to you, "She certainly was terrific today."
_____ B. Say, "It was a good performance but not perfect. You'd better do some practicing on those high notes!"

On this item alternative A is scored on the Generosity scale and B on the Truthfulness scale.

Farquhar and Payne (1963) have described the development of an instrument aimed at assessing relative preference for statements correlated with occupational motivation. Beginning with a set of eight alternatives describing high achievement motivation and eight describing low achievement motivation, they constructed a 64-item pair scale by combining high and low motivation alternatives. Two sample items from the scale, the *Preferred Job Characteristics Scale,* follow:

I Prefer:
1. A job where my opinion is valued, or
2. A job with short working hours.

I Prefer:
1. A job which does not tie me down, or
2. A job where I could decide how the work is to be done.

In the first item, alternative 1 is the high-motivation alternative; and in the second, it is alternative 2.

Illustrative Forced-Choice Selection Items for the Affective Domain of the Taxonomy of Educational Objectives

It was suggested that the *Taxonomy of Educational Objectives* is a valuable source of ideas for test items. This is particularly true of ideas for affective measures, since valid and reliable materials in this area are so scarce. Items representing various levels of the Affective Domain follow. Each is keyed to a particular classification and objective in the Affective Domain Taxonomy.

1.1 *Awareness*

Objective: Awareness of works in literature.

Source: General Acquaintance Test in Literature (Chicago: Board of Examinations, University of Chicago, 1952), pp. 106–107.

Directions: The items in this test are arranged in sets of three, with five possible responses printed to the right of each group. For each item, blacken your Answer Sheet with letter corresponding to the response that best completes the statement begun on the left. In no case will the same response be correct for more than one item within a single group of three. There is no objection to careful and intelligent guessing here.

1. In *Man and Superman* by Shaw (D)
2. In *The Emperor Jones* O'Neill (B)
3. In *Winterset* by Anderson (A)

A. the hero's father has been executed.
B. the hero had been a pullman porter
C. the hero is a white ruler of a South Sea island
D. the hero finally becomes engaged to the heroine
E. the hero is finally hanged

4. In *The Inferno* by Dante (B)
5. In *Don Quixote* by Cervantes (D)
6. In *Faust* by Goethe (A)

A. the hero is accompanied by the devil
B. the hero is accompanied by a poet
C. the hero is accompanied by his father
D. the hero is accompanied by a servant
E. the hero is accompanied by an ambitious woman

2.3 *Satisfaction in Responding*

Objective: Pleasure in science activities.

Source: Adapted from *Interest Index; Test 8.2a* (Chicago: Evaluation in the Eight-Year Study, Progressive Education Association, 1939).

Directions: As you read each item below underline one of the four letters after the number of that item on the Answer Sheet.

Underline S if you feel you *do* get satisfaction from performing the activity.

Underline U if you are *uncertain* as to your reaction to performing the activity.
Underline D if you feel you *do not* get satisfaction from performing the activity.
Underline X if you have *never performed* the activity.

7. To experiment with plants to find out how various conditions of soil, water, and light affect their growth.
8. To study rock formations and to learn how they developed.
9. To visit an observatory to learn how astronomers study the stars.
10. To read about how distances to inaccessible places are measured, such as from the earth to the sun, the height of a mountain, etc.
11. To read about new scientific developments.

3.3 *Commitment to a Value*

Objective: Devotion to those ideas and ideals which are the foundation of democracy.

Source: Social Beliefs; Test 4.31 (Chicago: Evaluation in the Eight-Year Study, Progressive Education Association, 1944).

Directions: The statements in this test are expressions of opinions. They deal with unsettled questions, and *there are no right or wrong answers. Please express your point of view about them.* Indicate how you really feel about the issues expressed immediately after reading the statement. Do not pause too long on any one of them. Mark the Answer Sheet as follows:

A if you *agree* with the *whole statement.*
U if you are *uncertain* how you feel about the *whole statement.*
D if you *disagree* with the *whole statement.*

12. Freedom of speech should be denied all those groups and individuals that are working against democratic forms of government.
13. Negroes should not be allowed to fill positions involving leadership of white people.
14. The masses of the people have too little intelligence to vote wisely on important social issues.

4.2 *Organization of a Value System*

Objective: Development of dominant values.

Source: G. W. Allport, P. E. Vernon, and G. Lindzey, *Study of Values,* 3rd ed. (Boston: Houghton Mifflin, 1960).

Directions: Each of the following situations or questions is followed by four possible attitudes or answers. Arrange these answers in the order of your personal preference by writing, in the appropriate box at the right, a score of 4, 3, 2, or 1. To the statement you prefer most give 4, to the statement that is second most attractive 3, and so on.

15. In your opinion, can a man who works in business all week best spend Sunday

a. trying to educate himself by reading serious books.
b. trying to win at golf, or racing.
c. going to an orchestral concert.
d. hearing a really good sermon.

16. Viewing Leonardo da Vinci's picture, "The Last Supper," would you tend to think of it
    a. as expressing the highest spiritual aspirations and emotions.
    b. as one of the most priceless and irreplaceable pictures ever painted.
    c. in relation to Leonardo's versatility and its place in history.
    d. as the quintessence of harmony and design.

Comment: The profile obtained for this test is the basic datum for evaluation at 4.2. This profile consists of six fundamental values based directly upon the typology of Eduard Spranger: (1) Theoretical, (2) Economic, (3) Aesthetic, (4) Social, (5) Political, and (6) Religious.

5.1 *Generalized Value Set*

Objective: Respect for the worth and dignity of human beings.

Source: Problems in *Human Relations Test.* Cited in Paul L. Dressel and Lewis B. Mayhew, *General Education—Explorations in Evaluation* (Washington, DC: American Council on Education, 1954), pp. 229–237. Reprinted by permission of the publisher.

17. Tom and Bob, who know each other only slightly, were double-dating two girls who were roommates. A sudden storm made it impossible to go to the beach as planned. Tom suggested going to a movie. After making the suggestion, he realized Bob was without funds. As Tom, what would you do?
    a. Pay for the movie.
    b. Lend Bob money.
    c. Leave it up to the girls.
    * d. Get Bob to suggest something.
    e. Apologize to Bob for making the suggestion.

18. Your social organization has pledged a student who is not liked by some of the members. One of your friends threatens to leave the school organization if this person is initiated. What would you do?
    a. Talk to your friend.
    b. Do not initiate the prospective member.
    c. Get more members to support the prospective member.
    * d. Vote on the prospective member.
    e. Postpone the vote until the matter works itself out.

The Method of Summated Ratings (Likert Scales)

Beginning with a set of attitude statements representing both favorable and unfavorable attitudes, we can develop a scale using relatively uncomplicated procedures. Likert (1932) has shown that the assignment of integral (whole-number) weights to a set of response categories will yield scores that correlate very highly with those obtained from a Thurstone scale. The usual response categories are: Strongly Agree, Agree, Undecided, Disagree, and Strongly Disagree. For those statements judged to be favorable toward the attitude object, weights of 5 for Strongly Agree, 4 for Agree, 3 for Undecided, 2 for Disagree, and 1 for Strongly Disagree are assigned. For unfavorable statements, weights of 1 for Strongly Agree, 2 for Agree, 3 for Undecided, 4 for Disagree, and 5 for Strongly Disagree are assigned. Thus, the higher the numerical score the more positive the attitude.

An Illustrative Problem

Following are seven statements, adapted from Glassey (1945), that might prove useful in developing a scale of attitudes toward education. Other subjects, for example, reading, science, or social studies, could be substituted.

1. I am intensely interested in education.
2. Education does far more good than harm.
3. Education enables us to live less monotonous lives.
4. Sometimes I feel that education is necessary and sometimes I doubt it.
5. If anything, I must admit a slight dislike for education.
6. I dislike education because it means that time has to be spent on homework.
7. I go to school only because I am compelled to do so.

It is obvious that gradations of favorableness are reflected in these statements. We might even have a group of judges classify these statements as favorable, neutral, and unfavorable. If we can obtain, say, 80 percent agreement on their classification, we will have a basis for assigning scoring weights to the statements. We then administer the items to our target group and score according to the scheme outlined at the beginning of this section. We would assign high weights to agreement with favorable statements, and to disagreement with unfavorable statements. The neutral statements would not be scored but would serve as buffers. This process would be undertaken for a large pool of items.

Selecting Statements

The next step is to identify those statements that discriminate between individuals with very positive attitudes and those with unfavorable attitudes. The method used for selecting attitude statements is similar to the item-analysis procedures used in refining achievement tests (see Chapter 11). The procedure involves obtaining a total score on the instrument for each individual in the group. The top third of the scores is called the High Attitude group, and the bottom third is designated as the Low Attitude group. A good statement should, on the average, receive higher ratings from the High group than from the Low group. A table like Table 18-1 should be developed for each statement, and a mean rating calculated for the two groups. The larger the mean difference, the better the item. One must remember that the difference will sometimes favor the High group and sometimes the Low, depending upon whether the statement is favorable or unfavorable. The final scale is composed of

Table 18-1 Determination of Mean Differences in Ratings of Hypothetical High and Low Attitude Groups for Statement on Attitude Toward Education

Response Categories	Low Group Weight	Low Group Frequency (*f*)	Low Group *f*X	High Group Weight	High Group Frequency (*f*)	High Group *f*X
Strongly Agree	5	4	20	5	12	60
Agree	4	8	32	4	20	80
Uncertain	3	16	48	3	10	30
Disagree	2	14	28	2	6	12
Strongly Agree	1	8	8	1	2	2
Sums		50	136		50	184
Mean Rating		$\frac{136}{50} = 2.72$			$\frac{184}{50} = 3.68$	

those items with the greatest mean differences, keeping in mind that we want a full range of attitudes to be reflected. It would ideally include about 20–25 statements.

The Semantic Differential Technique

Another useful technique for assessing affective learning outcomes is derived from the work of Osgood, Suci, and Tannenbaum (1957). Based on the assumption that in written and spoken language the characteristics of ideas and things are primarily communicated by means of adjectives, considerable research has been undertaken to investigate the connotative meanings of concepts. The technique used in this research is the semantic differential, which is not a test procedure per se but a general method of obtaining ratings of concepts on a series of bipolar adjective scales. A page from a semantic differential might resemble the following:

Learning

Fast ___ : ___ : ___ : ___ : ___ : ___ : ___ : Slow

Good ___ : ___ : ___ : ___ : ___ : ___ : ___ : Bad

Worthless ___ : ___ : ___ : ___ : ___ : ___ : ___ : Valuable

Quiet ___ : ___ : ___ : ___ : ___ : ___ : ___ : Active

Strong ___ : ___ : ___ : ___ : ___ : ___ : ___ : Weak

Unpleasant ___ : ___ : ___ : ___ : ___ : ___ : ___ : Pleasant

The respondent checks the blank on the continuum that corresponds to his feelings about the stimulus word. Any number of stimulus concepts might be used: people, objects, abstract concepts, practices, institutions, and the like. Osgood and his colleagues have identified three major dimensions of the meaning of concepts: *evaluation, potency,* and *activity.* Sample adjective pairs related to each of these dimensions are:

Evaluation: Good–Bad, Fair–Unfair
Potency: Strong–Weak, Heavy–Light
Activity: Fast–Slow, Active–Passive

The strongest dimension by far is the evaluative. It has been shown in hundreds of studies—in the United States, cross-culturally, and cross-nationally—to describe individuals' dominant feelings about ideas and objects. It is recommended that, in exploring affective learning outcomes, only the evaluative dimension be used.

Developing a Semantic Differential

The steps to be followed in constructing a semantic differential are as follows:

1. *Identify the concept(s) to be rated.* The number and type of concepts to be chosen will, of course, depend upon intent. It is best to select a group of related concepts that can be viewed within the same frame of reference. The more homogeneous the set, the easier and more meaningful the contrasts. A group of concepts like *learning, teacher, school, study,* and *textbook* would constitute a relatively homogeneous set. A teacher may wish to investigate sentiments about the central concepts in a particular unit or course.

2. *Choose appropriate bipolar scales.* The choice of a set of scales should be dictated by relevance and representativeness. As was noted earlier, the semantic differential measures a concept's connotative meaning (its implications for the individual), not its denotative or descriptive meaning. One should *not* use adjectives, therefore, that provide physical descriptions (e.g., *rock:* Hard–Soft). In addition, the scales should be as representative as possible of the full range of sentiments likely to be associated with the concepts in question. Ideally, one would experimentally determine the scales most relevant to a given concept by trying out his own list and then perhaps undertaking a factor analysis. For a classroom teacher, this suggestion is impractical. A reasonable sample of evaluative scales has already been provided by Osgood, Suci, and Tannenbaum (1957). Following is a list of 28 adjective pairs that have been found to bear heavily on the evaluative dimensions of semantic scales:

Good–Bad | Beautiful–Ugly
Sweet–Sour | Clean–Dirty
High–Low | Calm–Agitated
Tasty–Distasteful | Valuable–Worthless
Kind–Cruel | Pleasant–Unpleasant

Bitter–Sweet	Happy–Sad
Empty–Full	Ferocious–Peaceful
Sacred–Profane	Relaxed–Tense
Brave–Cowardly	Rich–Poor
Clear–Hazy	Nice–Awful
Bright–Dark	Fragrant–Foul
Honest–Dishonest	Rough–Smooth
Fresh–Stale	Fair–Unfair
Pungent–Bland	Healthy–Sick

Consideration needs to be given to the difficulty level of the words. Obviously, students cannot use adjectives whose meanings they do not know.

3. *Design a response sheet.* Only one concept should appear on each page. The concept should be printed at the top of the page and the scales listed beneath. The polarity of scales should be alternated (e.g., good–bad, worthless–valuable). The ordering of scales on consecutive pages is fixed, but the order of concept presentation may be randomized. This latter suggestion, however, introduces difficulty in scoring. Osgood has found that a 7-point scale is effective. One may use 3-, 5-, or even 9-point scales. For younger children, a 5-point scale might be most suitable. Ordinarily, 10 to 15 adjective pairs would be sufficient for a group of about 10 related concepts. Subjects have no trouble, however, rating 20 concepts on 20 scales in an hour's time. The younger the group, the fewer concepts and scales should be used.

4. *Write instructions.* The cover sheet should include a general orientation to the task and perhaps a statement about why the data are being gathered. The significance of the scale positions should be spelled out, as well as the procedure for recording responses. It is also important to describe the attitude the examinee should take toward the task: highly motivated and candid, moving rapidly through the scales, expressing first impressions, making independent judgments of each adjective pair relative to the concept, and treating each concept independently. Some examinees, particularly younger ones, may experience some initial difficulty relating the adjective pairs to the concept. If this occurs, the students should be encouraged to proceed rather quickly and respond on the basis of first impressions. Do not try to explain the relation of an adjective to the concept, since this will probably invalidate the pupil's response. Elementary-school pupils typically view the semantic differential as a game and "play" it with vigor. The presentation of the task as a game can encourage freer responses from the pupils and thereby make for a more valid measure of the pupils' attitudes. For the very young, consideration might be given to oral administration, with the teacher reading the instructions, concepts, and pairs while the examinees read along with the teacher and respond.

An example of a relatively standard set of instructions for a semantic differential exercise follows.

The purpose of this activity is to measure the meanings of certain concepts by asking you to judge them against a series of descriptive scales. On each page you will find a different concept and beneath it a set of scales. You are to rate each concept on each of these scales.

Here is how you are to use the scales:

If you feel a particular concept is *very much* like one end of the scale, you should place your checkmark as follows:

Pleasant _X_ : ___ : ___ : ___ : ___ : ___ : ___ : Unpleasant
1 2 3 4 5 6 7

OR

Pleasant ___ : ___ : ___ : ___ : ___ : ___ : _X_ : Unpleasant
1 2 3 4 5 6 7

If you feel a particular concept is *quite close* to one end of the scale (but not extremely), you should place your checkmark as follows:

Rugged ___ : _X_ : ___ : ___ : ___ : ___ : ___ : Delicate
1 2 3 4 5 6 7

OR

Rugged ___ : ___ : ___ : ___ : ___ : _X_ : ___ : Delicate
1 2 3 4 5 6 7

If you feel a particular concept is *only slightly* like one end of the scale (but is not really neutral), you should place your checkmark as follows:

Sharp ___ : ___ : _X_ : ___ : ___ : ___ : ___ : Dull
1 2 3 4 5 6 7

OR

Sharp ___ : ___ : ___ : ___ : _X_ : ___ : ___ : Dull
1 2 3 4 5 6 7

If you feel that the concept is *neutral* on the scale (that both sides of the scale are equally associated with the concept) or if the scale is completely irrelevant (unrelated to the concept), you should place your checkmark in the middle space.

Happy ___ : ___ : ___ : _X_ : ___ : ___ : ___ : Sad
1 2 3 4 5 6 7

The direction toward which you check, of course, depends upon which of the two ends of the scale best describes your feeling about each concept.

Do not worry or puzzle over any one scale. It is your first impression of each concept that we want. On the other hand, please do not be careless because we want your true impressions. Do not try to remember how you checked similar items earlier in the scale. *Make each item a separate and independent judgment.*

Remember, you are judging the concept as *you* see it—not as we or others react.

Important:

1. Place your checkmarks in the middle of the spaces, not on the boundaries:

this   not this

___ : ___ : _X_ : ___ : ___ : ___ X ___ :

2. Be sure to check every scale. Do not omit any.
3. Never put more than one checkmark on a single scale.

5. *Score the scales and concepts.* In summarizing the responses quantitatively, the usual procedure is to assign values from 1 to 7 (or from 1 to whatever range of points is used) such that the interval closest to the adjective representing the negative pole (e.g., low evaluation) receives a 1 and the interval closest to the opposing adjective receives a 7. The successive integers represent gradations between these two points. An individual's score on each scale for each concept may be then computed in terms of the scale positions. If only the evaluative adjective pairs are used, a 7-point 10-scale differential for a single concept would yield a maximal "positive" score of 70 and a minimum score of 10. The responses obtained may be used to compare an individual's attitudes toward different concepts—for example, to a lecture on history versus a film. Similarly, one may compare two individual's ratings of a given concept. Students are generally interested in their ratings relative to those of other members of the class. The semantic differential is a relatively nonthreatening task, and anonymity is therefore probably not required. In addition, the ratings of groups of people can be arranged in order to assess differences in attitude between groups, or toward various concepts within the group. The same concepts may also be rated at different points in time to assess changes in attitudes that take place as a function of some treatment or intervention.

Free-Response and Opinionnaire Methods

The opinionnaire is a frequently used polling method of gathering opinion and attitude data. The term *opinionnaire,* as opposed to questionnaire, is used intentionally, to suggest an emphasis on feelings rather than facts. The use of a well-constructed opinionnaire tends to systematize the data-gathering process and to help insure that the relevant questions are asked, and all important aspects of the problem surveyed.

Advantages and Disadvantages of Questionnaire Methods

The questionnaire method, either open-ended or closed (structured), is frequently maligned. But as is often the case it is the user that should be castigated for improper use, not the method itself. Questionnaires, if properly constructed and analyzed, can provide very valuable information about affective variables. They are, or can be, efficient with regard to time for construction and obtaining responses from large or small groups of respondents, and are relatively inexpensive. They do require carefully crafted questions. The unstructured free-response questionnaires will use large amounts of time for content analyses of the responses. A great deal of subjectivity is involved in interpreting responses. Respondents also may "wander around" in answering your questions, so be prepared to separate the wheat from the chaff. Unfortunately, opinionnaires are often haphazardly constructed, without proper concern for the phrasing of questions, the means of summarizing and analyzing data, or pilot testing or tryout of the schedule. Bledsoe (1972) suggests six criteria for a "good" opinionnaire:

1. Brevity.
2. Inclusion of items of sufficient interest and "face appeal" to attract the attention of the respondent and cause him to become involved in the task.
3. Provision for depth of response in order to avoid superficial replies.
4. Wording of questions neither too suggestive nor too unstimulating.
5. Phrasing of questions in such a way as to allay suspicion about hidden purposes and not to embarrass or threaten the respondent.
6. Phrasing of questions so that they are not too narrow in scope, allowing the respondent reasonable latitude in his responses.

Opinionnaires are generally of two types: the "closed" or precategorized type and the "open" or free-response type. The former type very closely resembles the forced-choice methods described earlier in this chapter. Rating scales are also frequently associated with the structured opinionnaire (see Chapter 9 for further discussion of rating scales). It is recommended that the open-ended form of opinionnaire be adopted for classroom use. The use of such free-response questions allows the teacher to cover a wide variety of topics in an efficient manner. Analysis of the responses to free-response questions can, however, be quite time consuming and difficult. In preparing opinionnaires, some general cautions should be observed (Payne, 1951):

1. Spell out in advance the objectives, purposes, and specifications for the instrument. This task should be undertaken *before* questions are written.
2. Try to limit the length of the questionnaire (e.g., ten questions). If the student becomes impatient to finish, he is likely not to consider his answers carefully.
3. Make sure students understand the purpose of the opinionnaire and are convinced of the importance of responding completely and candidly.
4. If possible, use a sequence of questions. Green (1970) illustrates the advantages

of this approach with a series of questions that could be used to stimulate attitudinal responses toward labor unions in a unit of a social studies course.

   a. How have labor-management relations been affected by unions?
   b. How have working conditions been affected by unions?
   c. What means, if any, should be used to control unions?
   d. What effects have unions had on the general economy of the country?

5. Make sure students are motivated to answer questions thoughtfully.
6. Control the administration of the opinionnaire so as to prevent students from talking with one another about the questions before answering them.
7. Urge students to express their own thoughts, not the responses they think the teacher wants.
8. Be sure the directions are clear, definite, and complete.
9. Urge students to ask about questions that are unclear to them.
10. If possible, try out the opinionnaire with other teachers or a couple of students to identify and clear up ambiguous questions, difficult terms, or unclear meanings.

Content Analysis

A teacher will ordinarily undertake a content analysis of the responses to opinionnaire questions. *Content analysis* is a systematic, objective, and—ideally—quantitative examination of free-response material. In addition to examining opinionnaire responses, content analyses of textbooks, television broadcasts, essays, records of interpersonal interactions, plays, stories, dramas, newspaper articles, speeches, or propaganda materials may be undertaken.

Several steps in completing the content analysis of a questionnaire.

1. *Identify the units for the purpose of recording results.* The specification of units, which requires great care, may be undertaken before beginning the analysis if the teacher knows what to expect, or after a sample of the responses has been examined. A unit is usually a single sentence, although any brief phrase that summarizes an idea, concept, feeling, or word will suffice.

2. *Identify the categories into which the units will be placed.* For example, the unit might be a sentence and the category a type of sentence, for example, declarative, interrogative.

3. *Analyze all the content (or a representative sample) relevant to the problem.* A given piece of material could be sampled for a given student, or samples could be taken from a group of students.

4. *Seek to attain a high degree of objectivity.* The teacher may wish to complete an analysis or to put it aside and redo it (or a portion of it) later to check agreement of results. A comparison of the work of two teachers working independently could serve as another check on objectivity.

5. *Quantify the results, if at all possible.* The use of simple summary indices such as frequency counts and percentages can be very helpful.

6. *Include a sufficiently large number of samples to insure reasonable reliability.* The larger the sample of material(s) analyzed, in general, the greater the reliability.

An Illustrative Content Analysis

In an effort to evaluate the impact of an eight-week summer enrichment program for academically and artistically talented students, the author asked several questions such as the following on a participant follow-up opinionnaire:

1. What contribution, if any, did the program make toward your developing a positive attitude toward learning?
2. How suitable were the instructional methods?
3. To what degree did the program influence your desire to attend college?
4. What do you feel were the most beneficial dimensions of the program?

A content analysis of the last question yielded the following results (with a sample of 50 subjects):

	Frequency	*Percent*
a. Contact with individuals with both different and similar interests.	34	68%
b. Freedom for independent and in-depth study.	12	24%
c. The high quality of teachers.	9	18%
d. The availability of cultural events, films, speakers, and the like.	8	16%
e. Freedom to broaden interests.	5	10%

Not only were relevant dimensions of the program identified, but a ranking of the importance of these dimensions also become possible. The fact that this information came from the participants themselves helps insure the validity of the responses. If precategorized responses had been used, we might have biased the respondents.

Affective Measurement and the Diagnosis of Learning Difficulties

It was noted in the previous chapter that five major use-categories can be identified where affective measurement could make meaningful contributions. These are: classroom applications, screening and selection, counseling, research, and program evaluation. Standardized affective measures are most frequently used in screening, research, and counseling. Commercially purchased measures of self-concept, general personality, and interests and values can provide meaningful information helpful to the understanding of each student. These kinds of data are particularly useful in counseling, particularly when coupled with relevant data from the "cognitive domain," for example, scores from ability, aptitude, or achievement tests. In a counseling situation a student may wish to explore any or all of the following areas:

Area	*Question Explored*
Educational Planning	What educational plans are most realistic relative to my ability and resources? What can I do to maximize my likelihood of success in what kinds of training settings?
Career Planning	What are my vocationally relevant skills, competencies, and aptitudes? Where are my relative career interests and are my interests similar to those who are successfully engaged in particular occupations or jobs?
Life Planning	As I begin to inventory my life goals, how would I allocate time, effort, and resources to a variety of roles such as student, marriage partner, parent, and citizen?
Personal Development	What are my feelings about myself and what attitudes do I value?

It is also in the classroom setting where, with a little effort, teacher and student can work together to maximize student development and achievement. Anderson (1981) notes how the diagnostic process can be enhanced through use of affective measures. The process generally involves five steps.

Steps in Diagnoses of Learning Difficulty	*Process*
Identification	Use data from relevant achievement measure (classroom or standardized) to locate area(s) of depressed performance.
Hypothesis Generation	Apply both measures of ability and affect to create a list of possible causes of difficulty.
Assessment	Assess area thought to be primary cause.
Diagnosis	Contrasting of data leads to most likely cause(s).
Remediation	Application of relevant treatment.

Assume a sixth grade student is having difficulty in language arts, in particular, reading. Application of a standardized achievement battery indicates student is reading at a little below the fifth grade level (Grade Equivalent = 4.8). Further evidence indicates scholastic ability equating to a percentile rank of 62. Application of any number of "home-made" measures might be used to examine the affective component of learning. Following are some examples.

Forced-Choice Method

A paired-comparison scale could be devised to look at the "relative" interest the student has in reading. A series of items like the following could be devised:

I would like to:

a. read a book.
b. visit the zoo.

I would like to:

a. do some arithmetic problems.
b. have my teacher read us a story.

I would like to:

a. do a science experiment.
b. get a book as a present.

I would like to:

a. read a story to my classmates.
b. make a poster about health.

The student's "score" on such a device would be the number of times activities related to reading were preferred over other activities.

Semantic Differential

A semantic differential could be developed using either *book* or *reading* as the stimulus. It is assumed that appropriate directions have been presented.

Reading

Good ___ : ___ : ___ : ___ : ___ : Bad
Sweet ___ : ___ : ___ : ___ : ___ : Sour
Fair ___ : ___ : ___ : ___ : ___ : Unfair
Happy ___ : ___ : ___ : ___ : ___ : Sad
Nice ___ : ___ : ___ : ___ : ___ : Awful

Using this approach a "score" would be derived by treating each adjective-pair as a rating scale (1 to 5) and simply add the rating for the five pairs with "5" being at the positive (left) side. Maximum score = 25.

Rating Scale

A pictorial variation on the Likert method could be used to "scale" attitude toward reading (Solley, 1989). For example, see Figure 18-1:

Directions (Read to Student)

Each statement below describes a feeling toward writing. The Survey will help determine your attitudes toward writing. There is no right or wrong answer and you will not be given a grade. Answer each statement as honestly as you can by circling the puppy which best describes how you feel about the statement.

Puppy 1 = strongly agree
Puppy 2 = agree
Puppy 3 = undecided
Puppy 4 = disagree
Puppy 5 = strongly disagree

1. How do you feel when your teacher reads a story aloud?

2. How do you feel when you are asked to read aloud to your teacher?

Figure 18-1

Reading attitude survey

3. How do you feel about reading books for fun at home?
1.
2.
3.
4.
5.
The score would be the sum of the puppy ratings such that the higher the score the more positive the attitude (i.e., happiest puppy = "5" if statement is positive, or "1" if negative, vice versa, etc.).

Figure 18-1

(continued)

Opinionnaire (Free Response)

A series of open-ended questions could be created and either administered (a) orally to a group of students where they write answers, (b) on a form upon which students could respond, or (c) as an individual interview with the teacher recording the responses. After responses have been collected a content analysis is undertaken and a scoring scheme devised. It might be economical from a labor standpoint to create a global scale for each question using specific responses as anchor points on a continuum.

Let's assume that in our hypothetical case attitudes toward reading are found to be negative. Score interpretation in terms of absolute or normative standards could be used, for example, "Had attitude score which corresponded to 35% of maximum possible," or "Had percentile rank of 35 in class of 22." Bases such as data from contrasted groups or identifying neutral points on a scale could also be used. Inasmuch as attitudes are learned, emotionally toned behavioral predispositions they can be changed and modified. It is assumed that if we can help our hypothetical student develop more positive affect about reading that, since they have the ability, they can improve their performances. Changing attitudes and developing motivation are very difficult and challenging instructional tasks. Klausmeier (1985, pp. 394) has outlined a series of steps that can be followed in changing attitudes in a classroom setting.

Step in Classroom Attitude Change Process	*Activity*
Identifying Attitude to be Taught or Changed	Targets might be broad such as likes school, classmates, or teacher, or specific to a school subject such as reading, or very specific such as grammar. Activities can be expanded to include values (e.g., equality, self-respect), as well as attitudes.
Provide Pleasant Emotional Experiences	Shaping techniques using praise and providing for academic success can be used. Avoid using fear and anxiety as motivators (e.g., don't drink and drive).
Provide Exemplary Models	Modeling is very effective, particularly with the very young students (e.g., attractiveness of celebrity endorsements).
Extend Informative Experiences	Information and knowledge about object facilitates initial attitude acquisition, e.g., directed reading, observing.
Use Small-Group Instructional Techniques	Such techniques as (a) group discussion, (b) group decision making, (c) role playing, and (d) cooperative small-group activity have proved effective.
Encourage Deliberate Attitude Change	Student might be encouraged to actively recognize, then change, attitude through behavioral change, e.g., as in responding to those of other races.

Affective assessments can serve as indicators of the need for additional information about a learning difficulty or behavior problem. Does this diagnostic path allow affect and cognition to go hand in hand? We want to strive to build in the student feelings of competence and the freedom to be independent learners.

Thus ends a treatise on all you wanted to know about developing affective measures but were afraid to ask. It's a lot of work! But aren't most things that are important?

Case Study Application

Ideally one of the hoped-for outcomes of our Reading Education course would be a more positive attitude toward the reading process and its educational value. Educational outcomes in the affective domain are difficult to measure. Fortunately there are a variety of approaches that can be used to measure such objectives. One might, for example, create a semantic differential using such stimulus concepts as

Reading, Books, Language, and such bipolar adjective pairs as good-bad, fast-slow, strong-weak, fresh-stale, or beautiful-ugly. Perhaps a series of open-ended questionnaire items could be collected. Sentence completion items like, "When I read I ______________," or "Reading makes me feel ______________" might be subjected to content analyses.

Our exercise for this chapter involves two tasks. First, try your hand at writing twelve statements related to attitude toward reading, for example, "Reading is the most important thing a student must do." These items will be aimed at our undergraduate students. Use the approach described under the heading, "The Method of Summated Ratings (Likert Scales)" in the present chapter. Refer back to the chapter section titled "Writing Items for Self-Report Affective Measures" for criteria that are useful in creating and editing attitude statements. Remember the interest is to "scale" an attitude domain. Therefore you will want to include statements that reflect positive, neutral and negative gradations of attitude. Use the Strongly Agree, Agree, Uncertain, Disagree, Strongly Disagree response format.

The second part of the exercise is to complete an item analysis of the attitude statements to be found in Table 18-2. The responses of our eighteen sample reading education students to twelve statements have been summarized in Table 18-2. After

Table 18-2 Summary of Actual Responses of Eighteen Students to Twelve Attitude Statements

	Attitude Statement											
Student	1	2	3	4*	5	6	7	8	9*	10	11	12
S_1	3	5	3	2	4	5	5	4	2	5	5	4
S_2	3	3	2	3	2	3	2	1	1	2	1	2
S_3	2	4	2	3	3	5	3	1	3	3	4	3
S_4	5	2	3	3	2	3	2	3	3	2	5	2
S_5	2	2	2	4	3	2	3	2	3	2	3	2
S_6	4	2	3	5	4	3	2	3	3	4	3	2
S_7	3	4	3	2	3	4	2	3	1	3	3	5
S_8	2	2	4	4	3	3	3	3	2	4	2	4
S_9	4	3	2	5	2	2	2	2	2	1	3	4
S_{10}	4	4	3	1	2	3	2	3	5	4	2	2
S_{11}	4	5	2	2	2	5	2	3	2	5	3	3
S_{12}	3	3	2	3	2	3	4	3	3	4	3	2
S_{13}	5	5	2	2	2	3	3	3	2	3	3	2
S_{14}	3	3	2	4	2	3	4	4	2	2	4	1
S_{15}	4	3	1	2	2	5	2	5	4	5	2	2
S_{16}	1	5	2	2	4	2	4	3	4	3	5	1
S_{17}	4	4	2	3	4	2	5	3	2	5	3	4
S_{18}	1	4	2	4	4	2	3	1	3	2	3	1

*Negatively weighted items, that is, SD = 5, D = 4, U = 3, A = 2, SA = 1. These items need to be reversed when obtaining individual student scores.

obtaining a score for each student you might want to sharpen your statistical skills and (a) create a frequency distribution, (b) calculate the mean, and (c) calculate a standard deviation. The item analysis procedure for the attitude statements is virtually identical with that used in conjunction with achievement test items. A "high" and a "low" scoring group, representing divergent degrees of attitudes toward the objective in question, are identical. In this case it is attitude toward reading. For the exercise use the high scoring six and the low scoring six individuals. The responses of each group are compared for each statement. Statements may be retained, modified, or rejected. The first step is to "score" the instrument for each student, then identify the "high" and "low" scoring groups. Then tally the responses to each item and complete the discrimination analysis.

You might even want to try your hand at a reliability analysis by using one of the split-half methods described in Chapter 12.

Content Review Statements

1. There is a wide range of verbal and nonverbal measures of affective variables, among them:
   a. Amount of time, money, and energy spent on a particular activity.
   b. Formal verbal responses to such scales as the semantic differential, Likert, and Thurstone scales.
   c. Reaction time.
   d. Amount of knowledge about a particular referent.
   e. Examination of personal documents.
   f. Sociometric measures.
   g. Projective techniques.
   h. Observational and performance measures.
   i. Physiological measures.
   j. Memory measures.
   k. Simulation.
2. In building verbal measures of affective variables, the developer should use statements that are:
   a. Couched in the present tense.
   b. Nonfactual.
   c. Singularly relevant to the object.
   d. Representative of a wide range of feelings.
   e. Simple, clear, direct, and short.
3. Attitude statements and inventories can be developed from free-response questions submitted to students.
4. Most methods of developing affective measures initially involve the identification of a series of statements reflecting gradations of favorableness or affect, from which a representative set is selected.
5. Forced-choice methods require selection between two or more alternatives that reflect either (a) gradations of favorableness or (b) different content, actions, or decisions that can be correlated with variations in feelings.

6. Forced-choice methods tend to produce instruments that yield more uniform distributions of scores and are efficient, easily scored, objective, reliable, and less fakeable than other instruments.
7. The Affective Domain Handbook of the *Taxonomy of Educational Objectives* contains excellent suggestions on the content and format of affective measures.
8. The method of summated ratings employs a 5-point scale (strongly agree, agree, undecided, disagree, and strongly disagree) with statements reflecting positive (favorable) or negative (unfavorable) affect.
9. By the method of summated ratings, statements are selected for the final form of the instrument that discriminate between individuals with high positive scores and those with high negative scores.
10. In developing affective measures, it is best to begin with at least three times as many items as the final form is expected to contain.
11. Judges should agree at least 80 percent of the time on whether a given statement is favorable or unfavorable.
12. In administering an affective inventory, one should urge subjects to express their initial reaction.
13. The semantic differential technique is a generalized method that uses pairs of bipolar adjectives to evaluate the connotative meanings of concepts.
14. The opinionnaire and other free-response methods may profitably be used to gather affective data.
15. Opinionnaires should be brief, relevant, comprehensive, nonthreatening, and concise.
16. Content analysis is a valuable tool for examining the data gathered with an opinionnaire or the free-response method.
17. Standardized affective measures can profitably be used to assist in educational, career, and life planning, and personal development.
18. The diagnosis of a learning difficulty involves the process of identifying, hypothesizing, assessing, diagnosing, and remediating.
19. Changing attitudes in the classroom involves attitude identification, creating supporting emotional environment, modeling, informing, discussing, and encouragement.

Speculations

1. What methods of assessing affective objectives do you prefer to use and why?
2. What are the advantages and disadvantages of using the following approaches to measuring affective outcomes: (a) attitude scales, (b) semantic differential, and (c) opinionnaires?
3. In what ways are writing achievement test items similar to writing attitude items?
4. How can affective measurement help in the diagnosis of learning difficulties?

Suggested Readings

Berdie, D. R., Anderson, J. F., & Niebuhr, M. A. (1986). *Questionnaire: Design and use.* (2nd ed.) Metuchen, NJ: Scarecrow Press, Inc.

Gable, R. K. (1986). *Instrument development in the affective domain.* Boston: Kluwer-Nijhoff. The author has collected together recent research and recommendations for instrument development in the affective domain. Very readable but not for the beginner.

Green, B. F. (1954). Attitude measurement. In G. Lindzey (Ed.), *Handbook of social psychology* (pp. 335–369). Reading, MA: Addison-Wesley.

Oppenheim, A. N. (1966). *Questionnaire design and attitude measurement.* New York: Basic Books.

Osgood, C. E., Suci, C. J., & Tannenbaum, P. H. (1957). *The measurement of meaning.* Urbana, IL: University of Illinois Press. More than a description of a technique, this very important work also introduces the reader to psycholinguistics.

Following are "collections" or compendia of instruments in the affective domain. Most are "fugative," that is, they are not commercially available.

Chunn, K., Cobb, S., & French, R. P., Jr. (1975). *Measures for psychological assessment.* Ann Arbor, MI: Survey Research Center, University of Michigan.

Lake, D. G., Miles, M. B., & Earle, R. B. (1973). *Measuring human behavior: Tools for the assessment of social functioning.* New York: Teachers College Press.

Robinson, J. P., & Shaver, P. R. (1973). *Measures of social psychological attitudes.* Ann Arbor, MI: Survey Research Center, Institute for Social Research, University of Michigan.

Shaw, M. E., & Wright, J. M. (1967). *Scales for the measurement of attitudes.* New York: McGraw-Hill.

Walker, D. K. (1973). *Socioemotional measures for preschool and kindergarten children.* San Francisco: Jossey-Bass.

Bev's Diary

Ah, a kinder and gentler topic: feelings. At last somebody is really concerned about attitudes and interests in education. It's exciting—I can see it in my students. How they feel does affect how hard they work. Their interests are important. I can use that information to help select materials for them to read and study. It's more fun for them and it makes my job easier.

Another side of the affective thing is what it means to be a good citizen (an old-fashioned term, I guess) in today's society. Schools can help students look at themselves and learn what kind of people they want to be. To help them make decisions about all the seemingly daily crises that they face in the early years—drugs, sex, job, and marriage. Attitudes toward these issues can be explored.

It's getting toward the last marking period. I know I'm legally required to give grades; it's a tough time but part of the job. Everybody I know would like to get high marks, but while all students may have been created equal, they all don't put forth equal effort.

Part Seven

Applications of Measurement Data

When asked what makes a job rough
A teacher replied it's so tough
To give the right grade
And not be afraid
When praying is not nearly enough.

To evaluate can be most subjective
From some it will bring forth invective
But with clever designs
And the right paradigms
The results are almost always objective.

Chapter 19

Using Measurement Data in Reporting and Marking

The need for informative reporting and marking procedures may be more acute today than at any time in the history of our nation's schools. Increased experimentation with innovative teaching methods and organizational systems is accompanied by a demand for effective communication among those engaged in the educational enterprise. Obviously, students need to be apprised of their progress. In addition, data are needed to help teachers plan for effective instructional experiences. This need takes on increasing importance as more and more schools implement individualized instruction and mastery learning programs, which require the continuous monitoring and feedback of progress information. Parents, too, are taking an increased interest in the schools. Their need to be informed should be met with the best techniques available.

Purposes of Marking and Reporting

Many educators decry the use of marks (or grades—we will use the terms interchangeably) for any purpose. It is claimed that grades do not motivate, but are rather quite detrimental to the student psyche and, in fact, have a negative impact.

If grades are reliable, valid, and representative of the degree of success achieved in working toward important goals, then information about progress in developing competencies (knowledge and skills) is related to future academic, occupational/vocational, and "life" success. Yes, grades do represent extrinsic rewards but so do most other recognitions for achievement from salary increases to ribbons, plaques, and trophies.

A noticeable degree of tension is exhibited by students and teachers, and to some extent by parents, as marking time rolls around. This tension is especially characteristic of beginning teachers, and can generally be attributed to their lack of experience in assigning marks and reporting student progress. The summation of complex human behavior into a simple index, in the form of a letter or number mark, may be presumptuous. If, in addition, marks are *not* based on a rational philosophy of education and a set of operational definitions of expected learning outcomes, their meaning will be obscure and ambiguous, and their purpose(s) will be subverted.

Communicating to Students and Parents

Marks provide useful and efficient data that can be used to communicate with students and their parents. Marking and reporting are essentially information-processing activities, and might be likened to elements in a communications network. Marks are merely the means by which a teacher communicates his or her evaluation of the progress each student has made toward a specified set of educational goals. As in any communications system, the message, that is, information about achievement, may be incorrectly transmitted to the receiver because of faulty encoding or decoding or because of the presence of "noise" or "static" in the network.

Students have a right and a need to learn about their progress. In addition to achievement data in the form of rank in class, grade equivalents, standard scores, and percentile ranks, students seem to desire more "subjective" and criterion-referenced evaluations of their performances. They want to know if their work is outstanding, good, acceptable, or unacceptable. The teacher is probably in a better position than anyone else to integrate the many factors in learning and achievement, and to communicate his summary to the student.

Parents, too, have a right and need to learn of the educational progress of their progeny. Marks are sensible summarizing appraisals which parents can use to counsel their child about his school work and future educational and vocational plans.

Communicating to Present and Future School Personnel

Just as the results of standardized achievement tests can be used to evaluate the overall progress of a particular instructional program and school, so can distributions of marks indicate trends related to progress. Such data are useful in making decisions about promotion, graduation, transfer, and future education.

Indices of past achievement are probably the best single indication of future achievement. College admissions personnel, therefore, view marks as generally indicative of the level of performance to be achieved by individual students admitted to their institution. Marks serve as academic currency in the college marketplace, although their exchange and conversion properties are limited.

Promotional decisions should, of course, never be made on the basis of marks alone. In fact, Holmes (1989) has shown that requiring a student to repeat a grade results in very little improvement in achievement, and only compounds "social" promotion. In a summary (meta-analysis) of sixty-three studies it was found that, on the average, retained children are worse off than their promoted counterparts using both academic and personal adjustment criteria. Little research has been focused, however, on the effect of retention *plus* intensive remediation. Retention usually just means "doing it over again."

Motivating Student Learning

The research literature reveals evidence that marks may function to reinforce or inhibit learning. Although we would ideally like learning to result from intrinsic motivation, the gross extrinsic force exerted by marks must be acknowledged.

In considering the motivational function of marks, it is important to define the basis on which marks are assigned. If a mark simply indicates status at a particular point in time, it is doubtful that most students will feel challenged to work for higher marks. If, however, marks reflect improvement or achievement relative to ability, students may be spurred to greater efforts.

Guiding Future Instruction

It is well known that past achievement is the best predictor and prognosticator of future achievement. Information on skills and knowledge already acquired and developed, then, is immensely helpful in designing future educational programs for individual students, groups, or classes. Data on important affective educational outcomes can also serve as a basis for planning meaningful student experiences. The data from criterion-referenced assessment and "goal cards" can be extremely helpful if carefully examined.

Recent Developments and Issues in Marking and Reporting Procedures

The last several decades have seen many changes in the grading and reporting practices prevalent in our schools (Geisinger, 1982; Thomas, 1960; Cureton, 1971; Terwilliger, 1971; Natriello & Dornbusch, 1984). Among the changes are the following:

1. Reporting progress not just status.
2. Including character traits as well as achievement (e.g., work habits, personal development, etc.).

3. Selected application of pass/fail systems.
4. Detailed reporting of competencies or skills (especially at the elementary school level) rather than simple letter grades in subject areas.
5. Attempts to take into account student ability in assigning grades.
6. Expanding the size of grade scale.
7. Encouraging more comments back and forth between teacher and parent.
8. Developing "contracting" grade systems where individual teacher and student pairs negotiate objectives, methods, evaluation, and standards.

Some of these practices were tried and found deficient or of limited applicability. Ebel (1965), for example, has proposed an ability-adjusted mark distribution model which turns out to be a basic variation on the normal-curve model; it simply results in a higher percentage of higher grades in higher ability classes. This causes some teachers philosophical problems.

Another system of limited applicability is the pass/fail approach. Although perhaps useful when the only intent is to evaluate the attainment of *minimal* objectives or standards, it may not be advantageous when faced with developmental objectives (greater range of difficulty and complexity) (Terwilliger, 1989). There is some evidence that students may not maximize their efforts under the pass/fail system, and that in fact student achievement levels may decline (Gold, Reilly, Silberman, & Lehr, 1971).

Individual grade/work contracts seem like an inherently fair way to approach teaching-learning-assessment tasks. There are some distinct advantages of using this approach to the management of instruction through the use and clarification of objectives. It can foster positive relations between student and teacher and clarifies expectations. On the negative side is the considerable amount of paperwork required and the loss of data for comparative ranking purposes. The method probably should not be used in public school settings, but if it is it should be on a limited basis. Application of contracts is better used at professional levels for personnel evaluation and supervision (Swanicki, 1981).

A contemporary problem in grading is "inflation." This is primarily a function of the assignment of a limited number (usually two) of high grades (usually A and B). Millman, Slovarek, Kulick, and Mitchell (1983) have noted that reliability tends to suffer if grade inflation is present. The causes of inflation are many. Among these are (a) a shift from norm-referenced to individually-referenced performance standards, (b) increased use by administrators of instructional effectiveness ratings on faculty made by students, and (c) general shifts to less rigorous grading standards. In general grades have become less of an incentive in a motivational sense, and the focus has been retargeted on performance and what the individual can do and what they know. This has given rise to more testing and the "certification" by exam.

An example of an improved and informative report/progress card is displayed in Figure 19-1. Note in particular the flexibility which allows for traditional grades as well as specification of factors contributing to that grade. In addition to cognitive outcomes, some attention is given to the student's affective development.

	First Quarter			Second Quarter			Third Quarter			Fourth Quarter		
LANGUAGE ARTS	Excellent Achievement	Work is Satisfactory	Improvement Needed	Excellent Achievement	Work is Satisfactory	Improvement Needed	Excellent Achievement	Work is Satisfactory	Improvement Needed	Excellent Achievement	Work is Satisfactory	Improvement Needed
READING												
Working in readiness activities												
Shows growth in vocabulary												
Reads with understanding												
Uses word attack skills												
Reads orally with expression and meaning												
Reads for enjoyment												
READING												
PENMANSHIP												
Manuscript ________ Cursive ________												
Working in readiness activities												
Forms letters correctly												
Spaces properly												
Writes neatly												
PENMANSHIP												
ENGLISH												
Applies basic rules of grammar												
Spells correctly in written work												
Shows growth in creative expression												
ENGLISH												
SPEAKING AND LISTENING												
Speaks clearly and distinctly												
Expresses ideas well												
Listens attentively												
Recalls with accuracy												
MATHEMATICS												
Working in readiness activities												
Forms numerals correctly												
Understands the meanings of numbers												
Counts and writes in more than one sequence												
Uses symbols and terms correctly												
Reads, writes, and solves equations												
Reasons well in solving problems												
Knows and understands number facts												
MATHEMATICS												
SCIENCE												
Shows curiosity												
Applies observation techniques												
Demonstrates understanding and makes application												
Bases conclusions on facts and experiences												
SCIENCE												

Figure 19-1

Representative elementary school report form

	First Quarter			Second Quarter			Third Quarter			Fourth Quarter		
	Excellent Achievement	Work is Satisfactory	Improvement Needed	Excellent Achievement	Work is Satisfactory	Improvement Needed	Excellent Achievement	Work is Satisfactory	Improvement Needed	Excellent Achievement	Work is Satisfactory	Improvement Needed
SOCIAL STUDIES												
Contributes to activities and discussions												
Has interest in current events												
Shows growth in understanding of people												
Understands charts, maps, and graphs												
Reports information accurately and effectively												
SOCIAL STUDIES												

ACHIEVEMENT IN SUBJECT AREAS:

A - Excellent
B - Good
C - Fair
D - Poor

	First Quarter			Second Quarter			Third Quarter			Fourth Quarter		
MUSIC AND ART												
Participates in music												
Participates in art												
HEALTH AND PHYSICAL EDUCATION												
Practices good health habits												
Participates in organized games and free play												
WORK AND STUDY HABITS												
Works independently - uses time wisely												
Uses materials wisely												
Works well with the group												
Takes pride in work												
Follows directions												
PERSONAL GROWTH												
Accepts responsibilities												
Practices self-discipline												
Practices good sportsmanship												
Respects the rights and property of others												
Shows courtesy and consideration												
Shows growth in self-confidence												
ATTENDANCE												
Date of Report												
Days Present												
Days Absent												
Days Tardy												

Figure 19-1

(continued)

MATHEMATICS GOAL RECORD CARD 2

Pupil ________ Teacher ________ Year ________

	Check
Addition combinations 10 and under (automatic response)	
Subtraction combinations 10 and under (automatic response)	
Can count to 200	
Can understand zero as a number	
Can understand place value to tens	
Can read and write numerals to 200	
Can read and write numeral words to 10	
Can read and write number words to 20	
Use facts in 2-digit column addition (no carrying)	
Roman numerals to XII	
Can tell time:	
Half hour	
Quarter hour	
Calendar (months, days of week, dates)	
Coins and their equivalent value to 25¢	
Recognition of 50¢ coin and $1.00	
Recognize and use ½, ¼, ⅓ of a whole	
Addition facts to 18 (aim for mastery)	
Subtraction facts to 18 (aim for for mastery)	
*Can identify simple plane figures:	
Quadrilateral	
Pentagon	
Hexagon	
Octagon	
*Can use compass to bisect line segment, construct triangles, and construct perpendiculars	
Word problems: (check one)	
1. Can set the problem up	
2. Can understand process involved	
3. Can notate work problems	
*(Goals starred are not essential for all students)	
Comments:	

Figure 19-2

Sample grade two mathematics goal card

Another reporting device is the *goal card.* A goal card, primarily useful at the elementary school level, is simply a listing of skills, knowledges, or competencies with a place to indicate mastery or progress. The unique feature of goal cards is their specificity, for example, can construct simple plane figure with straight edge and compass, can set up word problems, can use facts in 2-digit columns addition (no carrying), and so forth. Bauernfeind (1967) has noted six major advantages of using goal cards:

1. Goal cards help students "see" their progress as they acquire information and develop skills.
2. Goal cards help the teacher specify objectives and arrange them in a logical way.
3. Goal cards are an effective way to communicate with parents and the general public. They serve as an excellent basis for a parent-teacher conference.
4. Goal cards can contribute to planning for instruction, particularly if individualized programs are desired.
5. Goal cards facilitate communication among educators, for example, the Grade 1 arithmetic teacher with Grade 2 teachers, or the regular teacher with a substitute teacher.
6. Because they emphasize important objectives, preferably specified in behavioral terms, goal cards can serve as a sound basis for classroom assessment.

See Figure 19-2 for a sample Grade 2 mathematics goal card.

Recommendations for Grading Practices

After an extensive review of the available but sparse research literature on grading and marking, expert suggestions, and current best practice, Stiggins, Frisbee, and Griswold (1989) have made the following recommendations for assigning grades.

Recommendation	*Reason*
1. Students should be informed of procedures and standards to be used.	Professional (ethical) obligations, perhaps even logical requirement.
2. Acquisition of knowledge and skills should be basis for grade.	Teacher and student agree on clear basis for grade.
3. Attitude should *not* be used as basis for grade.	Trait difficult to define and assess.
4. Learning ability should *not* be used as basis for assigning grades.	No fair or universal way to factor in ability into grade.
5. Motivation and effort should *not* be used as basis for grade.	Not primary academic objective. Effort does not equate to knowledge or skill.
6. Interest in subject matter should *not* be used as basis for grade.	Difficult to define and of questionable legitimacy.
7. Personality (temperament, disposition, character) should *not* be used as basis for grade.	Are not evaluatable traits relative to curriculum.

8. Do *not* use formative assignments for grades.	These are part of instructional process.
9. Rely primarily on summative measures as basis for grade determination.	Frequent data give most reliable picture of progress.
10. Paper and pencil exams can provide valid and reliable bases for grades.	Permit measurement of variety of learning outcomes.
11. Oral exams should be used very sparingly.	Method is of questionable reliability.
12. Performance observations may be reliably employed as partial basis for grade.	Some instructional outcomes can only be assessed through observation.
13. Collect data frequently in concise units.	Frequency is positively related to reliability.
14. Data should be gathered which is maximally valid, reliable, and cost-effective.	Self-monitoring of quality control seldom done.
15. Weight components in accordance with announced specifications.	If weights are not controlled by grader, grades will not be valid.
16. District, school, and teacher grading policies need to be communicated.	Everyone should be held accountable for the same standards.
17. The normal curve model should *not* be used to assign grades.	Life is not normally distributed.
18. "Fixed percentages" grades are acceptable if there is a link between percentage and material to be required.	Reference should be on percent of material, not percentage of individuals obtaining a particular grade.
19. Do not simply aggregate raw score points for assigning grades.	This recommendation relates to number 15 which suggests that different outcomes have different weighted values.
20. Borderline grade cases should be reviewed in light of additional achievement information.	Let us not lose sight of the fact that graders are fallible.

Most of these recommendations reflect common-sense approaches, but common sense is frequently overlooked when we engage in the often emotional task of assigning grades.

Decision Points in Establishing Marking Systems

Despite tremendous technical and theoretical advances in education and psychology during the past century, particularly in regard to quantitative methods, we are still unable to recommend a perfectly viable system for assigning marks that will satisfy the majority of educators. This is true partly because most people consider marking a philosophical decision-making process, rather than a statistical one. This view leads to the treatment of marks as "evaluations" representing value judgments about students' learning and achievement. Others resolve the problem by considering grades as "measurements." Information about a student's progress toward a specified set of instructional objectives is gathered, combined in appropriate ways, and summarized as a mark, usually a letter (A through E) or number (1 through 100). Such marks are viewed as summarizations of data, rather than value judgments. This view of marking has some intrinsic appeal because it seems to relieve the teacher of the burden of making subjective judgments. Teachers can say, "Look, I'm just reporting how well my students achieved. I'm not making judgments about them." Despite the psychological comfort that may be derived from such a philosophy, the problem has really not been resolved. The teacher continually makes value judgments about what to teach, how to teach, and the like, and how "measurement" will be reported unavoidably rests on a subjective decision by the teacher.

Failure on the part of an instructor, department, school, or school system to specify the basis upon which marks are assigned can only result in chaos. Look, for example, at interschool differences in marking practices. A survey of 129 high schools completed by Educational Testing Service indicates the diversity of marking policies and practices in effect: (a) 22 percent of the schools in the survey had no fixed policy governing the assignment of marks, (b) 27 percent reported that an absolute standard of achievement was used, (c) 29 percent marked students on achievement in relation to ability, and (d) 16 percent said that marks represented achievement with respect to others in the class. Apparently marks mean different things to different people. The purpose of assigning marks is obviously obscured if uniform policies are not adopted. Among the more important decisions that must be confronted in developing policy statements on marking are the following questions.

Should an Absolute or Relative Standard Be Used?

Because most of the data of education and psychology do *not* conform to the requirement of a ratio scale—that is, a zero score has an absolute meaning—the use of an absolute scale to assign grades must be used with caution. Because a student responds correctly to every item on a test does not mean that he knows all there is to know about a particular subject. Such a score does not represent 100 percent comprehension. Tests are only samples of behavior, and the use of a percentage of the total number of items on a test, or of the raw total number of points it is possible to obtain over a semester's work, should be used with some caution as a basis upon which to assign marks.

An allied problem is that a fixed method of marking is frequently imposed by school administrators and boards of education. The usual method requires specification of a fixed percentage, for example, 65 percent, as a passing grade. Furthermore, an instructor is frequently limited in the percentage of certain grades he may assign. Such limitations actually require the instructor to predict the difficulty level of the items on his tests and predetermine the shape of the final distribution of scores, so that a specified number of students will fall into each achievement category. Such a task is almost impossible, even for the most highly trained professional test developer. Such an imposition of fixed percentages requires the teacher to play "catch-up" at the end of the semester. He may provide bonus points for projects or construct very difficult or very easy tests (without considering what they are supposed to measure) until the "correct" number of marks has been achieved.

The ability levels of classes as a whole do vary, and it would therefore seem reasonable to allow the performance of the class to determine the distribution of marks. A reference point, however, is needed. One might use a measure of central tendency—either the mean or the median—as a starting point for assigning marks. The former, however, being an arithmetic average, is unduly affected by extreme scores, and because classroom tests frequently yield asymmetrical distributions, the mean is probably an unwise choice. The median is generally considered the most representative measure of central tendency of all the scores in a distribution, and its selection makes sense, at least from a logical standpoint. If one assigns marks on a relative basis, a more logical starting point than the mean or median is needed. Such a starting point could be derived from the table of specifications and list of objectives for the course. Minimal requirements and competencies to be achieved could be identified, translated into expected scores, and then used to assign marks.

Should Level of Achievement or Effort Form the Basis of Marks?

Even under the most ideal conditions, marks are ambiguous. It would seem, then, that expanding the content base of a mark to include such variables as effort, perseverance, and assiduousness could only serve to further cloud already murky waters. Is it reasonable for us to assign a higher mark to a student who "tried harder" but attained the same level of achievement as several of his peers? Probably not. Effort should be rewarded, both formally and informally. The teacher can positively reinforce a student's efforts to learn. That a student is working hard should be communicated to parents. A marking and reporting system that treats achievement and effort separately is recommended. Within the achievement domain do not overlook the significant weight that can be given to homework.

Should Growth or Status at a Particular Point Form the Basis for Marks?

Assigning marks on the basis of improvement over the semester has great intrinsic appeal, and intuitively appears to be a fair and unbiased approach. Consider, for example, two students, X and Y. Both have shown a growth of 35 points, according to a pre- and post-test, in a course in American history. Student X, however, was below Q_1 to begin with, while student Y was above Q_3. Does the growth of these two students represent the same thing? Obviously not, either relative to content and skills resulting from instruction as measured on the tests, or in terms of final level achieved.

Marking on the basis of final status, particularly when measured by a comprehensive terminal examination, has much to recommend it. A final-status index is responsive to individual differences in learning rate and is more reliable than growth scores.

Should a Letter or Number Marking System Be Used?

Both letter and number systems of marking have enjoyed wide popularity, and each has its strengths and weaknesses. The letter system, which usually uses the symbols A through E, theoretically emphasizes the distinction between marks as measurements and as evaluations. The letter grade represents a translation from a number base, resulting from a combination of test scores, ratings, and the like, and it is assumed that the degree of excellence achieved is better represented by a letter. Letter marks have a common meaning for most people, and for this reason should probably be retained. One disadvantage of letter marks is that they must be converted to numbers if they are to be added or averaged. In addition, the use of only five categories of marks to some extent masks individual differences, that is, we lose information. The Bs received by five different students may not mean the same thing, either in terms of level (there are high and low Bs) or of content and proficiencies.

The number system of marking has great appeal for many people. It allows for a greater range of marks than is provided by five letters. One possible source of interpretive error is that the number system implies a greater degree of precision in measuring educational achievement than is warranted by the data. Does the use of a wide range of number marks really mean that fine discriminations among individuals are possible? No! We can probably do a reasonably good job of ranking individuals in the class, but differences of two or three points are not very meaningful. In summary, a grading or marking system which embodies the following is recommended:

ABSOLUTE STANDARDS
+
ACHIEVEMENT
+
STATUS
+
LETTER MARKS

Combining and Weighting Data

The process of assigning marks, like the tests that make up the major data base for grades, can be norm-referenced or criterion-referenced. Norm-referenced marks are *relative* and criterion-referenced marks are *absolute*. A relative mark is based on a student's standing in the group and tends to be based on fixed percentages of grades assigned. As opposed to the relative approach, the absolute method sets performance standards for each grade category. In either system it is necessary to take into account the relative importance of the various outcomes in a course. Perhaps a project that requires integration of a large number of knowledge and skills (e.g., a map construction) or a major research paper should receive considerably more weight in an achievement composite than several quizzes. Some method to take these different weights into consideration needs to be applied.

In order to assign marks, it is generally desirable to derive a composite score distribution weighting individual measurements obtained over, for example, a semester's work, in the appropriate proportions. There are a number of problems related to the combination of separate measures into a single composite measure for each individual student, not the least of which is the fact that test scores tend to weight by their variabilities. For example, if an instructor wishes to combine scores on the midterm exam with those on the final exam to form a composite, he is more than likely simply to add the two scores. Let us further assume that he wants each exam to contribute 50 percent to the composite score. If, however, the standard deviation of the final exam is 20, and that of the midterm 10, the final exam contributes *twice* as much as the midterm to the composite. An allied problem is a logical dilemma: Are we justified in combining scores from a number of different sources, representing different learning outcomes, into a composite? Strong arguments can be made pro and con. Assuming an underlying variable called "achievement in such and such a course," we are probably justified in ranking students in terms of overall performance. On the other hand, most of the methods of combining data assume that the measures to be combined are independent of each other—a tenuous assumption at best. If for no other reason than the practical exigencies of the educational assessment situation, deriving composite scores is justified.

Four methods of deriving composite scores will be described in this section. The first three apply primarily to the assignment of norm-referenced grades. Many methods have been investigated and it has been found that they tend to yield similar results. Keep in mind that the pooled appraisal of competence represented by the composite is a *relative* measurement, not an absolute one. It permits comparisons among individuals and judgments involving "more" or "less." But the real or absolute meaning of the scores is often obscured in a composite score.

Weighting with Standard Scores

A relatively straightforward method of combining scores is through the use of standard scores. The reader will recall from Chapter 10 that the use of standard scores is advocated because it allows a legitimate comparison of an individual's scores on different tests. This is an acceptable procedure because the use of a standard transformation puts all tests on a common score base. The standard score system suggested here is the Z transformation, and can be expressed as follows:

$$Z = 10\left(\frac{X - M}{S}\right) + 50, \qquad (10\text{-}9)$$

where

X = an individual's raw score
M = the raw score mean and
S = the raw score standard deviation.

The mean of the Z scores is 50, and the standard deviation is 10. Converting all the measures that one wishes to combine into standard scores will equate their means to an arbitrary value of 50, but, more important, it will adjust the individual scores in terms of the standard deviation. It should be reemphasized at this point that deriving a composite score requires that we work with the variabilities of the distributions, as weights are proportional to the variabilities. In this regard, the means are irrelevant in obtaining weighted scores.

How are these standard scores used to obtain composite scores? Refer to the data in Table 19-1. Assume that an instructor wishes to combine two quizzes and a final exam. In addition, he wishes to weight the final three times as heavily as the two quizzes. The first step is to determine the means and standard deviations for the three sets of scores (see columns 1, 2, and 3 of Table 19-1). The estimated standard deviations ($\hat{S}$) derived from the scores of the high- and low-scoring one-sixth of the distribution are very good estimates of the actual standard deviations. Next, Equation 10-9 is used to determine Z scores for every student on every test (see columns 4, 5, and 6 of Table 19-1). Finally, after applying the appropriate weight to Z_F, the composite scores are determined by addition. At this point, any of the marking procedures described in the next section may be applied. It should again be noted that in addition to providing a convenient method of eventually combining scores, standard scores themselves may be useful in test interpretation.

Weighting with Adjusted Raw Scores

An efficient method of equating the standard deviations of a number of measures is to divide each raw score in a particular distribution by its own standard deviation. Such a procedure automatically adjusts each raw score in relation to the variability of the total distribution. The adjusted raw scores for the three exams represented in Table 19-1 are summarized in Table 19-2.

The mere fact that the "adjusted raw score" procedure bypasses computation of the raw-score mean and standard scores may be enough to recommend it. The results obtained through the use of standard scores or adjusted raw scores yield the identical ranking of students.

Table 19-1 Hypothetical Test Data Illustrating Derivation of Composite Scores Using Standard Scores

	Raw Scores			Standard Scores			Composite[a]	Rank of Composite
Student	Quiz 1	Quiz 2	Final Exam	Z_1	Z_2	Z_F	Z_c	
S_1	38	48	93	69	62	65	326	2
S_2	36	53	98	66	68	68	338	1
S_3	34	47	94	62	61	65	318	3
S_4	33	53	89	61	68	62	315	4
S_5	32	42	82	59	56	56	283	6
S_6	31	45	85	57	59	59	293	5
S_7	30	38	77	55	52	53	266	8
S_8	29	40	74	53	54	50	257	9
S_9	27	43	79	50	57	54	269	7
S_{10}	26	34	72	48	48	49	243	11
S_{11}	26	35	72	48	49	49	244	10
S_{12}	26	34	69	48	48	46	234	12
S_{13}	25	32	70	46	46	47	233	13
S_{14}	25	30	68	46	44	46	228	14
S_{15}	24	29	65	44	42	43	215	15
S_{16}	23	26	60	43	39	40	202	17
S_{17}	22	28	63	41	41	42	208	16
S_{18}	20	22	61	37	35	40	192	18
S_{19}	19	24	55	36	37	36	181	19
S_{20}	16	22	48	30	35	31	158	20
M =	27.1	36.2	73.7					
S =	5.6	9.6	13.2					
$\hat{S}^b$ =	5.7	9.3	13.2					

[a] Composite obtained with following expression, $Z_c = Z_1 + Z_2 + 3(Z_F)$.

[b] $\hat{S}$ = Sum of scores for the highest scoring one-sixth of the distribution, minus the sum of the scores for the lowest scoring one-sixth of the distribution, divided by one-half the number of students.

Weighting by Common Denominator

Test scores weight by their variabilities. If the variabilities are approximately equal then the importance weights can be applied directly to the scores. What does it mean to be approximately equal? One rule of thumb suggests that if one standard deviation is less than one and a half times as large as another then we can probably treat them as equals. Consider the standard deviations of Table 19-1: 5.6, 9.6, and 13.2. The standard deviation of 9.6 and 13.2 are more than 1.5 times as large as the

Table 19-2 Derivation of Composite Scores Through Use of Adjusted Raw Scores (Based on Actual Raw Scores and Standard Deviations of Table 19-1)

	Adjusted Raw Scores $\left(\frac{X}{S}\right)$			Composite[2]	Rank of Composite	Mark[3]
	(1)	(2)	(3)	(4)	(5)	(6)
Student	Quiz 1	Quiz 2	Final Exam[1]			
S_1	6.79	5.00	21.13	32.92	2	B
S_2	6.43	5.52	22.27	34.22	1	A
S_3	6.07	4.90	21.36	32.33	3	B
S_4	5.89	5.52	20.22	31.63	4	B
S_5	5.71	4.38	18.63	28.72	6	B
S_6	5.54	4.69	19.31	29.54	5	B
S_7	5.36	3.96	17.49	26.81	8	C
S_8	5.18	4.17	16.81	26.16	9	C
S_9	4.82	4.48	17.95	27.27	7	C
S_{10}	4.64	3.54	16.36	24.54	11	C
S_{11}	4.64	3.65	16.36	24.65	10	C
S_{12}	4.64	3.54	15.68	23.86	12	C
S_{13}	4.46	3.33	15.90	23.69	13	C
S_{14}	4.46	3.13	15.45	23.04	14	C
S_{15}	4.29	3.02	14.77	22.08	15	D
S_{16}	4.11	2.71	13.63	20.45	17	D
S_{17}	3.93	2.92	14.31	21.16	16	D
S_{18}	3.57	2.29	13.86	19.72	18	D
S_{19}	3.39	2.50	12.50	18.39	19	D
S_{20}	2.86	2.29	10.91	16.06	20	F

[1] Final exam adjusted raw obtained by dividing each raw score by the standard deviation, and multiplying by 3.

[2] Composite obtained by summing entries across columns.

[3] Mark determined by relative approach: 7% A, 24% B, 38% C, 24% D, and 7% F.

5.6 for Quiz 1. A reasonable adjustment to make the distributions more or less equal in variability would be to multiply Quiz 1 by 2 and leave the Quiz 2 and Final Exam scores alone. We could then apply the importance weights of one, and three respectively. The conversion equation to get an appropriate weight composite would be:

$$C = 4(Q_1) + (Q_2) + 3(FE)$$

The "4" for Q, comes from the "2" variability adjustment and the "2" importance weight. The advantage of this method is that it does not require calculation of standard scores and one can work directly with the raw scores.

Everything considered, however, using adjusted (by the standard deviation) raw scores is probably the easiest given the ultimate intent of weighting.

Weighting with Absolute Scores

If performance or achievement is expressed as a percentage of the maximum possible there still exists a need to weight the various elements in a program of study. Criterion-referenced or absolute scores all have a base of 100. For example, a raw midterm exam score of 35 on an 80-item exam where each item was worth one point would be 44 percent, and a quiz made up of six, three-point credit completion items would convert a raw score of 11 to an absolute score of 61 percent. Nitko (1983) suggests that absolute or criterion-referenced scores can be weighted simply by (a) multiplying each percent score by the desired weight, (b) adding the adjusted weights for each student individually, and (c) dividing by the total of the combined weights.

This procedure is illustrated in Table 19-3. Each of the three components is converted to a percent, weighted by a multiplier, added together, and then averaged by dividing by five, the sum of the weights. Using this method assumes that the absolute scores are based on individually representative sampling from well defined and homogeneous domains. In addition the question of variability is not directly addressed inasmuch as the focus is on mastery, not how one student compares with another.

Three Marking Models: A Don't, a Maybe, and a Do

Before discussing the assignment of marks, several words of caution are in order. First, the use of quantitative procedures does not eliminate the human factor from marking. Marking decisions are still basically philosophical, evaluative, and judgmental; they can and do engender guilt. Second, the meaning ascribed to marks, be they letters or numbers, really rests on arbitrary conventions. The measures we use to assign marks must have meaning with respect to expected changes in students if the resulting marks are to have any meaning. Finally, the very act of condensing a multidimensional performance into one of five categories results in the loss of information and reliability.

The Inspection Model (A Don't)

A method of assigning grades that is perhaps more widely used than acknowledged is the inspection method. It generally involves examining the distribution of composite scores in the hopes of finding "natural breaks" or "cutoff points," and represents the zenith of marking on a relative curve. The observed distribution of scores, then, in a sense determines the percentage of marks to be assigned. Experts argue that these "natural breaks" in distribution are unreliable. Because of so many arbitrary

Table 19-3 Illustration of Assigning Absolute Marks

Student	Raw Scores			Percent Scores[1]					
	Quiz 1	Quiz 2	Final Exam	Quiz 1	Quiz 2	Final Exam	Composite[2]	Composite Percent[3]	Mark[4]
S_1	38	48	93	76	87	93	442	88	B
S_2	36	53	98	72	96	98	462	92	A
S_3	34	47	94	68	85	94	435	87	B
S_4	33	53	89	66	96	89	429	86	B
S_5	32	42	82	64	76	82	386	77	C
S_6	31	45	85	62	82	85	399	80	C
S_7	30	38	77	60	69	77	360	72	C
S_8	29	40	74	58	73	74	353	71	C
S_9	27	43	79	54	78	79	369	74	C
S_{10}	26	34	72	52	62	72	330	66	D
S_{11}	26	35	72	52	64	72	332	66	D
S_{12}	26	34	69	52	62	69	321	64	D
S_{13}	25	32	70	50	58	70	318	64	D
S_{14}	25	30	68	50	55	68	309	62	D
S_{15}	24	29	65	48	53	65	296	59	F
S_{16}	23	26	60	46	47	60	273	55	F
S_{17}	22	28	63	44	51	63	284	57	F
S_{18}	20	22	61	40	40	61	263	53	F
S_{19}	19	24	55	38	44	55	247	49	F
S_{20}	16	22	48	32	40	48	216	43	F

[1] Based on points: $Q_1 = 50$, $Q_2 = 55$, FE = 100
[2] Weighted: $Q_1 = 1$, $Q_2 = 1$, FE = 3 (Total points possible = 5 × 100)
[3] Composite Percent = Composite/5
[4] Using the Percentages from page 483.

decisions that need to be made and the lack of a sound interpretive base, it is not a recommended procedure.

The Norm-Referenced or Relative Model (A Maybe)

In using the so-called norm-referenced (group or relative) model for assigning marks, several assumptions of varying degrees of credibility are involved. First, the distribution is based on some arbitrary model or curve (sometimes unfortunately a normal curve) and assumes that achievement is distributed in a fixed way and that if the resulting distribution does not match the model, it is a result of sampling error. Second, it is assumed the sample means and standard deviations are the best estimates of the means and standard deviations of the population of which this particular class represents a sample. These assumptions involve about as much subjective judgment as any teacher must make in order to mark.

A typical relative model in the "normal curve" distribution of marks is presented in Figure 19-3. There are at least two ways that this curve may be used to assign marks. First, the instructor may mark off appropriate standard deviation units along the score scale, and assign the appropriate marks to them. Second, the percentage of marks dictated by the normal curve may be assigned the class. Will either procedure insure that the normal curve assumptions have been met? Yes, if and only if the underlying class distribution is normally distributed, an unlikely event.

The usual "relative" model involves simply assigning a fixed and arbitrary percentage of grades. Typically the percentage does not follow a normal curve. The school board in consultation with parents, teachers, and school administrators should set the guidelines for establishing marks. Gronlund and Linn (1990) have suggested, based on no scientific data and making no assumption about the shape of the distribution that perhaps for an introductory course the following flexible distribution (percent of students receiving grade) could be used to begin development of a relative marking system:

A = 10–20%
B = 20–30%
C = 30–50%
D = 10–20%
F = 0–10%

Consideration must be given to school educational philosophy, ability level of student body, performance level, and the purpose of assigning the grades.

To illustrate a normal curve model marks have been assigned to the students in Table 19-2 using the grade distribution of Figure 19-2. No matter the level of performance, the same distribution of marks is made.

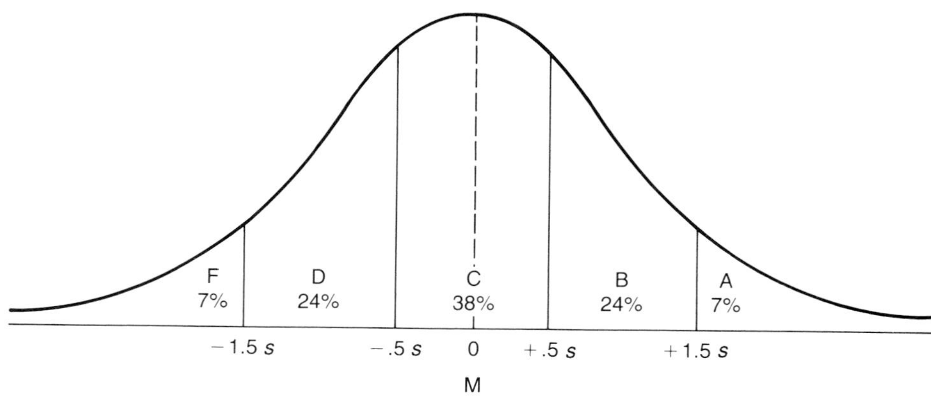

Figure 19-3

Hypothetical distribution of marks based on standard deviations

Absolute Standard Grading (A Do)

Basically the idea is to assign marks on the basis of proportions of objectives mastered or points earned. The percentage can be arbitrary, as it is in most systems, or based on an examination of content, objectives, skills, knowledge, or competencies. The question always is, "Does 80 percent mean that the individual has mastered 80 percent of the requirements?" This is a difficult measurement question to answer. It is the teacher who should set standards and specify outcomes that will equate to particular grades. It is virtually impossible to dictate uniform meaning to marks at the school or system level across subject areas and marks. In a real sense each mark is a case study, the meaning of which is the result of the interaction among student, teacher, and instructional program.

One of the problems in using the absolute approach in the public schools is when administrators require fixed performance percentages for grades, the teacher is being asked to equate or fix percentages of outcomes, that is, to build instruments which will equate to the percentages previously specified. To be able to build instrumentation to meet this requirement is a very challenging task even for a very skilled measurement professional.

Using the so-called absolute system involves applying prespecified criteria (expressed in terms of percent of points achieved) to student performance data. For example:

Mark	*Percent Correct*
A	91–100
B	81–90
C	71–80
D	61–70
F	60 and below

The percentages are usually fixed by boards of education, but with input from teachers, school administrators, and parents. Application of a variety of standard setting procedures can also be made (Jaeger, 1989). These procedures are similar to those involved in establishing standards for criterion-referenced and mastery tests.

Determining the composite upon which to base an absolute mark is easier than assigning a relative mark. Since the focus is on absolute levels of individual performance, percent scores (score points possible) only need to be aggregated in appropriate proportions. If, for example, you simply wish to have four bits of information each contribute an equal amount, simply add them. If, however, you wish the first bit to contribute twice as much, simply multiply it by two. If mixed percentages are desired, reduce the proportion to a common denominator and apply the weights. For example 35 percent–25 percent–40 percent–10 percent translates to 3.5–2.5–4–1, and for five measures which are desired to be weighted 30 percent–20 percent–10 percent–20 percent–20 percent would translate to 3–2–1–2–2.

An illustration of the "absolute assignment of marks is presented in Table 19-3. The group did not fare particularly well, with six Fs being assigned. Is this bad?

Surely in a sense only mastering 60 percent of the content does not reflect a high level of performance or competency. The absolute system does represent an approach to the maintenance of standards, yet still allowing *everyone* to achieve high marks if they work hard.

In comparing the distribution of marks in Tables 19-2 and 19-3 we find the following:

Mark	*Relative (Table 19-2)*	*Absolute (Table 19-3)*
A	1	1
B	5	3
C	8	5
D	5	5
F	1	6

It is at the low end of the achievement scale where the discrepancy is now apparent. How can we change the distribution of marks? Maintain the marking standards but make the tests easier, change the standards, get the students to work harder, or do a better job of teaching?

The last two approaches make the most sense.

Dishonest Ways of Marking

We cannot leave the topic of marking without pointing out some of the pitfalls that await the unwary, unthinking, or unmotivated grader. Palmer (1962) has provided us with seven danger signs that need to be heeded if we are to grade successfully.

Do not fall victim to grading by:

1. *Abdication*, that is, don't because of overwork or lack of effort, tailor courses to tests or rely on tests developed by other teachers or textbook publishers.
2. *Employing the carrots and clubbing system*, that is, don't add bonus credit for good behavior or avoidance of the prejudices of the teacher.
3. *Default*, that is, don't, because of a deep-seated hatred of grading and testing, base a final grade on a single exam in which a single misstep could spell disaster.
4. *Becoming a zealot*, that is, do not set the student racing with a vengeance and make the course an ordeal, endurance contests, or problem in survival in which you measure everything short of classroom posture.
5. *Changing rules in midgame*, that is, don't strew the line of march with booby traps and obstacles aimed at tightening up the standards after the game has started.
6. *Becoming a psychic grader*, that is, don't believe you have powers inaccessible to ordinary humans, allowing only you to "see" how much a student has learned without using any measurements.
7. *Anchoring everyone in a system of impossible perfection*, that is, don't overlook the fallibility of human-as-student or set yourself up as guardian of standards.

In short, don't fall victim, as the Dean did in the following limerick, to basing marks on irrelevancies:

There was a young girl at McMaster
Whose head was alfalfa and plaster
But she looked like a queen
And she smiled at the dean
So he graded her paper—and passed her.

On the Philosophy of Marking

It is incumbent upon all teachers, at every level of instruction, to spell out for their students the basis upon which marks will be assigned. It must be assumed that the practice of marking, regardless of the problems of accuracy and reliability, will continue for many years to come. Despite instructors' disagreements with the whole notion of marking, they have obligations to assign the most valid and reliable marks possible.

The many and important decisions that are made about students every day, and throughout their educational and occupational careers, dictate such a recommendation. Instructors who pursue a "no-grade" philosophy abrogate their responsibility as educators to communicate with each student about his or her progress.

There is no solution to the marking problem that would prove to be satisfactory to all concerned. Suffice to say that the assignment of marks constitutes a powerful system of reward and punishment, which can be used to bring about some highly desirable behavioral changes. Such a point of view implies the expenditure of a significant amount of time and effort in arriving at student marks. But preoccupation with marks, on the part of either teacher or student, must be considered unhealthy. Keeping in mind the limitations of marks, the basis of their assignment, and the fact that many significant outcomes of education are neither subject to marking nor markable (e.g., attitudes, values, interests) should lead to a proper perspective. Marks represent an integral, fallible, potentially meaningful, though perhaps irritating, element in the educational process.

Case Study Application

Among the most dreaded times of the teaching quarter, semester, or year is marking time. The marking of those important, but for the most part subjective, decisions can indeed be stressful. Whatever approach an instructor takes to the assignment of marks it should be rational and based on reliable data. Let us review for just a moment. It was noted earlier that there are two basic approaches to the assignment of marks: *absolute* and *relative*. The absolute approach specifies the percentage of "points" or credits that must be achieved to receive a certain mark. It kind of represents a "percent of perfection." The following absolute system is typical:

Mark	*% Points Needed*	*Meaning*
A	91–100	Excellent/Outstanding
B	81–90	Very Good
C	71–80	Average to Good
D	61–70	Below Average
F	60 and Below	Failing

This represents a 10-point range for each grade category. Other sizes are obviously possible, for example, an 8-point range where A = 93 − 100, B = 85 − 92, and so forth. Nowhere is it chiseled in stone that all grade categories have to be the same size. Decisions relating to grading standards should be joint ventures between teacher, school administrators, the Board of Education, and parents. It is important that if the "absolute" approach to marking is taken, that it be in the context of a criterion-referenced or at least objectives-referenced instruction-measurement system. The *relative* approach employs standards that relate to percentages of people rather than percentages of points. For example:

	Midterm Exam	*Final Exam*	*Lesson Plan*
Total Possible Points	80	80	40
Student			
1. Chelsea Dean	47	35	23
2. Denise Muth	58	74	38
3. Shawn Glynn	58	74	38
4. Tuni Fish	52	39	33
5. Jim Nastike	51	52	26
6. C. J. Huberty	55	56	35
7. Seymour Clearly	58	40	30
8. Allen Carlyle	58	76	39
9. Dixie Smith	55	76	38
10. Dean Creighton	59	62	31
11. Michael Allen	57	58	32
12. Jeffrey Allen	62	65	34
13. Karen Ann	68	80	37
14. Dee Pressed	52	53	24
15. Lawayne Chaplin	57	61	29
16. Joe Lynn	62	68	27
17. Jarred David	65	78	37
18. Pam Lynn	62	69	33

There are obviously other kinds of data that might be included in the final course evaluation. Perhaps a term paper or project grade, the results of quizzes, or the results of practice teaching. The 18 scores will need to be converted in some way so that they can be weighted in the specified way for the relative mark part of the exercise. Converting the scores to Z scores (Mean = 50, SD = 10) is probably the easiest. Rounding to the nearest whole number is suggested.

Mark	*% of Students Receiving Mark*
A	7
B	24
C	38
D	24
F	7

These percentages are assigned regardless of the distribution or level of performance. As was the case with the *absolute* method, these percentages can be changed by committee decision. The data used to assign relative marks must be appropriately weighted which means they could be made-up standard scores or adjusted raw scores.

Following are scores from three measures that will be used to make up the final mark in our reading education course. Weight them in such a way that the contribution will be as follows:

Midterm Exam	*Final Exam*	*Lesson Plan*
40%	40%	20%

Assign marks to all 18 students using both the absolute and relative methods, and compare the results. For the absolute system use the 10-point range, and for the relative grades use the 7–24–38–24–7 percent distribution.

Content Review Statements

1. Students have a need and a right to be apprised of their progress in school.
2. It is the responsibility of every teacher to develop valid and informative marking and reporting procedures.
3. The advent of individualized instruction and mastery learning programs intensifies demand for the development of viable reporting systems.
4. Marking and reporting systems should be based on sound and integrated philosophies of education, and on defensible technical procedures.
5. Marking and reporting programs serve the broad purposes of:
   a. Communicating to students and parents.
   b. Communicating to present and future school personnel.
   c. Motivating student learning.
   d. Guiding future instruction.
6. Recent developments in reporting procedures can be characterized as increasingly concerned with:
   a. Student behavior.
   b. Affective outcomes.

   c. Student needs at various levels.
   d. Student achievement relative to ability.
   e. Free-response instruction questions.
   f. The involvement of all those concerned with students in developing the reporting system.
   g. Computer processing of reports, allowing for more, and more detailed, information to be communicated.
7. Issues related to marking and reporting include:
   a. The development of pass/fail systems.
   b. The evaluations of contract plans.
   c. Grade inflation.
8. A goal card, listing instructional objectives, can be used effectively as part of the reporting system.
9. Current recommendation for marking practices emphasizing the use of frequently gathered multiple summative measures of cognitive achievement.
10. Decisions about marking procedures focus on the issues of:
    a. Absolute versus relative standards.
    b. Level of achievement versus effort.
    c. Growth versus status.
    d. Letter versus numerical marks.
11. It is generally recommended that an absolute system of marks, using a limited number of categories and relying on an individual's level of achievement, be applied.
12. Marks lack meaning unless reasonable procedural uniformity is achieved within and across classes, departments, and schools.
13. A mark should reflect a variety of areas of achievement, for example, test scores, class contributions, homework, projects, and similar data.
14. The weight of each component in a composite mark is determined by the variability of the separate component scores.
15. The "inspection model" of marking relies on the instructor to identify naturally occurring breaks in the distribution of composite scores which tend to be unreliable and is therefore not recommended.
16. The "relative model" of marking defines fixed percentages of students to receive specified marks, and sometimes assumes a normal distribution of achievement that rarely occurs.
17. An absolute system of marks holds the student responsible for specified levels of mastery.
18. Marks represent an integral, fallible, potentially meaningful, though perhaps irritating, element in the educational process.

Speculations

1. Do you think marks and achievement reports can be used to help involve parents in the education process of their children? How?
2. How should effort and attitude be treated as part of school reports?

3. What are the comparative advantages and disadvantages of absolute and relative marking systems?
4. Are relative and absolute marks compatible in the same school system? Under what conditions?
5. What are the comparative advantages and disadvantages of alphabetical and numerical marking systems?
6. What would school be like without marks?
7. On what basis do you decide to fail a student?
8. What suggestions can you make for improving the basis and process of assigning grades?
9. How do you decide on the weights for the different components of a mark?
10. Should the distribution of grades be about the same in all the sections of classes taught by (a) the same teacher, and (b) different teachers in the same department? Why or why not?

Suggested Readings

Carey, L. M. (1988). *Measuring and evaluating school learning.* Boston: Allyn and Bacon. Chapter 13, "Grading and Reporting Student Progress" contains an excellent description of how to create recording systems for day-to-day achievement indicators, and how to format and summarize the results.

Geisinger, K. T. (1982). Marking systems. In H. J. Mitzell (Ed.), *Encyclopedia of educational research* (5th Edition). New York: Macmillan. An excellent summary of the limited research that has been completed on its grading process, as well as an overview of the variety of systems used in the schools.

Gronlund, N. E. (1985). *Measurement and evaluation in teaching* (5th Edition). New York: Macmillan. Chapter 17, "Marking and Reporting" is a good how-to-do-it introduction. The chapter also addresses parent conferences.

Kubiszyn, T., & Borich, G. (1987). *Educational testing and measurement.* Glenview, IL: Scott, Foresman. Chapter 9 is a very readable overview of the basics.

Oosterhof, A. C. (1987). Obtaining intended weights when combining student scores. *Educational Measurement: Issues and Practice,* 6 (4), 29–37.

Terwilliger, J. S. (1971). *Assigning grades to students.* Glenview, IL: Scott, Foresman. An excellent overview of both practical and technical issues in the marking process.

Chapter 20

Curriculum Evaluation and Program Effectiveness

Most educators agree that measurement and evaluation are integral components of the instructional process, with the primary area of application being the assessment of learning outcomes. The kinds of outcomes, however, considered legitimate in American schools appear to be an ever-changing phenomenon. Several seemingly contradictory trends are evident. On the one hand, there appears to be a push on the part of society to force the schools back to a basic skill development orientation. The often heated rhetoric about reading, math, and minimum competencies attest to this public concern. From another standpoint the schools appear to be taking over many of the educational responsibilities that were historically considered the prerogative of parents and other socializing agencies of society. Such areas as sex education, human relations (including marriage), and strands of values, morality, and ethics are now addressed in the schools. These affective concerns among a variety of others require evaluation and pose many methodological and political problems.

On the contemporary educational scene tests continue to be used in traditional ways to (a) aid in directing curriculum emphasis, (b) yield valuable diagnostic data, (c) provide valuable information for a variety of administrative decisions, (d) stimulate and motivate student learning, and (e) aid in academic and vocational selection and guidance. General achievement test batteries are being applied throughout the grade range, diagnostic tests are being applied in the early grades, in special education, and in hospital and clinic settings, and selection tests are being used at institutions of higher education for undergraduate, graduate, and professional school students. An increasing use of tests can be found in the area of program and project evaluation. With the "accountability movement" rampant and virtually all funding agencies, especially at the state and Federal levels, requiring documentation of program impact, great numbers of educational and psychological measurements are being made.

With changes in goals and objectives, and accountability, come sociopolitical problems. Educational institutions, from the elementary grades through professional school, tend to reflect changes in society. Social forces from a variety of political, legal, religious, or economic origins generally find manifestations in curriculum reform, modified instructional systems, professional training programs, or school assessment practices. Many of these forces are at work in today's schools. Such factors as civil rights, the feminist movement, recession/inflation, and consumer awareness impinge on school practice.

It is the intent of this chapter to provide an overview of how evaluation and measurement procedures can be used to assess the impact of the aforementioned societal/cultural forces on curricula and programs. A secondary concern is with illustrating how those societal/cultural forces impact on the evaluation design process. Programs are here being defined as total school or system programs, new curricula, or innovative projects.

The Nature of Educational Curriculum, Project, and Program Evaluation

People are always evaluating. We do it every day. We buy clothing, a car, or refrigerator. All these decisions require data-based judgments. Educators make decisions about the effectiveness of curricula and/or programs, the progress of individual students toward specified goals, and efficiency of instructional methods. The most generally accepted definition of educational evaluation involves the idea of the assessment of merit, or the making of judgments of value or worth. The process employs both quantitative and qualitative approaches. One theme of this book has been that the making of informed value judgments requires the availability of reliable and valid data, and the exercise of rational decision making. This is as true about programs, projects, and curricula as it is about individuals. Good evaluations require sound data!

There are lots of models to help us develop rational approaches to evaluation (Madaus, Scriven, & Stufflebeam, 1983). Some of these models are very complex and involve the use of extensive resources. Is it any wonder then that the appeal of Wolf's (1969) five models is so great? These are the:

COSMETIC METHOD. You examine the program and if it looks good it is good.

Does everybody look busy? The key is attractive and full bulletin boards covered with projects emanating from the project.

CARDIAC METHOD. No matter what the data say you know in your heart that the program was a success. It is similar to the use in medical research of subclinical findings.

COLLOQUIAL METHOD. After a brief meeting, preferably at a local watering hole, a group of project staff members conclude that success was achieved, and no one can refute a group decision.

CURRICULAR METHOD. A successful program is one that can be installed with the least disruption of the ongoing school program. Programs that are truly different are to be eschewed at all costs.

COMPUTATIONAL METHOD. If you have to have data, analyze the hell out of it. No matter the nature of the statistics, use the most sophisticated multivariate regression discontinuity procedures known to humans.

In reality, unfortunately, these methods are quite popular, due in part to the complex nature of high quality evaluation, being labor-intensive and often expensive. In addition, the press of political considerations will often preclude the conduct of rigorous "scientific" evaluation.

Curriculum Evaluation as an Example of Educational Assessment

Revitalized interest in the teaching-learning process during the past several decades or so has resulted in a plethora of new curricula. The impetus to curriculum development has come from both subject-matter scholars and educational researchers—from the former because of new knowledge and insights into the structures of the disciplines, and from the latter because of new insights into the relation of the learning process to the organization and presentation of knowledge. The development of any new curriculum creates associated problems of evaluation.

Overall program effectiveness, cost, variables influencing effectiveness, and relevance are a few of the areas in need of assessment. Educational evaluation is probably of greater concern today than at any time in history due to the massive amounts of knowledge that our citizens must transmit and process, as well as to the complexity of this knowledge. Evaluative techniques adequate for assessing the effectiveness of small units of material are significantly less satisfactory when applied to larger blocks of information, the learning of which is highly complex and involves prerequisite learning, sequential behaviors, and perhaps other programs of study. The traditional use of experimental and control groups (as examined by contrasting gross mean achievement scores in a pre-post treatment design study), although generally valuable, tends not to provide sufficiently detailed information upon which to base intelligent decisions about curriculum effectiveness, validity, efficiency, and the like. Guba (1969) has lamented the failure of the evaluation designs for a group of government research proposals, for example, to meet even minimal requirements. The desire or need to compromise evaluation designs results in far too many "no significant differences." Guba notes, for example, that the practitioner seeking information about the success of his program is "inviting interference." This is a situation incompatible with control. If we lack control, experimental designs and methods of data analysis are considerably less applicable (Payne, 1982c). Most applied studies are done in natural settings, and natural educational settings are anything but controlled. But it is in these relatively unstructured and uncontrolled situations that evaluation and decisions must be undertaken. The field of curriculum evaluation is developing in response to the requirements of decision making.

Curriculum evaluation will play many roles, contingent upon the demands and constraints placed on it. Heath (1969), for example, suggests three broad functions performed by curriculum evaluation:

1. *Improvement of the curriculum during the development phase.* The importance of formative evaluation is emphasized. Strengths and weaknesses of the program or unit can be identified and enhanced or strengthened. The process is iterative, involving continuous repetition of the tryout evaluation-redesign cycle.

2. *Facilitation of rational comparison of competing programs.* Although differing objectives pose a large problem, the description and comparison of alternative programs can contribute to rational decision making.

3. *Contribution to the general body of knowledge about effective curriculum design.* Freed from the constraints of formal hypothesis testing, curriculum evaluators are at liberty to search out principles relating to the interaction of learner, learning, and environment.

A question remains about the ways curriculum evaluation differs from pure research, or the straightforward evaluation of learning. Following is a list of variables that may clarify the emphases unique to curriculum evaluation:

1. *Nature of goals.* The objectives of curriculum evaluation tend to be oriented more to process and behavior than to subject matter content.
2. *Breadth of objectives.* The objectives of curriculum evaluation involve a greater range of phenomena.
3. *Complexity of outcomes.* Changes in the nature of life and education, and the increased knowledge we now possess about the teaching-learning process, combine to require objectives that are quite complex from the standpoint of cognitive and performance criteria. The interface of cognitive, affective, and psychomotor variables further complicates the process of identifying what must be evaluated.
4. *Focus of total evaluation effort.* There is a definite trend toward increasing the focus on the total program, but this is in addition to the continued emphasis on individual learners.
5. *Context of education.* Curriculum evaluation should take place in a naturalistic setting, if possible. It is in the real-life setting, with all its unpredictable contingencies and uncontrolled variables, that education takes place. We must evaluate and make decisions in the setting in which we teach.

The following statement summarizes well the nature of contemporary curriculum evaluation:

> Curriculum evaluation can be viewed as a process of collecting and processing data pertaining to an educational program, on the basis of which decision can be made about the program. The data are of two kinds: (1) objective description of goals, environments, personnel, methods and content, and immediate and long range outcomes; and (2) recorded personal judgments of the quality and appropriateness of goals, inputs, and outcomes. The data in both raw and analyzed form can be used either to delineate and resolve problems in educational programs being developed or to answer absolute and comparative questions about established programs. (Taylor & Maguire, 1966)

The broad general description allows the final curriculum evaluation plan to take on any form dictated by its requirements.

Evaluating School Effectiveness

Sometimes instead of focusing on curriculum it is desirable and necessary to look at the educational program of the entire school. The last several decades have seen a significant increase in what has been popularly termed "school effectiveness research." The data resulting from such studies have been used for a variety of purposes. Among these are (a) performance prediction, (b) program evaluation, and (c) resource allocation. All of these applications are aimed at the improvement of the quality of education in our schools. Both the general public and professionals are concerned about education as can be attested to by the myriad of commission, committee, and panel reports. Legislation has been enacted that is aimed at strengthening the monitoring of student achievement and the universal application of legal school standards. The development of appropriate methodologies focused on implementing these provisions is a difficult and complex task.

There are many contributors to the complexity of these tasks, not the least of which is the extremely heterogeneous nature of student populations and schools. Variations in such educationally relevant variables such as school system tax base, teacher competency, and student ability make the applications of evaluation standards extremely difficult. Some of these relevant variables are under the control of the school system, others are uncontrolled.

Although flawed, one of the frequently used methods to investigate contributors to school effectiveness is the input/output approach, sometimes called the "education production function" model. Using the school as a unit of analysis, an extensive cluster of variables from meta-analyses (syntheses of research studies) has been identified by Glasman and Biniaminov (1981) as having very significant impacts on educational effectiveness. All of the following variables have shown significant relationships with student outcome data to varying degrees.

Student Background Characteristics

A. Family Background
   Family size
   Median family income
   Parental occupational index
   Quantity and value of family possessions
   Parent education level
   Cultural index
B. Student Background
   Sex (varied with subject area)
   Attendance in kindergarten
   At age-for-grade

Sociodemographic Characteristics of Student Population

C. Racial Composition
   Percent white student body
   Socioeconomic composition
D. Student Attendance Characteristics
   Degree of student turnover
   Days present
   Quality of schooling index
   Tardiness
E. Student Attitudes
   Locus of control
   Self-concept
   Academic aspiration

School Conditions

F. Services
   Tracking
   Number of books per student
   Age of school buildings
   Size of school site
   School enrollment
G. Expenditures
   Library expenditure
   Materials and supplies expenditure
   Administrative expenses
   Instructional expenditures
   Extracurricular expenditures
   Total expenditures
H. Staff
   Administrative manpower
   Auxiliary manpower

Teacher turnover
Teacher salary

Instructional Personnel

I. Teacher Background and Personal Characteristics
Percent teachers with advanced degrees
Type of undergraduate degree
Teaching experience
Verbal achievement
Race of teacher
Sex of teacher

J. Teacher Assignments
Teacher time in major
Teacher load
Teacher time in discipline

K. Teacher Attitudes
Job satisfaction

In still another meta-analysis Walberg (1984) identified nine significant factors which influence learning and which therefore relate directly to the productivity of America's schools. He identified the following factors:

Student Aptitude

1. Ability or prior achievement
2. Developmental level (age or maturation)
3. Motivation/self-concept

Instruction

4. Engaged learning time
5. Quality of instructional experience

Environmental Factors

6. Quality and quantity of home support
7. Characteristics of peer group support and interests outside school
8. Nature of classroom social group
9. Use of out-of-school time, especially TV

All of these variables must be measured in one way or another. Some lend themselves to measurement by testing, but all must be evaluated with regard to their impact on learning. The first three factors are generally unalterable, although some intervention programs have shown positive effects on student motivation and self-concept. Most of the remaining factors are heavily influenced by economics, political and social forces, and therefore to some extent are controllable. Since parents can play a significant role in enhancing and reinforcing learning it should be obvious to educators that they, educators, can't accomplish all education on their own.

Multiple correlation (regression) is a frequently used technique to examine prediction of school effectiveness. The techniques typically involve using several predictors and analyzing their independent contribution in estimating a single criterion variable. In a massive study of the achievement expectancies for 1,102 Chicago public schools, Bargen and Walberg (1974) found two major contributors to the prediction of student performance using the school as a unit of analysis at grades 4, 6, 8, and 11. These two factors were teacher quality and past student achievement. Teacher quality was indexed by salary, years of experience, verbal ability, and attitude toward teaching. After controlling for socioeconomic status these investigators calculated squared multiple correlations ranging from .67 to .94 (where the maximum = 1.00). The teacher quality factor was particularly potent at the elementary school level. In almost all studies, however, it was found—as is so often the case in life—that the best predictor of current or future achievement is past achievement.

The kinds of questions to be asked are many and varied. The varieties of variables that need to be identified, researched, and analyzed represent a significant challenge for school personnel.

Kinds of Evaluation Questions

The kinds of questions to be addressed by curriculum and program evaluators will, of course, be dictated by the information requirements of decision makers, and the nature and state of reforms or innovations that are proposed or have been implemented. Some questions might be considered *formative,* for example, how can we improve the materials used in the elementary mathematics curriculum? Or questions might be *summative* in nature, for example, should the current approach to the teaching of writing be continued? In any event the evaluation question should be based on objectives or goals. We need goals and objectives to help us frame the right evaluation questions. "If you don't know where you are going you may end up in the wrong place."

Following is a list of sample evaluation questions that might be asked. The list and kinds of questions are limited only by the creativity of the evaluator (Payne, 1982a).

Focus Category	*Sample Evaluation Question*
1. General Needs Assessment	Are the general system objectives in mathematics being met in our elementary schools?
2. Individual Needs Assessment	Are the career information needs of our graduating students being met?
3. School Services	Are our school psychological services perceived as adequate by students?
4. Curriculum Design	What effect has the implementation of the new way of organizing the mathematics courses over the school year had on student achievement?

5. Classroom Process	Are teachers following the prescribed teaching techniques in using the new Muth Affective Education Program?
6. Materials of Instruction	Is the drug abuse filmstrip/tape program more effective than the current combination of lecture and programmed materials?
7. Monitoring of Student Progress	Is our current monitoring performance and records system adequate in identifying those students in need of academic counseling?
8. Teacher Effectiveness	To what extent has teacher's verbal reinforcement techniques resulted in a decrease in student retention?
9. Learner Motivation	Has the tracking system based on post–high school aspirations resulted in changes in learner motivation?
10. Learning Environment	What changes in classroom climate, as perceived by students and faculty, have accompanied the introduction of the new position of assistant principal?
11. Staff Development	Did last week's staff-development program on creating behavioral objectives for competency-based education result in improved teacher skills?
12. Decision Making	To what extent have central office decisions in the last 24 months resulted in lower costs and improved student attitude toward school?
13. Community Involvement	Is community involvement in the instructional program a good thing?
14. Board of Education Policy	Are system policies effectively communicated to relevant personnel?
15. School Outcomes	To what extent are major cognitive, affective, and psychomotor outcomes being accomplished on a schoolwide basis?
16. Resource Allotment	Are projected allotments in the budget adequate for anticipated needs?
17. Instructional Methods	Do students have a positive attitude toward the Bennett Word Processing Program?

There is a tremendous variety of potential tasks represented here and they would require a great variety of measurement techniques. Among those would be traditional multiple-choice (or true-false and essay) achievement measures, questionnaires, surveys, attitude scales, observations, interviews, and perhaps cost-effectiveness analyses. The key to successful evaluation, however, is a systematic process.

Steps in the Evaluation Process

There will probably never be total agreement on the nature and sequence of steps in the evaluation process. The kind of evaluation questions being asked, availability of resources, and time lines are some of the factors that would dictate the final form of the process. Basically, the process boils down, with some exceptions, to an application of the "scientific method." Some evaluations might simply require the retrieval of information from records in files, while others might require pilot or field studies. Such studies might be as simple and informal as sitting with a student and listening to him or her as they work through a new unit on long division or it might be something as complex as a 20 percent sample achievement student survey study of all major physics objectives at the ninth grade level.

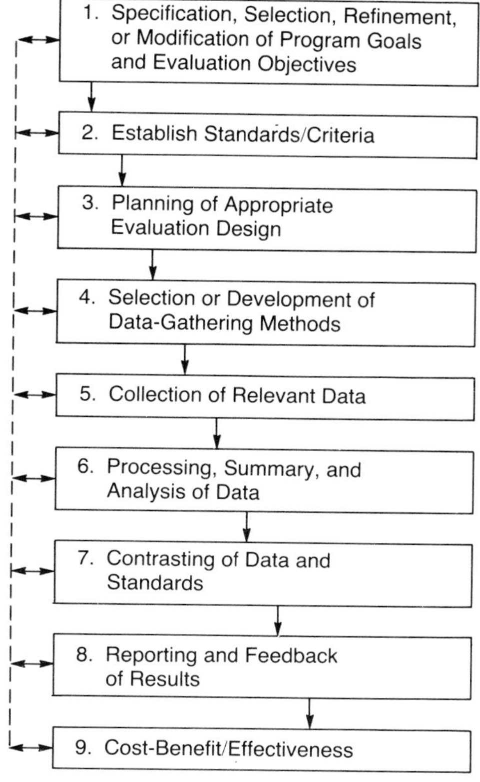

Figure 20-1

Overview of usual steps in curriculum evaluation process

Figure 20-1 contains a brief outline of the usual steps in conducting an evaluation, particularly a curriculum evaluation study. Only the major activities are identified. The dotted lines indicate that information may be shared between blocks (activities/processes), and that decisions are continuously being modified and revised. The sequence of activities in Figure 20-1 may be followed directly and exactly if summative evaluation is the role being played by evaluation, or periodically and systematically repeated if formative evaluation is the primary intent.

All of the steps are important, but one of particular interest in developing a comprehensive evaluation program is Standard Setting. The specification of criteria may be the most important part of the evaluation process. The question asked is: "On what basis do I make a value judgment?" The criteria might relate to an individual (Did Rick learn 75 percent of today's vocabulary words about plants?), or group or institution (Did 80 percent of the students in grade five in the county learn 80 percent of the capitals of 50 major countries?). We then gather data to evaluate the objectives. The reader is referred to the section on Standard Setting in Chapter 16 for further elaboration of this important topic.

Another step, but a frequently overlooked one, in the evaluation process is cost analysis. There are costs associated with effective education, both monetary costs and costs in terms of human resources. The cost-benefit question (Did it benefit the individual or society?) and cost-effectiveness question (Was the investment worth the dollars expended?) can be answered after the overall evaluation has taken place. An evaluator may be faced with the problem of finding that Method A of teaching the dangers of drug abuse is as effective as the current approach, Method B, but takes half the classroom time. Unfortunately, the data revealed that Method A costs a third again as much as Method B. Cost versus effectiveness questions are difficult to resolve.

In order to be successful evaluations must take place in a supportive environment and climate. This is critical. All the wonderful data in the world won't do any good if they aren't going to be used. Another critical factor is the skill of the evaluator. Evaluators come in all shapes and sizes. After declaring that evaluators range from the "knee-jerk conservatives" to the "wild-eyed liberals," Niehaus (1968) describes the different kinds he has observed.

> There is the myopic nit picker who seems to have an anxiety compulsion to try to measure the difference between the tickle and itch. There is the cautious creeper who is terrified at the thought of any type of innovation. There is the free swinger who arrived as his (sic) evaluation through some weird mixture of ESP and dianoetics and whose ignorance is bolstered by emotion. There is the anxiety evaluator, the worrier, who lives under a perpetual state of existential threat and who feels that if what he evaluates does not coincide with his preconceived and doctrinaire attitude, all is lost. There is the belaborer of the obvious who after a sizable expenditure of time and effort comes up with a ponderous announcement of something which has been obvious all along—something like the man who suggested, upon first viewing the Grand Canyon, "Something must have happened

here." There is also the circumstantial evaluator who uses a hundred words to do the work of one. He gets his observations wound up into such a cocoon that no one can figure out just what he is trying to communicate. (p. 333)

The "new generation" of evaluators, if they are to function effectively, must be even more generalist than their predecessors. In addition to being master of some fairly sophisticated quantitative and qualitative skills, the evaluator must be a little bit of a sociologist, economist, social psychologist, anthropologist, philosopher, and psychologist. The evaluator must be blessed with a strong self-concept, high tolerance for ambiguity, and the patience of a United Nations arbitrator.

Managing Evaluations

Evaluations don't just happen; they have to be very carefully planned. Figure 20-2 contains a diagram showing the relation between major kinds of evaluation questions and elements involved in managing the evaluation process. The left margin represents four general categories of evaluation questions. The categories are adapted from Stufflebeam's CIPP model (Stufflebeam *et al.*, 1971). A brief description of each component question category with an example follows:

Category	*Description*	*Sample Question*
Context (Goals)	Evaluation of goals, needs, and problems (needs assessment of goals)	What proportion of seventh grade students are reading at grade level?
Input (Designs)	An elaboration of the competing approaches to solving the problem or meeting the need	What are the relative advantages and disadvantages of the Pappas, Gordon, and Lynn techniques for teaching basic computational skills to at-risk elementary students?
Process (Activities)	Evaluation of the implementation of programs, activities projects, and curriculum, processes (Fidelity)	Are teachers in School A following the prescribed procedure in using the new math methods?
Product (Outcomes)	Evaluation of general and specific outcomes and products	Are scores on the eighth grade hygiene test given in the spring meaningfully higher than those obtained in the fall?

Phase / Component	Identification of Information Needs	Decision Rule Criteria	Information System Specifications	Data Collection	Data Organization & Reduction	Data Storage and Retrieval	Data Analysis	Reporting
CONTEXT To depict deficiencies in educational opportunities	Socio-economic status Current status Norms desired Mastery desired Cost-Effectiveness	Significant disparity between status and norms or desired mastery level	Sources(s) Type of Information Time Requirements Criticality Sample Requirements Quantity Accessibility	Census Data Demographic Study Standardized Tests Pupil Grades Pupil Attendance Dropout Data Attitude Survery Opinionnaire Locally constructed tests	Manual Man-Machine • general programs • special programs	Data Bank Knowledge File Machine Manual	Statistical Analysis Content Analysis Depth Study Case Study	Formal Reports Written Tabular Informal Reports Oral-group Oral-one-to-one
INPUT To acquire and assess alternative solution strategies	Available solutions to problem Data on prior trials Relationship to context	Feasibility Sufficiency Validity Viability Barriers Tensions Cost-Effectiveness	Source(s) Type of Information Time Requirements Criticality Sample Requirements Quantity Accessibility	Review of literature Interviews: LEA personnel, experts, community leaders, parents, residents Pannels, seminars, group meetings Transfer from other information centers Observations of demonstrations	Manual Man-machine • general programs • special programs	Data Bank Knowledge File Machine Manual	Statistical, Cost and Case Study Comparison of prior outcomes of alternatives Consultants for feasibility, barriers, tensions Force Field Analysis Educator jury for context, validity	Formal Reports Written Tabular Informal Reports Oral-group Oral-one-to-one
PROCESS To monitor for • a priori barriers • unanticipated problems • progress	Barriers to success Interactive tensions Problem areas Progress benchmarks	Acceptability Utilization Integration Assimilation	Source(s) Type of Information Time Requirements Criticality Sample Requirements Quantity Accessibility	Logs Observations Interviews Group Interviews Group Debriefing Other Instruments: • Attitude Scale • Acceptance Scale • Facilitant-Restraint Scale • Structured Questionnaire	Manual Man-Machine • general programs • special programs	Data Bank Knowledge File Machine Manual	Content Analysis Statistical Analysis	Formal Reports Written Tabular Informal Reports Oral-group Oral-one-to-one
PRODUCT To measure outcomes in relation to objectives	Project outcomes • achievement level • attitude • mastery • cost-effectiveness	Mastery level desired Achievement level desired Growth desired Attitude desired	Source(s) Type of Information Time Requirements Criticality Sample Requirements Quantity Accessibility	Standardized Tests Pupil Grades Attitude Scale Attendance Level Dropout Rate	Manual Man-Machine • general programs • special programs	Data Bank Knowledge File Machine Manual	Statistical Analysis • pre-post • experimental-control Population Analysis Accounting	Tabular Statistical

Figure 20-2

Evaluation management plan using CIPP question categories (Merriman, 1972)

These four categories of evaluation questions, in fact, describe four types of evaluations that logically describe a comprehensive evaluation system. They could be represented as follows:

Context	Input	Process	Product
Evaluation Goals	Evaluation Designs	Evaluation Activities	Evaluation Outcomes

These four evaluation types correspond to the previously described question categories: Goals, Designs, Activities, and Outcomes. Implementation of a program or project would usually take place between Input and Process. All four kinds of evaluations may be required in a given project, or perhaps only one type may be needed.

Across the top of Figure 20-2 are the basic operational processes employed in conducting an evaluation like those outlined in Figure 20-1. In each cell are representative activities that might be undertaken by an evaluator.

Criteria for an Effective Evaluation

After an evaluation has been completed we must evaluate it in order to determine how much confidence we can have in the results. Eleven criteria will be described that can be used to conduct an assessment of an already-completed evaluation project (a meta-evaluation). The criteria might also be used to help plan an evaluation study. Although used here in the context of program evaluation and curriculum evaluation the criteria also are directly appropriate for student evaluations. The eleven criterion categories are as follows:

Meta-evaluation Category	*Evaluation Questions*
Internal Validity	Are we sure that the treatment (or project, activity, curriculum) is the factor that will bring about the effect?
External Validity	Will results of evaluations generalize to other samples and/or situations?
Reliability	Are the data and information consistent and replicable?
Objectivity	Is there agreement on the meaning of the data?
Relevance	Are the data gathered maximally serving the purpose(s) of the evaluation?
Importance	Are the most important data being gathered relative to the needs of stakeholders?

Meta-evaluation Category	*Evaluation Questions*
Scope	Was the evaluation comprehensive and did the information represent the full spectrum required to meet decision-maker needs?
Credibility	Are the evaluation, the evaluator, and data of highest quality and do they meet highest professional and ethical standards?
Timeliness	Did or will decision makers get the data they need or will need?
Pervasiveness	Does or did everybody get the data who needs or needed it?
Efficiency	Were/are the data gathered in the most efficient manner with regard to money, time, and personnel?

It is obvious that to reach these criteria in the maximum is a very difficult task, but at least they (the criteria) represent targets toward which we can aim our evaluations. For a more comprehensive set of criteria the reader is referred to a publication by the Joint Committee on Standards for Educational Evaluation (1981).

Evaluating Instructional Materials

If instructional materials (e.g., textbooks, slide tape programs, learning activities, computer or videodisc programs), are being developed locally or by the national agencies responsible for education there exists an invaluable opportunity to conduct field tests to assess their effectiveness. The process outlined in Figure 20-1 could be used to gather data on the impact of the materials, activities, or procedures. The focus would probably be on payoff evaluation in terms of the extent to which the innovation brought about the desired effects. Many instructional materials are purchased from commercial publishers but they are more difficult to evaluate because of the interaction with the local curriculum. Whether the materials are developed in-house or by outside agencies, there are at least four major attributes that need to be looked at in order to make a preliminary assessment. They are:

Objectives: Are there actual objectives, stated in operational form, and aimed at the use of the materials? In addition, both general and instructional objectives should be available. Hopefully, the objectives flow from some relevant conceptual framework or theory. Are relevant problem-solving and creative skills addressed?

Scope and Sequence: The organization of the material should be such that it follows some conceptually developed pattern, which was based on a task analysis or other relevant research. Is a recommended sequence specified, which is responsive to a variety of individual or system needs?

Methodology: Are a variety of approaches and media used? Is the mode that is used based on a rational match of instructional intent and student readiness in the sequence? Is the methodology relatively straightforward, not requiring extensive, complicated preparation?

Student Evaluation: Are procedures provided whereby student progress and achievement may be assessed? Are the procedures available at different levels? Are the evaluation procedures compatible with the objectives and methodology?

To these attributes we might add cost, appearance, and attractiveness to student and teacher, durability and ease of production, and—if special materials are required (e.g., in science activities)—accessibility.

Evaluations can be informal and take place on a small scale. Teachers do it every day when they try out a particular activity with a particular student who is having a particular problem. They might be as extensive as the National Assessment of Educational Progress. No matter the size or cost, evaluations, if conducted efficiently and professionally, can yield results that will help improve the educational process.

Case Study Application

The measurement knowledges and skills you have developed to this point will have lasting meaning and utility only to the extent to which you are able to apply them in generating information for decision making. We can obviously use those knowledges and skills in assessing student achievement. We can also use them in building instruments to evaluate educational innovations. Let's try a hypothetical evaluation project to help reinforce both the ideas of instrument development and project evaluation.

It was a dark, rainy, overcast, dreary day when you were called into your department head's office. As head of the reading education department she had been contacted by a major instructional materials developer and solicited to serve as a field-testing site for a new set of six computer-assisted instruction modules aimed at teaching the teaching of reading techniques to prospective teachers. There are eight classes of the relevant course available next quarter. Enrollment averages about 20–25 students per class. The Dean and department head request that you take on this project (for no extra compensation as is usually the case) citing the benefits of visibility for the department and college, possible publications, and presentations at professional meetings. You meet with the developer of the computer-assisted instruction modules, department head, and Dean and evolve the following modest evaluation questions:

1. Will the new CAI reading education modules result in increased knowledge about techniques for the teaching of reading?
2. Will the new CAI reading education modules result in greater learning than the currently used traditional techniques?
3. Will the new CAI reading education modules result in positive attitudes toward computer-assisted instruction about the teaching of reading?

Try your hand at designing an evaluation project aimed at answering these questions. You may wish to outline what measures you would need and how you would go about developing them. Consider how and when you would collect data. There may be some useful ideas in Figure 20-1. In addition, the following Metaevaluation Scale for Evaluation Designs is presented for possible application while you are creating your design and then again after you have finished.

METAEVALUATION SCALE FOR EVALUATION DESIGNS (FORM B)*

	Extent to Which Standard Has Been Met (Circle)			
Context & Setting	*Low*	*Med.*	*High*	*N/A*
1. Appropriate audiences/stakeholders have been identified and involved in planning the evaluation. (U)	L	M	H	N/A
2. Evaluation is politically viable. (F)	L	M	H	N/A
3. Rights of human subjects and confidentiality issues have been addressed. (P)	L	M	H	N/A
4. Obligations of all parties involved in the evaluation have been stated formally. (P)	L	M	H	N/A
5. Potential areas of conflict of interest have been addressed. (P)	L	M	H	N/A
Evaluation Questions				
6. The purpose and object(s) of conducting the evaluation have been specified. (U)	L	M	H	N/A
7. Evaluation objectives have been specified. (U)	L	M	H	N/A
8. The most *important* information is to be gathered. (U)	L	M	H	N/A
9. Information of sufficient *scope* is to be collected. (U)	L	M	H	N/A
Design				
10. Evaluation procedures are practical. (F)	L	M	H	N/A
11. Legal constraints have been explicated. (P)	L	M	H	N/A
12. Evaluation design appears to be cost-effective. (F)	L	M	H	N/A

(continued)

	Extent to Which Standard Has Been Met (Circle)			
	Low	*Med.*	*High*	*N/A*
Sample(s)				
13. An external control unit (group, class, school) has been identified where appropriate and feasible. (F)	L	M	H	N/A
14. A data collection/management plan/diagram has been presented. (A)	L	M	H	N/A
Instrumentation				
15. Psychometric qualities of newly constructed instrumentation will be assessed. (A)	L	M	H	N/A
16. Data sources have been adequately identified. (A)	L	M	H	N/A
17. Data on validity of instrumentation have been presented. (A)	L	M	H	N/A
18. Data on reliability of instrumentation have been presented. (A)	L	M	H	N/A
Data Collection				
19. Issues of internal validity have been addressed. (A)	L	M	H	N/A
20. Sampling procedures are justified and described and the unit of analysis specified. (A)	L	M	H	N/A
21. Qualitative methods used in data collection and analysis have been described. (A)	L	M	H	N/A
22. There is sufficient control over data collection to avoid bias. (A)	L	M	H	N/A
Data Analysis				
23. Data analysis procedures have been described. (A)	L	M	H	N/A
24. Data analysis procedures are appropriate. (A)	L	M	H	N/A
Reporting				
25. Standards/framework for data interpretation have been specified. (U)	L	M	H	N/A
26. Provision has been made for reporting results to appropriate audiences. (U)	L	M	H	N/A
27. Provision has been made for utilizing evaluation results. (U)	L	M	H	N/A

*Based in part on an adaptation of *Standards for Evaluations of Educational Programs, Projects, and Materials* (McGraw-Hill, 1981).

NARRATIVE LEGEND FOR METAEVALUATION SCALE FOR EVALUATION DESIGNS

The attached metaevaluation scales for examining an evaluation design utilize four general types of criteria. The type of criterion involved in the scale is designated by a U = Utility, F = Feasibility, P = Propriety, A = Accuracy. Utility criteria or standards generally refer requirements that an evaluation yield data and practical information that is needed by the primary audiences of the evaluation. For most projects these audiences will be of two types. The first type of audience would be the local educational agency where the evaluation was implemented and where the needs analysis revealed the deficiency leading to the adopting or adapting of an educational innovation. This innovation might be a specific prescribed procedure such as the XYZ method of teaching reading or a process whereby a new method could be developed or process evolved, for example, improving school climate. The second type of audience would be a funding agency (public or private) which supported the development of the innovation. In this sense the funding agency serves as a surrogate for the public and the educational profession.

The second general category of criteria, Feasibility, contains standards that are aimed at insuring that the evaluation will be realistic, prudent, diplomatic, and frugal.

The third standards category, Propriety, is used to describe standards that focus on the legal, ethical, and general concerns for human welfare and rights of the individual. Invasion of privacy and confidentiality are of paramount concern.

The Accuracy standards reflect the typical and traditional technical requirements for sound evaluation. These criteria include such basic considerations as instrument reliability and validity, and adequacy and appropriateness of data analysis and reporting.

The metaevaluation scale has two forms. Form A is organized around the four standards just described. Form B collects the items under the usual elements of an evaluation design: Context and Setting, Evaluation Questions, Designs, Samples, Instrumentation, Data Collection, and Data Analysis.

An "Evaluation Adequacy Score" is derived by (a) converting judgments about standards to ratings (L = 1, M = 2, H = 3, N/A = does not get included), (b) adding the ratings (excluding the N/A), and (c) dividing the sum in "b" by 3 × the number of items receiving a rating other than N/A.

Content Review Statements

1. Society's changing needs have resulted in changing requirements of our schools.
2. Measurement and evaluation are aids to decision making.
3. Measurement and evaluation are increasingly being used to meet the needs of accountability.

4. Curriculum evaluation data can help:
   a. Improve educational experiences
   b. In the comparisons of alternative programs
   c. Us understand factors which contribute to educational success
5. Curriculum evaluation differs from research with regard to:
   a. Nature of goals—more process-oriented
   b. Breadth of objectives—greater variety
   c. Complexity of outcomes—more involved
   d. Form/Intent—decision oriented
   e. Context—naturalistic setting
6. Curriculum evaluation is the process of collecting, processing, summarizing, assessing the merits, and reporting effectiveness data.
7. Total school effectiveness is significantly influenced by such factors as:
   a. Student ability
   b. Instructional quality
   c. Sociodemographic variables
   d. School conditions
8. Steps in the evaluation process include
   a. Goal specification
   b. Standard setting
   c. Designing
   d. Instrumentation
   e. Data collection
   f. Data processing
   g. Interpretation
   h. Reporting
   i. Cost analyses
9. Evaluations can focus on curriculum or program:
   a. Goals (Context)
   b. Designs (Input)
   c. Activities (Process)
   d. Outcomes (Product)
10. Evaluation quality should be judged against criteria related to:
   a. Internal validity
   b. External validity
   c. Objectivity
   d. Relevance
   e. Importance
   f. Scope
   g. Credibility
   h. Timeliness
   i. Persuasiveness
   j. Efficiency
   k. Reliability

11. Instructional materials should be evaluated with regard to their:
    a. Objectives
    b. Scope and sequence
    c. Methodology
    d. Provision for evaluation

Speculations

1. Where should the standards for evaluating school effectiveness come from?
2. What does metaevaluation mean and what are its components?
3. What are the usual steps in the evaluation process?
4. What does CIPP stand for? Translate CIPP into a personal professional application.
5. What are the main factors to be considered in evaluating instructional materials?

Suggested Readings

Kosecoff, J., & Fink, A. (1987). *Evaluation basics: A practitioner's manual.* Beverly Hills, CA: Sage.

Patton, M. Q. (1986). *Utilization-focused evaluation.* Beverly Hills, CA: Sage. Light, but right on target. If the results aren't used it was a meaningless evaluation.

Popham, W. J. (1988). *Educational evaluation* (Second Edition). Englewood Cliffs, NJ: Prentice Hall. Who said textbooks can't be informative as well as entertaining?

Stufflebeam, D. L., *et al.* (1971). *Educational evaluation and decision making.* Itasca, IL.: F. E. Peacock. This reference is for the student who *really* wants to find out about the CIPP evaluation model.

Talmage, H. (1982). Evaluation of programs. In H. E. Mitzel (Ed.), *Encyclopedia of educational research* (Fifth Edition) (pp. 592–611). New York: Free Press. A nice succinct overview of the general dimensions of program evaluation.

Worthen, B. R., & Sanders, J. R. (1987). *Educational evaluation (Alternative approaches and practical guidelines).* New York: Longman. Lots of very useful suggestions, checklists, and advice on how to do it.

Bev's Diary

Well, it's over! The final exam and project actually weren't too bad. The exam seemed to be relevant and balanced, and was a fair test. I had plenty of time to finish the exam and review my answers. Just listen to yourself—you're talking that "text talk." Maybe that isn't so bad; it must mean I learned something. I internalized a lot of information. Oops, there's one of those text terms again. You know a secret, Diary, I actually enjoyed most of it. If nothing else, you learn to appreciate how much effort needs to go into making a good test, and what a positive influence it can have on teaching and learning. Well, what will the end-of-course limerick be? How about this?

> I once thought all tests were most pitiful
> And taking them an experience most unmerciful
> But I studied this fine text
> Learning each chapter and next
> I began to see them as really most helpful.

And you know another secret, Diary, I might even take an advanced measurement course. Please don't tell anybody!

Appendix A

Normal Deviates (z) Corresponding to Proportions (*p*) and Products (*pq*) of a Dichotomized Unit Normal Distribution

Proportion (*p*)*	Deviate (*z*)	*pq*	Proportion (*p*)*	Deviate (*z*)	*pq*
.99	2.326	.0099	.49	− .025	.2499
.98	2.054	.0196	.48	− .050	.2496
.97	1.881	.0291	.47	− .075	.2491
.96	1.751	.0384	.46	− .100	.2484
.95	1.645	.0977	.45	− .126	.2475
.94	1.555	.0564	.44	− .151	.2464
.93	1.476	.0651	.43	− .176	.2451
.92	1.405	.0736	.42	− .202	.2436
.91	1.341	.0819	.41	− .228	.2419
.90	1.282	.0900	.40	− .253	.2400
.89	1.227	.0979	.39	− .279	.2379
.88	1.175	.1056	.38	− .305	.2356
.87	1.126	.1131	.37	− .332	.2331
.86	1.080	.1204	.36	− .358	.2304
.85	1.036	.1275	.35	− .385	.2275
.84	.994	.1344	.34	− .412	.2244
.83	.954	.1411	.33	− .440	.2211
.82	.915	.1476	.32	− .468	.2176
.81	.878	.1539	.31	− .496	.2139
.80	.842	.1600	.30	− .524	.2100
.79	.806	.1659	.29	− .553	.2059
.78	.772	.1716	.28	− .583	.2016
.77	.739	.1771	.27	− .613	.1971
.76	.706	.1824	.26	− .643	.1924
.75	.674	.1875	.25	− .674	.1875

Proportion (p)*	Deviate (z)	pq	Proportion (p)*	Deviate (z)	pq
.74	.643	.1924	.24	− .706	.1824
.73	.613	.1971	.23	− .739	.1771
.72	.583	.2016	.22	− .772	.1716
.71	.553	.2059	.21	− .806	.1659
.70	.524	.2100	.20	− .842	.1600
.69	.496	.2139	.19	− .878	.1539
.68	.468	.2176	.18	− .915	.1476
.67	.440	.2211	.17	− .954	.1411
.66	.412	.2244	.16	− .994	.1344
.65	.385	.2275	.15	−1.036	.1275
.64	.358	.2304	.14	−1.080	.1204
.63	.332	.2331	.13	−1.126	.1131
.62	.305	.2356	.12	−1.175	.1056
.61	.279	.2379	.11	−1.227	.0979
.60	.253	.2400	.10	−1.282	.0900
.59	.228	.2419	.09	−1.341	.0819
.58	.202	.2436	.08	−1.405	.0736
.57	.176	.2451	.07	−1.476	.0651
.56	.151	.2464	.06	−1.555	.0564
.55	.126	.2475	.05	−1.645	.0475
.54	.100	.2484	.04	−1.751	.0384
.53	.075	.2491	.03	−1.881	.0291
.52	.050	.2496	.02	−2.054	.0196
.51	.025	.2499	.01	−2.326	.0096
.50	.000	.2500	.00	0.000	.0000

*Can also be read as q, where $q = 1 - p$.

Appendix B

Relationships Among *T* scores, z scores, and Percentile Ranks When Raw Scores Are Normally Distributed

z Score	*T* Score	Percentile Rank	z Score	*T* Score	Percentile Rank
3.0	80	99.9	−3.0	20	0.1
2.9	79	99.8	−2.9	21	0.2
2.8	78	99.7	−2.8	22	0.3
2.7	77	99.6	−2.7	23	0.4
2.6	76	99.5	−2.6	24	0.5
2.5	75	99.4	−2.5	25	0.6
2.4	74	99.2	−2.4	26	0.8
2.3	73	99	−2.3	27	1
2.2	72	99	−2.2	28	1
2.1	71	98	−2.1	29	2
2.0	70	98	−2.0	30	2
1.9	69	97	−1.9	31	3
1.8	68	96	−1.8	32	4
1.7	67	96	−1.7	33	4
1.6	66	95	−1.6	34	5
1.5	65	93	−1.5	35	7
1.4	64	92	−1.4	36	8
1.3	63	90	−1.3	37	10
1.2	62	88	−1.2	38	12
1.1	61	86	−1.1	39	14
1.0	60	84	−1.0	40	16
0.9	59	82	−0.9	41	18
0.8	58	79	−0.8	42	21
0.7	57	76	−0.7	43	24
0.6	56	73	−0.6	44	27

z Score	*T* Score	Percentile Rank	*z* Score	*T* Score	Percentile Rank
0.5	55	69	−0.5	45	31
0.4	54	66	−0.4	46	34
0.3	53	62	−0.3	47	38
0.2	52	58	−0.2	48	42
0.1	51	54	−0.1	49	46
0.0	50	50	0.0	50	50

Appendix C

Selective List of Test Publishers

Addison-Wesley Publishing Company, 2725 Sand Hill Road, Menlo Park, CA 94025
American College Testing Program, P.O. Box 168, Iowa City, IA 52240
American Guidance Service, Publishers' Building, Circle Pines, MN 55014
American Testronics, P.O. Box 2270, Iowa City, IA 52244
Bobbs-Merrill Company, P.O. Box 7080, 4300 West 62nd St., Indianapolis, IN 46268
William C. Brown Co., 2460 Kerper Blvd., Dubuque, IA 52007
California Test Bureau/McGraw-Hill, Del Monte Research Park, Monterey, CA 93940
Committee on Diagnostic Reading Tests, Mountain Home, NC 28758
Consulting Psychologists Press, 577 College Avenue, Palo Alto, CA 94306
Educational and Industrial Testing Service, P.O. Box 7234, San Diego, CA 92107
Educational Testing Service, Princeton, NJ 08540
Houghton Mifflin Company, One Beacon Street, Boston, MA 02107
IOX Assessment Associates, Instructional Objectives Exchange, P.O. Box 24095, Los Angeles, CA 90025
Institute for Personality and Ability Testing, 1602 Coronado Drive, Champaign, IL 61820
Jastak Associates, Inc., P.O. Box 4460, Wilmington, DE 19807
Macmillan Publishing Co., 866 Third Ave., New York, NY 10022
National Computer Systems, P.O Box 1416, Minneapolis, MN 55400
Personnel Press, 20 Nassau Street, Princeton, NJ 08540
Psychological Assessment Resources, P.O. Box 98, Odessa, FL 33556
Psychological Corporation, 555 Academic Court, San Antonio, TX 78204-0952
Riverside Publishing Company, 8420 Bryn Mawr Avenue, Chicago, IL 60631
Scholastic Testing Service, 480 Meyer Road, Bensenville, IL 60106
Science Research Associates, 155 North Wacker Dr., Chicago, IL 60606
Scott, Foresman, 44 East Erie St., Chicago, IL 60025

Sheridan Psychological Services, P.O. Box 6101, Orange, CA 92667
Slosson Educational Publishers, P.O. Box 280, East Aurora, NY 14052
Stanford University Press, Stanford, CA 94305
Stoelting Co., 1350 S. Kostner Avenue, Chicago, IL 60623
Teachers College Press, 1234 Amsterdam Avenue, New York, NY 10027
Western Psychological Services, 12031 Wilshire Boulevard, Los Angeles, CA 90025

References

Aaron, R. L., & Gillespie, C. (1990). Gates-MacGinitie reading tests (3rd ed.). In R. B. Cuder, Jr. (Ed.), *The teacher's guide to reading tests.* Gorsuch Scarisbrick, Scottsdale, AZ.

Adams, G. S. (1964). *Measurement and evaluation in education, psychology, and guidance.* New York: Holt, Rinehart & Winston.

Aiken, L. R. (1988). *Psychological testing and assessment* (6th ed.). Boston: Allyn and Bacon.

Airasian, P. W., & Madaus, G. F. (1972). Functional types of student evaluation. *Measurement Evaluation in Guidance, 4,* 221–233.

Airasian, P. W., & Madaus, G. F. (1983). Linking testing and instruction: Policy issues. *Journal of Educational Measurement, 20*(2), 103–118.

Alderman, D. L., & Powers, D. E. (1979). *The effects of special preparation on SAT-Verbal scores.* Research Report RR-79-1, Princeton, NJ: College Entrance Examination Board.

Alkin, M. C. (1972). Accountability defined. *Evaluation Comment, 3*(3), 1–5. Los Angeles: University of California at Los Angeles Center for the Study of Evaluation.

Allen, G. J., Elias, M. J., & Zlotlow, S. F. (1980). Behavioral interventions for alleviating test anxiety: A methodological overview of current therapeutic practices. In I. G. Sarason (Ed.), *Test anxiety: Theory, research and application* (pp. 150–186) Hillsdale, NJ: Lawrence Erlbaum.

Allport, G. W. (1962). *The use of personal documents in psychological science.* New York: Social Science Research Council.

Allport, G. W., Vernon, P. E., & Lindzey, G. (1970). *A study of values.* Boston: Houghton Mifflin.

American Psychological Association. (1981). Ethical principles of psychologists. *American Psychologist, 36*(6), 633–638.

American Psychological Association. (1986). *Guidelines for computer-based tests and interpretations.* Washington, DC: APA.

American Psychological Association, American Educational Research Association,

& National Council on Measurement in Education. (1985). *Standards for educational and psychological testing.* Washington, DC: American Psychological Association.

Amidon, E. J., & Hough, J. B. (Eds.) (1967). *Interaction analysis: Theory, research and application.* Reading, MA: Addison-Wesley.

Anastasi, A. (1988). *Psychological testing* (6th ed.). New York: Macmillan.

Anderson, L. W. (1981). *Assessing affective characteristics in the schools.* Boston: Allyn and Bacon.

Angoff, W. H. (1971). Scales, norms and equivalent scores. In R. L. Thorndike (Ed.), *Educational measurement* (2nd ed.) (pp. 508–600). Washington, DC: American Council on Education.

Angoff, W. H., & Anderson, S. B. (1963 February). The standardization of educational and psychological tests. *Illinois Journal of Education,* 19–23.

Anrig, G. R. (1987). ETS on "Golden Rule." *Educational Measurement: Issues and Practice, 6*(3), 24–27.

Applebee, A. N., Langer, J. A., & Mullis, I. V. S. (1989). *Crossroads in American education.* Princeton, NJ: Educational Testing Service.

Atkin, J. M. (1968). Behavioral objectives in curriculum design: A cautionary note. *The Science Teacher,* 35 (May), 27–39.

Atkinson, J. W. (1958). Towards experimental analysis of human motivation in terms of motives, expectancies, and incentives. In J. W. Atkinson (Ed.) *Motives in fantasy, action, and society* (pp. 288–305). Princeton, NJ: D. Van Nostrand.

Bahrick, H. P. (1964). Retention curves: Facts or artifacts? *Psychological Bulletin,* 61, 188–194.

Baker v. *Columbus Municipal Separate School District* (1971). 329 F. Supp. 706 (N.D. Miss).

Bangert-Downs, R. L., Kulik, J. A., & Kulik, C. C. (1983). Effects of coaching programs on achievement performance. *Review of Educational Research,* 53(4), 571–585.

Bargen, M., & Walberg, H. J. (1974). School performance. In H. J. Walberg (Ed.). *Evaluating educational performance* (pp. 239–254). Berkeley, CA: McCutchan.

Bass, R. K., & Dills, C. R. (Eds.) (1984). *Instructional development: The state of the art II.* Dubuque, IA: Kendall/Hunt.

Bassham, H., Murphy, M., & Murphy, K. (1964). Attitude and achievement in arithmetic. *The Arithmetic Teacher,* 11, 66–72.

Bauernfeind, R. F. (1967). Goal cards and future developments in achievement testing. *Proceedings of the 1966 Invitational Conference on Testing Problems.* Princeton, NJ: Educational Testing Service.

Beatty, L. S., Madden, R., Gardner, E. F., & Karlsen, B. (1984). *Stanford diagnostic mathematics test* (3rd ed.). San Antonio, TX: The Psychological Corporation.

Berk, R. A. (Ed.) (1982). *Handbook of methods for detecting test bias.* Baltimore: Johns Hopkins University Press.

Berk, R. A. (1986a). A consumer's guide to setting performance standards on criterion-referenced tests. *Review of Educational Research, 56*(1), 137–172.

Berk, R. A. (Ed.) (1986b). *Performance assessment: Methods and applications.* Baltimore: Johns Hopkins University Press.

Bersoff, D. N. (1981). Testing and the law. *American Psychologist, 36*(10), 1047–1066.

Bledsoe, J. C. (1972). *Essentials of educational research* (2nd ed.). Athens, GA: Optima House.

Block, J. (1965). *The challenge of response sets.* New York: Appleton-Century-Crofts.

Bloom, B. S. (Ed.) (1956). *Taxonomy of educational objectives. Handbook I: The cognitive domain.* New York: David McKay.

Bloom, B. S. (1970). Toward a theory of testing which includes measurement-evaluation-assessment. In M. C. Wittrock & D. E. Wiley (Eds.), *The evaluation of instruction: Issues and problems* (pp. 25–69). New York: Holt, Rinehart & Winston.

Bond, L. (1981). Bias in mental tests. In B. F. Green (Ed.) *New directions for testing and measurement: Issues in testing—coaching, disclosure and ethnic bias,* No. 11 (pp. 55–77). San Francisco: Jossey-Bass.

Bonney, M. E., & Hampleman, R. S. (1962). *Personal-social evaluation techniques.* Washington, DC: Center for Applied Research in Education.

Borman, W. C. (1986). Behavior-based rating scales. In R. A. Berk (Ed.), *Performance assessment: Methods and applications* (pp. 100–120). Baltimore: Johns Hopkins University Press.

Bracey, G. W. (1987). Measurement-driven instruction: Catchy phrase, dangerous practice. *Phi Delta Kappan, 68*(9), 683–686.

Brennan, R. L. (1983). *Elements of generalizability theory.* Iowa City, IA: American College Testing Program.

Brophy, J. E., & Good, T. L. (1986). Teacher behavior and student achievement. In M. C. Wittrock (Ed.), *Handbook of research on teaching* (3rd. ed.) (pp. 328–375). New York: Macmillan.

Broudy, H. S. (1970). Can research escape the dogma of behavioral objectives? *School Review, 79,* 43–56.

Bunderson, C. V., Inouye, D. K., & Olsen, J. B. (1989). The four generations of computerized educational measurement. In R. L. Linn (Ed.), *Educational measurement* (3rd. ed.) (pp. 367–407). Washington, DC: American Council on Education/Macmillan.

Caldwell, O. W., & Courtis, S. A. (1971). *Then and now in education: 1845–1923.* New York: Arno Press. (Original work published 1925.)

Campbell, D. T., & Fiske, D. W. (1959). Convergent and discriminant validation by the multitrait-multimethod matrix. *Psychological Bulletin, 56,* 81–105.

Cannell, J. J. (1988). Nationally normed achievement testing in America's public schools: How all 50 states are above the national average. *Educational Measurement: Issues and Practice, 7*(2), 5–9.

Cattell, R. B., Heist, A. B., & Stewart, R. G. (1950). The objective measurement of dynamic traits. *Educational and Psychological Measurement, 10,* 224–248.

Chase, C. I. (1983). Essay test scores and reading difficulty. *Journal of Educational Measurement, 20*(3), 293–297.

Chase, C. I. (1986). Essay test scoring: Interaction of relevant variables. *Journal of Educational Measurement, 23*(1), 33–41.

Chivdo, J. J. (1987). The effects of exam anxiety on grandma's health. *The Education Digest, 52,* 45–47.

Chunn, K., Cobb, S., & French, R. P., Jr. (1975). *Measures for psychological assessment.* Ann Arbor, MI: Survey Research Center, University of Michigan.

Churchman, C. W. (1959). Why measure? In C. W. Churchman & P. Ratoosh (Eds.), *Measurement definitions and theories* (pp. 83–94). New York: John Wiley & Sons.

Cohen, J. (1960). A coefficient of agreement for nominal scales. *Educational and Psychological Measurement, 20*(1), 37–46.

Cole, N. S., & Moss, P. A. (1989). Bias in test use. In R. L. Linn (Ed.), *Educational measurement* (3rd ed.) (pp. 201–219). New York: Macmillan.

Conoley, J. C., & Kramer, J. J. (Eds.) (1989). *The tenth mental measurement yearbook.* Lincoln: University of Nebraska Press.

Cook, W. W. (1951). The functions of measurement in the facilitation of learning, E. F. Lindquist (Ed.), *Educational measurement.* Washington DC: American Council on Education.

Corey, S. M. (1937). Professed attitudes and actual behavior. *Journal of Educational Psychology, 38,* 271–280.

Corey, S. M. (1943). Measuring attitudes in the classroom. *Elementary School Journal, 43,* 437–461.

Cottle, W. C. (1966). *School interest inventory.* Boston: Houghton Mifflin.

Cottle, W. C. (1968). *Interest and personality inventories.* Boston: Houghton Mifflin.

Cox, R. C. (1971). Evaluation aspects of criterion-referenced measures. In W. J. Popham (Ed.), *Criterion-referenced measurement: An introduction* (pp. 67–75). Englewood Cliffs, NJ: Educational Technology Publications.

Cox, R. C., & Graham, G. T. (1966). The development of sequentially scaled achievement tests. *Journal of Educational Measurement, 3,* 147–150.

Cox, R. C., & Vargas, J. S. (1966). A comparison of item selection techniques for norm-referenced and criterion-referenced tests. Paper read at annual meeting of the National Council on Measurement in Education, Chicago: ERIC Microfilm ED010517.

Cox, R. C., & Wildemann, C. E. (1970). *Taxonomy of educational objectives: Cognitive domain—An annotated bibliography.* Pittsburgh: University of Pittsburgh, Learning Research and Development Center Monograph No. 1.

Crocker, L., & Algina, J. (1986). *Introduction to classical and modern test theory.* New York: Holt, Rinehart & Winston.

Cronbach, L. J. (1946). Response sets and test validity. *Educational and Psychological Measurement, 6,* 475–494.

Cronbach, L. J. (1950). Further evidence on response sets and test design. *Educational and Psychological Measurement, 10,* 3–31.

Cronbach, L. J. (1951). Coefficient alpha and the internal structure of tests. *Psychometriks, 16,* 297–334.

Cronbach, L. J. (1960). *Essentials of psychological testing* (2nd ed.). New York: Harper & Row.

Cronbach, L. J. (1963). *Educational psychology,* (2nd ed.). New York: Harcourt Brace Jovanovich.

Cronbach, L. J. (1971). Test validation. In R. L. Thorndike (Ed.), *Educational measurement* (pp. 443–507). Washington, DC: American Council on Education.

Cronbach, L. J. (1990). *Essentials of psychological testing,* (5th ed.). New York: Harper & Row.

Cronbach, L. J., Gleser, G. C., Nanda, H., & Rajaratnan, N. (1972). *The dependability of behavioral measurements: Theory of generalizability for scores and profiles.* New York: John Wiley & Sons.

Cronbach, L. J., & Meehl, P. E. (1955). Construct validity in psychological tests. *Psychological Bulletin, 52,* 281–302.

Crooks, T. J. (1988). The impact of classroom evaluation practices on students. *Review of Educational Research, 58*(4), 438–481.

Cross, L., & Frary, R. (1977). An empirical test of Lord's theoretical results regarding formula scoring of multiple-choice tests. *Journal of Educational Measurement, 14,* 313–321.

Cross, L. H., Impara, J. C., Frary, R. B., & Jaeger, R. M. (1984). A comparison of three methods for establishing minimum standards on the National Teacher Examination. *Journal of Educational Measurement, 21,* 113–130.

Crowne, D. P., & Marlowe, E. (1960). A new scale of social desirability independent of psychopathology. *Journal of Consulting Psychology, 24,* 349–354.

Crowne, D. P., & Marlowe, E. (1964). *The approval motive.* New York: John Wiley & Sons.

CTB/McGraw-Hill (1987). *Comprehensive tests of basic skills.* Monterey, CA: CTB/McGraw-Hill.

CTB/McGraw-Hill (1988). *California diagnostic reading tests.* Monterey, CA: CTB/McGraw-Hill.

CTB/McGraw-Hill (1990). *Early childhood system.* Del Monte Research Park, Monterey, CA.: CTB/McGraw-Hill.

Cureton, E. E. (1960). The rearrangement test. *Educational and Psychological Measurement, 20,* 31–35.

Cureton, E. E. (1966). Kuder-Richardson reliabilities of classroom tests. *Educational and Psychological Measurement, 26,* 13–14.

Cureton, E. E., Cook, J. A., Fischer, R. T., Laser, S. A., Rockwell, N. J., & Simmons, J. W., Jr. (1973). Length of test and standard error of measurement. *Educational and Psychological Measurement, 33,* 63–68.

Cureton, L. W. (1971). The history of grading practices. *National Council on Measurement in Education: Measurement News, 2* (Whole No. 4).

Debra P. v. *Turlington* (1979). 474 F. Supp. 244 (M.D. Fla.).

Debra P. v. *Turlington* (1984). F. Suppl. No. 83-3326.

Deri, S., Dinnerstein, D., Harding, J., & Pepitone, A. D. (1948). Techniques for the diagnosis and measurement of intergroup behavior. *Psychological Bulletin, 45,* 248–271.

Dick, W., & Carey, L. (1990). *The systematic design of instruction* (3rd ed.). Glenview, IL: Scott, Foresman/Little, Brown.

Diedrich, P. B. (1964). *Short-cut statistics for teacher-made tests* (2nd ed.). Evaluation and Advisory Service Series, Pamphlet no. 5. Princeton, NJ: Educational Testing Service.

Directory of selected national testing programs (1987). Phoenix, AZ: Oryx Press.

Domino, G. (1971). Interactive effects of achievement orientation and teaching style on academic achievement. *Journal of Educational Psychology, 62,* 427–431.

Dressel, P. L. (1954). Evaluation as instruction. In *Proceedings of the 1953 invitational conference on testing problems.* Princeton, NJ: Educational Testing Service.

Dressel, P. L. (1960). Measurement and evaluation of instructional objectives. In *Seventeenth Yearbook of the National Council on Measurements Used in Education,* 1–6. New York: NCME.

DuBois, P. H. (1970). *A history of psychological testing.* Boston: Allyn and Bacon.

Dunning, G. M. (1954). Evaluation of critical thinking. *Science Education, 38,* 191–193.

Dusek, J. B. (1980). The development of test anxiety in children. In I. G. Sarason (Ed.), *Test anxiety: Theory, research and application.* Hillsdale, NJ: Lawrence Erlbaum.

Dyer, H. S. (1967). The discovery and development of educational goals. In *Proceedings of the 1966 Invitational Conference on Testing Problems.* 12–24. Princeton, NJ: Educational Testing Service.

Ebel, R. L. (1956). Obtaining and reporting evidence on content validity. *Educational and Psychological Measurement, 16,* 269–282.

Ebel, R. L. (1965). *Measuring educational achievement.* Englewood Cliffs, NJ: Prentice Hall.

Ebel, R. R., & Frisbee, D. A. (1991). *Essentials of educational measurement.* (5th ed.). Englewood Cliffs, NJ: Prentice Hall.

Educational testing service test collection catalogs (1989). Phoenix, AZ: Oryx Press.

Edwards, A. L. (1957a). *The social desirability variable in personality assessment and research.* New York: Dryden.

Edwards, A. L. (1957b). *Techniques of attitude scale construction.* New York: Appleton-Century-Crofts.

Eisner, E. W. (1967). Educational objectives: Help or hindrance? *School Review, 75,* (3), 250–260.

Embretson, S. E. (Ed.) (1985). *Test design: Developments in psychology and psychometrics.* New York: Academic Press.

English, H. B., & English, A. (1958). *A comprehensive dictionary of psychological and psychoanalytical terms.* New York: Longman.

Equal Employment Opportunity Commission (EEOC) (1966, 1970, 1978). Washington, DC: EEOC.

Evertson, C. M., & Green, J. L. (1986). Observation as inquiry and method. In

M. C. Wittrock (Ed.), *Handbook of research on teaching* (3rd ed.) (pp. 162–213). New York: Macmillan.

Eyde, L. D., Moreland, K. L., & Robertson, G. J. (1988). *Test user qualifications: A data-based approach to promoting good test use.* Washington, DC: Science Directorate, American Psychological Association.

Fabiano, E. (1989). *Index to tests used in educational dissertations.* Phoenix, AZ: Oryx Press.

Farquhar, W. W., & Payne, D. A. (1963). Factors in the academic-occupational motivations of eleventh grade under- and over-achievers. *Personnel and Guidance Journal, 42*(3), 245–251.

Fisher, T. H. (1980). The courts and your minimum competency testing program—A guide to survival. *Measurement in Education, 11*(1), 1–12.

Fitzpatrick, R., & Morrison, E. J. (1971). Performance and product evaluation. In E. L. Thorndike (Ed.), *Educational measurement* (2nd ed.) (pp. 237–270). Washington, DC: American Council on Education.

Flanagan, J. C. (1937). A proposed procedure for increasing the efficiency of objective tests. *Journal of Educational Psychology, 28,* 17–21.

Flanagan, J. C. (1951). Units, scores, and norms. In E. F. Lindquist (Ed.), *Educational measurement* (pp. 695–763). Washington, DC: American Council on Education.

Frisbee, D. A., & Friedman, S. J. (1987). Test standards—Some implications for the measurement curriculum. *Educational Measurement: Issues and Practices, 6*(3), 17–23.

Furst, E. J. (1981). Bloom's Taxonomy of Educational Objectives for the Cognitive Domain: Philosophical and educational issues. *Review of Educational Research, 51*(4), 441–453.

Gagné, R. M. (1985). *The conditions of learning.* New York: Holt, Rinehart & Winston.

Gagné, R. M., & Briggs, L. J. (1979). *Principles of instructional design* (2nd ed.). New York: Holt, Rinehart & Winston.

Gallagher, C. E. (1965). Why house hearings on invasion of privacy? *American Psychologist, 20*(11), 881–882.

Galton, M. (1987). Structured observation. In M. J. Dunkin (Ed.), *International encyclopedia of teaching and teacher education* (pp. 142–146). Elmsford, NY: Pergamon.

Gardner, E. F., & Thompson, G. G. (1963). *Investigation and measurement of the social values governing interpersonal relations among adolescent youth and their teachers.* U.S. Office of Education Cooperative Research Project 259A (8418).

Geisinger, K. F. (1982). Marking systems. In H. E. Mitzel (Ed.), *Encyclopedia of educational research* (5th ed.) (pp. 1135–1149). New York: Macmillan.

Ginsburg, A. L., Noell, J., & Plisko, V. W. (1988). Lessons from the wall chart. *Educational Evaluation and Policy Analysis, 10*(1), 1–12.

Glaser, R. W. (1963). Instructional technology and the measurement of learning outcomes: Some questions. *American Psychologist, 18,* 519–521.

Glasman, N. S., & Biniaminov, I. (1981). Input-output analyses of schools. *Review of Educational Research, 51*(4), 509–539.

Glassey, W. (1945). The attitude of grammar school pupils and their parents to education, religion, and sport. *British Journal of Educational Psychology, 15,* 101–104.

Gold, R. M., Reilly, A., Silberman, R., & Lehr, R. (1971). Academic achievement declines under pass-fail grading. *Journal of Experimental Education, 39,* 17–21.

Golden Rule Insurance Co. et al. v. *Washburn et al.* (1984). No. 419-76 (Ill, 7th Jud. Cir.).

Goldman, B. A., Saunders, J. L., & Busch, J. C. (Eds.), (1974–1982). *Directory of unpublished experimental measures.* (Vols. 1–3). New York: Human Sciences Press.

Goldman, L. (1961). *Using tests in counseling.* New York: Appleton-Century-Crofts.

Gorow, F. F. (1966). *Better classroom testing.* San Francisco: Chandler.

Green, J. A. (1970). *Introduction to measurement and evaluation.* New York: Dodd, Mead.

Greenbaum, W., Garet, M. S., & Solomon, E. R. (1977). *Measuring educational progress: A study of the national assessment.* New York: McGraw-Hill.

Griggs v. *Duke Power Co.* (1968). 292 F. Supp. 243 (MD NC).

Gronlund, N. E., & Linn, R. L. (1990). *Measurement and evaluation in teaching* (6th ed.). New York: Macmillan.

Guba, E. G. (1969). Significant differences. *Educational Researcher, 20,* 4–5.

Guerin, G. R., & Maier, A. S. (1983). *Informal assessment in education.* Palo Alto, CA: Mayfield.

Guilford, J. P. (1954). *Psychometric methods.* (2nd ed.). New York: McGraw-Hill.

Guilford, J. P., & Fruchter, B. (1978). *Fundamental statistics in psychology and education* (6th ed.). New York: McGraw-Hill.

Guion, R. M. (1965). *Personnel testing.* New York: McGraw-Hill.

Gulliksen, H. (1950). *Theory of mental tests.* New York: John Wiley & Sons.

Haney, W. (1981). Validity, vaudeville, and values: A short history of social concerns over standardized testing. *American Psychologist, 36,* 1021–1034.

Harmon, L. W. (1989). Counseling. In R. L. Linn (Ed.), *Educational measurement* (3rd ed.) (pp. 527–544). New York: American Council on Education/Macmillan.

Harrow, A. J. (1972). *A taxonomy of the psychomotor domain.* New York: David McKay.

Hawes, G. R. (1972, April). Twelve sound ways to announce test results. *Nations Schools, 89*(4), 45–52.

Hayward, P. (1968). Evaluating diagnostic reading tests. *The Reading Teacher, 21*(6), 523–528.

Heath, D. H. (1972). Aesthetics and discipline. *School Review, 80*(3), 353–371.

Heath, R. W. (1969). Curriculum evaluation. In R. L. Ebel (Ed.), *Encyclopedia of educational research* (4th ed.) (pp. 280–283). New York: Macmillan.

Helmstadter, G. C. (1964). *Principles of psychological measurement.* New York: Appleton-Century-Crofts.

Hively, W. (1974). Introduction to domain referenced testing. *Educational Technology, 14,* 5–9.

Hively, W., Patterson, H. S., & Page, S. H. (1968). A universe-defined system of arithmetic achievement tests. *Journal of Educational Measurement, 5*(4), 275–290.

Holmen, M. G., & Docter, R. F. (1972). *Educational psychological testing: A study of the industry and its practices.* New York: Russell Sage Foundation.

Holmes, C. T. (1989). Grade level retention effects: A meta-analysis of research studies. In L. A. Shepard & M. L. Smith (Eds.), *Flunking grades: Research and policies on retention* (pp. 16–33). London: Falmer Press.

Hoover, H. D. (1984). The most appropriate scores for measuring educational development in the elementary schools: GE's. *Educational Measurement: Issues and Practice, 3*(4), 8–14.

Hopkins, C. D., & Antes, R. L. (1990). *Classroom measurement and evaluation* (3rd ed.). Itasca, IL: Peacock.

Hopkins, K. D., Stanley, J. C., & Hopkins, B. R. (1990). *Educational and psychological measurement and evaluation.* Englewood Cliffs, NJ: Prentice Hall.

Jaeger, R. M. (1989). Certification of student competence. In R. L. Linn (Ed.), *Educational measurement* (3rd ed.) (pp. 485–514). New York: Macmillan.

Jaeger, R. M., & Tittle, C. K. (Eds.) (1979). *Minimum competency achievement testing: Motives, models, measures and consequences.* Berkeley, CA: McCutchan.

Joint Committee on Standards for Educational Evaluation. (1981). *Standards for evaluations of educational programs, projects, and materials.* New York: McGraw-Hill.

Joyce, B., & Weil, M. (1986). *Models of teaching* (3rd ed.). Englewood Cliffs, NJ: Prentice Hall.

Kahl, J. A. (1965). Some measurements of achievement orientation. *American Journal of Sociology, 4,* 669–681.

Kellaghan, T., Madaus, G. F., & Airasian, P. W. (1982). *The effects of standardized testing.* Boston: Kluwer-Nijhoff.

Kelley, T. L. (1939). The selection of upper and lower groups for the validation of test items. *Journal of Educational Psychology, 30,* 17–24.

Kelley, T. L., *et al.* (1988). *Stanford achievement test series.* San Antonio, TX: The Psychological Corporation.

Keyser, D. J., & Sweetland, R. C. (Eds.). (1988). *Test critiques* (2nd ed.). Kansas City, MO: Test Corporation of America.

Kirkpatrick, J., Ewen, R. B., Barrett, R. S., & Katzell, R. A. (1968). *Testing and fair employment.* New York: New York University Press.

Klausmeier, H. J. (1985). *Educational psychology* (5th ed.). New York: Harper & Row.

Krathwohl, D. R., Bloom, B. S., & Masia, B. B. (1964). *Taxonomy of educational objectives. Handbook II: The affective domain.* New York: David McKay.

Kropp, R. P., Stoker, H. W., & Bashaw, W. L. (1968). The validation of the taxonomy of educational objectives. *Journal of Experimental Education, 34,* 69–76.

Krouskopf, C. J. (1964). A construct validation of a classroom test. *Journal of Educational Measurement, 2,* 131–133.

Kuder, G. F., & Richardson, M. W. (1937). The theory of estimation of test reliability. *Psychometrika, 2,* 151–160.

Kulik, C. C., Kulik, J. A., & Bangert-Downs, R. L. (1990). Effectiveness of mastery learning programs: A meta-analysis. *Review of Educational Research, 60*(2), 265–299.

LaPiere, R. T. Attitudes vs. actions. (1934). *Social Forces, 14,* 230–237.

Larry P. v. *Riles* (1979) 495 F. Supp. 926 (N.D. Cal.) *appeal docketed* No. 80-4027 (9th cir., Jan. 17, 1980).

Lathrop, R. L. (1961). A quick but accurate approximation to the standard deviation of a distribution. *Journal of Experimental Education, 29,* 319–321.

Lenke, J. M., & Keene, J. M. (1988). A response to John J. Cannell. *Educational Measurement: Issues and Practice, 7*(2), 16–18.

Lennon, R. T. (1954, September). Testing: Bond or barrier between pupil and teacher. *Education, 75,* 38–42.

Likert, R. (1932). A technique for the measurement of attitudes. *Archives of Psychology,* no. 140.

Linn, R. L., & Drasgow, F. (1987). Implication of the Golden Rule settlement for test construction. *Educational Measurement: Issues and Practice, 6*(2), 13–17.

MacDonald, J. B., & Walfron, B. J. (1970). A case against behavioral objectives. *Elementary School Journal, 71,* 119–128.

MacGinitie, W. H., & MacGinitie, R. K. (1989). *Gates-MacGinitie reading tests* (3rd ed.). Chicago: Riverside.

Madaus, G. F., Scriven, M. S., & Stufflebeam, D. L. (1983). *Evaluation models.* Boston: Kluwer-Nijhoff.

Mager, R. F. (1962). *Preparing objectives for programmed instruction.* San Francisco: Fearon.

Mantel, N., & Haenszel, W. (1959). Statistical aspects of the analysis of data from retrospective studies of disease. *Journal of the National Cancer Institute, 22,* 719–748.

Marshall, J. C., & Powers, J. M. (1969). Writing neatness, composition errors, and essay grades. *Journal of Educational Measurement, 67,* 97–101.

Martuza, V. R. (1977). *Applying norm-referenced and criteria-referenced measurement in education.* Boston: Allyn and Bacon.

Mayo, S. T. (1970). Mastery learning and mastery testing. *Measurement in Education, 1*(3), 1–4.

McClung, M. S. (1978). Are competency testing programs fair? Legal? *Phi Delta Kappan, 59,* 397–400.

McMorris, R. F. (1972). Evidence on the quality of several approximations for commonly used measurement statistics. *Journal of Educational Measurement, 9*(2), 113–122.

Medley, D. M. (1982). Systematic observation. In H. E. Mitzel (Ed.), *Encyclopedia of educational research* (5th ed.) (pp. 841–851). New York: The Free Press.

Mehrens, W. A., & Kaminski, J. (1989). Methods for improving standardized test scores: Fruitful, fruitless or fraudulent? *Educational Measurement: Issues and Practice, 8*(1), 14–22.

Mehrens, W. A., & Lehmann, I. J. (1987). *Using standardized tests in educatio* (4th ed.). New York: Longman.

Mehrens, W. A., & Lehmann, T. J. (1991). *Measurement and evaluation in education and psychology.* (4th ed.). New York: Holt, Rinehart & Winston.

Merriman, H. O. (1972). Evaluation of planned educational change at the local education agency level. In P. A. Taylor & D. M. Cowley (Eds.), *Readings in curriculum evaluation* (pp. 225–230). Dubuque, IA: William C. Brown.

Messick, S. (1980). Test validity and the ethics of assessment. *American Psychologist, 35,* 1012–1027.

Messick, S. (1981). Evidence and ethics in the evaluation of tests. *Educational Researcher, 10,* 9–20.

Messick, S. (1989). Validity. In R. L. Linn (Ed.), *Educational measurement* (3rd ed.). New York: Macmillan.

Messick, S., & Jungeblut, A. (1981). Time and method in coaching for the SAT. *Psychological Bulletin, 89,* 191–216.

Metfessel, W. S., Michael, W. B., & Kirsner, D. A. (1969). Instrumentation of Bloom's and Krathwohl's taxonomies for the writing of educational objectives. *Psychology in the Schools, 6,* 227–231.

Michael, W. B., Michael, J. J., & Zimmerman, W. S. (1988). *Study attitude and methods survey.* San Diego: Edits.

Millman, J. (1981). Student performance as a measure of teacher competence. In J. Millman (Ed.), *Handbook of teacher evaluation* (pp. 146–166). National Council on Measurement in Education. Beverly Hills, CA: Sage.

Millman, J., Bishop, C. H., & Ebel, R. (1965). An analysis of test-wiseness. *Educational and Psychological Measurement, 25,* 707–726.

Millman, J., & Darling-Hamond, L. (1990). *The new handbook of teacher evaluation (Assessing elementary and secondary school teachers).* Newbury Park, CA: Sage.

Millman, J., & Greene, J. (1989). The specification and development of tests and achievement and ability. In R. L. Linn (Ed.), *Educational measurement* (3rd ed.) (pp. 335–366). New York: American Council on Education/Macmillan.

Millman, J., Slovarek, S. P., Kulick, E., & Mitchell, K. J. (1983). Does grade inflation affect the reliability of grades? *Research in Higher Education, 19*(4), 423–429.

Mills, C. M. (1983). A comparison of three methods of establishing cut-off scores on criterion-referenced tests. *Journal of Educational Measurement, 20*(3), 283–292.

Mitchell, J. W., Jr. (Ed.) (1990). *Tests in print.* Lincoln: University of Nebraska, Buros Institute of Mental Measurements.

Moore, R. W., & Sutman, F. X. (1970). The development, field test and validation of an inventory of scientific attitudes. *Journal of Research in Science Teaching, 7,* 85–94.

Mullis, I. V. S., & Jenkins, L. B. (1988). *The science report card.* Princeton, NJ: Educational Testing Service.

Myers, A. E., McConville, C., & Coffman, W. E. (1966). Simplex structure in the grading of essay tests. *Educational and Psychological Measurement, 26,* 41–54.

nal Council on Measurement in Education. (1990). *Standards for teacher competence in educational assessment of students.* Washington DC: NCME.

ıal Commission on Testing and Public Policy (1990). *From gatekeeper to teway: Transforming testing in America.* (Executive summary.) Chestnut Hill, MA: Boston College.

Natriello, G. (1987). The impact of evaluation processes on students. *Educational Psychologist, 22*(2), 155–175.

Natriello, G., & Dornbusch, S. M. (1984). *Teacher evaluative standards and student effort.* New York: Longman.

Niehaus, S. W. (1968). The anatomy of evaluation. *The Clearinghouse, 42,* 332–336.

Nitko, A. J. (1980). Distinguishing the many varieties of criterion-referenced tests. *Review of Educational Research, 50*(3), 461–485.

Nitko, A. J. (1983). *Educational tests and measurement: An introduction.* New York: Harcourt Brace Jovanovich.

Nitko, A. J., & Hsu, T. (1984). A comprehensive microcomputer system for classroom testing. *Journal of Educational Measurement, 21*(4), 377–390.

Odell, L. (1981). Defining and assessing competence in writing. In C. R. Cooper (Ed.), *The nature and measurement of competency in English* (pp. 95–138). Urbana, IL: National Council of Teachers of English.

Osgood, C. E., Suci, G. J., & Tannenbaum, P. H. (1957). *The measurement of meaning.* Urbana, IL: University of Illinois Press.

OSS (Office of Strategic Services) Assessment Staff. (1948). *Assessment of men.* New York: Holt, Rinehart & Winston.

Otis, A. S., & Lennon, R. T. (1988). *Otis-Lennon school ability test.* San Antonio: The Psychological Corporation/Harcourt Brace Jovanovich.

Palmer, O. (1962). Seven classic ways of grading dishonestly. *The English Journal, 51,* 464–467.

Parents in Action on Special Education v. *Hannon* (1980). 506 F. Supp. 831 (N.D. Ill.).

Payne, B. D. (1984). The relationship of test anxiety and answer-changing behavior: An analysis by race and sex. *Measurement and Evaluation in Guidance, 16*(4), 205–210.

Payne, D. A. (1963). A note on skewness and internal consistency reliability estimates. *Journal of Experimental Education, 32,* 43–46.

Payne, D. A. (Ed.) (1980). *Recent developments in affective measurement.* San Francisco: Jossey-Bass.

Payne, D. A. (1982a). Portrait of the school psychologist as program evaluator. In C. R. Reynolds & T. B. Gutkin (Eds.), *Handbook of School Psychology* (pp. 891–915). New York: John Wiley & Sons.

Payne, D. A. (1982b). Measurement in education. In H. Mitzel (Ed.), *Encyclopedia of educational research* (pp. 1182–1190). New York: The Free Press.

Payne, D. A. (1982c). Diary of a mad evaluator. *Educational Evaluation and Policy Analysis, 4*(4), 543–545.

Payne, D. A., Wells, R. A., & Clarke, R. R. (1971). Another contribution to estimating success in graduate school: A search for sex differences and comparison between three degree types. *Educational and Psychological Measurement, 31*(2), 497–503.

Payne, S. L. (1951). *The art of asking questions.* Princeton, NJ: Princeton University Press.

Popham, W. J. (1969). Objectives and instruction. In W. J. Popham (Ed.), *Instructional objectives* (pp. 32–52). Chicago: Rand McNally.

Popham, W. J. (1987a). The merits of measurement-driven instruction. *Phi Delta Kappan, 68*(9), 679–682.

Popham, W. J. (1987b). Preparing policymakers for standard setting on high-stakes tests. *Educational Evaluation and Policy Analysis, 9*(1), 77–82.

Popham, W. J. (1990). *Modern educational measurement* (2nd ed.). Englewood Cliffs, NJ: Prentice Hall.

Popham, W. J., Cruse, K. L., Smart, C. R., Sandifer, P. D., & Williams, P. L. (1985). Measurement-driven instruction: It's on the road. *Phi Delta Kappan, 66*(9), 628–634.

Popham, W. J., & Husek, T. R. (1969). Implications of criterion-referenced measurement. *Journal of Educational Measurement, 6,* 1–9.

Postman, L., & Rau, L. (1957). Retention as a function of the method of measurement. *University of California Publications in Psychology, 8,* 217–270.

Prescot, D. A. (1957). *The child in the educative process.* New York: McGraw-Hill.

Price, J. R., Martuza, V. R., & Crouse, J. H. (1974). Construct validity of test items measuring acquisition of information from line graphs. *Journal of Educational Psychology, 66*(1), 152–156.

Priestly, M. (1982). *Performance assessment in education and training: Alternative techniques.* Englewood Cliffs, NJ: Educational Technology Publications.

Randall, J. A. (1936). The anecdotal behavior journal. *Progressive Education, 13,* 21–26.

Raths, L. E. (1938). Evaluating the program of a school. *Educational Research Bulletin, 17,* 57–84.

Reigeluth, C. M. (Ed.) (1983). *Instructional design theories and models: An overview of their current status.* Hillsdale, NJ: Lawrence Erlbaum.

Reisman, F. K., & Payne, B. D. (1987). *Elementary education: A basic text.* Columbus, OH: Charles E. Merrill.

Remmers, H. H., Gage, N. L., & Rummel, J. F. (1965). *A practical introduction to measurement and evaluation* (2nd ed.). New York: Harper & Row.

Remmers, H. H., & Silance, E. B. (1934). Generalized attitude scales. *Journal of Social Psychology, 5,* 398–312.

Reynolds, C. R., & Brown, R. T. (1984). Bias in mental testing: An introduction to the issues. In C. R. Reynolds & R. T. Brown (Eds.), *Perspectives on bias in mental testing* (pp. 1–40). New York: Plenum.

Rice, J. M. (1914). *Scientific management in education.* New York: Hinds, Noble & Eldredge.

Richardson, M. W., & Kuder, G. F. (1939). The calculation of test reliability coefficients based on the method of rational equivalence. *Journal of Educational Psychology, 30,* 681–687.

Ricks, J. H., Jr. (1956). How accurate is a test score? *Test Service Bulletin No. 50.* New York: Psychological Corporation.

Ripple, R. E. (1965). Affective factors influence classroom learning. *Educational Leadership, 22*(7), 476–480.

Riverside Publishing Co. (1983). *Improving test-taking skills.* Iowa City: Riverside.

Roid, G. H. (1989). Item writing and item banking by microcomputer: An update. *Educational Measurement: Issues and Practice, 8*(3), 17–20, 38.

Rokeach, M. (1968). *Beliefs, attitudes, and values: A theory of organization and change.* San Francisco: Jossey-Bass.

Rosenshine, B. (1985). Teaching functions in instructional programs. *The Elementary School Journal, 83*(4), 335–351.

Salmon-Cox, L. (1981). Teachers and standardized achievement tests: What's really happening? *Phi Delta Kappan, 62*(9), 251–258.

Sarason, I. G. (Ed.) (1980). *Test anxiety: Theory, research and applications.* Hillsdale, NJ: Lawrence Erlbaum.

Sarnacki, R. E. (1979). An examination of test wiseness in the cognitive test domain. *Review of Educational Research, 49,* 252–279.

Saupe, J. L. (1961). Some useful estimates of the Kuder-Richardson Formula Number 20 reliability coefficient. *Educational and Psychological Measurement 21,* 63–71.

Schmidt, W. H. (1983). Content biases in achievement tests. *Journal of Educational Measurement, 20*(2), 165–178.

Scriven, M. (1967). The methodology of evaluation. *Perspectives of curriculum evaluation.* Monograph No. 1. Chicago: Rand McNally.

Scriven, M. (1972). Pros and cons about goal-free evaluation. *Evaluation Comment, 3*(4), 1–7.

Seddon, G. M. (1978). The properties of Bloom's Taxonomy of Educational Objectives for the Cognitive Domain. *Review of Educational Research, 48*(2), 303–323.

Shaw, M. E., & Wright, J. M. (Eds.). (1967). *Scales for the measurement of attitudes.* New York: McGraw-Hill.

Shertzer, B., & Linden, J. D. (1979). *Fundamentals of individual appraisal.* Boston: Houghton Mifflin.

Shoemaker, D. (1973). *Principles and procedures of multiple matrix sampling.* Cambridge, MA: Ballinger.

Simpson, E. J. (1966). The classification of educational objectives: Psychomotor domain. *Illinois Teacher of Home Economics, 10,* 110–144.

Simpson, R. H. (1944). The specific meanings of certain terms indicating different degrees of frequency. *Quarterly Journal of Speech, 30,* 328–330.

Sirotnik, K. (1974). Matrix sampling for the practitioner. In W. J. Popham (Ed.), *Evaluation in education: Current applications* (pp. 451–529). Berkeley: McCutchan.

Smith, E. R., Tyler, R. W., *et al.* (1942). *Appraising and recording student progress.* New York: Harper & Brothers.

Snelbecker, G. E. (1985). *Learning theory, instructional theory, and psychoeducational design.* New York: University Press of America.

Solley, B. A. (1989). *The effects of cogni*
children's narrative writing. Unpublishe
Georgia, Athens, GA.

Spielberger, C. D., Gorsuch, R. I., & Lushene
state-trait anxiety inventory. Palo Alto, CA: Co

Stake, R. (1967). The countenance of educational evalu
ord, 68(7), 523–540.

Stake, R. (1975). *Evaluating the arts in education: A respo*
bus, OH: Charles E.Merrill.

Stanley, J. C. (1964). *Measurement in today's schools* (4th ed.).
NJ: Prentice Hall.

Starch, D., & Elliott, E. C. (1912). Reliability of grading high s
English. *School Review, 20,* 442–457.

Starch, D., & Elliott, E. C. (1913a). Reliability of grading work in histo
Review, 21, 676–681.

Starch, D., & Elliott, E. C. (1913b). Reliability of grading work in mathem
School Review, 21, 254–257.

Steel, R. P., Mento, A. J., Davis, C. L., & Wilson, B. R. (1989). Psychometr properties of a measure of sense of competence. *Educational and Psychological Measurement, 49*(2), 433–446.

Stiggins, R. J., Frisbee, D. A., & Griswold, P. A. (1989). Inside high school grading practices: Building a research agenda. *Educational measurement: Issues and practices, 8*(2), 5–14.

Stufflebeam, D. L. *et al.* (1971). *Educational evaluation and decision making.* Itasca, IL: Peacock.

Subkoviak, M. J. (1988). A practitioner's guide to computation and interpretation of reliability of indices for mastery tests. *Journal of Educational Measurement, 25*(1), 47–55.

Super, D. E. (1970). *Work values inventory.* Boston: Houghton Mifflin.

Swanicki, E. F. (1981). Contract plans: A professional growth-oriented approach to evaluating teacher performance. In J. Millman (Ed.), *Handbook of teacher evaluation.* Beverly Hills, CA: Sage.

Swanson, B. B., Payne, D. A., & Jackson, B. (1981). A predictive validity study of the *Metropolitan Readiness Test* and *Meeting Street School Screening Test* against first grade *Metropolitan Achievement Test* scores. *Educational and Psychological Measurement, 41,* 575–578.

Sweetland, R. C., & Keyser, D. J. (1983). *Tests.* Kansas City: Test Corporation of America.

Taylor, P. A., & Maguire, T. O. (1966). A theoretical evaluation model. *Manitoba Journal of Educational Research, 1,* 12–17.

Terman, L. M., & Merrill, M. (1937). *Measuring intelligence.* Boston: Houghton Mifflin.

Terwilliger, J. S. (1971). Assigning grades to students. Glenview, IL: Scott, Foresman.

Terwilliger, J. S. (1989). Classroom standard setting and grading practices. *Educational measurement: Issues and practices, 8*(2), 15–19.

rogress (2nd ed.). New York: David

microcomputer test scoring and pro- per presented at meeting of American gton, DC.

surement and evaluation in psychol- hn Wiley & Sons.

measurement of attitude. Chicago:

968). Effects of promised reward multiple-choice vocabulary test. te for Studies in Education, On-

onal objectives and theories of *Analysis, 2*(2), 5–23.

ram. *The Clearing House, 25,*

ing the objective test. In E. F. Lind- *surement* (pp. 329–416). Washington, DC: Ameri- Education.

A. E., & Anderson, H. A. (1935). The reliability of an essay examination in English. *School Review, 43,* 534–539.

Tversky, A. (1964). On the optimal number of alternatives at a choice point. *Journal of Mathematical Psychology, 1,* 386–391.

Tyler, R. W. (1933). Permanence of learning. *Journal of Higher Education, 4,* 203–204.

Tyler, R. W. (1964). Some persistent questions on the defining of objectives. In C. M. Lindvall (Ed.), *Defining educational objectives* (pp. 77–83). Pittsburgh: University of Pittsburgh Press.

Tyler, R. W. (1973). Testing for accountability. In A. C. Ornstein (Ed.), *Accountability for teachers and school administrators.* Belmont, CA: Feardon Publishers.

United States v. *State of South Carolina* (1977). 445 F. Supp. 1094 (DSC).

Vernon, P. E. (1961). *The structure of human abilities.* (2nd ed.). London: Methuen.

Wainer, H. (1986). Five pitfalls encountered while trying to compare states on their SAT scores. *Journal of Educational Measurement, 23*(1), 69–81.

Wainer, H. (1989). The future of item analysis. *Journal of Educational Measurement, 26*(2), 191–208.

Walberg, H. J. (1984, May). Improving the productivity of America's schools. *Educational Leadership,* pp. 19–27.

Walbesser, H. H. (1965). *An evaluation model and its application.* Washington, DC: American Association for the Advancement of Science.

Wall, J., & Summerlin, L. (1972). Choosing the right test. *The Science Teacher, 39,* 32–36.

Webb, E. J., Campbell, D. T., Schwartz, R. O., Sechrest, L., & Grove, J. B. (1981). *Nonreactive measures in the social sciences* (2nd ed.). Boston: Houghton Mifflin.

Wechsler, D. (1974). *Wechsler intelligence scale for children—revised.* San Antonio: The Psychological Corporation/Harcourt Brace Jovanovich.

Wolf, R. M. (1982). Validity of tests. In H. E. Mitzel (Ed.), *Encyclopedia of educational research* (pp. 1991–1998). New York: The Free Press.

Wolfe, R. M. (1969). A model for curriculum evaluation. *Psychology in the Schools, 6,* 107–108.

Woodcock, R. W. (1987). *Woodcock reading mastery tests—revised.* Circle Pines, MN: American Guidance Service.

Worthen, B. R., & Sanders, J. R. (1987). *Educational evaluation.* New York: Longman.

Wynn, C. (1973). Pros and cons of behavioral objectives. *Georgia Educator,* 3(3), 12–14.

Yalow, E. S., & Popham, W. J. (1983). Content validity at the crossroads. *Educational Researcher, 12*(8), 10–14, 21.

Yelon, S. L., & Scott, R. O. (1970). *A strategy for writing objectives.* Dubuque, IA: Kendall/Hunt.

Glossary of Measurement, Evaluation, and Testing Terms*

ACADEMIC APTITUDE TEST	A measure of the native and acquired abilities needed for schoolwork.
ACHIEVEMENT TEST	A test that measures the extent to which an individual has "achieved" something—acquired certain information or mastered certain skills—usually as a result of specific instruction or general schooling.
ACQUIESCENCE	The tendency to "agree" with true items on a true-false test. Personality interacts with the test to produce a response style and results in invalidity. Also the tendency to select central or middle values on a rating scale.
ADAPTIVE TESTING	Computer-assisted test administration where presentation of items is dictated by examinee's responses to previous items or ability.
AFFECTIVE	Pertaining to attitudes, interests, values, feelings, preferences, likes, pleasures, confidence, pride, and satisfaction.

*This Glossary initially inspired by and selected excerpts taken from *A Glossary of 100 Measurement Terms* (Test Service Notebook No. 13, Undated, Harcourt Brace Jovanovich), and *A Glossary of Measurement Terms* (1959, CTB/McGraw-Hill).

AGE NORM	Values or scores representing typical or average performance of individuals classified according to chronological age.
ALTERNATE-FORM RELIABILITY	A measure of the extent to which two equivalent or parallel forms of a test correlate in measuring whatever they measure.
ALTERNATIVE	See *distractor.*
AMBIGUITY ERROR	Rating errors introduced when different raters interpret the same terms differently, for example, what is "average" or how frequently is "sometimes."
ANALYTIC SCORING	Breaking down a communication, e.g., an essay, into component parts, e.g., grammar with a differentially weighted scoring guide.
ANECDOTAL RECORD	Summary written description of student observation.
ANTICIPATED ACHIEVEMENT	Expected or predicted performance or achievement based on past performance or aptitude/ability measures.
APTITUDE	A combination of abilities and other characteristics, native or acquired, known or believed to be indicative of an individual's ability to learn in a given particular area. Thus, "musical aptitude" refers to that combination of physical and mental characteristics, motivational factors, knowledge, and other characteristics that is conducive to the achievement of proficiency in the field of music. Motivational factors, including interests, are sometimes distinguished from aptitude, but the more comprehensive definition seems preferable.
APTITUDE TEST	A measure usually cognitive or psychomotor of the likelihood of an individual's benefitting from a training program.

ARITHMETIC MEAN	The sum of a set of scores divided by the number of scores (commonly called *average* or *mean*).
ARTICULATED TESTS	A series of tests that provides different levels for different ages or grades, constructed and standardized so that the same or comparable elements or objectives are measured at all levels. Well-articulated tests are characterized by considerable interlevel overlap in order to test the wide ranges of abilities and achievements in any given grade or class. On a well-articulated series of test batteries, a given grade group achieves the same derived scores whether a lower or higher level of the test is used.
ASSESSMENT	The systematic evaluative appraisal of an individual's ability and performance in a particular environment or context. Characterized by synthesis of a variety of data.
AVERAGE	A general term applied to measures of central tendency. The three most widely used averages are the *arithmetic mean*, the *median*, and the *mode*.
BALANCE	The degree to which the proportion of items measuring particular outcomes corresponds to the "ideal" test or to that suggested by the table of specifications.
BATTERY	A group of tests standardized on the same population, so that results on the several tests are comparable (integrated norms). Sometimes loosely applied to any group of tests administered together.
BEHAVIORAL OBJECTIVES	Statements of intended educational outcomes defined in terms of criteria for student performance, sometimes specifying the conditions under which the behavior is to be observed. Akin to "performance" and "competence" objectives.

BIAS	Systematic, but invalid, advantage or disadvantage for particular group or subgroup based on irregularities in test content, administration, or interpretation.
BIMODAL DISTRIBUTION	The tendency of a frequency distribution to reflect two identifiable scores or regions along the score scale.
BISERIAL CORRELATION	A frequently used method of expressing the relationship between an artificial dichotomy (e.g., high/low) and a continuous variable. Often used to correlate responses to items and total test scores.
CEILING	The upper limit of ability that can be measured by a test. Individuals are said to have reached the ceiling of a test when their abilities exceed the highest performance level at which the test can make reliable discriminations.
CENTILE	A value on the scoring scale below which a given percentage of cases is located. Any of 99 values that divide a distribution into 100 equal units. The synonym *percentile* is regarded by some statisticians as superfluous. (See *percentile.*)
CENTRAL TENDENCY ERROR	The reluctance to give extreme ratings, either positive or negative.
CHANCE SCORE	The most likely score to result from guessing. (See *correction for guessing.*)
COACHING	Instruction and practice on test tasks like those to be encountered on a criterion measure (e.g., Scholastic Aptitude Test). Also includes general practice on test-taking strategies.
COEFFICIENT ALPHA	A generalized measure of internal consistency for items on a continuous response scale. Specifically the average degree of interitem correlation. (See *internal consistency.*)

COEFFICIENT OF DETERMINATION	The square of the correlation coefficient (times 100) reflecting the overlap or common variance. Usually between predictor and criterion measures.
COGNITIVE	Pertaining to such mental abilities as recall, comprehension, problem solving, and synthesis, and the sensing and processing of information.
COMPLETION ITEM	A test question calling for the completion of a phrase or sentence one or more parts of which have been omitted; a question for which the examinee must supply (rather than select) the correct response.
CONCURRENT VALIDITY	See *criterion-related validity.*
CONSISTENCY	See *reliability.*
CONSTRUCT VALIDITY	The degree to which a test measures given psychological qualities. By both logical and empirical methods the theory underlying the test is validated. Arguments for construct validity must be based on theory and empirical evidence. Examples of such methods are correlations of the test score with other test scores, factor analysis, study of the effect of speed on test scores.
CONTENT VALIDITY	The degree to which the content of the test samples the subject matter, behaviors, or situations about which conclusions are to be drawn. Content validity is especially important in an achievement test, and is determined with reference to the table of specifications and objectives. Examples of procedures to measure content validity are textbook analysis, description of the universe of items, judgment of the adequacy of the sample, review of representative illustrations of test content, intercorrelations of subscores, and solicitation of the opinions of a jury of experts.

CONTRAST ERROR	The tendency of a rater to judge a ratee in a direction opposite that of the rater, e.g., "Nobody is as neat and clean as I am."
CONVERGENT VALIDITY	The extent to which two different measures of the same criterion are correlated. (See *discriminate validity.*)
CORRECTION FOR ATTENUATION	An estimate of the effect of lack of perfect test and criterion reliability on validity or the correlation between the test and the criterion.
CORRECTION FOR GUESSING	A reduction in score for wrong answers, sometimes applied in scoring true-false or multiple-choice questions. Many doubt the validity or usefulness of this device, which is intended to discourage guessing and yield more accurate measures of examinees' true knowledge. It is assumed that if an examinee guesses on an objective test, the number of resulting wrong answers will be proportional to the number of alternative responses to each item.
CORRELATION	The relationship or "going-togetherness" between two sets of scores or measures; the tendency of scores on one variable to vary concomitantly with those on another, e.g., the tendency of students with high IQs to be above average in reading ability. The existence of a strong relationship—that is, a high correlation—between two variables does not necessarily indicate a causal relationship. (See *correlation coefficient.*)
CORRELATION COEFFICIENT (r)	The most commonly used index of relationship between paired facts or numbers, indicating the tendency of two or more variables or attributes to rank themselves, or individuals measured on them, in the same way. A correlation coefficient (r) may range in

value from -1.00 for a perfect negative relationship through 0.00 for none or pure chance to $+1.00$ for a perfect positive relationship, and summarizes the degree and direction of the relationship.

CRITERION — A standard by which a test may be judged or evaluated; a set of scores or ratings that a test is designed to correlate with or to predict. (See *validity.*)

CRITERION-REFERENCED TEST — A test whose items are tied to specific objectives. Usually used when mastery learning is involved. Variability of scores is of little consequence. Emphasis is on an individual's performance relative to an absolute rather than a normative standard, i.e., an individual's performance is compared with an a priori criterion instead of with the performance of other people.

CRITERION-RELATED VALIDITY — The degree to which test scores correlate with measures of criterion performance. Measures of criteria may be gathered concurrently (concurrent validity)—for example, correlation of the distribution of scores for men in a given occupation with those for men-in-general, correlation of personality test scores with estimates of adjustments made in counseling interviews, or correlation of end-of-course achievement or ability test scores with school marks—or at a later time—for example, correlation of intelligence test scores with course grades, or correlation of test scores obtained at beginning of the year with marks earned at the end of this year.

CROSS-VALIDATION — The process of determining whether a decision derived from one set of data is truly effective by applying the decision process (or strategy) to an independent but relevant set of data.

CULTURE-FAIR TEST — An idealized test where the influence of such potentially biasing factors as sex, race, religion has been attenuated. Examinees should not be penalized because of the lack of uniform socio-cultural experiences.

CURRICULUM EVALUATION — The process of collecting and processing data for decision making about the merit of an educational program. Such data may include (1) objective descriptions of goals, environments, personnel, methods, content, and results, and (2) recorded personal judgments of the quality and appropriateness of goals, inputs, and outcomes.

DECILE — Any of the nine percentile points (scores) in a distribution that divide it into ten equal parts; every tenth percentile. The first decile is the 10th percentile, the ninth decile the 90th percentile, and so on.

DERIVED SCORE — A score that has been converted from a qualitative or quantitative mark on one scale into the units of another scale (e.g., standard score, percentile rank, intelligence quotient).

DEVIATION — The amount by which a score differs from some reference value, such as the mean, norm, or score on another test.

DEVIATION IQ — A measure of intelligence or "brightness" based on the extent to which an individual's score deviates from a score that is typical for the individual's age. Usually expressed as a standard score. (See *intelligence quotient.*)

DIAGNOSTIC TEST — A test used to identify specific areas of weakness or strength and to determine the nature of deficiencies; it yields measures of the components of larger areas of knowledge and skills. Diagnostic achievement tests are most commonly developed for the skill subjects—reading, arithmetic, and spelling.

DIFFERENCE SCORE — The difference between two test scores. When the difference scores are from pre- and post-measures the gain or change scores tend to be unreliable.

DIFFERENTIAL PREDICTION — Prediction among populations or subpopulations (or subsamples) with combinations of predictors and criteria.

DIFFERENTIAL WEIGHTING — The elements of a composite are differentially weighted according to empirically determined weights or on the basis of presumed importance, e.g., items on a test or subscore in a battery.

DIFFICULTY INDEX — The percentage of some specified group, such as students of a given age or grade, who answer an item correctly or score in a particular direction.

DISCRIMINATE VALIDITY — If a test is in fact not correlated with a measure with which it is hypothesized not to correlate, it is said to have discriminate validity.

DISCRIMINATION INDEX — The ability of a test item to differentiate between individuals who possess a given characteristic (skill, knowledge, attitude) in abundance, and those who possess little of it.

DISTRACTOR — Any of the plausible but incorrect choices provided in a multiple-choice or matching item. Sometimes called a foil, alternative, or option. The choice is "distracting" and appears attractive to the less knowledgeable or skillful examinee, thereby reducing the efficacy of guessing.

DISTRIBUTION — An ordered tabulation of scores showing the number of individuals who obtain each score or fall within each score interval. (See *frequency distribution.*)

DOMAIN REFERENCED — Scores are based on a percentage correct of a sample of items correlated with a specified universe of objectives.

DUAL STANDARDIZATION — The procedure of norming or standardizing two tests, e.g., a group intelligence test and an achievement battery, simultaneously on one sample, thereby integrating the two instruments.

ERROR OF ESTIMATE — See *standard error of estimate*.

ERROR OF MEASUREMENT — Inconsistent or random errors (e.g., effect of guessing) which decrease the reliability of measurement. Technically or theoretically the difference between an individual's "true" score and an obtained score. (See *standard error of measurement.*)

EQUIVALENT FORMS — Any of two or more forms of a test whose content and difficulty are similar, and that yield very similar average scores and measures of variability for a given group.

EVALUATION — The process by which quantitative and qualitative data are processed to arrive at a judgment of value, worth, merit, or effectiveness.

EXPECTANCY TABLE — Usually a two-way grid or bivariate table expressing the relationship between two (or more) variables by stating the probability that individuals who belong to each of a set of subgroups defined on the basis of another variable. A method of expressing the validity of a test, if one of the variables is the predictor and the other the criterion.

EXTRAPOLATION — As applied to test norms, the process of extending a norm line beyond the limits of the data in order to permit interpretation of extreme scores. This extension may be accomplished mathematically by fitting a curve to the obtained data or by less rigorous graphic methods.

FACE VALIDITY — The acceptability of the test and test situation by the examinee and, to some extent, the user in light of the apparent uses to which the test is to be put. A test has face validity when it appears to measure the variable it purports to test.

FACTOR — A hypothetical trait, ability, or component of ability that underlies and influences performance on two or more tests, and hence causes scores on the tests to be correlated. Strictly defined, the term *factor* refers to a theoretical variable derived by a process of factor analysis from a table of intercorrelations among tests, but it is also commonly used to denote the psychological interpretation given to the variable—i.e., the mental trait assumed to be represented by the variable, such as verbal or numerical ability. (See *factor analysis.*)

FACTOR ANALYSIS — A set of methods for analyzing the intercorrelations among a set of variables, such as test scores. Using factor analysis we may attempt to account for such interrelationships in terms of underlying factors, preferably fewer in number than the original variables. Factor analysis reveals how much of the variation in each of the original measures is associated with each of the hypothetical factors.

FOIL — See *distractor.*

FORCED-CHOICE ITEM — Broadly, any multiple-choice item that requires the examinee to select one or more of the given choices. The term is best used to denote a special type of multiple-choice item in which the options are (1) of equal "preference value"—i.e., chosen equally often by a typical group—but (2) of differential discriminating ability—i.e., such that one and only one of the options dis-

	criminates between persons high and low on the factor that this option measures.
FORMATIVE EVALUATION	The use of evaluation data to modify, revise, and generally improve an educational program during its developmental stages. (See *summative evaluation.*)
FREE-RESPONSE ITEM	Examinees construct or supply the answer or response. Response may be very brief, e.g., word or numeral, or somewhat extended, e.g., sentence or paragraph.
FREQUENCY DISTRIBUTION	An ordered tabulation of scores showing the number of individuals who obtain each score or fall within each score interval.
GENERALIZABILITY	The extent to which a test produces comparable results over situations, populations, administrators, or locations. The key is the search for the relationship between a sample of scores relative to a universe of scores. Intricate statistical procedures may be applied.
GENEROSITY ERROR	See *leniency error.*
GRADE EQUIVALENT	The grade level for which a given score is the real or estimated average. A grade equivalent of 6.4 is theoretically the average score obtained by students in the fourth month of the sixth grade. Grade equivalent score units are subject to much distortion due to variations in curriculum, individual aptitude, and learning.
GRAPHIC RATING SCALE	A scale that presents the rater with a continuum of phrases describing degrees of a particular trait. The rater makes a judgment about an individual or object with reference to the trait and indicates his or her opinion by placing a mark on a line.

GROUP TEST — A test that may be administered to a number of individuals simultaneously by a single examiner.

GUESSING — See *correction for guessing*.

HALO EFFECT — The biased effect of a gross or global overall general impression of an individual on the rating of specific traits. The effect in practice is usually positive.

HISTOGRAM — A graphic representation of a frequency distribution using vertical bars to represent the different frequencies for scores or groups of scores.

INCREMENTAL VALIDITY — The increase in relationship between the predictor(s) and the criterion measure when another predictor is added to the set.

INDIVIDUAL TEST — A test that may be administered to only one person at a time.

INTELLIGENCE QUOTIENT — A now-outmoded index representing the ratio of a person's mental age to his chronological age (MA/CA) or, more precisely, especially for older persons, the ratio of mental age to the mental age typical of chronological age (in both cases multiplied by 100 to eliminate the decimal). More generally, IQ is a measure of "brightness" that takes into account both the score on an intelligence test and age. (See *deviation IQ*.)

INTERNAL CONSISTENCY — The extent to which items on a test are correlated with each other, implying the measurement of a common content skill, behavior, or other factor.

INTERPOLATION — In general, any process of estimating intermediate values between two known points. As applied to test norms, the term usually refers to the procedure used in assigning values (e.g., grade or age equivalents) to scores between the successive average scores actually obtained in the standardization process. In reading norm tables, it is necessary to interpolate to obtain a norm value for a score between the scores given in a table.

INTERQUARTILE RANGE — The score difference corresponding to the difference between the Third and First Quartile (75th and 25th percentiles).

IPSATIVE MEASUREMENT — Intra-individual comparison in which a given variable score is limited by scores on the other variables; the sum of scores across all scales is the same for all examinees. A forced-choice format is used.

ITEM — A single question or exercise in a test.

ITEM ANALYSIS — Any of several methods used in test development and refinement to determine how well a given test item discriminates among individuals differing in some characteristic. The effectiveness of a test item depends upon three factors: (1) the validity of the item with regard to an outside criterion, curriculum content, or educational objective; (2) the discriminating power of the item with regard to validity and internal consistency; and (3) the difficulty of the item.

ITEM RESPONSE THEORY — See *latent trait theory*.

ITEM SAMPLING — A procedure used in standardization of tests and curriculum evaluation. Instead of requiring all individuals to respond to all items, subgroups take subsets of items. For example, instead of requiring 100 individuals to answer 70 items, 10 groups of 10 individuals each answer 7 items.

KEY — See *scoring key*.

KUDER-RICHARDSON FORMULA(S)	Formulas for estimating the reliability—specifically, the internal consistency—of a test from (1) information about the individual items in the test, or (2) the mean score, standard deviation, and number of items in the test. Because the Kuder-Richardson formulas permit estimation of reliability from a single administration of a test, without dividing the test into halves, their use has become common in test development. The Kuder-Richardson formulas are not appropriate for estimating the reliability of speeded tests.
LATENT TRAIT THEORY	Statistical procedures are used to relate an individual examinee's score to an estimated hypothetical latent trait. Several models are used in item analysis, calibration, and test scaling as part of the standardization process.
LENIENCY ERROR	The tendency to rate more favorably those whom one knows best.
LIKERT SCALE	A method of scaling attitudes in which a respondent indicates his degree of agreement to disagreement to a series of propositions about people, places, ideas, activities, concepts, or objects.
LOGICAL ERROR	The tendency to give similar ratings to those traits that appear in the mind of the rater to be logically related to each other, e.g., assertiveness vs. aggressiveness.
MASTERY TEST	A test of the extent to which a student has mastered a specified set of objectives or met minimum requirements set by a teacher or examining agency. Usually a criterion-referenced measure. (See *criterion-referenced test.*)
MATCHING ITEM	A test item calling for the correct association of each entry in one list with an entry in a second list.

MEAN	The sum of a set of scores divided by the number of scores.
MEASUREMENT	The process of quantifying according to a standard. The assignment of numerals to represent objects, individuals, or phenomena.
MEDIAN	The 50th percentile; the point that divides a group into two equal parts. Half of a group of scores falls below the median and half above it.
MENTAL AGE (MA)	The age for which a given score on an intelligence test is average or normal. If a score of 55 on an intelligence test corresponds to a mental age of 6 years 10 months, 55 is presumed to be the average score that would be achieved by an unselected group of children 6 years 10 months of age.
MINIMUM COMPETENCY TEST	Measures of basic skill and competencies in subject areas (and writing) used to make graduation, certification, and promotion decisions.
MODE	The score or value that occurs most frequently in a distribution.
MULTIPLE-CHOICE ITEM	A test item in which the examinee's task is to choose the correct or best answer from several given options.
MUILTIPLE CORRELATION	The relationship between one variable and the weighted sum of two or more other variables.
MULTIPLE REGRESSION	A method of combining two or more predictors to estimate a single criterion measure. For example, freshman grade point average may be predicted from a combination of high school rank, intelligence test score, and interest inventory scores.
MULTIPLE-RESPONSE ITEM	A type of multiple-choice item in which two or more of the given choices may be correct.

N	The symbol commonly used to represent the number of cases in a distribution, study, or other sampling. The sum of the frequencies = *N* for population and *n* for a sample.
NORMAL CURVE EQUIVALENT	A normalized standard score with a mean of 50 and a standard deviation of 21.06.
NORMAL DISTRIBUTION	A derived curve based on the assumption that variations from the mean occur by chance. The curve is bell-shaped, and is accepted as a representational model because of its repeated recurrence in measurements of human characteristics in psychology and education. It has many useful mathematical properties. In a normal distribution curve, scores are distributed symmetrically about the mean, thickly concentrated near it and decreasing in frequency as the distance from it increases. One cannot tell if a particular distribution is "normal" simply by looking at it, but must determine whether the data fit a particular mathematical function.
NORMALIZED STANDARD SCORE	Normalized standard scores are made to conform to standard score values of a normal distribution curve by use of percentile equivalents for the normal curve. Most frequently expressed with a mean equated to 50 and a standard deviation equated to 10. (See *T* scores.)
NORM-REFERENCED MEASURE	A measure used to distinguish among members of a group by comparing an individual's performance with the performance of others in the group.
NORMS	Statistics that describe the test performance of specified subgroups, such as pupils of various ages or grades, in the standardization group for a test.

Norms are often assumed to be representative of some larger population, such as pupils in the country as a whole. Norms are descriptive of average or typical performance; they are not to be regarded as standards or desirable levels of attainment. Grade, age, percentile, and standard score are the most common types of norms.

OBJECTIVITY — Consistency in scoring. Objectivity is a characteristic of a test that precludes differences of opinion among scorers as to whether responses are to be scored right or wrong. Such a test is contrasted with a "subjective" test—e.g., the usual essay examination to which different scorers may assign different scores, ratings, or grades. Objectivity is a characteristic of the scoring of the test, not its form. An objective test is one in which the method of gathering data does not distort the phenomenon being measured.

OGIVE — A smooth curve resulting from the plot of cumulative frequency or cumulative frequency expressed as a percentage of the total against individual scores.

OMNIBUS TEST — A test (1) in which items measuring a variety of mental operations are combined into a single sequence rather than grouped together by type of operation, and (2) from which only a single score is derived. Omnibus tests make for simplicity of administration: One set of directions and one overall time limit usually suffice.

OPTION — See *distractor*.

PERCENTILE — One of the 99 point scores that divide a ranked distribution into groups each of which is composed of 1/100 of the scores. Also, a point below which a certain percentage of the scores fall. For example, the median (the 50th percentile) is the point in a distribution below which 50 percent of the scores fall.

PERCENTILE BAND — The percentile ranks corresponding to the score points that are one standard error of measurement above and below an observed test score. This describes a range within which an individual's true score is likely to fall.

PERCENTILE RANK — The percentage of scores in a distribution equal to or lower than the score in question. If a person obtains a percentile rank of 70, his standing is regarded as equaling or surpassing that of 70 percent of the normative group on which the test was standardized.

PERFORMANCE TEST — A test usually requiring motor or manual response on the examinee's part, and generally but not always involving manipulation of concrete equipment or materials, as contrasted with a paper-and-pencil test. The term is also used to denote a work-sample test, which simulates the behavior about which information is desired. A work-sample instrument may use paper and pencil to test skills such as accounting, shorthand, and proofreading.

PERSONALITY TEST — A test intended to measure one or more nonintellective variables. Personality traits include: so-called *personality inventories* or *adjustment inventories,* which seek to measure a person's status on such traits as dominance, sociability, and introversion by means of self-descriptive responses to a series of questions; *rating scales,* which call for self- or other-administered rating of the extent to which a subject possesses certain characteristics; situation tests, in which the individual's behavior in simulated lifelike situations is observed and evaluated, with reference to various personality traits, by one or more judges; and opinion or attitude inventories. Some writers also classify interest inventories as personality traits.

POINT-BISERIAL CORRELATION — Used to describe the relationship between a true dichotomous variable (e.g., sex) and a continuous variable. Also used in item analysis.

POWER TEST — A test intended to measure level of performance and to sample the range of an examinee's capacity, rather than the speed of response; hence a power test has either no time limit or a very generous one.

PRACTICE EFFECT — The influence of previous experience with a test on a later administration of the same or a similar test, usually resulting in an increase in score. Practice effect is greatest when the time interval between testing is small, the content of the two tests is very similar, and the initial test administration represents a relatively novel experience for the subject.

PREDICTIVE VALIDITY — See *criterion-related validity*.

PRODUCT-MOMENT COEFFICIENT — See *correlation coefficient*.

PROFILE — A graphic representation of an individual's or group's scores on several tests, expressed in uniform or comparable terms. This method of presentation permits easy identification of areas of strength or weakness.

PROXIMITY ERROR — A rating error which results in inflated correlations between traits just because they are rated at about the same time or are adjacent to one another on a response form.

Q-SORT	A technique used to measure personality, requiring the subject to sort a large number of statements into piles representing the degrees to which they apply to him.
QUARTILE	One of three points that divide the cases in a distribution into four equal groups. The first quartile is the 25th percentile, the second quartile is the 50th percentile or median, and the third quartile is the 75th percentile.
RANDOM SAMPLE	A sample of a population drawn in such a way that every member has an equal chance of being included. That is, the sample is drawn in a way that precludes the operation of bias in selection. One goal of such a sample is, of course, that it be representative of the total population, so that sample findings may be generalized to that population. (However, a random sample may still be atypical and unrepresentative of the population.) A great advantage of random samples is that formulas are available for estimating the expected variation of the sample statistics from their true values in the total population; in other words, we know how precise an estimate of the population is represented by a random sample of any given size.
RANGE	The difference between the highest and lowest scores, plus one, obtained on a test by a particular group.
RATING SCALE	A data-gathering method involving the use of numerals or phrases in conjunction with points along a continuum. A given instrument may include several such scales.
RAW SCORE	The first quantitative result obtained in scoring a test. Usually the number of right answers, the time required for performance, the number of errors, or

a similar direct, unconverted, uninterpreted measure.

READINESS TEST — A test that measures the extent to which an individual has achieved the degree of maturity or acquired the skills or information necessary to undertake some new learning activity successfully. Thus a *reading readiness test* indicates the extent to which a child has reached the appropriate developmental stage and acquired the prerequisite skills to profitably begin a formal instructional program in reading.

RECALL ITEM — An item that requires the examinee to supply the correct answer from his own memory, as contrasted with a *recognition item*, which requires him to select or identify the correct answer.

RECOGNITION ITEM — An item requiring the examinee to recognize or select the correct answer from among two or more given answers.

REGRESSION EFFECT — The tendency for a predicted score to be relatively nearer the mean of its series than is the score from which it was predicted to the mean of its series. For example, if we predict school marks from an intelligence test, we will find that the mean of the predicted school marks for all pupils who have IQs two standard deviations above the mean will be less than two standard deviations from the mean of the school marks. There is a regression effect whenever the correlation between two measures is less than perfect.

RELEVANCE — The extent to which specific items are in fact measures of specific objectives. In a real sense relevance is a function of item validity usually demonstrated by professional judgment.

RELIABILITY	The extent to which a test is accurate or consistent in measuring whatever it measures; dependability, stability, and relative freedom from errors of measurement. Estimation of reliability generally involves examination of internal consistency, equivalence of forms, or stability of scores over time.
RELIABILITY OF DIFFERENCE	The extent to which a difference between scores is consistent, e.g., the extent to which differences between pre- and post-test scores on one form of a test are related to pre- and post-differences on another form of the test.
REPRESENTATIVE SAMPLE	A sample that accurately represents the population from which it is selected with respect to characteristics relevant to the issue under investigation—e.g., in an achievement-test norm sample, representation might be according to pupils from each state, various regions, segregated and nonsegregated schools, and so on.
RESPONSE SET	A test-taking attitude whereby examinees wish to present a particular picture of themselves, e.g., faking good or bad.
RESPONSE STYLE	Predisposition to respond in a particular manner as a function of the *form* rather than the *content* of the question. For example, when in doubt on a true-false test the tendency is to agree when guessing, thereby agreeing with authority.
SCALED SCORE	A unit in a system of equated scores corresponding to the raw scores of a test in such a way that the scaled score values may be interpreted as representative of the mean performance of certain reference groups. The intervals between any pair of scaled scores may be

	interpreted as differences in terms of the characteristics of the reference group.
SCATTER DIAGRAM	A bivariate frequency distribution where pairs of scores are plotted on coordinate axes. A graphical representation of relationship.
SCHOLASTIC APTITUDE	See *academic aptitude test.*
SCORING KEY	The standard against which examinee responses are compared. List of correct or expected answers.
SELECTION ITEM	See *recognition item* and *multiple-choice item.*
SEMANTIC DIFFFERENTIAL TECHNIQUE	A method requiring individuals to express their feelings about a concept by rating it on a series of bipolar adjectives, e.g., good-bad, strong-weak, and fast-slow. The format is usually a seven-interval scale, and three major dimensions are generally measured: evaluation, potency, and activity.
SEMI-INTERQUARTILE RANGE	One-half of the difference between the third and first quartile (75th and 25th percentiles).
SKEWNESS	The tendency of a distribution to depart from symmetry or balance around the mean. For example, a positively skewed distribution may have more extreme low scores than high scores, causing the mean to be higher than the median.
SOCIAL DESIRABILITY	A source of invalidity on self-report affective measures whereby respondent answers in a predominantly socially desirable way, e.g., always saying "No" to items like "I have never stolen anything in my life," an item, although desirable, but rarely true.
SOCIOGRAM	A diagram of interpersonal relationships within a group in terms of friendship choices and rejections.

SOCIOMETRY — Measurement of the interpersonal relationships prevailing among the members of a group by means of sociometric devices, e.g., the *sociogram.* An attempt is made to discover the patterns of choice and rejection, to identify the individuals most often chosen as friends or leaders ("stars") or rejected by others ("isolates"), and to determine how the group subdivides into clusters or cliques.

SPECIFIC DETERMINERS — Two classes of ambiguous words that invalidate test items, particularly true-false items. One set (*some, might, could, sometimes*) tend to call for a True response. The other set (*never, always*) tend to call for a False response.

SPIRAL OMNIBUS TEST — Test where different kinds of item formats are used with different content throughout the test and the items increase in difficulty level as examinee progresses through test.

STABILITY — As applied to the examination of reliability, the method involves administering the same test to the same group on two different occasions, and correlating the scores. (See *reliability.*)

STANDARD DEVIATION — A measure of the variability of dispersion of a set of scores. The more the scores cluster around the mean, the smaller the standard deviation.

STANDARD ERROR OF ESTIMATE — An expression of the degree to which predictions or estimates of criterion scores are likely to correspond to actual values (standard deviation of the criterion times the square root of the quantity, one minus the correlation coefficient squared). A method of expressing the validity of the test. All other things being equal, the smaller the standard error the better the validity.

STANDARD ERROR OF MEASUREMENT — A measure of the estimated difference between the observed test score and the hypothetical "true score," i.e., errorless score (standard deviation of the test times the square root of one minus the reliability coefficient). A method of expressing the reliability of a test. All other things being equal, the smaller the error of measurement the higher the reliability. Used in estimating the true score.

STANDARD SCORE — A general term referring to any of a variety of "transformed" scores in terms of which raw scores may be expressed for reasons of convenience, comparability, ease of interpretation, and the like. The simplest type of standard score expresses the deviation of an individual's raw score from the average score of his group in relation to the standard deviation of the scores of the group. Thus:

Standard score (z) = raw score (X) − mean (M) ÷ standard deviation (S)

Standard scores do not affect the relative standing of the individuals in the group or change the shape of the original distribution. More complicated types of standard scores may yield distributions differing in shape from the original distribution; in fact, they are sometimes used for precisely this purpose.

STANDARDIZATION SAMPLE — The reference sample of those individuals, schools, or other units selected for use in norming a test. This sample should be representative of the target population in essential characteristics such as geographical representation, age, and grade.

STANDARDIZED TEST — A systematic sample of performance obtained under prescribed conditions, scored according to definite rules, and capable of evaluation by reference to normative information. Some writers restrict the term to tests possessing the above properties whose items have been experimentally evaluated and/or for which evidence of validity and reliability is provided.

STANINES — A unit that divides the norm population into nine groups. Except for Stanines 1 and 9, the groups are spaced in half-sigma units, with the mean at Stanine 5 and those scoring the highest at Stanine 9. Stanines are usually normalized standard scores.

Stanine	1	2	3	4	5	6	7	8	9
% in Stanine	4	7	12	17	20	17	12	7	4

STENCIL KEY — A scoring key which, when positioned over an examinee's responses in a test booklet or on an answer sheet, permits rapid identification and tabulation of correct answers. Stencil keys may be perforated in positions corresponding to those of the correct answers, so that only correct answers show through, or they may be transparent, with the positions of the correct answers identified by circles or boxes printed on the key.

STRIP KEY — A scoring key on which the answers to items on any page or column of the test appear in a strip or column that may be placed beside the examinee's responses.

SUBTEST — A collection of items in a battery or test that have distinct similar characteristics or functions. A separate score is usually provided.

SUMMATIVE EVALUATION — The use of evaluation data to determine the effectiveness of a unit, course, or program after it has been completed. (See *formative evaluation*.)

SUPPLY ITEM	See *free-response item* and *completion item*.
SURVEY TEST	A test that measures general achievement in a given subject or area, usually with the understanding that the test is intended to measure group, rather than individual, status.
T SCORE	A derived (normalized standard) score based on the equivalence of percentile values to standard scores, thus avoiding the effects of skewed distributions, and usually having a mean equated to 50 and a standard deviation equated to 10.
TABLE OF SPECIFICATIONS	Usually a two-way grid summarizing the behavioral outcomes and content of a course or unit of instruction. Percentages in the cells of the table indicate the importance of subtopics dictated by value judgments, instructional time spent, and the like. Used to guide achievement test development and selection. The specifications may also call for particular types of item, behaviors, and the like. Tables of specification are also used in the development of tests other than proficiency measures.
TAILORED TESTING	See *adaptive testing*.
TEST	A systematic procedure for gathering data to make intra- or interindividual comparisons.
TEST-WISENESS	Competency in test-taking skills and ability to outwit inept test constructor, e.g., ability to spot *specific determinees* and respond appropriately.
TEST-RETEST RELIABILITY COEFFICIENT	A type of reliability coefficient obtained by administering a test to the same sample a second time after an interval and correlating the two sets of scores. (See *stability*.)

TRUE SCORE

The average score on an infinite series of administrations of the same or exactly equivalent tests, assuming no practice effect or change in the examinee during the testings. A score for which errors of measurement have been averaged.

VALIDITY

The extent to which a test does the job for which it is used. Thus defined, validity has different connotations for various kinds of tests and, accordingly, different kinds of evidence are appropriate: (1) The validity of an achievement test is the extent to which the content of the test represents a balanced and adequate sampling of the outcomes of the course or instructional program in question (content, face, or curricular validity). It is best determined by a comparison of the test content with courses of study, instructional materials, and statements of instructional goals, and by critical analysis of the processes required to respond to the items. (2) The validity of an aptitude, prognostic, or readiness test is the extent to which it accurately indicates future learning success in the area in question. It is manifested by correlations between test scores and measures of later success. (3) The validity of a personality test is the extent to which the test yields an accurate description of an individual's personality traits or personality organization. It may be manifested by agreement between test results and other types of evaluation, such as ratings or clinical classification, but only to the extent that such criteria are themselves valid. The traditional definition of validity—"the extent to which a test measures what it is supposed to measure"—fails to acknowledge that validity is always specific to the purposes for which the test is used, that different kinds of evidence are appropriate to different types of tests, and that final responsibility for validation rests with the test interpreter and user. (See *content, construct,* and *criterion-related validity.*)

VARIANCE — The aggregate amount of variability in a set of scores. The square of the standard deviation or the average of the squared deviations about the mean.

WORK LIMIT TEST — A test that allows sufficient time for all or nearly all pupils to complete their work. (See *power test.*)

WORK SAMPLE TEST — A high-relevance performance test that provides for an actual tryout of examinees' behavior in a realistic setting.

Name and Title Index

Subject Index